Modern Chinese Literature
in the May Fourth Era

Harvard East Asian Series 89

The East Asian Research Center at Harvard University administers research projects designed to further scholarly understanding of China, Japan, Korea, Vietnam, Inner Asia, and adjacent areas.

Contributors

John Berninghausen
Cyril Birch
Yü-shih Chen
Ching-mao Cheng
Milena Doleželová-Velingerová
Irene Eber
Michael Egan
Yi-tsi M. Feuerwerker
Douwe W. Fokkema
Merle Goldman
Leo Ou-fan Lee
Perry Link
Bonnie S. McDougall
Harriet C. Mills
Paul G. Pickowicz
Ezra F. Vogel
Ellen Widmer

Modern Chinese Literature in the May Fourth Era

Edited by Merle Goldman
*Sponsored by the
Social Science Research Council*

Harvard University Press
Cambridge, Massachusetts,
and London, England
1977

Preparation of this volume has been aided by a grant from the Ford
Foundation

Library of Congress Cataloging in Publication Data
Main entry under title:

Modern Chinese literature in the May Fourth Era.

   (Harvard East Asian series   ; 89)
   The chapters are drawn from the conference which was held at Endicott
House in Dedham, Mass., Aug. 26-30, 1974 and from a workshop that
preceded it at the Harvard East Asian Research Center.
   Includes index.
   1. Chinese literature—20th century—Congresses. I. Goldman, Merle. II.
Social Science Research Council. III. Harvard University. East Asian Research
Center. IV. Series.
PL2253.M6   895.1'09'005   76-47652
ISBN 0-674-57910-0

To Jaroslav Průšek,
whose work made this book possible

Preface

"Modern Chinese Literature in the May Fourth Era" was a topic in search of a conference. As soon as the Social Science Research Council announced that such a conference was to be held at Endicott House in Dedham, Massachusetts, August 26-30, 1974, there was an enthusiastic response. Many scholars and graduate students had been working in this field in isolation and welcomed an opportunity to share their ideas with others. The chapters in this book are drawn from the conference and from a workshop that preceded it at the Harvard East Asian Research Center.

This book is not an encyclopedic survey of May Fourth literature. Rather, it shows the dynamics of change, discloses new material, and gives new interpretations. Consequently, there is no attempt at complete coverage. Some very important writers such as Guo Moruo, Lao She, and Ba Jin do not have chapters devoted to them, but they have already been subjects of full-length books. Others, such as Shen Congwen and the nonleftist writers associated with the Crescent Moon group, are topics of forthcoming studies. Also absent are several fine fiction writers, dramatists, and poets about whom no books have yet been written. It is hoped that this volume will act as a stimulus for major works across the wide and varied spectrum of May Fourth literature.

Our inquiry is directed backward and forward in time, as well as at May Fourth literature itself. Thus, Part One focuses on some of the forces—foreign as well as traditional—that affected not only the writers but also the whole generation of intellectuals that lived through the May Fourth era. In literary and intellectual history that era spans the period from the fall of the Manchus to the promulgation of Mao Zedong's "Talks at the Yenan Forum on Literature and Art" in May 1942. "May Fourth literature" refers to the literature written in that period, particularly the 1920s and 1930s. Part Two deals with representative writers and their works produced in the May Fourth atmosphere. Lu Xun is given disproportionate attention because of his preeminent position and influence. Part Three concludes the book with discussion of countertrends, criticism of May Fourth literature, and a perspective on May Fourth literature in relation to what existed before and what emerged afterward.

The workshop, the conference, and this book have been a group effort. Many people whose writings are not included in this volume have contributed significantly through questions, papers, and criticisms, including: Gary Bjorge, Lloyd Eastman, Lars Ellström, Donald Gibbs, Michael Gotz, Patrick Hanan, Donald Holoch, C. T. Hsia, Joe Huang, Ted Huters, Jeffrey Kinkley, Julia Lin, Lin Yu-sheng, William Lyell, William MacDonald, David Pollard, Adele Rickett, Robert Ruhlmann, Tao Tao Sanders, Richard Schirach, Benjamin I. Schwartz, Zbigniew Slupski, A. Tagore, Constantine Tung, Ranbir Vohra, Roxane Witke, and Wong Kam-ming.

Special thanks must also be given to Anna Laura Rosow and Elaine Baxter, who handled the workshop and conference arrangements and correspondence; Ellen Widmer, who was the rapporteur and has contributed valuable editorial assistance; Martin Robbins, who edited the papers and provided useful suggestions; Christopher C. Rand and Lucy M. Harris, who typed the manuscript and compiled the transliteration table; and Patrick Maddox, the representative of the Social Science Research Council. Gratitude must also be expressed to Milena Doleželová-Velingerová, Don Rimmington, William MacDonald, and Wayne Schlepp, who helped plan the conference, and especially to Ezra Vogel, whose commitment, enthusiasm, and ideas helped make the workshop and conference the stimulating beginning to this and future works.

With some exceptions, such as place names, the *pinyin* system of transliteration is used. Though in many cases it is as arbitrary as the Wade-Giles system, this system, now prevalent in the People's Republic of China, was used because it is typographically more consistent. Also, it is our hope that this book will lead to an appreciation of May Fourth literature in China as well as outside of China and among general readers as well as scholars of modern China.

Merle Goldman
Cambridge, Massachusetts

Contents

Modern Chinese Literature
in the May Fourth Era

Pinyin–Wade-Giles Conversion Table of Selected Names, Places, and Terms

Ba Jin (Pa Chin)
baihua (pai-hua)
Beida (Pei-ta)
Bing Xin (Ping Hsin)
Cao Yu (Ts'ao Yü)
Chen Duxiu (Ch'en Tu-hsiu)
Chuangzao she (Ch'uang-tsao she)
Ding Ling (Ting Ling)
Du Fu (Tu Fu)
Gongchandang (Kung-ch'an tang)
  (Communist party, CCP)
Guo Moruo (Kuo Mo-jo)
Guomindang (GMD) (Kuo-min
  tang)
guwen (ku-wen)
Hao Ran (Hao Jan)
He Qifang (Ho Ch'i-fang)
Hu Shi (Hu Shih)
Jiang Guangci (Chiang Kuang-tz'u)
Li Boyuan (Li Po-yüan)
Li Dazhao (Li Ta-chao)
Liang Qichao (Liang Ch'i-ch'ao)
Lu Xun (Lu Hsün)
Mao Dun (Mao Tun)
Mao Zedong (Mao Tse-tung)
Qu Qiubai (Ch'ü Ch'iu-pai)

Rou Shi (Jou Shih)
Shen Congwen (Shen Ts'ung-wen)
Tian Han (T'ien Han)
Wen Yiduo (Wen I-to)
Wenxue yanjiu hui (Wen-hsüeh
yen-chiu hui)
wenyan (wen-yen)
Xiao Jun (Hsiao Chün)
Xiaoshuo yuebao (Hsiao-shuo yüeh-pao)
Xin qingnian (Hsin ch'ing-nien)
Xu Zhimo (Hsü Chih-mo)
Ye Shengtao (Yeh Sheng-t'ao) (also
  known as Ye Shaojun [Yeh Shao-
  chün])
Yu Dafu (Yü Ta-fu)
Zhang Henshui (Chang Hen-shui)
Zheng Zhenduo (Cheng Chen-to)
Zhou Enlai (Chou En-lai)
Zhou Yang (Chou Yang)
Zhou Zuoren (Chou Tso-jen)
Zhu Ziqing (Chu Tzu-ch'ing)

Introduction

The May Fourth Movement began as a demonstration on May 4, 1919, against the Peking government, which had complied with the decision of the Western powers at Versailles to cede the province of Shantung to Japan. This demonstration provoked others, including the May Thirtieth movement of 1925. But the May Fourth movement was more than the opening attack on domestic weakness and foreign imperialism. It stimulated and galvanized an incipient cultural movement, growing since the late nineteenth century, that was directed at throwing off the weight of China's Confucian tradition and absorbing Western culture. This cultural movement culminated in the early decades of the twentieth century in a literary flowering that was one of the most creative and brilliant episodes in modern Chinese history.

With the rejection of tradition and increasing internal chaos, China's intellectuals and youth in different ways sought to assert a new order. Some, like Mao Zedong, Li Dazhao, and Chen Duxiu, responded with political action. Others, like Lu Xun, Mao Dun, and Guo Moruo, responded by creating a new literature that would establish new values and a new consciousness. Their purpose, like that of their political counterparts, was to "save" China and to integrate her into the modern world. In this effort, these writers avidly devoured the literature and thought of the Western world, searching for models for their creative expression. Though Versailles may have shaken their faith in the Western powers, it did not shake their belief that Western culture was relevant to China's needs. In varying degrees, they absorbed all the main trends in Western culture — romanticism, realism, naturalism, and symbolism. In a short period, they fashioned a modern literature.

The formative process was not easy. Though the traditional styles of

1

literature were consciously discarded, the influence of tradition lay heavily on the May Fourth writers. As Ezra Vogel points out in "The Unlikely Heroes: The Social Role of the May Fourth Writers," these writers were schooled in that tradition. Further, the values and standards of Western literature that Chinese writers aspired to imitate and absorb had been produced by a society and culture totally remote from China. Most difficult for these writers was the fact that they were personally caught up in the political crises of the time. The cooperation between the Guomindang and the Chinese Communist party in launching the Northern Expedition in 1926 to unite the country was broken in 1927 by Chiang Kai-shek's bloody coup against the Communist party in Shanghai. The coup not only sent the Communist party underground but split the Guomindang into the left wing in Wuhan and the Chiang Kai-shek wing in Shanghai. These events, plus the Guomindang's weak response to Japanese encroachments in Manchuria in the early 1930s, led the majority of May Fourth writers, under their acknowledged leader Lu Xun, to the Communist party either as members or sympathizers. Though after 1927 many of them became discouraged by the possibility of change, they believed even more intensely that China needed a total revolution to survive.

Their increasing radicalization was intensified by their own personal experiences. Most of them gathered in Shanghai, the mecca of China's young writers in the 1920s and 1930s. They were attracted not only because Lu Xun was there but also because the foreign settlements in Shanghai offered some free movement and some opportunities for opponents of the Guomindang government to publish dissenting views. Harold Isaacs, who lived in the foreign settlements, has described the atmosphere in his introduction to *Straw Sandals*.[1] Alongside a teeming native population lived the usual colonial groups: the privileged caste of foreigners, a wealthy native upper class and large white-collar class living off the foreign enterprises, and rival gangs involved in smuggling, gambling, and prostitution. Moving among these groups were political dissidents — and most of China's writers. Their position was precarious. Not only were they financially insecure but also their increasingly radical and pro-Communist statements exposed them to attack. Guomindang agents, conniving with the foreign authorities, destroyed their publishing houses and bookstores and subjected them to censorship, intimidation, kidnapping, and even murder. Despite such repression, the restraints of total political control and civil war did not entirely silence them. As Isaacs explained, because of the inefficiency "narrow openings remained in this system through which much did pass."[2]

As they committed themselves to a leftist position in the late 1920s and 1930s, a number of important writers shifted the focus of their work from their own personal experience and individual vision to more ideological and programmatic themes. Writers like Mao Dun and Ding Ling moved from stories of individuals and individual consciousness to panoramic treatments of class consciousness and great social and economic forces. Portrayals of contradictions within the individual were replaced by portrayals of contradictions within society. This pattern followed a trend apparent in the West, but their shift of focus was more a result of their own experiences in China. Some writers at this time even questioned the value of the Western literature they had adopted so uncritically. Yet here, too, there were "openings." Despite their growing disillusionment, their aesthetic and cultural tastes, as Bonnie McDougall discusses in "The Impact of Western Literary Trends," were still conditioned by Western standards. Furthermore, as the essays on Mao Dun by John Berninghausen and Ding Ling by Yi-tsi Feuerwerker demonstrate, although their work had become highly politicized, these writers still expressed the individuality and creativity that had characterized their work in the mid-1920s.

The explosive events and chaotic environment in which they participated and lived appeared to kindle rather than stifle their creative energies. The May Fourth literary outburst burned for over two decades until it was smothered by the bombing of Shanghai in 1937 and the dispersion of most writers to the hinterlands as they fled the Japanese and the Guomindang. Gradual implementation of Mao's dictum that politics control art presented in his "Talks at the Yenan Forum on Literature and Art" in 1942 finally extinguished the lingering glow of May Fourth literature.

The "Extrinsic" versus the "Intrinsic" Approach

The contributors to this book — scholars of Chinese literature as well as historians and social scientists, — regard the political, social, economic, moral, and artistic forces of the May Fourth era as inextricably mixed together in the May Fourth literature. Several different approaches are appropriate for analyzing this literature, and the various essays emphasize these differences. Most combine the "extrinsic" and "intrinsic," the historical and literary, approach to May Fourth literature. Some, however, stress that the "extrinsic" approach, which interprets literature in its sociopolitical and biographical context, gives more insight into the literature and the times. Others maintain that because literature is being studied, the "intrinsic" approach, which treats literature in its own terms, is more illuminating.

Those who emphasize the "extrinsic" approach believe that the literary works of the 1920s and 1930s go deeper than any other sources in revealing the conflict between tradition and change in the May Fourth era. These works provide unique insights into the convulsive social and human changes that accompanied the transition from the disintegrating old society to the revolutionary new one. The writers' lives, as well as their work, were microcosms of their civilization in transition. Reared in the Confucian tradition, they became adults in an age of revolution that exposed them to new and foreign ideas. They witnessed civil and foreign wars, were involved in the political conflicts of the times, and suffered personal anguish. Their efforts to understand these events and the tensions between the old and the new are reflected in their works. It could be said that as Trollope and Dickens depicted England's Victorian age and Turgenev and Tolstoy described the nineteenth-century landed Russian elite, the May Fourth writers portrayed the Chinese urban, upper- and middle-class world in transition to a new society.

Some writers, as Yü-shih Chen's essay on Mao Dun points out, allegorically reproduced specific political events in fiction. The Chinese Communist experience in the Nanchang Uprising and the effort to break with the Comintern are symbolically depicted in Mao Dun's story "Gulingzhi qiu" (Autumn in Kuling). But most works deal more generally with the political and social events of a generation in an age of turmoil. Indeed, many works are stories of youth trapped in and rebelling against the traditional society. Some of them may have been autobiographical, but they are also biographies of their generation. Their frustrations and dreams are also the frustrations and dreams of an entire generation's search for meaning and purpose in a China these writers described as prostrate, morally bankrupt, politically disjointed, oppressed by warlords and bureaucrats, and humiliated by foreign powers. Their works express their generation's indignation with what Lu Xun called the "man-eating" traditional society. They are filled with their excitement and enthusiasm for revolution and subsequent disillusionment when it was not realized, their vacillation in time of violent struggle, their desperate pursuit of personal happiness, and their emotional and mental agitation as they broke from Confucian morality. Theirs was a mixed and contradictory picture, but a true picture of their times and of the circles in which they lived.

Ezra Vogel writes that the May Fourth writers were more successful in interpreting their times than in changing them. "They could not solve problems but in their writings they could capture the drama." Yet the essays of Leo Ou-fan Lee and Harriet Mills on Lu Xun and those by Feuerwerker on Ding Ling and Berninghausen on Mao Dun also show that, as the most sensitive and articulate spokesmen, they not only interpreted but also guided their generation. They were rebelling against their Confucian heritage, but they were a part of it because they believed that as literati they had a responsibility to lead. At the same time, their view of themselves was also inspired by the Western image of the writer standing outside of society so that he can criticize and reform it. Also, like their Chinese predecessors, they assumed that society's essence was found in its culture and literature. If the revolution were to succeed, cultural change was even more important than political and economic change. As intellectuals and writers, they regarded themselves — and were regarded by their contemporaries — as the primary molders of society. They used their literary works as weapons to win personal, national, and revolutionary change. Some of them, as Mills points out in her study of Lu Xun, became frustrated by the ineffectiveness of their literary weapons to achieve change and turned from creative work to direct political commentary. Perhaps Lu Xun's subtle ironies could no longer fully express the massive social and political upheaval.

Though their literary weapons may not have achieved the revolution they sought, their efforts helped engender the revolutionary spirit that made possible the end of one civilization and the beginning of a new one. Their highly articulate and emotionally charged perceptions not only reflected reality but because of their power also helped to change that reality. Making their readers conscious of what the readers had not yet perceived led them toward change. The May Fourth writers provided the symbols, images, and models for their generation. True, many of their characters, such as Lu Xun's Ah Q and Yu Dafu's protagonist in "Chenlun" (Sinking), are submissive, passive, and self-deluding. A number of famous works show the society's diseases without prescribing remedies. But revealing the diseases and pains of their society challenged their readers to find cures. Ding Ling's stories of unattached, sexually liberated young women living in the city induced her readers, as Feuerwerker demonstrates, to liberate themselves from the old mores and to realize their own identities.

Because most May Fourth literature is both politically committed in statement and documentary in nature, there is a body of scholarly

5

opinion that tends to minimize its artistic value. This opinion views much May Fourth literature as sentimental, verbose, and florid. May Fourth literature was written quickly and lacked the careful analysis of responsible literary critics. Yet, other scholars counter that literature that had the power to capture the imagination of a generation of educated youth must have had other qualities than the ability to record history or move readers to tears. According to Milena Doleželová-Velingerová and her student Michael Egan who were trained in the Czech school of literary analysis, works that could convey the seething political and social turmoil of the time so dramatically that they provoked readers into action must have artistic merit. Historians, social scientists, and biographers can explain why writers have certain views toward their society and how literary works express their times. But these scholars stress that because writers create literature, their work should be ultimately judged by artistic standards. May Fourth literature, like all literature, did more than illustrate a period's political and social realities. The writers developed an aesthetic and a style of their own to express the events, attitudes, and human relationships of China in the 1920s and 1930s. The fiction form they used was not merely a structure that covered the materials. Through organization, language, metaphor, symbols, allegory, contrast, color, use of time, and psychological nuance, they arranged the material in their own terms.

By their analysis of several literary works, Doleželová, Egan, Berninghausen, Feuerwerker, and Birch demonstrate that May Fourth literature has artistic qualities beyond reflecting social reality. Not all the writers were successful, but nearly all sought in their writings to express not only political views but artistic skill. Feuerwerker, for example, shows that while Ding Ling was committed to using literature to achieve sexual and political liberation, she was also obsessed with perfecting her literary technique, even when her work asserted a specific political line. Most May Fourth writers collected, filtered, reorganized, and subjected to artistic control their nation's and their own experience. The result was a unique artistic rendering of reality.

Those scholars trained in the Czech school, specifically in structuralism, also argue that a genuine understanding of a piece of literature is not gained from examining its biographical references, its social and political setting, or even its ideological viewpoint. It is to be found in analyzing its structure, because the structure reveals the writer's true feelings and thoughts. Doleželová's study of the structure of Lu Xun's short story "Medicine" not only reveals Lu Xun's literary skill but his vision of the world. He used dialogue fragments to disclose information indirectly and nonlinear time shifts to merge past, present, and future. The mundane conversation among the superstitious customers of a tea shop suggest, explain, and belittle the great changes going on around them. The characters' perceptions as expressed in snips of dialogue and the momentous events they reveal are related in counterpoint. The events of revolution and martyrdom are interwoven with expressions of ignorance and superstition in a structural counterpoint that subtly reveals the conflict between tradition and revolution. As Doleželová demonstrates, content is an integral part of the form, but the form is also an integral part of the content. Patrick Hanan has written elsewhere that the very obliqueness and suggestiveness of Lu Xun's work produce its powerful impact.[3] Whether the subtlety of the work indicates the threat of censorship or whether it derives solely from his aesthetic imagination, there is no question that Lu Xun was a conscious artist. He shaped a literary technique learned from the West and from his own heritage into a rare artistry.

Other May Fourth writers also consciously used such modern literary techniques as nonchronological time, juxtapositioning of contrasts, and psychological insight. Egan analyzes Yu Dafu's use of these techniques in his story "Sinking." He also shows that Yu, like Lu Xun, exploited the contrast between illusion and reality and used color impressionistically to create mood. The result was a work that was emotive without being explicit. The supposedly realistic writer Mao Dun, as Berninghausen and Yü-shih Chen demonstrate, specifically described the large political happenings through evocative images, ambiguous allegory, and subtle symbols. Even in Ding Ling's writings, which contain so much of her own life experience, there is, as Feuerwerker points out, a boundary between fact and fiction, experience and story. The seemingly haphazard depiction of events in some of her works reflects fluctuating moods and deep emotions. The style expresses the content, giving the random quality of her use of detail an aesthetic purpose and coherence.

Those who emphasize the "intrinsic" approach effectively prove that May Fourth literature was the product of individual inspiration and artistry. Yet they also affirm that the materials filtered through the writer's imagination and art were the social, political, economic, and international urgencies of the era. Both the "intrinsic" and "extrinsic" approaches are valid because May Fourth writers had a commitment to both art and society. Therefore, in analyzing May Fourth literature, it is necessary to adopt approaches that are not strictly literary, historical, or sociological. Because of the close relationship between literature and society, a creative synthesis of all these approaches is needed in order to understand May Fourth literature as well as the May Fourth era.

It is true that for some writers this dual commitment to both art and society was to become a contradiction: Lu Xun decided to abandon creative literature, while the poet He Qifang retreated from his social commitment. Nevertheless, most writers, even Lu Xun in his political commentary and He Qifang in his more abstract poetry, sought to strike a balance between their commitment to their aesthetic standards and their political vision. Some stressed social content, others artistic technique. But as these essays demonstrate, May Fourth literary works as a whole projected an individual yet generalized, unique yet representative, conceptual yet realistic picture of life in a society undergoing revolutionary change. Because these works were artistically compelling as well as socially relevant, they, more than the era's political doctrines and slogans, captured the imagination and transformed the outlook of a generation of educated Chinese youth.

Foreign versus Native Influences

Another major area of debate focuses on the nature of the May Fourth movement — whether it was an inherent development that had been evolving since the late Qing period or whether it was fomented by the influx of foreign ideas in the early twentieth century. There is general agreement that there were both foreign and native influences on May Fourth literature, but disagreement comes over the degree of influence.

Those associated with the Czech school emphasize that May Fourth literature evolved from a transformation of literature and language under way since the nineteenth century. According to this group, the May Fourth movement was merely the catalyst for a development that would have occurred without the inflow of Western ideas. The May Fourth writers were conscious iconoclasts in their rejection of traditional conventions and modes of writing, but in practice their rejection was far from total. Although they sought foreign inspiration, Dole-želová in her chapter "The Origins of Modern Chinese Literature," shows their debt to China's popular literary tradition and to late Qing changes in the language and function of literature. In fact, in the eighteenth century, Chinese novels such as *Hong lou meng (Dream of the red chamber)* had already dealt with emotional relationships. And, as

Doleželová points out, by the late Qing period a number of Chinese novelists had dispensed with the traditional episodic structure linked by the actions of the hero and had developed a coherent plot with fewer characters. Late Qing also saw an increase in fiction written in the colloquial language (*baihuawen*) at the expense of the traditional literary genres of poetry and the essay written in the classical language (*wenyan*). Similarly, Lee explains that Lu Xun's early interest in the "unorthodox" Chinese folklore tradition stimulated his interest in Western literature. Ideologically, he was committed to total iconoclasm, but creatively he still clung to some features of the popular and even the orthodox tradition. These essays substantiate, therefore, the connection between traditional literature and modern literature. Further, because the literary tradition was already changing, the preconditions existed for the emergence of a dynamic new literature. May Fourth writers were attracted to Western literature because they had already been exposed to similar themes and devices in their own literature. Thus, their fascination with foreign sources was less the cause than the effect of changes already under way.

Other contributors agree that native preconditions had to exist before change could be absorbed. But they argue that the Western impact in the early twentieth century accelerated the literary changes that Doleželová described in the late Qing from minor, desultory, and disconnected trends into a major and dominant movement. Though educated men had read and even composed vernacular literature much earlier than the Qing, there had been few major changes in the narrative techniques and purposes of that literature. This group of essayists contends that the literature of the 1920s and the 1930s was not simply literature that had evolved from the late Qing, nor did it derive from innovations within the popular tradition. The Western impact brought with it new genres, techniques, approaches, and ideas that transformed late Qing trends in language and genre reform into a movement of unprecedented creativity.

Undoubtedly, much of the May Fourth writers' discussion of Western literature and theory was superficial. Ellen Widmer's chapter "Qu Qiubai and Russian Literature," suggests that portions of Qu's early analyses of Russian literature may simply have been paraphrases of Russian sources. Nevertheless, though Qu's study of the subject stemmed from concerns that were primarily nationalistic, in the process he absorbed many of the ideas and techniques of Western literature. Irene Eber in "Images of Oppressed Peoples and Modern Chinese Literature," shows how the spirit of nationalism was commu-

9

nicated to China through the translation of the works of the oppressed peoples in Europe. Even the Japanese influence, according to Ching-mao Cheng in "The Impact of Japanese Literary Trends on Modern Chinese Writers," went beyond transmitting Western literature in translation. Japanese writers such as Mori Ōgai and Natsume Sōseki directly influenced Chinese writers. Further, as Perry Link discusses in "Traditional-style Popular Urban Fiction in the Teens and Twenties," the native preconditions for a new literature may not have existed if the Western impact had not encouraged the establishment of commercial publishers, an increase in literacy, the growth of an urban middle class, and the publication of newspapers with literary supplements.

The modern short story, the major genre of the May Fourth writers, was also an import from the West. Doleželová explains that the old literary forms could no longer express the reality of twentieth-century China. The Western short story proved more appropriate. Unlike the novel, it did not have a plot with a beginning and an end, but revealed a slice of life where the conflict was less in the action than in the character's mind. This genre could more effectively reflect an individual's inner conflicts as he moved from the old to the new society. As Feuerwerker comments, in order to articulate the individual's inner conflict, the self had to be dramatized. Consequently, the focus on the individual's consciousness also brought in another Western import — the first-person narrator.

The May Fourth writers were attracted to these Western techniques because of their own needs and because their own literary tradition did not supply the means to express them. They may not have read Freud, but because of their own concern with psychological motivation as they themselves broke the bonds of family and tradition, they were drawn to the Western use of psychological insight to depict individual emotions and interpersonal relations. Most May Fourth writers were also intrigued with European and Russian literature's focus on social issues, but some rejected Western realism and naturalism as a means to deal with social questions. They chose other Western models. Douwe Fokkema shows that Lu Xun's ironic view of reality led him to the semiromanticism of Gogol and Andreyev. Andreyev's fusion of symbolism and realism, which Lu Xun stated "dissolves the difference between the inner world and outward manifestation," was a model that attracted Lu Xun. His indirect method of narrative, Hanan believes, was drawn from Andreyev.[4]

As one group of essays demonstrates that May Fourth literature was less discontinuous with the past than heretofore believed, another group demonstrates that contact with Western culture continued longer than previously thought. It has been generally accepted that after the early 1930s the trend toward the left and the obsession with mass and proletarian literature turned most writers away from the West, except for Soviet and Marxist literature. Yet McDougall argues that interest in Western literature did not disappear in the 1930s. Most writers became fervently anti-imperialist and pro-Marxist but were attracted to Western cultural models long after the turn toward the left. According to Widmer, this was even true of Qu Qiubai, one of the strongest exponents of anti-imperialism. He rejected May Fourth literature as too foreign for China but continued to be emotionally drawn to Western literature, particularly nineteenth-century Russian literature. As Mao Zedong rightly observed during the Cultural Revolution, Western culture and literary influence were deeply ingrained in the consciousness of the May Fourth intellectuals.

Nevertheless, in the study of the May Fourth literary movement, as in the study of modern Chinese history, there has been a move away from an emphasis on foreign influence toward an emphasis on native influence as a decisive force of change. Criticizing this trend, Paul Cohen, in an article published elsewhere on reform in the late Qing, explains that whereas previously there was an overemphasis on foreign influences, now there is an excessive emphasis on native forces. He cautions that "one can sin by defining the importance of one locus of emphasis in terms of the relative unimportance of another — and alternative — locus."[5] This polarization occurs in these essays. Yet what emerges from them, despite their different emphases, is that May Fourth literature was a hybrid that fused native and foreign influences. It was affected by both cultures but was not merely derivative. There is no question that the West's role was enormous in shaping China's intellectual life. At no other time, even in the period of Buddhist influence, was China so exposed to an alien culture. There is also no question that the impetus for change was already in motion before the May Fourth period. Consequently, new perceptions and new techniques were absorbed into a movement ready to accept them. The complex interaction between Western themes and Chinese material, and between Western techniques and Chinese inclinations, triggered the May Fourth creative explosion.

The Impact of May Fourth Literature

Some Western scholars, as well as China's present leadership, are skeptical of the relevance of May Fourth literature to China's problems in the early decades of the twentieth century. They question whether a literature concerned with a small circle of middle-class, urban intellectuals and written in a Western-oriented language and style, totally divorced from the experience of the Chinese masses, could reflect a society in revolution. They suggest that the elite who monopolized Chinese literature were even more alienated than the traditional elite because they were immersed in a foreign culture and engaged in artificial, self-conscious experiments. In some ways, they had less contact with Chinese realities than the old literati.

Some of these criticisms were expressed in the early 1930s by Qu Qiubai, the first Marxist to criticize the May Fourth movement. He called May Fourth literature an aberration, a foreign import without roots in China. Because of the May Fourth writers' total rejection of their own culture and their uncritical embrace of Western culture, including Marxism, the trickling down of culture to the common people that occurred in the West did not happen in China. As a result, intellectuals and writers were unable to communicate with the masses. To correct this situation, Qu exhorted writers to develop a style and content that was related to the realities of the masses and that could be understood by the ordinary Chinese. Paul Pickowicz interprets Qu's criticisms and proposals as creative efforts to adapt foreign aesthetics and foreign theory, including Marxism, to China's realities. In his chapter "Qu Qiubai's Critique of the May Fourth Generation: Early Chinese Marxist Literary Criticism," Pickowicz finds that Qu pioneered in the "Sinification" of Marxist literary thought. Qu was censured by the Chinese Communist party for his failings as a political leader, but his criticism of the May Fourth writers and his proposals to "Sinify" modern Chinese culture were accepted by many Chinese revolutionaries and emphasized by Mao Zedong in his "Talks at the Yenan Forum on Literature and Art" and in the Cultural Revolution.

The urban Butterfly literature described by Perry Link had more connections with the ordinary Chinese than May Fourth literature. Butterfly literature was a persistent trend from the pre–May Fourth period through the 1920s and the 1930s into the post–May Fourth period. In fact, as Link shows, the popular literature tradition continued in the guise of Butterfly literature. The content certainly was not revolutionary, but Butterfly literature reached large numbers of people, at least in the cities, primarily because its models were drawn for the most part from China's own vernacular tradition. Butterfly stories were easy to read because their direct, traditional-style vernacular was more accessible to the ordinary Chinese than the more

Westernized May Fourth vernacular. The syntax, vocabulary, and narrative were closer to the tales of the traditional storyteller enjoyed by the common people than the more Westernized grammar, vocabulary, and style of the May Fourth writers. Furthermore, like traditional popular literature, the stories were action-packed and the characters were usually all good or all bad. The purpose of Butterfly stories was escapist, but their characters exemplified a conservative attitude toward popular Chinese values and a hostile or ambivalent position toward the alien culture of the West. Thus, Butterfly literature was a link between premodern popular literature and present-day mass literature.

Despite its immense importance in recording and fomenting revolutionary change and its debt to tradition, May Fourth literature is regarded by Cyril Birch as an anomaly in China's cultural history. His chapter "Change and Continuity in Chinese Fiction," underlines its anomalous position by viewing May Fourth literature in perspective. He compares the characters, style, grammar, and ideas of a May Fourth piece of literature with both those of a traditional piece and those of a post-1949 piece. Within this context, there is greater continuity between pre–May Fourth and post–May Fourth literature than between either of these and May Fourth literature. Pre–May Fourth and post-May Fourth literature resemble each other in their optimistic, easily understood reflections of the ideals of society. They also resemble each other in their heroic characters, in the role of an impersonal order, and in their sense that society is organized in a specific way. Individual personalities do not transcend the roles the characters play in their society. In contrast, May Fourth characters are principally nonheroes. As they confront new realities, their individual personalities transcend their assigned identities. Besides the content, May Fourth literature is anomalous in style. Though Doleželová has shown continuities with late Qing literary style, the subtleties, ambiguities, psychological complexities, and subjectivity in May Fourth fiction have little place in traditional or post-1949 literature.

Although Birch, like Qu Qiubai, argues that May Fourth literature was an anomaly, he does not conclude as did Qu that because it was an anomaly, it was irrelevant and not revolutionary. In fact, Birch's paper regards May Fourth literature as a revolutionary force and post-1949 literature as relatively more conservative in respect to traditional values and style. Though May Fourth literature may have been an anomaly, that does not mean, as Qu and others have stated, that it had no roots in Chinese soil. Several essays in this book show that nothing was accepted in China for which the soil was not prepared. Obviously, the soil had already been cultivated enough by the intellectual and social ferment of the times to accept the roots of May Fourth literature. How else can we explain the potency of May Fourth characters, plots, and language and its power to inspire and guide a generation of youth? That the May Fourth mode of literature was rejected in the post-1949 period does not mean it was still a foreign substance. Its rejection did not occur spontaneously but was dictated by political authority. It is impossible to know if today's prescribed literature is any more representative of the desires of the masses than May Fourth literature. If current controls over culture and literature were loosened, Benjamin Schwartz has suggested, May Fourth trends would reappear.

May Fourth writers may have failed to achieve what they sought through literary means, but if they failed, it was not so much because of their revolutionary shortcomings and talents but because of the world in which they lived. Not only were they constrained by the weight of their own tradition and the increasing stridency of debate, didacticism, and factionalism, but also they were given too little time to develop their talents before being buffeted and dispersed by the Japanese invasion and civil war. Perhaps most important, their literary weapon was inadequate to deal with the crises of the time and actually achieve revolution. Literature can voice protest, fury, and resistance. It can also prepare the way for revolution and provoke response to change. But it cannot conduct the actual revolution.

Though May Fourth literature did not accomplish the revolution its authors sought, it stood apart from what came before and what came after as a revolutionary movement. Its writers showed courage and zeal in experimenting with content and technique. They produced works of unprecedented and varied creativeness. Some were of lasting significance. Tragically, their potentialities were unfulfilled. Yet, seen in the larger context of China's recent history, their works exemplified the struggle, idealism, revolutionary qualities, and at times even the brilliance they so avidly pursued.

Part One

The Native and Foreign Impact

Changes in literature were under way in China in the nineteenth century before the May Fourth movement. Milena Doleželová-Velingerová shows in "The Origins of Modern Chinese Literature" that in the late Qing period there were already evolutionary changes in literary genre and in the use of the vernacular before the movement to vernacularize the language in 1915–1919.

In the early decades of the twentieth century, Western cultural currents converged on this rippling stream and transformed these ripples into a literary torrent of unprecedented vitality and freshness. Bonnie McDougall in "The Impact of Western Literary Trends" describes the varied course of the Western inflow. At first the impact was overwhelming. It subsided in left-wing circles in the late 1920s, but remained strong among a small group of less politically oriented writers. Then, in the early 1930s, Western intellectual currents found their way again into left-wing literary journals and organizations and remained vigorous even when May Fourth writers increasingly identified with communism and Soviet literary theories.

Ching-mao Cheng in "The Impact of Japanese Literary Trends" describes how Western culture flowed into China by means of Japanese translations and Japanized Western theory. But Japan was not merely a conveyor of Western culture, though that was extremely important. Some of Japan's own cultural influence — both in style and content — washed off in the process of transmission.

Douwe Fokkema and Ellen Widmer show that the Russian cultural impact took different forms with different writers, implying that May Fourth cultural and literary borrowings were not as indiscriminate as they appeared. The Russian literature that attracted Lu Xun, Fokkema points out, was not the standard realist literature of the nineteenth

15

century. Rather, it was the pre- and postrealist writers like the partial romanticist Gogol and the symbolists like Andreyev who caught Lu Xun's attention. Fokkema attributes Lu Xun's mythological emphasis, multilayered meanings, and indirect narrative techniques to the influence of these Russian writers.

Whereas Lu Xun was drawn to Russian symbolism, the Communist literary theorist Qu Qiubai was drawn to the Russian realists Pushkin, Turgenev, and Tolstoy. Widmer's case study of Qu depicts a phenomenon that McDougall describes in general — the contradiction between Qu's demand for literary works that promote the proletarian revolution and his great appreciation of Russian literature of the gentry era.

Irene Eber shows that May Fourth writers were also attracted to the literary works of the oppressed peoples of Europe because their own concerns were similar to the concerns of these peoples — aggression, national identity, social inequality, the urban poor, and toiling peasants. They also looked to these works for literary techniques and experiments with language that would give them as wide an audience as possible.

Historical evolution in combination with radical changes provoked by the Western impact mark the transition in China from the traditional to a new society. The same forces mark China's transition from the traditional to a new literature.

1.

The Origins of Modern Chinese Literature

Milena Doleželová-Velingerová

Until about ten years ago, it was mainly the political and social forces and the influence of Western literature that were studied to clarify the formative process of modern Chinese literature. Although the contribution of external factors is indisputable, there are intrinsic factors that were equally indispensable for the formation of a new literature: the evolution of domestic literary traditions and the evolution of a new literary language. In particular, the development of modern Chinese literature — especially in its beginning — was characterized by the dominance of two phenomena: the *baihua*, or vernacular language, and fiction. This situation contrasts sharply with that of premodern times, when *wenyan*, the written classical language, was the paramount and most prestigious literary language, and poetry and the essay were the most esteemed literary genres. It is because of these sudden changes, as well as the iconoclastic character of the May Fourth movement, that the Chinese literature of the 1920s and 1930s generally has been treated as a phenomenon disconnected from the literary tradition. The year 1917, when Hu Shi and Chen Duxiu published their two famous articles on literary reform, has been accepted as a convenient starting point for modern Chinese literature.[1] But a closer look at the years immediately preceding the rise of the new literature reveals substantial changes in the literary and language situation. Moreover, these changes had been coming for several decades and were largely realized during the late Qing era.

The rise of modern Chinese literature, therefore, should be understood as part of a continuous process into which even the most discontinuous revolutionary periods and strongest foreign influences have to be integrated.[2] Equally significant is the close connection between the developments of language and literature. A better understanding of these developments will explain why fiction, the outcast in traditional Chinese literature, became the dominant literary genre in modern Chinese literature.

The Rise of the Modern Standard Language

During the late teens and twenties, young Chinese intellectuals fervently discussed the creation of a modern Chinese literary language.[3] Their discussions clearly show that the solution of the language problem was necessary to create a modern literature. But in studies dealing with modern Chinese literature, the language problem has been largely neglected and poorly understood. Generally, the rise of modern standard Chinese has been presented in a rather simplified form — the substitution of a "living" language (baihua) for a "dead" language (wenyan). This simplification assumes that the language of literature is the only use of language and ignores the development of language in other fields of communication — administration, journalism, science, the humanities, education, and so forth. In other words, the language situation in premodern China was complicated by the fact that several classical and vernacular language forms were being used concurrently to fulfill specific communicative functions. Like every nation in the early stages of modernization, however, China had to create a standard literary language from among these numerous parochial forms that could be used for both written and oral communication and in all human activities.

In the middle of the nineteenth century, there were three languages or language forms, each with a limited number of functions: wenyan, baihua, and various southern local dialects *(tuhua)* and koines *(fangyan)*, regional dialects whose status was raised to that of a common language in a larger area.[4]

Wenyan was exclusively a written language used for literature and philosophical, historical, educational, political, journalistic, and scientific writings, as well as personal correspondence. As mentioned earlier, it was the most prestigious language form in premodern China because of its use in poetry and essays, which were the core of orthodox literature according to Confucian aesthetics and the traditional division of literature. Wenyan, however, lacked a standard pronunciation; it could be pronounced according to any of the various dialects.

The northern vernacular language (baihua) was spoken as well as written. The spoken form (commonly called *guanhua* or Mandarin until the early twentieth century) originated as a medium of oral communication between imperial officials who were recruited from various regions in China and could not easily communicate because of the great differences among Chinese dialects. Based on the dialect of the administrative center, Peking, spoken baihua during the nineteenth century became widely used among bureaucrats and businessmen and spread throughout northern China, acquiring the character of a koine. Its pronunciation, however, continued to reflect its origin in Peking. Also, its function was limited to a medium of communication for administration, law, business, and trade.

The written form of northern baihua, called *baihuawen*, had become a well-established and sophisticated language by the middle of the last century, principally because it was used in novels, drama, and storytellers' written narratives. The baihuawen used in the famous novels of the eighteenth and nineteenth centuries, for example, closely approximates the northern spoken baihua.

The widespread southern koines, such as Cantonese, Wu, and Min, assumed roles similar to those of northern baihua. In their spoken forms, they functioned as common languages among businessmen, and in their written forms, they were used for plays and storytellers' written narratives. By about 1850, the most conspicuous difference between northern baihua and the various southern koines was the size and the location of the geographical areas to which they belonged. But in the second half of the nineteenth century, the southern regions became more prosperous and important than the northern areas, so that one of the southern koines could conceivably have challenged the northern baihua as a standard language for the whole of China.

Thus, the distribution of the three main forms of language cannot be described in terms of a simple oral-written polarity. Rather, each form was assigned a particular function in everyday activities and a particular genre in literature. Moreover, because this assignment corresponded to the current class stratification of Chinese society, it remained very stable.

During the period from 1870 to 1890, however, the demarcation lines separating the three language forms began to blur. The process was accelerated by an active movement for language reform, triggered by the domestic political reform movement and by acquaintance with the language situation in Japan and the West. The theoretical and practical efforts undertaken by late Qing reformers and writers at the turn of the century were aimed at using written baihua in fields previously occupied by wenyan. Characteristically, the movement started in the south, where China first became familiar with Western techniques and cultural concepts, and where the need for mass education was felt most urgently. The surprising fact that the southerners began to promote the northern language form clearly indicated the advantages of northern baihua over the southern language forms.

Actually, the vernacular had already somewhat expanded its function twenty years before the movement for written baihua began. In the 1870s written baihua was used in journalism and various other fields, challenging the previous "monopoly" of wenyan. The language situation at the turn of the century, therefore, cannot be explained only as the result of the language reform movement. Rather, the conscious efforts of the language reformers for the recognition of the vernacular stemmed from actual changes in the language situation and, of course, these efforts accelerated the development.

The first field where written baihua was adopted concurrently with wenyan was journalism. Until the third quarter of the nineteenth century, foreign missionaries largely used a language they called "easy *wenli*," which conformed to classical syntax but was restricted mostly to familiar characters and phrases. In the 1870s missionaries began writing in baihuawen, and several vernacular societies were founded to publish religious periodicals.[5] At the same time, newspaper editors tried to reach a wider readership. When the famous *Shen bao* (Shanghai news), began publication in 1872, the editors announced that they would write not only for the educated but also for "peasants, laborers, businessmen, and merchants." In 1876 *Shen bao* was enriched by a supplement, *Min bao* (People's news), a paper for "women and working men." This supplement was probably the first newspaper using a pure written baihua.[6]

By the turn of the century, written baihua was being used in the revolutionary press, and in journals for women,[7] not only for news items but also for the popularization of and education in history, geography, school reform, industry, and science. This development led to a necessary adoption of new terms in written baihua. In 1913 A. H. Mateer was able to compile a lexicon of the new terminology in written baihua. The glossary contained hundreds of expressions covering administration, medicine, sciences, and the military, as well as terms for objects imported from the West.[8]

Here and elsewhere many new terms were borrowed from languages — such as Japanese — that used Chinese characters and that had already incorporated translations of Western concepts and artifacts. The Chinese would borrow translated expressions in their character form and ascribe to them their appropriate baihua pronunciation.[9] In this way, for example, *diguozhuyi* (imperialism), *anshazhuyi* (terrorism), *lixian* (constitution), and many other terms entered the Chinese vocabulary. In this respect, the journal *Yishu huibian* (Collected translations), published in Japan by Chinese students during the first years of the twentieth century, played a major role. Many outstanding works by German, French, American, English, and Japanese political thinkers and economists appeared here for the first time in Chinese. Such Western texts, however, were invariably translated from Japanese translations, which accelerated the adoption of political and economic terms from the Japanese.[10]

The Japanese influence was also strong in the field of modern education. Chen Ronggun, who studied primary school education in Japan in the late 1890s, opened a textbook publishing house in Macao after 1898, when the failure of the reform movement prevented his return to China. From his textbooks Chen Ronggun eliminated the texts of the classics. Instead, he wrote *Furu sanzishu* (A primer for women and children), with texts in written baihua describing daily life.

Another reformer, Shi Chongen, who directed the famous publishing house Biaomeng in Shanghai at the beginning of the twentieth century, promoted written baihua in schools and business. He compiled illustrated textbooks with facing texts of the classics and their baihua translations. Besides issuing the first up-to-date illustrated written baihua dictionary, he also published a manual for business letters in written baihua to meet the increased need for a common business language.

The power of the vernacular to convey ideas and to influence people was soon recognized by more than just the reformers. A great many popular books in written baihua were published, mostly for a female readership. But often they were not media for progressive ideas. Instead, most of these publications were translations or explanations of the classics in vernacular, instructions about education in the family, or women's journals.

As mentioned earlier, various reformers in the last decades of the nineteenth century promoted language changes. Some of them were inspired by observing that in the West and in Japan the written language was close to or, as they assumed, identical with the spoken language. The unity of written and spoken language was advocated as early as 1887 by the diplomat, reformer, and poet Huang Zunxian. He pointed out that such a unity existed in various countries of the East and West, and that it was the cause of widespread literacy.[11] In 1898 Qiu Tingliang formulated for the first time the slogan "honor baihua, discard wenyan" (*chong baihua er fei wenyan*). He believed that because the written baihua is much easier to learn than wenyan, its adoption would destroy the caste of old-fashioned scholars. It would make memorization by rote unnecessary and preserve the teachings of the sages, for the classics translated into written baihua could then reach the people. In Qiu's opinion, the introduction of written baihua into schools and textbooks would liberate children's intellectual potential. In three or four years they could be well educated in Chinese and foreign subjects both old and modern and also gain a general knowledge of science. If books on agriculture, commerce, and handicrafts were translated into written baihua, any village boy could profit from them for the rest of his life. Qiu Tingliang stated vehemently that "wenyan is the matchless vehicle for keeping the nation in ignorance. Baihua is the matchless vehicle for giving knowledge to the nation . . . To sum up: if wenyan flourishes, learning will perish; if baihua expands, learning will thrive. If learning does not thrive, there will be no nation."[12]

The few scarce sources on spoken northern baihua (guanhua) that are available inform us that because of the nationwide strengthening and expansion of spoken baihua, by the turn of the century 70 percent of all Chinese-language speakers were able to speak guanhua (apart from their local dialects). The term "guanhua" was at that time understood to mean "common" rather than "administrative" language.[13]

In the 1890s and the first decade of the twentieth century, first efforts were also made to provide transliterations of spoken baihua (guanhua) pronunciation.[14] Letters of the Latin alphabet or original symbols were used for this purpose.[15] It was hoped that transliteration would facilitate reading and learning and lead to a codification of spoken baihua (guanhua) pronunciation, an important factor in the formation of modern Chinese.

The developments just described can be considered the beginnings of a major historical change in Chinese language, which was to affect every area of verbal communication in China. Although at the turn of the century wenyan was still used for orthodox literature and nonliterary texts and showed remarkable adaptability in creating neologisms for foreign and scientific terms,[16] in the competition to become a modern multifunctional language, wenyan was heavily handicapped. It lacked an oral form, which is essential for easy communication and mass education in any modern nation. Consequently, the dominant position of wenyan began to be challenged by northern baihua, both in its frequency of use and in the unorthodox theoretical ideas of language reformers. It became obvious to them that wenyan hindered the development of the Chinese nation-state.

Southern koines did not become bases for a national language for different reasons than in the case of wenyan. Like northern baihua, they had both written and oral forms. But the decisive factor in the competition between northern baihua and the southern koines does not rest in this oral-written dichotomy. The decisive factor was the spectrum of functions that northern baihua and southern koines assumed during the second half of the nineteenth century and during the late Qing period. As opposed to northern baihua, none of the southern koines surpassed its regional radius because they never functioned as a nationwide administrative language and, therefore, lacked the political prestige enjoyed by spoken baihua (guanhua). As written languages, the southern koines did not achieve the artistic variability and sophistication of northern baihuawen. Local drama *(difang xi)* and storytellers' written narratives, the major literary genres in which koines were used in the nineteenth century, were primarily intended to be performed orally and not read as independent literary works. Even the new drama of the late Qing period was exclusively spoken; it was performed orally in local dialects or koines and never recorded in the written form.[17] When several late Qing novelists tried to write novels in one of the southern koines, their experimental attempts proved to be abortive. This was both because of the difficulties of transcribing the pronunciation of koines in Chinese characters and because of the limited number of readers who were able to understand the texts. The written form of the southern koines was not cultivated enough to challenge the artistic superiority of northern written baihua, which had been used for centuries in novels, drama, and storytellers' written narratives.

Compared to wenyan and southern koines, northern baihua had several advantages as the most serious candidate for a national language. It had both oral and written forms, and its functions had expanded into nonliterary communication during the second half of the nineteenth century. Moreover, northern baihua could provide the emerging national language with a relatively unified system of pronunciation that at that time, as we have seen, could already be codified. These developments, and the efforts of the language reformers, gave the written baihua new social status. Having reached its verbal and artistic maturity during the past two centuries in the works of northern novelists, playwrights, and storytellers, by the end of the nineteenth century, and especially during the first decade of the twentieth century, northern baihua had gained a prestige that was acknowledged even among the predominantly southern late Qing novelists. Undoubtedly, this theoretical and practical nationwide recognition of northern written baihua was an important factor in the formation of modern standard Chinese.

Although many detailed studies are needed before we can reach any definite conclusion, it would seem that at the turn of the century written baihua and spoken baihua (guanhua) were actually merging into one language. Still, at this time, a national language *(guoyu)* that could be used for communication, both literary and nonliterary, written and oral, was more an ideal than a reality. It is therefore not surprising that by the second decade of the twentieth century there were strong efforts to make this ideal into a reality. These efforts culminated at the Central Congress of Pedagogues in Peking, held only a few months before the Revolution of 1911. The document adopted by the pedagogues defined the main features of the postulated standard national language as follows:

1. In order to function as a national language, guoyu cannot be based on any "natural" local dialect but must be a standardized "artificial" language;
2. In pronunciation it will take as its model the phonemic system of the Peking dialect [which implied guanhua];
3. Its grammar will prefer forms more or less common to all dialects; and
4. Its vocabulary can be enriched by expressions and idioms borrowed from various existing spoken forms of Chinese.[18]

It is no exaggeration to call this document "the charter of the movement for linguistic reform."[19] Its concept of the national language is surprisingly consistent and bears many similarities to modern theories of standard language. It represented a program based on a clear understanding of the language situation in China, and generally, it was followed with only a few adjustments.

Yet these language theoreticians, ardently struggling to establish a "living" language as the national language at a time when wenyan was generally but erroneously considered a dead language, could not quite develop a suitable blend of linguistic forms that would be welcomed by a majority of writers. Their program of reform was only a partial solution. Nevertheless, their efforts show the great progress that had occurred in the late Qing period. The fact that a single, multifunctional, modern standard Chinese was to a great extent achieved in the twenties and thirties and that its acceptance was relatively smooth was because of movements like theirs that ought to develop premodern baihua into a new literary language.

Literature during the Late Qing Period

An intriguing phenomenon of the beginnings of modern Chinese literature is the dominant position and artistic maturity of fiction. Such was achieved not only in the works of famous authors like Lu Xun, Ye Shengtao, Bing Xin, and others, but also in the short stories of "meteoric" writers, such as Li Min, Pan Xun, and Sun Lianggong, whose names and very limited literary work are today forgotten.[20] This dominance and artistic excellence is even more striking when compared with the daring, but seldom successful experiments of modern poets in the early twenties and with the surprisingly slow arrival of modern drama in the late twenties.

The reason for fiction's dominance in the modern literary scene is sometimes attributed to the sudden revolutionary change in the hierarchy of literary genres that is supposed to have taken place in the twenties as "a perfect parallel to the social struggle going on in the country at the same time." As the gentry declined, so poetry and the essay, the epitomes of the traditional literature, lost their eminent positions. Their replacement by fiction, which in Confucian aesthetics was never regarded as proper literature, reflected an increased literacy in China's society.[21]

This explanation is not fully satisfactory, even if we concede for the moment that a sudden revolutionary change in literary hierarchy occurred. The parallels between changes in the literary and social hierarchies do not explain why drama, occupying the same low position in traditional literature as fiction, did not become an equally leading genre in modern Chinese literature. Furthermore, the sudden changes in the hierarchy of genres may only be theoretical ones, caused by the inappropriate comparison between Confucian theory and the real literary situation. Poetry and the essay had been assigned the highest positions because they were the only conveyors of the doctrines and moral principles of the Confucian sages. Fiction and drama were excluded from literature because they were stubbornly considered pure entertainment with no didactic value, even though the prominent dramatists and novelists expressed strong, though sometimes veiled, ideological messages. The conventional Confucian aesthetic hierarchy obscures the real literary situation and the changes that occurred in the drama and novel, particularly after the seventeenth century. Thus, when we study the literary situation in historical perspective, it becomes obvious that shifts in the hierarchy of literary genres were taking place long before they became conspicuous in the modern period.

By the late Qing period all three major literary genres had undergone some significant alterations. The character and the depth of these alterations varied. Within the framework of Qing literature, still mostly dominated by tradition, the innovative trends and features might not appear of crucial importance. But studied in connection with the modern period, these changes in particular genres indicate the causes of fiction's dominance in the modern literary scene.

At the turn of the century, a movement calling for "new" literature appeared in all three genres. The movement was more or less spontaneous in nature, and although in some cases there was a conscious ideological formulation, it did not achieve the high level of theoretical, organizational, and practical coherence associated with the May Fourth movement. For this reason it did not bring about the radical transformations that were accomplished in the twenties, though it did create the necessary preconditions for those transformations.

Late Qing "new" literature had certain common features, which can be summarized as follows:

    1. The prominence of political and social themes, and a concentration on private emotional feelings and relationships — features reminiscent of the early romantic period in European literature.

    2. The striving for a simpler, more lucid, and more readable style in fiction and poetry, partly achieved by discarding the most restrictive features of the tradition.

    3. The introduction of structural changes — minimal in poetry, radical in fiction — and the appearance of a completely new literary form, the spoken drama.

These literary developments were reflected in each of the major genres.

The New Poetry A new style called *xin pai shi* emerged around 1895 and culminated in 1902–1904 in the *shijie geming* (revolution in poetry). About forty poets participated in this "revolution," producing some five hundred poems, many of which appeared in the political newspaper *Xin min congbao* (New people journal).[22] Because of ossified patterns, latter-day wenyan poetry had lost the emotional spontaneity of the original models of classic poetry. Therefore, these new poets emphasized the necessity for authentic emotions, the emotions genuinely experienced by the poet himself. Huang Zunxian's verse, for example, expressed impressions experienced during his extensive travels, such as "Lundun da wu xing" (A walk in London fog). "Baizeng zumu Li taifuren mu" (When visiting the tomb of Lady Li, my grandmother) described his deep sorrow over the loss of a happy childhood.[23] Kang Youwei's "Tristia" expressed his personal melancholy during his exile from China.[24]

Political and social themes were best exploited in the novel, but they also appeared in poetry. Some of the new poets (Huang Zunxian, Liang Qichao, Kang Youwei, and Tan Sitong) were involved in political activities, and their political, social, and patriotic verse is therefore based on authentic personal experience.[25]

Besides the employment of fresh themes, attempts were made toward a simpler poetic style. Negatively, the most "difficult" features, especially classical allusions, were avoided. "For me the words of the classics do not exist," proclaimed Huang Zunxian, "I don't dare to insert them into my poetry."[26] Positively, Huang Zunxian delighted in "the working in of all sorts of materials, including local dialects and proverbs."[27] Moreover, poetry was now open to new words from modern life and civilization.[28] Still, Huang Zunxian's renowned statement "Wo shou xie wo kou" (my hand writes as my mouth speaks) did not mean that he wanted to justify writing poems in the vernacular. He wanted only to liberate wenyan from the sterile and largely incomprehensible sediment of classical books and to adjust its vocabulary and syntax to the new themes and style. But that "new" style was still bridled by classical vocabulary that could not adequately express the new modern themes. It remained for a later generation of poets to create poetry in a more appropriate — vernacular — language.

Structurally, the poetry of the period seems to have been characterized by the resurrection of some old forms (*gushi, lisao, yuefu*) rather than by the creation of new ones. A detailed formal study of the poetry of that time is needed in order to determine to what degree old forms were subject to change. Some structural shifts can be expected at a

27

time when authenticity becomes the most desired value in poetry. In this connection, Huang Zunxian's wish "to write poetry in the same flexible and melodious way as did the *guwen* [old style] writers"[29] could hardly be accommodated within an inflexible structure. Furthermore, Huang Zunxian's active interest in folk poetry[30] is of major significance: it shows that he was able to find new poetic values completely different from those of the classics.

The New Drama Spoken drama made its appearance in China between 1900 and 1920[31] but was preceded by attempts to reform the classic Peking opera (*jingxi*). As one example of such attempts, a group of Chinese actors, who had seen several performances of Western drama in Japanese theaters at the turn of the century, founded the Xin wutai (New Stage) in Shanghai about 1910, striving to create a Westernized dramaturgy to replace the formalism of the old opera. They abandoned the symbolic movements, masks, and costumes and introduced Western props, "realistic" acting, and contemporary costumes. The result was a strange hybrid. In order to make spoken drama acceptable to the Chinese public, the actors incorporated many features of traditional opera into the transplanted literary form, such as music and stylized arias. Like the first Chinese translation of Western fiction, this experiment was a "paraphrase" in Chinese terms of foreign content and themes.

At about the same time as the New Stage was founded, another more idealistic movement for new drama, which aimed at a complete separation from classic Chinese theater, was being organized among a few Chinese exchange students in Japan. With help and guidance from a few famous Japanese performers and directors of Western drama, the Chun liu she (Spring Willow Society) was initiated in 1906.[32] Despite their serious intention to introduce to Chinese audiences true Western dramatic literature, this student group seems to have had no concrete plan for transplanting Western drama into Chinese theaters. Its approach was to abandon everything traditional and adopt a spoken delivery, realistic gestures, and contemporary costumes.

Only in the themes of the new-style drama was there a trend to adjust Western drama to Chinese contemporary conditions. The new plays fell roughly into two categories: dramas with a clear political and social message and "sentimental" plays. Because at the beginning the new drama lacked original texts, many late Qing novels and translated novels were adapted for the stage. A social message was clearly stated in the adaptation of Li Boyuan's *Guanchang xianxing ji* (The bureaucrats: a revelation) and in the theatrical version of Harriet Beecher Stowe's

Uncle Tom's Cabin (called *Hei nu yu tian lu* [Black slave cries to heaven]). Social and sentimental themes were combined in the adaptation of Zeng Pu's novel *Nie hai hua* (The flower in the sea of sin). The Revolution of 1911 quickly found expression in original dramas such as Ren Tianzhi's *Huang jin chi xue* (Gold and blood) and *Gonghe wansui* (Long live the republic).[33]

The "sentimental" stream also used adaptations. The very first play performed by the Chun liu she in 1907 was an adaptation of Lin Shu's translation of *La dame aux camélias*. Two years later the same group performed Sardou's *Tosca*, whose combination of sentimental and patriotic themes was obviously appealing to the audiences. It was only natural that Wu Woyao's "novel of sentiment," *Hen hai* (Sea of woe) was rearranged for the stage and performed around 1910 by a new theatrical group founded by Ren Tianzhi and Wang Zhongsheng.

When the Chun liu she moved to Shanghai in 1911, the new drama was enthusiastically welcomed and many new theatrical groups were founded; the atmosphere on the eve of the revolution was ideal for cultural experimentation. But enthusiasm alone could not guarantee the solid growth of the new drama. The height of the new drama, around 1911, was very short-lived, and its rapid decline invites a number of speculations. The famous playwright Hong Shen explains that the new drama was never put into script form and that the handling of Western props was inept. Furthermore, the actors of the newly founded groups, who believed Western acting to be easy and equal to "natural" behavior, were not sufficiently trained or prepared for their performances. They were not motivated by artistic ideals but only by hopes for money and fame.[34]

Although these facts explain the situation in part, there are more basic reasons why the new drama did not survive for more than a decade. First, knowledge of Western drama, its texts and techniques, was superficial. Second, the movement for the new drama, though coinciding with the movements for the new poetry and the new novel, began under different leadership. Instead of men of letters, poets, novelists, and political reformers, the new drama, especially after 1911, was written and produced by actor companies under the financial and often directorial supervision of profit-seeking entrepreneurs. Such companies were more concerned with theatrically pleasing adaptations than with a serious study of different Western plays and their aesthetic principles. Thus, in spite of the efforts to introduce occidental modes of acting, props, and costumes, Chinese actors, poorly acquainted with the demands of Western drama, relied heavily on traditional operatic

29

practices. In line with the old tradition, it was felt to be sufficient if the actors knew only the synopsis of a play. The "text" was then created and recreated by the actors as they performed. This old practice worked satisfactorily as long as the actors had mastered their acting techniques and had understood the basic structure of the play. But neither the art and technique of Western acting, nor the literary structure of Western drama, was sufficiently familiar to the actors. Consequently, the majority of the actors' performances were unavoidably amateurish and verbally ineffective.

This survival of an actor-centered, extemporaneous rendering of a theme may be one reason why no outstanding playwrights emerged in this early period. There was not yet a need to write new plays in a literary form. An equally important reason was the difficult problem of language. According to Hong Shen, the theatrical groups of the pre–May Fourth period used local, mostly southern dialects,[35] again following the tradition of local Chinese operas. Baihua was used only as a rare and rather unsuccessful experiment. The new drama could not, therefore, become a part of the new cultural movement, which insisted that literature be based on a language used nationwide.

The mere spoken use of dialects, the lack of an established written language, and a poor knowledge of the "grammar" of Western drama appear to have been the major drawbacks for late Qing new drama becoming the immediate predecessor of modern Chinese drama, *huaju*. Around 1916 this new drama began withering away. It is a telling example of the inability to transplant foreign culture or literature when the domestic conditions are unfavorable to its acceptance.

The New Novel Compared with poetry and drama, the situation of the novel at the turn of the century was basically different. In the eighteenth century, the Chinese novel had already undergone a period of development that substantially changed its character and status. Themes concerning emotional relationships and social criticism had been incorporated, and its language had already evolved far beyond that of historical documents or popular storyteller tales, which were the early novel's prime sources. The novel had become a sophisticated literary medium in which a developed form of vernacular language could encompass many aspects of the classical language. Moreover, the authors of novels were themselves literati, members of the educated establishment, and so were the recipients of their works. Accordingly, during the 1700s the novel was fast becoming accepted in educated circles. Its rise in status probably served to exclude the reader of popular literature, but this exclusion was counterbalanced by an increase in the novel's intrinsic literary value. For these historical reasons it is clear why the literary and language reformers of the late Qing period looked to the novel as a solution to the literary and language crisis.

In connection with this change in literary esteem, the novel's place in the development of a standard Chinese language must be especially emphasized. Certainly, its acceptance by the literary establishment could have led the novelists to use the language of the orthodox literature, wenyan. Indeed, during the nineteenth century and into the first decade of the twentieth century, there was a trend to write novels in the classical language. For the end of that period we can cite Su Manshu's *Duan hong ling yan ji* (Lonely swan) and Lin Shu's *Jing hua bi xue lu* (The jasper blood shed for the country). Also, most foreign novels were translated into wenyan, because it was still felt that they represented a different literary form from the Chinese novel.

But writing novels in wenyan could not be sustained. It was in conflict with developments in other areas toward a standard national language. Consequently, a new literary species, the late Qing novel, came to play a significant role in the expansion of written baihua, because of both its quantitative growth and its new sociopolitical themes.

In contrast to the eighteenth-century novel, the late Qing novel was the embodiment of a programmatic literary outlook. Its spokesmen viewed the novel as a major way to enlighten and educate the people about new social and political institutions. This theory, which strongly influenced the subsequent development of novel writing, had both traditional and modern origins. It grew from observations about the social function of the Chinese novel in the past, the character of its language, and the social function of the novel abroad.

In their 1897 article "*Guowen bao* fuyin shuobu yuanqi" (Reasons for printing fiction in the *National News*), Yan Fu and Xia Zengyou argued that the Chinese novel had exerted a much deeper influence on the Chinese people than the classics or historical works. The novel's strength can be explained by its clear and understandable language — close to the colloquial — and by its evocative, artistic rendering of dry historical facts. Since the Chinese novel had influenced the people in the past, it could be used to enlighten them in the present. In Europe, America, and Japan, fiction already performed this function, which should be an incentive to Chinese authors.[36]

Liang Qichao's 1898 article "Yi yin zhengzhi xiaoshuo xu" (A preface to the translation and publication of political fiction),[37]

31

characterized the Chinese novel as the most powerful teacher of the Chinese past. Unlike the classics and historical works, it could be read even by a poorly educated man. Giving foreign fiction credit for major changes in public opinion and for political progress in America, Europe, and Japan, Liang called for a *xiaoshuo geming,* a revolution in the novel. He wanted to use the novel for political education purposes to counteract the mostly negative values of the old Chinese novel (banditry in *Shuihu zhuan* [The water margin], lust in *Hong lou meng* [Dream of the red chamber]).

Hopes for increasing the novel's social impact were strengthened rather than diminished after the failure of the Hundred-Day Reform in 1898. It became obvious that China's salvation would not be the imperial court but an enlightened nation. Understandably, then, the most consistent statements on the late Qing theory of fiction were published in the first decade of the twentieth century.

One of the most important pronouncements was Liang Qichao's 1902 article "Lun xiaoshuo yu qunzhi di guanxi" (On the relationship between fiction and the rule of the masses).[38] His ideas are a curious blend of Japanese theory on the political novel, Buddhist concepts, and the domestic literary strain that emphasized the emotions. "The novel is the greatest conveyance of all literature" because "it possesses an astonishing potentiality to effect the Way of man." This potential is manifested by the four powers, all of which can stir the emotions: the power to suffuse (*xun*), the power to permeate (*jin*), the power to excite (*ci*), and the power to elevate (*ti*). In the past, however, the Chinese novel had misused its powers. It was necessary to create a "new novel" because only a new kind of novel could help transform the nation.

In response to this call for social *engagement* hundreds of late Qing novels were written. But not only social themes were used. The emotional themes of poetry and drama also appeared in many novels, giving rise to a type called *xie qing xiaoshuo,* "novel of sentiment." The term was coined by the main proponent of the genre, Wu Woyao. True, the ethics of Wu's sentimental relationships were still rather traditional and emphasized Confucian values. But the main importance of his *Sea of Woe* and *Jieyu hui* (Ashes of destruction) was that the theme of love was joined with, and in the second novel surpassed by, the social theme. Apparently, the novels of this time could not escape being "engaged literature."

As already mentioned, some late Qing novels revealed important changes in the structure of the genre as a whole. One change — the shortening of the novel — might seem superficial but in fact had a significant and historical effect. In the majority of late Qing novels, the number of chapters was much fewer than the one hundred or so of the traditional novel; sometimes a novel consisted of only eight, ten, or twelve chapters.[39]

An analysis of Wu Woyao's *Sea of Woe*[40] indicates that the shortening of the novel was an exterior sign of deeper structural change. To a great extent, the novel discarded the traditional plot pattern, where relatively self-contained episodes were organized in a "string" sequence, linked only by the progress of the main hero. Instead, it developed a unified, coherent plot. This change in plot, in turn, led to a substantial change in the number of characters. Instead of a great number of transient characters, the action was carried by only a few protagonists. This made it possible to focus on the psychological makeup and emotional life of a small number of roles.

Translations from Abroad   Foreign influence in the formation of modern Chinese literature, though widely affirmed, is generally overemphasized. Characteristically, foreign literature "imported" in translation during the late Qing period was mainly fiction. But instead of being overwhelmed by foreign literary modes, the domestic literary situation strongly influenced which works were to be translated.[41] The current literary expectations among Chinese readers explain the fact — at first sight surprising — that no French realist novelists, such as Balzac, Flaubert, or Zola were translated, and that the great Russian realist novels of Gogol, Turgenev, Tolstoy, Goncharov, and Dostoevsky remained unknown in China until the May Fourth period and later. Instead of European realism, the Chinese showed a preference for translation of adventure fiction (Conan Doyle's detective novels, Sue's *Les mystères de Paris*) and sentimental stories (*La dame aux camélias*). And the most frequently translated works were by authors such as Scott, Hugo, or Dickens, who combined the depiction of sentiment with social, historical, or pseudo-historical events.

Somewhat earlier the Japanese novel had developed traits similar to those of the late Qing novel: the political novel emerged in the late 1860s and the romantic novel at the end of the nineteenth century. It is therefore not surprising to find that many of these Japanese novels were soon available in Chinese translations.[42] Their acceptance was certainly facilitated by adaptations that catered to the taste and experience of the Chinese reading public. In contrast to the popularity of these translations, the commercial failure of Lu Xun and Zhou Zuoren's endeavor is most significant. In their 1909 *Yuwai xiaoshuo ji* (Collection of foreign fiction) they concentrated on the nineteenth-century European short story, including works by Chekhov, Andreyev, Garshin, Sienkiewicz, Maupassant, and Wilde. But at that time, Chinese readers were apparently not prepared to accept a completely new and alien genre — a short story that did not narrate the plot "from the beginning to the end" but that presented a "slice of life," whose action was concentrated on the psychological crises of its heroes.

The basic changes in the language and literary situation required to produce a modern literature were initiated and generally accomplished during the late Qing period. What seemed to be a sudden domination of baihua in literary and nonliterary texts in the May Fourth period cannot be regarded as the success of a few individuals inspired by foreign models. Rather, the formative process of modern baihua should be considered a further stage in a language evolution that was accelerated by appropriately timed theoretical and practical efforts on the part of Chinese writers, linguists, and critics. In this further stage modern Chinese language drew from and creatively remolded two major linguistic forms, premodern baihua and classical wenyan and absorbed certain influences from foreign languages.

During the first decade of the twentieth century, also, poetry, drama, and fiction underwent various changes as the result of literary reformers' conscious imitation of Western and Japanese models. But the internal historical development of the three major traditional literary genres had its own impact on the formation of modern Chinese literature.

As we have seen, the late Qing new poetry and the late Qing new drama had certain disadvantages that prevented them from being important in the early period of modern literature. Poetry was still expressed in the traditional wenyan, which was an obstacle in a period that demanded a greater accessibility to literature. Creating modern Chinese poetic language and prosody was complicated, for it required completely new poetic forms to accommodate modern written baihua. Because the potential model for creating modern poetry in written baihua — folklore poetry — was neglected and unexplored, and because the old prosodic forms conducive to wenyan did not suit baihuawen, it was quite a long time before modern poetry could come close to artistic maturity.

From the viewpoint of the nineteenth century, drama might have challenged fiction in the modern period as the dominant literary genre. In works like *Taohua shan* (The peach blossom fan) and *Changsheng dian*

(The palace of eternal youth), the southern drama, which had developed in the early Qing period, had shown itself to have a potential for artistic excellence similar to that of fiction in premodern times. Like the novel, southern drama was accepted by the literary establishment; late Qing theoreticians placed the drama on coequal terms with fiction, apparently discerning its comparable merits.

The unexpectedly minor role of drama in the initial period of modern Chinese literature was probably due to two factors. First, the new kind of drama that sprouted in the late Qing period had no domestic tradition like that of the southern drama; it was a completely new and imported form, one that could not be easily accepted by a wide audience. Second, its language was a serious disadvantage. At a time when baihua was gaining nationwide prestige, using regional dialects did not help the new drama compete for the leading position among other literary genres. These factors might explain why modern Chinese drama, huaju, developed so surprisingly late. The modern dramatists faced the same difficult problems as the modern poets: the creation of a completely new form and a completely new language.

Fiction's dominance in the early stage of modern Chinese literature was not accidental. It can be explained by three major factors: (1) traditional fiction was written in baihuawen, the language form that became central in the development of modern Chinese literature; (2) during a relatively long and uninterrupted period of development, fiction written in baihuawen acquired both thematic and stylistic features that made it best suited for a new literature; and (3) during the late Qing period, fiction was given an elaborate theory, which raised its status in the intellectual community. Fiction was not only accepted and read, but it was also advocated by theorists as the best way to enlighten the people.

As a result of these linguistic, stylistic, and ideological developments, modern Chinese fiction was not merely a continuation of traditional Chinese fiction but came to demonstrate radically new narrative structures. This is especially apparent in the emergence of the short story as the most prestigious literary genre in the May Fourth period. Thus, we see that the birth of a new literature was possible only because of mutual adaptation between traditional genres and changes in literary attitudes, especially those that flourished at the turn of the twentieth century. Both historical continuity and intrinsic changes mark the origins of modern Chinese literature.

2.

The Impact of Western Literary Trends

Bonnie S. McDougall

From its introduction toward the end of the Qing dynasty to the outbreak in 1937 of the war against Japan, Western literature enjoyed an enormous popularity among the new intellectual class in China. The enthusiasm for this literature was neither passive nor superficial, and in the twenties and thirties, literary theory and criticism were studied almost as intently as the literary works themselves. Toward the end of the twenties, the impact of the West slackened, and there was a noticeable reduction in demand for translations lasting from about 1926 to 1934. First, the overemphasis on Western culture in the early twenties brought its own kind of disillusionment, and the inferiority of the translations being produced was no longer as easily tolerated.[1] Second, the growth of Soviet literature and Marxist literary criticism reduced the value of the older European tradition in Chinese eyes: its criticism, open and implied, of liberal Western culture was welcomed in the antiforeignism that followed the May 30 Incident of 1925 and Western resistance to the Northern Expedition of 1926–1927. If decline was caused by these factors, then renewal can be explained along similar lines. Around the early thirties, Chinese writers began to realize that their writing was not yet skilled enough to satisfy the reading public: importing modern Western literature was necessary to meet the immediate demand for realistic and naturalistic work, and translations of older masterpieces were needed to improve the quality of writing. Internationalism received new encouragement through the Comintern, the League of Nations, and more stable relations between the Chinese government and the Western powers. Finally, a new kind of Western writing with more appeal to the Chinese was emerging. Disenchantment gave way to a new fascination.

The resurgent interest in Western literature in the thirties was soon arrested by the outbreak of war against Japan, and once again the years of military and civil turmoil that followed made the concerns of Western literature remote from Chinese needs. The elitist nature of the Western influence became more apparent as the importance of mass action was realized, and writers redefined their roles in terms of the nature and needs of a mass audience. This was a reversal of the situation in the early twenties and thirties, when writers generally based their attitudes to life and society on roles or models described in Western literature. Here, the paramount concern was the writer's image of himself as a creator, and generally the effect was to glamorize and heroicize the role of the writer in society.

The focus of European aesthetics when Chinese writers first came into contact with it was turning away from the art object (as in classical Chinese aesthetics) and toward the artist. In the post-Renaissance period, the artist had reemerged first as a named individual and creator, and by the late eighteenth century as an independent figure in society. One of the first signs of Western literary influence in China, then, was the new respectability of the professional writer. Although writing has existed in China as an independent profession attached neither to scholarship nor to government service, it was not the approved position in Confucian orthodoxy. As late as 1898, Liang Qichao argued the propriety of a statesman openly engaged in writing fiction, and not, more respectably, poetry and classical prose; he hardly considered the possibility that a serious-minded, educated man might wish to write political fiction and still prefer to remain outside any government office or institution.[2] By 1907, however, Lu Xun could envisage just that: the poet as prophet, leading the people to political reform and social justice, and yet standing outside society instead of expressing his ideas within the bureaucracy, as older Chinese poets like Du Fu (712–770) wished. Lu Xun pointed to Western poets like Shelley, Pushkin, and Petöfi, who appealed directly to the public through the power of literature, and quoted from Western philosophers such as Carlyle, Nietzsche, and Brandes to dispel the apathy or corruption that seemed to affect Chinese writers faced with a government in which nobody could believe.[3] The traditional ideal may have suited a stable society in which the profession of government service, or its opposite, the recluse's withdrawal, was still honorable, but in the present situation, Lu Xun sought to encourage idealistic rebellion among the younger intellectuals by presenting literature itself as a way for a conscientious patriot to serve best his country and its people.

With the continued disintegration of social roles after the republic was established, and encouraged by the proliferation of various publishing activities, many young and ambitious intellectuals were attracted to writing as a career. If the living was precarious, the other main alternatives — teaching or service in some kind of warlord administration — were hardly much better.[4] But having established that his role was to write, the writer had then to explore the relevance of his role in society — in particular, his participation or lack of it in the current political situation.

In most societies, a writer has at least three not necessarily exclusive roles: critic, reformer, and entertainer. To these traditional roles, all known in China, the May Fourth writer added several more described or adopted in the West. One of the earliest to appear was the role of prophet: in the Lu Xun version described above, the poet is possessed by a kind of demonic power enabling him to see into the future and guide his people toward it. A decade later, Guo Moruo again quoted Carlyle and Goethe to show that poets and prophets possessed the power of creation, like nature itself, because they were so closely in tune with the inner workings of the cosmos. The mission of the new poet, according to Guo, was therefore to express unimpeded his intuitions on the nature and essence of all phenomena, creating poetry as things are created in nature. To prepare himself for this solemn task, the poet must immerse himself in nature and society and cultivate his aesthetic perception and philosophical understanding. Only when he is complete as a man will his poetry achieve perfection.[5]

Under the influence of German romanticism, Guo was here asserting both the importance of the poet in regard to society and at the same time his obligations in society. After his return to China in 1921, Guo suffered some disillusionment over many of his more exuberant ideals, but his views on poetry remained much the same. In 1923 he adopted the expressionist theory of the indissoluble connection between art and life: art is expression, expression is life. Since creativity implies change, the creative artist is by nature revolutionary: "All true revolutionary movements are art movements; all sincere activists are true artists; and all sincere artists are true revolutionaries."[6] Three years later, yet another justification of the poet in society appeared: drawing on the European medieval theory of "humors" that determine personality types, Guo classed writers in general as the melancholic type. The writer's sensitivity to the flow of human affairs enabled him to anticipate social change in his work, acting as a kind of literary barometer.[7] What made the theory especially attractive, Guo noted, was that a writer with a pure proletarian background had yet to appear in China: the writer with a petty bourgeois background therefore required some special ability to achieve the necessary imaginative leap and produce the proletarian literature required.

Guo's pseudo-materialistic view of the writer's temperament developed alongside his growing interest in Marxism. By the twenties, two rival schools of Marxist thinking had arisen in regard to the writer's role in society. One school simply regarded the writer as a worker like all others; the other made him out to be a heroic figure, in the vanguard of the revolution or, alternatively, its standard-bearer. The standard-bearer theory was adopted by the League of Left-Wing Writers at its inauguration in 1930.[8] By then, however, Lu Xun at least had lost his faith in the inspirational and prophetic ability of Chinese writers, and switching to the other school, preferred to see the writer as the servant of the people. The importance attributed to writers within the left-wing movement was nevertheless hardly questioned during the thirties; it was only in Yenan in 1942 that Mao Zedong was finally able to humble these "heroes without a battlefield."[9]

Less exalted and more familiar figures to the Chinese were the writer as reformer or social critic. Social criticism in literature was a fundamental part of the great tradition. Its antecedents were respectably immersed in antiquity and its line of inheritance strengthened particularly during the Tang and Song dynasties. To the May Fourth reformers, the role of social critic seemed to have degenerated during the Qing dynasty to the defense of conventional morality as embodied in the slogan "wenyi zai dao" (literature as a vehicle of the Way). Several new Western-derived theories were proposed to revive this role, such as the naturalistic theory that literature was a reflection of society. Mao Dun, one of the earliest proponents of this theory, on the whole considered the reflection of society an involuntary feature of any literary work. A reflection can be more or less accurate, however, and Mao Dun counseled the writer to familiarize himself with his social background both by personal experience and by scientific research. When the reflection is thus more accurate, then to the extent that society is rotten and corrupt, the author automatically becomes a social critic.[10]

The explanation of Taine's historical method, on which the above argument is based, came to Mao Dun in watered-down versions in English and American college textbooks, where the author's personality was given equal weight with the determinants race, environment, and epoch. Many of these texts stressed the importance of personality in a kind of "prism" theory wherein the value or pleasure of a literary work is derived from the author's individual perception of life. Since Mao Dun, however, regarded personality or individual character itself as largely determined by race, environment, and epoch, its effect on a literary work was limited. He noted that some literary works seem to transcend reality rather than reflect it but failed to account for this transcendence and ignored the possibility that the writer's perception may be distorted or misleading and yet still capable of producing valuable literary work. The simplicity of the reflector theory encouraged young writers to voice their criticisms of society, though it tended also to discourage the development of individual sensibility. (It also helped indirectly to foster the intentionalist fallacy that became so widespread in modern Chinese literature, that literature can be judged according to the intention of the author; in other words, a consciously political author can produce only propaganda, while products of the so-called artistic types must necessarily have a high literary value. After Mao Dun became more explicitly Marxist in his literary doctrines after 1924–1925, he found it necessary to give more stress to the factor of personality in order to lighten the sternness of other Marxist critics.[11])

If the reflector theory has the advantage that the writer becomes a simple "literary worker" whose diligence is automatically rewarded by results, difficulties arise as soon as it is modified to allow the author to stand outside society and criticize it in a more active way. The writer as crusading reformer or revolutionary required a different kind of justification, which in the end was derived as much through personal experience and actual models as through theory. Ba Jin, for example, was convinced of the power of literature to change people's lives through his own response to books like Kropotkin's *An Appeal to the Young* and Kampf's *On the Eve*, as well as from the response of his own readership.[12] His examples came from Western literature, since before Liang Qichao few native writers were able so persuasively and dramatically to exert this kind of influence. Guo Moruo cited the contributions made to the French and Russian revolutions by writers, and more recently, the effect of Galsworthy's play *Justice* on English social reform.[13] The expressionist view of literature held by Guo Moruo and Yu Dafu in the early twenties also encouraged writers to adopt a revolutionary role, now with examples from contemporary German literature.[14] In practice, expressionism is, however, highly individualistic and hence unstable: it can encompass a wide variety of attitudes, from primitivism to aestheticism, and justify political theories from communism to fascism. Thus, Guo Moruo, who in 1923 condemned propaganda in art as a violation of the artist's inner integrity, by 1926 was taking part in propaganda work for the Northern Expedition.[15] Yu Dafu, in contrast, after a sometimes halfhearted left-wing phase that lasted about five years, resigned from the League of Left-Wing Writers in the early thirties and joined forces with Lin Yutang; at the same time, he went back to writing poetry in classical Chinese forms.[16]

A slightly different kind of social criticism was envisaged by the *Xueheng* (Critical review) group, which was formed in order to counteract the prevailing May Fourth fashion of "attacking everything Chinese, despising our national culture, agitating many unnecessary and even harmful changes in social life and customs, looking with scorn and contempt upon all religious and moral teaching, tending toward ignorant and bigoted and licentious individualism and away from any discipline, system and order." Appealing to works such as Matthew Arnold's *Culture and Anarchy* and Irving Babbitt's *Rousseau and Romanticism* and *The New Laokoön*, their theoretical justification was the "contagion" theory that contact with "the best that is known and thought in the world" would result in the spiritual elevation of the individual and ultimately the salvation of society; over this process the critic presides like a doctor, prescribing cures and fighting contamination.[17] In *Culture and Anarchy*, Arnold also employed the time-hallowed metaphor of "the purging effect wrought on our minds by culture," but catharsis is not often mentioned by the early May Fourth writers. Though many of them quoted from Arnold freely, probably few had themselves read any of his works; only the *Critical Review* group seems to have assimilated the basic conservative values of his views on culture and society.

Few writers were willing to admit that the artist can also serve the community as an entertainer. The word "entertainment" has in English a meretricious ring, though in common usage tragedy as well as comedy is included under this heading. The Chinese equivalent, "literature to console us in our grief and to entertain us when we are happy," also came into disrepute during the twenties as a hopelessly inadequate description of the function of literature. In the twenties, only a few brave individuals like Zhou Zuoren, Lao She, and Shen Congwen dared to declare this their chosen role, and the magazine *Yusi* (Thread of talk) was one of the few that presented Western literature to its readers without the usual accompaniment of theory, criticism, and biography. By the thirties, this group had divided into two directions. One was the frankly trivial, represented by Lin

Yutang's magazines *Lunyu* (Analects) and *Renjianshi* (This human world), in a supposedly English humorous style. The other was those who wrote for their private amusement or for a limited circle of friends. Zhu Guangqian fell back on the "psychological" function of literature to show that the proper social role of the writer was to ignore society's demands. Detachment was required precisely because the writer should concern himself with the proper functioning of the human mind, not with problems of society. Quoting I. A. Richards, Zhu wrote that the function of poetry is not simply to assuage grief or to enhance a life of leisure but to bring to people in general new and varied experiences of life so that they may absorb the vitality that sustains life and extends its meaning.[18] Zhu seemed to think that poets have a special ability to perceive what other people cannot, for instance, to perceive joy in grief, though, after Croce, he denied that poetic intuition can be separated from the actual creation of poetry.[19] By exposing the expressionist fallacy of the "dumb poet" (as held for example by Guo Moruo), Zhu emphasized the need for writers to refine both their perceptions and their use of language. To employ his special talent, the writer must remain detached from his material so that he may approach it with a fresh and "aesthetic" eye. Here, Zhu quoted the theory of "psychical distance" as advanced by a British psychologist, Edward Bullough. Bullough's intention was to defend literature against realism; Zhu gave the impression that he was defending literature against the demands of political activists, particularly from the left.[20]

Other writers sought exemption from the demands of ordinary life by claiming that their proper function as poets was solely to create beauty. The poet He Qifang, for example, held up Archimedes as a model of devotion to his particular duty: when soldiers came to arrest him, his only concern was to complete his drawing of a perfect circle.[21] In reaction against the popular theories of the twenties, He Qifang found in T. S. Eliot that poetry was not a turning loose of emotion, nor the expression of personality, but an escape from emotion and personality.[22] Like Shelley, he sometimes felt that he was simply a harp through which a wind passed calling forth sounds whose origin was not known to him; like Shelley, he sometimes sang to cheer his own solitude with "sweet sounds," but unlike Shelley, or Eliot either, his ambition did not go beyond these sweet sounds or the escape from self. One of his characters in self-explanation confesses that his talent is to play the lute, and in an age like the present that demanded the strident clamor of the trumpet, he could only put aside his lute and fall into hopeless despair.[23] Sometimes there is a more urgent need to escape: his poems and essays of the period 1934–1935 dwell on the theme of illusion, calling on Valéry and the subtle masters of Tang and Song. By suggesting the confusion between illusion and reality, he hoped to avoid reality altogether, though he was always aware of the dangers in doing this. In the end, he put down his lute.[24]

Not only did Chinese writers in general look to Western models, regardless of their political beliefs, but in the source of their inspiration a great deal of overlapping took place. For example, the Literary Association, which was known chiefly for its interest in modern realistic literature, also contained in its journals translations and studies from Western classical, medieval, and romantic literature, while the conservative *Critical Review*, which happily adopted Babbitt's criticism of both romanticism and realism, still featured writers such as Edgar Allan Poe, Shelley, Hugo, and Paul Bourget, and shared Arnold with romantics and realists alike. Nor can one draw a simple graph consigning realists to left-wing literature and romantics to the right. Flamboyantly romantic at its inception, the Creation Society soon turned toward the left, but even its politicization after the May Thirtieth Incident of 1925 failed to curb its passion for Western individualistic and decadent literature of the late nineteenth and early twentieth centuries. In the first issue of the new *Chuangzao yuekan* (Creation monthly) in March 1926, the young French-educated Mu Mutian and Wang Duqing ridiculed the prosaic attitude toward literature adopted by the early May Fourth reformers and introduced in their letters and in their own work pure poetry and symbolist *correspondance* into Chinese poetry; even Musset and Vigny were linked with the new age, along with Verlaine and Rimbaud. The first issue also contained an article by He Wei on the death of individualism in art, citing Mallarmé, Kandinsky, dadaists, and futurists all as examples of extreme individualism developed in reaction to the oppression of an unjust society. The spirit of Byron is invoked in several articles, one by Liang Shiqiu before his conversion to classicism. And when Jiang Guangci began his series on Russian literature after the October Revolution, affirming the importance of art as a revolutionary activity, his own choice of subjects fell on the more experimental and individualistic writers: Blok, Bedny, Ehrenburg, Essenin, and the Serapion brothers. Even when Guo Moruo formally renounced romanticism for proletarian art in his famous "Geming yu wenxue" (Revolution and literature), he still kept art in the vanguard of the revolution.

Urging Chinese writers to oppose imperialism and strengthen revolutionary literature, he stressed that Chinese literature had to keep up with trends in European literary development that had become worldwide.[25]

On the whole, Chinese writers at this time regarded Western literature as superior to their own classical and folk tradition.[26] A collective admission on this scale is remarkable, especially when applied to crucial questions of social identity, yet it was possible for the Chinese to sustain their tremendous enthusiasm for Western literature without falling into a crippling sense of inferiority. One reason for this lies in the general trend in Europe and America at the close of the nineteenth century to regard cultural as well as biological phenomena as universal. The impetus for this kind of thinking came from the Darwinian theory of evolution and was immensely encouraged by the increased ease of communication in the late nineteenth and early twentieth centuries. It was at this time that anthropology began to make spectacular progress, showing the similarities underlying completely different cultures. At the same time, Jung's concept of a "collective unconscious" encouraged research into myths and legends, and many collections of folktales from all over the world were compiled. In China, Zhou Zuoren and others took up the study of mythology,[27] and collections of folk and fairy tales were featured in both Literary Association and Creation journals. The development of new theories in history, anthropology, and psychology all tended to encourage the conviction, common among Western intellectuals in the twenties and reflected in China, that identification with mankind as a whole was a more progressive and enlightened way of thinking than identification with any particular race or nation.[28]

Another aspect of increasing "world consciousness" was the appearance of several books or series in the West presenting general outlines of world history or culture. These were commissioned by the Home University Library and similar organizations to cater to the growth of mass education in England and America in the twenties.[29] Comparative or world literary studies became a recognized genre by the early twentieth century,[30] and the vast amount of world literature translated into English since the late nineteenth century also contributed to the ease with which Chinese writers slipped into their world identities.[31] Through English and Japanese in the twenties, nearly all of world literature, past and present, became available in twentieth-century China. The writer's view of his role in introducing Western literature was not simply as an educator but as a participant and even an innovator. Influenced by Western universalistic thinking, he saw himself as an heir to world literature, which he should reveal to his fellow Chinese and advance by his own contributions. This was not only his response to Western literature, it was also his conditioning by Western thought itself.

Internationalism was also present in the Western literary theories adopted by the Chinese, both romantic and realist. Universalistic thinking in romanticism goes back at least as far as Goethe's philosophy of pantheism and his enthusiasm for non-Germanic culture. This was quickly translated by other romantics into a fondness for the exotic (as in the poetry of Byron and Pushkin, for example) or sparked off a new interest in the humble localities of the writer's origins, as local color lost its tinge of vulgarity and took on a new literary value in the work of Burns, Scott, Daudet, Petöfi, and Mickiewicz. This tendency persisted into realism and became one of its major strengths, as colorful descriptions gave way to a truer portrayal of life in poorer regions all over the world. Both romantic and realist writers could at times be accused of patronage, of presenting a picture of lowlife for the diversion of the educated classes, but at their best they appealed equally to the people they wrote about and to an international audience. Chinese writers, whether espousing realistic or romantic doctrines, all came under the influence of this national/international strain in modern Western literature.

Pride in internationalism, enthusiasm for the recent and the very new in literature, concern for the literatures of smaller countries in the Western world and beyond it, a tendency toward synthesis in regard to literary schools — all of these characteristics of May Fourth literature can be shown to spring from Chinese needs but were also partly conditioned and made acceptable by similar attitudes fashionable in the West. What is basic to the Western literary impact on China is that by the twenties, China had become tied to the rest of the world, subject to whatever social changes affected it. Though only a small section of Chinese society was as yet directly affected by these changes, the young and articulate intellectuals in all parts of China were able to perceive and assimilate these events through the immense quantity of information that came pouring in.

A fine example of the parallel rise and fall of literary trends in China and in the West can be seen in the Crescent Society, which of all the literary societies best sustained an interest in contemporary Western literature from the mid-1920s to 1933. Its journal, *Xinyue yuekan* (Crescent monthly),[32] was originally edited by three poets, Wen Yiduo,

Xu Zhimo, and Rao Mengkan, but in its second year of publication, the editorial board was expanded to bring in people more concerned with general political and social problems. At one stage, these articles nearly outweighed the literary ones, and a new magazine was planned for them; however, the original format persisted. *Crescent Monthly's* unifying theme was its commitment to the Western ideal of individual liberty and its conviction that China could survive only by adopting Western values as exemplified in England and America.[33] In 1929–1930, Hu Shi clashed openly with the Guomindang government over its abandonment of Western-style democracy, and in an article in the September 1929 issue of *Crescent Monthly*, attacked the Guomindang for having betrayed the spirit of May Fourth.[34]

The pro-Western stance is equally evident in the literary side of *Crescent Monthly*. For instance, the book review section was usually divided into two parts, for local and overseas publications, but the local publications were often Chinese translations of Western or Japanese books, so that most of the books reviewed were Western. To counterbalance this somewhat, a few of the Western books reviewed were concerned partly or wholly with China, such as Eunice Tietjen's *Poetry of the Orient* (1928) and F. H. Pritchard's *From Confucius to Mencken* (1929). The overseas publications section was particularly up-to-date, usually listing books published within the last two years. Studies and translations of Western literature were prominently featured in every issue, ranging from Shakespeare and Marguerite de Navarre to O. Henry and Joseph Conrad. By 1931, with Xu Zhimo's death and the virtual retirement of Wen Yiduo, and with attacks from left-wing writers and the Guomindang, the Crescent group became more and more isolated. It had upheld a kind of literary ideology that was also declining in the West: that literature is a form of art suited to the expression of subtle philosophical and psychological intuitions about the nature of the world and man. This attitude was handed down to Crescent readers from romantics and Victorians like Blake, Shelley, Browning, Hazlitt, Tennyson, Hardy, and Bridges, and further refined by Bloomsbury writers such as Virginia Woolf and Katherine Mansfield; A. A. Milne and J. M. Barrie produced rather diluted versions of the tradition.

In the twenties, it had seemed that psychological literature would replace the prosaic realism of Arnold Bennett and H. G. Wells, but Virginia Woolf herself remarked sadly in 1935 on the brief life-span of the new movement and the apparent invincibility of grim realism.[35] The causes of its decline can be traced from the new movement's main preoccupations. First came the psychological problems of the individual, who is either outside society or in a low-key conflict with it. The writers' sense of the desolation of modern society is profound, but their writing did not concern itself with current social movements. Virginia Woolf, for instance, took part in many political and educational activities, but in her novels, the individual's problems of love, the family, and identity entirely overshadowed any suggestion of social unrest. Her main characters, like herself and her friends, may at times be poor, but their level of poverty excluded dirt, disease, and the domestic slavery of women. Second was the new movement's preoccupation with style: the decade was a time of technical experiment and innovation. (Lawrence was the only one who seemed content with the conventional forms of the nineteenth-century novel.) George Orwell suggests that the major reason for the pessimism, rejection of active political involvement, and obsession with style is simply that the whole period of 1910 to 1930 was a prosperous one, especially the twenties: "They were the golden age of the *rentier*-intellectual, a period of irresponsibility such as the world had never before seen."[36] A similar charge could be leveled at the Crescent writers after 1928, with newly secure academic incomes and landlord family holdings behind them.

In the thirties, the literary climate in England changed with the appearance of poets like Auden, Spender, C. Day Lewis, and Louis MacNeice, and novelists like Isherwood and Lehmann. According to Orwell, "if the keynote of the writers of the twenties is 'tragic sense of life,' the keynote of the new writers is 'serious purpose.' " By 1934 or 1935, it was considered eccentric in literary circles not to be more or less left wing, and between 1935 and 1939, the Communist party had an almost irresistible fascination for any writer under forty.[37] These changes were closely linked with the conflict in Europe between Communist and fascist states, and in England and America, with the conflict between capital and labor. The Comintern's activity in assembling and organizing the socially conscious writers cannot be ignored, but the actual social struggles and unrest were the major reasons for the political literature of the thirties.

The demise of the Crescent group, therefore, was not so much due to inadequacies of its talent or organization as to the inevitable result of its anachronistic political beliefs and literary attitudes. Its response to Western literature must command admiration. Its members came to it not as eager apprentices, nor as conscientious literary workers doggedly surveying world trends. Writers like Hu Shi and Xu Zhimo, who had lived abroad for several years, considered themselves natural heirs to the civilization of the whole world, particularly the countries where they had studied; as personal friends of Western writers and scholars, they did not seem to feel that being Chinese was an advantage or disadvantage in literature. Hu's conviction that China had to accept fully the new "world culture," for instance, did not hinder his pioneering investigation of traditional Chinese fiction. Wen Yiduo, the most nationalist of the three, nevertheless dedicated his life to art under the direct influence of Western romanticism. As his dislike for Western society and the Westernization of Chinese intellectuals mounted, his commitment to art for the sake of art, like his embattled counterparts' in the West, grew more intense. In his poetry criticism, Wen deplored the excessive use of Western allusions in the poetry of Guo Moruo, though in his own work the same blend of exotic and local color appears. At the same time, he appealed to both Chinese and Western sources on such major parts of his general theory as the necessity of form in poetry.[38] Soon after the founding of *Crescent Monthly*, the contradiction between Wen's cultural nationalism and Western-style aestheticism became too acute for him to resolve; for nearly a decade, he ceased writing poetry and withdrew from his formerly active literary life. Nevertheless, in its early years, the great achievement of the Crescent Society was its ability to harmonize Western and Chinese culture; influences beyond anyone's control brought it to an end.

The second half of the twenties showed a definite decline in the exploration of Western literature, particularly in regard to countries like England and France. In the middle and toward the right of the political spectrum, a few survivors from the early twenties persisted in their original formats. *Critical Review* continued until 1933 under the same editorship, and up to the end produced translations from Plato, Babbitt, and Shakespeare, plus an occasional poem from French or English romantics, alongside its *wenyan* poetry and its articles on the shortcomings of the new literary movement. *Xiaoshuo yuebao* (Short story monthly) continued until the end of 1931 under the editorship of Zheng Zhenduo; though characterized by younger left-wing writers as having become escapist and cut off from social reality, it could probably have survived even longer were it not for the destruction of the Commercial Press in the Shanghai bombing of 1932. At the end of its life the mixture remained much the same: articles and translations from classical Greece and Rome, modern Europe, Russia, and Japan.

Writers from the Soviet Union appeared alongside the older generation but were not given any special prominence. The literary news
column, now edited by the very well-informed Zhao Jingshen, gave
roughly the same space to the smaller European, Asian, and Latin
American countries as to western Europe, the Soviet Union, and the
United States. But the former domination of foreign literature was
reduced and more space made available to promising new writers like
Ba Jin, Lao She, and Shen Congwen.

Meanwhile, the growing strength of the Soviet Union and the
productions of Soviet writers and critics were attracting the attention
of Chinese writers. Many began to study Marxism and to translate,
usually from English or Japanese versions, postrevolutionary Russian
literature and criticism. Hitherto uncommitted writers like Lu Xun and
Guo Moruo helped set the trend toward greater Chinese interest in the
Russian experiment, while in the articles of Mao Dun, already a
Marxist of some years' standing, there appears increasing reference to
Soviet critics in place of his former English and French masters.

Although in accounts by individual writers this change had clearly
started in the period 1924–1927, its effects were slow in appearing in
the literary magazines. One reason was that many writers, including
Mao Dun and Guo Moruo, became heavily involved in political
activities at the time of the Northern Expedition. Another was that very
few could read or translate directly from the Russian, so that there was
a time lag of up to four or five years, since left-wing literature had not
yet extended fully into the Western world. *Creation Monthly*, for
instance, continued to publish romantic French poetry up to 1928, and
when it did begin to include more material from the Soviet Union, it
ran up against the harsh if capricious Peking censorship and was
banned. A more serious attempt was made by Lu Xun to introduce
Soviet literature and criticism: between 1926 and 1930 he arranged the
publication of two magazines, *Mangyuan* (Wilderness) and *Weiming*
(Unnamed), and the series Weiming congshu (Unnamed Library) for
this purpose. Not all the authors in Weiming congshu were Soviet
writers: they include Gogol, Dostoevsky, and Andreyev as well as
Jonathan Swift, the Japanese critic Kuriyagawa Hakuson, and the
Dutch writer Frederik van Eeden. Unfortunately, as Lu Xun later
wrote, translations then were popular neither with readers nor
publishers, and the Peking authorities showed their displeasure by
closing the press down at least once.[39] Lu Xun also set up *Benliu*
(Torrent) for the more systematic introduction of non-Russian
Western writing, commenting that foreign writers usually had to wait

either for an anniversary or for the award of a Nobel Prize to gain mention in Chinese journals. In *Torrent*, translations generally outweighed Chinese contributions, and relatively few Soviet writers were included; instead, old May Fourth favorites like Ibsen, Turgenev, and Baroja could be found alongside more unlikely and exotic items like poems by Swinburne, Symons, and Apollinaire; illustrations were by Arthur Rackham and Raoul Dufy. There was no sign of any systematic selection. *Torrent* was broad enough to bring in the talents of Yu Dafu and Lin Yutang: the latter's contribution was a selective translation of Van Wyck Brooks's "Our Critics and Young America" (1924).[40] Brooks begins with a comparison between the nascent literatures of Ireland and America, both suffering from the dominance of English literature and criticism: this was obviously relevant to the situation in semicolonial China. He then denounces the shallowness of American cosmopolitanism and its misapplication of the Arnoldian doctrine of "knowing the best that has been thought and said *in the world*," but these passages Lin discreetly omits as inapplicable to Chinese conditions. Lin Yutang was often criticized by his contemporaries for his antiquarian leanings, but he was also one of the most dedicated internationalists in modern China.

Soviet influence showed up more clearly in the Sun Society (Taiyang she) publications. *Haifeng zhoubao* (Seabreeze weekly), which published seventeen issues between January and April 1929, featured original work by Chinese writers and critics, but translations from Soviet literature, articles by and about Soviet writers, and news from the Soviet Union dominated all else. Occasional non-Russian writers were included, invariably left-wing writers like Barbusse, Upton Sinclair, John Reed, and writers from eastern European countries like Poland. In contrast, *Dazhong wenyi* (Mass literature), edited by Yu Dafu, tried a more balanced, internationalist approach. In its two special issues on "newly arisen literature" (March and May 1930), reports on new writing came from Germany, France, England, America, and Japan as well as from Russia. In its translation section, Soviet authors were dominant, but American, German, French, Japanese, and Korean writers were also represented. Chinese writing, both original and critical, made up the larger part.

By 1930, when the League of Left-Wing Writers was set up, the Soviet Union had become the dominant if not the exclusive target of attention by writers in all sections of the left-wing movement. The league's own journals fell into two categories. The first, represented by *Baerdishan* (Partisan) in April and May 1930, and *Shizi jietou* (Crossroads) from December 1931 to March 1932, consisted solely of articles on current issues, not necessarily literary, with only an occasional poem for relief. There are no translations, no articles on overseas literary trends, no Western names scattered across the pages (though one reader had to ask what "baerdishan" meant). There are, however, passing references to Western literature (such as the development of proletarian poetry in nineteenth-century Germany and England), and resistance to cultural imperialism was carefully aligned with proletarian internationalism. *Crossroads* published an article on translation that stressed the importance of translating from world proletarian literature, especially from the Soviet Union; apart from introducing these works to the Chinese public, the author believed that translations were also necessary to enrich the vocabulary and grammar of modern vernacular Chinese writing. This article sparked off the two leading articles in the league's next publication *Wenxue yuebao* (see below), on mass literature and on translation, with Qu Qiubai and Lu Xun respectively arguing the disadvantages and advantages of Westernization.

The league also published journals with a more international emphasis. The first issue of *Qianshao* (Outpost) in April 1931 was a special one to commemorate the five martyrs executed by the Guomindang government; the journal was immediately closed down. It reappeared in August under a new name, *Wenxue daobao* (Literary guide). This issue carried letters of protest against the executions from writers and literary organizations in Germany, Austria, America, England, and Japan. A further international petition was drawn up by the International Union of Revolutionary Writers in Moscow, with signatories from twelve countries in Europe and America. Announcements and reports from the IURW were given prominence throughout the eight issues of the magazine, along with reports on proletarian literature in Germany and Russia and communications from left-wing associations in America and Japan.

Literary Guide was closed down in November 1931, and succeeded in June 1932 by *Wenxue yuebao* (Literature monthly). More in the style of the now defunct *Short Story Monthly, Literature Monthly* carried poetry, fiction, and drama by well-known writers such as Ba Jin, Mao Dun, and Tian Han. It also contained translations from Soviet and eastern European writers, but the proportion of native to foreign works, compared to *Short Story Monthly*, was much greater, and excluded western European literature entirely. Notes on the literary scene in other countries were mainly from the Soviet Union and America.

Though wider in literary appeal than any of its league predecessors, *Literature Monthly* proved no better at survival, and after its closure in December 1932, the league ceased publishing its own journals.

Beidou (Big dipper) was a roughly contemporaneous independent left-wing journal edited by Ding Ling. The amount of original writing was greater than in *Literature Monthly*, and translations of foreign literature were kept to an even barer minimum — basically one item per issue. There was a column for introductions that had notes on traditional Chinese literature but was mainly about modern Western writers: Barbusse, Zola, Dreiser. In later issues a column on world literature appeared, mostly with news from the Soviet Union and America. There were also a few articles from Japanese writers and reports on Japanese proletarian literature, and the irrepressible Mu Mutian managed to slip in a long article on Villon. The dominant foreign country mentioned was still Russia. Another independent left magazine, *Xindi yuekan* (New earth monthly), had a similar approach, though its circulation probably did not extend much beyond the circle of its editors, a group of Beida students. It carried only a few translations, but there were several articles on literature by Japanese left-wing writers.

On the whole, Western literature was poorly served by the left during the years 1928 to 1933. The total number of translations from Western writing was significantly reduced, and the focus of interest became much narrower: the only authors who appear with any frequency are Barbusse, Sinclair, Dos Passos, Michael Gold, and J. R. Becher. Eastern European writers were featured only occasionally, but the Soviet Union was well represented with translations, articles, news, and comments: no other single country had previously dominated the literary scene to such an extent. Another new development was the growing interest in Japanese literature for its own sake: proletarian literature had flourished there much earlier than in China or elsewhere in the world. Theoretical articles on left-wing literature were also just as likely to be from Japanese as from Soviet authors. In part, this can be attributed to wider Chinese access to Japanese material, but the main reason is probably the vigor of modern Japanese literature. Non–left-wing journals, like *Short Story Monthly* and later *Xiandai wenxue* and *Wenyi yuekan* (for these, see below), also shared this growing interest. In the West, left-wing literature was most advanced in America and Germany, and writers from these countries were best represented in left-wing journals; very few English writers were mentioned.[41] Nevertheless, one of the most striking features of left-wing publications, particularly after the formation of the league, is their total rejection of national chauvinism and insistence on proletarian internationalism. By the thirties, left-wing writers in most Western countries had formed well-organized groups, mostly with strong links to the Soviet Union and support from the Comintern. The appearance of the league in China from the disarray of the splinter groups of the late twenties was primarily in response to increasing government oppression, but it was also part of a worldwide trend.[42]

Harassed by censorship, the league and other left-wing journals were generally short-lived, but at this time middle- and right-wing publications were not doing well either. *Short Story Monthly* in 1931, *Thread of Talk* in 1932, *Critical Review* and *Crescent Monthly* in 1933 — all came to an end. It was not only Soviet books that were banned: Sinclair, Strindberg, and even Maeterlinck were banned in the thirties.[43] In general, these were not easy years. One short-lived attempt to fill the gap left by *Short Story Monthly* was *Xiandai wenxue* (Contemporary literature), published in Shanghai in 1931. The editor, Ye Lingfeng, was an evident Europhile with a weakness for Latin tags; while the journal published mainly original work by Ye and his friends, its first stated aim was to introduce Western literature, both recent and from the past; the editor had to be reminded by a reader to include news from the Chinese literary scene. In its translations and articles, it included writers from pre- and postrevolutionary Russia, America, England, Italy, Poland, Japan, and Korea. Most of the western European writers discussed were from the nineteenth century, like Balzac and Tolstoy, but contemporary figures like James Joyce, Valéry, and Sinclair Lewis also put in a brief appearance. Whether it failed to gain an audience or for some other reason is not clear, but the journal even for those days was very short-lived. Lacking the breadth of *Short Story Monthly* or the depth of *Crescent Monthly*, it expired after only two issues.

Of the warring factions of 1930 to 1933, the League of Left-Wing Writers demanded proletarian internationalism, the Crescent Society advocated liberal-democratic internationalism, and even the nationalist and conservative groups drew on Western models to defend their positions. Which faction should be considered the true heirs of the May Fourth new literary movement? The left-wing writers could claim that by broadening the literary movement to include the masses, by active participation in current political and social struggles, and by introducing literature in the tradition of realism and social reform, they carried forward the true spirit of May Fourth. The Crescent and other writers in the middle could counterclaim that their liberal-democratic ideals, their continued promotion of Western literature, and their readiness for intellectual speculation and literary experimentation more strictly adhered to the actual practice of the early new literary movement. The conservatives, of course, were consistent in their opposition to literary reform. What remains the intriguing question is the resurgence of interest in contemporary Western literature that took place in the left-wing movement in the years from 1933 to 1937.

After the closing down of *Literature Monthly* at the end of 1932, league members began to contribute to broader-based journals, reaching a wider audience and in less danger of government censorship. The most prominent of these journals was *Wenxue* (Literature). It had no formal connection with the league but has been described as "the most durable and influential leftist magazine of its time."[44] In its first issue (July 1933), Western literature was present but not predominant. In the first item, a collection of short articles under the general title of "Wusi wenxue yundongzhi lishide yiyi" (The historical significance of the May Fourth literary movement), Yu Dafu and others acknowledged the very great importance of Western literature in enriching modern Chinese culture. Of the other articles, only one referred specifically to the West: Liang Zongdai's article on Montaigne. Western references occurred mostly in a series of notes, many of them seemingly quite irrelevant to modern Chinese concerns: for example, Fu Donghua's note on the difference in sympathies between Aeschylus's tragedy *Prometheus Bound* and Shelley's lyrical drama *Prometheus Unbound.* Subsequent issues gave more attention to Western literature, but the same curious note of seeming irrelevance persisted. In some cases, however, that irrelevance was more apparent than real. In the July 1934 issue, there is a well-researched article on Theodore Dreiser by Wu Lifu and an equally serious study of J. M. Barrie by Gu Zhongyi, who had previously adapted Barrie's *The Twelve Pound Look* (1914) for *Crescent Monthly*. This play is a one-act, watered-down and updated version of Ibsen's *A Doll's House,* in which the redeeming social message that useful employment is better for women than idle luxury compensates somewhat for the patronizingly arch treatment of the characters. Another unlikely author to appear in *Literature* is Noel Coward. On the occasion of Coward's visit to China in 1935, the editor commissioned the playwright Hong Shen to write an article on him for the May issue, and for the following one Hong also prepared a translation of *The Vortex* (1923). Like Oscar Wilde,

Coward is not an author one would easily associate with the new literary movement, especially in its left-wing phase, but *The Vortex* is in fact a serious, even bitter drama about hypocrisy and moral decay in self-styled artistic circles. Although the names of Barrie, Coward, and Wilde are primarily associated with light comedy, the social criticism in their work was apparent to their Chinese as well as Western contemporaries.

Other items are more difficult to defend. Volume 3, number 2 (August 1934) lists the twenty books published in America between 1875 and 1935 that sold over a million copies. There is no suggestion that this list should be the basis of a translation program, and more than half the titles listed are distinctly inferior, such as the more recent best sellers by Gene Stratton Porter. The September issue reproduced, without comment, a survey conducted by the British *Observer* on the best-loved animals in literature: Rosinante, Rab, Brer Rabbit, Rikki-Tikki-Tavi, the Cheshire cat, Black Beauty, Modestine, the hound of the Baskervilles, Nana, and Owd Bob. The irrelevance of this information to the Chinese literary movement is remarkable. It could be explained as simply a fondness for list making, or else as a comment on mass literature in England and America.

The systematic introduction to Western literature continued to pose a major problem throughout 1934 and 1935. In July 1934, *Literature* drew attention to a new American journal, *The Literary World*, which not only published stories from all over the world but also listed major articles on literature in current European periodicals. This feature had two uses for a Chinese audience, according to *Literature*: as a guide to current journals and to indicate the latest trends in literary studies. In 1935 *Literature* decided to systematize its treatment of foreign literature with a series of detailed critical studies on past and present writers with translated excerpts from their work. Apart from Hu Feng's essay on Lin Yutang, all these studies were on Western writers (Schiller, Keats, Hugo, Hans Christian Andersen, Jókai Mór, Mark Twain, Isaac Babel, and Noel Coward), and apart from Babel and Coward, they were chosen simply because an important anniversary of their birth or death happened to fall in 1935. In 1934 there had been some discussion in *Literature* of the "literary inheritance" of the modern Chinese writer. Alarmed by the increasing Westernization of Chinese intellectuals, some contributors criticized current *baihua* writing as a new kind of *wenyan;* others defended the popularity of world literature, claiming that "the masterpieces of world literature form part of our own precious heritage." Their enthusiasm prevailed. *Literature* declared

1935 "the year of translation," and for the January issue, Fu Donghua contributed an elegant translation of Keats's "Ode to a Nightingale," and Mao Dun translated Andersen's "Snowdrop." There was also much talk of the need for a properly planned translation program. Lin Shu was criticized for having chosen his material at random, based on his personal taste; so was the unbalanced selection in the recently published Second Series of the Commercial Press Wanyou wenku (Universal Library).[45] In the end, *Literature* failed to adopt any program itself.

Meanwhile, *Literature* continued its commentary on the latest literary news from all parts of the world. Aldous Huxley's *Beyond the Mexique Bay* (1934) was recommended chiefly for its reminiscences of D. H. Lawrence, though the editor also commented that since Lawrence's death, Huxley must rate among the top two or three living English writers. The easy assumption of Lawrence's fame in China is unexpected, since he was seldom mentioned in journals during this period, and Huxley hardly at all. Yet the satiric analyses of a leisured class by the one author and the powerful descriptions of an awakening class by the other make both Huxley and Lawrence natural candidates for *Literature's* attention. News from countries outside Europe, Russia, and America continued — Mexico's development of a written vernacular language is sympathetically noted — but the twenties' concern for "poor and oppressed" countries seemed to have faded slightly. One final example of the lingering belief in Western culture among left-wing writers may be seen in the manifesto published in *Literature* in July 1935. Entitled "Women duiyu wenhua yundong de yijian" (Our opinions concerning the cultural movement), it was supported by seventeen organizations and 148 individual writers, including Lao She, Ye Shengtao, Fu Donghua, Zhao Jiabi, and Zheng Zhenduo. To counteract the government-supported movement for a renewal of classical studies in schools, the manifesto advances two propositions: first, China must continue to learn from the West; and second, it must also shape its social and literary policies to answer the needs of the whole people, not just an elite. The general conclusion was that the twin ideals of nationalism and internationalism should be supported and regarded as complementary rather than contradictory policies.

From this brief survey of *Literature*, it can be seen that for a left-wing magazine, it was remarkably broad in its interests and sophisticated in its familiarity with Western literature. Some of the references to Western writers might have been no more than name-dropping, and the inclusion of one author instead of another due to chance rather than to any deep understanding. *Literature* also shows a tendency to descend into mere gossip on current literary trends. In part, this is the result of too great a respect for all aspects of Western culture, a kind of colonial hangover that gives rise to the kind of "cosmopolitanism" described by Levenson.[46] Despite continual demands for systematization, the overall pattern of Western literature in *Literature* is quite haphazard, making it impossible to discern any selection mechanism beyond the accident of birth or death. In individual cases, however, contributors to *Literature* such as Ma Zongrong[47] set about their studies in a serious and systematic way, and many seeming irrelevancies carried information or insights appreciated by Chinese audiences. What remains is the strong probability that Chinese writers and readers not only looked to Western literature for material of social relevance but that while immediate social and political problems were not too overwhelming, they also sought there stimulation, inspiration, and pure enjoyment.

The widespread nature of this renewed enthusiasm for Western literature can be seen in the sudden spate of new literary journals that appeared between 1933 and 1935. Starting on June 1, 1933, the same date as *Literature*, the Peking magazine *Wenyi yuebao* (Literature and art monthly) was designed to fill the gap left by *Northern Dipper* and *Literature Monthly*. Like them strongly left wing in character, it also featured Western writers like Barbusse, Sinclair, and Sherwood Anderson as well as Soviet Russian writers. The Russian emphasis still dominated, and perhaps for this reason, the magazine had folded by the end of the year. Its last issue announced the publication of a new journal, *Wenxue jikan* (Literature quarterly), edited by Zheng Zhenduo and Jin Yi. *Literature Quarterly* was welcomed by *Literature* and the two seemed to be on friendly terms, operating from Peking and Shanghai respectively and sharing the same Shanghai distributor (the left-wing Shenghuo shudian). They also drew on overlapping groups of writers (Lao She, Jin Yi, Zheng Zhenduo, Bian Zhilin, and Wu Zuxiang), though *Literature Quarterly* has been identified as more independent from the left than *Literature*. In their attitudes to Western literature they are much the same, and in both publications Lawrence and Joyce, or Eliot and Richards, appear more frequently than Soviet writers and critics. *Literature* was more interested in Marxist and realistic criticism of the content and background of literature, and *Literature Quarterly* in technical problems of literary creation — it also saw itself more consciously as the successor to *Short Story Monthly*.

Following *Literature Quarterly* several other literary journals were established in the northern cities and other major centers in China, leading *Literature* to comment that 1934 should be known as "the year of journals." In 1935 two new magazines devoted to translations appeared, one of them edited by Lu Xun; *Literature* noted that the bad name once given to translations seemed to have disappeared. Finally, the success of *Wenyi yuekan* (Literature and art monthly) in Nanking should be mentioned, for it is the only literary journal that lasted right through the thirties. Like *Crescent Monthly*, it promoted the universal nonclass character of literature but at the same time also maintained that literature could not cut itself off from the age (though it might transcend it) and survive. Its three aims were to develop the national spirit, to introduce contemporary thinking from all over the world, and to create a new Chinese literature on the basis of the May Fourth literary revolution. From its very beginning in 1930, it emphasized the literature of "weak and small nations": Bulgaria, Yugoslavia, Sweden, Norway, Ireland, and India. The motive was clearly political, despite statements like "in the garden of literature there are no national boundaries." The point is repeated twice that China and other weak nations can achieve national liberation and world peace through literature that expresses the national spirit. Alongside these lofty national/international aims was an equally strong interest in the more decadent aspects of nineteenth-century French literature: poems by Verlaine and Baudelaire, articles on Verlaine (by Arthur Symons), on Maupassant (by Tolstoy), and on Huysmans (based on Symons and others). To add further atmosphere, the magazine was decorated throughout with line drawings of partially clad women and misshapen little men and enclosed between covers of Beardsley-like silver nudes against a black background. Its favorite English author was Thomas Hardy, and it preferred older Russian literature to Soviet writing. It was so successful that its editors were able to set up a weekly as well, and *Literature and Art Monthly* in the years up to September 1937 managed to attract contributors of the caliber of Shen Congwen, Ba Jin, Lao She, Zang Kejia, He Qifang, and Bian Zhilin. It lost its exotic covers over the years and reduced its Western content slightly but maintained its broad outlook and identity with oppressed nations. It was one of the very few journals to continue during the war, publishing first in Hankow and later in Chungking.

The impact of Western literature in China in the twenties and thirties above all fostered a sense of internationalism among Chinese writers. Partly stimulated by the riches offered in this literature, internationalism was also a concept from the West, not perhaps so much from overt explication as from the examples of cultural internationalism prevailing in Western literary scholarship. The persistence of traditional Chinese attitudes in the new generation should be acknowledged, but it was significant that even traditional attitudes required the sanction of Western defenses.

The kind of internationalism adopted in China was also, on the whole, "inter-national" rather than cosmopolitan. That is, Chinese writers envisaged a family of nations in which each country contributed in its own unique way to a world culture, making it much easier for Chinese writers to feel that their own contributions could be worthwhile. The emphasis on the literature of the poor and oppressed countries in the twenties and the attention given to "the people" or the proletariat also helped maintain the spirit of a "community of nations."[48] Despite their country's semicolonial status and technological backwardness, Chinese writers could still feel that their national background was not a disadvantage in terms of their contribution to world literature. On the contrary, by writing about actual conditions in China, poor and backward as they were, the writer would be bringing China into the mainstream of world literature, as Irish and Polish writers had done. The two strands of nationalism and internationalism appear tightly intertwined. During the late twenties and the thirties, internationalism was further strengthened and politicized by the introduction of Marxist thinking and the activities of the Comintern. Internationalism also persisted among non–left-wing writers, so that we find Zhu Guangqian defending traditional Chinese culture with reference to contemporary Western scholarship while at the same time criticizing the same Western scholarship from his own experience in traditional Chinese literature.[49]

In general, Western literature also encouraged reformist and modernist attitudes among Chinese writers. But Western influence was both widespread and multifaceted: left-wing writers saw themselves as prophets, reformers, and revolutionaries; liberal democrats saw themselves as defending the independence of writers from governments and political parties; conservative or right-wing writers were confirmed in their private escapism and conservatism, all by selecting the appropriate authorities. China's political and economic ties with the rest of the world, and the sensitivity of Chinese writers to literary movements abroad, made the development of literary movements in China very nearly parallel and contemporary with movements in other countries, such as England and America. This contemporaneity tends to be masked for present observers in that we now judge the twenties and thirties in both China and the West from the standards of our own generation, influenced by forty or fifty years of critical study and by our own preoccupations. Joyce and Kafka, for example, were by no means heroes of their generation or typical of the time, and Chinese literary judgments on them and lesser figures also should be seen against contemporary opinion in the West. The very immediacy of the Chinese reaction may have hindered their deeper understanding of the course of Western literature so that Chinese judgments on contemporary literature had insufficient historical background and experience. Although for these and other reasons, it is easy to ridicule certain aspects of the Western impact in China or to undervalue its seriousness, it is hard to avoid being impressed by the energetic and sensitive response of Chinese writers of this period to Western literary trends. In their aspirations and also in their achievements, the writers of the May Fourth movement brought China into world literature and underlined the necessity for the new literary movement to be studied in the world context, not as an isolated phenomenon unique to China.

3.

The Impact of Japanese Literary Trends on Modern Chinese Writers

Ching-mao Cheng

"The modern Chinese literary world has for the most part been constructed by students returned from Japan," Guo Moruo once unabashedly declared. The major writers affiliated with important literary societies were students returned from Japan, he explained. Some good writers had studied in Europe and America, and some talented ones had emerged from within the country, but their efforts and achievements not only were much less extensive than the Japanese-educated writers, they also remained largely under that influence. "Such being the case," Guo concluded, "the new literature of China can be said to have been baptized by Japan."[1] Statistics prove his claim. Most Chinese writers who were active and influential during the twenties and thirties had studied in Japan.[2]

Because of its humiliating defeat in the Sino-Japanese War (1894–1895), China was forced to realize that Japan, earlier regarded as its faithful cultural disciple, had become an advanced country. Beginning in 1896, Chinese students were sent to study in Japan. This decision was initially an unpleasant necessity rooted in the hope that China could modernize itself by following the Japanese example. As time passed, especially after the Russo-Japanese War (1904–1905), many Chinese became genuinely impressed with Japan's remarkable modernization since the Meiji Restoration (1868). Some even reasserted the false conception of linguistic and ethnic affinity (*tongwen tongzhong*) with the Japanese, indulging themselves in the glory of Japanese victory as if they had won it. To find out why Japan could be so successful while China suffered repeated failures, more and more Chinese students went to Japan under either government (central or provincial) or private sponsorship. In the 1906–1907 academic year, their estimated number exceeded ten thousand.[3]

Responding to Chinese eagerness to learn, the Japanese were as eager to teach. But the massive presence of Chinese students bewildered many Japanese and undermined their efforts to educate them and their justification to do so. A famous "cultural critic" wrote cynically in the November 1902 issue of the influential *Taiyō* (The sun) magazine: "Having stolen Western civilization and haughtily assumed it to themselves, and having conceitedly become more and more proud of themselves after the victories in the Sino-Japanese War and Boxer Incident [1900], the Japanese nowadays tend to look arrogantly upon themselves as the teachers of China."[4] The so-called "Western civilization," and little else, was what the Chinese wanted most to learn from Japan — second hand, of course. To most Chinese, then, Western civilization meant little more than practical learning, acquiring technological skills useful at home: military tactics, engineering, medicine, politics, economics, and education. No wonder that nearly all Chinese students, even those who were to become prominent in the new literary movement, majored in these practical disciplines — by their own choice or under instruction from the government.

Why were so many Chinese studying in Japan later attracted to literature? Major modern Chinese writers like Lu Xun, Zhou Zuoren, Yu Dafu, and Guo Moruo became involved in literary activities while studying something else in Japanese universities. To explain this unusual phenomenon, there is a much-quoted statement from Lu Xun's autobiography:

> By the time I graduated from a Tokyo preparatory school, I had decided to study medicine. One of the reasons was that new medical science, I was convinced then, had contributed a great deal to the success of Japan's modernization. I therefore entered the Sendai Medical School, where I studied for two years. That was the time when the Russo-Japanese War was going on. I happened to see in a newsreel a Chinese who was about to be decapitated [by the Japanese] for serving as a [Russian] spy. I felt then that China had to promote a new literature before doing anything else.[5]

After watching the newsreel, he said, he suddenly realized that medicine was not a pressing need, because the people of an unenlightened and weak country, no matter how physically healthy they were, would serve only as the senseless spectators for public executions. Lu Xun concluded that China must first transform the spirit of its people and that "the best way for spiritual transformation was through literature."[6] This well-known turn in Lu Xun's life from medicine to literature typifies the experience of many Chinese students who abandoned their original careers for literature because their deepest concern was the "spiritual transformation" of their people.

The idea that literature can produce "spiritual transformation" was not new in China. Chinese tradition, particularly Confucian teaching, had long considered literature as an important vehicle of moral teaching, indispensable to the official and intellectual activities in the service of one's country. In this connection, the most quoted passage had been from Cao Pi's (187–226) essay "Dianlun lunwen" (On literature): "Literature is a great undertaking in the building of a state, a splendid enterprise that can be immortal."[7] Modern Chinese intellectuals saw that literature had fostered social and political change in Japan and Western countries. So they revitalized the ancient Chinese idea of literature's important function and gave it a new emphasis. Rather than focusing on poetry and the essay, two of the most respected traditional literary genres, this renewed interest in literature was distinguished by its enthusiastic promotion of fiction, which had always been publicly despised for being vulgar despite its wide audience in private circles.

One person initially responsible for this change was Liang Qichao, and the literary trends of Meiji Japan helped shape his views of fiction. Often considered the most influential intellectual force in the two decades prior to the May Fourth movement (1919), Liang was in exile in Japan from the failure of the 1898 reform until the Republic of China was established in 1912. Before exile, he had served as chief editor of *Shiwu bao* (Current affairs journal) under the influence of Huang Zunxian, whose *Riben guozhi* (Japanese history [1890]) was probably the most responsible for changing Chinese attitudes toward Japan. Liang had already observed in *Current Affairs Journal* that "the reform of Japan has relied heavily on popular songs and novels, for nothing else can better serve to entertain children and enlighten the people."[8] Immediately after arriving in Japan as an exile in 1898, he started *Qingyi bao* (The China discussion), and later, *Xinmin congbao* (New people journal) and *Xin xiaoshuo* (New fiction) in 1902, to continue his campaign for China's enlightenment. Barely two months after his arrival in Japan, he wrote in the first issue of *The China Discussion* (October 1898):

The genre of the political novel originated in the West. . . Formerly, in European countries, at the beginning of any reform or revolution, their leading scholars, wise men, as well as people of virtue and principle often described their own experiences and political views in novels. . . Indeed, political fiction should be given the highest credit for the daily progress of political conditions in America, England, Germany, France, Austria, Italy, and Japan. A celebrated English scholar said, "Fiction is the soul of the people." How right! How right!

Liang Qichao then spelled out his plan to translate and serialize in *The China Discussion* foreign political novels "that are of instructive value to the current situation of China," so that "patriots of our country can read them."[9]

To prove he was not just talking, Liang translated *Kajin no kigū* (in Chinese, *Jiaren qiyu*, Romantic encounters with beautiful ladies), a political novel by Shiba Shirō (better known as Tōkai Sanshi, 1852–1922). This was serialized in thirty-five installments, starting with the first issue of *The China Discussion*. He had just barely begun learning Japanese then, but his translation was praised by some Japanese as "really great, even better than the original."[10] Later, another famous Japanese political novel, *Keikoku bidan* (in Chinese, *Jingguo meitan*, Praiseworthy anecdotes of statesmanship), by Yano Ryūkei (1850–1931), about the heroic and successful struggles of the Thebans against Spartan encroachment in ancient Greece, was anonymously translated and serialized. Apparently not satisfied with translations alone, Liang wrote several novels and plays of his own. Among the best known is *Xin Zhongguo weilai ji* (Future events of new China [1902]). This book was evidently inspired by the Japanese *miraiki* (accounts of the future) novels like *Mōsō miraiki* (Fanciful accounts of the future [1878]) by Baitei Tōjin, *Nijūsannen miraiki* (Accounts of the future twenty-three years [1886]) by Suehiro Tetchō, and *Nippon no mirai* (The future of Japan [1887]) by Ushiyama Kakudō.

Liang Qichao's obsession with fiction, particularly political fiction, led him to publish another journal, *New Fiction*, in the winter of 1902. After four years of closely observing Japanese literary circles and with some ability to read Japanese, he declared in his opening article for the new journal's first issue that "fiction is the highest form of all literature" and called for a "revolution in fiction" (*xiaoshuojie geming*). If the Chinese wanted to reform their popular education, modernize their morality, religion, government, customs, learning, art, as well as their mind and personality, they had to start with new, modernized fiction. Why? "Because fiction has a power beyond imagination to control humanity."[11]

Though he was exiled for over a decade, Liang Qichao's influence was felt throughout China — not only in big cities but also in remote villages in all provinces. Nearly all political and cultural leaders of the succeeding generation gratefully acknowledged, on occasion, their indebtedness to Liang Qichao for his intellectual stimulation and the inspiration gained largely through reading his overseas publications smuggled into China.[12]

His contribution to the development of modern Chinese is greater than is generally realized today. Qian Xuantong actually called him "one of the creators of new literature" and credited his surpassing insight in "importing Japanese sentence structures, employing new terms and common sayings in writings, and treating drama and novel as equals to expository essays."[13] Zhou Zuoren agreed with Qian in appraising Liang Qichao's contribution in terms of Japanese-Chinese literary relations:

> Speaking of the recent development of Chinese fiction when compared with that of Japan, we can find some similarities and differences between the two countries... Formerly, fiction writing was always considered a "low-down occupation" in China and was never respected until after the last year of the nineteenth century when, with the publications of *China Discussion* and *New People* journals, Liang Qichao began to talk about the "Relations between Fiction and Popular Education," and published *New Fiction* as a result. This important reform movement is very similar to what took place in the early Meiji era.[14]

Another look at Liang Qichao's position in the formation of modern Chinese literature was offered by Masuda Wataru, possibly the most informed Japanese scholar of modern Chinese literary history. He said, "It is not extravagant to state that the 'literary revolution' is a 1917 version of the 'revolution in fiction.' "[15]

Certainly, Liang deserves such praise. His contribution to and subsequent influence on modern China as a journalist, educator, and reformer compares to that of Fukuzawa Yukichi (1834–1901), the first and strongest advocate of *bummei kaika* (civilization and enlightenment) in Meiji Japan. But he distinguished himself from Fukuzawa by his unusual emphasis on the utility of political fiction. In the sixty-ninth issue of *The China Discussion*, its editorial board (possibly Liang Qichao himself) stated that novels like *Praiseworthy Anecdotes of Statesmanship* and *Romantic Encounters with Beautiful Ladies* published so far in the journal were "the harbingers of Chinese political fiction."

One might similarly say that *New Fiction* was the forerunner of Chinese fiction periodicals. After its inception in Yokohama, Japan, in 1902, it not only published many memorable works but also set the example for many similar magazines that soon appeared one after another in China, such as *Xiuxiang xiaoshuo* (Illustrated novels [1903]), *Yueyue xiaoshuo* (Monthly novels [1906]), and *Xiaoshuo lin* (The forest of fiction [1907]). Working toward a common goal established by *New Fiction*, these magazines together published a great number of political and social novels, or what Lu Xun called *qianze xiaoshuo* (exposure or reprimand fiction).[16] This is reminiscent of a similar phenomenon in late Tokugawa and early Meiji Japan, *kanzen-chōaku shōsetsu* (encourage-the-good-and-reprimand-the-evil novel).

The best time for Japanese political fiction is generally said to have been between 1880 and 1890. First, it is considered a manifestation of the *jiyū minken* (democratic) movement of the early Meiji era. Many a Japanese intellectual then, in or out of office, tried to express his social and political views in fiction as a means of informing the people and influencing government attitudes and policies. Second, the popularity of political fiction was a result of an increased number of translated or adapted works of Western literature since the Meiji Restoration. The most popular Western authors at that time were Sir Thomas More, Shakespeare, and Edward George Bulwer-Lytton; Alexandre Dumas (*père*), Victor Hugo, and Jules Verne; as well as Russian nihilists.[17] Few of these authors are political novelists in the strict sense, but their works were more often than not given titles with a strong political flavor. One translation of Shakespeare's *Julius Caesar* was entitled *Kaisa kidan: jiyū no tachi nagori no kireaji* (roughly, A tale of Caesar: the lingering sharpness of the long liberty sword). Dumas's *The Memoirs of a Physician* became *Kakumei kigen: nishi no umi chishio no saarashi* (The origin of revolution: bloody winds on the western sea); Verne's *Martin Poz* won a rather sentimental new name, *Seiji shōsetsu: kajin no chi'namida* (A political novel: blood and tears of a beauty).

By 1898, when Liang Qichao arrived in Japan, the peak of Japanese political fiction had been past for nearly a decade. The younger generation was experimenting with various newly imported literary theories and modes. Reacting partly to the prevailing political fiction, Tsubouchi Shōyō (1859–1935), generally called the theoretical architect of modern Japanese fiction, published his influential *Shōsetsu shinzui* (The essence of fiction) in 1885. He rejected utilitarian views and promoted literary autonomy and realism. Two years later, Japan's first modern novel in the Western realistic mode, *Ukigumo* (Drifting cloud), was published by Futabatei Shimei (1864–1909). Subsequently, many Western literary ideas, techniques, and modes — romanticism, neo-romanticism, naturalism, and symbolism — successively or concurrently dominated literary practice and in one way or another helped shape modern Japanese literature over the next two decades.

But Liang Qichao seems to have been completely ignorant of these new developments while in Japan. Actually, his lifelong interest in Japanese literature never went beyond political fiction. This is not difficult to explain. For one thing, his concept of fiction is essentially one of utility. No less significant is his inability to read Japanese in the colloquial style, which became the prevailing mode of literary expression. Most political novels were written in the so-called *kambun kuzushi* (broken Chinese) style. Since Chinese characters made up over 80 percent of any given text, it was actually classical Chinese *(wenyan)* as customarily rendered *(kundoku)* into Japanese. So, when a Chinese wanted to read such material, he simply picked out all the Chinese characters and rearranged them in Chinese grammatical order to form a fairly understandable, if not very polished, classical Chinese text. But Japanese is a highly inflected language — Chinese characters alone cannot transcribe all the suffixes, prefixes, and conjunctions. Many Chinese at that time (as now) often do not fully grasp the complexities of Japanese grammar and make many mistakes in translating *kambun kuzushi* material into Chinese. Liang Qichao, for one, made many misreadings and mistranslations in his renderings of Japanese works. Nevertheless, he boasted on more than one occasion that "if one is well versed in Chinese writings, one can read all Japanese books with no difficulty after only one year of study."[18]

Zhou Zuoren systematically introduced the new development of Japanese literature since the appearance of Shōyō's *The Essence of Fiction* and Shimei's *Drifting Cloud*. His lecture in April 1918 on the advancement of modern Japanese fiction was published in the first volume of *Xin qingnian* (The new youth), in July. Significantly, this lecture was given at the very early stage of China's new literary movement — roughly one year after Hu Shi's "Wenxue gailiang chuyi" (Preliminary suggestions for literary reform) and Chen Duxiu's "Wenxue geming lun" (On literary revolution). It preceded Lu Xun's "Kuangren riji" (Diary of a madman), the epoch-making work of modern Chinese fiction, by one month.

In his article, Zhou Zuoren first argued that "Japanese culture can perhaps be characterized as one of *creative imitation*" instead of the commonly held Chinese view that "Japanese civilization is a daughter of China." After briefly summarizing Japanese fiction from the *Tale of Genji* up to the Meiji political novels, he outlined the "new fiction" — beginning with *Drifting Cloud*, which he called a work of realism and "art for life's sake." Then, with copious commentary, he traced various trends of Japanese fiction by school, circle, genre, or ideas. Chronologically, these are: Kenyū-sha (The Fellow Students' Society), which advocated the doctrine of "art for art's sake"; Bungaku-kai (The Literary World), which represented a group who imitated European romanticism; the *kannen shōsetsu* (ideological novels), *hisan shōsetsu* (tragic novels), and *shakai shōsetsu* (social novels), which shared a common concern for the moral conflicts of the individual with family and society and looked for some solutions. *Shizenshugi* (naturalism), another advancement in realism, flourished after the Russo-Japanese War, influenced by French naturalists like Zola and Maupassant; *yoyū-ha* (the dilettante group), headed by Natsume Sōseki (1867–1916) and including Mori Ōgai (1862–1922), was not an organized society but a term for writers who thought that leisurely observation of life was the best attitude toward literary endeavors. Finally, *shin-shukanshugi* (neo-subjectivism), an antinaturalism movement, had two distinct inclinations, *kyōrakushugi* (hedonism), which was promoted by some naturalist-turned-decadent writers like Nagai Kafū (1879–1959) and *risōshugi* (idealism), begun by a group of young idealists whose ideological base mixed Western democracy, evolution, socialism, liberalism, and Tolstoyan humanism.[19]

Zhou Zuoren's introductory lecture on all aspects of Japanese fiction up to his time thoughtfully reflects his wide readings in Japanese literary works and studies — certainly an unusual achievement for a Chinese youth at that time. Although he no doubt used some secondary Japanese sources, his comments are generally judicious and often to the point. His purpose was not merely to inform the Chinese about what had been happening in Japan but, more importantly, to show what the Chinese could learn from the successful example of the Japanese. Recognizing the inevitable differences between the two countries because of distinct cultural and social backgrounds, he emphasized and reemphasized their similarities of purpose and direction in modern development. Given the similarities, he asked, why had the Japanese accomplished so much but the Chinese so little? In his view, "This is simply because the Chinese are unwilling to imitate and unable to imitate." His article concluded:

If we want to remedy the sick condition [of our fiction], *we have to free ourselves from the past tradition and, before anything else, imitate others wholeheartedly.* Only through the process of imitation can we hope to create an original literature of our own. Japan is an example. As mentioned earlier, the condition of Chinese fiction at this moment is similar to that of 1884 or 1885 in Meiji Japan. The surest and most appropriate task for us right now is, therefore, to promote the translation and studies of foreign works. . . In sum, *if we Chinese want to develop our new fiction, we ought to start from the very beginning.* What we need most at this particular point is an *Essence of Fiction* — a book that explains what is fiction.[20]

Zhou Zuoren later became known as a pro-Japanese writer with a genuine love and admiration for traditional Japanese culture, but his assertion here that the Chinese should follow the Japanese example was not that much different from what Liang Qichao had advocated. The only difference was that Zhou Zuoren was more interested in literature's intrinsic value than its sociopolitical functions. In other words, by imitating the Japanese, he hoped that China, too, "can produce many works of originality and create a new literature of the twentieth century."[21]

The desire to "create a new literature of the twentieth century" was certainly the common goal and task of China's literary revolution. Although 1917 is usually regarded as the beginning of this new movement, as Chen Duxiu said, "the spirit and tendency of the literary revolution have been brewing for a long time."[22] Historically, its origin can be traced back to the "revolution in fiction" or still earlier to the "revolution in poetry" of the late nineteenth century.[23] In any case, many intellectuals, like Hu Shi in the United States and Lu Xun and Zhou Zuoren in Japan, were ready for the eventual literary revolution. In 1917 the new literary movement was formally and forcefully launched when Hu Shi published his famous "eight principles," better known as *ba bu zhuyi* (eight-don'ts-ism), as his suggestions for "literary reform," and Chen Duxiu called for "literary revolution" with his more positive "three great principles." The movement gained further momentum from the May Fourth Incident of 1919. As part of a broader cultural and intellectual revolution, it helped cause unprecedented social and political changes in modern China.

With the outburst of the literary revolution, *New Youth* could not publish all the new writers. More journals and newspaper supplements were begun or supervised by newly formed organizations of various purpose and direction. The best-known and most influential of the writers' groups were the Wenxue yanjiu hui (Literary Association or, more precisely, Association for Literary Studies), Chuangzao she (Creation Society), Yusi she (Thread of talk Society), and Xinyue she (Crescent Society). At first the literary revolution stressed and partially accomplished the destruction of the old tradition. Then Hu Shi suggested a "constructive literary revolution" and published his *Changshi ji* (A book of experiments) — a collection of modern poetry, historically important but inferior, to show that there could be "a literature in the national language and a national language suitable for literature."[24] A few years later, Xu Zhimo and his Crescent Society followers were creating a new poetry. But the biggest contribution to constructing a new literature was made by the writers and critics affiliated with the Literary Association and Creation Society, nearly all students returned from Japan.

Since so many Japanese-trained writers were so important in this new phase of the literary movement, some questions should be asked: Why did Japanese literary trends influence Chinese writers? In what way and to what extent?

Before answering these questions, it is useful to know the Chinese view of Japanese literature. Their attitude had changed little since the time of Liang Qichao, who said, "There is no Japanese learning which is not from the West."[25] Most Chinese writers tended to believe the stereotype that modern Japanese literature was nothing more than an imitation of the West. They refused or failed to appreciate its originality. Zhou Zuoren's remark, quoted earlier, that Japanese culture is one of "creative imitation" is perhaps the most generous, but it is his own view and by no means represents any measurable change in general Chinese attitudes. Then why did Chinese students keep going to Japan? As stated before, few went to Japan with literary studies in mind, and those who became interested in literature in Japan often focused on Western literature or Western-influenced Japanese literature. Japan's remarkable success in modernization, of which literature was an inseparable part, impressed them. They were eager to know what and how the Japanese learned from the West and hoped to follow the successful Japanese experience — as a shortcut to Western literature.

For this reason, most Japanese works translated and introduced in China were on, or related to, Western literary works and theories. Many European works were retranslated from Japanese translations, which were often retranslations from English. Although some modern,

Japanese novels and short stories were translated, they were chosen less for their Japanese qualities than because they could offer examples of Western-influenced literary creations by the Japanese, so as to encourage the Chinese to do the same. In any case, the primary emphasis during the first decade of literary revolution was on introducing literary theories. As a result, Chinese literary circles were inundated by Western literary terminology. Li Helin wrote of this situation:

> During such a short period of twenty years [1917–1939], due to the impact of Western literary trends of the past two to three hundred years on the one hand, and because of the drastic changes in domestic and international political, economic, social, and cultural conditions on the other, Chinese literary thought currents have more or less reflected the contents of almost all the literary schools of European countries since the eighteenth century: namely, romanticism, naturalism, realism, decadence, aestheticism, symbolism, expressionism . . . as well as neo-realism (also known as social realism or dynamic realism). But, while it took Europe two to three hundred years to develop these ideas or schools, we have tried to swallow all of then in "twenty years!" Therefore, unlike various European literary ideas, which are better defined and more lasting, the sequence and duration of these "isms" or "schools" in China are rather inconsistent — some exist simultaneously, while some simply vanish as soon as they appear.[26]

Certainly, introducing Western literary thought was the work of various individuals and groups. But much of the task was carried out by Japanese-trained students through Japanese studies of Western literary theories and literary history.

Indeed, after Zhou Zuoren's article on modern Japanese fiction, a vigorous effort was made to import foreign works and ideas. Western literature was the main goal, but since the returned students from Japan did most of the work, it is not unreasonable to assume that Western-influenced Japanese literature was a convenient channel, or at least a point of comparison, for further inquiries into Western origins. Of the two major writers' groups, the Literary Association emphasized translation projects, while the Creation Society concentrated on introducing Western literary ideas or movements. Consequently, an increasing number of new, Japanese-coined literary terms became part of Chinese and, because their meanings were not clearly explained and understood, caused much confusion. Commenting on the excessive preoccupation with terminology by members of the Creation Society, Lu Xun sarcastically observed:

> We can hear so-and-so are promoting such-and-such isms — like Cheng Fangwu's high-flown talk about expressionism, Gao Changhong's self-appointment as a futurist, etc. — but we have never seen a single work of any such-and-such ism. They boastfully hang up the sign-board, only to end up with twin declarations of the opening and bankruptcy of their shops. No wonder, then, as soon as Western literary theories were put up on stage, they seem to have already made an exit.[27]

Here, Lu Xun sounds as if he were against introducing Western literary theories or "isms." Rather, he had an instinctive disgust for empty talk. He is simply annoyed with people who arrogantly applied Western standards to denounce translations or creative works of others while doing little work of their own. Actually, he was one of the most studious translators. Throughout his life he did much to familiarize the Chinese reading public with foreign literary trends and works, many of them Japanese.

Regarding the introduction of Western literary theories in the early 1920s, China faithfully followed Japan's example. All Western theories imported to Japan at some early date briefly appeared on the Chinese literary scene. But even in theory, the results were very different despite the fact that both countries followed similar paths in theoretical pursuits and constructions. Despite the great need for a Chinese *Essence of Fiction*, which Zhou Zuoren urged should be written, China has failed so far to produce one of comparable magnitude and significance. Some have said that because the Chinese are a practical people, they are too practical to waste time and energy in abstract theoretical contemplations. Although such a contention may contain some truth, the real reason lies elsewhere. Mao Dun (1896–), while editing *Xiaoshuo yuebao* (Short story monthly), the major organ of the Literary Association, often discussed the kind of literature China most needed. "The real literature is no more than the literature that reflects the times," he stated. "I am of the opinion that true literature must deal with social life — a literature that is concerned with mankind. In an oppressed country, the aspect of social conditions ought to be stressed still more."[28]

Such views were by no means Mao Dun's alone. They were shared by almost all modern Chinese writers, including members of the Creation Society. Consisting exclusively of Japanese-educated students at its inception, the Creation Society was first known for its inclinations toward romanticism and "art for art's sake," as opposed to the Literary Association's assertion of realism and "art for life's sake." But this distinction was deceptive and is less substantial than usually assumed. Cheng Fangwu, the Creation Society's leading theorist, mentioned in an early article that "responsibility toward the times" is the first of three "missions of the new literature." He added, "Our epoch is being filled with hypocrisy, sin, and ugliness! Our lives are being suffocated with filthy air! To smash the status quo is the mission of new writers."[29] This view was summed up by a statement that Lu Xun quoted in one of his essays: "Men of letters are not allowed to be idle spectators in the times of greatest social change."[30] With such ideals, it is no surprise that Lu Xun began his literary career by translating works written by the writers of "the oppressed nations," such as eastern European countries like Russia, Poland, and the Balkan states, rather than translating the more famous and fashionable western European or Anglo-American authors. Later, as a creative writer, Lu Xun confessed he always cherished the idea of "enlightenment" for the improvement of human life: "When selecting material, I often turn to the unfortunate people of sick, abnormal society, hoping that, by exposing the people's pains and bitternesses, I could remind others of the pressing need for treatment."[31]

This strong sense of social and epochal mission may have been the most important factor affecting the general direction of modern Chinese literature, and it led to a development quite different from that in Japan. When the Chinese writers started, in the late teens, to create a new literature, Japan had generally finished introducing various Western literary theories and was already undertaking what Zhou Zuoren called "creative imitation" of Western models. Beginning approximately thirty years later, and in an apparent, if unspoken, competitive spirit, the Chinese writers simultaneously had to learn Western literary theories and create literary works of their own. It first seemed that many Chinese writers were trying to absorb all the Western theories that Japan had accumulated over several decades. That effort was rather short-lived, and, in the end, halfhearted at best. Unlike their Japanese contemporaries' wholehearted, almost puritanical pursuit and application of Western theories in the agonizing experiment of "cutting Japanese feet to fit Western shoes," the Chinese simply invited the theories in and then either let them float in the air or shelved and forgot them.

There were a series of literary debates, but they were usually centered on the merit or demerit of certain theories in terms of sociopolitical function rather than in terms of literary values. This was largely caused by the times and circumstances. As Takeda Taijun rightly pointed, out, "The Chinese writers devoted to the literary revolution had to swallow the immense sense of indignity for their A Q-esque existence before they could yearn after the far-off Western literature."[32] The Japanese writers were fortunate to live in a country that had enjoyed economic and technological advancements as well as a series of military victories at the expense of its Asian neighbors. But the Chinese writers suffered from continuous national defeats and humiliations, which they felt were caused not only by foreign imperialism but by the backwardness of their own people and society. While the Japanese writers were absorbed in discovering the meaning of literature and seeking emancipation, assertion, and perfection of *jiga* or *jiko* (selfhood) at an abstract level, their Chinese counterparts were preoccupied with down-to-earth worries over the fate of endangered *dawo* (the big self, nationhood) in their struggle to enlighten their people and save their country. Thus, the most fundamental question the Chinese writers asked was not "what is literature?" but "what is its use?" Their concept of literature did not outgrow the preliterary revolution stage of political or exposure fiction. With such an overriding sense of social and national mission, Chinese writers could unite themselves for nonliterary activities at times of national disasters, like the war against Japan, with little soul-searching about their integrity as men of letters.

The impact of Western literary theories introduced through Japanese channels or directly from Western sources did not fundamentally change the Chinese utility concept of literature. But Chinese writers, consciously or unconsciously, seem to have taken Zhou Zuoren's suggestion: follow the Japanese example of "creative imitation" in fiction writing. What was meant by "creative imitation" in Japanese fiction?

Obsessed with Western literary ideas and tirelessly working to imitate Western models, the Japanese writers certainly succeeded in creating a modern literature as extraordinary as it is impressive. In a critical appraisal of pre–World War II Japanese literature, Okuno Takeo, a contemporary Japanese literary critic and historian, wrote the following summary:

> Since the Meiji era when modern European literature was introduced, Japanese writers have fought an agonizing battle against the inconsis-

tency between conceptions and reality. If a modern literature is to be created from the Japanese experiences in a society yet to acquire its modernity, the resultant literature will necessarily be devoid of vitality and removed from reality. On the other hand, once a complete interpenetration with Japanese reality is attempted, it is no longer a modern literature. This is indeed the inescapable fate the Japanese writers have to confront within a backward society. As a result, Japan has produced many contradictory and contorted literary works one after another. There are, for example, unscientific, unsubstantiated romantic naturalism (Tayama Katai, Shimazaki Tōson, Tokuda Shūsui); solitary, self-closing, and feudalistic modern egoism (Mori Ōgai, Natsume Sōseki, and the like); sophisticated and realistic idealism (Shirakaba School); as well as *watakushi-shōsetsu* (I-novel) produced in and by a group of exiled fugitive slaves; personal and impersonated Marxist literature; and a modernistic literature of new techniques prepared with moss-grown ideas.[33]

This passage illustrates the general tendency of Japanese critics and writers to use a Western, or Japanized Western, point of view. Their addiction to Western concepts and terminology, their habit of abstraction and classification and their concern with the backwardness of their society are the main reasons there are so many inconsistencies and contradictions in modern Japanese literature. In this respect, fortunately or not, the Chinese writers have avoided a similar confusion because of their halfhearted reception of Western literary ideas.

Of all the literary movements in modern Japan, naturalism is undoubtedly the most important to date. Reflecting the commonly accepted view of Japanese literary scholars, Nakamura Mitsuo, a contemporary literary scholar, stated, "Naturalism is the most important pivot in the history of modern Japanese fiction. It is the conclusion to Meiji (1868–1912) literature, and has served as the foundation of Japanese literature since the Taishō era [1912–1926]."[34] What is Japanese naturalism, and why is it called by Okuno Takeo "unscientific, unsubstantiated romantic naturalism"?

Zhou Zuoren observed that Japanese naturalism at first was directly influenced by French naturalism. Sometime around 1900, Zola was particularly popular among the young Japanese literary aspirants who emerged to rival the then dominant romanticist group. Zola's voluminous novels and *Le roman expérimental* were widely circulated, mostly in English translation, and faithfully followed. In the epilogue to his

Chigoku no hana (Hell flowers [1902]), a historically significant but aesthetically unsuccessful experiment on Zolaesque scientific naturalism, Nagai Kafū stated, recalling passages in *Le roman expérimental*, "There is no doubt that part of a human being is beast by nature. . . I wish to concentrate on describing without reserve the whole truth of this darker side: the lust, the violence, and the brutal force that we have inherited from our ancestors and from our surroundings."[35] Despite his enthusiasm and sincerity, Kafū and most of his fellow aspirants simply could not handle the scientific objectivity of what the Japanese call Zolaism. They turned to more digestible and flexible models in other naturalists like Flaubert, Maupassant, and the Goncourt brothers. Gradually, they dissociated themselves from the naturalistic movement.

Interestingly, the older generation of romanticists picked up what the young Zolaists had left undone. They gave Japanese naturalism a new momentum and a different direction. In their drive to update and upgrade the quality of their writing, Japanese writers had to learn the major European literary trends as fast as they could. Nearly all of them had to go through one "ism" after another to catch up to the European literary world. With the former romanticists then leading the naturalistic movement, Zolaesque scientific theories were dismissed as impracticable in Japan's backward society. Instead, by a clever, possibly unconscious twist in the implication of the word "nature" *(shizen)*, naturalism was given a new dimension of meaning: the principle of inward reflection and the subjective expression of human "nature" in isolation from objective realities. Included in this subjective vision of reality were the Japanese romantic traits of self-confession and lyrical expression. What resulted was a unique form of Japanese naturalism. This was characterized by a Rousseauesque morality of unrestrained self-revelation, intensive lyricism, and occasional self-pity, and by a sentimental search for the so-called *kindai jiga* (modern selfhood). Hence, the term *watakushi-shōsetsu* or the I-novel.

Watakushi-shōsetsu, a product of the very private, self-contained womblike world of the modern Japanese writer, is indeed "the paradox in the history of modern Japanese literature," as Edwin McClellan pointed out. For "side by side with the development of so-called 'realism' has been this extraordinary subjective element of watakushi-shōsetsu."[36] This trend was started by the publication of *Hakai* (Broken commandment), in 1906, by Shimazaki Tōson (1872–1943) and *Futon* (Quilt) in the following year by Tayama Katai (1871–1943). Despite early reputations as romanticists, as soon as their works appeared, both writers were hailed as true naturalists, the epoch-making writers of modern Japanese literature. Consequently, the principles of objective, impersonal observation and presentation of human conditions as inspired by realism and naturalism were never thoroughly realized. The social, political consciousness heightened by earlier political fiction was totally lost in the dubious search for "modern selfhood." The autobiographical genre of watakushi-shōsetsu became the mainstream of Japanese literature. Though started by so-called naturalists, or to be exact, romantic naturalists, this peculiarly Japanese literary mode prevailed in the coming generations.

The peak of Japanese naturalism is usually said to be the decade after the Russo-Japanese War, also the peak of Chinese students studying in Japan. It can be assumed that this movement exerted some influence on the Chinese writers then in Japan. Indeed, once the literary revolution had begun, translations of Japanese naturalistic theories and works began to appear in Chinese literary circles. In 1921 Shimamura Hōgetsu's article "Bungeijō no shizenshugi" (Naturalism in literature and art, 1908) was translated into Chinese by Chen Wangdao. Others like Xie Liuyi, Li Zhichang, and Wang Fuquan also introduced, among other things, naturalism based on secondary Japanese sources.[37] Even Lu Xun translated a study of naturalistic theory and technique by Katayama Koson (1878–1933).[38] In addition, Katai's *Quilt (Mianbei)* and Tōson's *Shinsei (Xin sheng*, A new life), as well as a number of short stories had their Chinese versions.

Because these translations and introductions were mostly done by members of the Literary Association, these writers were often accused of being influenced by Japanese naturalism. One of the prime "suspects" was Lu Xun. In a critical review of Lu Xun's *Nahan* (A call to arms), Cheng Fangwu slighted "Diary of a Madman" and other short stories in that collection as "the kinds of documents stubbornly promoted by naturaists." He added that:

> The author [Lu Xun] studied in Japan earlier than I did. During his stay in Japan, naturalism was prevailing in the Japanese literary world. There seems to be no doubt that the author was influenced by naturalism at that time. It is only natural, then, that the author has now produced a number of naturalistic works, by which a gap in the evolutionary process of our country's literature has been filled.[39]

This speculation is unsubstantiated and has been disproved by thoughtful Japanese scholars — to their great disappointment.[40] Recalling his life with Lu Xun in Japan, Zhou Zuoren might have had Cheng Fangwu's speculation in mind when he said, "Yucai [Lu Xun] . . . never paid close attention to the works of Shimazaki Tōson and the like. When naturalism was in vogue, he did glance through Tayama Katai's *Quilt* and Satō Kōroku's [1874–1949] *Kamo* [Duck], but he showed no interest at all."[41] The same can also be said of Zhou Zuoren himself, even though he knew Tōson and wrote an essay on him.[42] True, the Literary Association generally did favor and promote realistic or naturalistic fiction. Mao Dun, for example, declared at one point that "modern Chinese fiction must start a kind of naturalistic movement." But his kind of naturalism is closer to the French original than the Japanized version.[43] Regarding the Literary Association, the influence of Japanese naturalism, or its resultant genre of watakushi-shōsetsu, was minimal if not nil. In this sense, Zheng Boqi, another founding member of the Creation Society, was correct when he said, "Realism promoted by the Literary Association has been inclined toward Russian humanism and failed to realize the goal of naturalism."[44]

Ironically, some influences from the Japanese naturalistic watakushi-shōsetsu can be detected in the writings of the Creation Society, despite their openly critical attitude toward any kind of naturalism, Western or Japanese. All its first members were studying in Japan when the idea of founding a literary society was being conceived and finally realized in 1922 — not necessarily as a rival but as an alternative to the Literary Association. Thus began the so-called Chinese romantic movement. Compared to the followers of the Literary Association, members of the Creation Society studied in Japan roughly ten years later, so they personally observed modern Japanese literature at its height. Accordingly, they were better informed and more familiar with its various trends in the teens. The teens in Japanese literary history was a period of democratic and liberal ideas, of idealism and humanism, and of the rise and fall of every conceivable Western-influenced thought current, new and old. Nevertheless, beneath all the new developments was the persistent, swelling undercurrent of the naturalistic, autobiographical watakushi-shōsetsu.

During its early stages, the Creation Society was crying for the "creation of our selfhood," seeking inspiration from writers popular then in Japan: Rousseau, Goethe, Heine, Byron, Shelley, Keats, Whitman, Hugo, Spinoza, Bergson, Nietzsche, Rolland, as well as the European symbolists, expressionists, and futurists.[45] What the Creation members hesitated to mention was their affinity also to wataku-shi-shōsetsu in their writing. Generally, their prose literature, particularly fiction, is largely autobiographical, intensely personal, and often embellished with emotional, lyrical, and melancholic moments, recalling the common characteristics of watakushi-shōsetsu. Guo Moruo's "Muyang aihua" (Sad story of a shepherdess [1925]), Ye Lingfeng's "Nuwashizhi yinie" (Evil descendants of the goddess Nuwa [1925]),[46] and Wang Yiren's "Liulang" (Wandering [1924]) are a few examples.

One of the best examples is Yu Dafu's "Chenlun" (Sinking [1921]), a short story about a lonely, frustrated Chinese student in Japan who engaged in nightly masturbation for momentary relief and finally drowned himself in the sea. As C. T. Hsia pointed out, "though a third-person narrative, 'Sinking' is unabashedly autobiographical." Here is his general appraisal of the writer's works:

> In that sense, the whole body of Yu Dafu's fiction, with the few exceptions in the proleterian mode, constitutes a Rousseauist confession. In one of his essays, Yu Dafu declares that all literature is autobiographical, but characteristically he fails to emphasize the kinds of subtle transformation to which a great writer invariably subjects his personal experience. His own practice testifies to the predominance of a literal imagination fascinated by the narrow world of his private sensations and feelings.[47]

In the retrospective essay to which Hsia apparently referred above, Yu Dafu stated clearly and with utmost confidence:

> The saying that "all literary work is nothing but the author's autobiography [zixuzhuan]," I feel is absolutely true! Objective attitude. Objective description. No matter how objective you are, if and when a pure objective attitude, a pure objective description is possible, then there will be no use for the talent and soul of an artist; and the reason for the existence of the artist will disappear.[48]

This passage reflects the general defense made by Japanese watakushi-shōsetsu writers against the critics who accused them of being too subjective, too personal, and too indifferent to the outside world. Most revealing is Yu Dafu's use of the term zixuzhuan (jijoden in Japanese, a term preferred by Japanese naturalist writers over watakushi-shōsetsu when referring to the very private autobiographical nature of their

81

creative works).

"Sinking" is usually considered the beginning of decadent literature in modern China. Decadence *(tuifei)*, like so many other borrowed foreign concepts, was often misunderstood and condemned for its negative spiritual and moral perversity without its positive merits being fully acknowledged. Because of its "decadent" qualities, "Sinking" was denounced by some self-righteous moralists for its indecent exposure of the hero's voyeuristic, self-abusive acts as well as possible evil effects on the reading public. In the middle of this controversy over "Sinking," Yu Dafu said, "Those who have never lived in Japan will never quite understand the true value of this work; those who have no sincerity in dealing with literature and art have no right to criticize this work."[49] The reason behind this pronouncement, especially the first point, is not very clear. It may imply that unless one had lived in Japan, as the author had, he could never comprehend the gravity of an inferiority complex, despair, and the other psychological distresses suffered by the hero of "Sinking." But it might also indicate that Yu Dafu was defending himself with the Japanese watakushi-shōsetsu in mind, indignant at critics ignorant of contemporary Japanese literary trends who did not recognize the true significance of this work. There is no question that the Japanese impact on Yu Dafu was profound.

Despite unfavorable criticism, Yu Dafu did not lack sympathetic and enthusiastic followers, especially within the Creation Society circle. Some emerging young writers gratefully acknowledged their indebtedness to him. Wang Yiren expressed on occasion that he felt possessed by Yu Dafu whenever he was holding his pen.[50] Partly inspired by Yu Dafu's works, and partly influenced by more translations of Japanese modern novels, watakushi-shōsetsu–like fiction became very popular in the middle of the 1920s, particularly in the Shanghai area. This sudden new phenomenon provoked disapproval from a number of well-known writers. Perhaps on behalf of the majority of the Literary Association and Thread of Talk Society, Mao Dun criticized the prevailing sentimentalism, self-pity, and lack of social consciousness in Chinese literature, caused largely by misconceptions of Western decadence, aestheticism, and individualism. He agreed that "China nowadays is in a time of distress" but argued that "sentimental literature of distress has no place in art! If we are forever trapped in the confines of sentimental literature, then the future of new literature is indeed a cause for anxiety."[51]

Guo Moruo was worried, too. Being on the defensive, he cleverly blamed the influence of Japanese literature while ignoring the fact that this new trend was launched largely by his group, including himself and, of course, Yu Dafu. Characteristically, Guo slighted modern Japanese literature in the harshest terms possible:

> Aspects like depiction of extremely limited personal life; like taking pleasure in toying with extremely trifling lyrical diction; and even like absorption in sensual pursuits of the demimonde... All of these sicknesses of the bourgeois literature have in totality been spread to China. These sicknesses are what make the Japanese literary world fail to produce great works.

Another cause of Japanese failure, Guo added, was "the very absence of epochal spirit." Thus, he urged his fellow writers, "Let's forsake the foreign influences and, at the same time, let's reform our own life so that we can strive to become social men."[52] These words were written in 1928, some years after Guo Moruo and most of his fellow members had changed their public stance from romantic to revolutionary. Guo's extraordinary denouncement of Japanese literary achievement and its undesirable spread to China further confirms the influence of the Japanese naturalistic watakushi-shōsetsu on a group of Chinese writers.

Yet, if Yu Dafu's "Sinking" is somehow deeply indebted to the Japanese watakushi-shōsetsu genre, at the same time, it contains elements distinctly characteristic of modern Chinese literature. Unlike the modern Japanese writers, who were allowed to confine themselves in a womblike world, or a "paradise of the exiles" (*ruzan no rakudo*) to borrow Nagai Kafū's expression,[53] Yu Dafu, or the protagonist of "Sinking," his alter ego, was deprived of any spiritual asylum, not to mention an ivory tower. One of the few persons who showed a genuine appreciation of the meaning and significance of "Sinking" was Zhou Zuoren, undoubtedly the first Chinese writer to take sexual psychology and behavior seriously. Zhou, basing his argument on Albert Mordell's *The Erotic Motive in Literature* (1919), emphatically stated that "though it is a literature for the initiated, 'Sinking' is a work of art." It might be amoral, but contained nothing immoral, for it shared common themes with "all naturalistic and decadent works." Then Zhou continued:

> It seems more correct to say that what is described in this collection, "Sinking," is the common agony of a youth. The conflict between the will to live and reality is the source of all agony. Discontented with

> reality and yet unwilling to escape into emptiness, man can only
> continue to seek unattainable pleasure and happiness in this hard and
> cold reality. This is what makes the sorrow of modern man different
> from that of the romantic period.[54]

This passage pointed out not only the agony of the "Sinking"
protagonist, but, by implication, the agony of Yu Dafu as well as most
modern Chinese writers.

The protagonist's frustration and despair are identifiable with the
frustration and despair of his own time and country. Embodying
national humiliation in times of domestic division and outside
imperialist oppression, living abroad where racial prejudice is a fact of
life, the young protagonist alienates himself from his fellow Japanese
students and even turns away from his overseas compatriots and his
family back home. His image of the motherland becomes a distant
abstraction, one he can no longer grasp with certainty. He can only cry
repeatedly and in vain, "China, O China, why don't you become
powerful!" But China is as powerless as the hero. In his total
helplessness, his sense of inferiority takes the form of revenge: revenge
on the Japanese, revenge on his countrymen, and finally revenge on
himself by jumping into a foreign sea. Just as he is about to commit
suicide, the protagonist cries in desperation, "Motherland O Motherland! My death is your fault! Hurry up and become rich! Become
strong! You still have many children suffering in bitterness."[55] These
final words, echoing the madman's last wish, "save the children," in Lu
Xun's "Diary of a Madman," reveal the pervasive concern of most
modern Chinese writers, regardless of literary "isms" or political
belief. Despite similarities in development and evident indebtedness,
this is why modern Chinese fiction distinguished itself from its
Japanese counterpart. In this sense, the Western muses, even in
Japanese garments, seem to have failed in securing for themselves a
permanent niche in the heart of most Chinese writers, despite the fact
that they were once enthusiastically invited to provide inspiration.

The "modern agony" Zhou Zuoren referred to in his remarks on
"Sinking" describes the mental state of modern Chinese intellectuals.
Its very existence explains to a great extent why the Chinese writers are
so attracted to Kuriyagawa Hakuson (1880–1923), something that
never fails to amaze the Japanese. Once popular, but obscure since his
death, Hakuson was neither an original thinker nor a great writer. He
does not even appear in all the voluminous comprehensive anthologies
of modern Japanese literature published to date. But as a university

professor of English literature, and as an occasional essay writer, Hakuson was a successful and convincing transmitter of Western literary ideas. His theoretical work, *Kumō no shōchō* (Symbols of agony, 1921), based on his simplistic contention that "agony or frustration arising from the suppression of human vitality is the foundation of literature and art, and the way to express it is symbolism in its broad sense" was a creative synthesis of his extensive knowledge of Western literary tradition.[56] His collected essays, *Zōge no tō o idete* (Outside the ivory tower, 1920) and *Jūjigai o yuku* (Toward the crossroads, 1925), were the intimate record of his intellectual contemplation of topics ranging from literary and cultural to the social and philosophical problems that confronted the Japan of his times. Each of these works was widely circulated in China in at least one translation.

Kumen (kumō in Japanese, meaning agony, bitterness, or anguish) is one of the most frequently encountered words in modern Chinese writings, indicating that it is a widespread mental characteristic of modern Chinese. Obviously, even the title of Hakuson's *Symbols of Agony* strongly appealed to Chinese intellectuals who sought ways to release their agony, anguish, and bitterness in those times of national and individual misfortune. When they asked themselves what they could and should do as intellectuals and "social men," Hakuson's very titles of his two other books, *Outside the Ivory Tower* and *Toward the Crossroads* helped provide the answers. Modern Chinese writers simply could not live in the security of an ivory tower even if they wanted it; they found themselves at an intersection of their history, trying to find the right direction to follow for themselves and their society.

Lu Xun, who translated both *Symbols of Agony* and *Outside the Ivory Tower*, wrote in the epilogue to the latter about his agony at being a confused observer at the Chinese crossroads. He urged his readers to forsake their historical burdens and follow Hakuson's example of fearless criticism of his own people and country:

> Indifferent, moderate, compromising, hypocritical, narrow-minded, self-important, conservative, and so on — all these prevailing [Japanese] traits pointed out by the author [Hakuson] make one wonder whether he was not actually talking about the Chinese as well. Especially remarks like halfheartedness, indecisiveness in doing things; doing everything in the direction from the soul to the body; leading a ghostly life, and so forth. . . Since the author has determined this is a serious illness and, after diagnosis, has prepared a prescription, and because China is a country infected with the same disease, we can borrow it for

young men and women for their information and treatment. If quinine can treat malaria for the Japanese, then it certainly will work for the Chinese.[57]

Characteristic of a former medical student, Lu Xun's argument here is made concrete with medical analogies. Here, that early optimistic view of late Qing reformers — if Japan can reform so can China — still moved Lu Xun and many of his contemporaries. Evidently inspired, or to be precise, reinspired by Hakuson, Lu Xun started a magazine *Mangyuan* (Wilderness) in 1924, while translating *Outside the Ivory Tower*. He hoped to create a climate for "cultural criticism and social criticism," in order to "continue to tear off the mask of the old society."[58]

Because of the apparent enthusiasm with which he translated Japanese works and retranslated Western works from Japanese, Lu Xun was once ridiculed as "a writer forever after the Japanese" in the Tientsin *Yishibao Daily*. This ridicule was published in 1935 when Lu Xun was retranslating some modern Russian novels and Marxist literary theories from Japanese versions. "Soviet Russia is not very far away from China, but why do we have to learn of the Russian through the hand of the Japanese?" the accusing reporter Zhang Luwei questioned. "We don't see many in the Japanese crowd who really understand the new spirit of Russian literature. Why then insist on searching for our nutrition from superficial Japanese intellectuals? A shameful affair, indeed."[59] Such anti–Lu Xun sentiment was by no means isolated. It could be an expression of widespread anti-Japanese sentiments caused by increased and continuing Japanese aggression (the May Thirtieth Incident, 1925; the Mukden Incident, 1931; and the North China Incident, 1935). One response to such national crises was the fast conversion of many writers of different literary affiliations to the united effort to save China from Japanese conquests.

Under such conditions, even the "cultural criticism and social criticism" advocated by Lu Xun seemed inadmissible in the Chinese literary world. Members of the Creation Society dramatized their change to revolutionary literature during the latter half of the 1920s by advocating Marxist proletarian literature. In the meantime, writers of other groups, Lu Xun and his followers in particular, were also moving toward a revolutionary stance. Thus, a common ground was set for the formation of the League of Left-Wing Writers in 1930. As Japanese aggression intensified, most Chinese writers forgot their differences and joined in such organizations as the United Association of Chinese

Writers' Anti-Aggression Associations (1938), founded for the common pursuit of *kangzhan wenyi* (literature and art in the War of Resistance).

During the same period, parallel development occurred in the Japanese literary world. Though refraining from using the term *kakumei* (revolution), the so-called *puro bungaku* (proletarian literature), with its focus on Marxist theories, is essentially similar to Chinese revolutionary or proletarian literature. In the 1920s, members of Shinkankakushugi-ha (the Neo-Impressionist School) dramatically declared their conversion to the proletarian cause, and a nationwide leftist writers' organization was formed in 1928, known as NAPF (Nippona Artista Proleta Federacio). Overall, the Japanese leftist writers were less influential than their Chinese counterparts in politics and mass education. Mostly because of government suppression, many left-wing writers had to change their literary stance once more and collaborate with the Japanese military government's aggression under various organizations such as Dai-Nippon bungaku kenkyū kai (Literary Research Association of Great Japan, 1938), Nippon bungaku hōkoku kai (Japanese Literature in the Service of the Country Association, 1942), and Dai-Tōa bungakusha taikai (The Greater East Asian Literary Workers Assembly, 1942).

With such fast-changing developments in both countries, the literary relations between Japan and China became less and less close. But before the all-out war between the two countries, some Chinese writers, in promoting the proletarian revolutionary literature, relied as usual on some Japanese translations and studies of Marxist theories. Besides Lu Xun, it is well known that Guo Moruo was introduced to Marxism by Kawakami Hajime (1879–1946), one of the earliest and most effective intellectual spokesmen for communism. Likewise, other Japanese-educated writers like Cheng Fangwu and Yu Dafu were all indebted to Japanese sources for their new literary and political activities. But once the two countries were fully at war, all cultural relations suddenly ceased. This ended nearly a half century of Japanese impact on modern Chinese literary and intellectual undertakings.

This general survey clearly indicates that Japan had contributed a great deal to modern Chinese literary development, mostly as a channel for Western influence. This is particularly obvious in literary theory. Also, Japanese naturalistic fiction, especially the watakushi-shōsetsu autobiographical type, helped bring about the so-called "decadent" fiction in the early twenties. However, its influence was rather short-lived. Besides the decadent writers affiliated with the Creation Society, Lu Xun seems to have been attracted to Natsume Sōseki and Mori Ōgai, the two most important writers in modern Japan, who were removed from ever-changing literary trends. In this connection, Zhou Zuoren indicated that "Lu Xun's short stories are considerably influenced by Sōseki as evident in his light touch of satire and irony, though there is no apparent stylistic resemblance between them."[60] This supposition is supported by Lu Xun's occasional assertion of a *yuyu* (leisurely, dilettante) attitude in literary pursuits (Sōseki was a self-styled *yoyū-ha* or dilettante writer) and his translation of Ōgai's "Asobi" (Play), an autobiographical story of a dilettante.[61] Yet his interest in dilettantism was no more than a yearning, an unattainable luxury for Lu Xun and his fellow writers.

The only Chinese writer deeply influenced by Japanese literature for any length of time was Zhou Zuoren. Because of his lasting attachment to Japanese culture, evident even during the Japanese occupation, he was gratefully called by Japanese *chi'nichi-ka* (bosom friend of Japan) and scorned by his countrymen as *qinripai* (pro-Japanese element). However, his main interest was in premodern Japanese literature, such as haiku, Edo fiction, *kyōgen*, and discursive essays. As a real friend of Japan, he wrote numerous articles on Japanese traditional culture and customs that reveal his sincere but futile efforts to promote mutual understanding between the two nations.

To conclude, it is appropriate to quote a typical Japanese opinion of Lu Xun regarding Japanese influence that characterizes the Chinese attitude in general: "He is indifferent to Japanese literature. His interest in Japanese literature (in the broad sense) is always its function as an introducer of foreign literature. To put it strongly, he acknowledges only the utility value of Japanese literature."[62]

4.

Lu Xun: The Impact of Russian Literature

Douwe W. Fokkema

The influence of the great Russian writers on modern Chinese literature is a well-known fact. Tolstoy, Dostoyevsky, Gogol, Chekhov, Andreyev, and others were widely read in China and translated, as has been mentioned in all major studies dealing with the subject.[1]

But how can knowledge of the dissemination of Russian literature in China help us to understand modern Chinese literature and, in particular, the work of Lu Xun? The wide circulation of Russian fiction divulged a particular way of thinking and literary expression to the Chinese reading public, including the writers. They were impressed not only by the themes treated in Russian literature but also by the way the thematic material was presented. As Russian literature affected also the formal structure of modern Chinese fiction, we need to know more about that Russian influence to understand the modern Chinese literary conventions.

A system of conventional signs as used in communication is usually called a code.[2] The New Culture movement introduced a new cultural code in China, which in various aspects differed from the old Confucian code. It reorganized the existing material and introduced new priorities, sometimes by means of foreign examples. Russian literature, like other foreign influences but perhaps more strikingly, served as a lever to destroy the existing cultural system and to reorient the readers toward a new cultural system. As soon as the new system, which, of course, differed from that of nineteenth-century Russia, had been established, there was no need any more for *this type* of disorientation by means of *this particular* foreign influence. As is well-known, Russian influence gradually subsided, especially after the Hundred Flowers period (1956–1957).

Douwe W. Fokkema

Serving as a lever to break up the traditional system, Russian literature introduced a number of new values, which can be distinguished roughly into three major groups: romanticism, realism, and symbolism and decadence. The romanticist and symbolist values are overrepresented in the Russian texts that Lu Xun admired and translated; the values of realism are underrepresented in his translations. In effect, this may provide a clue to the interpretation of Lu Xun's creative writings.

The complex of romanticist values is analyzed by Lu Xun in his early essay "Moluo shi li shuo" (The power of Mara poetry [1907]) [I,55–103].[3] It deals with romanticist concepts of literature, taking its cue from Byron but speaking as well of Pushkin, Lermontov, and Gogol, who, in recent Soviet criticism,[4] are stigmatized as exponents of realism, at least for some parts of their career, but who, in fact, often resorted to romanticist devices. Among these are nature symbolism, mystification, the cult of heroism, and the irrational predilection for absurd exaggeration and irony. It is significant that the romantic hyperbole or irony may serve to enhance the role of the narrator at the cost of conventional (classicist) or "objective" views of related events.[5] The concept of Mara fits well in this pattern. Mara is the Buddhist name of a demon of destruction and rebellion and can be equated with Satan. Lu Xun mentions that Byron has been considered a "satanic" poet and applies the term to "all those poets who were firmly determined to rebel, who devoted their energy to action and were disliked by their contemporaries."[6]

Lu Xun's preference for the power of Mara served as a criterion when he judged Russian literature or selected Russian texts for translation. In an article on Lu Xun, Zhou Zuoren mentions that his brother was deeply impressed by Gogol's stories "The Diary of a Madman" and "How Ivan Ivanovich Quarreled with Ivan Nikiforovich," and by his satiric play The Inspector General.[7] This preference for Gogol is borne out by his translation activities. In 1934 Lu Xun translated Gogol's "The Nose" [XVI,656–697], one of the most absurd stories ever written. One year later, the novel Dead Souls [XX,41–603] followed, which relates the bizarre fraud of Chichikov, who intends to buy up "dead souls" (that is, the names of serfs who had died since the last census and for whom their owners continued to pay tax) in order to get money by pawning them. Apparently, the morbid nature of much of Lu Xun's writings can be traced back to European romanticism with its tendency toward absurdity and mystification. This does not exclude indigenous influences as noticed by T. A. Hsia.[8]

Lu Xun was not particularly interested in the complex of realist values extant in Russian literature. He translated nothing from the writings of Tolstoy, Turgenev, or Dostoyevsky, leaving the translation of *War and Peace* to Guo Moruo and of Turgenev's *Fathers and Sons* to Chen Yuan.[9] In 1934, Lu Xun rendered one story by the satirist M. Ye. Saltykov-Shchedrin (1826–1889) into Chinese [XVI,714–739], and one year later, he translated several stories by Chekhov [XVIII,751–819] including "A Bad Boy," "An Inscrutable Character," and "She Was It." But these are comic parables filled with symbolism and can hardly be called realist. Characteristically, "An Inscrutable Character" contains an ironic reference to Dostoyevsky. If the assumption that Lu Xun neglected the mainstream of Russian realism is correct, it should be made explicit which qualities of realism were depreciated by Lu Xun and, after him, by other writers.

Realism as a period concept or period code of European literature can be characterized as being geared toward an objective representation of social reality. Realism can also be regarded as didactic, moralistic, and reformist, as René Wellek indeed has done.[10] Realism divides people into various types and is antiheroic.

The objective representation of social reality was not a value that inspired Lu Xun. With no intimate knowledge of Russian society, he could not judge the degree of objectivity displayed by Tolstoy or Turgenev. Moreover, the realist interpretation of the world is dependent upon a consistent belief in God, or fate, or science. It strikes the European reader as detached and objective, but probably had an alienating effect among the Chinese. It destroyed the Confucian world model. If realism stood for integration in Europe, the Russian realist novel produced ideological disintegration and reorientation in China. In having that effect, the Russian realist novel did not fulfill its assertive role and was not interpreted or *decoded* as realist. Its disintegrating function, however, could easily be surpassed by other European fiction, which more effectively destroyed Confucian conventions.

The didacticism inherent in Russian realism was more favorably received. Whereas the moralistic and reformist elements in European realism were incorporated in a more general tendency toward objective representation, it appears that in China the didactic values were isolated from the ideal of objective representation, which was misunderstood anyhow. As we shall see, this can be observed also in the writings of Lu Xun.

The idea that human beings can be distinguished in types also fell

Douwe W. Fokkema

on fertile soil. But one wonders whether the ideal of the antiheroic, which is closely associated with the norm of the objective representation of social reality as well as with the differentiation of human beings into types, was acceptable to the Chinese. Although heroic figures like Juehui in Ba Jin's *Jia* (Family [1933]) are rare in Chinese literature of the 1920s and 1930s, the role of the Chinese *writer* as a spokesman for the oppressed and humiliated can be called heroic, particularly in the case of Lu Xun. The ideal of realism and naturalism that the writer be merely a humble observer who must report on a world that exists independently of his creative sensibility[11] did not fit into the Chinese cultural context, which called for action and a revaluation of values. One of the few exceptions to this rule is Mao Dun, who had made a close study of naturalism[12] and experimented with the device of detached reporting in *Ziye* (Midnight [1933]).

A formal characteristic of European realism is the all-inclusive narration.[13] Nothing escaped the author's attention. Everything could be described, from the depth of a soul to the trivialities of society. In European realism, this influenced the form of the novel, which usually was lengthy, and of the short story, which had to be penetrating and concise. But in Europe, the all-inclusiveness of the narration was supported by the integrated realist world view, which in China was interpreted as criticism and disintegration of the existing, predominantly Confucianist, system. In the Chinese cultural context, the consistent world view was missing, or at least was called into question. Therefore, the aspects of Russian realism that were rooted in a consistent world view could not successfully be imitated. The result was a paucity of realist novels in China, and if short stories aimed at realism, they easily risked indulging in trivialities void of meaning or psychological analysis without a social context.

Of all major realist values, it is apparently only the didacticism and the typicality of characters that, without much qualification, were accepted as ideals by the Chinese writers (including Lu Xun) and their reading public. The acceptability of these two values was certainly enhanced by certain qualities of traditional Chinese literature. The Chinese readers were all too familiar with moralism and schematic characterizations in literary and operatic texts. It appears that only those realist values were absorbed that fitted into the traditional pattern.

The complex of symbolist values conveyed by Russian literature is represented in Lu Xun's translations of M. F. Artsybashev (1878–1927), L. N. Andreyev (1871–1919), and V. M. Garshin (1855–1888). Applying the term "symbolism," often reserved for poetry, also to fiction of the late nineteenth and early twentieth century follows a suggestion made by René Wellek.[14] Chekhov's stories negated certain realist values. This was even more so with Artsybashev, Andreyev, and Garshin. Lu Xun translated Garshin's stories "Four Days" [XI,215-232] and "A Very Short Novel" [XVI,592-601], Artsybashev's story "Happiness" [XI,302-312] and his novel *Worker Shevyryov* [XI,585-749], as well as various stories by Andreyev [XI,191-215, 235-270]. These take up almost three hundred Chinese pages in the 1973 edition of Lu Xun's *Complete Works*. The majority of these translations was done in about 1920.

Artsybashev's novels were extremely popular in the early decades of this century, but gradually his rather unsuccessful variations on Dostoevskian themes were judged in a less positive way. His fiction is characterized by eroticism, sensualism, and nihilism. On the one hand, he was inclined to reject all values; on the other hand, he seemed convinced that a social revolution was unavoidable. Pessimism was the result of this dilemma. In *Worker Shevyryov,* written before World War I, the question is discussed whether the revolution should be made by peaceful means or should resort to violence and terrorism. Aladev, a former anarchist, has been converted to the Tolstoyan belief in peaceful means. His antipode, Nikolai Shevyryov, who has been sentenced to death but escaped, is a cynic who exposes all Christian and human values as hypocrisy and self-deception. When Shevyryov is almost arrested, Aladev, who lives in the same house, becomes involved and decides, against his own convictions, to shoot at the police. He happens to have a bomb in his room, and he uses it against the intruders. As a nice example of symbolism, one of the first police bullets goes through the portrait of Tolstoy on the wall. Aladev dies in the fight, but Shevyryov escapes. He is discovered by the police and escapes again for a while. Finally, he manages to enter a theater and, as a true terrorist, from one of the boxes begins to fire on the audience, in this way expressing his contempt for the people who continue to enjoy themselves while there is so much unhappiness and injustice in the world. One must conclude that *Worker Shevyryov* is full of symbolism. The story (fabula) is weak and simple. The various episodes are only loosely connected, and if they are related, it is through their common theme of human greed and cruelty. Some episodes are fantastic, such as the hallucinations or dreams of Nikolai Shevyryov, who engages spirits in discussion. The novel as a whole seems to be a defense of terrorism. Both heroes finally resort to violence, which leaves them no hope to escape; they only destroy themselves and others.

Andreyev's fiction is of similar inspiration. He, too, did not shun rhetorical effects, although in using them, he showed to have taste, which Artsybashev often lacked. His range of themes is wide and varied. His work is full of madmen and utterly desperate characters. Death is not a fate that threatens one or two particular human beings but that destroys millions and millions, thus becoming an abstraction rather than a constituent element of the story. Like Artsybashev, Andreyev emigrated after the Bolshevik Revolution. Lu Xun's high opinion of Andreyev was by no means an exception in China.[15]

Although Garshin died in 1888 (by committing suicide), he comes close to symbolism, both in style and themes. His famous story "The Red Flower" deals with a madman in a lunatic asylum who is obsessed by the desire to challenge and defeat the evil of the world. He believes that all evil is contained in three poppies growing in the hospital garden and uses all his cunning and energy to pick the flowers. Thereupon he dies from exhaustion, happy and certain of having attained his end. The story is a parable, but one full of bitter irony. Lu Xun did not translate this particular story, but, as he himself observed, a Chinese translation had appeared by 1929 [XVI,602].

Lu Xun's preference for symbolism is confirmed by his translation, in 1923, of the novel *De Kleine Johannes* (Little John [1886]) by the Dutch author Frederik van Eeden (1860–1932) [XIV,5–212]. This novel refutes materialism and naturalism in the style of a fairy tale.

Symbolism is less compatible with social commitment than realism or romanticism. Its concern is nonsectarian, nontemporal, and nonnational. Its main theme is "the confrontation between human mortality and the power of survival through the preservation of the human sensitivities in the art forms."[16] The affiliation with metaphysics and music and the ambiguity of indirect communication seem to deprive the symbolist writer of the possibility of speaking clearly of matters that are pertinent to the problems of the day. Lu Xun explains in his famous essay "Zhu Zhong E wenzizhi jiao" (China's debt to Russian literature [1932]) [V,53–59] that in Andreyev's writings one finds terror *(kongbu)* and in Artsybashev's works, despair and deceptive exaggeration *(juewang he huangtang)*. Why were these authors translated at all? Perhaps the crude and sensual symbolism of Artsybashev could be charged with social significance by the Chinese reader. After all, it certainly disturbed the conventional norms more than realist fiction, and anything that significantly weakened the Confucianist establishment was welcomed. This would give one more example of the general rule that information encoded in a particular text can be decoded differently against the background of an alien context.

Siegfried Behrsing investigated the criteria Lu Xun used to select his translations and suggested that many works were translated for reasons other than their literary qualities.[17] First, Lu Xun had to rely on what had been translated in Japanese or German, the only two foreign languages he knew. (This, of course, would not exclude the possibility of translating any of the larger works of Tolstoy, Dostoyevsky, or Turgenev.) Second, Lu Xun is supposed to have favored translations conveying social criticism. But he seems to have had little knowledge of the complex social conditions in the countries where his sources originated. In practice, it turned out that not all social criticism was necessarily "progressive." Behrsing concludes that stories translated by Lu Xun often are sentimental rather than revolutionary. Third, Lu Xun probably selected certain texts for translation for the somewhat arbitrary reason that he liked their illustrations.

In spite of these pertinent observations, Behrsing tends to obscure the fact that Lu Xun may have used artistic criteria to select his material. A way to interpret large parts of the many-sided writings of Lu Xun would be overlooked if it were suggested that his work can be reduced to social criticism. Modern literary theory based on information theory postulates that the literary text has been encoded several times.[18] For instance, Lu Xun's "Kuangren riji" (Diary of a madman [1918]) [I,277–292] can be read as the story of an individual, as a mythological explanation of human existence, and as a political satire. The one interpretation is significant against the background of the two other possible interpretations. The question whether Lu Xun is primarily a creative writer or a social critic is solved if one accepts the theory that, in literature, several structures overlap and that a literary text can be decoded in various ways, depending on our knowledge of the codes and the social context of author and reader. Or, in more familiar terms, the ambiguity of much of Lu Xun's creative work, which leaves open the possibility of both a political and mythological interpretation, enhances their informational content and is precisely the reason why his writings are so well disposed to being received as literature.

Our interpretative competence can be enlarged by extending our knowledge of the codes that have been used by the writer when he encoded his text. It may be concluded that Lu Xun was attracted by romanticist and symbolist values. Of realist values, only the didacticism and the typicalness of characters attracted him. His growing interest in socialist realism *avant la lettre,* such as fiction by A. A. Fadeyev [XVIII,262–624], A. S. Yakovlev [XVIII,11–251], A. S. Serafimovich [VII,792–806], and many other Soviet writers [volume XIX] confirms that Lu Xun was congenial to these writers' subjectivist attempt to impregnate social reality with a teleological significance. The common factor in romanticism, symbolism, and, with some qualification, also early socialist realism, is the writer's role as a creator of worlds and myths. Considering the cultural vacuum that was threatening Chinese society, this concept appealed to Lu Xun and many other Chinese writers more than the realist ideal of detached description based on a given, unshakable interpretation of the world — widely accepted in nineteenth-century Europe but out of place in twentieth-century China.

The impact of romanticist and symbolist values on Lu Xun is not restricted to choosing texts for translation, but they also constitute a subcode that should not be neglected in the interpretation of his creative writings. This can be illustrated by an analysis of three of his most well-known stories: "Diary of a Madman," "A Q zhengzhuan" (The true story of A Q [1921]) [I,359–417], and "Shang shi" (Regret for the past [1925]) [II,276–305].

Lu Xun's "Diary of a Madman" has often been mentioned as being inspired by Gogol's story of the same name, first published in 1835. In Russian classicist literature, madmen played almost no role. One may find them in adventure novels, where they appear as laughable, comic figures. But a different role is assigned to them in romantic literature.[19] The madman is not bound by social conventions, and in the period of romanticism, he is called upon to uncover the essential in the human soul. Chinese cultural history also provides instances of a respectful role for the madman, notably in the representation of the Taoist eccentrics. But the madman of the romanticist code is different. He may present an interpretation of the world, whereas the Taoist outcast aspires after metaphysical values.

Both Gogol's and Lu Xun's "Diary of a Madman" present an interpretation of the world and convey social criticism, though in different degrees and of different purport. The form of the stories is similar. Lu Xun's story differs from Gogol's in that it quite normally introduces the existence of the diary as being written by a sick man who has been cured since. As a result, the world of madness and the world of sanity are distinctly separated. On the basis of the contents of the diary in Lu Xun's story, we conclude that an insane man provides us with a healthier and more penetrating interpretation of the world than would a normal man. Lu Xun's madman is, so to speak, less mad than Gogol's Poprishchin. The latter's diary begins rather normally, then proceeds through a stage of comic ambiguity (the speaking and letter-writing dogs) to the end, with Poprishchin's presumption that he is the king of Spain and with his fear that the earth will land on the moon. A characteristic difference between the two stories is that Lu Xun's diary entries have no dates, whereas the dates in Poprishchin's diary gradually become completely nonsensical, thus providing an indication of the degree of madness and thereby a clue to the interpretation. It is in conformity with the romanticist code that the most revealing passage in Gogol's story appears in an entry that the date announces as being quite mad. Here, Poprishchin, who has been tortured in the madhouse, calls for his mother: "Dear mother, save your poor son! Shed a tear on his tormented head! See how they torture him! Embrace your son who has been left by everyone! There is no place for him in this world! He is chased by everyone! Mother, take pity on your sick child."[20]

This kind of self-concern is lacking in Lu Xun's story. Here, too, the climax occurs in the last entry. However, the writer of the diary does not call on others to save himself but to save the children. "Perhaps there are still children who have not eaten men? Save the children." [I,292]. Lu Xun was certainly inspired by Gogol's "Diary of a Madman." He made use of several of its devices, notably that of letting the truth be spoken by the madman, but the kind of social criticism has a quite different aim. The story conveys the message that the children of the world should be saved, not the writer of the diary. This interpretation is in striking conformity with the old Chinese legend of how Tang Taizhong escaped death.[21]

The impact of Russian literature on the work of Lu Xun seems to transcend the realm of imitation. One of the principal devices Lu Xun appears to have borrowed from nineteenth-century Russian literature is that of introducing a point of view that does not coincide with that of most readers and departs from the prevailing literary tradition. In Lu Xun's work, the "aesthetics of identity" (conformity with the traditional norm) is replaced by the "aesthetics of opposition."[22] It is generally assumed that his work, at least to some extent, departs from the Chinese literary tradition, and it seems that it distinguishes itself from that tradition precisely because it thwarts the expectations of the readers more than they are used to. It wakes and shocks them by means of alienating devices that, for instance, prevent the reader from identifying himself with the main character, which may be a madman, or a crook (Kong Yiji), or a petty thief (A Q), or even an oversentimental, shortsighted lover (Zhuansheng). Crooks, bandits, and sentimental lovers had been represented in traditional Chinese literature but, as a rule, from either an acceptable or plainly rejectable point of view.

Lu Xun's underdogs are ambiguous and difficult to accept, yet they reveal an important world view. This is a new element in Chinese literature, mainly inspired by Russian literature, which has immortalized the madman Poprishchin and the fraud Chichikov (Gogol), the idling Oblomov (Goncharov), the idiot Myshkin (Dostoyevsky), the lunatic in "The Red Flower" (Garshin), the terrorist Shevyryov (Artsybashev), and, of course, Ivan the fool (Tolstoy). None of them is a plainly rejectable character. They all belong to the vast category of the humiliated and oppressed, like most of Lu Xun's characters.

A Q is a despicable bastard who repeatedly cheats and is being cheated but never will admit that he has lost face. Again and again he sees reasons to hope that chances will turn in his favor. He expects much of the successful 1911 revolution. But he soon learns that the new lords are the same as the old ones, except that they have new titles. Finally, A Q is charged with stealing and, without much ado, sentenced to death. In fact, he was not guilty in this particular case. He had wanted to participate in robbing his former boss, but no one had asked him to participate. Even in the revolution, he had remained an outcast.

If the story is considered to contain a political message — a criticism of national weakness — such an interpretation may be regarded as correct, but not complete. The romanticist convention in nineteenth-century Russian literature that the truth can or even must be spoken by the underdog or outcast (admired by Lu Xun) suggests that it is also possible to interpret A Q as the seer, the only person disposed to reveal the truth. Indeed, his insights that the new establishment hardly differs from the old leaders, and that also after the revolution there is no justice, cannot be expressed by someone who fits into the new, or old, social system. It is the most devastating criticism of society if the truth appears to be spoken only by madmen or petty frauds.

Lu Xun's heroes cannot and need not have a political program. Their wisdom will be restricted to "saving the children" ("Diary of a Madman"), or teaching a child ("Kong Yiji"), or not telling the truth to someone one has loved ("Regret for the Past"), or the vague idea that anyone can be considered guilty and might be put in jail ("The True Story of A Q"). The fact that a simple but sane philosophy is expressed by outcasts and underdogs acquires a significance that should not escape our attention.

Zhuansheng ("Pure life") is an outcast, too. "Regret for the Past," with "Zhuansheng's Notes" as a subtitle, again can be interpreted as a piece of social criticism, but it has also mythological significance. It exemplifies the gradual estrangement between two people who initially seem all too well disposed to love each other. Zhuansheng, from whose point of view the story is told, is not the kind of person with whom the reader immediately sympathizes. He seeks the reasons for his own unhappiness and ill fate with others and boasts of his own capacities. His remorseful insight that he never should have told Zijun, the girl with whom he has lived, that he did not love her any more comes too late, only after her death. His belated sentimentality seems out of place. Yet the story's implicit meaning is all too clear. He should have loved Zijun with more care. Of course, tragic love has been described in Chinese literature before. What first comes to mind is *Hong lou meng* (Dream of the red chamber). But the difference between Jia Baoyu and Zhuansheng is that the latter does not fully deserve our sympathy.

The number of examples can easily be multiplied. Wei Lianshu in "Guduzhe" (A solitary man [1925]) [II,245–276] is called a strange man of a different kind *(yige yilei)*, and yet, has an extraordinary feeling for appropriate relations with friends and family. In "Zhufu" (Benediction [1924]) [II,139–163], Xiang Lin's wife shows an exemplary loyalty to her first husband and her son, who was killed by a wolf, but the people make fun of her or feel awkward in her presence. In "Yao" (Medicine [1919]) [I,298–311], the main characters suffer from superstitious beliefs, yet they have an extraordinary compassion. "Medicine," as Lu Xun himself has explained, was inspired by the "grim coldness of Andreyev."[23]

The heroes in these stories are all outcasts and underdogs, in varying degrees. Lu Xun's device of making them the main spokesmen released him from the obligation to present an elaborate critique of social conditions in China and made the implied social criticism all the more effective. Through the indirectness and ambiguity of his method, Lu Xun could maintain his integrity as an artist and become more or less immune to censorship, at least as far as his creative writings were concerned. Although social criticism is not very explicit in Lu Xun's stories, the *formal* device of choosing the point of view of the idiot or petty fraud has the *semantic* effect of social criticism of the establishment, where apparently, no wisdom at all is to be found. If related to its European origin, this device is romanticist rather than realist. From a political point of view, as a result of its vague and general nature, the implied social criticism is highly subversive and not restricted to criticism of the Guomindang rule.

Therefore, the attitude of the Chinese cultural leaders toward the creative writings of Lu Xun and other Chinese writers using the same device, sometimes less rigorously, indicates how much censorship was imposed. Other approaches may have validity here, but an analysis of the main characters in novels of the late 1920s or 1930s may reveal why recently there has been a campaign in the Chinese press against "the literature of the thirties."

The heroine of Mao Dun's *Hong* (The rainbow [1930]), Mei, is first a sensitive and ardent lover, and second a revolutionary. One of the principal characters in Ba Jin's *Qiyuan* (Leisure garden [1944]) is Mr. Yang, formerly the owner of a luxurious house and beautiful garden, but at the time of the main story an outcast, who, like A Q, lives in a temple. Xiangzi, the main figure in *Luotuo xiangzi* (Rickshaw boy [1937]), who becomes the victim of his own stubborn toiling, fits into this category. They all are defeated, or, as in the case of Miss Mei, haunted by wavering and uncertainty. In short, they are not "positive heroes." Positive heroes are rare in fiction of the 1930s.

After 1949, the situation gradually changed. First, the Chinese writers were cut off from the legacy of nineteenth-century Russian literature. This process began about 1960 with the criticism of Tolstoy.[24] It was completed in 1966 with the dismissal of Zhou Yang, who once translated *Anna Karenina* from the English version (although this was by far not the only reason for his political liquidation). The criticism of Russian prerevolutionary literature originated in political and ideological arguments but was also related to literary conventions such as that of making outcasts or underdogs into major spokesmen in fiction.

The prevailing ideological argument viewed most of nineteenth-century Russian literature as a product of the "theory of human nature" *(renxing lun)*, and, as such, a denial of the principle of class war. The criticism conveyed in nineteenth-century Russian literature is often directed against every kind of society, and therefore is mytho-logical rather than political. The condemnation of society as a whole leaves no place for a strict division into positive and negative forces. The mythological condemnation of all human relations in Russian literature is supplemented by the vague idea that all human beings can be saved. This all-inclusive condemnation and possible salvation results from a subjective interpretation of the world and is part of the romanticist code. Clearly, it is incompatible with the idea of class struggle.

The next step was a severe criticism of the "literature of the thirties" and a ban on the 1957–1958 edition of Lu Xun's *Quanji* (Complete works, edited by Zhou Yang and others) during the Cultural Revolution. A subjectivist attitude, like that of all-inclusive condemnation and possible salvation prevalent in Russian literature, was expressed in Lu Xun's poem "Yingde gaobie" (Farewell to a shadow [1924]) [I,468–471], which ends as follows: "I alone shall go. Not only shall I be without you, but also there will be no other shadow with me in the dark. I shall perish alone, and the whole world will belong to me." Since this subjectivism may turn against all norms except its own, it fits into the "aesthetics of opposition." Evidently, many of Lu Xun's writings fall into this category. "Anyone can be put into jail," concludes A Q. All children should be saved (regardless of their class origin), writes Lu Xun's madman in his diary. Of course, Lu Xun's creative work cannot be banned as easily as Russian fiction. Every nation wishes to have a national literature, if only for reasons of pride or political expedience. His writings remain subversive all the same.

The reprinting of Lu Xun's *Complete Works* in Peking in 1973 signals an easing of cultural control that has also been indicated by other events. It is significant that his writings are again on the shelves of Chinese bookshops. If Chinese readers are allowed to buy his works, they can become acquainted with values that depart from the present social norms. Indirectly, they can become acquainted with the world of European romanticism, Chekhov's vignettes, the symbolism of Andreyev, and, by inference, with the idea that there are various possible world interpretations. If anything, this runs counter to the claim of objective truth usually upheld by Marxism.

5.

Qu Qiubai and Russian Literature

Ellen Widmer

Considering how seriously Qu Qiubai took his role as leader of the proletarian literature movement in the early 1930s and how single-mindedly he warned his fellow intellectuals against overinvolving themselves with foreign literatures, it may seem surprising that he also maintained a serious interest in the classics of nineteenth-century Russia. This interest was more than a youthful enthusiasm. During the winter of 1933–1934, just before leaving Shanghai to join Mao Zedong in the Kiangsi Soviet, Qu was translating Pushkin's *The Gypsies*. Nor was it a purely "tenderhearted" passion (to borrow the vocabulary of T. A. Hsia[1]), something totally at odds with his role as revolutionary. In a major statement on proletarian literature, "Puluo dazhong wenyide xianshi wenti" (Practical problems of proletarian mass art), published by the League of Left-Wing Writers in April 1932, Qu said; "China still now does not have 'Turgenev's enjoyable language' (Lenin's expression). China's proletarian literature must take on the job of creating such a language."[2] The following September, he reiterated this point in *Wenxue yuebao* (Literature monthly): "Not only do works of literature function artistically to move the masses; they also serve the broader purpose of setting high standards of writing. The 'beautiful, enjoyable language' of Pushkin, Tolstoy, and Turgenev is useful even today and makes suitable textbook material."[3]

Qu's interest in Russian literature may have meant different things at different times, but until almost the end of his life it was closely integrated with his proletarian concerns. His writings on the subject afford an opportunity to see how Russian literature complemented — and how it may finally have clashed with — his plans for literary revolution in China.

Early Writings on Russian Literature

Literature was always very close to Qu Qiubai's heart. As a boy he loved to read, and by his teens·he had begun to write poetry. Precocious too was his preoccupation with reform — of China, of literature, and of China through literature. Legend has it that he celebrated the first anniversary of the Chinese republic (when he would have been just over twelve) as if it were a day of mourning; and we know from Qu's own account that he was briefly interested in reforming classical studies by reviving the Modern Text School. Not long after, Qu began studying Buddhism, hoping thereby to find new ways, in his words, of "saving China by cultural means."[4]

It is hard to say whether Russian literature was ever seen as the answer to the prayers of Qu's Buddhist phase or whether it merely supplanted that phase. Qu's initial exposure to Russian studies came in 1917, via the National Institute of Russian Language in Peking. Although his entrance into the college had nothing directly to do with his hopes of saving China, it was soon thereafter that news of the Russian Revolution began to fill him with excitement and to invest his language learning with new interest. The next few years saw him developing this interest in two ways. During the winter of 1918–1919, he joined Li Dazhao's informal study group on the Russian Revolution and Marxism;[5] and in May 1919 he began publishing short translations of Russian authors: Tolstoy especially, but also Gogol, M. N. Albov (a follower of Dostoyevsky), and N. N. Zlatovratsky (a writer of populist novels).[6] By 1920, before his first trip to the Soviet Union, Qu had begun to comment on the value of Russian literature. These early comments are our best evidence of the ways in which the political and the literary sides of his interest in Russia were connected.[7]

It is clear, first of all, that both derived from his hopes for political reform in China. Here Qu was following Li Dazhao in his belief that nineteenth-century Russia and contemporary China had a great deal in common — the same backwardness and the same "Asian spirituality." While these characteristics had come across as disadvantages in the prerevolutionary writings of Lenin and Trotsky, they became, in Li's analysis, the explanation for Russia's great success in leaping ahead of the capitalist world to form a society more progressive and more "spiritual" than anything that had come before. For Qu as for Li, the Russian Revolution had shown that China could expect a similar sort of transformation, perhaps on an even grander scale.[8]

Qu's interest in Russian literature seemed to take this analogy as its point of departure. His recent exposure to materialist thinking, presumably in Li's study group, left him far less overtly optimistic than he had been in his Buddhist phase about the ability of "cultural means" such as literature to contribute to social change. In fact, he asserts the contrary at several points in these articles, that literature can only reflect social change, not cause it. Nevertheless, his arguments gradually work themselves back to the earlier view. The chain of causation does indeed begin with social change, as Qu argues in his "Eluosi mingjia duanpian xiaoshuo ji, xu" (Preface to Collected short stories by famous Russian writers), but social change has the effect of causing people's thinking to change, and once their thinking has changed, they start to want new kinds of literature. Regrettably, China does not yet have a literature that will give expression to the changes that are taking place in Chinese society. In the meantime, the search for a new kind of literature is best rewarded by a close look at the literary side of the Russian model, especially that is, at Russian literature of the nineteenth century, the time that Russia was most like China.[9]

Russian literature takes on added importance, in Qu's analysis, once Chinese readers begin to respond to the new translations. Qu's note to his translation of Gogol's *The Servants' Room* elaborates on the complexities of his response. When a society first begins to change, Qu feels, it does so slowly, leaving people with the feeling that there is a good deal more to be done. Under such circumstances, the reader may sense that there is still something wrong with society but not know exactly what. Here, reading can help him to clarify his understanding in ways that mere wondering cannot. This is because he is presumably contributing to the wrong in many ways of which he is not conscious. Inevitably, his vested interests in the status quo make it difficult for him to come to terms with the harmful consequences of his own behavior, however much he may feel he wants social reform. For Qu, good literature operates rather like modern psychiatry, although the analogy would not have occurred to him. Unlike straightforward exposure, a good understated piece of satire such as Gogol's can play tricks with the reader's sympathies, helping him to work around his own resistance and to press for further reforms. Though literature operates initially at the request of society, its power lies in this ability to "alter philosophies of life and break down social customs."[10] Thus has Qu circumvented his doubts about the relevance of literature to reform. Writers such as Gogol, Pushkin and Turgenev, Qu reasons, once asked the same kinds of questions about society that China is asking now. Until Chinese literature starts to turn its attentions in similar directions, Russian writings such as theirs can help to steer the reformist instincts of Chinese readers into constructive channels and to accelerate the process of social change. They can also inspire Chinese writers to develop an indigenous modern literature, one that will answer even better than Russia's to the needs of the Chinese people.

Qu is clearly impressed with the literary qualities of Russian literature, which make it such a good catalyst for the self-reform of readers; but at least as attractive, in his view, is the similarity of the issues with which it deals to those with which Chinese readers are beginning to concern themselves. Here the politicalness of Qu's approach to literature is nearly matched by the literariness of his approach to politics, for he has put Russian literature in a key position — on the boundary between China's backward (though "spiritual") present and the Russian-style revolution to come. When one considers what this analysis does for those few Chinese who know Russian, it is plain that Qu's hopes of "saving China by cultural means," imported cultural means included, have not really been abandoned.

"Russian Literature before the October Revolution"

In 1921–1922, during his first visit to the Soviet Union, Qu undertook his principal study of Russian literature. The original manuscript has been lost, but a revised version was published in 1927 in Jiang Guangci's *Eluosi wenxue* (Russian literature), under the title "Shiyue gemingqiande Eluosi wenxue" (Russian literature before the October Revolution).[11] It is this version that now occupies close to eighty pages of Qu's collected works. There is no way of knowing what the original was like, but the version that we have does not convey the impression of consistently focused, original research. It is a very general, often superficial, account of trends in all areas of Russian literature from prehistory to the October Revolution of 1917. Its organization, moreover, is often quite haphazard, and there is good reason to think that Qu may have pieced it together from one or more studies in Russian.[12] Yet it seems to fit in well with Qu's other writings on Russian literature, and for all of its drawbacks, it is still his most extended study of the subject. We must, therefore, consider its arguments in some detail.

Qu's analysis of Russia's literary history falls into four major divisions: (1) premodern literature; (2) modern literature up to the liberation of the serfs in 1861; (3) modern literature from the liberation of the serfs until the turn of the century; (4) Gorky and the prerevolutionary beginnings of proletarian literature.

The most important point that Qu has to make about Russia's premodern literary forms is that they eventually succumbed to modernization — in the wake of a complex of economic and political reforms that were being introduced into Russia during the eighteenth century. While these economic and political changes were the result of increased Russian contacts with Europe, the great triumph on the literary front was that writers began to revolt against excessive Frenchification in the literature of the Russian aristocracy and to develop a version of the spoken language that would serve for literary expression. The early leaders of this movement were scientists and historians like M. V. Lomonosov (1711–1765), not literary men, but their work set the stage for the "great" *(weida)*, modern period of Russian literature that was to be the nineteenth century. For Qu, the greatness of this new literature lay in its ability to "apply the ideals of the culture to real life, to reflect real life in a literary form."[13] By bringing the written language into contact with the spoken, in other words, these reformers had made it possible for literature to draw closer to the feelings and aspirations of the people, "to say what the people wanted to say but could not."[14] In drawing closer to the feelings and aspirations of the people, literature was getting ready to serve as a tool of reform.

The first great modern writer to emerge, in Qu's opinion, was Pushkin. Pushkin's genius lay, for Qu, in two places — his writing style and his commitment to write about real events. For Qu, Pushkin's use of language was both a remarkable reflection of the common idiom and an instrument of such astonishing beauty that it set the standard for years to come. Pushkin erred, Qu notes somewhat sourly, by immersing himself too enthusiastically in European romanticism and by taking himself too seriously, but he had a redeeming sense of duty toward the common people. This meant that his characters were often ordinary men, drawn in a lifelike manner; or, if they were "superfluous"[15] gentry like Eugene Onegin, living parasitically off the labor of peasants and idly acquiring useless knowledge, they at least showed some signs of being ashamed of themselves. In any case, Qu feels, Pushkin's style and his characters were suffused with a Russian-ness new to Russian literature. For the first time in history, Russian literature had something to set it apart from European traditions and something to be proud of.

Qu does not suggest that Pushkin's writings made much of a direct contribution to social, political, or economic reform. That is to say, they were stronger on "reflecting real life in a literary form" than on "applying the ideals of the culture to real life." Still, they were the first to introduce a number of important lines of development — realism, national spirit, beautiful vernacular, psychological sensitivity, awareness of social issues, and, of course, the "superfluous man" — whose combined influence would eventually help to bring about the liberation of the serfs. Gogol may have been the real father of Russian realism in Qu's view, and he may have done more to awaken reformist sentiments among his readers. Lermontov (1814–1841) may have contributed at least as much to the development of the "language of the average educated member of society."[16] Turgenev may have done more to paint the peasants' outlook on life and to expose the evils of landlordism, while his "superfluous men" may have shown the evils of superfluity more clearly. Thus, they may have provided more direct encouragement for those gentry, like Alexander Herzen (1812–1870), who were beginning to devote their lives to reformist causes. Still, it was Pushkin who had set these trends in motion. In Qu's opinion, the differences between Pushkin's and Turgenev's work was as much a reflection of changed social reality as it was a matter of improvements in literary techniques. Techniques, though, *had* also improved, making it easier for literature to sum up reformist urges among the Russian people and "quietly lead on revolutionary youth."[17] With literature's help, the liberation of the serfs had become, before long, an inevitability.

Liberation ushered in the second major phase of modern Russian literature as Qu saw it. Without serfs, the gentry no longer enjoyed the privileges they once had, and power was passing down the social ladder to the class next in line, the bourgeoisie. As far as Qu is concerned, the Russian bourgeoisie was a sorry lot, insistently money-minded and indifferent to their common cause with other Russians, let alone to human decency. As idealistic ex-nobles and their offspring streamed to the villages to expiate the guilt of centuries of domination, they collided head on with the new money-mindedness, which doomed many of their efforts to failure, leaving them frustrated and disillusioned. Nevertheless, Qu argues, the insistence of these "conscience-stricken nobles" on social service required of literature that it too move closer to the people. Further, a new iconoclasm forced writers to look again at the gentry literature of Turgenev and his generation, which suddenly looked less true to life than it once had.

Instead, populist authors and critics, such as Zlatovratsky (1845–1911, whom Qu had once translated) and Chernyshevsky (1828–1889), stepped in to capture the reading public, and postliberation literature enjoyed tremendous circulation even when artistic quality was not first-rate.

Meanwhile, upper-class writers, such as Tolstoy, Dostoyevsky, and Chekhov, it seemed to Qu, were falling out of step with Russia's march toward social reform. If their distaste for the bourgeoisie was perfectly justified, some of their other concerns were less so. Tolstoy's escapist fantasies about the innate goodness of the peasantry, Dostoyevsky's probings of the individual psyche, and Chekhov's dim, depressed vignettes — all are taken as evidence of important shortcomings in these writers' outlooks. Still, their hearts were basically in the right place, with the people, and their writings did at least as much as Pushkin's had done to put Russian literature on the map. If they did nothing to further social progress directly, the accuracy and beauty with which they mirrored the contradictions of their day were still enough to qualify them for membership in the great tradition.

As social conditions went from bad to worse at the end of the nineteenth century, Qu maintains, it was only Gorky who was able to rise above the bleakness of reality and inspire firm hope in the future. Gorky, it seems, was writing of a new sort of Russian, the city man and the laborer, who felt anger, not despair, at bourgeois outrages and who drew strength from the conviction that the proletariat would rule the world. In language, too, Gorky's writing was refreshingly innovative, for it made use of a "new vernacular," closer to the language of the working class than anything that had appeared in writing before. Otherwise the early twentieth century was a literary disaster, in Qu's opinion, with hopeless utopians and Europophilic pure-art artists undoing most of the progress that Gorky's work had ushered in. Nevertheless, it was not hard for Qu to bring his study to an optimistic conclusion. The Russian Revolution was approaching, and Gorky's innovations would soon receive due recognition under the new, proletarian phase of great Russian literature.[18]

"Russian Literature before the October Revolution": Two Ellipses

While China is not mentioned directly in this study, it seems reasonable to assume that Chinese problems were still as much at issue as they had been in 1920. Qu may not have conceived of "Russian Literature before the October Revolution" as a preview of China's literary future, but it is surely an important amplification of his earlier views on the general relationship between literature and social change in China and Russia. Moreover, since Qu's later thinking on Chinese literature often seemed to return to the same broad pattern of analysis, it is all the more important to consider two respects in which this analysis seems strangely elliptical.

The first concerns the treatment of the Russian masses. Qu was perfectly aware when he wrote this study that illiteracy had been widespread in Russia up until and even after the revolution. In another work of the same time, a diary called "Chidu xinshi" (History of the heart in the red capital), he makes the point that "before the revolution 70 or 80 percent of the Russian people were illiterate."[19] Yet in "Russian Literature before the October Revolution," Qu gives the impression that the great success of Russian literature was its ability to draw so many Russians into the process of change. The development of a modern Russian literature came in response to the wishes of "ordinary people" (pingmin), we are told. Pushkin felt a duty to serve "the masses" (yongzhong), so he wrote of ordinary life. Herzen "popularized" (tongsuhua) Western science, social thought, and literature. After the liberation of the serfs, literature became more socially conscious and readership expanded enormously.[20] Yet in reality, as Qu knew, these developments were completely over the heads of all but 10 or 20 percent of Russian society.

It is not only when Qu talks of "people" in these contexts that he seems to mean something more elite. The popular Russian language he praises Lomonosov and Pushkin for developing was really the language of the "average *educated* member of society," it turns out, and only with Gorky does the written language really make contact with the language of the streets. Finally, Qu has made "Russian culture" synonymous with gentry culture, so much so that it is said to collapse along with the gentry at the end of the nineteenth century.[21] The real progress of prerevolutionary Russian literature, in Qu's scheme of things, is still confined almost entirely to the "philosophies of life" of the enlightened Russian aristocracy and their immediate associates, the nonaristocratic intelligentsia. The masses are not really included until after the revolution.

Of course, in theory there is no reason that Russian gentry authors, or some of them anyway, could not have perceived what the masses truly wanted. We have, however, the comments of Tolstoy on Pushkin in *What Is Art?*, a book whose ideas are taken up rather indirectly in "Russian Literature before the October Revolution." According to Tolstoy:

When fifty years had elapsed after Pushkin's death, and simultaneously, the cheap edition of his works began to circulate among the people and a monument was erected to him in Moscow, I received more than a dozen letters from different peasants asking why Pushkin was raised to such dignity. And only the other day a [man] called on me who had evidently gone out of his mind over this very question. He was on his way to Moscow to expose the clergy for having taken part in raising a [monument] to Mr. Pushkin. Indeed, one need only imagine to oneself what the state of mind of such a man of the people must be when he learns from such rumors and newspapers as reach him that the clergy, the Government officials, and all the best people in Russia are triumphantly unveiling a statue to a great man, the benefactor, the pride of Russia — Pushkin, of whom till then he has never heard. . . He tries to learn who Pushkin was, and having discovered that Pushkin was neither a hero nor a general, but was a private person and a writer, he comes to the conclusion that Pushkin must have been a holy man and a teacher of goodness, and he hastens to read or to hear his life and works. But what must be his perplexity when he learns that Pushkin was a man of more than easy morals, who was killed in a duel, *i.e.,* when attempting to murder another man, and that all his service consisted in writing verses about love, which were often very indecent.[22]

This view makes a rather abrupt contrast with Qu's notions about Pushkin's closeness to the people, for the common man, if we can believe Tolstoy, not only had no idea that Pushkin existed for many years after his death but would not have approved of him if he had. Tolstoy may also be wrong, of course. The point is that Qu's observation about Pushkin was made without the slightest suggestion that the Russian masses, given a chance, might have seen things differently. If Qu actually ever read *What Is Art?*, he had long since filtered out such implications.

The absence of the masses is not readily apparent in "Russian Literature before the October Revolution," most likely because Qu himself was not aware that they were missing. Having adopted the view that progress means decreasing the distance between writers and society, and secure in the knowledge that a proletarian revolution emerged from concerns Russian literature had fostered, he assumes that Russian literature was getting closer to the masses; but he fails to realize that the masses were not getting much closer to literature. In contrast to Russian leftists like Lenin and Kropotkin, whom Qu admired,[23] he seems unaware that "to apply the ideals of the culture to real life, to reflect real life in a literary form" is quite a different process during the "conscience-stricken gentry" phase, when literature

111

is only *about* "the people," and the proletarian phase, when "the people" become more intimately involved. Thus, Qu is not fully aware, one suspects, of the potential conflict between the kind of mass appeal he claims to want for literature and the kinds of stylistic beauty and reformist human love that creep into his definition of greatness. If literature had really been "mass" in a society like Russia's where literacy was low, it could hardly have been complex enough to be beautiful, for the time being at least, by an aristocratic standard. Further, if society were truly egalitarian, there would no longer be any reason to put the burden of reform on those humanistic gentry for whom good style was most important. Since Qu was later to make such a point of insisting that writers meant "masses" or "proletariat" when they talked about "the people,"[24] his apparent indifference to the problem here is all the more significant.

One does not have to look beyond "History of the Heart in the Red Capital" for possible explanations. There Qu is far more candid about his attitudes toward the old Russian gentry than in "Russian Literature before the October Revolution." To take one example:

> The intellectuals of the Russian gentry used to hate bourgeois culture more than anything. Now they are all about to become pitiful, backward members of the bourgeoisie. Although . . . although . . . [sic] those "conscience-stricken gentry," those youngsters who went "to the people," have contributed more than a little in the area of social thought to the welfare of the working people during the past generation. And among the leadership of the Communist party, there are many who were gentry at an earlier date. A month ago, I met an English Communist party member who knew a good deal about Russian literature. He said that the bourgeoisie did not contribute anything to Russian culture. [Russian] historians, literary people, and social thinkers were almost all gentry.[25]

In "Russian Literature before the October Revolution," Qu could not have expressed such opinions so openly, it would seem; but here, in the more intimate diary format, he presents the gentry not as "backward members of the bourgeoisie," twice upstaged by the forward march of the dialectic, but as potentially superior, both in their claims to represent Russian culture and in their devotion to mass interests. So devoted were they, in fact, that they could even lead Communist parties.

What Qu seems to have established in "History of the Heart in the

Red Capital" is a set of polarities, justified in theory more or less but also emotionally meaningful. On the one side are the "conscience-stricken gentry," loyalty to the nation, the "Asian" spirit of cooperation among the people, and love of nature; on the other are the bourgeoisie and their grasping commercialism, excessive admiration for Europe, individualism, and indifference to nature. The one side is good, appealing, harmonious; the other, offensive and out of balance. In "History of the Heart in the Red Capital," though not in "Russian Literature before the October Revolution," Qu seems to attribute the gentry's superior virtues to their roots in the countryside. Thus, it was far easier, in his view, for the gentry to speak on behalf of the rural masses than it would have been for the urban bourgeoisie; and once commercialism swept through the countryside, it was the gentry who took greatest offense. Under such circumstances, the gentry became the natural allies of the masses and very likely their leaders as well. Though many of them sold out to temptation and joined the ranks of the bourgeoisie, those who remained true to their enlightened gentry values did not. Perhaps many of them erred in the direction of conservatism, but as a rule they tried to do what was best for the nation.[26] This is how their "great" Russian literature could speak for all the Russians, in Qu's view. This is why "Russian Literature before the October Revolution" could be so tolerant of writers like Tolstoy and Chekhov even when their writings failed to herald the proletarian future. Despite the attempt in "Russian Literature before the October Revolution" to relate value in literature to social change, it was somehow all right for gentry literature to go on promoting gentry ideals after the liberation of the serfs because these ideals seemed to speak so well for all Russians.

One might say that there was more than a grain of truth in Qu's emphasis on gentry contributions. The Russian bourgeoisie was, after all, a rather fleeting phenomenon, and the Communist party did indeed draw heavily on the talents of upper-class Russians. However, Qu also seems to have had a vested interest in insisting on the natural identity of reform-minded gentry thinking with the mass viewpoint. "History of the Heart in the Red Capital" is filled with analogies linking China, the Chinese gentry, and Qu Qiubai himself to nineteenth-century Russia, the Russian gentry, and the Russian "superfluous man." All had faced or were facing the destructive energies of capitalism; all had confronted or were confronting the threat of over-Westernization and its consequences: the weakness of the semi-colony, the shame of the collaborationist, the isolation of the individual. In all cases the answer was "proletarianization" *(wuchanjiejihua)*. "Proletarianization" could be expected to bring the same strength and dignity to China that it had brought to the Soviet Union; but even before that glorious day, the anticipation of a proletarian future could do a lot for a frustrated intellectual. As Qu explains:

> I earnestly hope that I can be an embryo of the new culture of mankind. The basis of the new culture lies in combining two cultures, the Western and the Eastern, which have been opposed in the past and which now, since the beginning of the Communist era, can begin to complement each other . . . Make no mistake about it, I am only the smallest, most infinitesimal foot soldier; but I am a fighter through and through. Since I became a foot soldier, I have enrolled in the vanguard of the world cultural movement, which is about to open a new path for the culture of all mankind and which will bring new luster to China's more than four thousand years of moral and material splendor.[27]

Qu was quite open about the difficulties and fears he experienced as he contemplated surrendering his ex-gentry identity in favor of the mass movement. Still, he felt that the only alternative was to become a "superfluous man" or, worse, an out-and-out scoundrel; and this he could not, or would not, do. Rather than wallow in "superfluous" despair, it was much more attractive to imagine that he, like some members of the Russian gentry, could become "embryos of the new culture of mankind." And if he saw anything wrong with the presence of an ex-gentry member among the vanguard, he was not alone in overlooking it. Certainly, Qu had to play down his hopes that he would lead, not follow mass interests. He saw his role as transmitter to China of the Russian example in "earthshakingly important" terms; but its importance was defined by the relevance of the Russian example to the interests of the Chinese masses.[28] Yet in assuming an identity of interests between upper-class reformers and the mass movement, Qu had found a way to hang onto some part of his gentry consciousness. By interpreting Russian literature as an arm of revolution — in Russia and in China — Qu could go on involving himself in pursuits like literature and translation (not to mention party leadership) that most of "the people" could not share; moreover, he could do so in good conscience.

The other outstanding ellipsis in "Russian Literature before the October Revolution" appears in Qu's attitude toward literary artistry. As we have seen, artistic considerations were not completely missing in his appreciation of Russian writings, despite the emphasis on social change. Pushkin's beautiful prose, Gogol's realism, Chekhov's irony — all are entered into the record of greatness alongside more tangibly reformist achievements. "Greatness," as we have seen, is literature's ability to "apply the ideals of the culture to real life, to reflect real life in a literary form" — a definition vague enough to encompass both reformist and artistic considerations. In practice, as Qu works through his study, it is evident that sheer ideological correctness, such as that of Chernyshevsky and Zlatovratsky, does not move him nearly as much as the beautiful humanism of Tolstoy and Dostoyevsky, nor does it seem to outweigh the subtle moodiness of an art such as Chekhov's. Tolstoy, Dostoyevsky, and Chekhov, whose work is not given highest marks for ideological orientation, are specifically called "great" at least once; Chernyshevsky and Zlatovratsky never are. Ironically, though it was the connection with proletarian revolution that had earlier provided Qu's justification for taking up Russian literature, it is literary standards, as often as not, that seem to prevail in his assessments. Qu may not be inconsistent here — the value of a writer like Tolstoy may still be linked, ultimately, to revolution. Yet in view of the road-to-revolution approach of "Russian Literature before the October Revolution," it is curious that the revolution itself is not presented as the direct result of Russian literature, while the greatest literature is often not the most demonstrably reformist. Here Qu's submerged sensitivity to the pleasures of literature seems to strain against the logic of his master plan.

"History of the Heart in the Red Capital" is once again elucidating. Inserted between entries in the diary are translations — from Gorky, to be sure, but also from Lermontov and Tiutchev (1803–1883). By a purely political standard, both Lermontov and Tiutchev fall well below the average for approved authors in "Russian Literature before the October Revolution," though both are highly praised for their writing styles. Lermontov's lyrics are presented without comment in the diary, but it is obvious that they were put there because Qu enjoyed them; and Tiutchev is introduced as someone whose spiritual qualities are "extremely Eastern."[29] The diary also shows Qu enjoying Russian literature in other ways — reflecting on Turgenev's *Nest of Gentlefolk* when he sees some ex-gentry in a Moscow coffee shop, paying a long and sentimental visit to Tolstoy's former estate, recollecting Herzen as he thinks about the differences between the bourgeoisie and the gentry.

Gentry images, it turns out, are doubly applicable in Qu's emotional life; for whenever his comfort in the possibility of gentry leadership breaks down, as it does with disconcerting frequency, he has only to reach for that other, "superfluous" set of associations from Russian literature. In Qu's words, "Alas! Regret, lamentation, sorrow. . . I used to regard myself as unusual, but looking back, can I find anything unusual about me? How ridiculous! 'What indeed can you do? Why not identify yourself with the masses?' Reason has reached a conclusion, but the force of inertia is too great."[30] This passage, from an entry in the diary entitled "China's 'Superfluous Man' " (mostly about Qu himself), is prefaced by a long quotation from Turgenev's *Rudin;* and elsewhere in the diary Qu quotes *Crime and Punishment* in about the same way — as if the "superfluous" figure's concerns were the same as his own.[31] Underneath the surface, one suspects, Qu was just as moved by these heroes as were less politically radical writers, such as Yu Dafu, and found them just as relevant to his personal concerns. Despite his refusal to side with them in "Russian Literature before the October Revolution," he was obviously conscious of sharing many of their problems. Of course, even at his most "tenderhearted," Qu never basked in superfluity the way Yu did.[32] His constant preoccupation with serving society compelled him to neutralize his weaknesses even if he could not turn them into advantages. Still, it was not just that the Russian gentry had successfully transformed themselves into proletarian leaders (in many cases) that attracted him to their writings. It was also that they had so beautifully captured the image of superfluity before discarding it.

If this diary is reliable indication, Qu's sober assessment of the political value of literature in "Russian Literature before the October Revolution" had very little to do with the ways in which he himself experienced this literature. Instead of simply forcing him to think more about the masses, as it was supposed to do, "great" Russian literature seemed to provoke a strong personal response, not always pleasant but always deeply meaningful. This, surely, is the reason that Qu was so willing to make so many allowances for good writers in "Russian Literature before the October Revolution." Enjoying the expressive powers of "great" Russian literature as he did, it was hard to turn his study into pure social science. Lermontov, Tiutchev, Tolstoy, Dostoyevsky, and Chekhov were all authors he very much admired. By employing a standard of evaluation that gave some credit to literary excellence, he could be realistic about their contributions to revolution and still grant them the honor he wanted them to have. Moreover, by applying a political standard that changed over time, he could praise writers like Turgenev on both reformist and literary grounds, even though their politics could not have seemed particularly revolutionary by the time Qu wrote. Like other leftists, Qu would have to remove Tolstoy, Turgenev, and the others from his list of heroes before too much longer,[33] but in 1921–1922, it was still not heresy to praise them.

The differences between Qu's private and his public writings at this time suggest that even in 1921–1922, he felt some pressure (no doubt at least partly self-imposed) to tone down his identification with the Russian gentry and his love of Russian gentry literature.[34] His private faith in the salutary social effects of gentry self-reform had to be redefined as popular progress for "Russian Literature before the October Revolution" before it would fit in. His private love of the literary side of Russian literature had to be combined with a reformist standard in his less intimate writings before it seemed acceptable. By identifying the gentry as "the people" in "Russian Literature before the October Revolution," Qu had temporarily postponed the painful realization that mass and gentry interests were not always compatible. By combining literary and nonliterary standards in his definition of literary value, he had sidestepped the task of choosing between them. The fact that "Russian Literature before the October Revolution" is stricter in its application of proletarian principles than "History of the Heart in the Red Capital" can probably be taken as evidence of the direction in which Qu felt his thoughts ought to be moving. If "Russian Literature before the October Revolution" is not without its contradictions, this is surely a reflection of the intellectual and emotional difficulty of the adjustments Qu was making.

The Return to China

Upon Qu's return to China in 1923, he began to apply himself to the task of creating a new, modern Chinese literature, though political activities were beginning to consume more and more of his time. In general, the goals he sought for Chinese literature were based, as before, on the values he had found in Russian literature, or rather, in the progression of Russian literature to its Soviet phase. Evidently, however, his awareness of the implications of mass illiteracy was growing during this period. His first article to consider the question seriously, "Huangmoli" (In the wasteland [1923]), gives a rather negative picture of the extent to which modern Chinese literature had reached the masses. Most interesting here is Qu's imaginary dialogue with a worker who had not been able to understand some of Qu's own writings from six months earlier because the language was too obscure for him.[35] Apparently, by this time Qu had begun to shed the belief that an intellectual literature, however well-intentioned, could reach the Chinese people if it did not adjust to their level.

Whether this new insight extended retroactively to nineteenth-century Russian literature or not is harder to say. Qu's literary translations were beginning to be more of Gorky in the mid-1920s, evidence perhaps that he was beginning to see nongentry Russian literature as a more appropriate model for China than Pushkin, Gogol, or Tolstoy. On the other hand, though Qu may have been branching out toward proletarian literature by this time, there is no reason to believe that he had completely abandoned his former faith in the old kind of Russian-style literature that could "alter philosophies of life and break down social customs." On the contrary, we know that he suggested to Guo Moruo in 1925 or 1926 that Guo translate Tolstoy's *War and Peace* because the book made such a good case against "Napoleonic individualism."[36] Qu could scarcely have wasted much thought on the dangers of "Napoleonic individualism" among workers and peasants even if he had dreamed that any of them would have the stamina to read Guo's projected translation. Certainly, Qu was not yet ready to abandon his personal interest in the Russian classics, nor was he prepared to surrender his earlier conviction that they might do some good for Chinese society as a whole.

The Years of League Leadership

Qu's efforts at writing and translating literary materials flagged between 1925 and 1930, the period when he was most active politically. After gaining and losing the chairmanship of the Communist party, Qu returned to the Soviet Union for some Comintern work in 1928–1930. Shortly after his return to China, his expulsion from the Central Committee left him free to pick up the cultural task where he had left off, and before long he had become a leader of the League of Left-Wing Writers.[37] Actually, it was not quite where he had left off; for radical leaders were no longer content, as Qu and others had once been, to wait one hundred years for China to catch up with its Communist future. Disagreement ran high over timing and methods, but literature was now supposed to reach the broad masses directly, not just to write about them. For anyone professing to be a leftist, literature's days of concentrating exclusively on "changing the philosophies of life" of highly literate readers were over. Besides, by the early 1930s, Qu had had a second look at the Soviet Union. There, policies to reach the masses culturally had been developing for more than a decade — Qu himself had helped with a program to develop a Latin alphabet for the Chinese-speaking peoples of the USSR during the late 1920s. These and other programs were apparently enough to dispel whatever doubts orthodox Marxists may have felt about the feasibility of using "cultural means" to direct, encourage, and propagandize social change. Thus, when Qu advised in "Practical Problems of Proletarian Mass Art" that the purpose of mass literature was to "unite the feelings of our team in the class struggle, to forge a fighting spirit in the consciousness, the thoughts, and the so-called philosophies of lives of the masses,"[38] there can be no doubt that this time he really meant the masses. "Agitka" (agitational propaganda), the first type of "literature" recommended to the Chinese proletarian literature movement in this article, came straight from Soviet practice and had no other purpose than to rouse mass opinion.

Naturally, the role of intellectuals was to be severely curtailed in the new order of things. "Practical Problems of Proletarian Mass Art" insists that literature should be proletarian in viewpoint, and efforts to develop *mass* proletarian literature (proletarian literature written or communicated in forms the masses could understand) should take precedence over literature addressed to the Europeanized intellectuals. Qu did not deny that intellectuals would have to go on authoring proletarian literature for many years to come, but he severely limited their freedom to innovate, leaving little room for the kind of intellectual, Russian-style literature he had once favored. Form, content, and language in Qu's new master plan were to serve the masses directly, not just their upper-class allies. While he was vague about who could decide what sorts of literature best served the masses, he was well aware that serving them would not be easy for highly educated authors. Thus it is highly unlikely by this time that he would have jumped so easily as before to the conclusion that Pushkin's work, or the work of other Russian intellectuals, had automatically reached the common man just because the author hoped or thought it would. Qu's program for the 1930s included the provision that writers test their works in "tea houses, vacant lots, factories, back alleys, and intersections" to see whether the masses liked them or not.[39] Furthermore, many of his translations and "adaptations" from Russian and Soviet literature between 1931 and 1933 were specifically designed to appeal to the mass imagination. It was no doubt also in the spirit of reaching as many people as possible that Qu revised his 1922 translation of Gorky's "Philistine Hymn," putting it into more colloquial Chinese.[40]

Qu seemed, in other words, to have completely "proletarianized" his interest in Russian literature by this time.

To a certain extent, Qu's previous background in Russian literature was still serving him well in the 1930s. The goals of the proletarian literature movement, as he presented them, included many of the elements that had gone into his appreciation of Russian literature: realism, vernacular style, artistically arranged content, and the commitment to guide and heighten readers' social consciousness. While the original model may have been Russian, the power of the model lay in its insistence that literature should cater as closely as possible to national needs and ways of speaking. But now that the target of reform had moved from the well-educated consciousnesses of the upper classes to the barely accessible minds of the Chinese proletariat, the direct usefulness to China of intellectual, Russian-style literature was less self-evident.

Nevertheless, instead of abandoning his now outmoded interest, Qu seemed simply to assign it to a less prominent place in his thinking. Even in the 1930s he was capable of referring to elite Russian readers as the "common people" of Russia, and though the nineteenth-century Russian gentry was relegated to unflattering bourgeois status in some of his analyses,[41] his old admiration for "conscience-stricken gentries," Chinese as well as Russian, can still be detected. His celebrated "*Lu Xun zagan xuanji* xuyan" (Preface to *Selected essays of Lu Xun* [1933]) is a case in point.[42] There, Qu builds the argument around a quotation from Alexander Herzen, which praises the Decembrist revolutionaries of 1825 as principled sons and daughters of the Russian gentry, whose righteous stand is explained by their closeness to nature. Similarly, says Qu, Lu Xun's consistent dedication to mass causes can be explained by his links to the countryside. Because Lu Xun's gentry family was on the decline, Qu argues, he mingled with the common people when he was young and felt close to them. After the May Fourth movement, when many intellectuals took the bourgeois academic route of Hu Shi, Lu Xun remained more involved with the people; and after the anti-Communist purges of 1927, he was among the group that moved left to proletarian literature. As always, Qu would have denied that gentry status, declining or otherwise, was a guarantee of good behavior. Yet even though good behavior was, more than ever, defined as a person's willingness to think in terms of the masses, Qu's old emphasis on the gentry and its special potential to find itself in the mass movement seems to have remained at the back of his mind.

Further, despite Qu's firm injunction that China's new literary language should be as close as possible to the spoken language of the proletariat, he continued to worry about the lack of a "beautiful, enjoyable" literary language such as the one Lomonosov and Pushkin had brought to Russia. Understandably, Qu failed to reiterate the point that this language, in contrast to that of Gorky, was based on the speech of the "average *educated* member of society"; but it is quite clear that he was operating with such an assumption in mind. As "Practical Problems of Proletarian Mass Art" puts it, "The standard is: when a work is read to a laborer he can understand it. From there we can open up new vistas so that the workers and peasants can gradually organize their own capacities for artistic language and . . . can gradually progress and create 'enjoyable Chinese' . . . like Turgenev's 'enjoyable [Russian].' "[43] Normally, as in the above passage, Qu seems to be saying that once the proletariat have learned the fundamentals of reading, they can set about creating a beautiful written language. At other times, though, he seems to reverse the order, harking back to the arguments of "Russian Literature Before the October Revolution" that the "beautiful, enjoyable language" is a *prerequisite* for full literary contact with the masses. "Practical Problems of Proletarian Mass Art" also contains this second sort of emphasis: "In the seventeenth and eighteenth centuries in Russia, the Europeanized gentry only read Church Slavonic scriptures and French novels while the ordinary people [*pingmin*] read Russian. China still needs a second revolution in writing like that begun by Lomonosov and completed by Pushkin. Otherwise, revolutionary intellectuals will not speak the same language as the popular masses."[44] Evidently, Qu had not completely eradicated the old way of thinking, in spite of his increased emphasis on the proletariat; and his confusion about timing here can probably be taken as evidence that he had not quite come to terms with all the implications of the new proletarian order. None of this could be considered heresy, and there is no reason to think that it was so perceived by Qu's contemporaries. It is just that Qu's public commitment to "proletarianization" in the 1930s had not completely eliminated his old interest in the contributions of the Russian gentry, an interest with which "proletarianization" was less than fully compatible.

Qu was silent by this time about the benefits to China of "great" Russian writings, except as examples of beautiful language. It is impossible to know from Qu's public pronouncements whether it was just his prudence in the face of possible criticism. Qu does not spell out his reasons for thinking that the styles of Pushkin, Turgenev, and Tolstoy made such compellingly useful models (via translation) that the less than fully revolutionary content of their works could be disregarded. However, his posthumously published translation of Pushkin's *The Gypsies,* which he began in 1933 and never quite finished, may be a clue that he was still attracted to Russian literature for personal reasons, whatever he may have felt about its ability to contribute to Chinese society. *The Gypsies* is a long narrative poem about a sensitive young man who flees conventional society to join a troop of gypsies, then finds himself unable to get along in gypsy society as well. Somehow this piece seems all wrong in terms of Qu's literary directives for the thirties. Its social message, what there is of one, is subtle and debatable; and a good deal of the interest lies in the theme of jealous love. It would be hard to imagine what Qu saw in the piece: whether he identified with the hero's antisocial tendencies as Pushkin may have done, whether he took the ending as yet another illustration of the evils of superfluity, or whether he was simply moved by the love story.[45] Whatever the case, this translation seems to indicate that Qu's private interest in Russian literature in the 1930s was in some conflict with the directives that he was issuing as leader of the proletarian literature movement.

"Superfluous Words"

Taken by themselves, such scant indications of Qu's abiding fascination with the "great" Russian tradition would mean very little, and they pale in any case alongside the record of his persistent and seminal contribution to the proletarian literature movement, both in Shanghai and, after 1933, in Kiangsi. Had Qu not been captured by Guomindang soldiers in February 1935, had he not chosen to write the prison diary "Duoyude hua" (Superfluous words), the case might have looked very different. Yet it now seems virtually certain that Qu did write "Superfluous Words." This contention, long denied by left-wing critics from Lu Xun on, was confirmed during the Cultural Revolution by Zhou Enlai himself, and Qu subsequently fell from the posthumous state of grace he had been accorded until that time.[46]

This is probably as Qu would have wished it. "Superfluous Words" is his confession of ineligibility for the kind of martyrdom that his impending execution seemed likely to inspire; and he naturally fell back on the old "superfluous" image complaining once again that his gentry upbringing had left him too weak and indecisive to cope with the strains of political activity. There are no direct quotations from

Russian literature in this confession, though the choice of title and the tenor of discussion resound with the despair of men like Rudin. To some extent Qu seems to have gone overboard in demonstrating the shallowness of his commitment to mass interests. His expulsion from the Central Committee may well have been the deflating experience he says it was. Nevertheless, it is difficult to imagine that he could really have worked so hard and so creatively on behalf of the proletariat if his attitude was really as poor as he says it was.

In any event, "Superfluous Words" leaves no doubt that Russian literature had sustained him all along. He speaks of it in his confession as the one field in which he had always felt at home, the one field in which he still might have something to offer.[47] Not once does he specifically refer to any tension between this interest and his more clear-cut proletarian sympathies. However, he leaves no doubt that his overall point of view was never fully that of the proletariat: "My gentry consciousness, deeply buried and hard to detect as it was, in fact never disappeared."[48] Perhaps Qu would have also agreed that there was something of the gentry in his early writings on Russian literature and in his lingering attachment to Russian masterpieces in the 1930s. Of interest is this passage toward the end of "Superfluous Words":

> In recent years, I have reread some literary classics, both Chinese and Western, and I believe that I have had some new experiences. From these works, you understand human life and society rather intimately. You understand people of differentiated characters, not in general classifications, such as "good man," "bad man," or "bureaucrat," "commoner," "worker," "rich peasant," and so forth. What are revealed before you are human beings in flesh and blood, with distinct personalities, though they are still placed in certain relations to production and in certain social classes. This, I suppose, is the first step I have taken to advance from a mere "man of letters" to real appreciation of literature. But is it too late? It is![49]

Here to be a "mere man of letters" is still the minus it always was but the alternative is "real appreciation of literature," not "proletarianization."

One would like to know whether Qu had embarked on these "new experiences" by the time he was writing articles like "Practical Problems of Proletarian Mass Art." If so, the strain of contradiction must have been almost unbearable. Whatever the case, this excerpt supplies a somewhat more hospitable context for Qu's *Gypsies* translation than do any of his writings for the League of Left-Wing Writers. The confession also makes it clear that the conflicts we have observed in Qu's work on Russian literature in the 1920s and 1930s — between literature about the people and literature of the people, between literature's literary and nonliterary values — were conflicts of which Qu himself was sometimes aware. "Russian Literature before the October Revolution" had obscured the conflicts by identifying the interests of the Russian gentry with those of the masses and by blending literary and nonliterary components in its definition of literary value. Qu's public writings of the 1930s had all but eliminated the gentry side of the Russian model and the literary side of the value of literature. Still, the conflicts had not gone away.

This is not to say that they were irreconcilable, that Qu's "tender-hearted" interests of old were totally at war with his role as revolutionary. On the contrary, he was able to draw several sorts of conclusions from the Russian example, some more political, some more literary, some mass-centered, and some "superfluous." While his love of Russian literature had occasionally worked against the more conspicuously "proletarian" side of his nature, his conscience lay with the proletariat, and he made heroic efforts to serve them until his capture. Like other Chinese leftist writers of his time, and perhaps ahead of most of them, he gradually let his wish for a beautiful, modern Chinese literature yield before the greater need to educate the masses. If his compromises were not always successful or satisfying, at least they were made. Yet if in the end his imprisonment rekindled or intensified the old "superfluous" image, he was no doubt giving way to feelings that had often lain just below the surface.

"Superfluous Words" is not a complete reversal of Qu's "proletarian" stance, for he still maintains that "proletarianization" should be the answer for "superfluity" generally and for China as well. It is just that by 1935 Qu had come to feel that the new proletarian order left little hope for himself or for the others of his generation who had been raised as members of the gentry. Consistent too, in a way, is Qu's continuing interest in the social side of literature. The list of books worth rereading in the final section of "Superfluous Words" features Gorky's *Klim Samgin*, Tolstoy's *Anna Karenina*, and Turgenev's *Rudin*, alongside Lu Xun's "A Q zhengzhuan" (The true story of A Q), Mao Dun's *Dongyao* (Vacillation), and Cao Xueqin's *Hong lou meng* (Dream of the red chamber).[50] None of these are frivolous books, certainly. All contain a mixture of social and literary concerns, of the sort that appealed to Qu in "Russian Literature Before the October Revolution."

None, however, would have been suitable for the mass proletarian audiences on which the league had come to place greatest emphasis. Qu may have removed himself from the ranks of the proletariat by 1935, and he may have begun to approach literature in a more literary fashion; but his tastes were not too different from what they had been in the early 1920s. It was just that such tastes were now seriously out of date in left-wing circles.

Qu seems also to have returned at the end to another of his earlier views, that a literature addressed solely to intellectuals was still worth writing. This at least is one inference that might be drawn from his tentative, last-minute bequest of some of his prison writings to Ye Shengtao as material for a novel.[51] Too much the "superfluous man" to think of making further contributions to the mass literature movement, Qu now proposed to step directly into the pages of intellectual fiction: to be for Ye what Rudin had been for Turgenev. Had a novel indeed emerged from the prison writings, Qu might well have found a kind of posthumous peace with that small group of highly literate readers whose philosophies of life had once seemed so crucial to China's future.

6.

Images of Oppressed Peoples and Modern Chinese Literature

Irene Eber

The impact of translated Western literary works on the development of modern Chinese literature is an indisputable fact. Most twentieth-century writers and intellectuals were also translators. The specific nature, however, of the relationship of translated literature to the works that were written still remains largely undefined. A further complication of the role and function of foreign works in Chinese translation is that translation activity was not only a literary phenomenon. Insofar as the translation of foreign works coincided with the emergence of new intellectual, social, and political movements in twentieth-century China, translators adapted their works to the larger aims of these movements. Therefore, artistic and aesthetic considerations frequently were a secondary concern.

Among Western literary works, those of the so-called small and weak peoples (*ruoxiao minzu*) are of special interest. Whether in fiction, drama, or poetry, their works explored new literary techniques and themes, and experimented with language directed at as wide an audience as possible. To the Chinese translators and writers, works that dealt with social injustice and oppression, national identity and emancipation, the urban poor and the toiling peasants were particularly attractive. This interest in the fate of oppressed peoples led to an interest in their writers and literature, and the latter, in turn, supported a variety of ideas that were a part of the New Culture and new literature movements.

Late Qing Background

Several developments at the turn of the century facilitated the dissemination of information about the condition of small and weak, or oppressed, peoples. Among these were the growth of a publishing industry, discussions of and attempts at using vernacular Chinese, and the demand for the creation of a new literature. All three were interrelated and did not take place in isolation from one another. In addition, nationalistic and political concerns led to a more careful scrutiny of oppressed people's literary figures and their works, particularly in Japan, where translations from Western literature were readily available.

The spectacular growth of modern Chinese journalism at the end of the nineteenth and early into the twentieth century — that is, of the treaty-port newspapers — is well known. Publishing became profitable. Though most of the newspapers and journals were at first sponsored by Westerners, control soon gravitated into Chinese hands. Also, around the turn of the century, newspapers added special supplements (*fukan*). In the early years of the twentieth century, these became full-fledged literary journals and included popular fiction. It is, furthermore, important that the volume of publishing presupposed the existence of a market — a literate or semiliterate reading public — in the treaty ports and peripheral areas. Hence, when translations began to be prepared, there was not only the means for production,[1] but also a consumer market.

That Chinese ought to be written as it is spoken was suggested by various individuals prior to and after the turn of the century. Huang Zunxian was an early proponent of vernacular, as was Liang Qichao. Even Yan Fu grudgingly conceded in 1897 that the spoken language (*koushouzhi yuyan*) can be used for writing on nonliterary topics.[2]

The relationship between these sporadic calls for language reform and the appearance of a large variety of newspapers and journals which called themselves vernacular (*baihua*) is difficult to ascertain. It is also not certain what precisely the "vernacular" in the title meant. Thus, Zhou Zuoren, writing in 1932, commented that vernacular then and now are two different matters:

> I consider the vernacular of that time as compared with the vernacular of today in two points dissimilar: first, today's vernacular is "the language written as it is spoken," and the fact is that the vernacular of that time was translated eight-legged [*bagu*] vernacular. Secondly, the attitude was different. Today, when we write literature . . . no matter toward which people [the writing is directed] . . . we use vernacular. [But] . . . at that time, the ancient style [*guwen*] was used for gentlemen and vernacular was used for underlings.

Moreover, the use of vernacular at the end of the nineteenth century was a political demand; today, wrote Zhou, vernacular is no longer related to politics.[3]

Aside from the fact that increased publishing tended to support the spread of different kinds of vernacular, the new journals and weeklies also introduced Chinese readers to peoples who, like themselves, were oppressed by the major powers. Thus, Poland's sorry condition under Russian, Prussian, and Austrian rule was repeatedly mentioned. In 1904, the newly founded *Dongfang zazhi* (Eastern miscellany) carried a glum article on Poland's three partitions, in 1772, 1793, and 1795. Polish language and literature are forbidden; there is neither freedom of speech nor of publishing. Poland and China, the author sadly noted, are equally weak and ashamed of their condition.[1] At various times the persecution of Jews, a people without a country, was mentioned.[5] A lengthy article in 1905 tried to explain the ways in which the Zionist (*Xunshan*) organization was trying to help Jews.[6] Occasional notes are found concerning blacks in America. In his *Xinmin congbao*, (New people journal) Liang Qichao noted that finally, forty years after the Civil War, capable blacks were being employed, showing America's move toward freedom and common rights.[7] An article in 1906 about Booker T. Washington is particularly interesting for mentioning the work-study program at Tuskegee with its emphasis on literacy and learning a trade.[8]

Along with the increased diversity of a rapidly developing publishing industry, intellectuals were calling for a new fiction and literature. The change in late Qing fiction is discussed elsewhere. What is important here is that the genre of political fiction was singled out as being important in social and political reform. At issue here is not only the centrality of fiction in change, as Liang Qichao insisted,[9] but also that what was generally defined as political fiction was, in fact, revolutionary fiction.

The literature which had as its theme revolution, national emancipation, and freedom was created by writers of all kinds of peoples who were oppressed by the large powers. Lin Shu and his collaborators may have chosen to translate such writers as Dickens, Conan Doyle, H. Rider Haggard, Scott, or Hugo, whose works complemented current literary tastes, but it was their anti-Manchu and national revolution sentiment that led Lu Xun and his brother Zhou Zuoren, some years after they arrived in Japan, to turn to the fiction of small and weak peoples.[10] Years later Zhou recollected his gradually developing interest in small and weak people's literature:

Originally I studied sea transportation, and I had few opportunities to relate this to literature. Later, because of my enthusiasm for the problem of national revolution, I went to hear Zhang Taiyan's lectures. At that time, Mr. Zhang regularly incited against the Manchus, and he lectured on this topic. Later on again, because I paid attention to the literature of national revolution, I connected this literature with that of weak and small peoples. Among all kinds of works, like those of the Dutch, the Poles, the Jews, and the Indians, there were some that described the country's internal decadent conditions. There were some that described the deeply grievous loss of their country's independence. And when I read these, they had a deep effect on me, because they also made highly interesting reading.[11]

At the same time, Lu Xun pointed to the importance of the Pole, Adam Mickiewicz (1798–1855), and the Hungarian, Sándor Petöfi (1823–1849), as unconventional men and patriots. These are the Mara poets to Lu Xun, together with Byron, Shelley, and Pushkin, unique and unconventional poet-activists. They teach China that the new tide (*xin chao*) cannot be stopped. Just as these Mara poets heralded a new age for their people, so a new culture (*xin wenhua*) will come to China.[12] Lu Xun saw them as great men who yearned for light and freedom, and therefore, inevitably led their people.

For information about Poland and Mickiewicz, the Zhou brothers used Georg Brandes, *Poland: A Study of the Polish People and Literature*. A selection of works by authors from small European countries existed in German translation, in the Reclam Universal-Bibliothek series. In spite of the limited materials available to them, the Zhou brothers published their translations *Yuwai xiaoshuo ji* (Collection of foreign fiction) in 1909. The book sold only a few copies. The various reasons for its failure need not concern us here. More significant was the motive for making these works available in Chinese. According to Zhou Zuoren's preface to the 1920 edition, the translations were prepared because of a vague plan of transforming society through literature and art. Chinese readers should be introduced to the new literature of foreign countries. Nationalism, patriotism, heroism, love of one's oppressed country, and unconventional and fearless men trying to bring light and freedom — these were the themes that struck those Chinese who read about and translated the literatures of small and weak peoples. As yet, the people, the masses, and specifically, the peasantry, figured very little or not at all in either the accounts or translations.

The more systematic translation and popularization of oppressed people's literature at a later time was based on these various late Qing developments. An expanding publishing industry, together with language innovations that reached an increasing number of readers, made it possible to publicize the oppressed condition of different kinds of peoples like Jews, blacks, Poles, or Hungarians. Their writers and their works, too, dealt with national revolution and national identity, thus supporting similar ideas among Chinese intellectuals. Concern with peoples so very remote gradually enabled Chinese to enter the world of other peoples. How to relate their own efforts to those of other peoples was a recurring topic of discussion among writers and translators.

Views on Oppressed People's Literature in the Twenties

The beginning of a systematic interest in the literature of oppressed peoples is a part of the literary revolution and New Culture movement of May Fourth. Using either English or Esperanto translations (the latter had some vogue in China before and certainly after 1912), Chinese translations and discussions about this literature fused with the need to write a new and different literature.

Those writers who discussed the literature of oppressed peoples stressed that cultural consciousness and identity as well as cultural change could not be separated from linguistic change and literary creativity. They also saw an inherent connection between literary creation and national renaissance. This made the literature of oppressed peoples, especially from the nineteenth century, significant. The May 1921 "Manifesto of the *Literary Ten-Daily*" insisted not only on the "importance and power" of literature as well as its avant-garde features but also asserted the necessity of introducing foreign literature to China. Acquaintance with world literature, it was stated, will give Chinese literature new life and will lead to renewed efforts to create a Chinese literature. The article cites the Irish, Poles, Jews, and Hungarians as examples of peoples who formerly had no hope. But then they awakened to a renaissance (*fuxing*). Only China still seemed in a long, deep sleep.[13]

In February 1921, one month after the Wenxue yanjiu hui (Literary Association) assumed editorial control of *Xiaoshuo yuebao* (Short story monthly) its new editor, Mao Dun, wrote that it would not suffice to introduce only the literature of strong peoples. The objectives of the new literature movement also required understanding the new literature movements of others, like those of the Irish and the Jews. But, he insisted, this must lead to the actual creation of a new Chinese literature.[14]

The Celtic Revival, or the Irish Renaissance, as it is sometimes called, particularly captured the imagination of Chinese writers. Mao Dun alluded to this in his discussion on Irish literature and world progress. "It is no longer valid," he wrote, "to think in terms of one particular people's progress. All must assist one another in their development of civilization [*wenming*]."[15] Zheng Zhenduo more explicitly saw Ireland's literary renaissance as a particular renaissance within a world context. Zheng explained that the Irish are different from the English, being a people (*renmin*) of Celtic ancestry with their own culture, arts, and learning. Their literary renaissance is coupled with their struggle for independence and freedom.[16]

New literature movements, renaissances, and a desire for national independence may have been common characteristics of the literature of oppressed peoples. In addition, however, there were also particular aspects. Different historical backgrounds and varied social conditions gave a unique stamp to each people's literature. Mao Dun seemed especially sensitive to the particularity of various oppressed people's literature.

He pointed out that Polish and Jewish literature were different from Russian literature, because, unlike the latter, Jews and Poles did not have a country (Poland was reconstituted as a nation only after World War I), and they daily felt the hand of the stronger people. Thus, the Polish writer Henryk Sienkiewicz (1846–1916), in spite of his sympathetic portrayals, shows the Polish peasant as stubborn and crafty. Jewish writers, in turn, portray a hopelessness, and Jewish literature generally reflects the longing for their ancestral country. David Pinski's (1872–1959) short play, *A Dollar*, ridicules man's brutish nature, and Sholem Asch's (1880–1957) *The God of Vengeance* and his *Uncle Moses* commiserate with the ruin of man caused by religious notions. Hungarian literature is again different. It is patriotic and yearns to express the country's old culture, as in the work of Petöfi. These literatures are angry because they are about a chaotic world. Chinese writers, Mao Dun said, will have to portray the chaos of their world.[17] Moreover, both the Jews and the Poles were old peoples, though by the nineteenth century they had had no status in Europe for a long time. But because they were not willing to become "second-rate," they generated new thoughts and ideas which shocked the world into new ways of thinking and forced it to acknowledge their existence. Because both peoples had outstanding writers who portrayed their people's life and thought, they are an example to China.[18]

Finally, writing on "Shehui beijing yu chuangzao" (Social background and creativity) Mao Dun said, "I feel that literature that is representative of the life of society is true literature and is literature that has a relationship to human beings; in oppressed countries, it is even more important to pay attention to social background."[19] The importance of language and literary creativity to developing national consciousness and identity was frequently pointed out. The introductory essay to the October 1921 issue of *Short Story Monthly* specifically stated which Slavic peoples have a spoken-language (*yuyan*) literature. Poland particularly represented a case where the literary renaissance (*wenxue fuxing*) was related to linguistic developments. In spite of Poland's loss of independence in the eighteenth century, Poles preserved their language and eventually created a literature in Polish. By these means, Poland assured her survival.[20]

Yiddish literature provided another instructive example. Until the latter part of the nineteenth century, Jews wrote literature in Hebrew, that is, in their old literary language (*wenyan*), according to Mao Dun. At that time, however, they began to use the spoken language, Yiddish, for literary purposes, and thus introduced a revolution in the written language (*wenzi geming*).[21] Mao Dun apparently did not realize that even though Yiddish opened a new chapter in Jewish letters, it by no means supplanted Hebrew, which, in fact, underwent a revolution of its own.

How language created new departures in literature was also referred to when writing about the poetry of Blacks in America. The well-known literary critic and historian Zhao Jingshen discussed Paul Laurence Dunbar's use of dialect and language in the twentieth century.[22] It was also noted that the Irish do not have a national language (*guoyu*) and must, therefore, use English. Nonetheless, "they are returning to their own poetry and songs, and their new literature is permeated by a patriotic spirit because they use the strength of new learning."[23]

The literature of oppressed peoples was said to be a literature of realism and, at times, a literature of realism and romanticism. Regarding Polish literature, Zheng Zhenduo pointed out that even though romanticism had kept Poland's national aspirations alive, Poland's great contribution was the development of nineteenth-century realistic literature.[24] Although Sienkiewicz was sometimes called the foremost representative of realism, the Yiddish masters, such as Pinski, or Y. L. Peretz (1852–1915), the first writer to adhere strictly to the method of realism, were said to portray the plight of the impoverished classes with exceptional sympathy.[25]

The combination of realism and romanticism was at times also praised. According to Mao Dun, it was a "countercurrent" in Irish literature: "It seeks a new road apart from realism. We all know that realism . . . still contains many elements of theory . . . [and] modern literature has already become separated from reality. . . Although the Irish new literature is a product of the late nineteenth century, it has already combined realism and romanticism into one."[26] J. M. Synge's excellence as a "peasant writer" is a case in point, as Mao Dun noted in his article on the Irish literary countercurrent. Zheng Zhenduo, on the other hand, concluded that contemporary Irish writers were moving from romanticism to realism, which accounted for the excellence of Irish literature.[27]

Nonetheless, to Mao Dun, new literary trends, utilizing the motif of the common man and peasant, were expressed through romanticism-realism. He attributed Sienkiewicz's greatness to the fact that his works united romanticism and realism. "In Sienkiewicz's works," wrote Mao Dun, "can be found the highest ideals and the lowest brutality man can inflict upon man." Thus tempered by romanticism, Sienkiewicz's fiction is not simply objective. Fiction, according to Mao Dun, should describe the good in human beings, not only the bad. He also implied that Sienkiewicz's realism was probably mellowed by a Christian morality that permeates all his works.[28]

Whether a literature was realistic, moved from romanticism to realism, or was a combination is significant. Self-conscious inquiry into the nature of literary change took place. It was recognized that a romantic epic poem like Mickiewicz's *Konrad Wallenrod*, a romantic exaltation of national heroes and great men which had moved a previous generation, no longer excited the imagination. When Zhou Zuoren spoke of realistic literature as popular literature in his well-known essay "Rende wenxue" (Human literature), he touched the main issue. Realistic literature was more than an observation of the world without illusions. Its emergence was also related to the discovery of commoners and peasants. The moment they were recognized, rather than romantically or idyllically idealized, the question of class, social injustice, and social reform entered into literature. Writers and people, particularly commoners and peasants, met in one social reality in eastern Europe — whether it was Yiddish, Polish, or Hungarian literature. This meeting produced new and different conceptualizations. In this sense, such realistic literature was more than a descriptive method. It was a reorientation in subject matter and treatment.

When the literature of oppressed peoples was first read and translated by Chinese writers, no comparable literature was being produced in China, as Mao Dun stressed repeatedly. This literature, therefore, must be seen in relationship to attempts at creating a new literature. Moreover, writers and intellectuals of the twenties, on the whole, subscribed to the tenets of biological and social evolution, which were also applied to literature. The evolutionary nature of Chinese literature was described by Hu Shi, Lu Xun, and Mao Dun in the early twenties. Criteria of literary criticism were not eternally existent, Mao Dun explained. They were relevant to a certain time, and changed as the times changed. Still, literary evolution did not cause the writer to move from one approach to another. Literature could be both romantic and realistic. At least, this is what Mao Dun was trying to convey in 1919 when he wrote:

> During the last year our critics sent romantic literature to the devil and they extolled realistic literature to the skies. This is the way of people who do not understand the principle of literary evolution. In the foundations of romantic literature there is liberty of thought, a forceful creative spirit which after ten thousand generations conserves its values and thus will remain forever an element of literary evolution... The critical and popular spirit particular to realistic literature will forever imbue literary works with a new spirit... Though realistic literature does not deserve to be honored to the utmost limit... romantic literature suffers injustice if held in undue contempt.[29]

By defining the course of other people's literature, and by ascribing an evolutionary process to literary creation, Chinese literature and writers could become a part of this process. Europe may have taken a century or more, but in China, it was possible to telescope the evolutionary development into a few years.[30] Perhaps Zhou Yang did not exaggerate all that much when he wrote years later that China was fortunate because the works of small and weak peoples (*ruoxiao minzu*) exerted the greatest influence on Chinese literature during the May Fourth period.[31]

Translations and Translating in the Twenties

Most of the works translated can be grouped into definite categories of themes. The largest category by far is that of social injustice as it affects the urban poor or peasants. Frequently this theme is coupled with antiwar, antireligion, or antitradition sentiments. Another category deals with the peasantry and the social injustice element is secondary to questions of national identity and national assertion. Children's stories, usually told through the eyes of a child, form a third category. Still another large category of translated works has as its theme the philosophy of life, or *weltanschauung*. Smaller categories include works that are entertaining, tales of the marvellous, and those which are descriptive of the middle class.

A number of themes were avoided, that is, they were not translated, even though they were contained in works from which other translations were prepared. Such, for example, is the theme of romantic love. Where love between the sexes is an element, the work chosen usually subordinates this to the social problem portrayed. For example, in Pinski's play *Forgotten Souls*,[32] the story's romantic aspects are completely submerged by the idea of self-sacrifice and waste of human life. Prior to the fifties, proletarian subjects were also generally avoided. This is rather surprising, because much Yiddish literature deals with working-class life in America, especially sweatshop stories, and Polish literature also depicts the horrors of the early textile industry. Perhaps these topics were too remote from the translators' lives. Another theme not found is anti-Semitism — probably equally remote, or altogether incomprehensible.

On war and social injustice, there is Marya Konopnicka's (1842–1910) angry battle cry, her poem "Now when the King . . ."[33] The stark and painful simplicity of the Polish original has been successfully transferred to the Chinese via the English translation. King and peasant go to war. The king is neither wounded nor killed and returns triumphantly. The peasant, however, dies and is buried in a pit. A poem of only six verses, each shows the contrast between the fate of the nobleman and the peasant. Social injustice and peasant plight are superbly portrayed in two Polish stories, "Twilight"[34] by Stefan Zeromski (1864–1925) and "The Trial"[35] by Wladislaw Reymont (1868–1925). Both stories deal with peasant exploitation, the first by the corrupt bureaucratic establishment. In both cases, grinding poverty and continuous subjection to injustice lead to peasant brutalization. Peasants become sullen, crude, and cruel. But where in "Twilight" the peasant passively accepts his fate, in "The Trial," the peasant actively resists. Social injustice and the urban poor are the subject of many of Pinski's works. In his one-act play *The Cripples*,[36] he angrily denounces society which does not have a place for the incapacitated. In his story "Tale of a Hungry Man,"[37] he describes the utter hopelessness of the urban poor. Among children's stories, there is "A Pity for the Living"[38] by Sholem Aleichem, the master recreator of children's thoughts, fears, and joys, and the puzzling world of adults.

The most widely publicized story dealing philosophically and mythologically with love and beauty was Sienkiewicz's "Be Blessed."[39] It has, as do a number of his stories, an Indian setting, and is a fanciful tale describing how, because of the power of Krishna, the lotus, personified as a beautiful maiden, came to live in the heart of the poet Valmiki. There, it took the form of happiness, compassion, beauty, and light. The story was translated three times and published in five different publications. One may conjecture that the story was appealing because it handled a clearly philosophical issue in a fictional setting. Technique, an important issue to be sure, should not be overstated though because this is also a lyrical and poetic story. Perhaps the technique, subject, and style combined to make this a uniquely attractive work.

Some observations regarding these translations may be useful. In the twenties, only brief works, short stories, plays (especially one-act plays), and some poetry were translated. But it was not until the fifties that novels began to appear in quantity. Some of these were still nineteenth-century works, but most were of more recent date, from the war years, or shortly thereafter. Hence, the novels of an earlier period, although read by those who could, were not made available to Chinese readers.

Translations in the twenties may have had a wider circulation than is apparent at first glance. Many stories and plays were translated several times (often under different titles) and by more than one translator. Some were republished several times in different journals and anthologies. Frequently, the two or three translations vary significantly, not only because more than one translator is involved but also because different works served as sources for the translations. Because republications or retranslations appeared in several publications, no doubt they had a fairly wide circulation.

The task of translation was not a simple matter. A way to clarify a completely different cultural milieu to the Chinese reader had to be found. Such clarification was necessary for specific customs, expressions, religious observances, or religious symbols. At times, translators apparently did not understand what they were translating. At times

137

they tried to explain the unfamiliar. Several methods were used. An unfamiliar term might be footnoted with a careful explanation. Among translators, Wang Luyan (Wang Heng, 1901–1940) took special pains with such clarifications. If the translations had been prepared from English, a translator might also add the English equivalent. Still another method was to coin a new phrase or term, which may or may not have been clear to the reader. Most frequently, however, translators chose a familiar and near-equivalent term. It would appear that when a translator transliterated without explanation, he did not know the meaning. In those cases, the story's essence may have been lost to the Chinese reader.

Chinese translators, by translating from translations, necessarily worked with preselected materials. Their choice of works to translate was dictated by availability and influenced by the opinions of others who had made the initial selection. This was also true for English language works, such as Irish or black American literature, where they could use only whatever was available. Nevertheless, this should not be taken to mean that everything available was indiscriminately translated. On the contrary, whenever Chinese versions are traced to the sources from which they were taken, it becomes obvious that translators practiced considerable selectivity. Translations were not prepared at random. Moreover, the fact that translations can be grouped into categories of themes further supports the assumption that translators tried to adapt the works they chose to the larger aims of the new culture movement and the literary revolution.

Oppressed Peoples, Their Literature, and World Politics in the Thirties

In the twenties, the literature of oppressed peoples conveyed a variety of ideas. Some of these were new, while others corroborated or supported prevalent New Culture and literary revolution thinking. By the end of the twenties, and certainly in the first half of the thirties, changes occurred. There were fewer discussions about this literature and less translating. Even more importantly, these oppressed peoples were seen from different perspectives.

A part of the reason, no doubt, is found in the changing political climate following the Guomindang–Chinese Communist split, and the establishment of the Nanking regime in 1928. Among intellectuals, there was increasing polarization and shifting concerns. Very few, if any, translations were printed in right-wing literary journals, though those of the left did continue to publish a fair number of translations of oppressed peoples. The spirit of May Fourth, which had spoken in many voices, was running its course. Moreover, after the Commerical Press building in Shanghai was bombed out in 1932, *Short Story Monthly* also ceased publication. As a result, the major journal whose editors had shown a nearly constant interest in this literature ceased publication. To some extent, its place was taken by the influential *Wenxue* (Literature), published from 1933 to 1937, but there was a significant difference in emphasis.

This difference is clearly conveyed by the special issue devoted to the literature of oppressed peoples that appeared in 1934. For example, in addition to the customary Polish, Hungarian, Czech, or Yiddish literature translations, *Literature* also printed examples of Arab and Slovak literature. The issue, furthermore, contains an impressive annotated English language bibliography that lists works on Arabic, Persian, Brazilian, Latin American, Hungarian, as well as Slavic literature.[40] No longer were oppressed peoples seen as existing only in Europe. Most significant, however, was Hu Yuzhi's introductory article, which placed them and their writings within a new political context. Whereas earlier the political issues were national revolution and political independence, now the problem was stated in terms of imperialist oppression, and the attempt was made to understand more clearly who oppressed peoples actually were. The three categories into which Hu divides oppressed peoples need not concern us here, save for his assertion that, without exception, their free development was being stifled by strong and powerful countries. They share one further characteristic, namely that the content of their literature, art, and scholarship consists of opposition to imperialism and an enthusiastic search for emancipation. Why might these facts be important to the Chinese? Because, explains Hu, these peoples are so numerous among the world's population that research concerning them should not be just a curiosity; when it is undertaken, opposition to imperialism and emancipation should be kept in mind.[41]

How does Hu see their political status in relationship to literary creativity? Jewish literature, he wrote, holds one of the most important places among small and weak people's literature. Although after World War I, the British created a Jewish homeland in Palestine, most of the Jews still live under imperialist oppression, and recently they have begun to be persecuted in Germany. Irish literature, similarly, has had a brilliant history in world literature. Throughout, the Irish rebelled against British imperialism with little success. Also, in the past few hundred years, the Irish have had a remarkable movement to preserve Celtic culture. The Armenians are an ancient people who have lived under Turkish imperialist oppression. Similar to the Jews, they are scattered throughout the world and their literature is appreciated everywhere.[42]

To Hu, being oppressed by imperialism and desiring emancipation is different from demanding national revolution and cultural self-awareness. This difference, certainly more of degree than kind, may suggest that Hu was already thinking of prescriptive rather than descriptive literature. The line is very thin between realistic writing as descriptive, expository literature and realistic writing as prescriptive, didactic literature that offers a remedy for evils depicted. One may quarrel with René Wellek's narrow definition of realism, but there is some validity to his statement when he writes, "It is a simple fact of literary history that the mere change to a depiction of contemporary social reality implied a lesson of human pity, of social reformism and criticism, and often of rejection and revulsion against society. There is a tension between description, truth, and instruction."[43] Other writings also show that oppressed status implied something different from what it had been in the twenties. In a book entirely devoted to small and weak peoples, Zheng Zhang emphasized that oppressed peoples show a common characteristic in their literature, art, and scholarship. In spite of their dissimilarities, they all search for emancipation from imperialism and long to oppose it.[44]

Themes of social injustice continued to be translated in the thirties.[45] Nonetheless, it is in the translation of Claude McKay's poem "If We Must Die"[46] that the leftist political emphasis found more forceful expression. Defiant and no longer acquiescing, the Chinese translator joined the Black poet:

> Like men we'll face the murderous, cowardly pack,
> Pressed to the wall, dying, but fighting back![47]

At the turn of the century, treaty-port cosmopolitanism, an expanding journalism, and a new generation óf Chinese intellectuals combined in bringing the condition of weak and small peoples to the attention of Chinese readers. Increasingly, some of the intellectuals tried to understand these people's desire for national revolution, emancipation, and identity through the efforts of their writers and works. Acquaintance with oppressed people's literature seemed to shed light on the desire for change in China.

In the twenties, such vague notions came to be more concretely expressed in conjunction with the May Fourth movement. Nineteenth-century small and weak people's literature was translated in quantity, and its writers — their literary techniques, language, and motives for creating a new literature — were the subject of extensive discussions. Hence, Chinese writers and translators saw their own attempts at creating a new literature within a larger context. They were not laboring in isolation, nor were the movements, of which literature was a part, divorced from intellectual movements elsewhere. The creation of new literature together with national emancipation and a renaissance implied a universality of common concerns with those who were oppressed. Together with this, however, came a growing realization that each of these peoples was different, and that each people's literature expressed its individuality as a people, a culture, and as a nation. Awareness of the particular characteristics of the various literatures, in turn, underscored the necessity for writing a new and distinctly Chinese literature. The images of oppressed peoples as perceived by Chinese writers affirmed for them the validity of their own efforts in creating modern Chinese literature.

Part Two

The May Fourth Writers

Ezra Vogel sets the stage for the discussion of some representative writers of the May Fourth era by exploring the sociological and political forces that turned these writers, whom he characterizes as "unlikely heroes," into "heroes." Though overwhelmingly from the upper classes, because of the chaos of the times and their profession, they lived most of their lives close to the poverty level. They were not active revolutionaries or politicians, but they emerged as the conscience of their generation as they articulated the national stirrings and created the ideological and spiritual base for a new society.

Preeminent among the "unlikely heroes" was Lu Xun, who is discussed here from three different perspectives. Leo Ou-fan Lee combines the Eriksonian psychohistory and intellectual history approaches to analyze the familial, social, and cultural influences that affected Lu Xun's formative years. Harriet Mills traces the changes in Lu Xun's writing from fiction to satire as his political disillusionment deepened and as he turned increasingly to the left after 1929. Milena Doleželová-Velingerová presents a textual analysis of one of Lu Xun's short stories, "Medicine," that reveals the subtlety and symbolism of his literary technique.

A variety of approaches is also used in the treatment of China's foremost "realist" writer, Mao Dun. John Berninghausen characterizes the protagonists of Mao Dun's early work as individuals committed to the revolutionary struggle while seeking personal liberation from their tradition and the harsh realities of their own existence. This contradiction in the lives of Mao Dun's protagonists reflected the contradictions in the lives of many of the May Fourth writers. Yü-shih Chen reveals that the political events of the period, specifically, events involving the Chinese Communist party, with which he was associated, were depicted allegorically in Mao Dun's writing.

Yi-tsi Feuerwerker shows that China's most important woman writer, Ding Ling, transformed into literature her own life experiences as a woman breaking away from the old social mores. At the same time, Ding Ling sought to produce works of literary value that were distinct from the mere reflection of social disruption. Michael Egan examines in close detail two stories of the less politically oriented, Japanese-influenced writer Yu Dafu. In his analysis of Yu's work, Egan reveals some of the innovative literary methods used by a number of the May Fourth writers.

These May Fourth writers and others who are not discussed here represent different approaches to literature. Yet most of them were confronted with a similar dilemma — how to use their literature to achieve China's modern transformation without sacrificing their desire to create good art and to achieve personal fulfillment.

7.

The Unlikely Heroes:
The Social Role of the
May Fourth Writers

Ezra F. Vogel

In their youth, the writers who emerged in the outburst of nationalism after May 4, 1919, hardly seemed to have the makings of heroes. They were trained in the Confucian classics to become orthodox literati. With successful examinations, they might have become distinguished officials, scholars, or local notables, but not heroes. They may have delighted in the popular tales of knights-errant and relished stories of bandit leaders, but they themselves were reserved, reflective, hesitant, and pedantic, lacking in determination and willpower. Yet the May Fourth writers somehow became heroes. How are we to understand this transformation in the writers and their relation to their audience and their society?

The Moral Intellectuals

The Indecisive Young Dreamers   Even after the 1911 revolution, when the content of education began to change, the traditional student role remained largely intact. The semiautobiographical or fictionalized biographical accounts of early May Fourth writers recount remarkably similar childhood experiences. The future writers began their schooling before the 1911 revolution by reciting and memorizing the classics and other texts remote from daily life. Compared to the more organized schools of Europe and Japan, the atmosphere of their classrooms was likely to be informal. Their early teachers were often vague and pedantic. However hazardous it may be to generalize about personal qualities in a country as diverse and dynamic as modern China, these accounts reflect striking personal similarities in their responses to this early education. Indeed, the system produced compliance and escapism, not fortitude and determination. Exceptions like Mao Zedong did become rebels. Most future writers, like other students, were subdued by the system. They may have fought boredom with petty mischief, but they did not have the passion or determination to become fighters. They were indecisive and irresolute — like the protagonists in their well-known works: Ye Shengtao's *Ni Huanzhi*, Lao She's *Lihun* (Divorce), Qian Zhongshu's *Wei cheng* (The Besieged City), or even Ba Jin's *Jia* (Family).

The authors and their protagonists shared visions — of educational reform, of love, of "poetic sense." But how quickly they became discouraged when their visions were not realized. They were more reactors than initiators. When they encountered difficulties they were more likely to muddle along (*hunguoqu*) than to stand firm. Perhaps they were immobilized by the overwhelming difficulty of effecting real social change in a complex, degenerating society. But their remoteness from the fray was more than situational. Most likely, it stemmed from an ingrained sense of Confucian propriety and the general adherence to traditional authority in the wake of impending change. These qualities were hardly the stuff from which heroes are made.

The Moralists There have been studies of the political role of the May Fourth writers, but their role has been political only in a very special sense. Michel Crozier has distinguished between "action intellectuals," who may advise politicians on courses of action, and "moral intellectuals," who preserve moral purity by being more detached. The moral intellectual may take a strong moral stance on political issues. He may be active in his life and work, but he is peripheral to the practical workings of politics. The Chinese literati had been trained to be moralists and officials. Yet, even before the 1911 revolution, not all literati were action-oriented. Many had turned to scholarship or teaching. After 1911, the distinction between politics and scholarship, between politicians and moralists, became much sharper. The separation stemmed partly from the increasing occupational specialization that occurs in all modernizing societies. But it became especially marked in post-1911 China because the naked use of power by the warlords was increasingly separated from any base of moral legitimacy. In imperial days, local scholars could still be involved in local affairs. After 1911, men of letters could no longer span the gap between their moral orientation and the arbitrary political order.

Some Western-educated intellectuals tried to take an apolitical stance as scientists and technicians. Some opportunistic intellectuals of a more practical bent compromised and found places for themselves in the bureaucracy, politics, or the military in the quest for wealth and power in the new order. But those who became writers maintained their earlier moral mold. Incisively, they attacked the decadence and corruption they saw around them. As Michael Egan shows, even Yu Dafu, sometimes regarded as a degenerate writer, actually disapproves of his degenerate protagonist in "Chenlun" (Sinking) and undercuts him with mild ridicule. While this heightened sense of moralism was hardly unique to writers, by 1930, these writers became the most effective moral spokesmen. As Ching-mao Cheng points out, these writers, following Liang Qichao and Lu Xun, conceived a new moral mission: using literature to awaken the Chinese people to the evils of the status quo, to save the nation and the people. Their nonpragmatic moralism was rooted in the refined culture of a declining aristocracy resisting opportunistic new leaders who gained power less by training and refinement than by manipulations of military and economic power. But it was also fueled by new foreign intellectual currents that inspired individualism and opposition to the old political system. These writers advocated a moral social order, but they did not fight for it.

The Concerned Elitists The early May Fourth writers were overwhelmingly from elite families who did not share all the difficulties of the poorest layers of Chinese society. Lu Xun, Mao Dun, Ding Ling, Guo Moruo, Ye Shengtao, Shen Congwen, and others had fathers, grandfathers, or other close relatives in high official positions under the Qing. Nearly all of the writers' family fortunes and positions seriously declined after the 1911 revolution. Yet compared to journalists or the Butterfly writers, they retained a strong sense of elitism. At the same time, like traditional Confucian elites, they were concerned with the welfare of the common people. Perhaps because of their recent impoverishment, these writers had a deep, though sentimental identification with the downtrodden. Unlike the downtrodden, however, their elite status gave them the self-confidence to criticize the military-political leaders on behalf of peasants and workers who still considered direct expression of dissatisfactions beyond their station.

In no society does literature fully reflect the masses, but in early twentieth-century China, the gap between the illiterate masses and their impoverished elite defenders was especially great. For all their alienation from the praetorian political elite and their concern for writing "mass literature" in the 1930s, the May Fourth writers could not bridge the great social chasm that separated them from the rustic peasant, either in literature or life-style. The Communists' hero, Lu Xun, continued to wear his scholar's robe; more impoverished writers still rode in rickshaws. Even their contact with the masses was limited.

The "masses" in their stories were often drawn from family servants or from rickshaw pullers and shopkeepers who served them. Lao She knew urban artisans well, and Shen Congwen knew soldiers and border life, but they were exceptions. Later Communist writers like Zhao Shuli and the model Communist writer of the 1970s, Hao Ran, may not have been as skillful as the May Fourth writers, but they obviously wrote of peasants with more realism, depth, and subtlety.

The writers of the 1920s and 1930s were more at home describing the degradation of prominent families, the irrationality of pompous academics, the hypocrisy of Confucian moralists, and the rivalries among businessmen than they were describing the mundane life of workers and peasants. They could brilliantly depict exploiting landlords, speculators, tax collectors, and others so cruel to the masses. Nevertheless, as Perry Link shows, the writers whom the May Fourth authors condescendingly dubbed the Butterfly School had a much broader audience. The irony was that May Fourth authors, even when writing what they called "proletarian literature" in the 1930s, knew very well that they were not of the toiling masses and that their works were not read by the masses. Yet their moralism was directed in good part toward defending the cause of the masses.

The Degraded Moralists It is not unusual for righteous moralists to become heroes for a cause. But the May Fourth writers found it hard to muster the strident righteousness that makes for moral heroism. Part of the tragedy of China's twentieth-century writers is that they lacked the security and toughness to avoid compromises with their own moral standards. In "Guduzhe" (The misanthrope, perhaps better translated as "The loner"), Lu Xun describes the moral degradation of a fellow intellectual who could make a living only as a military adviser. Unable to get enough to live by begging, he comments on his new profession: "What a joy! Wonderful! I am now doing what I formerly detested and opposed. I am now giving up all I formerly believed in and upheld!" Such a case may have been extreme, but the need for intellectuals to eke out an existence while avoiding personal risks to their security called for many less dramatic but nonetheless painful compromises with their own moral integrity, and thus eroded their own basis of self-respect. As much as writers attacked others who violated moral standards far more outrageously, their own moral sensitivities kept them from being blind to their own limitations. It was this self-awareness that made it difficult for the writers in the 1920s and 1930s to flaunt the strident self-confidence of which moral heroes are made.

The Pseudoprofessionals

In the late Qing dynasty, the writer began to emerge in a new role. Not only did he assume a distinct position but, as opposed to the traditional storytellers, his association with the cause of nationalism gave him a new respectability. Although the writer assumed a new occupational role, the career line and the financial base for the role was never securely established. A few May Fourth writers were able to earn their living writing, but others translated, taught, borrowed, and skimped. Few supported themselves by creative writing. Unlike writers for the budding newspapers and popular magazines, they viewed their other employment not as an occupation but as a temporary expedient, for they were *wenren*, litterateurs.

There was no training program to determine entry into the community of litterateurs, defined only by a common culture. A broadly read young aspirant might try his hand at writing. If he lived in the provinces, he would move to a culture center like Peking or Shanghai. The distinction between men of letters and popular or journalistic writers was thin. Some writers moved back and forth across the line. But by the late 1920s, there were certain key individuals, periodicals, publishing houses, and literary societies at the core of the literary world. Men of letters and aspiring men of letters gravitated to them.

Some young aspirants got advice from literary greats like Lu Xun, or from sponsoring editors, but this was rarely more than words of introduction, encouragement, or sponsorship. The literary world lacked the kind of cultivation and training that master craftsmen provided in the artisan world. Sometimes skills were developed through specific literary groupings, where ways were discussed to raise standards, introduce foreign works, and evaluate literary contributions. But even such groups did not provide the systematic criticism of individual manuscripts necessary for a supervised cultivation of young talent.

By the late 1920s, the Chinese literary center had clearly shifted from the somewhat more scholarly academic atmosphere of Peking to the more cosmopolitan and free-swinging atmosphere of Shanghai. Living close by and reading each other's works, writers developed both a clearer sense of identity and a distinct style of life. Like avant-garde counterculture intellectuals everywhere, they attacked existing customs and tradition — in style as well as words. Some writers experimented with love outside marriage, flaunting their disregard for the traditional family system. Most writers lived apart from their parents, singly or in couples, in small rooming houses.

The culture of most writers was inseparable from the culture of poverty. They lived in the simplest of surroundings, sometimes without adequate food and clothing. They indulged in sentimentality and self-pity, as if banished from their rightful stations in life. Many, burdened with weariness or family responsibility, faded out of the role as quickly as they had entered.

In the late 1920s and 1930s, children of poorer gentry families or of fathers in commercial, clerical, and managerial work flocked to Shanghai to be writers. This later wave of writers represented a broader social base and described a broader slice of life. They wrote of their native provinces using some local dialect and local color. They attracted readers in the provinces, but they wrote for the growing audiences in the cities.

Even counterculture, avant-garde writers cannot entirely escape the culture and the organizational patterns of the society they criticize. In tightly knit Japanese society, where cliques were stronger and more permanent, arbiters of literary taste, the *bundan* (in Chinese, *wentan*), tightly controlled membership and ranking in the literary world. Chinese literary associations, like other Chinese organizations of the day, were looser, more eclectic, and changeable.

To be sure, certain semicliques had members who shared common experiences, attitudes, and life-styles, and they tended to remain close over a long period of time. One prominent semiclique, the Crescent Moon Society, consisted of liberal sophisticates who returned from study in Europe and America and found respectable academic positions in Peking. Another was the Creation Society, a group of poverty-stricken writers who had studied in intensely nationalistic, homogeneous Japan and gave up specialized technical training for literary careers. But even these, the most homogeneous of literary societies, did not maintain fixed membership or fixed publication with regular activities over many years.

More common than these semicliques of similar writers were groups that produced a publication or developed a publishing house. A publication was held together not only by its backers but also by its editor and associates. The selection of manuscripts and a group of authors for publications set a tone and style that provided some temporary coherence. Certain larger publishers, such as the Commercial Press, remained strong throughout the period, but even their literary magazines frequently changed. The League of Left-Wing Writers, formed in 1930, represented a definite point of view, but it never became a tightly knit, cohesive group.

Even within the literary capital of Shanghai in the late 1920s and 1930s, the literary world remained extraordinarily eclectic. In the late teens and early twenties, prominent writers tried to define the purposes of the new national literature. Mao Dun, for example, advocated that one should know enough about society to write vividly about concrete individuals while conveying an understanding of the dominant forces of the age. Lu Xun maintained high literary standards concerning the organization of stories, the economy of wording, and the vividness of expression. Despite the efforts of such leading writers, the looseness of Chinese society rendered it impossible for any group to set literary, social, and even moral standards that could be effectively enforced on the literary scene. Perhaps the ease of starting magazines and newspapers, the concern with sales, the breadth of editors' interests, and the general social disorganization made eclecticism inevitable. As a result, writing was often too undisciplined to be considered high quality by international standards.

Another reason why standards were so difficult to maintain was the lack of literary critics. Some writers, like Cheng Fangwu and Zhu Ziqing, wrote thoughtful literary criticism, but their criticisms hardly inhibited others or set expectations for what authors should write. Lu Xun wrote brilliant, savage attacks, but even his essays can hardly be regarded as serious literary criticism. Acceptance of a manuscript by an editor was much more important than comments by a critic — and editors remained eclectic.

More important than criticism in raising standards was the high achievements of individual writers. Lu Xun's "Kuangren riji" (Diary of a madman), "A Q zhengzhuan" (The true story of A Q), and other stories were an enormous breakthrough that set a new pattern for many lesser writers. Similarly, beginning in 1929, the publication of *Shi* (Eclipse) and other novels by Mao Dun raised the expectations of authors in longer works, as Cao Yu's *Leiyu* later set a new standard for dramatists. Whatever advances literature made were accomplished less through literary criticism or teaching than by the successes and the impact of these writers.

Despite the eclecticism and variable standards, there was a kind of loose intellectual community among writers. As individualistic as they were, they read each other's magazines, positioned themselves in relation to each other, and carried on at least indirect dialogues. In broad cultural perspective, their publications were parallel and similar.

151

Nevertheless, to the extent that an ethos constrained or elevated writing, the standards were more moral than literary. This was increasingly true in the late 1920s and 1930s as politics polarized and writers took political stances. With the sense of national crisis, political impact, not literary standards, became the overwhelming concern. The orthodox role of the writer, to serve the proletariat and the political line, was developed theoretically by Qu Qiubai in the early 1930s, practiced by Zhou Yang, and finally canonized in 1942 by Mao in "Talks at the Yenan Forum on Literature and Art." This sharpened the political purpose of writing and correspondingly narrowed the range of subject matter and plot from the time when Lu Xun sought to expose the evils of the old society. Although the participants were more conscious of their differences than of their similarities, this new intellectual, politicized community created the underpinnings for making the writer first a celebrity and then a hero.

The Celebrated Intellectuals

Like most good writers everywhere, the May Fourth writers were among the most sensitive and imaginative people of their time. Although many of them grew up in sheltered families and communities, they were among the first to become conscious of the problems of their nation, plagued by destructive warfare, flagrant inhumanity, and grinding poverty. They could not solve these problems, but in their writings they could capture the drama. They may have been impractical, but they were in touch with reality and even more with the subjective reality, the dreams and frustrations of the individual searching for meaning in an age of turmoil. Moreover, the initial opening of China to foreign life and literature gave this generation of writers a freshness and vividness that could not be repeated. If their naïveté made them overrespond, it nonetheless enabled them to consider an enormous range of ideas and ideals.

In Japan and many contemporary Western countries, the audience for avant-garde writers included those in positions of power and influence. In China of the 1920s and 1930s, the May Fourth writers, despite their scope and vitality, were somehow too alien and threatening to Nanking officials, Shanghai businessmen, or military leaders. They were occasionally "used" by politicians seeking a mouthpiece, but the overwhelming majority of their readers were educated youth. Earlier generations of Chinese had been moved by storytellers and later generations were to be moved by more dramatic media of radio, movies, and revolutionary operas. In this brief era in China before extended literacy and radio, the "reading generation" was composed of educated youth.

The emotional life of this "reading generation" centered on May Fourth literature to an extraordinary degree. In an era before personal counseling and the language of psychological analysis, no one came closer than the May Fourth writers to giving voice to inner feelings. Youths called themselves and each other by the names of well-known protagonists. Vernacular fiction was not new nor was identifying with protagonists; the Chinese public had long treasured characters in works like *San guo yanyi* (Romance of the three kingdoms), *Shuihu zhuan* (The water margin), and *Hong lou meng* (Dream of the red chamber). What was new was the range of characters, the subtlety of their development, the richness of detail, the conscious articulation of inner conflicts, and the up-to-dateness. For Western youth in the same era, the stars were "movie stars." For Chinese youth, the stars were fiction writers and their protagonists.

They were stars because they were among the first who denounced the burdens of the past. If Western movies provided Western youths with models for romance, May Fourth writers provided models of youth trapped by traditional society as they raised their first cries of anguished awareness. Lu Xun's "Diary of a Madman" became a beacon because it so vividly portrayed the madness of Chinese society that so many young people had sensed but not articulated. Ding Ling won a following with her "Shafei nüshi de riji" (Diary of Miss Sophie), not because of its literary quality, which borders on the sophomoric, but because of the shock value of an emancipated female character. There was an element of naïve sentimentality in the response of the educated Chinese youth, but the new stirrings of social awareness gave their identification with their "writer-stars" more "social significance" than Western youth who were moved by their screen stars.

In addition to antitraditionalism, the other theme that captured the young people's imagination was nationalism. In Meiji Japan, a strong government had captured the nationalist spirit by uniting the country against imperial powers. Japanese writers expressed the anguish inherent in Japan's nationalistic response to the challenge of the West by full-scale modernization. In republican China, in contrast, political leaders not only failed to unite the nation, but in their effort to achieve personal glory in an era of protean politics, they could not even maintain the mantle of moral legitimacy. The writers rather than the politicians captured the nationalist stirrings among the people by attacking the government for its failure to meet the challenge of the

West. They gave literature the moral purpose of creating the spiritual, ideological base for a strong modern nation.

From the beginning of the May Fourth period in 1919, leading intellectuals were already trying to define how a national language and literature could help create a modern nation. All modernizing countries strive to spread literacy and create a national literature that reaches a broader population. In the process, formerly elitist cultures are transformed and adapted to the needs of a broader populace, language becomes more standardized, and written language comes closer to the oral vernacular. In China, as in certain other cultures, such as the Irish or the eastern European Jewish, the written language just before this development diverged so greatly from the vernacular that a deeper effort was needed to bridge the gap. In all three cases, the solution was the same: a new vernacular literature, widely published and read. Of course, written language is never identical with spoken language, but in these three cases, the new burst of creativity constituted a genuine literary renaissance. In all these cultures, the new writing included poetry and the essay, but above all, the short story, the novel, and popular drama.

Certainly, each of the three cultures reflected a particular style. Eastern European Jews laughed at their own tragedy and foibles; the Irish gave vent to fanciful and imaginative creations; and the Chinese combined realism and sentimentality. Yet the major purpose of the new movements — the creation of new popular literature for a broader audience in order to awaken the people and heighten consciousness against an outside enemy — was remarkably similar.

Compared to Ireland and eastern European Jewry, China was a much more diverse society, with many more local dialects, with more severe social stratification, and more varied layers of culture. The most skilled Yiddish and Irish writers could reach a large portion of their society. But in China, with a more heterogeneous audience, it was impossible for elite authors writing with subtlety and sophistication to compete with the simpler and more popular writers.

May Fourth writers had a smaller audience than more popular Chinese writers, but they had higher standards and a more serious social purpose. The Butterfly writers more willingly accepted society as it was and wrote of how an individual might succeed or at least adapt to it. For all their inner tensions, the May Fourth writers were bound by the noblesse oblige of a moral elite. Like the Confucian moralists who preceded them, they wanted to uplift moral standards and improve the nation. They were more alienated from the existing society than popular writers, but they were also more deeply concerned with China's fate and its transformation. Yet despite their vision at the beginning of the May Fourth period, they were unable to complete the formation of a truly national culture. Cultural heterogeneity and the broad disparity in levels of culture remained serious problems long after the May Fourth period, even after a later generation of political rulers tried to abolish elite culture and replace it with a low common denominator of standardized culture.

In their efforts to create a new national language, the May Fourth writers, like nationalists elsewhere, did not hesitate to adapt tradition and incorporate foreign culture. Indeed, they were on the forefront of reevaluating China's past and introducing Western learning. They translated foreign literature, introduced new terms and concepts, and used a broader range of literary styles and techniques than earlier Chinese writers. May Fourth writers did not escape foppishness and faddism, but their broad experimentation was never very detached from a more serious purpose.

The writers enjoyed a much wider audience than natural or social scientists. They acquired a political role not only because they began writing in response to Liang Qichao and Lu Xun's call for literature to awaken the public but also because politicians, aware of their wider audience, cultivated them. Even warlords sometimes tried to enhance themselves and popularize their rule with men of culture, but their efforts were minor and unsystematic compared to the leftists, who early made efforts to cultivate a mass audience. Indeed, leftists were similarly organizing and mobilizing writers in all the East Asian countries at precisely the same time. When the League of Left-Wing Writers was organized in 1930, many writers who would not join the Communist party were at least willing to join in a popular front. In short, strident nationalism provided a new goal for the writer that was in keeping with the traditional moral role of the literati.

The Heroic Intellectuals

More than anything else, it was the danger from political repression and Japanese invasion that turned a generation of cautious, sensitive, and sometimes tortured writers into heroes in the 1930s. Lu Xun was cynical about revolutionaries in 1911, about the demonstrators of May 1919, and about his leftist students in early 1927. Even in the late 1920s he bemoaned the fate of writers under communism in Russia. But he was stirred by needless brutality and could wax poetic when talking about the ruthless shooting of a former student at Peking Normal

School. As John Berninghausen shows, even Mao Dun, later minister of culture in Communist China, had been disenchanted with young leftists, but became even more critical of the brutal forces of foreign imperialism.

With internal atrocities perpetrated by warlords, with repression by GMD officials desperately trying to maintain order, and then with the Japanese invasion, writers became bolder. The growing persecution of fellow writers was so outrageous as to dissipate their natural reserve and hesitation. If they lacked the personality to organize, they nonetheless displayed great courage. They remained moral intellectuals but their political stance became increasingly resolute and specific. By the 1930s they desperately sought to reach a broader audience. Harriet Mills points out that it was in this context that Lu Xun, disappointed with the impact of his short stories, turned increasingly to the "barbed" essay.

Writers were not the only ones facing capture and execution in an era of almost constant fighting and arbitrary police action. Soldiers, businessmen, and political leaders risked assassination. But it was the printed word that was the key vehicle for patriotic expression and the writers, already stars for a generation of educated youth, that were most vulnerable. In early 1931, after the execution of the writers who became known as the "five martyrs," danger pervaded the lives of Shanghai writers. Fear directed their lives. They moved, hid, changed their names, and developed disguises. They often lived in foreign concessions, which offered more hope of protection. Even while using pseudonyms, they wrote by analogy, using foreign stories and historical parables. To protect themselves from inside informants, they reduced or even cut off contact with fellow leftists. The mutual suspicion that resulted continued to fester and was to break out again between the same writers thirty years later during the Cultural Revolution. But despite their quarrels, they continued to stimulate their readers, to invigorate the nation. To their readers, they were living martyrs, fighting police brutality and the Japanese invasion.

Perhaps nothing, except foreign invasion itself, did more to stir Chinese nationalism than the works of the May Fourth writers. With the Japanese invasion, they finally reached a broader audience than the educated youth. A frightened populace looked for a clarion call to pull them together. The writer rather than the politician sounded the call. It was the writer who roused a generation, first the educated youth and later a broader public, to rally to the cause of its country.

The Posthumous Heroes Even though the writers played a political role, in some ways their deepest and most lasting impact was nonpolitical. They brought into the public consciousness a subtle treatment of personal concerns hitherto private or at best profane. Questions about sex, women's roles, family relations, the meaning of education, and philosophies of life had never before received the frank and thoughtful public airing they got from these creative writers. During the 1920s and 1930s, many writers wandered into dead ends. In retrospect, the outsider wonders how some absurd ideas were taken so seriously and how the readers could absorb so many stereotyped clichés. Yet, in the course of two decades the writers had led a generation of readers to new levels of personal awareness.

At the same time, May Fourth writers had led a generation of young dreamers to see how difficult it was to implement their visions. Just as post-Freudians in the West could never again accept the Victorian moralist who denied sexual drives, so the Chinese reader of Lu Xun could never again accept the pristine righteousness of a Confucian moralist who denied the existence of personal interests. Readers of Ye Shengtao's *Ni Huanzhi* could not again be so naïve about solving society's problems by educational reform. Nor could readers of Mao Dun's *Eclipse* be so naïve about the instant solution of problems by revolution. The writers and their readers became increasingly aware of the depth of China's difficulties and of the far-reaching changes needed to solve them. The writers helped radicalize a generation, but at the same time they also made them more sophisticated and knowledgeable about the world and their own feelings. They created a new culture that had an impact and continues to have an impact beyond the narrow circle of intellectuals.

Nevertheless, there is no denying that the visions of the May Fourth writers were not realized after 1949. As C. T. Hsia, Merle Goldman, Douwe Fokkema, Joe Huang, and others have pointed out, they helped rally a generation of youth to a political cause under which their own creativity could not prosper. The irony was even deeper. Under the banner of "proletarian literature," these children of declining aristocratic and middle-class families helped create a more truly "proletarian literature" with lower literary standards and simpler, more positive molds than they themselves could fit.

With notable exceptions of men like Lu Xun, who died in 1936, Yu Dafu and Wen Yiduo, who were killed in the 1940s, and Lin Yutang, who defected to the West, most writers remained in China after the Communist rise to power. Some continued to write in the early 1950s in an effort to adjust to a narrower range of acceptability. But by the late 1950s, for all practical purposes, they were dead as creative writers. The post-1949 regime's success in getting from them some measure of cooperation reflected their same old problem — their caution, ambivalence, and moral sensitivity. They were aware that they had enjoyed privileges not shared by the masses and that their championing of the masses had not been without condescension. They understood that tighter political control, however painful to them and their work, brought many benefits to their nation and its people. The political leaders used their ambivalence to gain their participation in the propaganda apparatus, even though their participation curbed their creativity and isolated them from their audience. They had gone full circle, from the reserved, cautious intellectual, to the hero, and back again. They remained heroes, no longer through interaction with their readers, but in the memories of their readers.

Within China, one writer among them has been canonized. Lu Xun, perhaps the greatest and certainly the most influential, died before his creative and egotistical independence required open denunciation. In 1949, Mao in "On New Democracy" praised Lu Xun in extravagant terms: "On the cultural front, he was the bravest and most correct, the firmest, the most loyal and the most ardent national hero, a hero without parallel in our history." Canonized by Mao, Lu Xun has never been subject to open public denunciation. His followers were denounced repeatedly, but he escaped. In 1957, when Ding Ling and her associates lost favor, and in 1966, when even Guo Moruo denounced all his previous works in order to stay in favor, Lu Xun remained a hero. He received more publicity during the Cultural Revolution, when his old quarrel with the party organization's cultural czar, Zhou Yang, was revived to justify that writer's fall and Mao's opposition to the party organization. From 1966 until the early 1970s, when virtually no other May Fourth writer's works were available on the market, selected works of Lu Xun were published and sold.

The canonization of Lu Xun has not ended the emotional impact of his works in contemporary China any more than the thought of Mao has lost its force for orthodox Chinese Communists, but there is an official interpretation. Lu Xun is revered for his attacks on the old Chinese society, not for his attacks on injustice in general. He is remembered for his call to arms, not for his depressed poetry. He is remembered for his denunciation of decadent scholars and gentry, but not for his denunciation of young leftists. Lu Xun is a hero, but he has been cast into a mold that includes only part of him.

In both China and Taiwan, most works of May Fourth writers are suppressed. In Taiwan, many May Fourth writers are considered too closely allied with the Communists. In China, many of these writers reprinted in the early 1950s are now considered not Communist enough. But it is clear from what was said in the Hundred Flowers Campaign of 1957 and the Cultural Revolution of 1966 that their audience in China has not forgotten them. From the energy that Taiwan authorities use to suppress May Fourth writers and from the interest that Taiwan residents show in May Fourth writers when they go abroad, it is clear that their former readers in Taiwan have also not forgotten them.

When writers are suppressed, even reading them becomes a sign of protest, an act of self-assertion against an orthodox political line. The open, colorful, and sometimes decadent era found in May Fourth writings reflects a radically different environment from the better-organized, politically and economically more successful but stultified environments of contemporary China and Taiwan. The reader of May Fourth works in Taiwan and China may be reading as nostalgia for things past, but the content still touches issues close to his heart that are not expressed in the available media. How many former readers still read the works surreptitiously is anyone's guess. For some people, living under tight political controls, May Fourth works symbolize the spirit of open criticism. For them, May Fourth writers have become a new kind of hero, unsung because of the danger of discussing them.

Few Westerners, besides China specialists, bother to read May Fourth literature. China specialists read them in the spirit of scholarly objectivity, searching for understanding. But for those interested in the vitality and fullness of modern China, nothing surpasses May Fourth literature. Just as history is a product of the era in which it is written as well as the period written about, so is our interest in literature related to our contemporary life. As Westerners raise doubts about their own countries — their moral decay, their ungovernability, their outdated institutions — the world of the May Fourth writers may seem less remote. And as the contact between China and the outside world grows and others outside China begin to show interest in things Chinese, it would not be surprising if these writers attract more enduring interest than some of the glossier propaganda or official histories. Perhaps because the May Fourth writers are more accessible to Western readers, there is in many of our relatively objective scholarly descriptions an underlying admiration of these writers — for they are also our heroes.

8.

Genesis of a Writer: Notes on Lu Xun's Educational Experience, 1881–1909

Leo Ou-fan Lee

In the celebrated preface to his first collection of short stories, *Nahan* (A call to arms), Lu Xun admits that his writing is drawn from personal memory. In a somber and melancholy tone he gives us a fragmentary but highly revealing account of how he became a writer. The autobiographical threads he weaves into the preface seem to tie his spirit "to the solitary days long past"[1] and suggest that the reader cannot fully understand his short stories without somehow coming to grips, as Lu Xun did, with significant events in his past.

Lu Xun's early years span both the "traditional" and "modern" periods of Chinese history. His emergence from a traditional milieu to become modern China's foremost writer came after long intellectual and psychological trials. His many years of education in China and Japan reflect changed perceptions of literature and the writer's role. His long journey to fame reveals a long mental evolution from traditional culture through science to literature. An analysis of his early background is important to understanding his development as a writer and his conception of literature.

The World of Chinese Tradition

It is well known that by the time Lu Xun (Zhou Shuren) was born, his family had outlived its fortunes. But even in its twilight, this large gentry family in Shaohsing, Chekiang province, still represented an impressive microcosm of Chinese tradition. However dilapidated, the residences of the Zhou clansmen formed large compounds of houses, gardens, ponds, high walls, pebbled corridors, lacquered gates, stone bridges, moss-grown paths, and courtyards. The Zhou clan had been divided and subdivided into several branches. These "houses" *(fang)* had such time-honored Confucian titles as "Wisdom," "Attainment,"

"Humanity," "Bravery," "Sincerity," and "Prosperity." Lu Xun, ironically, was born into the house of "Prosperity."[2]

Although Lu Xun's family was typical of many traditional Chinese gentry families, the relatively liberal attitude of his grandfather and his parents enabled him to pursue a traditional-style education that was somewhat less rigid than the orthodox pattern. He began at six by reading a history primer, *Jian lüe* (Outline of history) with a great-uncle. His grandfather felt that aside from learning how to read and write, the boy should first of all have a basic knowledge of Chinese history. Unorthodoxly, he also believed in the educational value of popular novels, especially the *Xiyou ji* (Journey to the west), his personal favorite, and encouraged his grandson to read them.[3]

In 1892, when Lu Xun was eleven, he was sent to a local tutor, with whom he studied intermittently until 1897. The normal classical education did not motivate him, despite his tutor's congeniality and considerable learning. The young Lu Xun was not too interested in practicing calligraphy, but he loved to draw and copy. The Confucian classics were much less appealing than books he obtained through his relatives: popular novels and romances, works on flora and fauna, books on painting, and, above all, the various accounts of fantasy, ghosts, and mythology.[4]

Interest in such areas was not unusual for traditional Chinese literati. But as William Schultz has pointed out, in prerepublican times "popular fiction, mythology, and fable and fantasy comprised a realm the child was rarely encouraged to enter."[5] That young Lu Xun was permitted — even helped — to explore this slightly unorthodox field had lasting consequences on his development. From the beginning Lu Xun never wholly embraced the intellectual substance of the "great tradition." He frankly acknowledged that "books of the Confucian and Mencian school . . . seemed to have nothing to do with me."[6] Though he had surely read the Four Books and Five Classics, he was not intellectually committed to the Confucian line of philosophers from Confucius and Mencius to Zhu Xi and Wang Yangming. Nor was he impressed by the eight *guwen* (classical-style) masters of prose of Tang and Song times or the "eight-legged" essay style used in official examinations. To him, reading histories was more enlightening than the classics and philosophers. He preferred unofficial histories *(yeshi)* and private accounts, which, in his view, give a less pretentious account of China's past than the official dynastic histories.[7] He was fascinated by the manners and mores of an age as described not so much in public records as in private miscellanies *(congshu)*. The first books he bought were said to be a collection of miscellaneous Tang works called *Tangdai congshu*. In his later research he was guided by an eclectic notion of pre-Song times that grouped together unofficial histories and biographies, romances *(chuanqi)*, personal notes *(biji)* and collections, as well as stories and novels under the general heading of *xiaoshuo.*[8] All these works are *zaxue*, or "miscellaneous learning." Lu Xun openly admitted that he was a *zajia*, a practitioner of *zaxue.*

These early intellectual pursuits led to his later interests in what may be called the "countertradition" in Chinese culture. In philosophy, he was "poisoned" by Zhuang Zi and Han Fei Zi.[9] In fiction, he was more attracted to pre-Tang works, where the great Confucian tradition had not yet had its full impact on literature. In poetry, he liked the ancient Qu Yuan and the late Tang poet Li He. In prose, his model was Xi Kang and other "neo-Taoist" literati of the Six Dynasties. For a while he read Buddhism extensively. This led him to sponsor the printing of the *Baiyu jing* (Sutra of a hundred fables). His studies with the great master Zhang Binglin (Taiyan) gave him impressive skills in *xiao-xue* — philology, particularly etymology — rather than training in *daxue* (classical studies).[10]

Lu Xun's inclinations toward the "countertradition" are closely related to his fondness for aspects of the "little tradition": popular tales and fables, folk religious practices, mythology, and village operas. In his collection of reminiscences, *Zhao hua xi shi* (Morning blossoms plucked at dusk), some of the most vivid descriptions are lavished on figures of the little tradition — the charming ghosts of Wuchang (the infernal agent) or Nüdiao (the ghost of a hanged woman). In contrast, his most vituperative remarks were made against the book *Ershisi xiao tu* (Twenty-four illustrated cases of filial piety), which exemplified to him the inhuman impact of the absurd moralities contained in the great tradition. A long essay in his reminiscences, "Cong baicao yuan dao sanwei shuwu" (From the hundred-plant garden to the three-flavored study), lyrically recalls the two worlds of his childhood: the playful and fanciful world of the little tradition, symbolized by the garden, and the uninspiring world of the great tradition, typified by his tutor's study. Of course, these two traditions are not mutually exclusive, either in Lu Xun's life or in Chinese culture. Lu Xun also effectively used his knowledge of the "countertradition" to reinforce his interest in the little tradition. He drew upon his favorite books of fantasy, such as *Yuli chaozhuan* (Stories of the ghosts of hell), to embellish the memory of these ghost figures of village operas.

In a seminal essay, the late T. A. Hsia has brilliantly demonstrated that Lu Xun's childhood world had a direct bearing on the many "aspects of darkness" in his art.[11] The world also had a deeper pertinence to Lu Xun's psychological makeup. The environment in which the young Lu Xun assimilated the two strains of Chinese tradition was itself filled with psychological tensions. The "Hundred-Plant Garden," the Zhou children's playground, held the mysteries of family lore. The old nurse warned the children never to go near areas where the long grass grew, because a snake fairy with a beautiful woman's face lived there, and whenever someone responded to her call, she would come to devour him at night.[12] The old nurse, A Chang, also bought Lu Xun an illustrated edition of the *Shanhai jing* (The classic of hills and seas) "with pictures of man-faced beasts, nine-headed snakes, three-footed birds, men with wings, and headless monsters who used their teats as eyes."[13] She told him gory anecdotes of massacres committed by the "long-haired rebels" (the Taipings). One of Lu Xun's great-uncles, who had tutored him for a year on Mencius, became insane and committed suicide by stabbing himself with a pair of scissors, setting himself on fire, and finally jumping off a bridge and drowning.[14] These figures and incidents that peopled a crumbling household exerted a haunting power on the psyche of a sensitive boy.

Outside the world of this decaying gentry family, the city of Shaohsing also had its darker and seedier side. Despite its scenic beauty, the landscape was dotted with what was popularly called the "three abundances," latrines, memorial arches, and graves.[15] Like many old cities in traditional China, Shaohsing's long history also bred a myriad of ritual practices of popular superstition that governed alike the lives of gentry and peasants. The young Lu Xun participated in an invocation ritual connected with the opening of a village opera performance of *Mulian xi* (The drama of Mulian), a popular opera that describes "the descent into hell of the Saint, one of Lord Buddha's disciples, to rescue his mother who is there receiving punishment for her sins."[16] The ritual called for a dozen boys to ride on horseback to the nameless graveyards at sunset and throw javelins at the graves. As a daring young boy, Lu Xun obviously enjoyed this ghostly pageantry with relish. But as he grew older and had to assume the increasing pressures of family misfortune, this phantasmagoric world may have haunted as much as delighted him. The prevailing mood of nostalgic warmth and childish glee in *Morning Blossoms* seems also permeated by a lurking sense of foreboding and doom. As recollected by the mature sensibilities of a middle-aged writer, Lu Xun's childhood was a mixture of blessing and curse.

The major shift in tone from light to darkness in Lu Xun's childhood memories, as he often indicated, is connected with his grandfather's imprisonment in 1893. The scandal caused a great transformation of family fortunes. Lu Xun was sent to live with his mother's family for a while, where he was sometimes called a beggar.[17] "Is there anyone whose family sinks from prosperity to poverty?" Lu Xun remarked in the preface to *A Call to Arms.* "I think in the process one can probably come to understand what the real world is like."[18]

By itself poverty may not have caused Lu Xun great emotional tribulation, but it was accompanied by a loss of family prestige. In the preface, Lu Xun describes himself standing in front of a pawnbroker's counter twice his height and receiving "money proffered with contempt"[19] — a subtle touch that accentuates the poignancy of his role as a scion of a disgraced and powerless gentry family. In a sense, both Lu Xun's grandfather and his father were victimized by the very system that had established the family prestige. His grandfather, a *jinshi* (metropolitan candidate or doctor), was jailed in Hangchow for seven years because of his involvement in bribery in the provincial examinations. His irritable temper worsened after his imprisonment. According to Zhou Zuoren's accounts, although the old man did not usually vent his anger on his grandchildren, he would curse loudly and bite his fingernails in tantrums that frightened everyone in sight.[20] Lu Xun's father was an even more frustrated scholar because he had failed several times to attain any degree higher than *xiucai* (licentiate or bachelor). When he was not bedridden, he often smoked opium and drank. He normally ate alone. Slight inebriation at the beginning of his meals often brought out his geniality, and he would gather the youngsters around him for stories of fox fairies from the *Liaozhai zhiyi* (Strange stories from a Chinese studio). But as he got drunker his face would turn pallid and his words would become more strained. As his mood changed the children would leave.[21]

With his grandfather stifled by officialdom and his father weakened by bad health and dissipation, the young Lu Xun had no strong and exemplary figure to emulate. It was not sheer accident that Lu Xun adopted his mother's maiden surname, Lu, as part of his pen name. Lu Xun's mother also came from a cultured gentry family from a nearby village. She had no formal education, but she had taught herself to read. She was considerably "emancipated" when she unbound her feet in response to the "natural feet" movement launched at the end of the nineteenth century.[22] But even with her stamina and strong will she could not substitute for a father figure in Lu Xun's mind. As the eldest son, Lu Xun may have felt the responsibility to redeem his father and grandfather. Especially after his father's death he felt a sense of duty to assume the role of a young father to his brothers and to restore the family name. Within a traditional Chinese "extended family," this psychological matrix does not necessarily lend itself to Oedipal conflicts. In the case of Lu Xun, it nurtured an early maturity — what Erik Erikson has called the "early conscience development":

> It is, in fact, rather probable that a highly uncommon man experiences filial conflicts with such inescapable intensity because he senses in himself already early in childhood some kind of originality that seems to point beyond the competition with the personal father. His is also an early conscience development which makes him feel (and appear) old while still young and maybe older in single-mindedness than his conformist parents, who, in turn, may treat him somehow as their potential redeemer.[23]

Erikson's insights, derived from his study of Gandhi, may prove equally relevant to Lu Xun in his relationship with his father. In a vivid reminiscence, Lu Xun recounted how his father made him recite twenty to thirty lines from the *Outline of History* before he could join an excursion to a village opera performance.[24] The incident actually illustrates the pathetic efforts of a disillusioned scholar to make his son fulfill what he himself had failed to achieve — the academic knowledge that led to officialdom, wealth, and prestige. Lu Xun's two brothers have argued in their later accounts that their father was not as strict as Lu Xun portrayed him,[25] but it was nevertheless natural for him to treat his intelligent eldest son as his "potential redeemer." In so doing, he also imposed on his son, as Erikson puts it, "a sense of being both needed and chosen ... and thus of carrying a superior destiny and duty."[26]

In another long reminiscent essay, "Fuqin de bing" (Father's illness), Lu Xun sarcastically describes how quacks of traditional herb medicine "treated" his father's illness. His father had fallen gravely ill possibly in late 1894 or early 1895, shortly after his grandfather's imprisonment.[27] For a long time the doctors could not determine the real disease. They sent the young Lu Xun to search for a variety of unusual medical "adjuvants" — "aloe root dug up in winter, sugarcane that had been three years exposed to frost, twin crickets and ardisia"[28] — to accompany their regular prescriptions. This was all futile. The patient vomited large quantities of blood. The doctors, diagnosing with the motto of their trade, *yi zhe yi ye* (to practice medicine is [to find] the intent), decided that because black could overcome red, black ink would quench red blood. So the sick man was ordered to drink ink. Gradually the backs of his feet became swollen and then also his legs, stomach, and chest. The imaginative doctors reasoned that since the folk term for this swollen state of the body was "expanded drum," a slice of the used "drum skin" should be able to cure it.[29] Finally, in 1896, after more than a hundred days of applying "drum skin pills," Lu Xun's father was attacked by paroxyms of asthma. By this time, everybody knew that death was near:

> Father labored for breath for a long time. It was painful for me even to listen to it. But no one could help him. Sometimes an idea would flash like lightning into my mind: "Better to end the gasping faster. . ." And immediately I knew that the idea was improper; it was like committing a crime. But at the same time I thought the idea rather proper, for I loved my father. Even now, I still think so.
>
> In the morning, a relative who lived in the neighborhood, a Mrs. Yan, entered. She was a woman well versed in etiquette and told us that we should not be idle while waiting. So they put new clothes on him. Then they burned some paper money and a certain *gaowang* sutra into ashes, wrapped the ashes in a piece of paper, and made him clutch it in his fists . . .
>
> "Scream, your father is going to stop breathing."
>
> "Father! Father!" I started calling.
>
> "Louder! He can't hear. Call him quickly!"
>
> "Father! Father!"
>
> His face, which had quieted down, suddenly became tense. He opened his eyes slightly as if he felt something bitter and painful.
>
> "Yell! Yell! Quick!"
>
> "Father!"
>
> "What? . . . Don't shout . . . don't . . . ," he said in a low tone. Then he gasped frantically for breath. After a while, he returned to normal and calmed down.
>
> "Father!" I kept calling him until he stopped breathing. Now I can still hear my own voice at that time. Whenever I hear it, I feel that this is the gravest wrong I have done to my father.[30]

This account, like most of Lu Xun's reminiscences, is half truth and half fiction. Zhou Zuoren recalled in his memoirs that the distant relative, Mrs. Yan, could never have been present at such an intimate moment. The whole episode of calling his father's soul may have been fabricated by Lu Xun for dramatic effect.[31] But the significant fact remains that more than twenty-five years after it had taken place, Lu Xun chose to perceive such an incident from a psychological perspective. The sarcastic tone of the essay changes to a sense of heightened trauma near the end, an indication that his father's illness and death must have propelled a psychological crisis in the young Lu Xun by bringing to a head all those dark forces of misfortune that figured in his childhood world.

Erikson calls this experience, following Kierkegaard, the "curse" in the lives of innovators with precocious and relentless consciences.[32] They grow up with "an obligation (beset with guilt) to surpass and to originate at all cost" so that they may exorcise their childhood "curse."[33] Thus they are, because of this curse, among the "chosen" few who will lead extraordinary lives. Lu Xun, like Gandhi, Luther, and the other "chosen," may have been subjected to such a psychological crisis. Of the childhood "curse" Erikson writes: "In adolescence this may prolong his identity confusion because he must find the one way in which he (and he alone!) can re-enact the past and create a new future in the right medium at the right moment on a sufficiently large scale."[34]

To find the "right medium" in literature took Lu Xun a decade. The period from 1896 to 1906 may be regarded as a period of "moratorium" in which he embarked on a long journey of what Erikson calls identity formation and identity confusion.[35] And this search for identity led him to the highly unorthodox route of new-style schools and Western science.

The World of Western Science

By the end of the Qing dynasty, the examination system was corrupted by irregular practices. But there were alternatives open to a disaffected member of the literati. He could become a private tutor, a medical doctor, a personal secretary (*muyou*), or a tradesman.[36] Entering a new-style school to learn foreign subjects was not only highly unorthodox but also undesirable. But this was Lu Xun's choice in 1898, two years after his father's death, when he left home and enrolled at the Kiangnan Naval Academy in Nanking. As he recalled his decision in the preface to *A Call to Arms*: "I wanted to travel a new path, to escape to a new place, and search for new kinds of people."[37]

Economic need was obviously behind this unorthodox choice. The naval academy offered full scholarships. Moreover, one of Lu Xun's distant great-uncles was an administrator at the academy and could provide a needed source of protection.[38] For his mother and grandfather, this "new path," though undesirable, was not too risky. But Lu Xun was not entirely confident in the beginning. The naval academy disappointed him: its curriculum was lax, its administration inept. Even the staff members themselves favored the old practice of civil service examinations. Lu Xun was lured back briefly to take the first-level district examination in 1898. Though he did reasonably well on the first test, he did not show up for the other tests. His mother was persuaded to hire an illegal "sit-in," but the imposter did even worse than Lu Xun might have. Thus ended Lu Xun's only halfhearted attempt at "making it" through the regular channel of success.[39]

Lu Xun's search for new identities began in a period of rapid transformation in his communal culture, and his experience, in many ways, typified his generation. Lu Xun entered the Kiangnan Naval Academy in 1898, when the reform movement under the leadership of Kang Youwei and Liang Qichao was strongest. The so-called Hundred-Day Reform failed, but "new learning" was quickly becoming widely popular. In 1899, when Lu Xun transferred to the School of Mining and Railways of the Kiangnan Military Academy, the reformist atmosphere was so open that the school principal would read Liang Qichao's *Shiwu bao* (Current affairs) daily as he rode to school in a horse-drawn carriage and ask his students to write compositions on George Washington.[40] Despite his initial misgivings about his "new path," Lu Xun soon felt he was at the center of a new educational current.

The curriculum at the School of Mining and Railways was much more satisfactory. Besides German and Chinese, "there were such subjects as science, geology, and mining ... all very refreshing."[41] Other subjects included mathematics, geography, mechanical drawing, and physical education. Lu Xun studied his new subjects with zest and seriousness. He copied an entire two-volume text, Sir Charles Lyell's *Principles of Geology,* together with its charts and graphs. Another habit developed in childhood — drawing — was put to good use in sketching railway tracks. A classmate of his later recalled that his drawings were both good and fast, and he invariably scored high in tests.[42] These new courses were a refreshing departure from the Chinese classics that had been forced down him as a boy. Western science was a novelty for Lu Xun, and the new scientific subjects a new branch of his miscellaneous learning, *zaxue.* But they were no longer just avocational interests.

Formal schooling was no longer boring, as a new area of his unorthodox interests became a legitimate academic discipline.

In his leisure hours, he continued his early habit of extracurricular reading. More miscellanies were added to his private collection, and assorted books on travel, agriculture, and history were bought, devoured, and sent home to his brother.[43] But the most significant stimulus to Lu Xun's intellectual development in this period came from a new body of modern works and translations different from any traditional works he had read before. Like most young intellectuals in urban centers at that time, Lu Xun came under the pervasive influence of Liang Qichao and Yan Fu. He pored over Liang's newspapers and journals and sent his brother bound volumes to read. He was immensely impressed by Yan Fu's translations, particularly of J. S. Mill's *On Liberty* and Huxley's *Evolution and Ethics*, which he recommended highly to his brother.[44] He was so fond of Yan Fu's elegant rendition of Huxley's prose that years later he could still recite the first passage from *Evolution and Ethics*: "Huxley sat alone in his room in the south of England. With the hills behind him and the pastures facing him, the scenery outside seemed as if spread out before his very desk. Thus he conjured up the time, two thousand years ago, before the Roman general Caesar had arrived. What was the scene here in those days? Perhaps only untouched wild grass."[45] In one of his reminiscences, Lu Xun recaptured the wonder he felt while first reading this work: "Ah! The world once produced a man like Huxley, who sat in his study and thought such refreshing thoughts. Thus as I read on breathlessly, 'survival of the fittest,' 'natural selection,' Socrates, Plato, and the Stoics all appeared one by one."[46]

Lu Xun's recollection indicates that this brave new world may have kindled his youthful imagination as much as it excited his intellectual curiosity. In Yan Fu's translation, Huxley's "Prolegomena" reads like fiction. It unveiled a landscape of exotic scenery and bizarre appeal much like Lin Shu's translations of Western adventure novels, which Lu Xun read with equal enthusiasm. He was certainly excited by the atmosphere of dynamism in this wonderland of the West and may have approached it with the same delight with which he had read traditional Chinese tales of fantasy and legend.

This social Darwinian world opened the mind of a young man to a bright vista, while the world of Chinese tradition was pushed into the shadows. During this Nanking period, Lu Xun's thought is filled with Manichaean contrasts between China and the West — contrasts that probably led to his later iconoclasm in the May Fourth era. Evolutionism became an important part of his intellectual convictions. Future generations, he believed, had to be better than the past, and the present generation had to know the tradition to open up new ways for the future.

Social Darwinism in itself does not support any political ideology. It can even be used, as in the United States, to justify conservatism. It was doubtful whether the twenty-year-old Lu Xun really understood Huxley's ethical message against impersonal evolution. But the incipient nationalism of a generation of Chinese intellectuals, Lu Xun included, turned social Darwinism into first a reformist and then later a revolutionary ideology. It gave coherence and sensibility to the large body of Western materials that were being introduced into China in the early twentieth century.

Having embraced this brave new world of Western science, Lu Xun was yet to sort out its specifics. At the mining school, he probably did not perceive the possible gap between his formal training and his informal self-education. In a way, his extracurricular readings of Yan Fu and Liang Qichao bolstered his new academic discipline. He was too carried away by the idea of science and technology as the key to national wealth and power to contemplate the possible implications of this utilitarian notion. It took several years of introspection in Japan for him to realize that acquiring a scientific discipline satisfied neither his temperament nor his ambition.

Lu Xun graduated from the School of Mining and Railways in January 1902. In March, he was sent to Japan on a government scholarship. The "new path" not only led his mind into new areas of knowledge but also guided him to a foreign land. Lu Xun was twenty-one in 1902 when he arrived in Japan, a wide-eyed adolescent eager for more Western science; he returned to China in 1909 a mature adult of twenty-eight, who had finally found his true vocation in literature.

Except for a year and a half at the Sendai Medical School, Lu Xun was something of a "nonstudent" or "dropout." During most of his eight years in Japan he had merely a pro forma student status. In his first two years, he was officially enrolled at the Kōbun Gakuin, a preparatory school set up for Chinese students to study Japanese. The easy routine there gave him enough time and energy for his extracurricular interests. After he left Sendai in 1906, he was again officially registered at a German language school in order, one suspects, to continue receiving scholarship money, while he spent most of his time in other activities. This was common for most Chinese students in Japan, whose numbers grew to more than ten thousand by 1906.

Therefore, Lu Xun enjoyed ample free time in Japan, but his life seemed to be dominated by a single-minded dedication to serious intellectual pursuits. While many of his compatriots fell for the charms of Japanese women, restaurants, tea gardens, or geisha houses, it is difficult to find anything sensual in Lu Xun's own writings about his Japanese period. "Eyewitness" accounts by his brother and friends confirm the impression of a serious, aspiring young man. They reported that Lu Xun ate simple Japanese food and wore his student uniform or Japanese clothes; he grew a moustache, started cigarette smoking, and liked to eat peanuts and drink milk shakes.[47] Although he lived on and off with Chinese students in Tokyo, he was severely critical of most of them, especially the rich dandies who loafed around Tokyo's pleasure quarters with their long queues coiled up on their heads.[48]

In his first two years in Japan he was still preoccupied with science; his intellectual mood continued to reflect his educational experience in Nanking. Drawing obviously on his previous studies at the mining school, in 1903 he published two articles in a Chinese student journal, *Zhejiang chao* (Chekiang tide), one on China's mineral resources, the other on Mme. Curie's discovery of radium. In both, Lu Xun expressed the utilitarian maxim that "scientific knowledge and its application comprise an indispensable prerequisite to national progress."[49] In the same year, he also made free translations of Jules Verne's *De la terre à la lune (Yuejie lüxing)* and *Voyage au centre de la terre (Didi lüxing)*. Treating Western science fiction most seriously, he wrote, "The fictional heritage in our country abounds in works dealing with sentimental, historical, satirical, and bizarre subjects. But only science fiction is scarce. This is one of the reasons for the primitiveness of our knowledge [of science]. Therefore, if we wish to fill in the gap of today's translations and to lead the Chinese people toward progress, we must begin with science fiction."[50]

Lu Xun's arguments in this preface closely followed those of Liang Qichao in his essay "Lun xiaoshuo yu qunzhi de guanxi" (On the relationship between fiction and the rule of the masses). For both Liang and Lu Xun in this period, fiction was an educational medium. Its literary and imaginative possibilities were subservient to its uses. While Liang Qichao mainly read political novels, Lu Xun's scientific background naturally led him to science fiction. Significantly, while arguing for the importance of scientific knowledge, Lu Xun referred to his earlier interests — traditional Chinese fiction with its "sentimental, historical, satirical, and bizarre subjects." In a less serious vein, he would have enjoyed science fiction as fantasy, as he had earlier enjoyed such works as *The Classic of Hills and Seas* and *Stories of the Ghosts of Hell,* or even Yan Fu's translation of Huxley's *Evolution and Ethics.* But Lu Xun still considered himself a man of science who used journalism and translation to popularize his cause, just as Liang Qichao used them to publicize his political theories and goals. The prospect of a literary career had not yet occurred to him, but in time, the study of science became a new orthodoxy, and gradually he began to feel its unpleasant weight.

One year after he arrived in Japan, Lu Xun cut off his queue — a symbolic act of cutting himself off from his fun-seeking compatriots in Japan. The event also inspired him to write a classical poem called "Zi chao" (Self-portrait):

> My heart has no tactic to dodge the magic arrow;
> My homeland is darkened,
>   like a millstone, in the storm of wind and rain.
> To the chilling stars I convey my thoughts, my people unaware of
>   my sorrow.
> With my blood I shall sacrifice myself to Emperor Xianyuan.[51]

According to Xu Shoushang, to whom Lu Xun gave the poem, the allusion to the magic arrow is Western and refers to Cupid's arrow — in this context probably Western science.[52] But the magic power of Western science only made Lu Xun more aware of the dark powers in his own people. To define his identity in this impending "storm of wind and rain" meant also to cast his fate with his own country, to shed his martyr's blood for the heritage bequeathed by the first ancestor of the Chinese race, Xianyuan. This poem is suffused with a melancholy patriotism similar to the mood of Qu Yuan's works. The juxtaposition of China and West in the imagery brings out a personal vision of a lone martyr, which Lu Xun conveyed throughout his later writings.

This celebrated poem vividly captures Lu Xun's mental state at that time. It also indicates the conflict between his study of science and his incipient nationalism. Like most conscientious Chinese students in Japan, Lu Xun was swept along by the tide of nationalism. The reformist atmosphere in Nanking gradually gave way to that of revolution. The various groups of revolutionaries in Japan were fighting for supremacy among themselves and against Liang Qichao's constitutional reformers. Lu Xun attended rallies, heard speeches, met and talked to revolutionaries, and read the mushrooming student journals published by provincial societies, particularly *Chekiang Tide,* the one from his own home province. But in this early period, Lu Xun's political loyalties were not yet clearly defined. Although he might have leaned toward the revolutionaries and later joined the Guangfu hui (Restoration Society),[53] his articles in 1903 still showed Liang Qichao's influence. In an essay on "Sibadazhi lun" (The spirit of Sparta) he followed Liang's much-used practice of citing Western history as an example for the inculcation of nationalism. Through a melodramatic account of Leonidas's defense of Sparta against Xerxes and his Persian invaders, Lu Xun conveyed a clearly didactic message: that Spartan bravery and self-sacrifice should become one of the "fundamental elements of a new national consciousness."[54] Lu Xun's nationalism in this article did not take a narrow political turn to revolutionary action. Rather, his idea of the Spartan spirit is reminiscent of Yan Fu's view of Herbert Spencer and Lin Shu's impressions of H. Rider Haggard's heroes. It essentially emphasizes a Faustian sense of dynamism in the West and calls for a release of individual energies for the good of the nation.[55]

Rather than being narrowly political or revolutionary, Lu Xun's nationalism expressed broad cultural concerns. According to Xu Shoushang, Lu Xun was obsessed during this period by three basic questions:[56]

1. What is the ideal nature of man?
2. What is lacking in the Chinese national character?
3. What is the root of China's illness?

Lu Xun's devotion to science led him to the intriguing possibility of finding the "scientific" origins of human nature and the Chinese national character. Reportedly, he talked to Xu Shoushang about studying medicine in order to find "solutions to these questions through science." But in their discussions, a sense of nationalism had led them to "unscientific" conclusions. They realized that "our nation was most lacking in honesty and love," and that the basic cause for China's illness was the historical fact that China had been twice enslaved by barbarians.[57]

Science might have an intellectual function as a medium of enlightenment, but the ethical and political dimensions of Lu Xun's solutions were beyond its power. Clearly Lu Xun's extracurricular reading and thinking in an atmosphere of growing nationalism gradually came into conflict with the goals of his scientific training. He had held both a broad intellectual view of science as enlightenment and a narrowly functional view of science as vocational discipline, considering the intellectual view an avocation that served the functional. But the way he asked his three questions betrays a strong "cultural-intellectualistic" mode of thinking. This was typical of traditional Chinese intellectuals, with their emphasis on the priority of a "change of basic ideas *qua* ideas" over social, political, and economic changes.[58] The intellectual "essence" of this "cultural-intellectualistic" view did not turn out to be scientific knowledge. Lu Xun's explorations, therefore, did not ultimately lead him to a Western positivist view of science but to a heavily traditional Chinese concern with culture and morality *over* science. Yet it took him another three years to break finally with science in favor of literature.

In September 1904 Lu Xun enrolled at the Sendai Medical School. As he stated in the preface to *A Call to Arms*, the seed for this action had been sown in his Nanking years. He had realized then the pernicious effects of traditional Chinese medicine and learned through translated histories that Japan's Meiji Restoration "had originated, to a great extent, with the introduction of Western medical science."[59] But the psychological roots of this decision could be traced to the "curse" of his father's death. "I dreamed a beautiful dream," Lu Xun wrote revealingly in the preface, "that on my return to China I would cure patients like my father."[60] From an Eriksonian perspective, studying Western medicine can represent a first step to exorcise the "ghost" of his father: every operation administered by the doctor Lu Xun would serve to "re-enact" the traumatic scene of his father's death, and every Chinese patient cured would enable him to purge a bit more of the "gravest wrong" that he felt he had done to his father. Lu Xun's "beautiful dream" is not merely an ideological statement; it could also be a psychological wish fulfillment.

There may also have been practical considerations. Medicine was one of the better disciplines that Japan offered to aspiring Chinese students. Lu Xun also wanted to avoid the Tokyo mob of Chinese dandies, according to Zhou Zuoren. So he chose Sendai in northern Honshu. Less prestigious than medical schools of the big universities, this school was relatively secluded. It was also free of tuition, entrance examination, and Chinese students.[61] In Sendai, Lu Xun lived alone in a boardinghouse near the prison by the Hirose River, known as "the horse's back" — one of the city's coldest spots.[62] To fend off cold weather he took a daily hot bath.[63] He was the only Chinese student there and had very few friends. This period of self-exile may have made him more introspective, strengthening his solitary temperament. A Japanese classmate described him:

> Lu Xun at the time was very quiet. I never thought he would become a great man. . . He seldom went out of his room, where he was always studying. I lost touch with him after he left for Tokyo and was surprised to learn that he had become the famous Lu Xun. "That man?" I thought. I remember how surprised he was when one day he finally realized that a frog's blood had gotten mixed in with his own blood during a laboratory session and said, "My blood is the same as frog's blood."[64]

At the end of the first school year, Lu Xun's highest grade — 83 — was in ethics. His other grades were mediocre, but his grade average of 65.5 was above the passing mark and good enough for a foreign student.[65] His lowest grade (59.3) was in an anatomy course taught by Mr. Fujino Gonkyūro, whom Lu Xun immortalized in a moving and memorable essay, "Tengye xiansheng" (Fujino *sensei*.)

Fujino was born in 1874, graduated from the Aichi School of Medicine, and attended the Tokyo Imperial University. He became an instructor at Sendai in 1901 and a professor in 1905. When the school was later incorporated into Tōhoku University, he was forced to "voluntarily resign" because he did not have the necessary qualifications to continue as a professor on the university level. He is reported to have died in 1945.[66]

When teaching at Sendai, Fujino walked to school every day, while other professors took the *jinrikisha* to work. His nickname was "Gon-san" (taskmaster), and he was noted for his harshness. He never smiled during lectures; his diagrams were drawn on the blackboard with careful precision. He began his anatomy lectures in reverential *kanbun* (classical Japanese) tones. Indifferent to fashion, he often wore a straw hat in winter, and was once mistaken for a beggar in a train. The various accounts that Japanese scholars have found show him as a quiet and somewhat eccentric man who kept his promises, held to his word, and took loving care of children.[67]

Lu Xun's portrait of "Fujino *sensei*" in his 1926 essay shows many more admirable traits in this Japanese teacher than his teaching style. Fujino's upright character, his solitary and eccentric ways, and his penchant for correctness (Lu Xun's grade of 59.3 was 0.7 below passing) were the major components of this unique personality. It was his singular persuasiveness and unobstrusive kindness that stayed in Lu

Xun's memory. His photograph hung in Lu Xun's study for many years — obviously the mirror of an exemplary man in whom Lu Xun could see something of himself. "I always remember him, I don't know why," Lu Xun wrote in 1926. "Of all the teachers I have known, he has made me feel the most indebted and encouraged."[68] Fujino was probably Lu Xun's first model teacher who compared in influence to the other great teacher in his Japan years, Zhang Taiyan. Although only seven years older than Lu Xun, Fujino may have appeared, in one sense, as something of a surrogate father to him. In a life previously lacking outstanding father figures, Lu Xun may have responded most gratefully to Fujino's offer to correct his class notes — a considerate gesture from a responsible teacher. Despite Fujino's effect on Lu Xun, it appears that Lu Xun did not make a similar impact. Fujino later said of his Chinese student, "His Japanese was not all that perfect at the time he entered, and he went through a lot of effort to understand the lectures. After the lectures I would correct what he did not hear correctly or whatever mistakes he had made. . . He was very diligent at the lectures. He was not among the excellent students. He probably came to my house to visit, but I don't remember."[69]

In 1905 the Japanese were deeply affected by the Russo-Japanese War, and its impact also extended to Sendai. Many of the medical-school teachers were drafted; students were mobilized; and others volunteered for hospital work. Thousands of Russian prisoners of war crowded the city streets. Japanese jingoism was at its height. A sign displayed at a Sendai store proclaimed more Japanese victories in China.[70] In 1906 the Treaty of Portsmouth was signed, and Japanese everywhere thought it was grossly unfair. Frustration and anger spread throughout the country. Xenophobia was very high in Sendai. In this highly charged political atmosphere, the famous news slide incident took place, an incident that decisively changed the course of Lu Xun's life.

A bacteriology professor had brought a slide projector back from Germany to Sendai to show slides of bacterial forms. When lectures ended early, he would show news slides of the Russo-Japanese War. One day Lu Xun was suddenly confronted with a picture of his fellow countrymen in Manchuria. One was accused of being a Russian spy and was about to be executed by the Japanese military as others stood around him to watch the spectacle. Of this incident, Lu Xun wrote:

> Before the term was over I had left for Tokyo, because after seeing these slides I felt that medical science was not such an important thing

177

after all. People from an ignorant and weak country, no matter how physically healthy and strong they may be, could only serve to be made examples of, or to become onlookers of utterly meaningless spectacles. Such a condition was more deplorable than dying of illness. Therefore our first important task was to change their spirit, and at that time I considered the best medium for achieving this end was literature. I was thus determined to promote a literary movement.[71]

Certainly, it was not only this incident that prompted Lu Xun to give up medicine for literature. Still, it culminated many frustrations suffered in these two years. He had not done too well at the medical school. The fact that his best subject was ethics demonstrated his greater insight into the moral and spiritual than the scientific. Lu Xun had been drawn toward the human mind and spirit in spite of his practical education. Moreover, his aesthetic inclinations — demonstrated in his childhood drawing — again revealed themselves. Once for an anatomy drawing assignment he placed a blood vessel in the wrong position out of artistic considerations.[72] His humanistic sensitivities may also have been irritated while dissecting the bodies of paupers, executed prisoners, or inmates who had died in prison.[73] Reportedly, when he first dissected cadavers he felt uneasy about cutting up the bodies of women and children.[74] Such personal concerns were gradually combined with his nationalistic feelings. The news slide incident was only a final catalyst that brought him face to face with his real self. Lu Xun's melodramatic description of this incident seems almost intentionally focused on this confrontation between himself as an "observer" in a foreign classroom and a larger, symbolic image of self as a "participant." In watching this mirror image (the news slide) he was transported to a more collective and pressing identity with his fellow countrymen.

Psychologically, the incident may be interpreted as triggering a second "crisis" in Lu Xun's life; he was compelled by both external and internal forces to confront his past. The "reenactment" of his childhood "curse" was extended by his premature "generativity crisis" to a whole "communal body" — those "weak in power, poor in possessions, and seemingly simple in heart," as symbolized by the ignorant Chinese in the slides. Lu Xun's poem ("Self-Portrait") had already indicated that his personal identity had to be defined in relation to a larger identity. He would have to surpass his father and find another "right medium" on a sufficiently wider scale than the practice of medicine.

Literature was not necessarily the best choice at the time in spite of Lu Xun's later rationalization. In a society in which literature had never been respected as an independent profession, Lu Xun was taking a considerable risk of becoming a failure like his father, a disillusioned scholar who had been neither useful nor influential in his society. It can be argued that literature may be even less efficient than education as a way to "change the spirit" of a nation. But in Lu Xun's mind, literature appeared as the most effective way to probe the human spirit and national character — areas where medical science clearly had not given satisfactory solutions. From the very beginning, Lu Xun's conception of literature carried with it the legacies of his "spiritual" experience, as well as his sense of nationalism.

The Theory and Practice of Literature

Although Lu Xun had decided to give up medicine, science was still very much on his mind after he left Sendai for Tokyo. His intellectual transition from science to literature was not as easy and clear-cut as he later described it. His 1907 essays indicate a continuing inner struggle between science and literature. He tried frantically to justify his decision, precisely because he still doubted its validity.

Following the direction of his earlier writings on science, Lu Xun wrote in 1907 an essay titled "Renzhi lishi" (The history of man), which traced the development of Western science from Thales through Cuvier and Lamarck to Darwin and Haeckel in an evolutionary framework. But in three subsequent essays, he began to question an unreserved faith in science.

In "Kexue shi jiaopian" (Lessons from the history of science), he warned against stressing science at the expense of moral, aesthetic, and religious values. World history, he argued, "does not march in a straight line, but twists and turns like a spiral; it ebbs and flows in successively big and small waves in a myriad ways." Both spiritual and material values have their proper function in human history. Thus, to consider only economic wealth and military power was to him merely "to be dazzled by the things at hand and refuse to go into the essence."[75] He stressed the importance of the spiritual ideals in scientific discoveries as well as the practical aspects. "Scientific discovery has often been motivated by powers beyond science. In other words, we can say that it is moved by nonscientific ideals." He concluded that mankind needed not only Newton but Shakespeare, not only Boyle but Raphael, not only Kant but Beethoven — "if you have Darwin, you must have Carlyle."[76]

179

Such forced didacticism seems to betray Lu Xun's own intellectual struggle. Having conducted an internal debate between art and science, he seemed finally to emerge somewhat in favor of the arts over the sciences. In his next essay, "Wenhua pianzhi lun" (On extremities in cultural development), his idealistic tendencies became abundantly clear and were framed mostly in intellectual elitism. He wrote that "cultures developed by modifying past practice to meet new needs. In the process deficiencies in the old were exaggerated and the pendulum swung to the opposite extreme." The legacy of the nineteenth century — material progress and majority rule — had come to a point where it required correcting: "Man was so dazzled by the objective material world that he scarcely cared whether he still retained the subjective inner spirit. The emphasis on the exterior and the abandonment of the interior, the pursuance of the physical and the renunciation of the spiritual accounted for the insatiable material desire with which the world's teeming masses were obsessed."[77]

Since the ignorant masses, obsessed with material desires, "had sunk into mediocrity," only those few "farsighted, combative" individuals who rose above the mundane crowd could react against these excesses. Lu Xun saw an important reaction under way that would bring about a civilization of the twentieth century significantly different from that of the nineteenth. Representative of this new trend were Stirner, Schopenhauer, Kierkegaard, Ibsen, and particularly Nietzsche. They also exemplified a type of "subjectivism" that probed the human spirit. This subjectivist ideal, he further argued, should be differentiated from the earlier eighteenth-century ideal of a harmony between the intellect and the emotions. For him, Hegel embodied the culmination of the intellect, whereas the romantic school of Rousseau and Shaftesbury embodied the supremacy of the emotions. But by the end of the nineteenth century, this ideal of the perfect man with a balanced combination of intellect and emotions could no longer be found. One must pin one's hope with "superhuman willpower," Lu Xun argued, on those fierce, combative, and indefatigable talents that stem from the emotional realm.[78] It is in this context that Lu Xun defined and advocated the Nietzschean concept of the Superman.

However valid Lu Xun's interpretation may be, the article represents a further attempt to justify the area of moral, spiritual, and aesthetic values that had become increasingly dominant in his mind. The juxtaposition of the realms of intellect and emotion is especially revealing because it corresponds to the dichotomy between science and literature that he had drawn at this time. Scientific knowledge was in the intellectual domain and values were in the emotional. Science as the pursuit of objective knowledge had degenerated into crass materialism. Thus, he rejected the trend fashionable among Chinese reformers to adopt only its material aspects. Rebelliously, he advised his compatriots: "If we want to work out a policy for the present, we must examine the past and prepare for the future, discard the material and elevate the spirit, rely on the individual and exclude the mass. When the individual is exalted to develop his full capacity, the country will be strengthened and will arise. Why should we be engrossed in such trivialities as gold, iron, congress, and constitutions?"[79]

In "Moluo shi li shuo" (The power of Mara poetry), Lu Xun went one step further: he openly defended the function of literature in the context of spiritual and aesthetic values. Literature was to nurture the human spirit. Literature had an emotional power to reveal the principles underlying the "subtle mysteries of life" in a way that science could not. He also rejected the "sociological" view in both China and the West that literature must be consonant with conventional morality. On the contrary, he argued, in the same elitist vein, that the practitioners of literature were often geniuses who rebelled against conventional morality and "ran counter to the common disposition" of their contemporaries.[80] They were the poets of "Mara" — a term Lu Xun borrowed from the Indian god of destruction — or Satan. Byron, in his view, was the archetypal Mara poet, who was followed by Shelley, Pushkin, Mickiewicz, Słowacki, and Petöfi. All of them were "strong, uncompromising, sincere, truthful, and scornful of convention. Their powerful utterances brought about a national rebirth, making their countries great in the world." At the end of the essay, Lu Xun asked, "Where are now the warriors of the world of the spirit? Where are those who raise their voices for truth, who will lead us to goodness, beauty, strength, and health? Where are those who utter heartwarming words, who will lead us out of the wilderness? Our homes are gone and the nation is destroyed, yet we have no Jeremiah crying out his last sad song to the world and to posterity."[81]

Lu Xun apparently saw himself as a "warrior of the world of spirit" and cast his lot with literature. "The Power of Mara Poetry" can be read as the first manifesto proclaiming his new role as a writer. It was intended originally to be published, together with the other essays written in 1907, in a new literary magazine called *Xin sheng* or *Vita Nuova* (New life). Borrowed from Dante, this revealing title symbolized Lu Xun's "new life" as a practitioner of literature. Unfortunately, none of the other Chinese students understood this special allusion; some even remarked jokingly that the term meant simply "novice students."[82]

The magazine would have two parts: theoretical articles and translations. A painting entitled *Hope* by the nineteenth-century English painter George Frederick Watts (1817–1904), would be included in the first issue.[83] *New Life* was probably intended to circulate among young intellectuals who were yet to be exposed to a journal devoted exclusively to pure literature. But *New Life* was ahead of its time. Most Chinese students in Japan preferred more practical subjects. Many studied law, political science, physics and chemistry, even police administration, "but no one studied literature or art."[84] There were only four "editors" involved in this literary endeavor: the Zhou brothers (Lu Xun and Zhou Zuoren), their friend Xu Shoushang, and another student, who soon left for England. *New Life* was aborted for lack of capital and support. The first issue never came out, and Lu Xun's essays were published in another provincial student magazine, *Henan* (Honan).[85]

Lu Xun's next project was translating Western fiction. The immediate motive may have simply been money. Translating a story and selling it to a magazine or publisher in China could add some additional income to his meager government scholarship. In the thriving publishing world of Shanghai, there was a growing demand for Western translations.

The Zhou brothers pooled their linguistic skills — in addition to Japanese, Lu Xun and Zhou Zuoren read German and English respectively — and often collaborated in the translations. By the end of 1907 they had finished translating *The World's Desire* by H. Rider Haggard and Andrew Lang. Zhou Zuoren did most of the translation, though Lu Xun helped transcribe the poems in the novel. The work was sold to the Commercial Press for two hundred dollars. Their second collaborative work was a novel about Ivan the Terrible by Aleksey Tolstoy. Zuoren wrote the first draft from its English translation, and Lu Xun then revised it. But the publisher rejected the manuscript because there already was a Chinese version.[86] As a result, the brothers began to explore more obscure works from "exotic countries." Generally, they sought the literature of Russia, Poland, Czechoslovakia, Serbia, Bosnia, Finland, Hungary, Romania, and modern Greece; and less often of Denmark, Norway, and Sweden. Most of these works were retranslations found in German magazines they purchased cheaply at Japanese bookstores. For introductory material they used general texts such as *Impressions of Russia* and *Impressions of Poland* by the Danish author Georg Brandes and *Hungarian Literature; An Historical and Critical Survey* by the Austro-Hungarian author Reich. Lu Xun's discussion of Polish and Hungarian literature in "The Power of Mara Poetry" was mainly drawn from these two books.[87]

These peculiar circumstances partly determined the unusual selection in the two volumes of *Yuwai xiaoshuo ji* (Collection of foreign fiction) published in February and June of 1909. The collection contained sixteen stories, one each representing England, America, France, and Finland; two were taken from Bosnian literature, seven from four Russian writers, and three from a Polish writer, Henryk Sienkiewicz.[88] Three-fourths of the collection was by Russian and eastern European authors.

The most obvious reason for Lu Xun's fondness for Russian and eastern European writers, as the Zhou brothers stated and numerous scholars have often reiterated, was that this literature was the literature of the "oppressed peoples" who displayed "a spirit of militant resistance."[89] But the underlying motive was not necessarily related to political radicalism. Lu Xun's sympathies in this period were by no means inclined toward socialism or Marxism. He was "either unacquainted with or uninterested in the socialist movement and its literary expression in Japan in the first decade of this century," as Harriet Mills has pointed out.[90] Rather, it seems likely that Lu Xun and Zhou Zuoren were trying to join in the general movement for nationalism. A book introducing literature from oppressed nations would naturally elicit echoes among nationalistic Chinese youth, who were the bulk of the reading public.

Another important reason for Lu Xun's choice of foreign writers has to do with his own literary tastes. According to Zhou Zuoren, Japanese translation of Russian literature at the time was not highly developed. The Zhou brothers bought the works of Turgenev, but never translated them. Naturalism was in vogue in Japan, but they merely bought a few works by Flaubert, Maupassant, and Zola, as well as Baudelaire and Verlaine. Japanese literature did not attract Lu Xun's attention, though he liked Natsume Sōseki and Mori Ōgai.[91] Lu Xun's favorite Russian authors were Gogol and Andreyev, whose works subsequently influenced him profoundly. He preferred Gogol's indirect and ironic approaches to reality and Andreyev's psychological symbolism. As Patrick Hanan has suggested, Lu Xun's literary tastes tended to focus on either prerealists or postrealists.[92] Thus, aside from Gogol and

Andreyev, Lu Xun liked Lermontov, Garshin, Sienkiewicz, Petöfi, Neruda, Vrchlický, and Päivärinta,[93] most of whom are either romantics or symbolists and have a generally humanistic tone. He also liked writers of fairy tales — perhaps an extension of his earlier interest in works of fantasy and science fiction. In this genre, his two favorite authors were the Russian Vladimir Korolenko and the Dutch writer Frederik van Eeden, whose book *De Kleine Johannes* (Little John) Lu Xun first learned of from a German magazine and later translated. Interestingly, the work is a fairy tale with a veiled attack on materialism and naturalism.[94]

Lu Xun's preferences for foreign authors were mostly guided by his literary temperament and linguistic background (German rather than English or French). He may also have been motivated by a desire to be up-to-date with the most recent trends on the European continent. By the first decade of the twentieth century, the height of realism and naturalism was over in Europe. Turgenev, Flaubert, and Zola were all passé. In Russia, the most popular writer was Andreyev. Two of the three works translated by Lu Xun for *Collection of Foreign Fiction* were by Andreyev (the third was "The Red Flower" by Garshin). Both of Andreyev's stories are heavily psychological and downright pessimistic; they hardly exude any "spirit of militant resistance." One of them, "The Lie," describes the infidelity of a woman who breaks her promise and goes to another man. Her lover, the narrator, suffers from her enigmatic lies and wants to win her back, "but mendacity is omnipresent and there is no hope." Another longer story, "The Silence," shows how an old couple, whose beloved daughter refuses to communicate with them and commits suicide, are themselves driven by her "silence" to madness and silence.[95] The work is suffused with a depressive atmosphere and a nihilistic mood in sharp contrast to the positive motives that allegedly inspired the translators. Andreyev's works impressed Lu Xun as "mystical and profound"; he detected in them "a blending of impressionism and realism" that reflected "the inner frustrations of the Russian people and the drabness of their lives."[96] The two stories must have appealed to Lu Xun for the simple reason that he thought they were good literature, literature that dealt with the suffering of the human spirit and explored, however pessimistically, the "national character" and "soul" of a different people.

Thus through his essays and translations published in this last period of his stay in Japan, Lu Xun's central conception of literature is fairly clear. By 1907 he had gone beyond Liang Qichao's view that literature is primarily a vehicle for political education. For Lu Xun, literature exemplifies a nation's spiritual essence. It not only gives the most profound reflection of "the ideal quality of human nature," but also the most searching examination of the "national character." It was this essentially cultural-philosophical view of literature that dominated Lu Xun's thinking and inspired his literary activities. Increasingly disgusted with the superficial utilitarianism of his era, he sought a deeper meaning in literature in order to find a diagnosis, if not a cure, for the "spiritual illness" of his people. The psychological undertones of such a "spiritual" inquiry also reflected the results of Lu Xun's own soul-searching in the long process of his identity formation.

In an essay written in 1933, Lu Xun claimed that he "had harbored no intention to elevate fiction to the garden of literature [*wenyuan*] but merely thought of using its power in order to change society."[97] This later rationalization seems to gloss over the important fact that he had wanted decidedly to elevate fiction to "high literature." His cultural-philosophical conception had turned literature itself into a serious intellectual activity more prestigious than "miscellaneous learning," which was his previous avocational interest.

Having established his theory of literature, Lu Xun met only with failure in his literary practice. His projects were less original than the ideas that justified and inspired them. His first project, to publish a literary journal, was not truly unprecedented. In China at the turn of the century, a number of enterprising treaty-port journalists — men like Wu Woyao and Li Boyuan — were rapidly making literary journalism a paying profession. But they did not have Lu Xun's intellectual pretensions; their works were still dictated by the tastes of urban popular culture. Lu Xun apparently modeled his *New Life* magazine after Liang Qichao's *Xin xiaoshuo* (New fiction), which commanded enormous respect and influence in intellectual circles. But perhaps he hoped that it would surpass Liang's journal in its literary quality and depth.

Lu Xun's translation project was one of the earliest instances of translating foreign short stories. The quality of the translation was comparable to Lin Shu's, though the Zhou brothers, knowing some Western languages, were more faithful to the originals than this classical stylist, who had to rely on the help of oral translators. The Zhou brothers had envisioned a systematic effort to cover the literatures of all countries in a multivolume compendium. The project was conceived, in a sense, very much in the *congshu* tradition, although Lu Xun's intentions went beyond the simple desire to translate and collect. In his preface to *Collection of Foreign Fiction*, Lu Xun advised his readers to "read into these inner voices and seek out the abode of their spirit."[98]

The sales of this two-volume translation were dismal. Only twenty-one copies of volume one and twenty copies of volume two were sold in Japan. The sale in China was entrusted to a fabric shop in Shanghai. Only about twenty copies had been sold when four or five years later the shop caught fire and the remaining copies, along with the original type, were lost.[99] The plans for the future volumes had to be abandoned. The failure crushed Lu Xun's literary ambition. For the next ten years he published few translations of Western fiction. It was not until 1918 that he was encouraged to make a third attempt at literary practice — creative — and succeeded brilliantly.

The World of Creative Writing

Lu Xun returned to China in August 1909, thus ending his educational experience in Japan. In the decade following his return, from 1909 to 1918, Lu Xun went into a prolonged depression. The failure of the 1911 revolution, the chaos of warlord politics, and especially the oppressive obscurantism of Yuan Shikai's government combined to inflict a heavy toll on his psyche. But it seems also that he never recovered from the fiasco of his initial literary endeavors in Japan. Of this, he wrote, "Only later did I feel the futility of it all. . . I felt if a man's proposals met with approval, it should encourage him; if they met with opposition, it should make him fight back; but the real tragedy for him was to lift up his voice among the living and meet with no response, neither approval nor opposition, just as if he were left helpless in a boundless desert. So I began to feel lonely."[100]

Although Lu Xun had found the right medium in literature, his literary identity was not created "at the right moment on a sufficiently large scale," as the above passage from his own recollection seems to indicate. While Confucius "stood firm" at the age of thirty, in the sense that he had solidified his identity and internalized his learning, Lu Xun at that age found himself in both external and internal turmoil. He returned briefly to science and taught biology and other subjects at three schools in Hangchow and Shaohsing. In 1912 he was invited by Cai Yuanpei to be a bureau head in the Ministry of Education in Peking to supervise libraries, museums, and galleries. In a revealing way, he also retreated into his past avocational interests: copying tombstone inscriptions, editing works by local Shaohsing notables of the past, collecting materials on early Chinese fiction, and reading Buddhist sutras. All these experiences represented a regression to roles he had already rejected — a science teacher, a bureaucrat, and a traditional scholar. Lu Xun's depression may have been deepened by such regression.

When the literary revolution catapulted him to nationwide fame, he was still burdened with the legacies of his past experience. "Kuangren riji" (Diary of a madman), published in 1918, had not been written on a casual impulse. It signaled an outburst of creative energies accumulated during a long spell of mental questioning and rumination. In a way, Lu Xun doubted with the "madman" the entire cultural heritage of his childhood. In spite of its apparent antitraditional message, the story, in both form and content, yields several clues to Lu Xun's own background. The protagonist, a victim of Chinese tradition, was drawn possibly on a real model, one of Lu Xun's distant cousins who had once suffered from paranoia.[101] But the feverish intensity of his mental state recalls Lu Xun's description of his father on his deathbed. In the beginning of the story, the narrator ceremoniously states that sections of the diary are copied out to "serve as a subject for medical research"[102] — certainly not for doctors of the human body but for spiritual explorers of the human soul. It is a fitting subject that combines Lu Xun's medical background and his literary interest. In its artistic conception, the story owes much to Gogol and Andreyev, Lu Xun's favorite Russian writers in his Japanese period.[103] Thus, Lu Xun's spiritual trials and difficulties had definitely shaped this pioneer piece of modern Chinese literature.

It may be possible to find two sides of Lu Xun's identity as a writer. As a leading intellectual of the May Fourth era he was future-oriented and "totalistic." As a literary man and a man of sentiment he still clung to memories of the past and to past forms. But Lu Xun's long journey to the role of a writer demonstrated that the two "persons" were closely intertwined and interactive. There was a tendency in his childhood years to set aside his literary interests as an avocation. But his intellectual pursuits had already shown those "countertraditional" tendencies that facilitated his departure from the world of Chinese tradition and his transition to Western science. His immersion in science in the Nanking period, reinforced by his reading of social Darwinism, provided a source for a future-oriented intellectual outlook based on evolutionism; it also led to his choice of medicine as a future vocation. But his interests in the spiritual aspects of human life had been present all along. His long period of identity confusion in Japan proved that his preoccupations could not be sufficiently fulfilled by medicine. Literature was an outlet for both his intellectual and psychological needs, but it cost him considerable mental anguish to make the final transition from science to literature. Each point of this transition was marked by a striking degree of tentativeness, coupled with trials and errors. Lu Xun was clearly not a man endowed with a farsighted understanding of his "revolutionary" destiny, as some of his blind worshipers have portrayed him.

Perhaps the most enduring legacy of Lu Xun's long and tortuous journey to literary fame is that he evolved a conception of literature — and his role in it — that was neither strictly utilitarian nor purely "autonomous." Literature, with its cultural and spiritual weight, should not be treated simply as a means of reaching a sociopolitical goal; nor should it represent a self-contained artistic world unrelated to the author and his society. In other words, creative writing to Lu Xun did not mean that his art was over and above everything else; nor did it imply that his literary role was subsidiary to his ideological convictions. Lu Xun was truly an "intellectual writer." His subsequent writings can be taken as evidence of his theory in practice, for they reflect his persistent exploring of a kind of collective consciousness to which he could relate his own personal experience. Thus, he freely resorted to symbols, character archetypes, capsule statements filled with metaphorical layers of meaning, and impressionistic descriptions filled with psychological insights. And he continued to respond to the type of foreign literature that was at once "realistic" and "symbolic."

Perhaps the eventual success of Lu Xun's works in China can be taken as a tribute to a supreme act of creative reenactment that merged his personal "curse" with the curse of a nation and made his cultural-spiritual inquiries meaningful to his fellow countrymen in their stage of history. For, as Erikson writes, "the mark of a creative re-enactment of a curse is that the joint experience of it all becomes a liberating event for each member of an awe-stricken audience."[104]

9.

Lu Xun: Literature and Revolution — From Mara to Marx

Harriet C. Mills

At two-thirty on the afternoon of October 22, 1936, a procession ten thousand strong left the International Funeral Parlor in the International Settlement of Shanghai to escort Lu Xun to his grave in the Chinese city. Their banners hailed "the soul of China," whose "pen was mightier than the sword." In the settlement, mounted Sikh policemen and armed patrolmen lined the route of march, which authorities had shortened for fear of possible leftist demonstrations. In the Chinese city, Chinese policemen with fixed bayonets stood guard. It was a guard mounted not in honor but in fear. It was not just Lu Xun the writer but Lu Xun the anguished patriot who was being interred — the Lu Xun who in his later years had shifted his hopes for China from the Guomindang at Nanking to the Communist opposition.

The Making of the Man

Politics did not concern the young Lu Xun.[1] The Zhous of Shaohsing — merchants, gentry, and officials — were basically conservative, and Lu Xun received a traditional education. But his real interest lay in art, in Tang and Ming fiction, in treatises on flora, fauna, and his native Shaohsing.[2] The indignities he felt as a poor relation shunted among relatives in the countryside during a crisis at home, and the suspicions he harbored of incompetence by the Chinese doctors treating his dying father disturbed him more than any ferment for political change. He grew up, he recalled, totally oblivious to the distinction between Manchu and Chinese.[3]

Lu Xun's modern schooling, first at the Naval Academy and then at the School of Mining and Railways in Nanking, began in May 1898, just a few months before the short-lived Hundred-Day Reform. Two years later, the Boxer Rebellion provoked foreign intervention and protests led by revolutionary intellectuals against the dynasty. Instead of joining these movements, Lu Xun read arguments for reform in Liang Qichao's *Shiwu bao* (Current affairs), which featured translations of Western literature as well as discussions of science. His decision to study medicine in Japan was a reaction to his reading, which had convinced him that Japan successfully modernized partly because of adopting Western medicine; he wanted China to modernize and be strong. If war came, he would serve as an army doctor, but he saw no role for himself as reformer beyond that.[4]

He arrived in Japan in the spring of 1902, and the sharp contrast between backward China and progressive Japan impressed on him the urgency of change at home.[5] But he ignored student political action groups in Tokyo and studied the intellectual heritage of the West, particularly the theory of evolution and social Darwinism he had recently met in Yan Fu's translation of Huxley. Struggle, adaptation, defeat, and survival — these were the basic laws of the natural and human world. Knowledge, particularly of science, Lu Xun felt, was the key to this adaptation and survival.

So he introduced his countrymen to the wonders of radium in an essay paraphrased from a Japanese source.[6] Drawing on his training at the Nanking School of Mining and Railways, he prepared *Zhongguo dizhi lüe lun* (Outline of Chinese geology)[7] and *Zhongguo kuangchan zhi* (China's mineral resources).[8] To these he appended strong pleas that China exploit her own resources rather than allow others to enrich themselves at her expense.

In Nanking, Lu Xun had led a somewhat bifurcated intellectual existence. His early interests in fiction, art, and other aspects of his native tradition persisted, but these private delights were inconsonant with the modern knowledge he was acquiring. The two worlds remained quite separate for him. But in Tokyo, a critical, if incomplete, fusion occurred. He had been in Tokyo only a few months when Liang Qichao's famous essay on the political utility of fiction appeared. This theory legitimized Lu Xun's old love of fiction, for it convinced him that the knowledge which China needed to survive could be imparted through fiction. And so, in 1903, he began with translations of science fiction, particularly that by Jules Verne. "Stupid yellow race," Lu Xun cried in a preface, "wake up!"[9]

But to survive, China must understand not only science but also the history that had produced the ravages of modern imperialism. The more he read in Western intellectual and political history, the more complex and, in a sense, the more hopeless the problem of China seemed. China must not only become informed but she must also be willing to absorb that knowledge and change. By 1906, medicine, at best a technical remedy for the human body, had become too limited for him and lost its appeal. He dropped out of medical school and returned to Tokyo to press his fight for Chinese rejuvenation in terms that were personally more congenial and intellectually more pertinent.

Back in Tokyo, he again had opportunities to ally himself with revolutionary fellow provincials like Zhang Binglin and the future martyrs, Qiu Jin and Xu Xilin, and organizations such as the Chekiang-based Restoration Society that were directly involved in political activities.[10] But Lu Xun generally remained aloof. His prodigious energies in his final Tokyo years (1906–1909) were devoted almost exclusively to trying to modernize the mind of China. He ignored the details of political systems and strategies. Instead, he read more widely than before in the background of Western intellectual and cultural history and in translations of Western literature, particularly works of the "oppressed peoples" of eastern Europe, whose predicament was reminiscent of China's.[11] He became convinced that poetry was as powerful an agent for reform as fiction. He spelled out his message for his countrymen in a series of essays, supplemented by a group of translated stories. He lectured his compatriots on the long, intricate history of science, and then on the physical development of man. He argued that including man and monkey in a common evolutionary scheme was neither cause for shame nor grounds for rejecting modern science. He valiantly attempted to explain the scientific perspective to a nonscientific readership, for he deeply believed that China, to survive, must be at home with science. He also expounded on questions affecting the strengthening and rejuvenation of China.[12]

First and foremost, Lu Xun vested his hope for salvation in the superior man. He carefully explained that this philosophy of "individualism" was not a program for selfish indulgence but a philosophy to free the creative potential of men like Stirner, Schopenhauer, Kierkegaard, Ibsen, and especially Nietzsche. To hamper the free development of such genius spelled disaster, because these rebellious, dissatisfied, and searching minds not only hastened the demolition of the past's outmoded processes but also pointed the way forward to new stages in man's ever-evolving struggle. Such men were at once great destroyers and great bringers of light. What was true in intellectual and philosophical terms was also true for literature. He called on China to produce Mara poets, poets of destruction and rebellion in the mold of Lakidisa of ancient India, of nineteenth-century figures like Lermontov and Pushkin in Russia, Arndt and Kerner in Germany, Petöfi in Hungary, Mickiewicz in Poland, and especially Byron. Such men spoke to the souls of their people. They inspired them, voiced their yearnings for progress, dignity, and independence, and so were powerful forces in various struggles for national liberation. What he feared most was that these creative individuals, these supermen or geniuses, would be crushed under what he called "the tyranny of millions of unreliable rascals."[13] Had not China's own Qu Yuan been rejected? Where now were her warriors of the spirit? Where, he asked, "are those who raise their voices for truth, who will lead us to goodness, beauty, strength, and health? Where are those who utter heartwarming words, who will lead us out of the wilderness? Our homes are gone and the nation is destroyed, yet we have no Jeremiah crying out his last sad song to the world and to posterity."[14]

Second, Lu Xun was no democrat during this period. However beautiful any ideal of social leveling and equality might be, to him it represented a lowering of standards, a sacrifice of brilliant individuals to the mediocrity of the masses. He wrote: "Right and wrong cannot be decided by the people; to let them decide would have no good result. National affairs cannot be decided by the people; to do so would not achieve peace and security. Only when the superman appears in the world will peace come and if not that, then at least a genius."[15] For him the "common masses" represented a mindless pressure for conformity that stifled men of genius or conscience. To entrust power to the masses would be to establish a regime more oppressive than that of the tyrants of old. In the past, he pointed out, victims of oppression could appeal to the masses, who on occasion would revolt against a dictator. But there could be no appeal from a government of the masses.

This was unquestionably his basic position on the dynamics of history. At the same time, an unfinished essay breaks down the masses in China into ruling and ruled, revealing a different perspective. Within this framework, his sympathy is clearly with the ruled peasantry, not with the ruling gentry. The peasant masses were long-suffering and hardworking people who could catch only a few moments of communal relaxation a year. Yet it was they — not the gentry — who kept alive appreciation of the power and beauty of nature. What others called folk superstition Lu Xun praised as an imaginative attempt by the untutored to explain observable natural phenomena. Their structure of belief, he contended, represented "the aspirations of people anxious to get beyond this limited and relative world to the world of the unlimited and absolute."[16] Men, he continued, must have something to rely on; religion — even folk religion — cannot be dispensed with.

Third, Lu Xun held a pendulum theory of political and cultural development. Societies change relentlessly through time; thus, there was no Golden Age to recapture. Every age was both old and new, a continuation and an evolution. As the pendulum swung between emphasis on the material and the spiritual, between autocracy and liberty, exaggerations occurred. Nineteenth-century Western thought was both a product of and a reaction to the French and Industrial revolutions. The Renaissance, the Reformation, and the French Revolution were all part of one long struggle on the political front against medieval theocracy and the divine right of kings. As the struggle went on, freedom of thought began to increase, and intellectual speculation and scientific inquiry flourished. The cry for liberty and equality came as a necessary reaction to the earlier tyranny of the autocrats. But these goals were in turn pursued, after the French Revolution, to the dangerous extreme of democracy, where all rights were held to rest in the people, whom as we have seen, he did not consider capable of intelligent decisions.

The Industrial Revolution had brought unprecedented prosperity as well as unbounded faith in materialism, but it had also unleashed forces that threatened to stifle the spiritual and artistic creativity of man that had nurtured that revolution. By the end of the nineteenth century, he asserted, "materialism's evil consequences had already become evident . . . mind and spirit progressively deteriorated; aims and taste degenerated into vulgarity."[17] Societies withered as they lost interest in the spiritual and became obsessed with the material; progress ceased. If the material alone is considered the foundation of civilization, Lu Xun said, "then does that really mean that an exhibit of machinery and a display of foodstuffs would suffice to conquer the world? If it is said that only the majority can determine right and wrong, then does that mean that a man living in a band of monkeys should live in trees and subsist on nuts? Even women and children would say no to this."[18]

What, then, was his prescription for China? For China to survive in the modern world, he felt that "of first importance is the establishment of man, and after man is established all things shall rise. We must honor the individual and free the spirit. If this is not done, China will wither and die in a generation. In the past China was materialistic and distrustful of genius . . . and so destroyed it with materialism and imprisoned it with mob rule. China's collapse was thereby hastened."[19]

Further, China must "examine the past and prepare for the future, discard the material and elevate the spirit, rely on the individual and exclude the mass . . . then the country will be strengthened and arise. Why should we be engrossed in such trivialities as gold, iron, congresses, and constitutions?"[20] By implication he was criticizing not only the Kang-Liang constitutional monarchists but also the self-strengtheners and the republicans as well. In his view, all of these overemphasized the material and underemphasized the creative individual and spiritual values. Even if the proponents of constitutions and congresses were sincere, he thought them ignorant, their recommendations ill-founded, and their approach as stupid as that of the chronic invalid who relies on prayer rather than the proper medicine. He opposed grafting new military and industrial techniques onto an essentially traditional society. Advocates of military reform, like those of commercial and industrial expansion, were, he suspected, more interested in what they might gain than in how China might benefit. He also attacked local ruling groups who, while vaunting a pseudo-modernity, were trying to suppress peasant superstitions as one cause of China's weakness. Such characters, Lu Xun cried, forget that it is the rulers who have been the great destroyers in Chinese history, not the ordinary peasants. "Get rid of the gentry," he railed. "Superstition can stay."[21]

In some very moving passages, he rejects the thinking that identified patriotism or love of country with glorification of military force rather than with the accomplishments of peace. Wistfully, he mentions Tolstoy's doctrine of passive noncooperation. He urges his countrymen to sympathize with rather than criticize countries like Poland and India which, like China, have been invaded by the militarily powerful. He calls on his homeland to become strong enough to defend herself but not to invade others. If she has strength to spare, let her help others as Byron helped Greece and the Pole Joseph Bem did Hungary. "But alas," he concluded, "although China is one of the countries that has been invaded, she has not awakened."[22]

Never again does Lu Xun engage in such systematic or sustained exposition of his intellectual and political beliefs. Clearly, the major elements of his later thought are already evident: (1) a preoccupation with national survival; (2) a faith in evolution; (3) a conviction of the primacy of the intellectual and spiritual over the material; (4) a philosophy of the political utility of literature; and (5) an awareness, as yet unfocused and unclarified, of class forces in society.

However persuasively Lu Xun may have expressed himself, however prophetic and significant his words may appear today, at the time, his efforts failed to convince. The essays attracted little attention and the magazine *Xin sheng* (*Vita Nuova* or New life), the dream of Lu Xun, his brother, and two friends, in which these treatises were to have appeared, never materialized. Two volumes of short stories from "small and oppressed peoples" that he and his brother translated sold less than two dozen copies.

The New Republic and *New Youth*

In Japan, Lu Xun was almost convinced that the right poetry and the right fiction could influence society enough to affect the very terms of the social struggle. In the special, highly charged atmosphere of Tokyo, it was easy for students to underestimate the vast intractableness of China. Yet after his return to China in 1909, he was virtually silent for almost a decade, sobered perhaps by a fresh exposure to her enormous problems. The overthrow of the Manchus in the fall of 1911 brought momentary hope. Significantly, his only "modern" literary effort of the 1909–1918 period, the short story "Huai jiu" (Looking to the past), which was international in form but classical in language, was written within a few months of this event.[23] But despite the enthusiasm with which he welcomed the revolution, his attempts to deal — at the request of his fellow townsmen — with the revolutionary troops of Wang Jinfa occupying Shaohsing proved frustrating. Within a few weeks, Lu Xun had left his hometown for good, convinced that only the surface trappings had changed.[24] He became a bureaucrat in the new Ministry of Education in Peking, specializing in art and popular education.

Like many other former advocates of reform in the next half-dozen years of incessant political chaos, Lu Xun returned to his early scholarly interests in the literary and artistic heritage of the homeland he wanted to preserve, stopping only rarely to correct or publish translations sent by his brother, Zhou Zuoren. Lu Xun had not rejected the theories of his Japan years, but evolution was a slow process.

As the movement for intellectual and social reform gathered momentum around Beida and *Xin qingnian* (New youth) in late 1917, Lu Xun became skeptical about its possible success.[25] He still believed in literature, but it was no longer the magic key to salvation. China was a black vat, an iron house in which her people were suffocating to death. Why should he try to awaken the dying when he had no help to offer, when all he knew was that "China was closer to ruin than to progress."[26] For eight months, he resisted all of his friends' efforts to involve him; but finally, early in 1918, he reluctantly joined them.

At the time, his actual contribution to this first cultural revolution was minor.[27] During the four years of the *New Youth*–May Fourth period, except for occasional appearances at planning sessions for *New Youth*, Lu Xun stood aside from the turbulent intellectual discussions and all associated social and political activities. He also wrote little. What he referred to as his "commissioned writing"[28] was written in support of his friends and consisted of just nine stories, two essays, five short poems, a few translations, and less than a page a week of miscellaneous reflections. The stories were jotted down in a night or two; the rest flowed quickly. In Japan, his message had been fresh and original, now he echoed his friends. That his stories and essays have endured where much that had greater impact at the time has been forgotten does not contradict Lu Xun's relative obscurity in those years. He wrote, as he had done in Japan, under a variety of pen names. Few outside his closest associates at Beida knew what he, Zhou Shuren, was actually writing. His brother, Zhou Zuoren was, in those years, the better-known writer.

It was Lu Xun's fiction, that is, the two-dozen-odd narrative sketches now printed in *Nahan* (A call to arms) and *Panghuang* (Hesitation), that gained the widest audience. They were mature models of a new form, and they set a standard probably not matched to this day. Although his first vernacular effort, "Kuangren riji" (Diary of a madman), indicts traditional Chinese society as a grand cannibal feast, the stories that followed are intensely personal, often gently satirical looks at the "way we were." They are caring and sad. They show what is wrong, but they do not goad or prod the reader, for Lu Xun had no program for action. He was no Dickens. The popularity of his work attests to the accuracy of his vision.

Why then did he stop writing fiction after 1926? Writing fiction, even "Diary of a Madman," was for Lu Xun an intimate, almost poetic experience through which to express some mood, some anger, some subtle picture. But apparently he could not use it to depict the reality of something external to him or his experience — to argue a case, to analyze a problem, or even to recapture history. From the mid-1920s to the mid-1930s his work on Yang Guifei, his proposed novel on several generations of a Chinese family in transition from traditional to modern society as well as a novel on the guerrilla regions, which his

Communist contacts urged upon him, all came to naught.[29] His slim volume *Gu shi xin bian* (Old stories retold) does not contradict this analysis. These were not *his* stories, but stories with which he was playing.[30] He called them facetious and used them as allegories to attack miscellaneous targets, frivolous and serious. His fiction never carried the brunt of his attack on Chinese society, although some hated features were reflected in it. After the mid-1920s, as his attack on Chinese society became less personal and more concerned with general principles, his storytelling died a natural, if regrettable, death. Unmatched as his stories are, it was the satiric essay, which he began to develop in these years, that increasingly over the next two decades expressed his strongest criticism.

In the *New Youth* period, he did not discuss the "big" political issues before China; his range was very narrow. There are more references to Yuan Shikai and the European war than to current Chinese developments. Publicly, he ignored the May Fourth movement. He stuck to what he called "minor questions."[31] He attacked the traditional family system and argued hard for women's rights and against the double standard of chastity. He struck at those who upheld the "national essence" (*guo cui*) and opposed the introduction of the vernacular as a literary medium. He ridiculed the advocates of spiritualism and the occult, while he praised science and the scientific spirit. Finally, his attack on the Chinese character came down hard on what he termed China's proneness to conceit and compromise and her steely resistance to change. He also deplored her national insensitivity to the rights of others. By what right, he asked, did China complain that Japan had swallowed up "*our* tributary, Korea?"[32]

But when it came to a blueprint for change, he was even less explicit than he had been in Japan and had nothing but rhetoric to offer: the more that is destroyed, the more mankind progresses; learn the difference between cannot and will not; better to worship Darwin and Ibsen than Confucius and Guan Yu. He still believed in evolution, in national self-criticism, in a future for mankind, even though he could not tell what it would be or how to reach it. To avoid discouraging the optimism of his young associates, he hid his own sense of futility.[33] His private views had modified significantly. For him, evolution no longer guaranteed China's national survival, only that of mankind as a whole. If China as a nation continued to exist, it would prove she had adapted; if not, she was not fit to survive.[34] Her old order was bound to collapse. Through reform and the acceptance of new ideas, she could minimize the impact of the disruption, but he thought such a positive response unlikely. He prophesied her future would be a "big mess." Yet he was not pessimistic: with work and determination China might well emerge among the survivors of the human race.[35] His basic prescription remained what it had been in Japan: knowledge, evolution, and science, but his weapon was new.

In place of the ponderous if passionate treatises he produced in Japan, Lu Xun had now moved to the very short, very tart, quick satirical jab. His reasons are clear. "The object of satire," he wrote years later, "is society, and so long as society does not change . . . satire will remain."[36] His satiric method consisted of capturing and exposing the "irrational, ridiculous, disgusting, or even detestable" element in a situation so commonplace that its preposterousness is completely overlooked and it no longer causes surprise. Satire, he said, must be true. For example, he wrote:

> It is very common for a young man in a Western suit to worship Buddha and even more common for a moralist to lose his temper . . . But if Satire takes photographs at this juncture of the young man kowtowing with his bottom in the air and the moralist scowling, these not only offend the eyes of those who see them but their own eyes as well, and such pictures are detrimental to their lofty schemes to advocate science or Confucian morality . . . But it is the art of satire to concern itself deliberately with such matters, bringing out their essence, even with exaggeration.[37]

He explained the bitter humor that results. "Tragedy," he contended, "shows how what is worthwhile in life is shattered, comedy shows how what is worthless is torn to pieces, and satire is a simplified form of comedy."[38] Elsewhere, he suggested that satire was like photography. A photographer could use a box camera to take the distant eroded hill or he could use an electronic microscope to probe infection close at hand. The satirist reveals what is; the cure he leaves to others. Satire can move from surface to core with flexibility and perfect focus. It can be cool or angry; it can involve much or little of the artist. It can raise questions it does not have to answer. If those questions were posed merely to convince readers that there are no answers and that nothing is worth doing in the world, then such a writer is a cynic, not a satirist. The line between heartless mockery and caring satire, he once observed, is paper thin. The aim of the satirist is positive. Lu Xun's doubts made him skeptical of immediate progress, but not a cynic, and satire could accommodate skepticism. It was these satirical essays that Chen Duxiu called Lu Xun's real contribution to *New Youth*.[39] Over the years they became his dreadful weapon of attack.

The Road to Involvement

The breakup of *New Youth* and the dispersal of the May Fourth forces together with the continuing political chaos depressed Lu Xun. China, he wrote in early 1922, had "no flowers, no poetry, no light, no warmth, no interests, not even any curiosity."[40] In 1923, even his family fell apart. At the end of that year, he predicted that China would never budge unless whipped with some enormous whip. But where the blow would come from and whether it be for good or ill he did not know.

The gloom affected all aspects of his work. His commentary is sparser, narrower in scope, and more petty in spirit than it had been earlier. What little there is consists largely of sneers at aspects of the literary scene and were ad hominem. Attacks on the concept of national essence become attacks on the editors of *Xueheng* (Critical review). Nowhere does he write of reform per se. Although the pace of his storytelling picks up a bit, its mood remains the same. This continuing sense of frustration shaped his translations. With no solutions of his own to propose, he spoke indirectly through others, particularly Russians and Japanese, who had faced problems of reform. He translated Artsybashev's *Worker Shevyryov* and the moral fables of Eroshenko, hoping that they would arouse hatred for despotic authority in his Chinese compatriots.[41]

By the fall of 1924, the horrors of civil war, inflation, floods, and refugees in the society around him, and a chilling desperation of the spirit within, became almost unbearable. Evolution now seemed too slow, and "he didn't much believe in it anymore."[42] Change required human effort. Although he had no program, he must do something. Had not his beloved Petöfi sung that despair, like hope, was but vanity?

The two years from this decision for action until August 1926, when he left Peking as a refugee, were critical in Lu Xun's development as a man and writer. He came to understand the importance of action and his practical radicalization began. To understand why, we must know something of the current warlord rivalries and the crisis at the Women's Normal College, where Lu Xun was a part-time instructor. These final years in Peking divide logically into two periods; both are extraordinarily productive. In the first, which ran between September 1924 and May 1925, he wrote more commentary than he had in the six and a half years since he first began in *New Youth*. The second fifteen months, from May 1925 on, were more productive than any comparable period in his life. But the emphasis in content and style is different, reflecting his shifting priorities. As the range of his activity and comment expanded, the solitary textual research into traditional literature, the primary focus of his intellectual effort since his return from Japan, declined. But behind this facade of frenetic activity, doubts and anguish persisted.

At the beginning of the first period, in late October 1924, the "Christian" warlord General Feng Yuxiang took Peking and forced the last Qing emperor from the imperial palace. He reluctantly agreed to a compromise arrangement with his rival, the Manchurian warlord Zhang Zuolin, to install an old Yuan Shikai supporter, Duan Qirui, as premier. It was an uneasy balance in which the real conflict between the more liberal Feng and the more conservative Duan-Zhang forces made for instability. The revolutionary government at Canton under Sun Yat-sen's Guomindang party, now supported by Soviet Russia, provided a rival center of power. In an unsuccessful attempt to negotiate a reunification between north and south, Sun came to Peking in December 1924. After his death there in early March, the tension between Zhang Zuolin's group and Feng Yuxiang surfaced again in a complicated struggle that lasted over a year. Meanwhile, on May 30, 1925, came the famous Shanghai incident, which set off waves of anti-imperialist sentiment in north and south.

Lu Xun expressed his reaction to all this in ways that were newer in style than in content. The highly complex and often obscure symbolism of the prose poem or poetic narration in *Yecao* (Wild grass) was well suited to projecting his very personal agony as he tried to come to grips with the society about him. But this style was short-lived. A second form, which persisted longer than the first but never became a major component in his work, was the informal, personal essay style of pieces like "Leifengtade diaodao" (The collapse of the Leifeng pagoda), in which discussions of Chinese conditions blend with talk about himself.

Although Lu Xun had decided by now that he must do something to nudge the slow pace of evolution, what he actually said in the final months of 1924 was largely a restatement of old themes. China was still a cannibal society, a vast hierarchy of repression where everyone had someone below to suppress. He was still gloomy about the Chinese national character. What else, he asked grimly, could explain how with " 'vast territory, abundant resources, and a great population' — with such excellent material, [we are] able only to go round and round?" He had no new remedies, but there is a new passion as he repeats his old reliance on knowledge or his now tempered enthusiasm for evolution. His hopes for change were still with the young. However slow the relentless progress of evolution, youth was the future. He called on his old gods, "Rousseau, Stirner, Nietzsche, Tolstoy, or Ibsen," who dared tear down that they might build, but he warned that destruction might not bring construction.[43]

In the winter of 1924–1925, Lu Xun began to take veiled note of current political events. In February 1925, as the fruitless negotiations for unity between north and south China dragged on, he wrote:

> I think that perhaps my nerves are cracking. Otherwise it it too frightening.
> I feel as if for a long time there had been no Republic of China. I feel that before the revolution, I was a slave. Not long after the revolution I was cheated by the slaves and became their slave.
> I feel there are many citizens of the republic who are enemies of the republic.
> I feel that everything must be done over . . .
> I feel that the wellsprings of the republic have already been lost although it has been only fourteen years.[44]

With the death of Sun Yat-sen on March 12, 1925, the Duan government in Peking moved swiftly to close pro-Sun newspapers and generally to restrict freedom of speech. On March 20, in a tribute to the fallen leader, Lu Xun angrily compared these small-minded politicians buzzing so greedily over the spoils to flies: "Buzz off, flies! You may have wings and you may be able to hum, but you will never surpass a fighter, you insects."[45] He cursed his luck at having been born in the wrong place at the wrong time and being forced to live under a "tyranny of fools." The Chinese, he concluded, had never been rated as men, "but at best only as slaves and this is still true today. Indeed, on many occasions we were worse off than slaves."[46] In some ways, Lu Xun had changed greatly. He had begun to talk, however symbolically, about selected current national events in which as a citizen he had a stake but in which he was not directly involved. His response, however, was still more emotional than prescriptive.

In the early weeks of May 1925, this changed. A dispute at the Women's Normal College, where he had been teaching part-time for several years, flared up. Lu Xun joined the fight, which though involved with principle, was basically a personal battle against personal adversaries for very personal goals. In the protracted struggle during the rest of 1925 and the opening days of 1926, Lu Xun supported a student-faculty faction (including his student and future wife, Xu Guangping) that opposed a conservative principal appointed and backed by the Minister of Education of the Peking government. The school was but one of the trouble spots in higher education in Peking at the time, but largely through Lu Xun's involvement, it became a symbol. As tension increased with the expulsion of student leaders in May and violent police attacks on the school and its attempted dissolution in August, Lu Xun became more and more critical of the Minister of Education, Zhang Shizhao, and those he viewed as Zhang's supporters. For this, Lu Xun was suspended for several months from his ministry job in 1925, to be reinstated only as the result of his legal challenge. In the end, when the school survived and a new principal had been appointed, Lu Xun finally resigned his teaching post there. In April 1926 he was listed among fifty dangerous radicals to be arrested. Not only had he criticized the government's educational administration but he had also bitterly protested the March 18, 1926, massacre of students demonstrating against any government concessions to heavy Japanese pressure. On what Lu Xun called "the darkest day since the founding of the Republic,"[47] one of his own students from the Normal College had been killed. From mid-April until early May, he went into hiding. In August, he left Peking for good to teach at Amoy University at the invitation of his old colleague, Lin Yutang.

Lu Xun wrote more on the Normal College and associated events than on any other topic in his life; nothing else so reflected concerns in his personal situation. His approach throughout was personal, his spirit, peevish, his temper, short, and his goals, opponents, and style, limited, but of far-reaching impact. Instead of illuminating the underlying issue of the confrontation between a dictatorial warlord government and a segment of the intellectual community, his pettiness narrowed the scope to the single case of the Women's Normal College. He was more anxious to destroy his antagonists as individuals than as types. Throughout, he was more polemicist than satirist. Polemicists, he wrote later, should be able to "wound or kill . . . without degrading themselves," content to pour out their emotion in battle yet able to reason and "stop at ridicule or at heated denunciation."[48] Satire was positive, polemics were negative. In this instance, Lu Xun came perilously close to polemics. Today few bother with the details of this complicated episode.

For all its pettiness, this dispute had at least three important results. First, through this confrontation with the education minister, Zhang Shizhao, Chen Yuan, professor of English at Beida, and other of Zhang's supporters, Lu Xun emerged before a segment of Chinese student readers of magazines like *Yusi* (Thread of talk) as a champion of their rights. Although his motivation was personal and limited, the wit he brought to it, together with the general rhetoric of concern for China that continued to permeate his writing, made the Normal College their school and the creator of A Q their spokesman and hero. Second, the battle crystallized for Lu Xun his disdain of the vaunted Anglo-Saxon code of objectivity, "fair play," and liberalism so touted by Chen Yuan and his British- and American-trained "gentlemen" associates. Was not Zhang, an old revolutionary turned reactionary, an Edinburgh graduate? And what had the University of London really taught Chen Yuan about "fair play"? Lu Xun's dissatisfaction with this group carried over a few years later to Chen Yuan's spiritual heirs in the Crescent Moon group. Lu Xun never felt comfortable with this tradition; he translated virtually nothing from it and did not cultivate its representatives in China. Third, in the course of this controversy, Lu Xun developed three new styles. One was a diary form that mixed trivia with acute observations on Chinese society past and present. Another was a reminiscent essay on his childhood and school days, into which he worked bitter references to the "gentlemen" of the *Xiandai pinglun* (Modern review). The third and most important was a sort of verbal sparring, where Lu Xun would gleefully seize upon some hapless word of an opponent, like Chen, and then twist it. Chen, as Lu Xun's chief target, would try to retaliate but with less effect. Lu Xun would then, once again, almost strangle Chen with a clever net woven of Chen's own verbiage, making him look pitifully stupid. This technique later developed into one of Lu Xun's most feared weapons, which he used frequently and to better purpose.

Lu Xun's advance toward radicalism, which was so strongly influenced by the Normal College affair and the bloody massacres of 1926, shows up in three other areas. First, he comments more directly than before on other events, from the May Thirtieth Incident of 1925 to the chaos surrounding the change of government between warlord factions in Peking in mid-1926.[49] His remarks reflect both deep anger and cool perspective. He cursed both the privileges of British imperialism in China and the perpetrators of the March 1926 massacre. But, he contended, to criticize British brutality without condemning the Chinese equivalent was blind. Second, he became increasingly involved with the pro-Guomindang, antiwarlord publishing world, a fact that cannot be explained away simply by his personal ties to some of the editors. Finally, Lu Xun shows a renewed interest in Soviet Russia and Russian literature. For several years there had been increasingly friendly interest in the Soviet Union among many Chinese intellectuals. For them, the 1919 Karakhan declaration renouncing all special czarist privileges in China contrasted sharply with the continuing defense of extraterritoriality and other privileges by the Western imperialist powers. Sun's open welcome of Russian assistance for his revolutionary government at Canton — to which much of China's youth looked for national salvation — was well known even in rival areas under warlord control. Peking newspapers carried dispatches and travel accounts from the Soviet Union. Some of the first students sent there to study were back by 1924, when Lu Xun began to buy books on Marxism, proletarian cultural theory, and literary developments in the Soviet Union. He read Trotsky, Blok, and Radek among others. Between the spring of 1925 and his departure from Peking the next summer, Lu Xun expressed his growing interest in Russia largely through prefaces and postfaces to translations done by some young friends of his in the Weiming she (Unnamed Society). Launched with capital contributed half by Lu Xun and half by his student associates, this society made a major contribution to the development of modern Chinese literature in the next five years, particularly through two book series edited by Lu Xun. Competency in things Russian distinguished the group; two of its five chief members had already returned from Russia, and two others were students of the language. Examination of Lu Xun's comments on the various volumes published by the group show that by the time he left Peking, he had a sketchy but sympathetic knowledge of recent developments in Soviet literature and that he was already thinking about the problem of the bourgeois reformer in a time of revolution.

What did Lu Xun have to say about his general philosophy of literature in this, his new era of involvement? Basically, little had changed. Literature was still for him an instrument of reform: "The world is changing from day to day; it is high time for our writers to take off their masks, look frankly, keenly, and boldly at life, and write about real flesh and blood. It is high time for a brand new arena for literature, high time for some bold fighters to charge headlong into battle!"[50] In addition, Lu Xun still found literature important in transmitting foreign ideas needed for reform, although he did not exaggerate its potential. "Everything is dark in China! No one can do anything." The chances for and against national survival were about equal. "If [we] really want to live on," he wrote, "[we] must dare to speak, laugh, cry, rage at, revile, fight, and defeat this accursed age in this accursed place!"[51] No matter how great the literature that followed, it would fade together with the problems that produced it.[52] Finally, Lu Xun took very seriously his conviction that the older writer was obligated to develop new talent. In addition to the Unnamed Society, Lu Xun, with some of his young student friends, in late April 1925 launched the *Mangyuan* (Wilderness), which he hoped would "bring forth new critics so that after my tongue is cut loose, there will be people to continue to speak, to tear away the false masks of our old society." As for his own work, he claimed that he wrote to make his enemies uncomfortable, and he preserved his writings as evidence of that struggle. Critical as he might be of others, he was even more critical of himself, he insisted. "Balanced and impartial talk," he contended, was the "equivalent, in fact, to not writing at all."[53]

To conclude from this review of these years of initial involvement that once Lu Xun had begun to act he put his doubts behind him ignores his anguish. He was still deeply torn between his more positive public stance and his private doubts. *Wild Grass* is a remarkably frank public reflection of this tension. There, the reformer is a fool. The traveller in "Guoke" (The passerby) muddles through, knowing neither name nor destination, only that he cannot turn back because "there's not a place without troubles, not a place without landlords, not a place without expulsion and cages, not a place without smiles on the face, not a place without tears outside the eyes. I hate them. I am not going back."[54] The world of *Wild Grass* is one of ice valleys and "Dead Fire" (*Si huo*), where amid the clatter of life, the tomb stands as the cold promise of salvation when all hope is gone and only the rictus of the corpse remains.

But it is the private correspondence with Xu Guangping that carried the straightforward, intimate record of his dilemma. "What I say," he told her, "is often different from what I think," for the simple reason that he did not want to infect others with a gloom he could not be absolutely sure was justified. Although he tried to insist to others that there must be a way out, he confessed he did not know what it was. "Life is rather like bitter tea." If one added sugar, "the bitterness remains but the taste is improved. The sugar is not easy to find. I don't know where it is."[55] He had neither direction nor compass. Nonetheless, he would stumble on "even through thick brambles." So he told

Xu Guangping: "My ideas are really not easy to comprehend all at once because there are many contradictions therein . . . of humanitarianism and individualism. Thus, sometimes I suddenly love people or suddenly hate them. Sometimes I do things for other people, sometimes I do things for my own amusement. Sometimes in the hope that life will be over as quickly as possible, I work very hard. I do not really know whether there is any other reason."[56] "You resist," he wrote Xu Guangping, "in the hope of a brighter future . . . But my resistance is simply to make trouble for the darkness." "I clearly know that a pen is useless but now I have only this . . . As long as there is a place to publish, I won't put it down . . . as long as my tongue and pen exist, they shall be used regardless."

Preparation for Radicalism

On August 26, 1926, Lu Xun and Xu Guangping left Peking together, she to teach at home in Canton, and he at Amoy on the invitation of Lin Yutang. A projected two-year separation turned into a mere four-and-a-half month interlude.[57]

Amoy was not important in the development of Lu Xun's thinking on the writer's role. Despite a warm welcome from students, whose literary endeavors he assisted, Lu Xun disliked the unfamiliar dialect and uncongenial community. He was torn between loyalty to Lin Yutang and an invitation to be dean of humanities at Sun Yat-sen University in Canton, where he would be near Xu Guangping. Canton soon won out.

In no mood to think of the present, as he waited out the dull weeks to his departure at the end of the term, Lu Xun turned back to scholarly studies, to preparing prefaces and postfaces for two collections of his Peking essays, and to more early reminiscences. His few informal essays were relaxed and chatty rather than polemic, more narrative than political. Four or five were in letter form, still another offshoot of the personal element that had entered his writing in late 1924. He turned back to the semiallegorical historical short story, a form he had experimented with once before and now used merely to vent some very private irritations that had no general social merit.[58]

How, he asked Xu Guangping in exasperation, could he write about Amoy when he did not understand the language or the situation? To describe events in China "exactly as they happen . . . would appear grotesque," "more incredible" than the wildest fantasy.[59]

By far the most interesting product of these months is his correspondence with Xu Guangping, which was published some years later.[60]

In it, Lu Xun emerges as often vacillating, temperamental, inconsiderate, and politically naïve. The progress of the Northern Expedition delighted him, but Xu Guangping's description of the tensions in the supposedly united Guomindang-Communist front in Canton surprised him, particularly as they affected the educational world. He had thought, he confessed, that in Kwangtung things at the university would be better. In the end, he accepted Xu Guangping's judgment that he would find allies in the fight against reaction. Although most of these had departed before he arrived, Lu Xun was unperturbed, content, he claimed, to assist in the development of literature at the university and in the city.

By the time of his arrival in Canton on January 18, 1927, Lu Xun found himself in an entirely new position, both personally and politically.[61] The host of disappointed students who followed him from Amoy to Canton, coupled with the extravagant welcome given him by the public and the press as a "revolutionary fighter," dramatized his public stature. As a university dean and major public official, he now had to make the hard decisions himself, rather than criticize those who did. For the first time, he faced the practical reality of the rivalry between the Guomindang and the Communists, and also learned of the factions on each side, as the various groups tried to cultivate him. For all the rhetoric, Canton, Lu Xun concluded, had not changed; at best it had a "revolution by government order."[62]

In the lectures he gave in response to public demand during his initial two weeks in Canton, Lu Xun formulated no new ideas. He repeated old *New Youth*-type arguments against trying to preserve traditional language and culture and reiterated his long-standing concerns about the futility of martyrdom in revolution.[63] He warned that Chinese aversion to change, which he had decried so often, had turned the once revolutionary Canton into nothing more than a resort where comfort and security — not struggles for justice — ruled.[64]

However, in a major address at the Whampoa Academy just a week before the April purges, he addressed himself for the first time formally to the topic of "Literature of a Revolutionary Period" ("Geming shidaide wenxue").[65] Although the speech reflects largely his Peking reading in Russian sources, his selection of the topic and its careful development before such an unlikely audience suggests that in the intensely political atmosphere of Canton, Lu Xun was beginning to think seriously about the relation between literature and the current revolution. Less sanguine than he had once been on the reform potential of literature, he now simply addressed himself to the question of what relation, if any, literature has to cataclysmic changes like revolutions.

Literature, he argued, is weak and ineffective. Revolutions are won by revolutionaries not writers. Only revolutionaries can write so-called revolutionary literature. Major revolutions affect literature, but the reverse, he insisted, is not true. Before a major revolutionary effort, protest literature can, in nations that understand the futility of pure complaint, become the voice of fury and resistance. In passive or oppressed countries like Egypt, Arabia, Persia, and India, it leads to nothing but silence and subjugation. When actual revolution occurs, literature disappears; people are too busy changing society to worry about literature. After a successful revolution, there are songs of victory and mournful dirges, both sure signs of real change. But, alas, he cried, China has "neither dirges for the old nor praise of the new . . . China has not changed."

Then he added a new note, which would receive more emphasis in the years ahead. The world, including China, he wrote, as yet has no people's literature. All literature is *for* and *by* the upper class. Literature *about* the lower classes is not a people's literature. The people, he insisted, have not spoken. "Only when [the workers and peasants] achieve true liberation will there be a real people's literature."

During the spring of 1927, relations between the Guomindang and the Communists deteriorated rapidly throughout China. In Shanghai, on April 12, Chiang Kai-shek responded to a recent series of strikes and uprisings with a bloody putsch against his former Communist associates. There were similar anti-Communist moves in Peking, and, in Canton, on the night of April 15, there began a roundup of some three thousand suspected Communists of whom about two hundred were killed. Some forty students were among those arrested, and one with whom Lu Xun had worked was killed.

Deeply troubled by the terror and by his inability to get his university colleagues to cooperate in some action to assist the arrested students, Lu Xun resigned after just two and a half months as dean. In the pervading atmosphere of fear, old associates began to avoid him; press attacks appeared; and he was placed under surveillance. It was his most painful lesson so far that might makes right; but, in the end, the bloodbath of Canton was to give the final push toward his search for a radical alternative.

For the next four and a half months, Lu Xun did some editing of his past work and a little translation. Then, suddenly, about the first of September, three weeks before he and Xu Guangping departed for

Shanghai, he began to discuss, candidly and critically, his confrontation with revolution in Canton. He went beyond the narrow framework of personal interest and ad hominem attacks of his later Peking days to focus on the disillusioning failure of the Guomindang-led revolution itself.[66]

Sadly, he was forced to accept the fact that the Guomindang had feet of clay and that its leaders appeared less interested in revolution than in power.[67] Opportunism, rather than concern for truth or justice, guided their actions. How could men like Chiang Kai-shek or Dai Jitao, who had once supported Sun's policy of cooperation with the Communists, now invoke his name against the same group? Did such men, he asked angrily, believe in anything? "Revolutionary" and "antirevolutionary" meant nothing. Those in power were "revolutionary"; those who were not were "antirevolutionary." In Peking, it had been the same: supporters of Zhang Shizhao were "enlightened" but his opponents were classified as "bandits."

The cruelty of the government suppression — "torture and wholesale extermination that should not exist among men in the twentieth century" — shocked him.[68] Likewise, he denounced the Guomindang's censorship and suppression of free speech. Even the Manchus had allowed laments, but today "everyone has to smile contentedly whatever his lot." To military censors, books with red covers as well as those already declared antirevolutionary in Russia were dangerous. The world, he went on, had forgotten that bayonets could control writers as well as soldiers. J. S. Mill had said that dictatorship made people cynical, but, Lu Xun added, he did not know that a republic made them silent.

Not only was Lu Xun's faith in Sun Yat-sen's party gone but also his belief in youth as the hope of the future was battered. His disenchantment had begun during his Amoy days, when he learned that a vicious campaign waged against him in the north by a young Peking writer he had befriended stemmed from the young man's jealous love of Xu Guangping. Lu Xun felt betrayed. To be so repaid for the advice and support he had given so generously to young authors was too much, and he threatened (emptily as it turned out) to stop assisting them. He would not be "cheated, bound, enslaved, or slandered" any longer.[69]

This personal and restricted disappointment became general and political in Canton. As he watched university students split into competing networks of informers, he had to admit they were, like their elders, divided, venal, and cruel. No longer could he believe that China would be more vibrant and alive when the young succeeded to power.

"Facts are facts; the bloody drama has begun and the actors are youth, and self-satisfied youth at that."[70]

There was nothing left. "I came with illusions that were dispelled by reality, leaving me only a sense of desolation."[71] Only doom and darkness lay ahead. Reform efforts would fail. It would be better to stay in bed and smoke. "My former attacks on society were also pointless. Society did not even know I was attacking." So, in an open letter of September 4, he declared, "Perhaps after this I shall have nothing more to say. What will come once the terror is gone, I have no way of knowing, but probably it won't be anything good. Nonetheless, I am trying to save myself with my old methods: the first is numbness, the second forgetting."[72] Much as he might long for such opiates, he knew that he had come too far to return to their solace. The year 1927 was not 1913, nor even 1917. The personal and political dilemmas had finally become one.

The Turn to the Left

Lu Xun spent his final nine years, from October 1927 to October 1936, in Shanghai,[73] where, for the first time, he earned his living only by writing.

His experience in Canton had proved to him conclusively that there had to be a new approach to China's problems. Emotionally and intellectually he had to find a convincing rationale to sustain hope. He began by expanding his earlier reading in Japanese on Russian literature and literary theory, but his motive was no longer intellectual curiosity. It was survival. After a few months, his attention shifted first to general discussions of Marxist social and political thought, then to economics and dialectics, and then to the Soviet experiment itself. Many of his old views fell into place. He now had a theoretical explanation for oppression, imperialism, for the inadequacy of evolution and the necessity of revolution, as well as for his conviction that literature and art were the prerogative of the privileged. He seems to have welcomed the idea that inevitable class struggle would result in a proletarian victory. In short, he accepted the Marxist interpretation of history as the study of shifting "economic relationships" and culture as derived from these relationships.[74]

Lu Xun understood fully that an appreciation of Marxism and even a sympathy with its goals did not change him from a bourgeois intellectual into a proletarian. But he believed that progressive intellectuals still had a role to play. His would be basically educational. Not only did he inform himself more thoroughly than before on Soviet literature and Marxist literary theory but through an extensive translation and editorial program he also made his findings available to others. But he never allowed his interest in Marxism to restrict his literary horizon. For him, Marxism was a new and helpful way to examine the world, not a creed to dictate what he should read or how he should feel about it. And so, during these years of transition, he continued to work on non-Marxist materials.

There is almost a sense of mission about his efforts in the Marxist realm. Appalled at the low level of the debate on revolutionary literature, he moved to introduce basic background material on Soviet literature. He translated two general compilations on Soviet literary policy, selections from earlier Marxist theorists, Plekhanov and Luna-charsky, as well as several articles by Japanese writers on the proletarian literary movement. He also translated short stories and novels from both the fellow-traveler and the proletarian traditions in the Soviet Union. A similar balance was built into a Russian translation series he agreed to edit in early 1930. He neither endorsed nor condemned the writers or positions he presented. Throughout, he maintained his aim was first to help China's ignorant and impatient young theorists inform themselves and second to demonstrate that despite what they might think, there was as yet no *one* true position, because there were still significant differences of opinion in Russia.[75]

A parallel effort focused on non-Soviet and non-Marxist literature. He deliberately kept the handsome, big monthly *Benliu* (Torrent), which he launched in 1928, free from the revolutionary literature debate then in progress. He used it primarily to further two of his long-standing goals: first, the development of new young writers, and second, the furtherance of a knowledge of world literature. Although some attention was paid to Russian authors, particularly those of the nineteenth century, the emphasis was on other literatures. Similarly, the magazine and translation series of the Morning Flower Society (Zhao hua she), which he organized in late 1928 with some young friends, concentrated on material from non-Soviet Europe.

It is from Lu Xun's comments on literature, which combine ideas he had long held with new or newly sharpened elements, that we can best piece together his views on society and literature during his 1927–1929 search for a new hope. A sharp increase in passing references to class conflict in society and to its impact on culture reflects a heightened conviction of the relevance of previously held views, if not new intellectual discoveries. During these years, he was not writing in

211

support of others but was basically publishing in journals he controlled or had close ties to. His remarks can be taken as a straightforward indication of what he was feeling.

What emerges is a familiar but newly militant activist view on literature's social function and the writer's social responsibility.[76] This view is tempered by his continuing frustration over the basic ineffectiveness of all literary effort. But he argued that revolutions *needed* literature *just because* it was literature in the same way they needed slogans, catchwords, telegrams, or textbooks. He objected to using "the class struggle as a weapon in art." More clearly than before he says that all literature is partisan and that the class nature of literature is inevitable, although he rejects any rigid economic determinism. For him, literature is shaped by its environment and cannot escape beyond its age. Literature fades with the age and circumstances that produced it. Thus, "proletarian literature is one part of the workers' struggle to liberate their own class and all other classes. They want the whole place, not one corner." It was good for the disadvantaged to seek redress. Why should the hungry love the full? Lu Xun shows how far he has come since 1917 when he approvingly quotes Radek's remark that in times of great social change, no writer can be merely an observer. Writers, he went on, must unmask tyranny. They cannot fall silent. Sympathy for the proletarian cause was fine but not enough. Even Tolstoy, whom Lu Xun admired, had proved ineffectual despite his prodigious labors, because he had not advocated the class struggle. As a petty bourgeois himself, Lu Xun believed he could be of service to the revolution, but he knew he could never write proletarian literature for its future victors. China, he never tired of insisting, had no real proletarian or radical revolutionary literature, only bombastic explosions by self-anointed spokesmen, and even these, all too often, ignored the minimum requirements of technical excellence that Lu Xun felt essential in literature.

It is worth repeating that although Lu Xun's blend of old and new views on the nature and function of literature now had strong Marxist overtones, it was closer to the liberal Marxism of Trotsky than to the rigidity of the Proletkult tradition. He disliked the theoretical disputes among Marxists. The dispute between Trotsky and his opponents over freedom in literature and the role of the party or government in literary matters was not a question of right and wrong or of what was correct or incorrect. Rather, it represented differing approaches to similar goals. Lu Xun chose not to confront the whole issue of "whether or not literature was considered as one wing of the political struggle," which was not an easy issue to resolve.[77] Fortunately, he died before he had to confront it.

Lu Xun's transition years were not easy. In addition to everything else, he was confronted with sniping from the Communist-affiliated Creation and Sun societies. He also clashed with the Crescent Moon group, heirs of the *Modern Review* tradition. It is not surprising that he wrote very little and that what he did write was a mixture of old and new elements. There are familiar calls for reform and old laments on Chinese society and character. But there are also explicit attacks on the Guomindang government as such, rather than on certain officials as individuals, as was the case in Peking. There are also scattered sharp protests on censorship and terror, topics that dominated his work after 1933.

Despite the Chinese Communist party's past interest in Lu Xun, its most vocal literary elements at this time either ignored or were hostile to him, even as he was drawing closer to their cause. He was partly attracted by his reading, but more importantly by the logic of the Chinese situation and the enthusiasm and dedication of young revolutionary friends. As one of them, Feng Xuefeng, recalls, Lu Xun came to his faith in the party as a political force, as the only viable center of opposition to the now discredited Guomindang, even before he came to his faith in its program.[78] By the end of 1929, Lu Xun, who had no specific program of his own, was ready to support the Communists.

The League of Left-Wing Writers

In the opening weeks of 1930, Lu Xun for the first time actively identified himself with a political movement. This was the period when the Li Lisan leadership of the Chinese Communist party was beginning to organize a series of "front organizations" in the literary and cultural sphere to create a mass base of support for a new Communist-led revolutionary drive to take over major urban centers. The party obviously needed to recruit sympathetic intellectuals of stature like Lu Xun, and at the end of 1929, it not only ordered the attacks on Lu Xun to stop,[79] but in February 1930 it won him as a nominal sponsor for the fledgling Freedom League. About the same time, he helped form a Communist-led literary organization which, at his insistence, incorporated the term "left-wing" into its title. On March 2, 1930, he gave the inaugural address to the League of Left-Wing Writers. Even Li Lisan himself held several talks with Lu Xun in these months. Lu Xun was now openly associated with the "left," if not directly with the Communist party. It was a logical continuation of his political evolution, and for the next two or three years, he gladly played the role of leading symbol of the Communist-led league. But he did not become involved in its practical political activities, for this had never been his style. As with *New Youth*, he had his reservations. But now it was a question of interpretation rather than basic disagreement on the outlook for possible success. To Lu Xun, the official party line that China was entering a high tide of revolution was nonsense, but he did believe that ultimately the revolution would succeed.[80] Revolutionary literature in China, he contended, was the function of a revolutionary setback, not success.[81]

The years in which Lu Xun was moving close to the party, as well as the 1930–1932 period when he was closest to it, form one of the most politically complicated chapters in Chinese party history. Not only did the party face increasing Guomindang oppression but it was torn by shifting alliances within its own Communist ranks. From such close associates as Feng Xuefeng, who worked in the Propaganda Department under the Central Committee, Rou Shi, a representative of the Congress of Delegates from the Argas Soviet held near Shanghai in late May and early June 1930, and still later from Qu Qiubai, who was finally driven from the top post in the party about January 1931, Lu Xun could have learned much about such external and internal problems of the party, but there is no indication that he bothered. His mere friendship with Communists was dangerous enough. Although he obviously knew of the problem of Trotskyism, there is, for example, absolutely nothing to indicate that he had the slightest inkling that the arrest and murder in early 1931 of his beloved disciple and friend Rou Shi may in any way have been connected to internecine party struggles.[82] The politically motivated murder of associates like Qiu Jin in Japan, his student in Peking, or the victims of the Canton massacre had always accelerated the radical thrust of Lu Xun's political development. Had Lu Xun suspected that Communist intrigue might have been involved in the sacrifice of the five martyred writers, he would never have intensified his support for the Chinese party and its Soviet ally thereafter. Thus his sympathetic but still highly intellectual support prior to February 1931 becomes, as we shall see, highly charged, angry, and emotional defense of the party thereafter.

The record of his support of the League of Left-Wing Writers and the development of his literary thinking is important. His main contribution to the development of the league was his unstinting editorial support for several of its unofficial and official publications.

Between January 1930 and January 1932, the unofficial organs he and companions like Rou Shi, Feng Xuefeng, and Qu Qiubai launched were (1) *Wenyi yanjiu* (Literary research), February 1930; (2) *Mengya* (Sprout), January to May 1930, and its successor *Xin di* (New earth), June 1930, which featured official league pronouncements, statements by the Proletarian Poetry Club and the Young Anti-Imperialist League, and some Lu Xun essays on literature as well as blunt criticism of certain league positions; and (3) *Shizi jietou* (Crossroads), basically a vehicle to express anti-Japanese sentiment. On the official level, he was one of thirty "editors" of *Baerdishan* (Partisan) in April and May 1930; and a year later, he was the inspiration, designer, and major contributor to *Qianshao* (Outpost), the league's memorial to its five martyred colleagues, Outpost's sucessor, *Wenxue daobao* (Literary guide), carried not only league documents but also some of Lu Xun's bitterest denunciations of the Guomindang terror. In short, between 1930 and 1932, Lu Xun published almost all of the little he wrote in organs associated with the league. In addition, he helped other left-wing groups with occasional speeches and appearances.[83]

Turning to the substance of Lu Xun's literary thinking, it becomes evident that in the fourteen or fifteen months before the execution of Rou Shi and his companions, Lu Xun's comments on literature were essentially an extension of the transition years just concluded. His opening address to the league in March 1930 was cautious rather than euphoric in tone.[84] He reminded his audience how easy it was for radical, enthusiastic, but unrealistic proponents of revolution to go "right" after a revolution or to become disillusioned to the point of suicide, like his favorite examples Esenin and Soboly. To succeed, he said, the league must broaden its battlefront, recruit new fighters, be flexible in its strategy, and achieve a genuine united front within its ranks, a unity it did not now have. Elsewhere, he made a special point of emphasizing the important contribution he felt "social science" could make to literature. "All we need at this stage," he wrote in the spring of 1930, are a "few solid intellectual critics who really understand social science as well as literary criticism."[85] Such men could impel literature and art along the correct path. A few days later, he remarked that belief in the class nature of literature did not necessarily imply support for the Soviet Union.

There are other indications in 1930 of this cool, realistic approach to literary problems confronting the left. Early in the year, during a discussion on the development of mass literature, Lu Xun was cautious. "If literature tries to bow to the masses, then it very easily tends to accommodate or flatter the masses," he declared. Therefore, he urged different levels of literature for different levels of readers, and he encouraged writers to produce easily intelligible works that could gradually raise the level of the masses. The ultimate solution, he cautioned once again, was political not literary. Any large-scale attack on the problem of mass literature "needs the aid of political power; one cannot walk on one leg and much passionate talk is only the self-solace of literary people."[86]

But after the execution of five martyrs, his tone changed radically. When emotions change, he observed, the degree of one's theoretical understanding is bound to change.[87] His praise of the Soviet Union became passionate and echoed official party and league calls for support. For the first time, he began to talk about *our* side. There were references now to the "sacred goal" of a "future classless society." The sooner the dictatorship of the proletariat succeeded, the sooner "nobody need starve to death." To achieve these goals, the revolution needed all the allies it could get. Therefore, he strongly opposed threats by the left against authors who did not come forward to assist in the struggle.

In the postmartyr period, Lu Xun also talked more positively, though somewhat inconsistently, about "proletarian literature." In the first outpouring of his anger, he wrote in April 1931 that the death of Rou Shi and his colleagues was a blow to the working class and to revolutionary literature. But, he went on, "proletarian literature will continue to grow ... because it belongs to the great ranks of the revolutionary toilers; and as long as the people exist and gain in strength, so long will this revolutionary literature grow."[88] A few weeks later, he described the revolutionary literature of the proletariat as the only literary movement in China. Like a tender shoot in the desert, it was growing cramped and crooked. In contrast to his position prior to February 1931, Lu Xun now wrote that "revolutionary literature had a genuine mass foundation," although he conceded it was not work by genuine proletarians but by bourgeois writers describing simply the evils they had experienced. Therefore, he welcomed the league's slogan, "Proletarianize the writers."

In the absence of genuine proletarian literature, the best that could be hoped for was a literature of exposure by bourgeois writers attacking their own class.[89] Who else could attack with such effect? He himself had begun that way. Accounts of lower-class suffering by bourgeois writers, while not proletarian literature, could prove valuable to later generations. But, he warned, writers who merely attack the old society without clear understanding of the basic problems may harm the revolution. Further, they must — with careful attention to literary technique — highlight the significant aspects of that experience, not merely set it down. Fellow-traveler literature had, he claimed, played a valuable role in catching one aspect of Soviet experience.

Lu Xun generally avoided theoretical debates within the league, but voiced occasional support for the league in selected disputes with outside groups, such as the conflict with the Crescent Moon over the class nature of literature, the Nanking government over the issue of its "Nationalist literature," and "Third Category" writers, left-leaning liberals outside the league, over the "independence" of the artist from politics. He spoke out rather more in connection with discussions by Qu Qiubai and others on the development of mass culture. Here he was trying hard to be a practical strategist. He identified three levels in the Chinese audience, each with needs to be met, namely, the illiterate, semiliterate, and educated.[90] There should be works written especially for the first group, who could also profit from plays, movies, and lectures. He had no suggestions for the second. For the third, which he knew so well, he recommended translations. Not only could translations spread vital new ideas to this strategic group but also they could give the Chinese language a much needed linguistic infusion. He agreed with Qu Qiubai that modern "written and spoken Chinese was too imprecise." To develop an adequate base for mass communication, Chinese needed to go on the "offensive." It should take over suitable dialect and classical elements, and adopt, test, and finally digest foreign grammatical structures and new vocabulary in order to stimulate new modes of thought and expression. Lu Xun also supported the adoption of popular literary and artistic forms — especially folk opera librettos and cartoon books — as a way to reach the masses. Ultimately, he argued somewhat expansively, out of opera librettos would come a Flaubert and from cartoon strips a Michelangelo. After all, was not the Sistine ceiling originally just a series of religious propaganda pictures?

Positive as Lu Xun's feelings toward the league in these years were, he was not uncritical of it and of the "mistakes" of its members and friends. He spoke openly and even gratuitously against Guo Moruo and Zhou Yang in attacks whose rumbles are still being heard. He charged bad planning in the revolutionary movement. Specifically, he argued that a lack of detailed analysis of Chinese society and habits had caused the mechanical adoption of totally unsuitable Soviet precedents. He wrote, "A fighter who wants to understand the revolution and the enemy should make the closest analysis of the foe confronting him. The same applies to literature."[91]

Lu Xun's basic views on society and literature were now complete.

Anger and Defiance

Suddenly, in January 1933, the militancy Lu Xun had been expressing for three years in journals of the League of Left-Wing Writers to a generally sympathetic but limited audience was redirected outward into regular newspapers and periodicals.[92] The shift was in response to external pressures and exhortations: first, the league and its press were now effectively curtailed by the government; second, the International Union of Revolutionary Writers was calling on its supporters around the world to carry their message to the mass bourgeois press; and finally, Lu Xun unexpectedly found an outlet in a mass circulation daily, the Shanghai *Shenbao*. He started writing furiously. From some forty pages of commentary in 1932, he went to more than five hundred in 1933. He maintained almost as fast a pace until his death, his emphasis now on public policy, particularly Guomindang censorship, government terror, and the policy of nonresistance to Japan. There were subsidiary themes — defects in the Chinese character, the government's attempted revival of Confucianism, and the classical language and popular reaction to it. This was the height of his satirical essay-commentary.

Although his closest associates had left Shanghai by early 1934, his faith in the Chinese Communist party remained strong. "As long as I have the strength, I hope to be able to help those who are working to benefit the Chinese masses,"[93] because, as he said elsewhere, a life dedicated to the masses grows and lives even after death.[94]

But even as his faith continued and his stature in international left-wing and Communist circles increased, the league and his relations with it in Shanghai were deteriorating badly. In the summer of 1936, the long-standing friction between Zhou Yang, secretary-general of the league, and Lu Xun finally erupted in the well-known debate National Defense Literature.[95] A little earlier, Zhou Yang, in response to the Communists' August 1935 call for a united front against Japan, had not only dissolved the League of Left-Wing Writers but had also organized a new group under the slogan "National Defense Literature." His association accepted as allies anyone who was anti-Japanese. Lu Xun refused to join. On the theoretical level, he was not reconciled to this approach, which he feared might pave the way for a new 1927-

type tragedy; on the personal level, he saw the move as a ploy by Zhou Yang to enhance his personal power in party cultural circles. Finally, Lu Xun proposed a counterslogan, "popular literature of the national revolutionary struggle," which was considerably more militant in stance than Zhou Yang's. Here, Lu Xun may in part have been reflecting the stiffer tone of the Communists' December 1935 Wayaobao Resolution, of which Feng Xuefeng, who had just returned to Shanghai from Yenan, would presumably have informed him. Whatever the doctrinal differences, the dispute was basically personal and, as such, it was an embarrassment to the Communist party. Finally, in October 1936, Lu Xun and twenty authors from both camps joined in a "Statement by those in Literary Circles on Unity, Peace, and Freedom of Speech." Lu Xun appeared the winner, as Zhou Yang and his principal supporters did not sign. But it was a Pyrrhic victory, for in a few days, Lu Xun was dead.

In the last years of his life, Lu Xun continued with his three other lifelong literary goals: introducing foreign literature, developing new talent, and editing constructive, high-quality literary magazines and books. In 1934, with Mao Dun and Li Liewen, he launched *Yiwen* (Translation), devoted largely to Russian and central and northern European literature.[96] The standards he set there for careful if somewhat "awkward" translation, supplemented with helpful background commentary, stand to this day, although his dream of a "series of planned translations" remained "only a dream."[97] The list of young authors he encouraged with prefaces and editorial guidance is also long. For still others, he arranged publication of their works, sometimes at his own expense. Not only did he preface and pay for publication of translations from the Russian by Cao Jinghua and Qu Qiubai, but his "Slave Series" brought out Xiao Jun's *Bayuede xiangcun* (Village in August), Xiao Hong's *Shengsi chang* (Place of life and death), and Ye Zi's *Fengshou* (Harvest). Finally, he edited magazines like *Hai yan* (Stormy petrel), whose title was an allegory for impending revolution and whose substance made its first issue in January 1936 a sellout in one day.

But the greatest contribution of his final years remained his sharp satirical essay-comment or *zawen*. For Lu Xun, the writer in times of crisis above all must be a fearless critic of society, tough and honest.[98] The brave man draws his sword against the strong; the coward goes against the weak.[99] Not only must the writer dare to call a prostitute a prostitute and a hero a hero but he must also challenge those who would make the prostitute a hero and the hero a prostitute. "The writer's task is to react and fight back immediately against what is harmful . . . to resist and attack." "Works," he added, "which are opiates will perish along with those who administer or take narcotics. The essays which live on must be daggers and javelins, which, with their readers, can hew out a bloodstained path to a new life." In the mid-1930s, Lu Xun strongly opposed a movement to promote the "humorous essay" led by his former friend, Lin Yutang, and his own brother, Zhou Zuoren, two of China's best-known essayists. Initially, these two proposed "humorous criticism" of society and public figures. "Humorous criticism," Lu Xun charged, was a contradiction in terms, especially a humor that Lin insisted had to be detached, charitable, and not indignant. Lu Xun warned that in China, "humor must become satire directed against society or degenerate into . . . common 'joking.'" He was right. Almost immediately, Lin announced his retirement from active commentary on the world to let his mind roam over all things great and small, from flies to the universe. To Lu Xun, this was a reprehensible attempt to avoid reality and an abdication of social responsibility.[100] Their work, he predicted, would degenerate into literary bric-a-brac, rather like party snacks, which, while tasty, do one no good.[101]

During the course of this 1934–1935 exchange between the entertaining *xiaopinwen* of Lin Yutang and the militant *zawen* of Lu Xun, Lu Xun predicted that the short satirical *zawen*, which as yet had no acknowledged place in Chinese literature, would soon become a recognized genre. He was right, and he was the one largely responsible. But ironically, it was soon disavowed by the very party that symbolized the dreams that had nurtured it.

As for his own work, Lu Xun said he wrote to expose injustice, tear down the masks of righteousness, and vent his indignation.[102] His own work made him shudder because it was like the "cry of an owl reporting things of ill omen"; the more correct the report, the more disastrous for China. It was a losing game. So, like a street peddler of rusty nails and broken crocks, he simply "spread out" his *zawen* hoping someone would find something useful. They were expendable.

His views had grown and shifted through the years, but always he was true to himself. At the end, he sought no accommodation with his enemies. "Let them go on hating me," Lu Xun wrote. "I have no sword," only a pen that is "not for sale."[103]

10.

Lu Xun's "Medicine"

Milena Doleželová-Velingerová

The short story "Yao" (Medicine), written in April 1919 at the beginning of his literary career, already shows the traits of Lu Xun's later work: a subject matter derived from personal experience, a forceful (but concealed) ideological message, and a polished narrative technique.[1]

Like other Lu Xun stories, "Medicine" has attracted critical attention because of its autobiographical elements and its ideology. The autobiographical features seem to endow Lu Xun's work with an extraordinary authenticity. Moreover, the discovery of ties between the author's private life and his literary work has promised to give a better understanding of both the author's personality and his writings.[2] Not surprisingly, in this age of ideological conflict Lu Xun's message has become a prime subject of discussion, summoning different and mutually contradictory interpretations.[3] But aside from such polemics, Lu Xun's narrative techniques have rarely been studied,[4] although his mastery of the written word and the short story genre has often been praised.

Analysis of the narrative elements of "Medicine," however, reveals the story's structural unity and its basic artistic principles and leads to a better understanding of the story's autobiographical elements and to a more substantial formulation of its ideological message. Such an approach is further justified by the character of Lu Xun's writing: his message is never explicit but is concealed in an intricate code that can be deciphered only if the organizing principles of the story's structure are revealed.

"Medicine" is one of those narratives whose autobiographical sources are well known. They relate to the bitter experiences of Lu Xun's childhood and youth. First there is his father's death at the hands of "quack" doctors. Forced to commute for years between his home and the local apothecary to fetch "cures" for his father, Lu Xun was deeply impressed by this family tragedy.[5] The second source, though not a personal experience, is still closely related to Lu Xun's life. The formidable woman revolutionary Qiu Jin, an outstanding Chinese political figure at the beginning of the century, came from the same town as Lu Xun, Shaohsing. In 1907 she was denounced by close friends and publicly executed near her home city.[6] Lu Xun, studying in Japan at the time of her execution, did not have any direct knowledge of the event but apparently learned of the incident at second hand.

To demonstrate the relationship between these autobiographical facts and the resulting literary work, a simplified synopsis of the story of "Medicine" is provided here. But instead of the *composition* of the story, the order of events as related in the text, we present the *disposition* of the story, the chronological sequence of events, as follows: Uncle Xia denounces his nephew Xia Yu to the authorities, because he fears that his relative's political activities may lead to the extermination of the whole family. He is awarded twenty-five taels of silver. Imprisoned, Xia Yu shows fearless conduct. Instead of breaking down during the investigation, he incites the jailer to revolt and proclaims that the great Qing empire belongs to all the Chinese people. Uncle Kang, who belongs to the town's underworld, informs Hua Old Shuan, the owner of a small teahouse, that Xia Yu will be executed. From the executioner Old Shuan buys a roll of bread, *mantou*, which is dipped in Xia Yu's blood at the moment of the execution. Old Shuan and his wife feed the mantou to their fatally ill son, Little Shuan, because they believe in its healing powers. A half year later, during the Qing Ming Festival in early spring, Little Shuan's mother accidentally meets Xia Yu's mother in the cemetery. The graves of their sons lie side by side, separated only by a path. Xia Yu's mother is puzzled by a circle of flowers decorating her son's grave. In her grief, she turns to a superstitious belief and asks a raven perched nearby to fly down and indicate the presence of her son's soul. But the raven fails to respond. On leaving the cemetery the two women are startled by the raven's loud caw as it suddenly takes off toward the horizon.

The story's disposition gives us basic information about Lu Xun's handling of the autobiographical material. To begin with, all references to the author are removed; there is no father, and there is no revolutionary from "our" town. These figures from the author's personal experience are transformed into the story's main characters, and their basic qualities, such as age and sex, are determined by structural considerations. Second, and more importantly, the two independent personal experiences become two story lines, linked together into one coherent plot. Unity is achieved not only because there are motifs common to both lines, such as the "medicine" and the mothers, but also because both story lines have the same organizing principles.

The first of these principles, information manipulation, governs how and when information about events in the narrative is to be introduced. Lu Xun demonstrates this principle in "Medicine" by temporarily withholding significant pieces of information from the reader. This delayed information release, a well-known mystery story technique, helps create suspense and tension in the plot.

The second organizing principle of "Medicine" is the creation of dynamic oppositions in the story structure. This principle brings significant components of the story into mutual opposition and allows the author to readjust their relative importance as the story progresses. Neither of these principles can be observed in the story disposition; rather, they appear to be organizing principles of the story composition. In other words, they are operations that transform the "natural" chronological sequence of events (as manifested in the disposition) into the "artificial" order of motifs, as given in the linear development of the text.

In its compositional order of motifs, the story has two clearly different units. The first unit consists of the first three sections of the story. It is characterized by unity of time, dynamism, and the prevalence of a narrative mode conditioned by certain protagonists. Unity of time is achieved in that the events narrated in the first three sections occur within a very short time span — only a few hours. Dynamism results from the multiplicity of action motifs (all significant events of Little Shuan's and Xia Yu's lives are narrated in this first unit) and from the tension created by delaying the release of background information. Finally, the narrative mode of the three sections is determined by the point of view of particular characters: in section one, the most important events are related as the observations and experiences of Old Shuan; in section two, as the observations and feelings of Little Shuan; and in section three, as the biased opinions and beliefs of Uncle Kang.

The second compositional unit of "Medicine" consists of only the fourth and last section, which, in all its basic structural features, contrasts with the first unit. Significantly, it is separated from the first unit by a considerable temporal gap: the first three sections take place in the fall, the fourth section in the spring. This fact alone indicates that the last section functions as an epilogue to the story. Rather than a series of action scenes, as in the first unit, the second unit is, basically, a static episode permeated by a lyrical and reflective mood. Furthermore, the narrative mode of the second unit is not determined by the point of view of a character but rather by an "objective," "hidden" narrator.

This binary compositional design does not correspond to the differentiation of the two story lines in the disposition; instead, both story lines are incorporated into one compositional frame. Within this common frame, they both are subject to the same organizing principles discussed above.

First, let us observe how the principle of information manipulation applies to the story lines. The information about both Little Shuan's and Xia Yu's fates is initially elliptic and fragmentary; background on the more important events and circumstances is introduced only gradually into the narrative. Not until section three is the erstwhile "mystery" of both story lines completely revealed.

In section one, the milieu and the characters are described in a terse, abbreviated sketch that provokes the reader's visual and sensual imagination; all we are allowed to see is a two-room teahouse on a gloomy, silent street, lit by a ghostly lamp in the dark of an early morning in autumn. The three most important characters in this section are also depicted with maximum economy; only those traits meaningful to the ensuing action are provided. Old Shuan is projected solely through his half-terrified yet hopeful state of mind, which seems to brighten as the sun rises and the sky grows light. But Old Shuan's excitement is not immediately explained; as he nervously pockets a package of silver dollars, one can only surmise that he is about to buy something of great value. The two remaining characters, Old Shuan's wife and son, are likewise known only by isolated references — her voice and his coughing. Neither characteristic is given particular significance at the time.

Besides this suggestive characterization, the action in section one is fragmented and difficult to comprehend. Presented through Old Shuan's deranged and incoherent perceptions, it reflects his excitement and terror. He observes "many strange people in two's and three's, wandering about like lost souls." The eyes of one "shone with a lustful light, like a famished person's at the sight of food." No explicit information about the execution is given. It is referred to only as a "sound," while the executioner is just "a man clad entirely in black . . . his eyes like daggers, making Old Shuan shrink to half his normal size." Most importantly, the object that the villager buys from the executioner is also mysterious. We perceive, at first, only its outward identity — a roll of mantou. Its metaphorical identity is only suggested to us by the phrase "a crimson substance," and its healing power is only vaguely hinted at, again through Old Shuan's giddy state of mind. " 'Whose sickness is this for?' Old Shuan seemed to hear someone ask; but he made no reply. His whole mind was on the package, which he carried as carefully as if it were the sole heir to an ancient house. Nothing else mattered now. He was about to transplant this new life to his own home, and reap much happiness."

Section two contains more definite information about the main characters and a more consistent description of the action. The fragments of section one gain more coherence. The question "Whose sickness is this for?," which seemed only to show Old Shuan's hallucinating mind, becomes a logical link between the first and the second sections. The gloomy picture of sick Little Shuan gives us an answer to the question, while the tender attentiveness with which his parents give him the mantou reveals to us the connections between the mantou and the child's coughing. But information about the substance that had transformed the mantou into a miraculous medicine is still withheld. Its disclosure is prevented by the particular point of view from which the action of this section is seen.

The most important stages of the action are related via the perceptions of Little Shuan, and, secondarily, those of a customer in the teahouse. Little Shuan is asked to stay away from the kitchen so that he cannot see what his parents are preparing. When he is given the mantou for his breakfast, "he had the oddest feeling, as if he were holding his whole life in his hands." And "his father and mother were standing at each side of him, their eyes *apparently* pouring *something* into him and at the same time extracting *something*." (Emphasis added.) The customer, struck by a strange odor permeating the teahouse, asks twice about the source of the smell but gets no answer. The narrator reveals that the parents prepared the mantou in the stove, but its "crimson substance" remains a secret.

Only in section three is this secret revealed — by Uncle Kang. In fact, he has so much additional information to provide the other characters and the reader that Uncle Kang can be rightly called a secondary narrator. He reports his information in response to questions from the occupants of the teahouse (Old Shuan and his wife, anonymous customers), who, with the exception of occasional comments on

Kang's revelations, remain relatively passive to the situation. To emphasize Kang's special narrative role, he is described in greater detail than the other characters. He is "a heavy-jowled man" and "his dark coarse cotton shirt was opened in the front, unbuttoned, and fastened carelessly by a broad dark girdle at his waist." His predatory mind is hinted at later when he boasts about his connection with the jailer.[7]

To heighten the tension of the story, the secret of the mantou is disclosed during the first part of his narrative in three gradual stages. In the first few sentences — shouted to attract the other customers' attention — Kang only alludes to the secret. But these sentences tell us that it was Uncle Kang who informed Old Shuan about the execution. In the second stage of his revelation, Kang indicates the close connection between the healing power of the mantou and the mysterious substance: "This is a guaranteed cure! Not like other things! Just think, brought back warm, and eaten warm!" Finally, the substance is directly identified. Significantly, it is also in this explicit declaration that Little Shuan's disease is given its real, frightening name: "A roll dipped in human blood like this can cure any consumption!"

Revealing the secret of the mantou marks a turning point in the development of "Medicine." The story of Little Shuan is closed. At the same time, the motif of human blood provides a link to the second story line — the events surrounding Xia Yu's execution.

This second story line, like the first, is subject to the principle of information manipulation. The execution being concealed in section one, it is only in section three that Uncle Kang tells of Xia Yu's fate. Continuing in his narrator's role, Uncle Kang reveals the revolutionary's name and the other missing parts of Xia Yu's story — how he was denounced by his uncle, how he incited the jailer to revolt, and how he proclaimed that "the great Qing empire belongs to us." Only now does the most important event of this story line, the execution, become clear. The reader can finally reconstruct what actually happened in the first compositional unit of "Medicine."

One aspect of the disclosure of the revolutionary's story deserves special mention. Both Uncle Kang's remarks and the comments of his listeners are totally negative. The revolutionary is a "young rogue," a "real scoundrel," a "rotter." The revolutionary's tragedy thus deepens. The "people" who were supposed to benefit from his actions have turned into his enemies and judges.

When the first compositional unit ends at the conclusion of section three, all necessary information about the two story lines has been given. The tension generated by the device of delayed information release is dissipated. But this is only a momentary respite. The second unit, the epilogue, brings an even more intense and persistent tension, because the information will not be revealed in the text; the reader will have to discover it.

The intensity of the epilogue is, again, generated by the principle of information manipulation. But here it operates in a fashion opposite to that of the first three sections: definite information is provided, but it has a concealed, symbolic meaning. In other words, the principle of information manipulation is now implemented by means of symbolic encoding. The reader must himself manipulate the symbols until the story's overall meaning is deciphered. In the first compositional unit, the unknown information is presented successively in the text, but in the epilogue, the unknown meaning has to be provided by the reader's own interpretation. The clue to such interpretation is given by the second organizing principle of "Medicine," namely, dynamic opposition. As mentioned earlier, this principle is manifested in the formation of contrasting pairs of structural components and in the readjustment of their relative importance in the course of the narrative. It is applied conspicuously to both story lines, which, as we have seen, are linked together by the motif of human blood. But in the epilogue, this binary character is demonstrated by other motifs: the graves of the two young men lying side by side are divided only by a thin path; they look like rolls of mantou, the substance that brought their fates together. The two mothers, although unknown to each other, are united in grief. And after Mother Hua crosses the path, they do not part.

The relationship of the two story lines is complicated, however, by the dynamism generated from these oppositions. The arrangement of the two lines undergoes a radical reversal in the course of the story. Up until the point in section three when the secret of the mantou is revealed, the story revolves around Little Shuan. But at this pivot the focus of the two story lines is altered and the emphasis shifts to Xia Yu. This transition is made clear in the last part of the teahouse conversation: while Uncle Kang tells about Xia Yu's execution, Little Shuan's paroxysm of coughing and his mother's anxious questions are heard in the background.

The principle of dynamic opposition governs not only the sequence of events in "Medicine" but also its thematic structure, which is dominated by two polar themes — darkness (superstition) and revolution. The whole first unit is dominated by the theme of darkness, as

227

both protagonists are victims of a benighted society. What is more, darkness obscures the character of the revolutionary's activity, which is misrepresented by Uncle Kang's biased report and by the comments of the villagers. It seems, at this point, that darkness has eliminated its opposing theme. But, at its very moment of triumph, its power begins to wane. First, the hunchback's comment at the end of section three — "Crazy" — echoes the other villagers' opinion about the revolutionary's "crazy" behavior in jail. But this comment is delayed and follows Uncle Kang's final words — "A guaranteed cure!" — with which he tries to console the cough-racked Little Shuan. Where the hunchback's comment occurs gives the utterance new, unintentional meaning, for it undermines the theme of superstition. Second, and more important, an unbiased reader will learn from Uncle Kang about the revolutionary's ideals and courage, and the theme of revolution thereby emerges in a positive light.

This latter theme, however, is given more prominent treatment in the epilogue. There, the reversal in the relative importance of the two main themes is first indicated by the change of seasons. Autumn, in the Chinese tradition, is an awesome period of the year, corresponding to the theme of darkness in the first three sections. In the epilogue, the coming spring foreshadows the dispersion of darkness and the emergence of new hope. Accordingly, the theme of revolution supersedes that of darkness. This is clearly implied when Xia Yu's mother says, "They all wronged you. . . I know, they trapped you.[8] But a day of reckoning will come, Heaven will see to it. Close your eyes in peace." This comment contrasts sharply with those expressed previously by the villagers. Coming from a grieving mother, it has much more textural and emotional weight; it transforms the victim of the darkness into a hero.

The character of the epilogue is primarily symbolic, and, therefore, the revaluation of the two themes is also expressed principally in symbolic form. Understanding these symbols in the epilogue is necessary to determine the final ranking of the themes and to formulate the story's ideological message. In accordance with our previous discussion, we find that the various symbols used are actually pairs of opposites, arranged so that one member of the pair has a special importance with respect to the other member. In other words, the meaning of the symbols is revealed in the opposition of properties assigned to the particular members of the pair.

The most obvious symbol in the epilogue consists of the two mothers. Here, the ranking of themes is shown in the fact that Little

Shuan's mother has a role subordinate to that of the revolutionary's mother. The former crosses the path and utters but two brief sentences, while the revolutionary's mother is a full, expressive character. The circle of flowers on her son's grave prompts her to ask the crucial question: "What does it mean?" Further, she is linked to the raven, the epilogue's most significant symbol, by her pleading that the raven fly down to show her son's presence. And, last but not least, she speaks of her son's fate and "a day of reckoning."

Other symbolic pairs are more obscure. In section three, the names of the two victims — Hua and Xia — may seem separately insignificant. But as a pair, they are two common appellations for China.[9] In the epilogue, the two most difficult symbols are the flowers on the graves and the raven. Many critics have already discussed the first of these, apparently because of Lu Xun's own comment in his preface to *Nahan* (A call to arms). But what has escaped attention is the fact that the "wreath" on Xia Yu's grave is purposely connected with the flowers on Little Shuan's grave. As with other graves in the cemetery, there are *naturally* growing spring flowers on Little Shuan's resting place; but the circle of flowers on Xia Yu's grave is arranged *artificially*. As Mother Hua observes, "They have no roots . . . they can't have bloomed here." As further evidence of a pairing of motifs, the flowers on Little Shuan's grave have a neutral, greenish tint, whereas the circle on Xia Yu's grave is composed of red and white blooms.

Certainly we could be satisfied with Lu Xun's own general interpretation of the wreath as an encouragement to "those fighters who are galloping on in loneliness."[10] Still, this encouragement can have a more specific form. In contrast to the naturally growing flowers, the wreath was the result of a *human* act, though it is not clear whose; the old woman says only that it could not have been playing children or grieving relatives. Perhaps the grave was honored by Xia's comrades. The shape of the wreath and its red and white colors may refer to a non-Chinese emblematic system, and, therefore, signify an act of people who had adopted non-Chinese customs and ideas. That the symbol raises these questions and leaves them without a definite answer may be the best interpretation possible.

A similar approach can be taken with the raven, which, because it appears at the end of the story, is a highly significant symbol. Just as the first unit of the story culminates with the full revelation of its characters' actions, so the second unit reaches its climax with the story's most obscure and, at the same time, most provocative symbol.

One might point out that the raven is just one bird, not a pair of symbols as we find in the rest of this carefully structured story. But a closer inspection reveals a hidden polarity. In fact, the raven appears in two contrasting scenes and serves a double symbolic function. In the first scene, the raven is completely passive and is associated with Xia Yu's mother's superstitious belief. According to Chinese legend, the raven can be read as a representation of filial piety, because a young raven feeds its old parents when they are unable to find food. But when the raven does not respond to the mother's call, its function as a symbol of superstition is negated. Now it can assume a new symbolic function, as shown by its strange behavior in the second scene.

Significantly, a pause separates the second scene from the first. Before the pause, the raven is still seen "on the rigid bough of the tree, its head drawn in, perched immobile as iron." But after the pause, the raven suddenly caws loudly, and the women see it "stretch its wings, brace itself to take off, then fly like an arrow toward the far horizon."

Here the reader must ask Mother Xia's question: "What does it mean?" The general structural principle of dynamic opposition that governs the other symbolic pairs and the underlying themes leads to an explanation. In the first scene, the raven symbolizes superstition (darkness), whereas in the second scene, it symbolizes the opposing theme of revolution. The second function of the raven, in effect, reinforces the final dominant position of the theme of revolution vis-à-vis the theme of darkness.

Choosing the raven to symbolize revolution might seem bold or even inappropriate. In both the Chinese and Western traditions the raven has mainly represented tragedy, death, fright, and the unknown. Yet it is well known that Lu Xun was never one of those writers who idealized violent change. And in 1919, when "Medicine" was written, he was just emerging from a deep depression caused by his disenchantment with the incomplete Revolution of 1911. He might have rightly felt that a true revolution is an event that reaches toward far horizons, and is, at the same time, awesome and frightening. The raven, then, can be an apt representation of this image of revolution. Through the story's organizational principle of dynamic opposition, the "double-faced" raven evokes a set of dual connotations around one of its basic themes.

Thus, we see that Lu Xun uses the principles of information manipulation and dynamic opposition to express the bizarre juxtapositions of a society in tumult. It is through a structural interpretation of

"Medicine" that one can identify these juxtapositions and, therefore, better formulate Lu Xun's ideological message. Indeed, the intended message reflects the binary nature of the story's organization, for the dynamic relationship between the themes of darkness and revolution culminates in the negation of the powers of darkness and the affirmation of a frightening, but cathartic symbol of revolution.

11.

The Central Contradiction in Mao Dun's Earliest Fiction

John Berninghausen

In the autumn of 1927, the thirty-one-year-old Shen Yanbing, already well known in Chinese intellectual circles as a critic, translator, editor, and politically active intellectual, began to write fiction. With the publication of his first work of fiction, the short novel *Huanmie* (Disillusionment), he adopted the Chinese word *mao dun* ("contradiction") as his pen name. Another writer and fellow member in the Wenxue yanjiu hui (Literary Association), Ye Shaojun (later known as Ye Shengtao), altered it slightly by adding the grass element to the character "mao," thus making it an actual surname and giving it a twist something like "Kontradiction" in English. Because most of his significant works from that time on were published under this name, he is best known as Mao Dun.

The key to Mao Dun's creation of his early protagonists and to understanding the works of fiction he wrote in 1927–1931 lies in the basic contradiction embodied in their lives. One side of that contradiction is their disillusionment with and continuing interest in "making revolution," however vague and immature their conception of revolution. The other side is typified by each protagonist's search for some personal fulfillment or liberation independent of the fate of a social class or the nation as a whole.

The Marxist critic Georg Lukács, in a passage particularly applicable to Mao Dun's early fiction, wrote that

> since human nature is not finally separable from social reality, each narrative detail will be significant to the extent that it expresses the dialectic between man-as-individual and man-as-social being. It is these tensions and contradictions both within the individual and underlying the individual's relation with his fellow beings — all of which tensions

increase in intensity with the evolution of capitalism — that must form the subject-matter of contemporary realism.[1]

The emphasis placed upon a central contradiction within a dialectical framework of literary analysis is a fruitful approach to Mao Dun; there is more than sufficient evidence within the texts themselves to warrant an approach that posits the dichotomy between making a revolution and seeking personal fulfillment as the central contradiction: the pursuit of personal liberation from economic insecurity, alienation, reduced social status, and the constrictions of traditional Chinese culture (especially those enforced upon women by family or social limitations) in order to save one's individual self *versus* devoting oneself to active participation in revolutionary struggle in order to build a more just society and save the nation are themes central to most of Mao Dun's early works.

It may well be that the division of various elements into categories (such as that of the political/historical/social/revolutionary in contradistinction to that of the personal/psychological/individual/romantic) required for this scheme of analysis involves a certain arbitrariness. This arbitrary effect is, however, no more pronounced in the application of an analytical framework that seeks to clarify by exploring the conflicting tensions within a unified contradiction than the arbitrariness inherent in any other mode of literary analysis. Splitting apart the two sides of an important contradiction in the process of undertaking a retrospective evaluation of the literary experience is one way of providing the limited focus necessary for critical analysis.

The insights to be gained during retrospective analysis subsequent to the initial, direct experiencing of a literary work in all its bold, vivid immediacy provide a major justification for literary criticism. That these insights will be conditioned by the application of preexisting "criteria of interpretation" or "analytic categories" is unavoidable. Nevertheless, the literary analyst must strive to select a mode or modes of analysis that fit the complex reality of the literature being analyzed. The underlying structure and meaning of Mao Dun's earliest fiction serves to draw the reflective gaze of systematic analysis toward a heightened awareness of the central contradiction embodied in these novelettes and short stories. Whether or not one is predisposed to accept what may be called a dialectical mode of analysis, the validity of this approach is demonstrated with reference to the increased comprehension and pleasure it affords the reader or critic by enhancing his or her awareness of the underlying bond linking the two sides of the central contradiction. Of course, the validity of this approach does not necessarily exclude the applicability or validity of any other.

Disillusionment after the Failures of the 1927 Revolution

> Ever since taking part in the demonstrations at her Provincial Girls' School last year, Jing had become very negative as she watched so many of her schoolmates gradually abandon the true objectives of participation in the movement as they began instead to run about with — fall in love with — those handsome young "society" men who were lending loud vocal support to the righteous cause. She felt they richly deserved the ridicule of others; it really did make her angry. She developed an extreme loathing for this type of "activism" and, ignoring the taunts of her enthusiastic schoolmates that she was weak-willed, she dropped out of things right in midstream, her illusions shattered and disappointed with everything.[2]

The first chapter of *Disillusionment* (Huanmie) takes up the pressing question that faces almost every protagonist in Mao Dun's early fiction — what to do with one's life. With few exceptions, the main characters in the fiction produced between the autumn of 1927 (when he wrote *Disillusionment* and the end of 1931 are between eighteen and twenty-five years old, educated in urban high schools and colleges, born into well-educated families of some means, and have not yet settled into a career or family responsibilities. Many of them are also pursuing romantic love or are attempting to marry by choice rather than be pressured into an arranged marriage. With this narrow range of class background, age, and life experience characteristic of Mao Dun's early protagonists, it is not surprising that his early plots revolve around the search for a proper place and role in society. It is, after all, a problem commonly faced by persons of that age in various societies and eras. Mao Dun reveals and clarifies this existential search by the more politicized and educated youth through the description of historical context, the development of plot, and the delineation of character. The conceptualization of this existential search is expressed by the words and thoughts of various protagonists as well as by the impersonal narrative. Though much caution need be exercised in relating a fictional world to the historical, there is no question that in Mao Dun's mind, and in that of his intended public, there was a direct relation between the two worlds. In this sense, Mao Dun was very much within the "realist camp," with its essentially mimetic theory of art, which took such a strong hold on fiction in the West during the middle and latter part of the nineteenth century.[3]

The first half of *Disillusionment* takes place in Shanghai in the late spring of 1926. The demonstrations mentioned in the passage quoted above refer to those that erupted in the summer of 1925 during the May Thirtieth movement. In the second half of the novel, a sadder but wiser Jing flees the disappointment of a disastrous first love affair by going with several idealistic former classmates to Wuhan, where she hopes to find herself by working for the good of China. She goes to work for the new revolutionary government that had been established there after the military successes of the first Northern Expedition. But she is once again disillusioned and disgusted with the opportunism, chicanery, and degeneracy she encounters. Working as a nurse in a hospital for wounded soldiers, Jing falls in love with Qiang Meng, a patient under her care. They are married, but her newfound happiness is soon spoiled when he is recalled to the front lines.

While writing *Disillusionment* in September and October of 1927 in Shanghai, Mao Dun decided to write two more short novels as the second and third parts of a trilogy. He wrote *Dongyao* (Vacillation) in November and December and *Zhuiqiu* (Searching) between April and June of 1928. These three tenuously interrelated novelettes were then published as a trilogy entitled *Shi* (Corrosion, also sometimes rendered "The eclipse" or "The canker"). Mao Dun tells us:

> I had decided . . . to write about the three different periods modern youth had gone through in the time of revolution: (1) the exuberance on the eve of revolution and the disillusionment when coming face to face with it; (2) the vacillation [wavering] during the intensification of the revolutionary struggle; (3) after the disillusionment and vacillation, the unwillingness to accept loneliness and still wanting to make a final search.[4]

The plot of *Vacillation* centers on political turmoil in an unspecified county seat (*xiancheng*) in Hupeh province during the first half of 1927, when it was governed by representatives of the Wuhan government. The protagonist, Fang Luolan, an educated young man in his early thirties, has been made the head of the Merchants' Association by the local left-wing GMD administration.[5] Fang is trapped between the conflicting interests of the local merchants (the bourgeoisie) and the clerks' union supported by the Peasants' Association (the proletariat). He is even more torn between his sense of loyalty to his pretty but somewhat traditional wife and his new love for a politically active, modern, and sexually liberated woman who has been sent out from Wuhan to work with the Women's Association.

In the third work, *Searching*, the locale shifts back to Shanghai. The several young protagonists, all former schoolmates at the same college in Shanghai where Jing was studying in the first part of *Disillusionment* are at loose ends in the spring of 1928 after having participated in the revolutionary struggle that had ended in failure and repression the previous year. In their various ways, they are searching for something meaningful to do with their lives, something to keep alive the ideals and dreams that were discredited by the previous year's experiences. Even the less idealistic and relatively pragmatic Wang Zhongzhao, who is struggling hard to build a career for himself in journalism, is denied a happy ending. In the highly pessimistic, melancholy, and loosely plotted *Searching*, the more idealistic and spirited protagonists who are still "searching" for a way to fulfill their ideal of finding themselves by doing something of service to their society suffer frustrations and unhappy endings almost as bleak as those of the more "decadent" characters.

The opening chapter of *Searching* has Zhang Manqing suddenly turning up in Shanghai after a year's participation in revolutionary work elsewhere. He is very depressed and detached, thus presenting a great contrast for those who knew him as a dedicated and idealistic student activist in the preceding years. His friend and former class-mate, Wang Zhongzhao, brings him to their alumni club and tries to cheer him up by pointing out that everyone else is just as depressed these days as Zhang. Wang tells Zhang that he will regain his courage and again transcend his era rather than just sleepwalk through it. Zhang responds that even if he does, he must seek a new direction. Questioning whether it's better to burst the bubble of illusion upon which all of one's dreams depend or to go on deceiving oneself, to allow oneself to dream those pleasant dreams, he answers his own question:

> As for me, I'd rather take the pain of disillusionment. That's why I hate the past year but also am grateful to it at the same time, grateful to that year of laughter and tears and mixed-up affairs. Me pessimistic? Yes, I admit that I am but it's not from the loss of my dreams. No, it's because of the sickness of our times that I see. But that's nothing more than the small price we had to pay for the experiences of this past year.[6]

Zhang's new direction is to pursue a career in education. Much like the madman in Lu Xun's "Kuangren riji" (Diary of a madman), Zhang Manqing apparently feels China's only hope lies in educating the children who are not yet old enough to have been corrupted by their feudalistic culture and Confucian hypocrisy. Zhang views his own generation as having already proved itself incapable of saving the nation, even though this generation has years to go before attaining the ripe old age of thirty.

Another former classmate, Zhang Qiuliu, with whom Zhang Manqing had been falling in love just before he went off to participate in the revolution, passionately rejects the new direction he is advocating. She insists that it simply won't do for them to bury themselves in study while living through such momentous events — the fiery movements of their time. Nor can they sell out to the corrupt life of money-grubbing nor become bandits and burglars:

> We're bored and stultified all day. We gather together here to mess around for a while, we go to dance halls to fritter away our evenings, and in times of greatest depression, we laugh and shout, we wildly hug and kiss. We're completely decadent, we carry on fast and loose, but all the while holding back our tears. Yet who of us is *willingly* wasting away his life like this? We still must go forward. That is what's behind this decision of ours to organize a new [activist] group.[7]

At first glance, the reader may imagine that Zhang Qiuliu will be the positive, activist, and healthy foil to Zhang Manqing. But she is soon discovered to be one of Mao Dun's sexually uninhibited and rebellious young women protagonists, not without considerable appeal but generally unsuitable in their hedonism, pessimism, and immaturity to function as "revolutionary heroines."

Before Mao Dun began to write fiction, he had temporarily departed Shanghai and his highly successful literary career there in the industrial, commercial, and literary center of China. A leading young critic, editor, and translator during the period from 1920 to 1925, he left in order to take part in the revolutionary movement.[8] Going first to Canton in early 1926 to work with other radical intellectuals in propaganda and education, Mao Dun soon returned to Shanghai. He left again to go to Wuhan, where he spent the first half of 1927 as editor of the *Minguo ribao* (Minguo daily newspaper). This gave him a good vantage point to observe the workings of the left-wing GMD-CCP alliance in carrying out the revolution. But when this early revolutionary government and the alliance upon which it was based collapsed in the late spring and early summer of 1927, he fled Wuhan in late July for the summer resort area of Kuling near Kiukiang, where Mount Lu provides relief from the heat. Although Mao Dun refers to this month in Kuling as *yang bing* (recuperating) in his famous essay "Cong Guling dao Dongjing" (From Kuling to Tokyo),[9] his post-1949 explanation that this was a euphemism for "hiding out" is entirely plausible. In any case, he was back in Shanghai at the end of August, out of work, no doubt blacklisted and in danger of arrest for his past involvement in the Wuhan revolutionary regime. It was under these circumstances, in a severely disillusioned state of mind about the revolution, that Mao Dun began to write fiction.

Mao Dun is typical of the writers who created the new, vernacular "modern Chinese literature" in the 1920s: he was born to a family of scholar-gentry background whose economic fortunes had declined. Not yet in his teens when the upward mobility offered by the imperial examinations ended, he received some modern education in a major urban intellectual center (attending a Peking University preparatory school from about 1913 to 1916) but apparently could not afford to go to college. While other modern Chinese writers went abroad for study, Mao Dun worked for the Commercial Press in Shanghai. Although he never actually traveled to Europe or America, his "journey to the West" through the reading of Western literary works proved to have a significant impact on him.

Having personally participated in the 1927 revolutionary experience in Wuhan and having witnessed its demise, a great tension had been created within Mao Dun. On the one hand he totally rejected any accommodation with either traditional Chinese society or the emerging right-wing GMD regime, both of which he considered backward, corrupt, and unjust. On the other hand he was reacting against the incompetence, stupidity, and hypocrisy he perceived to be at the root of the recent revolutionary failures. As a sensitive individual of literary bent who was forced to live in hiding in Shanghai that fall, Mao Dun chose to express this tension in the form of fiction. He may also have been in need of money and hoped to earn some by writing.

The search for an acceptable future by most of his early protagonists is impelled by their discouragement with the way in which the 1927 revolutionary movement had turned out and by their continued commitment to ideals and goals that would require a revolutionary solution to China's problems. Like Mao Dun, the cultural and political radical who had taken up writing fiction and invented them, these young protagonists had taken some active part in the May Thirtieth movement, the Northern Expedition in the latter half of 1926, or the Wuhan revolutionary government in the first half of 1927 — generally in the role of educated youth responsible for propaganda and public education work. While many of their fellow revolutionaries perished in the bloodletting by the military/police forces of the right-wing GMD now controlled by Chiang Kai-shek, these protagonists had somehow survived to suffer severe demoralization.

Not surprisingly, these early works, with their pessimistic tone and demoralized, often promiscuous, bourgeois protagonists, were very sharply criticized by Marxist literary critics. In the preface to his first collection of short stories, *Ye qiangwei* (Wild roses), in 1929, Mao Dun defends his practice of describing "the dark reality" and attributes true courage to those who can find the proof of a happier future within the "loathsome evil" of an unhappy present: "We have no need of lamentations for that which is already past nor empty glorification of that which lies ahead; rather we must focus our attention on reality, analyze reality, strip bare reality. But those who cannot see reality with any clarity still constitute a great number."[10]

It is easy to discern the stubborn independence and integrity of Mao Dun the writer striving for a realistic picture of the times as they are, however discouraging, rather than painting them as Mao Dun the revolutionary might wish them to be. This commitment to providing a picture of reality, whether social, psychological, historical, or economic, is central to Mao Dun's literary theory and practice right from the beginning. Ye Ziming uses the term "critical realism" to characterize Mao Dun's style during the early period of his fiction.[11]

A useful and succinct presentation of the theory of critical realism can be found in the work of the unorthodox Marxian critic Ernst Fischer, who traces the historical progression from romanticism to critical realism in his stimulating work *The Necessity of Art:*

> Out of the Romantic revolt of the lonely "I," out of a curious mixture of the aristocratic and plebian denials of bourgeois values, came *critical realism.* The Romantic protest against bourgeois society turned more and more into criticism of that society — without, however, losing the nature of the protesting "I" . . . The attitude has not fundamentally changed, only the method has become different, colder, more "objective," more distant.[12]

Although Fischer is writing about the development of fiction in Europe, Mao Dun was, as already noted, at least as influenced by Western realism as by native Chinese literary traditions. Perhaps the leading champion in China of nineteenth-century European realism and naturalism during the early years of the May Fourth period, Mao Dun specifically acknowledged Tolstoy and Zola to be two of his favorite writers. His style itself, with its impersonal, often detached tone and its verbose, sometimes awkward sentence structure and formidable diction, gives evidence of his indebtedness to European realism.

Through his style, he maintains a certain distance between the reader and the protagonist, even when the narrative enters into the thoughts of a protagonist. Some readers find this impersonal, "realistic" style somewhat too detached and perhaps a bit clinical in the attention given to detail (one indication of the influence of Zola and naturalism). However, this stylistic device of distancing, so prevalent in the critical realism of the modern writer seeking to expose social evils, is also consistent with the requirements of Mao Dun's overall thematic scheme. At least part of the motive force for his literary creation originated in the contradictory feelings about revolution and personal fulfillment he and many others like him were experiencing at the time. Maintaining sufficient distance between reader and characters/plot serves to draw the underlying contradiction into sharper focus.

One method of achieving this distance is the use of a secondary character, such as Teacher He in "Semang" (Color-blind), or Ke, the teacher-revolutionary in his 1931 allegorical novelette *San ren xing* (Of three friends), to provide a level-headed and telling critique of the protagonist. Using E. M. Forster's terminology, these two characters are so "flat" as to be almost disembodied. Yet for all their one-dimensional lifelessness and abstraction, they can keep the reader aware of an alternate and perhaps more objective viewpoint than that of the "rounded" protagonist. For example, the teacher-revolutionary He is the voice of the Chinese Communist party itself or one of its members.

Literary critics and scholars opposed to "extrinsic approaches" have a tendency to minimize any reliance on what a writer says about his intentions or even the writer's own interpretation of his work. Obviously, a biographical approach to the study of a writer and his works has its limitations, as does an investigation into the explicit and implicit values transmitted. The mechanical application of rigid ideological or moral yardsticks to literature generally fosters little appreciation for the wide range of thematic concerns in a work, still less for its form, its style, or its aesthetic impact. But it would be foolhardy to attempt an interpretation of Mao Dun's fiction without considering various ideological concerns or biases, however subtle and artistically integrated into the literary text these might be. Passages from his prefaces and postscripts, as well as essays such as "From Kuling to Tokyo," can provide helpful guideposts in identifying some of his symbols. They also serve as indication of deeply felt concerns that may lie behind the writer's invention and use of those symbols.

In his relatively long short story "Color-Blind" dated March 3, 1929, Mao Dun's protagonist is another intellectual youth who was in Wuhan with the revolutionary forces and returned to Shanghai in the spring of 1928. This young man, Lin Baishuang, torn between his somewhat weakened sense of political responsibility and a thirst for being in love, learns from his friend, Teacher He, that people have started to call him decadent for fooling around with romance. Lin Baishuang's only response to these criticisms that he is backward, vacillating, or going soft is an enigmatic smile and contemptuous pity for

> those brave men whose harsh censure was the same as had once been applied to them themselves; even more he felt sorry for them since it would probably not be long before they used these same words to praise themselves. How well he knew where these brave fighters had purchased their lottery tickets for the "society of the future" and how they believed that the grand drawing would be held in the next three years, how they were thus doing all they could to be "the early birds" in establishing themselves as heroes.[13]

While Lin Baishuang's or any other character's thinking should not be taken as identical to Mao Dun's, there is a striking resemblance between the lottery tickets Lin ridicules in "Color-Blind" and the vouchers Mao Dun derides in the preface to *Wild Roses*.

> Those who know how to have faith in the future are indeed fortunate and deserving of our praise. They should, however, be careful not to take "historical certainty" as a voucher issued for their personal happiness, nor should this voucher be peddled without restraint. The "social forces" that lack true conciousness and merely depend on this voucher as their morphine needle are nothing but houses built on sand

and lead to nothing but almost inevitable failure.[14]

The short story and preface were apparently written within two months of each other in the spring of 1929 during Mao Dun's almost two-year stay in Japan. Both forcefully express his disdain for those naïve radicals and CCP literary critics who he believed were clinging to a blind optimism due to the self-interest, dogmatism, and intellectual timidity that prevented them from confronting unpleasant truths. In the story, Lin derives a certain vindictive satisfaction in predicting ignominious reversals just ahead for the "brave fighters" who dare criticize him. Even Teacher He, who is still working hard for the revolution, speaks with cutting sarcasm about those revolutionaries who shout slogans yet change nothing. Still another example of Mao Dun's frequent and satiric descriptions of the gap between revolutionary ideals and frustrating, dismal reality is the ironic story "Nining" (Mud), dated April 1929. In it the peasants fear their young Northern Expedition liberators because of rumors about "communizing wives"; in the end two peasants, Old Huang and his third son, are summarily executed for no good reason when the warlord forces return. These examples suggest that Mao Dun's faith in an achievable revolution as China's salvation must have been quite shaken at this time.

As suggested earlier, Mao Dun was not the kind of man who was happy to take orders from anyone, including CCP literary men, about how or what he should write. Although a less than completely airtight censorship by the GMD gave him some leeway, nonetheless a certain minimum discretion was clearly a necessity. We should not mistake his independent stance or ambivalencies for downright opposition to making revolution, revolutionary goals, or the Chinese Communist party per se. There are some hints that may indicate a subtle expression of support for revolutionary forces, particularly in the works written after he went to Tokyo in the summer of 1928. Yet given the writer's own experiences and earliest works of fiction, it is certain that his feelings about many of the revolutionaries and the disturbing aspects of revolution in the making were highly ambivalent. Furthermore, we can safely assume that Mao Dun expected his intended audience (mainly urban-educated, bourgeois youth) to recognize and perhaps identify with his own ambivalent feelings as conveyed by his early protagonists.

John Berninghausen

Changing Times and Personal Insecurity

A characteristic of the bourgeois youth in Mao Dun's early fiction is their acute awareness of the rapidly and unpredictably changing times in which they were living. This awareness produced considerable alienation and increased their feelings of insecurity just as foreign imperialism and economic penetration of China greatly increased the nation's sense of insecurity.

At least two generations of Chinese intellectuals before Mao Dun had been absorbed in a painful and ultimately unsuccessful effort to adapt the traditional Chinese order and values to the extremely disruptive effects of the industrial revolution, expanding international trade, and imperialism. Yet the old order, Chinese traditions, and Confucian values receive scant attention in Mao Dun's fiction. Not only does he rarely attack or seek to discredit the "ugly reality" of old China, but also his infrequent use of popular Confucian sayings is so noticeable that it seems intentional.

Despite the relatively high class background of most of Mao Dun's protagonists, they are portrayed as being afflicted with a sense of insecurity in the late 1920s. Apparently they just did not know how or when they would be able to capitalize on their privileged cultural and educational (if not wealthy) backgrounds and secure a good job. Of course, this problem was somewhat more complicated than usual for many of them, who could only be satisfied doing work that would significantly contribute to the remaking of their society as well as providing a livelihood and position in society commensurate with their background and expectations.

In *Disillusionment*, Hui, a friend of Jing's who has spent the last two years studying abroad, is looking for a job in Shanghai. She sends Jing a letter that describes her problems:

> I've already been turned down for three different jobs. I never thought getting a job would be this tough. Now my elder brother is saying: "Most of the students who have studied in the West, no matter whether they got a B.A. or an M.A. or a Ph.D., are not able to find a job when they come back to China. So for someone like you who has only eaten a couple of years of foreign rice, even if you did pick up a smattering of foreign speech, the only thing you could do would be to work as an errand girl in a Western firm, but they don't employ girls for that sort of work."[15]

244

An even more alienated attitude toward education and its uselessness in getting a job is stressed in the novelette *Lu* (The road), written in early 1931. The main character, Huo Xinchuan (usually called Xin), is graduating from a college in Wuhan in the spring of 1930. The son of an impoverished scholar family, he is very worried about finding a job and is gently satirized as hoping to take the traditional way out for poor scholars in China: marrying the daughter of a wealthy family. Riding on a ferry back across the Yangtze River from Hankow to Wuchang at the start of the novelette, Xin is thinking:

> His father had long been hoping that he could make some money and help out the family. But how could the old man (being generally out of touch with things) ever figure out that even he, one of their school's more promising students, had less chance of finding a position than a skilled laborer? Couldn't he join the party [GMD] and go into government work and politics? Well, not only did you need someone to bring you in but you also had to be able to flatter people and claw your way upward. As for teaching, they had no close relative or friend in the Education Ministry or currently serving as the head of some college or school.[16]

This passage is interesting not only as a reflection of the anxiety and insecurity of young Chinese intellectuals at the time but also as an example of Mao Dun's style, in which he takes us inside the thoughts of a protagonist rather than have all characterization carried within description by the voice of the narrative. (His extensive use of the interior monologue was noted some years ago.[17]) The description of his protagonists' thoughts, emotions, and anxieties points up the social and political tensions of the time. Technical devices such as interior monologue and, occasionally, impressionistic mental imagery, make the psychological dimension of his realism fairly compelling.

Sometimes the sense of a rapidly changing world acutely felt by many of Mao Dun's characters is interpreted hopefully as a sign that there is a chance for successful revolutionary change; occasionally it is joyfully expressed by someone who welcomes the breakdown of traditional roles, values, and the status quo. These positive aspects of rapid change are both present in Mao Dun's first short story, "Chuangzao" (Creation). Xianxian has become independent of her husband, who tried to mold her into a "perfect wife" only to lose his control over his "creation." Bored with Junshi's complaints about how she's changed, the now politically active and sexually unabashed

Xianxian points out the impossibility of hanging onto the status quo: "Who knows! Yesterday it was one thing, today it's another, tomorrow another yet. As for the day after tomorrow, I myself haven't even caught a glimpse of what it will be like in my dreams. This is precisely the wonderful and contagious affliction of our times."[18]

More often, however, the rapid changes and apparently chaotic developments cause the type of anxiety and insecurity that Fang Meili, the twenty-eight-year-old wife of Fang Luolan in *Vacillation*, expresses in response to her husband's criticism that she has become less lively and gay than she had once been: "I don't know what I should do anymore. Don't laugh, Luolan, but the world is certainly changing too fast, becoming too complicated and contradictory and I really have lost my way in it!"[19] Later on, when Fang Luolan himself does not know what to do when faced with a conflict between the merchants and the store clerks, the same words once spoken by his wife run ironically through his mind.[20]

The sense of helplessness and alienation of those faced with an uncertain future and caught up in the machinery of modern times is graphically described by Lin Baishuang in "Color-Blind":

> What appears to the average person to be a hero is actually just a cog in the giant machinery of human history; not only am I acutely aware of my insignificance but I don't even feel like part of the giant machinery's operation. My place in this machinery of modern life is less than that of a tiny screw. No, I'm just a bit of waste metal that happened to fall into the works, being pushed about and ground down amid the countless cogs and axles.[21]

The above metaphor is a typical example of Mao Dun's use of tropes of machinery in his early fiction as a stylistic device effective in enhancing the reader's awareness of certain essential themes. Tropes (metaphors, similes, symbolic images) involving machinery or technology are frequently employed to stress the sense of insecurity engendered by the rapid pace of change. These tropes also serve to link his characters' feelings of uncertainty and alienation to the profound changes caused by the incursion of Western technology and the early stages of industrialization.

In the later part of *Of Three Friends*, Yun travels to Shanghai with his father's last fifty gold coins in his pocket. Having left home and his former life as a student behind him forever at the age of twenty-one, he realizes that his father's fondest hope that he should make a success of himself and regain the family's former land holdings and independent position is an impossible fantasy. As for his father's other request of him, however, that he must never forget their enemies, it is strongly implied that Yun will succeed in doing something about this, because he is going to link up with the revolutionaries in Shanghai. Musing on the deck of the ship, Yun thinks about how much the world has changed in his father's lifetime:

> When his father had been twenty-one years old, he had still never seen one of these small steamers plying this river, far less were there any dark shadows of airplanes passing overhead through the skies above their farmland. Nor were there any diesel-powered water pumps back then such as the ones now being used by fat Dong and other big landowners like him — foreign water wheels. The world had changed and thus Yun, who was himself now twenty-one, would never be able to comprehend everything around him as his father had once been able to do, he would never be able to encompass his whole world in his thoughts. Furthermore, it probably would not be too long before his father wouldn't be able to either.[22]

Mao Dun was quite taken with this symbolic imagery — the commonplace yet very powerful symbolism for a traditional agrarian economy and unalienated sense of a well-integrated existence being shattered by technological innovations and the increased pace of change. He employed variations of this imagery again the following year in "Dangpuqian" (In front of the pawnshop) and "Chun can" (Spring silkworms). Occasionally entire stories seem to have been constructed around an elaborate metaphor that had inspired the author and that was highlighted in the title, such as "Shi yu sanwen" (Poetry and prose) and "Color-Blind." Sometimes Mao Dun's use of extended tropes seems partly explainable by the need to liven up a frequently verbose and awkward style. Not infrequently does one stumble across an unexpected patch of lyrical description, typically a word painting of a natural scene, the weather, the lighting; alternatively, the writer uses a setting in which nature or some inanimate thing described is personified to reflect the protagonist's mood.

Of Three Friends, a somewhat schematic novelette, sets up three young men who have all attended the same high school as symbols for three different philosophical and political tendencies in the response of Chinese youth to their socioeconomic difficulties. Xu, the love-sick romantic student who becomes an impractical and idealistic altruist;

Hui, the cynical nihilist who does not believe in taking any political action until the giant cataclysm comes to sweep everything away and let China start over; and Yun, the pragmatic materialist who eventually joins the revolutionary forces in Shanghai after his peasant father is forced to sell off his land in order to ransom his son's life from a corrupt local despot.

After Yun's father has been ruined, despite a lifetime of hard work on the land, Hui and Yun meet on a boat traveling down the Yangtze to Shanghai. Hui has recently seen a peasant revolution in the countryside and explains to Yun why he is returning to the city:

> What I had been waiting for and hoping for all along finally came to pass [a violent upheaval], but it didn't look anything like what I had envisioned . . . People are people, not gods. What human beings can accomplish will not be miracles but just plain ordinary things, "vile" things . . . Yun, the fire's too hot, the blood's just too red and fresh.[23]

A letter from Yun reaches Hui two months later. This long letter enunciates, more clearly than ever before in Mao Dun's fiction, the arguments for devoting one's life to revolution. Having outlined the whirlwind changes sweeping the world with specific references to the incursion of Japanese imperialism into Manchuria, Yun claims that no one can be impervious to them:

> There's one kind of man in this world who, no matter how simple and stubborn, will change for the better when he feels the full force of reality's metal band begin to tighten around his head, just like my father. But there's another kind of person who, no matter how educated and intelligent, will only change for the worse under the whiplashes of reality and that's you, Hui.[24]

The message of *Of Three Friends* appears to be that the force of reality in China will not permit the younger generation to opt out of the revolutionary struggle. Since this novelette was finished in October 1931, and the last third of the work clearly reflects the upsurge of patriotic feelings in the wake of the Mukden Incident and Japanese military aggression in Manchuria, which took place in September, Mao Dun can be seen to have already grasped the great role anti-imperialist sentiment would play in winning over popular support to the side of more progressive or revolutionary political forces in China.

Love, Women's Liberation, and Personal Fulfillment

Just as his youthful protagonists desire to do something with their lives to bring about a better society, many of Mao Dun's early protagonists also struggle to escape from being trapped in traditional, corrupt, or personally constricting roles. As may be seen in the example of Mei in *Hong* (The rainbow) or in the case of Xianxian in "Creation," Mao Dun is most interested in the modern young woman's search for liberation, although it is a liberation of a personal not a collective nature. Likewise, Lin Baishuang and Fang Luolan seek romantic love and an exciting sexual relationship as important to their personal fulfillment.

Many critics and literary historians have noted the importance given young women protagonists in Mao Dun's fiction, especially the early fiction, and have praised his technical skill and psychological insight in depicting them. For the Western reader becoming acquainted with Mao Dun's early works only now — almost fifty years after they were written — there will be many shocks of recognition, even perhaps a sense of déjà vu, in this fiction from a different culture and historical background.

In an era when the concepts and social practice of women's liberation are finally merging to become a powerful and historic movement, the extensive treatment of the issues involving women's liberation in China, or at least, those issues as documented for us by Mao Dun's early fiction, can be quite striking. Marián Gálik notes: "In 1921–22 Mao Dun devoted much attention to the question of the emancipation of women . . . His theoretical studies and frequent meetings with women in the course of his revolutionary activity helped Mao Dun to be known in Chinese literature as having created true-to-life women characters of high artistic value."[25]

In the final scene of "Creation," the insecure husband, Junshi, picks up a carved ivory rabbit he gave his wife as a souvenir. The two Chinese characters *zhangfu* (husband) have been scraped out with a knife. Junshi remembers that his wife, Xianxian, has expressed disapproval of this term *zhangfu* as being too overladen with the stench of traditional Confucian morality. She said that it automatically called to mind phrases like *fu zhe tian ye* (your husband is your everything). She had suggested that *airen* (lover) was preferable, but Junshi had not previously realized that *zhangfu* had already been added to her list of proscribed words.

At the end of the story, Xianxian goes out for some unspecified political activism. She leaves behind the pointedly symbolic message that Junshi must hurry and catch up — she is not going to wait for him. This suddenly clarifies an apparently insignificant detail in the story's opening — the heading "Women and Politics" on a magazine propped up against a lamp in their bedroom. Indeed, the central theme of "Creation" is the personal liberation of Xianxian from a husband who represents the Confucian male chauvinism and backward-looking selfishness of Chinese men. It is also significant that Xianxian moves toward political activism, even though the exact nature of that activism is not made specific.

In "Creation," Mao Dun also strikes at Confucianism itself, not only by means of the protagonist's objection to Confucian sexism but also with a bit of deft satire as the story opens with his description of their bedroom:

> From the right-hand corner of a small desk covered with a dark green cloth next to the south window two half-opened red roses leaned out from a small light blue porcelain vase with the impudent air of saucy, smiling young ladies. They seemed to laugh derisively at the stack of books bound in the foreign style and sitting there stiff and correct in their formal attire on the opposite corner of the desk, hoping to make it abundantly clear to one and all by this upright Confucian bearing that they certainly were not those novels that needed to demean themselves by touching upon relations between the sexes.[26]

The extended metaphor, the personification, the naturalistic attention to detail, and a hint of the protagonists' class and personality in the description of scene are characteristic of Mao Dun's fiction, particularly when he took the time to write carefully and was not just hurriedly throwing something together for immediate publication. Less typical of his early fiction, however, is the almost whimsical satire, the deft sense of humor revealed here. This occurs much more often in the short stories written after 1932.

The protagonist in *The Rainbow*, Mei Xingsu (or just Mei), is perhaps Mao Dun's most ambitious psychological study of a single character. This relatively long work of nearly three hundred pages (written in Tokyo during April–June 1929) tells of a young woman's struggle to break free from the traditional role of the bourgeois wife and of her painful search for a personal identity in the time between the May Fourth Incident (1919) and the May Thirtieth Incident (1925). In this six-year period, a span of time longer than is generally encompassed in a single work by Mao Dun, Mei gets married but then leaves her husband, Liu Yuchum (an unassuming and hardworking businessman, he is devoted to her but understands neither her nor her resentment of a marriage arranged in the traditional fashion), supports herself for a while as a teacher but eventually leaves her home province of Szechuan to go to Shanghai. There she is drawn into the political turmoil of the May Thirtieth movement and by the end of the novel is on the way to becoming a revolutionary, or at least, a politically conscious and active modern woman. The development of her life, like that of Xianxian, links both sides of the contradiction between the liberation of the individual (the individual woman) and political responsibility (participating in the struggle to save China and make revolution). In both instances, the side of the contradiction involving personal liberation is stronger, and is given much more attention in the narrative, than the countervailing effort to find one's identity by involvement in collective political struggle. This latter side of the central contradiction is a potentiality only vaguely revealed at the end. In the cases of Jing in *Disillusionment* and Lin Baishuang in "Color-Blind," however, there is an almost manic-depressive fluctuation between the two extremes.

With the wider latitude and scope of a novel held together by a steady focus on one protagonist, *The Rainbow* finds Mao Dun taking the time necessary to depict much of the *process* of Mei's personal struggle. Spending the summer in Chungking after abandoning her marriage, Mei cares for a sick friend. She just lets the time slide by, day after day:

> She had long since used a burning anger and hatred to cauterize the hot, stinging tears of past sorrows. Even when some scene or object would accidentally provoke stirrings of the old resentments deep within the recesses of her heart, these would be instantly repressed by her unrelenting reason. She had already used the keen sword of her will to cut off all ties to her past. As for the future? Her daydreams about the future had always been very pale; for the present she had none at all. Thus she had no way to trick herself into feeling some sort of spurious happiness. No, she had only this monotonous gray present and could do nothing but passively let the present slip into the past, abandoning it forever to forgotten memories.[27]

But Mei, a heroine in the tradition of Ibsen's Nora, is stronger than this. Soon Mei tells her friend, Xu Qijun, that she is determined to take a lover and find her own way in the world. This worries Qijun, who now comprehends that:

> Mel's external serenity was not just laziness or irresponsibility but was instead a determination to "walk right into danger with her head held high." This "discovery" made her tremble, and moreover she could not help having some doubts for the new thinking that was normally quite easy for her to believe in: people are being awakened to a new awareness, are being called forward, are moving ahead, but not toward the light, toward darkness instead. The fighters who are shouting out their war cries to arouse the young have not prepared a bright and happy society into which refugees [from the old one] can be received.[28]

Skillfully portraying his heroine's vacillating moods, Mao Dun has successfully conveyed a sensitive and disturbing awareness of just how frightening it was for a young Chinese woman in the 1920s actually to put into practice the theories of "liberation" with which many modern young women identified. The way in which he articulated his protagonist's doubts and fears increases respect for Mao Dun's realism and admiration for his heroine.

The change in social values taking place in China at this time is exemplified by the desire of "modern youth" to arrange their own marriages or at least have veto power over unacceptable parental choices. Zhao Yunqiu, one of the two young women to whom Lin Baishuang is attracted, is in imminent danger of being married off against her wishes by a venal father. Lin becomes aware of this only when Li Huifang tells him about Zhao Yunqiu's problem. Li Huifang denounces Zhao Yunqiu's father for betrothing his own daughter to a military officer in Nanking who is already married: "When those old bureaucrats want to get back into an official position [government], there's simply no trick or scheme they won't use no matter what!"[29]

Although Mao Dun obviously sympathizes with these young women, he probably had somewhat ambivalent feelings about freedom of choice in love and marriage, just as he harbored conflicting feelings about revolution. In "Zisha" (Suicide), the protagonist, Miss Huan, has been given a handsome dowry *and* her freedom to choose a husband by the kind hearted and understanding aunt who raised her. She becomes involved with a young revolutionary who leaves her pregnant (although unknowingly), and she hangs herself, because neither she nor her society (at least in her mind) could accept this kind of reality, this outcome of her first independent action. Just as she is about to kill herself, her life rushes past her eyes: "She remembered how the tide of a new age had excited her soul when she was seventeen, how she had hungered for the glorious new future, dreamed of the happiness to come; how she had congratulated herself on the fact that she'd like to arrange her own marriage, how she had tentatively yet joyfully become acquainted with members of the opposite sex, but it had all turned out like this!"[30] To Miss Huan, all these concepts of freedom, liberty, and progress now seem fraudulent. It would have been better, she reflects, if they had arranged the marriage. Then she could have had at least as happy a life as that of her cousin's wife.

There is further evidence of Mao Dun's own contradiction regarding the modern liberated woman. He often uses two women characters as foils for each other and as the simultaneous objects of a male protagonist's attention. Zhao Yunqiu and Li Huifang in "Color-Blind" have already been mentioned. Zhao is "gentle, rational, inspirational, and knows how to love you," while Li is "vivacious, passionate, sexy, and knows how to make you fall for her." The same dichotomy occurs in *Vacillation*. Fang Luolan's wife, Meili, represents the traditional type of ideal Chinese woman. These are quite appealing to many of Mao Dun's male characters, some of whom are quite dubious about whether the liberated and politically active "new woman" is all that lovable even if she is sexually exciting. Fang Luolan's lover, Sun Wuyang, represents the experienced, self-confident, impetuous, and committed political activist who is also the personally and sexually liberated woman. Fang Luolan is a protagonist with whom the author seems to have identified more than with most other male characters;[31] Fang really begins to fall for Sun Wuyang only when he finds out that she is not only spontaneous and vivacious but is also gentle, charming, sensitive and has "a pure and refined soul."[32] Similarly, in *Searching*, Zhang Manqing says that his life has done a complete about-face. Instead of craving excitement and stimulation, he now wants a peaceful existence:

> I feel this new attitude I now have toward life has changed many of my ideas. Even in the realm of love, my ideal is now someone gentle and quiet, a woman who doesn't like empty talk and who is above paying attention to trivialities. That combative spirit of our female fellow students, so political with mouthfuls of "save the nation" and "save the people," those so-called political activist women don't appeal to me at all.[33]

Other women characters who are foils for each other in the dichotomy between old-fashioned virtue and reserved charm versus uninhibited sexuality and aggressive political/cultural activism are Jing Yong and Du Ruo in *The Road,* Jing and Hui in *Disillusionment,* and Biaomei and Cassia in "Poetry and Prose."

"Poetry and Prose" (written in December 1928), exposes the hypocrisy of some men's attitudes toward women and sex. A young man, Bing, has seduced Cassia (Gui), the physically attractive widow of a respectable man, and has been carrying on an affair with her for a few months. After receiving a gift of flowers from Biaomei, his younger cousin with whom he is now infatuated, Bing begins to feel disgust for Cassia. The title comes from the metaphor Bing uses to explain (and justify) his change of heart. Biaomei is now the "poetry" in his life whereas Cassia has lost her mystery. The "soul-trembling poetry" of the adventure and spiritual pleasure he experienced the first time they made love now seems merely physical and lascivious. She has turned into something mundane and ugly like "prose." Cassia knows Bing now despises her, but she doesn't intend to let him be rid of her so easily. She also knows that no matter what he says, he still cannot resist her physical allure, that he is an enormous hypocrite: "You mouth rhapsodies to some kind of poetic relations between the sexes, some kind of exalted, mysterious, and spiritual love, but the fact is that once you see some bare flesh, you're intoxicated by it, you go crazy over it, you pant and slobber just like a dog."[34]

Mao Dun delights in titillating the reader with erotic scenes, and on a more serious level, often appears to locate the personal fulfillment of some women characters with a nonconformist life-style and liberated sexuality, sometimes hinting at a revolutionary potential. Yet he does not project a happy or socially useful destiny for protagonists like Zhang Qiuliu and Wang Shitao of *Searching,* who are sexually promiscuous.

Realism and Objectivity

Mao Dun was very much a writer of his own time, and most of his fiction has a contemporaneous quality somewhere in between journalism and "instant history." Nearly every piece of his early fiction has at least a few historical references that demark a temporal setting only one or two years before publication. None of Mao Dun's male protagonists is obviously autobiographical nor do his plots seem to be autobiography disguised as fiction, "Autumn in Kuling" being the notable exception. Nevertheless, the writer and his readers meet on the common ground of their preoccupation with their *own* times.

At the end of the second section of his essay, "From Kuling to Tokyo," Mao Dun explains how he had closeted himself on the third floor of a house in Shanghai for about ten months writing the three novels of *Corrosion*. Already in 1928, having recently commenced his illustrious career as one of China's leading writers of modern fiction, he expresses his desire for objectivity: "The only thing I was concerned about was not allowing my individual subjectivity to sneak in, and moreover, to make the characters in *Disillusionment* and *Vacillation* respond to the revolution in a manner consistent with the objective situation of the times."[35]

The literary critics who were loyal to the CCP and wished to adhere closely to Soviet literary practice were quick to point out the absence of "positive heroes" or "model characters" in Mao Dun's early fiction. Qian Xingcun criticized him for overemphasizing the disillusioned and vacillating backward elements and for lacking the necessary sympathy and breadth of vision needed to describe adequately the great liberation movement of their time: "Since reality must have two aspects, and since any writer who is truly representative of the times must be a spokesman for either the "courageous true revolutionaries" or a spokesman for the "disillusioned, vacillating and backward types," the issue then becomes one of what it is that a writer of this era should do to fulfill his mission."[36]

It is true in Mao Dun's early fiction we find no hero of the externally cheerful, self-sacrificing, morally puritanical, unflinching and ruggedly handsome type all too frequent in the didactic allegories of socialist realism or revolutionary romanticism. Mao Dun had already given his answer to this particular problem in the preface to *Wild Roses*:

> Among the protagonists there is not a single courageous one worthy of veneration or fully awakened. It is, of course, true that there are some really courageous revolutionaries, some real revolutionaries, in this chaotic society, but there are far, far more who are not so brave nor so fully awakened. In my opinion, it is very good to write about a character who is beyond reproach and who can serve as a model for everyone. However, it is also a worthwhile thing to write about the tragedy or bleak demise of some 'ordinary people' and in this way open up people's eyes.[37]

Another explanation for Mao Dun's unwillingness or inability to create the type of heroic and exemplary protagonist some CCP critics were advocating may be related to his inclination to set up dialectical relationships with his characters. He either established two different characters as foils to each other, each representing one-half of a contradiction or conflict, or he embodied the contradiction in a single character, pulled first one way and then the other. In either case, the struggle that sometimes rages and sometimes simmers between the two sides of the contradiction makes for more interesting and plausible characters than romanticized, blameless, and heroic model protagonists, however inspiring their piously delineated virtues. For these latter, the only struggle can be one leading to inevitable victory over equally abstracted villains, who are totally evil and just as boring for the lack of any humane aspect as are the "model heroes" for lack of any serious flaw.

In Mao Dun's early works, the male protagonists usually represent and express the negative or passive side of youth's response to revolution. But after his return from Japan in April 1930 to Shanghai, Mao Dun immediately joined the newly founded League of Left-wing Writers. Possibly he then encountered a more sophisticated Marxist analysis of China's plight and of how the writer should serve the revolution. He doubtless came into close contact with many revolutionary intellectuals and CCP members in the league, where he was one of the leading activists.

Mao Dun's first attempts to write about nonbourgeois protagonists, or at least provide more "rounded" secondary characters belonging to a class background lower than his own, date from 1931 with the short story, "Xiju" (A comedy), and the schematic, allegorical *Of Three Friends*, completed that fall. Yun, the pragmatic son of a landowning peasant who becomes a revolutionary at the end of *Of Three Friends*, represents the writer's efforts finally to create a male protagonist embodying the positive side of his generation's ambivalent attitudes toward a Marxist revolution.

Although he had probably recovered sufficiently from his earlier disillusionment with the revolution to be willing to attempt a more "positive" message at this time, Mao Dun had difficulty integrating such a message or protagonist into his plot. Perhaps he was being circumspect in the face of GMD repression against left-wing writers or perhaps he had not yet found a satisfactory method of embodying the positive side of the contradiction into a character or plot that would be consistent with his own high standards of realism and objectivity. Perhaps both are true. His greatly increased skill in depicting both sides of a dichotomy developed rapidly after the return to his home area (T'ung-hsiang county in Chekiang province, where he was born in 1896) following the Japanese bombardment of Shanghai on January 28, 1932. This development partially accounts for the artistic advances in the works he wrote afterward.

Those young Chinese sufficiently well educated and sophisticated to read Mao Dun's ornate, highly literate style with ease, not to mention sufficiently cosmopolitan, alienated, and "modern" to want to read it, came mainly from a middle- to upper-class background. Naturally, Mao Dun's own class background and that of his limited audience made it difficult for him to create a convincing account of purely economic hardships sufficiently severe to bring China's bourgeois or petty bourgeois youth over a total commitment to revolution. Mao Dun's integrity as a realist writer striving to write about those things he had perceived and analyzed as objectively as possible thus precluded the use of simplistic *economic* inevitability being employed as the motive force driving his earliest protagonists into the revolutionary struggle. But the novelettes written in 1931, *The Road*, and *Of Three Friends*, are transitions between his early fiction and his more mature works of 1932–1942. A crucial element of this transition was precisely the increased attention given to economic forces in contrast with the heavily psychological focus on individual consciousness that marks the novels *Corrosion*, *Wild Roses* and especially *The Rainbow*.

In Mao Dun's works during the period from the autumn of 1927 to the end of 1931, two main themes (the theme of politics, recent history, and revolution intertwined with while simultaneously pulling against the theme of personal liberation, psychological alienation, and the individual's search for self-fulfillment) provide a central contradiction. While either of these two themes may dominate the narrative at any given time, they generally are interwoven in a convincing fashion. Mao Dun himself makes the close connection between love and politics quite explicit in his preface to *Wild Roses:*

> These five stories are clothed in the outer garments of "love." I, the author, have tried to show each individual's class "consciousness" by means of his or her behavior in love. This is not an easy thing to accomplish with the desired effect, but the open-minded and judicious reader will probably perceive that behind the depiction of love lie some significant issues.[38]

The protagonists vacillate between the two sides of the central contradiction and usually suffer some disillusionment in the attempt to serve the nation as youthful activists from a relatively well-educated background; equally do they find themselves disillusioned in their search for personal fulfillment and love. The protagonist of Mao Dun's first work of fiction, Jing in *Disillusionment*, starts out quite disillusioned with politics, tries to find herself in a love affair, thereby losing her virginity to the opportunist Bao Su (who happens to be a secret informer on the payroll of the reactionary forces), then bounces back from that disillusionment to join her friends in the revolutionary upsurge connected with the Northern Expedition:

> She already had visions of a new life — an exciting, glorious, ardent new life was waiting to welcome her with open arms. This young woman who had been vanquished on the field of love now turned her eyes in a new direction, her heart filled with the hope of finding her solace and the joy of being alive by "serving society."[39]

The character Lin Baishuang, in "Color-Blind," also portrays the interrelationship between love and politics when he is defending himself to Teacher He (a symbol for serious revolutionaries/CCP) by claiming that it is not because of love that he is depressed and politically inactive. The fact is, he insists, that the boredom and depression growing out of his disillusionment with politics and revolution was the cause of his search for excitement and romantic love.

It is in the second of his first three novelettes, namely *Vacillation*, that we encounter the two sides of this central contradiction linked together within the narrative in full force and with much artistic as well as ideological impact. An analysis of the way in which this novelette is structured reveals a step-by-step exposition of the background to both sides of the dichotomy between politics and love leading up to the pivotal sixth chapter, in which the precipitating events that actually set the plot on its course toward a resolution finally occur: (1) a detailed delineation of Fang Luolan's psychology and the process of Fang's growing infatuation with Sun Wuyang; and (2) the arrival of Shi Jun, who has been sent out from the central government (left-wing GMD/CCP) in Wuhan to adjudicate the political and economic disturbances in this area. Shi is an inexperienced but dedicated and educated youth. He makes the fatal mistake of believing that Hu Guoguang, Lu Muyou, and Zhao Botong are good revolutionaries when they are actually covert opportunists and reactionaries. The rest of the novel is an intricately interwoven development of these two strands that demonstrates the potential for fashioning an interesting plot out of the dialectical treatment of a plausible central contradiction.

Possibly Mao Dun wanted this basic dichotomy between romance and psychological realism versus politics and revolution to reflect the Marxist theory of the relationship between the world of ideas, consciousness, ideology (the "superstructure") and the world of economics, material production, material reality (the "base"). The case for such an interpretation becomes more persuasive if based on some later works. The scene in "Color-Blind" where Lin sees a big, modernistic, foreign-owned bank in Shanghai as a "temple of Mammon" may offer support for this notion of a "base-superstructure" analogy. As he stands there looking at some new buildings going up, Lin becomes absorbed in watching the clouds of sparks flying up from the smokestack of a small, chugging engine, sparks that seem to him like some free and vibrant new ideas.[40] Not only is this a trope of machinery but it may also be an indication that Mao Dun conceived ideas to be produced by economic, material change (such as Shanghai and industrialization represented). Indeed, it is not altogether impossible that the central contradiction in Mao Dun's earliest fiction, a contradiction anchored in his treatment of objective reality as he had experienced it and presented in an aesthetically compelling style, is symbolic of the contradiction he saw between idealism and materialism; out of this latter contradiction there would soon emerge a whole new generation — the increasingly patriotic and revolutionary youth who grew up in the later years of the May Fourth era.

12.

Mao Dun and the Use of Political Allegory in Fiction: A Case Study of His "Autumn in Kuling"

Yü-shih Chen

Mao Dun, one of the most versatile twentieth-century writers, now lives in semiretirement in Peking. He has withdrawn from the literary and political worlds that, until recently, he served and helped to shape. He has received official recognition first as a pioneer in a new literature that was eminently of its time, then as an untiring literary worker and a promoter of cultural exchange. Among other offices, he was elected chairman of the All China Association of Literary Workers (July 23, 1949) and was a member of the board of directors of the Chinese People's Association for Cultural Relations with Foreign Countries (May 1954). He was editor of *Renmin wenxue* (People's literature) (1949–June 1953) and of *Yi wen* (Translations) (1953). In 1949 he became first secretary of the Writers' Union Secretariat, and he served as minister of culture until 1965.[1]

The most productive years of Mao Dun's career as a writer, however, are long past. By 1950 he had written all his novels and nearly all his short stories and important essays. He had formed and revised his rather amorphous theory of literature. Although he has continued to write travel notes and personal reminiscences over the past twenty years and has talked to students on the principles of literature and literary techniques, his overall achievement as a major twentieth-century writer was established by the works that were in print before 1950.[2]

Mao Dun is committed to a belief in reality. No other twentieth-century writer has captured the drama of economic bankruptcy around 1930 in Shanghai — the nerve center of China's national economy — better than he. In *Ziye* (Midnight) and in the equally celebrated short stories "Lin jia puzi" (Lin's store), "Chun can" (Spring silkworms), "Qiu shou" (Autumn harvest), and "Can dong" (The last of winter days), the story of what happens to the city and the countryside in an era of national economic crisis is told with great power. Mao Dun's reputation as a major twentieth-century novelist of the realist school is largely the result of these works. It is also because of these works that he has received recognition as one of the foremost Marxist-socialist writers of the May Fourth generation, having been nominated, with Ba Jin, for the Nobel Prize in Literature in 1975.

As a realist, Mao Dun has been committed to questioning what constitutes reality. His polemical exchanges with the Creation Society in the early 1920s and with the radical left critics in the late 1920s, and his position in the controversial "mass literature" movement at the turn of the 1930s, underscore his scorn for any literary approach that is not based on realistic observation. He has been driven by his sense of the complexity of life — whether in the political, social, or literary arena — into repeated attempts to tackle problems from a new angle. Up to the end of his novelistic career in the late 1940s, Mao Dun continued to rearrange and rewrite his stories to incorporate new insights he had gained from history and from contemporary society. This attempt to revise his own understanding of the past can easily be mistaken for wavering conviction. Critics today, preferring ready formulas in literature to basic ambiguities, are not likely to appreciate the sensibility of a writer so tentative and many-sided. This may in part explain the lack of understanding and appreciation of the thematic matter that obsessed Mao Dun when he was writing his first novels — the trilogy *Shi* (Eclipse): *Huanmie* (Disillusionment [1927]), *Dongyao* (Vacillation [1928]), *Zhuiqiu* (Searching [1928]).

This corpus of works, together with a few short stories published between 1928 and 1933, evolves out of a common experience and deals with a common subject:[3] the role of the Communist movement in modern China. Moreover, all use a similar, symbolic technique. This symbolism was imposed on the writer by a double censorship, that of the government and that of the Chinese Communist party, which he was a member of — and a committed worker in — until 1927.[4] In these early works, covert criticism of party policy and action is expressed through plots that have disastrous denouements. The allegorical intent of these denouements, however, is often lost on the reader, if indeed the works are read at all. *Eclipse* is an exception. It has escaped neglect largely because of what might be called its psychological realism. It is still read and admired (though not as much as *Midnight*), but not for its allegorical purpose: to encapsulate the course of the multilineal Communist movement in China in the 1920s. Over the years this purpose has been lost to the public. Today *Eclipse* is read for its successful portrayal of the sensibility of revolutionary youth in that era of monumental historical change.

A case study, however, of Mao Dun's short story "Gulingzhi qiu" (Autumn in Kuling [1933]) illustrates that contrary to the common interpretation, Mao Dun's early fictional works are more than just stories of love and amateur politics among a group of young petty bourgeois intellectuals. The subject of "Autumn in Kuling" is the Nanchang Uprising of the summer of 1927, an epoch-making event in the history of Chinese Communism. Mao Dun was deeply involved, both politically and emotionally, with every phase of the uprising's planning and execution. Since his personal involvement with the course of the Chinese Communist movement during the years of the twenties accounts to a large extent for the structure and meaning of this story (and others written during the same period), it is imperative to fully appreciate his personal activities as a committed Communist coworker in this period before proceeding to an interpretation of his works.

Biographical Background

Shen Yanbing, better known by his pen name Mao Dun, was born in 1896 in Chekiang province. His father died when he was ten years old. In 1914 he matriculated in Peking University, but was forced to leave after three years of study because of financial hardship at home. In 1918 he got a job in the translation and compilation department of the Commercial Press in Shanghai. His career, like that of many men of letters at that time, began to divide into literature and politics.

Information is relatively plentiful about the role Shen Yanbing played in the literary world in the early 1920s, but there has been a tendency to overlook the role he played concurrently in the political arena. Between 1918 and 1920, when Shen was working for the Commercial Press and writing for current periodicals like *Xuesheng zazhi* (Student magazine), he developed an interest in socialist thought in general and in Communist literature in particular. He probably also joined a Marxist study group when such groups were being formed in Shanghai around 1920.

In "Wode xiao zhuan" (My brief biography), Shen wrote, "Before I was twenty-five, I lived a peaceful and stable life under the supervision of my mother. In the ten years since, my friends have exerted a great influence."[5] Shen was twenty-five in 1920. It is common knowledge that such literary celebrities as Zhou Zuoren, Zheng Zhenduo, Xu

Dishan, and Ye Shengtao were among his friends. Few are aware that during the same years Shen Yanbing was helping to found the Wenxue yanjiu she (Literary Association) and busy editing the reorganized *Xiaoshuo yuebao* (Short story monthly), he was also associating with an eminent circle of political activists, including Chen Duxiu, Li Da, Shi Zuntong, and other founding members of the Chinese Communist party.

Under pressure from the government, many of the May Fourth leaders left Peking in 1920 to continue their political activities in Shanghai. Chen Duxiu was one of the first to arrive in Shanghai to organize a Chinese Communist party. In the succeeding months he spoke to a number of young intellectuals and predicted to a friend in July that if the Shanghai party nucleus of the Chinese Communist party were to be formed immediately, Yu Xiusong, Shen Yanbing, and seven others would undoubtedly join. The Shanghai party nucleus was formed in August, and Shen Yanbing joined the party in the following year after the first congress.[6] His activities as a CCP member between 1921 and 1925 were divided between propaganda and the labor movement.

How much of a faithful believer in Marxism Shen Yanbing was in those days we do not know. As a party member, he gave the impression of being prudent, although there were incidents showing that he could also speak up against too much party discipline.[7] As a political activist, Shen organized and promoted labor movements and was acquainted with many leaders of the women's movement at the time.[8] The Secretariat of the Chinese Labor Unions was established in 1921, headquartered in Shanghai, and for many years was one of the most active CCP organizations. Shen participated in the workers' education program and helped organize strikes. In 1922 he was said to have lectured, like Liu Shaoqi, at the People's Girls' School, which was headed by Li Da, a writer who became the first propaganda director of the CCP. In 1923 and 1924 Shen taught fiction studies at the famous cadre-training center at Shanghai University while working in the labor movement, and it is likely that he was directly involved in organizing the May Thirtieth movement of 1925. His familiarity with the workers' life and his firsthand knowledge of events associated with the May Thirtieth Incident in Shanghai were given fictional expression in the factory scenes in *Midnight* and in the last chapters of *Hong* (The rainbow). Because of his personal involvement, his mixed feelings of enthusiasm and disappointment over the character Ni Huanzhi — who failed to respond positively to the May Thirtieth Incident in Ye

Shengtao's novel *Ni Huanzhi* — assume a new meaning over and above that of a disinterested literary critic.[9] Similarly, his angry outburst against the Creation Society members — notably Cheng Fangwu and Guo Moruo — for not having stepped out of their "snail shell" into the street when the May Thirtieth movement was happening all around them was precipitated also by motives stronger and more complex than a doctrinal feud between mutually antagonistic literary schools.[10]

Because of these and other radical actions, Shen Yanbing was forced to relinquish the editorship of the *Short Story Monthly* in 1923.[11] From 1923 to 1925, although he was still officially in charge of the section "Literary News from Overseas" in the *Short Story Monthly*, his literary activities were noticeably reduced. A blank thus appears in his literary output during the second half of 1925. Toward the end of that year, he "severed [his] professional tie with literature" and left for Canton to devote himself wholly to the revolution. One of the last pieces he finished before leaving for Canton was entitled "Lun wuchanjieji wenyi" (On proletarian literature).[12]

The years 1926–1927 were turbulent. These were also the years during which Shen Yanbing the revolutionary was transformed into Mao Dun the novelist. For the next time we meet him in a literary context is with the appearance of *Disillusionment,* the first part of the trilogy *Eclipse,* serialized in the September, October, and November issues of the *Short Story Monthly* in 1927. Under the striking pen name Mao Dun (Contradiction), the author of *Disillusionment* wrote with an immediacy and an exaltation that took the literary world by storm. *Vacillation* (January–March 1928) and *Searching* (June–September 1928) followed. Feverish, despondent, and neurotic, the as yet unidentified author of these works little resembled the Shen Yanbing of earlier days. The world reflected in the three novels linked under the title *Eclipse* was immensely different from the world that inspired the radical yet reasoned argument in his essays "Ziranzhuyi yu Zhongguo xiandai xiaoshuo" (Naturalism and modern Chinese fiction) and "Xin wenxue yanjiuzhede zeren yu nuli" (The duties and strivings of researchers in new literature). Looking into Mao Dun's life during the intervening years from 1925 to 1927 will probably yield a better understanding of that transformation than the inferences that can be made from the literary theories he adhered to at one time or another. This process of transformation is recorded by Mao Dun himself in his autobiographical essay "Ji ju jiu hua" (Remarks on the past [May 1, 1933]).[13]

"Remarks on the Past" is an important document on the nature and substance of Mao Dun's early fictional works. It not only reveals a dimension in his life up to 1928 that is central to our understanding of his writings but it also offers a way to understand the complex narrative style he devised to transmit his frequently censored ideas on a level more or less distinct from that on which his uncensorable narrative flow was developed. This narrative style uses facts as well as metaphors and symbols, and it advances plot simultaneously with political allegory. "Remarks on the Past" relates:

The year 1926 probably is a year I will never forget. Since the New Year's Day of that year, my life lost its tranquillity. I was one of the passengers on board the ship *Xingshi* [Awakened lion].[14] There were five of us traveling together.

Since I left school, I had worked as an editor in a book publishing company. This was how I became involved with literature. But from the time I stepped onto the *Awakened Lion* on New Year's Day in 1926, my professional tie with literature was severed.

Canton in those days was a huge furnace, an enormous whirlpool — a colossal *contradiction*.[15]

In March, this furnace, this whirlpool, violently "exploded."

In the middle of April, I returned to Shanghai. I had no job then, but was very busy. My health was much better in those days. Frequently, I ran around for a whole day and did not even feel tired; I even felt like doing something more afterward. So I began my research in Chinese mythology, a world apart from my daytime occupation. Nonetheless, I found it helpful to balance physical activities with research. Meanwhile, I thought of using what spare time I had left to try my hand at writing a novel. This was because the mentality and outlook of several females at that time attracted my attention. It was on the eve of the Great Revolution. Students with a bourgeois background and women intellectuals felt rather strongly that if they did not join the revolutionary party, they would be wasting their learning. Furthermore, they entertained strong illusions about revolution. They walked into revolution on the strength of those illusions. But all they did in fact was to stand on the periphery of revolution and look in. There were also females who sought revolution because they had been frustrated somehow and were indignant as a result — they added a dash of skepticism to their illusions. Standing shoulder to shoulder with them were still other, totally different types. Together, they presented very strong contrasts. And my urge to write a novel grew stronger by the day . . .

I remember one evening in August. I had just come out of a meeting and was on my way home. It was raining hard. There were no pedestrians and no automobiles; raindrops fell pit-a-pat on my umbrella. The person walking next to me was one of the females who had formerly attracted my attention. During the meeting, she had talked excessively. Her face was still flushed with excitement. As we walked, I suddenly felt inspiration surging inside of me. If at all possible, I think I would have grabbed a pen right then and there and begun to write in the rain. That night, after I got home, I was able for the first time to formulate an outline of the novel I had wanted to write.

This is how, once again, I resumed my traffic with literature on a "nonprofessional basis" after I had broken my "professional" tie with it.

The outline I had made at that time later became the first half of *Disillusionment.* A whole year went by from the time the outline was formed and the time I actually began writing. During that year, I was caught up in the torrents of the revolution. I never had the time to revise my outline. In January 1927 I arrived in Wuhan. I forgot all about the outline. I also forgot all about the fact that I ever had the urge to do creative writing. Wuhan at that time, too, was an enormous whirlpool, a colossal contradiction. And the females I had encountered in Shanghai also turned up in Wuhan. In this time of whirling crisis, their natures were exposed even more clearly . . . Finally, that colossal contradiction again exploded. I watched many people showing their ugly faces, and I watched many "modern females," who lost control of themselves, become depressed, go under. I left Wuhan and went to Kuling to recuperate. In the third-class cabin on board the ship *Xiangyangwan,* there was a berth with two light blue skirts for curtains. They were meant to obstruct people's view but had the contrary effect of arousing attention. In that crowded third-class cabin, I ran into two females whom I had met before in Shanghai and then in Wuhan. They were going to Kiukiang. They told me that there were quite a few acquaintances of mine aboard the same ship. The outline I had written and left in my apartment in Shanghai suddenly surged up in my consciousness. Since I had nothing to do, I let it occupy my mind again.

I stayed in Kiukiang for half a day and then went on up to Kuling. The first thing I did after settling in a hotel room was to pick up the old outline again. The result was the piece "News from Kuling" ["Guling tongxin"] . . . Less than four days after we arrived in the mountains, the two friends who came with me from Hankow left . . .

When we first arrived, a lot of old acquaintances were there. The Grand Hotel of Lushan was filled with people who had fled Wuhan. At the end of July, they left in separate groups. Then three others came, stayed only one day, and then took off to some cave in the deep white clouds to seek refuge from the din. The once bustling Lushan grew quiet. Two friends stayed on — both females. One was in the hospital and

I visited her. But we had exchanged no more than a few words when she lowered her voice and said, "This is not the place to talk." The other stayed at the Supervisory Department [*Guanliju*] as a temporary guest of Mrs. Lin. It was she who told me what had been going on in Lushan. When the autumn winds blew, I returned to Shanghai. I dug out the year-old outline from a pile of paper and read it over and decided that it had to be revised and cut.

I sat down and began to write. What came of it were *Disillusionment* and *Vacillation* . . .

Thus, it is not by coincidence that I made three females the protagonists of *Disillusionment*. Those who do not know me will probably try to guess who these three females are. They may even want to compile a "key." However, should they know me and my friends, male and female, they will probably understand that these three females are not three individuals but many individuals — they are three types. Miss Jing is the type that receives most of my attention. The other two are just for support and contrast. I admit that I have not portrayed any truly revolutionary female. For this, I deserve to be criticized.

"Remarks on the Past" is a mixture of fact, metaphor, and political allegory; it is not merely personal reminiscence or straightforward autobiographical account. Mao Dun had left the CCP in late 1927, but in "Remarks" he was still writing about the CCP and therefore had to use indirect methods of expression to protect himself and his friends. On the whole, he used the actual time and geographical location for the historical events presented: from March 1926 in Canton; April to December in Shanghai; January to July 1927 in Wuhan; and the end of July to early August in Kiukiang and Kuling. But what actually happened during this time and in these places is presented by him indirectly, not on a single level or in uniform terms. The cataclysmic events that swept Canton and Wuhan are presented in strikingly similar metaphors as "a huge furnace, an enormous whirlpool — a colossal contradiction" that "exploded." The policy-making process that went on first in Shanghai and then in Wuhan and Kuling, from which such events evolved and on which subsequent actions revolved, is presented in a much more complex narrative structure. Within this narrative structure, there is a realistic "cover" that involves Mao Dun's research in Chinese mythology and his retreat to Kuling. Then, there is an allegorical underpinning that appears in the form of "meetings" and "females."

To trace the extremely complex historical events that underlie this deliberately vague narrative is a necessary first step in understanding the similar narrative method in the short story "Autumn in Kuling," which develops around a voyage on the ship *Xiangyangwan* from Wuhan to Kiukiang that Mao Dun actually took. Such a conspicuous clue strongly suggests looking more deeply into his activities upon his arrival in Canton in January 1926 and into the larger historical events of 1926–1927.

Mao Dun in the Propaganda Department Mao Dun left Shanghai toward the end of 1925 and was in Canton in January 1926. From January to April, he served as secretary in the Propaganda Department in the Central Executive Committee of the Guomindang, first under its nominal chairman Wang Jingwei and then, after February 1926, under Mao Zedong who succeeded Wang as acting chairman.[16]

Prior to Mao Dun's arrival in Canton, the CCP had already passed the resolution requiring members to join the Guomindang. When Mao Dun arrived in Canton, the CCP had already gained a foothold in high-level Guomindang governmental organizations. The Propaganda Department in which he served was, predictably, under CCP control.

While the exact nature of the propaganda work Mao Dun did in Canton is not known for certain, he probably followed the expansion of the party activities from cell work to training school programs.[17] Under the cover of his job as secretary, he conducted training and educational programs for party cadres as well as ground-level organizing among the masses. This phase of his practical experience is amply reflected in his fiction. Party work for Mao Dun during the revolutionary years of 1926 and 1927 was frequently conducted within the schools; and schools provide the setting and antagonists for much of his early fiction. Fictional meetings among students in those schools — both in *Eclipse* and elsewhere — parallel party meetings, in which party policies and objectives were discussed and actions planned. This parallel between fact and fiction offers a significant new interpretation as to why meetings and personal relationships among students in Mao Dun's novels and stories receive so much attention from Communist writer-critics such as Qian Xingcun. When Qian criticized Mao Dun for obscuring the "main subject" in chapter 5 of *Disillusionment* with his "method of indirect presentation," the reference is exactly to one such "meeting" in one such "school."[18] And when Qian attacked Mao Dun for his interpretation of the women characters in *Searching*, it is obvious that Qian's criticism does not really apply to any valid literary issues in the work. Rather, it is directed to a larger historical frame of reference from which the women characters derive their symbolic meaning.[19]

Mao Dun himself mentioned more than once that during the revolutionary years he had been in close contact with the "leadership center," the "ground-level organizations," and the "masses."[20] "Between 1925–1927, I had considerable contact with the nucleus leadership center in the revolutionary movement. My post enabled me to have frequent dealings with ground-level organizations and the masses. Hence, by all accounts, I should have been able to have an overall understanding [of the revolutionary movement]." The knowledge that he had been a CCP member and a high-level party propagandist clarifies the content of this statement. The "leadership center" he referred to is the CCP Central Committee, and the "ground-level organizations" are local party cells. This fact reveals a personal perspective, previously unidentified, from which his early fictional works were written. The perspective is not one of a keen, disinterested observer, as previously assumed, but one of a committed coworker in the CCP who, having followed the party policy-making process from the inside, was in a privileged position to present to the world "an overall understanding" and "a penetrating analysis" of the revolutionary movement.

Hence, the revolution that Mao Dun has "observed and analyzed" in the three parts of *Eclipse* (and secondarily in other writings) corresponds not so much with the overall national revolution of 1926–1928 as led by the Guomindang in alliance with the CCP as with the Chinese Communist movement in its early stage. Only in this light are we able to explain Mao Dun's apparently deep emotional involvement with the dilemma and tragic fate of his fictional characters (who in real life are his comrades). And only this approach to the subject matter in his fiction explains why such prominent CCP leaders and leftist critics as Qu Qiubai and Qian Xingcun took so much interest in even the most minute details in his novels and short stories published between 1928 and 1933 — *Eclipse*, *Ye qiangwei* (Wild roses), and *San ren xing* (Of three friends). Such correlation between history and fiction finds further support in the following observations made by Mao Dun in September–October 1928, almost in ironical anticipation of the uproar raised over *Searching* by his comrades at a time when Communist development had suffered a devastating defeat, and misfortune had overtaken many of his old friends and commrades:[21] "One who will not be bent by external forces may lose his mind with disappointment at the perverse behavior of those he loves. One day such matters may become known. This is what gives my writings a deeply pessimistic hue, and colors them with a basic tone of lugubriousness and agitation."[22]

The metaphors of the twice-exploded contradiction Mao Dun referred to in "Remarks on the Past" are obviously related to developments in the Chinese Communist movement. Two dates stand out in relation to the "contradictions": March 20, 1926, and July 1927. Are these chosen by chance? It is scarcely necessary to recall that on March 20, 1926, and July 15, 1927, the Guomindang and the CCP confronted each other in two crucial tests of power. The March Twentieth Coup resulted in a setback for the Communist movement; the July 15th "Wuhan debacle" marked the split of the CCP from the Guomindang left, which was followed by a large-scale persecution and massacre of Communist members and followers. These two confrontations are the two explosions mentioned in "Remarks." They are viewed by Mao Dun as the inevitable consequence of the tension and conflict that arose out of a "colossal contradiction" that he captures in two striking images: an all-consuming "huge furnace" and an "enormous whirlpool." In their respective suggestions of burning violence and inextricable self-encircling action, they lead to an inevitable end.

The March Twentieth Coup, also known as the Zhongshan Gunboat Incident, marked the rise of Chiang Kai-shek to power and a notable reverse in CCP expansion.[23] In the series of negotiations that followed, Chiang Kai-shek demonstrated his desire to curb CCP development by requesting that important party members be removed from responsible Guomindang posts and by stipulating rigid restrictions on CCP participation in the Guomindang government. The CCP control over the Guomindang Propaganda Department was dissolved in early April. Shortly afterward, as Mao Dun described in "Remarks," he returned to Shanghai.

From mid-April to the end of 1926, Mao Dun continued to work in the CCP Propaganda Bureau in Shanghai. The "August meeting" in "Remarks" is both a profile of the Second Enlarged Plenum in Shanghai (July 1926) and a composite of the many meetings held earlier on the central controversy that preoccupied all ranking CCP members: the policy of collaboration between the Guomindang and the CCP. In this foreshortened representation, the reasserted "contradiction" — the collaboration policy — stretched out painfully and inevitably toward a second "explosion," the Wuhan debacle of July 1927.

The "Females" in Mao Dun's Literary Consciousness It is obvious from the early history of the Communist movement in China that the Comintern had a direct hand in formulating and directing the CCP policy toward the Guomindang and had interfered in many other party matters, such as the organization of mass movements and the interpretation of revolutionary tides.[24] In retrospect, one can say that the Comintern interpretation of the situation in China from 1922 to 1928 and its assigned strategy of collaboration with the Guomindang was inaccurate and erroneous, causing the events that befell the CCP on March 20, 1926, and in July 1927. It is inconceivable, therefore, that Mao Dun, who had held responsible positions in the Guomindang Propaganda Department, who was aware of every Comintern intrusion into CCP internal and external policies, and who had already person-ally witnessed the miscarriage of Comintern policy in China, should not have given the Comintern's role in the revolution years of 1926–1928 a prominent representation. The natural question to ask, then, is, in what image is the Comintern role cast? Who are the most prominent figures in the climactic scenes in Shanghai "on the eve of revolution," and in Wuhan in July 1927, as noted by Mao Dun in his recollection of those days? The answer is "the females."

It is the females in Shanghai with their special ideological outlook who attracted Mao Dun's attention. It is a female who, walking home with Mao Dun after the meeting in August 1926, reveals to us through her flushed face and excited talk what had happened in the meeting. The modern female acquaintances Mao Dun had known from Shang-hai and Wuhan days were on board ship when he retreated from Wuhan to Kiukiang. Another two female acquaintances were present when Mao Dun went to Kuling to recuperate from ill health. Who are these females, and what do they represent? They must represent something persistent and essential to Mao Dun's revolutionary expe-rience to deserve such intense concern. "Remarks" says that these females have to do with the revolution of 1926–1928, with ideology, and with types; they are composites of persons Mao Dun had known during the years he served as party propagandist.

The females in "Remarks" are symbolic participants in the actual revolutionary history of the 1920s. They present images of the dominant CCP leadership groups, including the group following Comintern policy, committed to conflicting political positions.

In Mao Dun's fiction, the main women characters are better realized than in his autobiographical essays like "Remarks." But in his fiction he so often shifts between the close-up of the individual, the movement of her group, and the analytic survey of the whole revolutionary history that to follow his trail, these works must be read on many different levels at once. In "Remarks on the Past," the women Mao Dun encountered on the ship correspond to the two female characters Old Ming encounters in "Autumn in Kuling" and serve as the bridge between the world of reality and the world of fiction in Mao Dun's life and works. In a sense, they are also our indispensable "key," especially when *Eclipse* and other novels and stories are concerned, to an enlightened reading of the themes and the meaning of characters and character relationships.

"Autumn in Kuling": A Case Study of History and Fiction

"Autumn in Kuling,"[25] the undated short story, was first published in installments in the journal *Wenxue* (Literature) in 1933.[26] In a footnote, Mao Dun revealed that the story originally had nine sections, but sections five to eight "for reasons unknown, disappeared the night after it was written." Mao Dun said, "I could have found them if I had wanted to look for them, but I did not feel like looking, nor was I up to rewriting the missing parts."[27] What he did instead was to move the original section nine to become the present concluding section five.

"Autumn in Kuling," in its present truncated form, reads as incoherently as one might expect. The few characters, because of the missing sections, appear nebulously drawn. As fiction, the story holds little interest. But in the light of several autobiographical passages in "Remarks," it offers a rare opportunity to observe closely how Mao Dun used fiction to satisfy his irrepressible urge to write about and examine contemporary history, despite all the practical difficulties of dealing with such sensitive matters in public. The four middle sections disappeared because the work was a thinly veiled report on current history.[28] The story's undeveloped form, moreover, becomes an advantage when connections between history and Mao Dun's fiction are sought. There are less concealment and fewer missing connections to uncover.

"Autumn in Kuling" opens with a scene in Hankow at Pier Six. The date is July 23, 1927 (given only in the author's own footnote). Three men are seen boarding the ship *Xiangyangwan* to go to Kiukiang. In the common cabin, they meet a number of old acquaintances and exchange ambiguous remarks on the current political situation and military developments. A light blue skirt strung up in the common cabin as a temporary screen calls their attention to the presence of two female acquaintances, also going to Kiukiang, where they will get trains to Nanchang.

In Kiukiang, the three men spend two very confusing and frustrating days. First, they have trouble finding the people they had arranged to meet. Then their plans change repeatedly in less than half a day. The two female acquaintances they met on board the ship appear, somewhat unexpectedly, in the same hotel. The train to Nanchang has been delayed because of army transportation.

The following scene in section five abruptly shifts to Kuling. A week or so has elapsed. Two of the three men are playing chess in a hotel. "Where do you think Old Song [the third man] and the rest of them are now?"[29] one of the two asks. "Don't they say that once beyond Fuchow, it will all be wild mountains? We are in the mountains all the same, but theirs over there must be much more interesting." The two men muse about their friend and about their own situation for a while. Finally, they decide to go back to Shanghai in two or three days.

The plot of "Autumn in Kuling," summarized above, tells very little about the events presented, and much less about the identity of the characters. There is much bustle in the story, but the way it is presented raises more questions than it clarifies. For example, the three men are not identified, the reason for their trip to Kiukiang is not known, nor is the meaning of their seemingly casual encounters with the females. The final episode in Kuling, instead of answering these questions as endings normally do, introduces its own unanswered mysteries — the business of Old Ming and Master Yun in Kuling, and of "Old Song and the rest" in the mountain area near Fuchow.

"Autumn in Kuling" has never attracted critics' attention and so has never been seriously studied. One reason is that the real story behind it has remained hidden; clues to an intelligible reading were lost when the middle sections mysteriously "disappeared." But the similar trip described in "Remarks on the Past" — a work published in 1933, the same year as "Autumn in Kuling" — rescues the story from being dismissed because of its obvious literary flaws. Mao Dun, too, had traveled from Wuhan to Kiukiang on a ship called *Xiangyangwan*. The exact date of his departure was not noted in "Remarks," but from a letter he published in the *Zhongyang fukan* (Literary supplement to the *Central Daily*) in Hankow on July 29, 1929, entitled "Yun shaoye yu caomao" (Master Yun and the straw hat), we know that he also left Wuhan on July 23, 1927, the same day that *Xiangyangwan* departed from Hankow in the opening scene of "Autumn in Kuling."[30]

Such striking and unexpected coincidences inevitably suggest a connection between the actual and the fictional trips. Other details, down to the very color of the woman's skirt strung up in the cabin, indicate that the two trips are one and the same trip. The light blue skirt that caught Mao Dun's attention in the third-class cabin in "Remarks" was also strung up in the common cabin in "Autumn in Kuling." In both cases, the skirt belonged to one of the two women Mao Dun and his characters in the story had known from their respective Shanghai school days. Later on in "Remarks," Mao Dun went from Kiukiang to Kuling; two of the three male characters also go from Kiukiang to Kuling. From Kuling, Mao Dun left in less than two weeks' time to go back to Shanghai; the two men also decide to do this at the end of "Autumn in Kuling."

The coincidence of such small details cannot be accidental. The author evidently links "Autumn in Kuling" to his autobiographical "Remarks" and relies on these links of detail to reveal the larger common historical context that was his main concern and real subject. Such reliance on external information to reveal the deeper subject matter and use of selected details to point out the larger historical framework occur repeatedly in Mao Dun's early fictional works. This is true of the stories in *Wild Roses* and their prefatory remarks. It is also true of the trilogy *Eclipse* and Mao Dun's two articles in defense of it, "Cong Guling dao Dongjing" (From Kuling to Tokyo [October 1928]) and "Du *Ni Huanzhi*" (On reading *Ni Huanzhi* [1929]). Therefore, to understand fully Mao Dun's early fiction, the usual approach to realistic literature is not enough. The work's historical background must be explored and grasped. The eventual interpretation must then carefully observe the distance originally built into these writings between the fictional form and the actual history represented.

"Autumn in Kuling" admittedly is not a successful story. But it is useful for the purpose of studying Mao Dun's fictional method. It is short and clearly identifiable with a relatively small cluster of historical events: the historic retreat of the Chinese Communists from Wuhan in the second half of July 1927 and the famous Nanchang Uprising of August 1. A comparison of the time, place, and sequence of events in the "Autumn in Kuling" to those of these two major historical events place one point beyond dispute: Mao Dun's early fictional works are fictional representations of current history, and the literary technique he employed in these works, far from being purely realistic, is broadly allegorical.

In terms of time, "Autumn in Kuling" begins on July 23, 1927, when the retreat was already under way and the plan for the Nanchang Uprising had been made final. It ends in Kuling around August 8, when the Nanchang Uprising had already been duly executed and the

Southern March to Kwangtung had commenced and reached its first stop in Fuchow.[31]

Hankow, Kiukiang, and Kuling are the actual settings of the fictional events in the order they occurred. Nanchang and Shanghai are mentioned in context as the two separate destinations of the retreating party after its members had gathered in Kiukiang. An intriguing feature that deserves special attention is the use Mao Dun makes of specific place names like Chengchou (section two in "Autumn in Kuling"), Mahuiling (section four), and Fuchow (section five) to anchor the political perspective of the story. These place names, some totally unknown to the general public, identify important military events in the history of the Chinese Communist movement at that juncture, serving as "emblems" of the historical Mahuiling events associated with these names. Mahuiling, in section four, signifies Chinese Communist troop movement during the Nanchang Uprising.[32] In section five, Fuchow signifies the Southern March to Kwangtung after the uprising.[33] Chengchou in section two evokes painful memories of Tang Shengzhi's betrayal (from the CCP point of view) of the revolutionary cause on May 29 and the Chengchou conference on July 10, which together foreshadowed the July 15 expulsion of the CCP from the Wuhan government.[34]

In his "On Reading *Ni Huanzhi*," Mao Dun complained that the author of *Ni Huanzhi* failed to make clear which political party Ni Huanzhi belonged to: "Ni Huanzhi at that time probably had already joined a certain political party. But from chapter 22 on, the activities of Ni Huanzhi do not clearly reflect his collective background; as a result, they become the insignificant actions of one individual. This greatly affects the basic orientation of this novel."[35] "Autumn in Kuling" presents a concrete example of how Mao Dun suggested the "collective background" of *his* fictional characters by placing their activities in historical time and place.

In "Tan wode yanjiu" (My understanding of fiction writing), Mao Dun discusses the significance of characters and character relationships in fiction writing: "The prime goal in fiction writing is people. One has to have people first before one can have a starting point . . . One cannot single out one character from the others and study him separate and apart . . . It is not sufficient to just have people; there have to be relationships among people. It is these relationships among people that constitute the theme in a work of fiction."[36]

Analysis of "Autumn in Kuling" should therefore stress not only the characters but also relationships among these characters. Because the story's theme, as Mao Dun indicated in the above statement, occurs not so much in any one individual character but in their interrelationships, once these interrelationships are shown, their "collective background" becomes clear.

There are three main characters in "Autumn in Kuling": Old Ming, Old Song, and Master Yun.

Old Ming worked in a newspaper office in Wuhan before he left for Kiukiang. He is said to have inside knowledge of why everybody is going to Kiukiang.

Old Song recently arrived in Wuhan from Shanghai. He is specifically introduced in the first section as an "exiled Guomindang member from Chekiang, and not an X dang [CCP member]."[37] It is said that Old Song "did not clearly understand" what he was sent to do in Kiukiang. But once there, he is the one most busily engaged in all sorts of ambiguous business. Toward the end of section four, he is ordered to attend a "meeting" in Nanchang, and in the concluding section, he is said to be in the "mountain area near Fuchow."

Master Yun is a somewhat elusive character.[38] The name Yun appears in a number of Mao Dun's writings. It is the name of a hero in *Of Three Friends*. It is also the name that appeared in the title of Mao Dun's July 29 letter from Kuling. There is even a Miss Yun in "From Kuling to Tokyo." Yun probably stood for something or someone very much in the foreground of Mao Dun's consciousness in the early years of his career as a novelist. But here in "Autumn in Kuling," aside from his ringing laughter, his sportive air, and his persistent presence throughout the story, nothing very positive can be said about him as a fictional character. The only clue to what he represents in "Autumn in Kuling," is his preoccupation with Lushan.[39]

Individually, none of these three characters seems particularly significant. But in examining their activities in the perspective of their "collective background" and their relationship with other characters in the story, a different picture emerges.

In section one, the common reason for their departure from Wuhan is presented first in the opening scene at the Hankow waterfront and then in a morose statement by Old Song. The juxtaposition of the Japanese gunboats in the river with the *Xiangyangwan* at Pier Six speaks silently of the tense political situation to Wuhan during the last hour of the CCP presence there. The departing *Xiangyangwan* signifies the retreat of the Communists and the ugly presence of the Japanese gunboats symbolizes that the GMD government at Wuhan had already compromised with the foreign imperialist powers and abandoned the original cause of the national revolution. Old Song's sullen complaint that he should not have come all the way to Wuhan from Shanghai to face this "rotten mess of a situation" represents the prevalent feeling among CCP members at that point.

In section two, there is a clear portrait of the political party the mutually acquainted *Xiangyangwan* passengers belonged to. Ostensibly, section two contains a number of trifling incidents on the night of July 23 in the common cabin. Actually, the two casual encounters between Old Ming and his acquaintances and the incidental glimpses of other passengers is Mao Dun's subtle way of delineating their "collective background." In the first encounter between Old Ming and the leftist youth Old Xu, Old Xu's conversation reveals the most recent political development that lead up to the Wuhan retreat. The same conversation also reveals something about the business awaiting the *Xiangyangwan* in Kiukiang:

> At Chengchou, I sent you a telegram. It was sent to the newspaper office. Did you receive it? Damm it! That Honan was certainly a godforsaken place. The Red Spear Society! The Blue Spear Society! And whatnot, you name it! The local bullies and evil gentry certainly had the run of the day there. But Old Ming, are you going to Kiukiang too? Damm it, we'll give them hell when we get to Kiukiang.[40]

Old Xu's excited and disjointed talk is presented not merely as a sketch of an overenthusiastic leftist youth, undoubtedly a common type in the revolutionary ranks at that time. Nor was he created to enliven the realistic cabin scene on board the *Xiangyangwan*, although he fulfills that function equally well. Over and above such realistic functions, Old Xu also presents the political past and future of the *Xiangyangwan's* voyage. Old Xu's remarks about the unenlightened people in Honan, on the resistance of the local secret societies to the unwelcome Communist propaganda, and on the "compromise" his Director Deng (Deng Yanda in the Political Department of the Fourth Army) eventually was compelled to make, succinctly summarize the political developments that caused the passengers to board the *Xiangyangwan* and go to Kiukiang in section one. "Give them hell" in Kiukiang refers to the prospective Nanchang Uprising. But to have Old Xu mention it in so offhanded a manner in his conversation with Old Song suggests that the passengers in the common cabin not only knew about the plan but were also participants in their different capacities.

The encounter between Old Ming and his two female acquaintances serves a similar purpose of underlining their common political background. Miss Wang is someone Old Ming had known from his former school days in Shanghai. Miss Tao is a member of the Committee for the Women's Movement in Hupeh. "School" and "Committee for Women's Movement" imply CCP policies. Miss Wang and Miss Tao are going to Kiukiang only to get a train for Nanchang: obviously that they are intimately involved in the Nanchang Uprising plan.

Thus, section two presents an overview of the people who constituted the political community in "Autumn in Kuling." There were Guomindang leftists like Old Xu, and women activists in the CCP like Miss Wang and Miss Tao (also symbolic representatives of party policies). Among the other passengers, there are other types like Old Li and his gang, as well as the young man who speaks with a heavy Cantonese accent. The name Old Li strongly suggests Li Lisan, who first conceived the idea of the Nanchang Uprising, and the young man with a Cantonese accent easily leads one to think of the CCP troops gathering near Nanchang from the Fourth Army, the main force in the uprising plan, which included many natives from Kwangtung. The ship's passengers are bound together in a common destiny by two significant factors: they share a common past (Shanghai and Wuhan) and they are heading toward a common future (Kiukiang).

Sections three and four deal primarily with the situation at Kiukiang. Section three is set in the early morning of July 24, after the arrival of the ship, and section four, the same evening. Gathering war clouds, which have long hovered on the not too distant horizon, are now descending over the city of Kiukiang.

In Kiukiang, soldiers are seen everywhere. They crowd the train station, pack the outgoing trains, march in the streets, and shout slogans like "long live XXX [Wang Jingwei?]! Down with XXX [Chiang Kai-shek?]!"[41] These scenes in sections three and four reproduce most realistically the motions and commotions in Kiukiang at the time.[42] These were the days immediately preceding the Nanchang Uprising. The Front Committee had already been formed. Its general headquarters was in Nanchang, and military operations had already begun. But the central political leadership in Hankow had not yet decided whether the uprising was advisable. The CCP Central Committee was still meeting secretly with Russian military advisers and representatives from the Comintern, and an envoy was sent by the CCP Central Committee as late as July 26 to halt the already initiated military action. Such lack of synchronization between the political and the military is depicted concretely by the great confusion and frustration Old Song and the two female characters experience in Kiukiang.

Interestingly, in sections three and four, all the important passengers on the ship get back together in the same hotel in Kiukiang. It looks as if Mao Dun had modeled the Huayang Hotel in "Autumn in Kuling" on the Grand Kiangsi Hotel in Nanchang, the general headquarters of the Front Committee for the Nanchang Uprising, for the collective activities of his fictional characters in Kiukiang.

In the concluding section five, what must have been the climax of the story — the Nanchang Uprising — is already over. Anything Mao Dun saw in Lushan or learned from his female acquaintance at the Supervisory Department as related in "Remarks" was deleted from the story. It is unfortunate that Mao Dun felt compelled to withhold this central drama after it was written. In the original, sections five to eight might have covered the exact time and action of the Nanchang Uprising and the initial stage of the Southern March (July 25 to August 8). Obviously, there was no conceivable way in which Mao Dun could have treated these events to the satisfaction of current censorship.

The execution of the retreat plan can be reconstructed from the itineraries of the three main characters in the story as Mao Dun published it. Old Song's itinerary — from Shanghai to Wuhan to Kiukiang, Nanchang, and Fuchow — traces the part of the retreat plan that actively involved the Nanchang Uprising and the Southern March. Old Ming and Yun's itinerary from Wuhan to Kiukiang and then Lushan-Kuling and Shanghai follows the retreat route of the CCP Central Committee from Wuhan via Kiukiang to Shanghai.

As a work of literature, "Autumn in Kuling" complies in many ways with Mao Dun's own views for modern Chinese fiction. Its subject matter is thoughtfully chosen: for a CCP member, what can be more important and deserving than an unprecedented attempt, as exemplified by the Nanchang Uprising, on the part of the Chinese Communist party to break free from Comintern interference and from the "suicidal" policy of collaboration with the Guomindang? Its theme reflects the spirit of a revolutionary epoch and is concerned with the life and destiny of more than just a few individuals. "Autumn in Kuling" may not be good fiction, but it gives convincing evidence of Mao Dun's early experimentation with political allegory couched in realistic terms.

13.

The Changing Relationship Between Literature and Life: Aspects of the Writer's Role in Ding Ling

Yi-tsi M. Feuerwerker

In 1951, six years before the antirightist campaign ended her literary career, Ding Ling wrote a brief essay instructing youth on how to regard the new literature that flowered after the May Fourth Incident. Somewhat defensively, she praised the revolutionary "relevance" and breakthrough achievement of the May Fourth writers and their works to an audience that seemed largely ignorant or perhaps contemptuous of both. The only writer she named was Lu Xun, whose "profundity, transcending any period in history, is as yet not attained by us." Then she went on to say, "How can our youth, because we have just begun to understand 'serve the people,' because we have taken a brief turn in the countryside or the factory, lightly write off with one stroke a great history and the literature produced by this history?" In fact, there were those who harbored "the prejudice that any writer who grew up under the influence of the new literature of May Fourth is no good."[1]

To anyone reflecting on her life, the fact that Ding Ling felt it necessary to plead for renewal of interest in May Fourth literature is not without its poignancy. In 1919 she had been a schoolgirl in Changsha, experiencing what she called the "great liberation" of the jump from classical to colloquial language in both reading and writing.[2] Seven years later, her brilliant literary career, which she did not refer to in this 1951 essay, began with the publication of her first stories. Now she was writing as one of the most prominent figures in the cultural hierarchy of the newly established People's Republic. But just six years later, she would be the target of the massive antirightist campaign that totally discredited her writing and ended her career. Thus, her brief essay not only indicates the range of decades, from the 1920s to the 1950s, spanned by her literary activities but also underscores the enormous changes that occurred between the

281

early and later phases of her thirty-year career. The essay's defensive stance also anticipates the fate of the writer who genuinely attempts to adapt to such changes yet persists in a serious commitment to literature.

Other veteran writers who began writing after May Fourth had survived into the 1950s, and a few — very few — have continued to be productive. But, because of her early successes, continual involvement, and later downfall, Ding Ling most concretely, almost telescopically, illustrates the terrible dilemma confronting the writer in the unfolding context of modern China's political history.

Her eventful life can easily trap one into concentrating on the life at the expense of the work. The drama of her biography is certainly there, ready to be exploited. Her rebellion against social and literary conventions was expressed by both her liberated life-style and her impassioned writings on the sexual frustrations of young women. This gave her an early notoriety as "farther out" because she was female. Many of her own stories and the reminiscences of her friends like Shen Congwen and Yao Pengzi unabashedly divulged information about her private life.[3] This is what sold. When she decisively embraced the Communist cause in the early 1930s, her writings changed distinctly and aroused strong controversy. The execution of her husband by the Guomindang drew outraged protests within China and from abroad. Her own arrest in 1933 and presumed martyrdom occasioned numerous memoirs, tributes, and new editions of her collected works. Then she mysteriously escaped to the border regions and submerged herself in literary and propaganda activities for the war and the revolution. Her fame made interviewing her a must for nearly every foreign correspondent who came to Yenan.[4] Some breathlessly told her life story as relayed by interpreters; others, with little, if any direct access to her original writings, hailed her as one of the foremost writers of modern China.

When the revolution triumphed, Ding Ling's exalted positions included membership on the powerful Committee on Cultural and Educational Affairs and vice-chairmanship of the All China Association of Literary Workers. She was also the editor of *Wenyi bao* (Literary gazette), the influential journal of the All-China Federation of Literary and Art Circles, and head of the Central Literary Institute, a training school for writers. Meanwhile, the Stalin Prize (second place) for her novel on land reform, *Taiyang zhaozai Sangganheshang* (The sun shines over the Sangkan River, 1948), signified international recognition of it as a great achievement in China's new socialist literature. Since the antirightist drive and her expulsion from the Communist party in 1958, Ding Ling has, in effect, disappeared from the Chinese scene; but, as the most celebrated victim of the government's intolerance of literary dissidence, her life has continued to be a subject of speculation abroad.

With such a life story, who needs fiction? But it must be as a fiction writer that Ding Ling merits critical attention. For the great interest of this life is that it was so continually and consciously transmuted into literature. The facts of Ding Ling's history can be left to the journalists and biographers, who, in any case, can be sure of very few of them. Well publicized as some of the events are, there are too many serious gaps and conflicting views about many others for a complete, authentic "life." While biography does provide one important context for the literary work, it becomes truly relevant only as it is metamorphosed into writing. To achieve this metamorphosis was in part the writer's role as Ding Ling saw it, and the margin between fact and story, experience and fiction, paper thin as it might occasionally be, nevertheless maintained a somehow distinct boundary between the two areas.[5]

The writings that reflect Ding Ling's views on the relationship between literature and life include two long novels (one unfinished), one novelette, a few negligible plays, a handful of poems, some volumes of critical essays, and some sixty short stories. The essays do not offer many usable theoretical statements of her literary ideas. With the notable exception of Henry James, few fiction writers have provided explicit formulations that are adequate to their mediating role between life and literature, or even to their own understanding of it, and Ding Ling was far from being, even remotely, a sophisticated literary theorist. Most of her essays were written in the late 1940s or early 1950s. What further limits their usefulness as a source of her ideas is that they are mostly speeches or articles produced for specific public occasions; they follow the general "line" on literature at any given moment. The few particular individual observations that can be distinguished (often because they were later attacked) come through only sporadically.

The largest and most significant source for Ding Ling's perception of the writer's role is her fiction. There are many passages, which can be excerpted and quoted, directly concerned with the problems of writing. In many of the stories, writers or people with literary interests are important characters, providing a gallery of writers' portraits that change with her political development. We may also observe the concrete effects realized through the handling of the narrator in her stories. This invented or implied author often provides insight into why and how life experience is processed into literature.

Life into Literature: Two Examples

Because of Ding Ling's belief in the interdependence between the man/woman and the writer, between experience and art, she will often — indeed, feels it is part of her obligation to do so — refer to real persons and events in her life or treat personal experiences, sometimes in their raw immediacy, in her fiction. She does not hold back from confronting herself in her writings even in moments of pity and agony, from exposing herself to the public in all her emotional vulnerability. In this impulse toward literary soul-baring Ding Ling was hardly alone — it was a typical phenomenon among May Fourth writers. But her techniques for making over the autobiographical into the fictional were both diverse and markedly her own. The two stories that take as their starting point the same traumatic event, the execution of her husband Hu Yepin, provide a contrast in narrative methods; significantly, both are also turned into occasions for demonstrating the importance of literature as a response to life.

The much-anthologized "Mouye" (A certain night),[6] published in June 1932, sixteen months after Hu's death, incorporates unverifiable details, some of which could only have been pieced together after the news of his execution leaked out some days later. On a bleak winter night (she remembers it had rained on February 7), after more than twenty days of confinement, twenty-five young men and women were machine-gunned in the courtyard of Longhua Prison. Ding Ling's account leaves them nameless, the central figure merely identified as a "warmhearted poet, faithful and hardworking." She imagines him briefly losing consciousness from the shock of the summary death sentence announced minutes before its execution, showing first uncontrolled fury and defiance, and then a calm acceptance and a feeling of solidarity with his comrades in death. Is this an idealized, romanticized presentation of an unbearable (to her) event? One would like to know whether "The Internationale" indeed was sung by the victims as the bullets tore into them.[7]

Ding Ling's grief and despair were described almost twenty years later in the very moving "Yige zhenshirende yisheng — ji Hu Yepin" (The life of an upright man — reminiscences of Hu Yepin),[8] but in the almost contemporary story "Mouye," the pain of his death was perhaps mitigated or depersonalized by an imagined re-creation of it.

This is one way that Ding Ling transmuted life into literature. Although she does not spare herself the brutal detail of the guard hitting Hu's chest with his rifle butt, the narrative is for the most part distant and impersonal in tone. When the prisoners have heard their sentence and are being led out, she writes:

> The sky was black, black without end. From that blackness came raindrops and lumps of snow, from that blackness came the wild roaring of the north wind. The earth was gray, like fog, the accumulated snow in the night reflecting a deathlike gray. People's shadows were black, moving silently across the snow. Guards, prisoners, the sound of shackles, the sound of bayonets, no one spoke, no one moaned, no one sighed or wept; toward the yard, that deep corner of the yard, the temporary execution ground, they moved without stopping.[9]

Hope for the revolution's eventual success is implied in the last sentences, but it is far off:

> In some places, one, or two, or three . . . some blood was flowing, dripping on the snow in the darkness.
> One could not tell when day would break.[10]

This conclusion evokes the title of the much less well-known second story, "Cong yewan dao tianliang" (From night till daybreak), actually written perhaps a year earlier than "A Certain Night."[11] A lone woman is on the way to her "so-called home" one evening. She is unidentified, but the story is filled with references to specific names and events in Ding Ling's life. The sound and sights of the city — the trolley wheels grating on the tracks, street lamps casting shadows of the new leaves at her feet, a child walking between two people, probably his parents — fill her with rambling and affecting thoughts as she walks. It is the anniversary of her younger brother's death years ago. She thinks of her grieving mother, who now takes care of her own young son, Xiaoping, born three months before his father's execution, and of the letter asking for more powdered milk, more money, so the child can eat and dress a little better. After she arrives at the house, which reeks of cooking oil and opium, she goes to her rented room upstairs and lies down. A line of *his* poetry comes to mind. She recalls that from the trolley window she had seen a profile so familiar that she had almost joyously called out to him, "Hey, Pin," before she had remembered and had to hold back her tears. Then she had gone into a department store and looked at children's clothes that she had no money to buy.

There she ran into Mrs. F, also fondling a child's pretty outfit, but she noticed that it was not bought. This chance encounter brings back memories of that fateful night when *he* had failed to return, and frantic with fear and anxiety, she had rushed about the city. She had finally reached the F's, but they did not hear or respond to her wild knocking or calling. (In "The Life of an Upright Man," this episode is also described, with the F's identified as Feng Naichao and his wife.) "How could Mrs. F have known that she could cause one who had hardened her heart to shed tears?" Other memories crowd her mind. Filled with sympathy for the mother who had to put back the dress, for the F's impoverished condition, but also with envy for their present happiness ("they are now as we once were"), she impulsively goes to a pawnshop, and with the five dollars she gets, buys a pink silk dress for the F's baby girl. In the morning the irrational behavior born of her self-pity is seen for what it is. She tears up the note to the F's, lets the pink dress fall onto the floor, and resumes writing a story. (From internal references, it can be identified as "Tian jia chong" [Tian Village]).

Unlike the distant, impersonalized "A Certain Night," "From Night till Daybreak" has all the immediacy of a straight, fresh transcript of personal experience. In this account of one night's happenings, actual names and places are mentioned; chance encounters, random thoughts, fluctuating moods, inconsequential behavior, all seem to occur naturally. In the end, though still filled with self-doubt, the narrator/author has seen through something of, and thus won a victory over herself. An apparent jumble of occurrences has in fact been skillfully organized into something that leads to insight and achieves aesthetic coherence. This treatment of her reaction to Hu Yepin's death thus illustrates a second way of transmuting life into literature.

The question of the relation between literature and life is one that no author can totally answer, an enigma that can be solved only in particular situations, day by day, work to work. These two stories attempt radically different solutions, indicated, for instance, by Ding Ling's uses of the narrator. While both are third-person narrations, in "A Certain Night" the narrator is invisible yet omniscient, paradoxically presenting events she could not personally have seen as if she had directly seen them.[12] The assumed attitude of impersonal detachment makes it possible for Ding Ling to keep out whatever private reactions, probably overwhelming, she may have felt toward the execution to create an objective image of tragic yet haloed martyrdom.[13]

In "From Night till Daybreak," a "subjective third person" becomes the dramatized "center of consciousness"[14] through which the story's narrated action is filtered. In fact what takes place within that consciousness *is* the action of the story. Whether or not we choose to consider this narrator as more closely identified with the author, and the events as more "personal," more "true to life" than in "A Certain Night," *within* this story, the narrator/author directly *enacts* a process of life as it becomes literature, a process of making moral and artistic sense out of seemingly random experience. Moreover, the story expresses explicitly Ding Ling's view of the role and importance of literature. At the end, after her lesson in handling life's pain, she goes back to her desk and tries to fill the blank manuscript paper. She has been writing about the act of writing itself, about the circumstances and self-discoveries that precede it. After all that has occurred, writing comes as a restorative, a reaffirmation. She writes to let herself — and she finds she now can — face life again and go on living.

It is striking to note how many of Ding Ling's stories conclude in the last paragraph with the main character physically picking up a pen or composing sentences.[15] He or she has overcome despair, has resolved a conflict, is making a fresh start, or has reached a state of acceptance or awareness. The act of writing asserts a new sense of order imposed on the chaos of reality. In presenting this image of the writer, Ding Ling provides a very concrete example in her own practice of what much of modern Chinese literature was trying to do. Great historic crises may not always produce literature adequate to their times, but for the generation of Chinese writers of the May Fourth movement, caught in the crisscross of literary, political, and social revolution, literature was their response to the horrors of what was happening around them. The crumbling of the old order, the humiliations of imperialism, the savagery of civil war, police terror, massacres, even when they were not, like Ding Ling, direct victims, were part of their personal internal experience. Writing would be their answer to the insoluble problems of their times, their attempt to grapple with the fearful intangibilities of their existence.

These literary efforts were not free from elements of self-indulgence and self-pity, and these no doubt hastened the day of disenchantment with literature itself. With the exception of Lu Xun, all the May Fourth writers began their careers when they were quite young. By the time Ding Ling wrote "A Certain Night," she had already published five volumes of short stories and one novelette; she was then twenty-five years old.[16] Those who dedicated themselves to literature in China in the twenties were collectively the youngest literary generation to make an impact in the history of a society where age and tradition had always held sway. To them the orthodox past was outmoded, done with, together with the closed literary and educational system that had helped to perpetuate it. A new literature, effected by their personal confrontation with new realities and governed by "realism," a modish doctrine expressive of their specially close relation to experience, was their goal. But historical developments prevented them from carrying through to middle age or literary maturity the self-discoveries and artistic experimentation they had so earnestly begun. Even before the war with Japan and the success of the Communist revolution, intellectuals and writers were becoming radicalized and increasingly skeptical about the merit and relevance of their literary work. In a situation where total revolution seemed the only way out, could literature continue as a luxury of the privileged few? The disillusionment with literature in the early 1930s perhaps came from having expected too much of it in the first place. To subordinate literature to political action might, for the moment, end the soul-searching over literature's place in the writer's life and his society. But with such a fundamental alteration of its premises, how should literature survive in the long run as a distinct activity, as the writer's personal engagement with experience?

Ding Ling's career offers a uniquely precise record of these developments in modern Chinese literary history. It also raises urgent questions about the writer's role and the validity of literature itself. Her preoccupation with getting immediate experience into words remained constant, but as the historical context she wrote in underwent successive stages of change, so did her life in literature.

Literature and the Subjective Self

Ding Ling was first a rebel and iconoclast. Her commitment to writing was made only when, after a period of restless experimenting, she had worked her way into a liberated, convention-defying style of life. This life-style strongly determined what she wrote. Although her interest in fiction was developed from early childhood and manifested itself when she was in high school, her energies were much more engaged in the exciting activities going on as the "waves of the May Fourth movement" hit her small town. She cut her hair, attended meetings, led demonstrations, and taught "abacus" at the evening school for the poor when she was barely taller than the desk on the platform.[17] This precocious activism soon led her to Shanghai and other cities, where she sporadically studied painting and literature, hobnobbed with anarchists, and generally lived an "emancipated" life. In Peking in the summer of 1924, she met a struggling young poet — a rare "person," a "piece of uncut unpolished jade" — and she and Hu Yepin soon were living together.[18] An idyllic picture of this relationship is presented in the affectionate *Ji Ding Ling* (Reminiscences of Ding Ling) by Shen Congwen.

A dedicated and prolific writer himself, one of Shen Congwen's concerns in his account was to locate the sources of Ding Ling's literary impulse in her character and her way of life. His observations must be read in conjunction with Ding Ling's own accounts of her early beginnings as a writer. While he and Hu Yepin (usually referred to as "the naval cadet") dreamed and planned to launch their own journal so they would not be at the mercy of callous editors, Ding Ling, at first, saw herself only on the sidelines as proofreader and account keeper. She was gradually drawn into writing but tried first to become an actress in Shanghai, influenced, says Shen, by the heroines in three French novels. Shen quotes her: "Would it not be worth it to go into that vast, expansive sea of men, find a brand-new life in which laughter and tears were mixed together, and take a chance on testing one's destiny?"[19]

Her failure as an actress became the basis of her first short story, "Mengke"[20] An innocent, sensitive girl arrives in the city, becomes disillusioned by its hypocrisy and emptiness, runs away from her relatives there to seek independence, and despite her suffering from the demeaning demands of her profession, becomes an actress. Whether or not Ding Ling was vicariously enjoying through this story the success denied herself of a beautiful film star who was the toast of "Shanghai's self-appointed writers, playwrights, directors, critics, and the pitiful minions who do the cheering for these people," she certainly spared herself Mengke's need to develop a greater and greater "capacity to tolerate rude humiliation."[21]

"Mengke" is not a very successful work, but it had the main ingredients of the characteristic situation in the early Ding Ling story: a lonely individual pitted against a hostile or uncongenial world, driven into intense awareness of her own sensibilities as she struggles to come to some sense of the self. At various times, Ding Ling described her feeling of personal frustration and despair and linked it both with her early motivation to write and the kinds of characters she wrote about: "Why did I begin to write at that time? I think it was out of loneliness. Dissatisfied with society, with no way of making it on my own, there was a lot I needed to say, but no one to listen. I wanted to do something but there was no opportunity, so since it was at hand, I took up my pen to analyze for myself this society."[22] Because of her suffering, Ding Ling says elsewhere that her "stories could not but be full of contempt for society and full of the stubbornness of the individual's lonely soul."[23] In one of her last pieces, she refers back to the people typical of the May Fourth period who "formed characters in my mind. These were all characters under heavy pressure, in conditions without help, feeling entirely alone, but still striving to find a way to go on. That kind of stubborn people. So when I first wrote stories, I wrote about characters like that."[24]

The most fully realized of these stubborn, lonely characters is Miss Sophie, who made Ding Ling's early fame, and with whom, unfortunately for her, she remained identified. Miss Sophie, to judge by her Westernized name and lack of family connections, is a woman leading a liberated existence in the big city. Her tuberculosis, which at one point requires hospitalization, further detaches her from regular occupation. She finds herself strongly attracted to a man who has the handsome "air of a medieval knight" but a despicable soul. While indulging in feverish fantasies of physical love, she acts perversely to undermine her conquest of him. The battle of self-contradictory impulses reaches a climax in a kiss, which represents for her both a victory and a degradation; she sends him away and is left to castigate herself in despair.[25]

The shock effect of frank descriptions of sexual desires and frustrations accounted for the work's initial impact. But in a sense, "Shafei nüshi de riji" (Diary of Miss Sophie) is also, as was Lu Xun's famous essay, about "what happens after Nora leaves." It concerns the absence of resources in an unreformed society for the individual who has broken away from conventional arrangements. Lu Xun is saying that without equal economic rights, Nora can have only a grim future. Ding Ling is investigating the chaos of personality, of which the inability to cope with sexual feelings is an important manifestation, when caught in the chaos of a disintegrating world. After the great struggle to leave home and the traditional village, and the wholesale repudiation of authority and outmoded values, the young men and women who made their way into the semi-Westernized coastal cities would seem to have achieved the freedom to explore the fullest possibilities of their feelings and being. But self-absorption in a vacuum leads only to a dead-end despair for which Sophie has no one else to blame: "I have wreaked havoc on myself. If a person's enemy is himself, how, oh heavens, can he seek vengeance and indemnity for all his losses?"[26] At the end of the story she is planning to go south, where no one knows her, to "squander away what's left of my life." Her self-pity is not unredeemed by an admixture of severe self-criticism, but whatever weaknesses the character might possess, her author is boldly asserting that she is worthy of attention in spite of what she is. This assertion, which makes Miss Sophie so much a symptom of her age, is advanced through Ding Ling's adoption of the nontraditional "I-narrator" form.

The fictional "I-narrator" (whose degree of identification with the author can vary widely) in diaries, letters, or other types of narrative, was introduced into Chinese literature through the inspiration of Western models, such as the extremely popular translation of *The Sorrows of Young Werther*.[27] It quickly became one of the most significant and characteristic new phenomena among the writers of the May Fourth decades. In traditional fiction, a highly restrictive system of values was held in common by both narrator and audience. The storyteller was "one of us," and from a vantage point external to the events could lay open and comment on his story, relying upon shared assumptions about human experience to carry his audience along with him. However, to Ding Ling and other subjectivist writers of the 1920s, such as Yu Dafu, Guo Moruo, and Lu Yin, the objective values of their world were felt to be dissolving, so the true subject matter of a story was not so much external events as the now idiosyncratic and problematical response by the individual to events. Their *"dramatization of I"* signified "the awareness of self in a special condition, in conflict with, in opposition to, in flight from, the world beyond the self."[28]

The "I-narrator" shifts the action from external events to the inner life of the character, whose ordeal is often self-induced, and whose tragedy, like Miss Sophie's, now lies within the self. Other stories of Ding Ling's early period, even when less self-centered, focus on characters who are similarly victimized by their own ambivalent or wayward responses to their situations — prostitutes dreaming of a different life they might have had, a country girl destroyed by her longings for the city's unattainable luxuries, overwrought female schoolteachers involved in petty lovers' quarrels, a woman socially ostracized by a love affair then betrayed by her lover, and several stories about women in the midst of disconcerting love affairs or contemplating suicide.[29] Whether in first or third person, the dramatization of a subjective interpretive consciousness is always the means of narrating the story.

If narrative conventions express the writer's sense of the self in relation to the world, they can be expected to undergo transformation when the writer is converted to a specific political ideology. In 1930 Ding Ling, with many other prominent literary figures, joined the League of Left-Wing Writers, and her work took a decidedly "proletarian" turn. At times she continued to focus on the individual consciousness, particularly in stories where the intellectual/writer adapts to the revolutionary cause. But more and more she turned to larger canvases and group scenes. In "Shui" (Flood),[30] she experimented with a new narrative method that Jaroslav Průšek has termed "pointillism."[31] Flashes of scenes and fragments of dialogue from anonymous voices present the process of mass consciousness-raising among peasants who are crushed by hunger and disaster. But the depersonalized "points" do not coalesce into an effective whole.[32] In her last major work, *The Sun Shines over the Sangkan River*, her technique is much more secure. Here she tries to integrate the characterizations and life histories of representative individuals in a small community so that under the leadership or catalytic action of political cadres they will be able to assume their proper roles in the culminating drama of the last chapters, the confrontation with the landlord Qian Wengui. How far Ding Ling had come in some twenty years from her early subjectivist phase to her final socialist-realistic phase can be seen by comparing a passage from this novel and one from the early story, "Diary of Miss Sophie." Illustrating two poles of narrative technique, both passages attempt to establish or introduce character as a prelude to action — action, however, that takes place in two different fictional worlds.[33]

For Miss Sophie, the outside world barely exists. It is her sense of isolation that intensifies her self-awareness and her despondency:

> I haven't written anything again for several days. Whether it's due to my sour mood or some nameless feeling, I don't know. All I know is since yesterday I have just wanted to cry. When others see me cry they imagine I am thinking of home, thinking of my illness; when they see me laugh, they think I am happy and congratulate me on the radiance of my health... But all so-called friends are the same; to whom can I confide my fond heart, which disdains tears yet is incapable of laughter? Furthermore, since I understand so well the various desires in the world I am unwilling to relinquish and the distress that results from every effort to pursue them, even I am no longer willing to be sympathetic toward this sorrow that comes on unrepentantly. How then can I take up a pen and express in detail all my self-accusation and self-hatred?[34]

The long, tortured, "Europeanized" clauses, each modifying or contradicting what went on before, show an obsessive introspection leading to mental paralysis. She is incapable of expressing herself, of being understood by her friends, and above all of taking practical action.

Whereas Miss Sophie "reveals" herself through the diary form, Dong Guihua (Cassia, a common rustic name) in *Sangkan River* is presented objectively by an omniscient narrator whose point of view represents the consensus of the community.[35] While only slightly longer than the first passage, this one tells us about Dong Guihua's history, her current situation in the village, and her readiness to play a progressive role in the coming struggle for land reform:

> The head of the Women's Association had come here from the north as a refugee over four years ago. A village relative brought them together and she started living with Li Zhixiang. It was to his advantage to marry her, since it would cost him nothing, and she saw that he was a straightforward man, so both sides agreeing, they married without much ceremony. She was a woman almost forty, very sharp, not a bad match for this thirty-year-old tramp. The two got on well, and gradually set up something like a household. People all said Li Zhixiang was lucky to get such a wife. She had suffered a lot, understood the cares and hardships of life, knew how to manage, was good-tempered. All the people who lived in the mud houses in that western section spoke well of her. Last year when Nuanshui Village was liberated and they wanted to set up a Women's Association, they picked her. She said she didn't know anything, and wasn't a native of the village, but it didn't do, and she was elected. When anything came up in the village, the cadres would ask her to call people to the meeting.[36]

Ideology is expressed through style, a reflection of the way the world is perceived and shaped. The necessary information about Dong Guihua is given briefly, in a matter-of-fact, everyday language enlivened by occasional colloquialisms which Ding Ling, as a southerner, had to learn. The straightforward sentence structure underlines the fact that unlike Miss Sophie, whose complex or perverse mental states are too much for her own understanding, much less that of her well-meaning friends, Dong Guihua is clearly known, firmly placed within her community through the eyes of those in her neighborhood. Later on, she herself will have some dark moments of doubt, but as is intimated in this passage, when the time comes, she will perform her role properly and carry her husband along.

Although complex human relationships and the unraveling of intrigues form important parts of Ding Ling's novel, the main action centers on how people, starting from mixed motives, backward notions, fear, and hesitation, struggle to reach a state of clearly defined political consciousness. People like Dong Guihua are the available human material, with all their limitations and potential, that help carry out the immense revolutionary experiments to be repeated throughout the late forties in north China. In a revolution where mass consensus and mass participation are central, the subjective states of each individual are of supreme importance but only within well-defined psychic areas or levels of experience. The dynamics of character development in the head of the Women's Association is not unlike that in Parcifal, whose character is explored not for its own sake, but is "limited by his developmental motif, his progress in Christian knighthood."[37] Dong Guihua's progress in revolutionary consciousness can be made clear and exemplary only if sexual feelings (such as those suffered by Miss Sophie) and similar irrelevancies are filtered out.

These changes in narrative form happened because the ambiguities and complexities of the subjective consciousness have no legitimate place in a revolutionary ideology. The individual writer no longer casts himself simultaneously as chief actor and spectator in a personal and precarious confrontation with reality. What had been a typical literary symptom of the old world's dissolution was eliminated with the establishment of the new. The writer has become a bit player in collective presentations where all actual experience is generalized, all plot outcomes predictably inspirational in the interest of enhancing communal feeling. Thus, the sublimation of individual energies into socially constructive channels has banished the self-doubting, anguished narrator and brought to an end the brief episode of subjectivism in the history of Chinese fiction.

But divisions in literature are seldom absolute. In spite of Ding Ling's strides toward socialist realism, she was attacked during the antirightist campaign in 1957–1958 for failing to rid herself of her early individualistic tendencies.[38] One running critical refrain, which dubiously blurred the distinction between life and literature, was that she herself continued to be the "incarnation of Miss Sophie's soul."[39]

The matter with "Miss Sophie" was not only that she was an "extreme individualist" but that she also posed specific problems as a woman. Feminism was at least an implied issue in the charges against her. Though not in the sense imputed to her by the critics, it certainly constituted a conscious and significant dimension in her literary career from the very beginning.

Literature and Feminism

Feminism, like "individualism," is a loaded word in a socialist context. How much should the specific female consciousness be stressed in a total social revolution? In discussing Ding Ling's feminism, I am not referring to women's rights but to her perceptions into the specific female condition and its treatment in her writings.[40]

Ding Ling's personal situation and concerns in women's emancipation were of the "second generation." The pioneering battles against the most flagrant institutionalized forms of oppression — arranged marriage, foot-binding, denial of education opportunities — had already been fought and won for her to some extent by her mother. The story of this extraordinary woman who at thirty, a widow with two small children, left her gentry family to study in the city and qualify herself to be an educator, is partly told in Ding Ling's unfinished novel *Muqin* (Mother).[41] The mother's effort to keep up in gym class, painfully running with freshly unbound feet, so movingly described by Ding Ling, was what made it possible for the daughter, at age thirteen, to lead fellow students in a demonstration at the Provincial Assembly to demand equality for women. What Ding Ling faced in her unconventional existence in the city were the much more pervasive and subtle discriminatory attitudes. Some of these she internalized, and she had to contend with them to establish herself as a writer and a person.

In the *Reminiscences* referred to above, Shen Congwen sought connections between Ding Ling's feminine identity and literary motivations. He found that Hu Yepin's effect on her budding literary efforts was mixed. It was supportive and restrictive at the same time, "a hothouse and cradle of this woman writer's soul."[42] It nurtured her talent but circumscribed her experience. It also inhibited her later on, when she could not easily accept her successes while Hu still went unrecognized. "In her victory she felt she had to say smilingly to old friends, 'This is all Pin's achievement, without the naval cadet there would have been no book.' "[43] Indignant at the rejection of Hu's manuscripts, she often tore up her own, or left them unfinished, in the belief that her work had won acceptance over his "just because she was a woman." Otherwise, according to Shen, she would have produced twice as many works between 1927 and 1930.[44]

On the other hand, Shen Congwen saw in Ding Ling a proud self-assertion against men that was necessary both to her writing and her revolutionary work. In Peking, he observes, she must have felt how commonplace and petty those "so-called writers" were in their conversations and thinking:

> If because of this, her pride went up, this pride was useful to her; it was indispensable. With some people pride would only limit the develop-ment of their work; this person, however, required just this bit of pride, and the disgust and contempt roused by the commonplace reasoning but swaggering behavior of males [nanzi] in general before she could perceive her own vocation and responsibility. Therefore, when she took up her pen to write, she produced In the Darkness, Wei Hu, Flood, Mother; when she felt she should put down that pen to go to receive a more serious education, without hesitation, without bravado, she went among the groups of the broad laboring masses.[45]

Whether or not Shen Congwen's reminiscences can be taken as wholly accurate, most of Ding Ling's stories up to 1931 focus almost obsessively on a young woman struggling somehow to assert her individual self in or through her female condition. In these early fictional works, because the protagonist is often female, the two concerns of the subjective self and feminism naturally overlap. The special awareness of self in its relation to the world can be dramatized through different narrative forms as discussed above; under the influence of ideology, the "feminist aspect" of Ding Ling's writings likewise went through successive stages of change.

The early stories are characteristically about a young woman in a complicated love situation outside of conventional arrangements. One indication that conventions have been shed is her preoccupation with her sexual feelings. The rhapsodies of these sexually aroused, uninhib-ited young women may seem tame (the sex act is only hinted at) by the standards of present-day nonsocialist writing, but to Ding Ling's contemporary readers, they were "bold," "modern," and "realistic." She did actually reveal aspects of female sexuality never before — and certainly never since — depicted in Chinese literature. What makes Ding Ling's writings unique among the general May Fourth effusions of love is not only that she was a woman somewhat more frank and daring than the rest but also that she often links sexual libertar-ianism with the individual woman's self-exploration. She is, moreover, able to see the resulting mixture with a degree of critical aware-ness. Ding Ling's assertive, self-conscious, sexually active female characters contrast sharply with the passive and suffering victims of blighted love who tearfully expire in so many other novels by contemporary women writers.

If her women indulge in fantasies of lovemaking, it is partly to assert their power. The "Salome-type" flirt in "Yige nüren he yige nanren" (A woman and a man)[46] knows that she is playing a role but cannot rest until "she can see another's soul acupunctured by her and vibrating in her palm." But the girl in "Ta zou hou" (After he left)[47] who arbitrarily sends her lover home at 2:00 A.M. in the rain, after musing on this evidence of her power over him, weeps from shame and remorse and despises herself for using her attractions like a prostitute. Another story describes a girl disengaging herself from an affair and returning to her writing.[48] Thus, as vulnerable as women are to love's temptations, they can often turn it into an occasion for the clear-eyed testing of the self. Love can also be a tender or passionate affair, as between the two half-starved writers in "Nianqiande yitian" (The day before New Year's)[49], and in the astonishing *cri de cœur* "Bu suan qingshu" (Not a love letter).[50] The second piece is an outpouring of passion for the only man who has "ever set my heart on fire" but renounced for the sake of Hu Yepin.

One reason for being strong and hard (*qiangying*) and asserting oneself is to counteract women's particular weakness, the feminine sensibility, which is emotional, high-strung, and given to melancholy or hysteria. Ding Ling wrote about women because she understood their weaknesses:

> but because of this, there has been much misunderstanding. Actually I strongly dislike these weak points in women, but like Fadeyev's writing about Mechik in *The Nineteen,* although he does his utmost to expose his faults, we can see where he sympathizes with him. I may not feel sympathetic toward the women in my writings, but I am unable to write in accordance with my opinion . . . at times what I write is the opposite of my original intention.[51]

She is torn between sympathy and criticism because she sees women suffering not only as victims of circumstances but of self-defeating sentimentalism as well. The insidious effect the feminine sensibility can have on writing is discussed in a story about a woman writer composing a story while working her way out of an emotional entanglement:

Today, she [Yecao] was feeling terribly vexed because she had injected some very fervent feelings into a very cool and rational woman and had, moreover, introduced a light layer of melancholy. This was really not the character in her imagination, but this was precisely a shortcoming of women that she could understand best. She didn't know what to do, to tear up the manuscript and rewrite it or to go on but without being sympathetic to this woman. She could not stop thinking about this vexing matter, gradually she thought of the social environment that caused women to overstress emotions, she thought how pitiable women were; then as she reflected, she began to loathe herself.[52]

But when Yecao meets her supplicating lover that night, she is strong enough to free herself of him, though not without some regret, and walks home to her writing "happily singing her new-formed phrases."

After 1930 love is rejected not in favor of literature but of political action. In the stories of this transitional "love and revolution" phase, the nature of the revolution to be embraced is vague and remote, while the pleasures of love to be renounced are still intimate, detailed, and self-indulgent. But once the total break is made with love, the unattached young women living a free life in the big city, struggling to articulate their self-awareness in relation to men, disappear as central characters in Ding Ling's stories. In the later works, women are of many ages, have specific occupations, are rendered in varied settings — destitute peasants fleeing a flood or ravaged by war, factory wives laundering in the streets, students helping in the fall harvest, as well as writers working on propaganda teams or collecting material for their stories. The sexual identity concerns are outgrown or irrelevant in the face of disasters and urgent collective tasks.

Still, to Ding Ling the special tragedy of woman's condition remained. Soon after she got to Yenan in 1936, she helped establish the Women's National Salvation Association, and was thereafter actively involved in women's activities. She no longer wrote to dramatize the struggles of the individual woman within herself but to attack hardships and discrimination particular to women in society — even when that society, as presented in her works of the time, is very progressive.

"Sanbajie yougan" (Thoughts on March 8) was an essay written in 1942 for the *Jiefang ribao* (Liberation daily), which Ding Ling edited. It compassionately presents the situation of women, who are always the object of attention or criticism, whether they marry or not, have children or not, or if they are divorced. In the old society, they might have been called "pitiful," "ill-fated," but today "it's her own doing," and "it serves her right":

> I am a woman myself, I understand better than others the shortcomings of women, but I understand even more their suffering. They cannot be above their times, they are not ideal, they are not forged of steel. They are unable to resist society's temptations and silent oppressions, they have all had a history of blood and tears, they have all had lofty emotions (whether they have risen or fallen, are fortunate or unfortunate, still struggling alone or have joined the crowd)... I wish men, especially those with position, and women themselves would see women's shortcomings more in connection with society.[53]

Her point is that women are oppressed even when they are supposedly equal and can choose their marital status. The story "Zai yiyuan-zhong" (In the hospital)[54] may have been a metaphor for Yenan. Yet bleak and disillusioning as the conditions were facing the young, idealistic female obstetrician, the story does end on the positive note of "growth through hardship." The heroine in "Wo zai Xiacun de shihou" (When I was in Xia village)[55] also looks forward to a better future. But one message of this deeply disturbing story as expressed in the words of one of its characters is "the misfortune [*daomei*] of being a woman." The writer, the "I," befriends a girl in Xia village who has just returned from a year in the Japanese army. Captured when the enemy attacked the village, she has been down in the "fiery pit" [*huokeng*]. Escaped and returned home, she is sent back among the enemy as a spy. Now severely ill with venereal disease, she is released from her secret mission for medical care. Her return causes great commotion in the village. Certain younger villagers recognize the heroism of her sacrifice. To others, she is both an object of prurient curiosity ("over a hundred men") and to be shunned as something "worse than a tattered shoe." Her body has been brutally exploited by both sides in the war — the physical use by one is the means to information by the other — but she must still be condemned according to the notions of chastity.

Seventeen years later, during the antirightist campaign, this story was attacked as a glorification of a prostitute in the enemy's camp and a blatant example of Ding Ling's own immorality. It was charged that when she was under arrest from 1933 to 1936, she sold out the Communist party by selling herself and living with a man who had been a spy for the Guomindang. Thus, she was herself guilty of violating the chastity code (*shijie,* to be disloyal or unchaste, used in both senses here).[56] "In the Hospital" was criticized for its "extreme individualism" for having, as the title of one article put it, located "Miss Sophie in Yenan."[57] "Incarnations of Miss Sophie" (Ding Ling herself being one of them) were being turned up in every work under attack. Her preoccupation with sex was seen as a reflection of bourgeois decadence and nihilism, her search for self-affirmation merely a selfish desire to "manipulate men," because "facts have long proved that it is the reactionary class that suppresses women's liberation, not males [*nanxing*] in general."[58] If there is no specific oppression of women as women in *any* society, neither is there the need to explore sexual relationships as a problematical dimension of human experience. Indulgence in sexual fantasy is moreover "a kind of opiate for youth . . . they will want to find the 'happiness' Sophie had from Ling Jishi's person and completely forget the class struggle of real life."[59]

The stream of puritanical outrage was directed against Ding Ling's personal life as much as her works. Since her early love relationships had been much gossiped about in Shanghai, the charges against her now were eagerly believed. It was one price she had to pay for combining literary avant-gardism, political protest, and, unforgivably, sexual emancipation together in her rebellion against authority and her own assertion of independence. But to hold Ding Ling completely "responsible" for the sexual fantasies of Miss Sophie is to obliterate altogether the dividing line between literature and life and to raise immediate questions about the role of the writer.

The Political Role of Literature

In a broad sense, all of Ding Ling's early writings or, for that matter, all the writings produced in the twenties and early thirties, were already intensely political. Even their most subjective outpourings clearly reflected the political and social changes going on around them and implied urgent questions of human worth and social attitudes. An increased awareness of the magnitude of China's problems, and of the need for total solutions, brought about the accelerated politicization of literature. This process was reinforced by factors in the writers' personal and literary situations.

There was no financial security in writing. It was a matter of bare survival — bargaining with petty publishers and fending off the insistent landlady. In an early story, Ding Ling portrayed the harassed writer "cooking and laundering oneself, spewing out one's own heart and blood to write, so someone can count up the words and pay out a little money to live on . . . meeting with cold indifference, like death, yet patiently walking this road of literature, which the materialistic times in its pursuit of petty profit does not deign to notice."[60] Poverty and lack of recognition made a writer acutely aware of the social context of his enterprise. It deepened his grudge against the present structure of the world[61] and pressed on him the question of what was the good of writing. It also made him ask himself how much affectation there was in his assumed role.

The May Fourth writers were conscious iconoclasts who had rejected classical conventions and modes of writing. But new literature cannot be created freely and directly in a vacuum. In part, they had to try molding a new tradition for themselves. The means available toward this end were the unfamiliar themes, symbols, conventions, and verbal patterns they extracted from the imperfect translations of Western literature that were circulating in their rather small and enclosed literary world. These superficial borrowings from the West, plus the glorified self-image of the rebellious artist, were initially useful and exciting in opposing the old system, but before long, their inadequacies in dealing with emerging new realities had to be admitted. In an often-quoted passage, Ding Ling, with characteristic forthrightness, goes straight to the core of this crisis in the writer's self-confidence. The character in her story is concerned above all about the effect of literature on its readers:

As for writing, I sometimes feel that it would not be much of a loss if we gave it up entirely. We write, some people read, time passes, and no effect whatsoever. What is the meaning of it then except we've gotten paid for it? Even if some readers are moved by some part of the plot or certain passages of writing — but who are these readers? Students of the petty bourgeois class above high school level who have just reached adolescence are most subject to melancholy. They feel that these writings fit their temper perfectly, expressing some melancholy that they can feel but not really experience. . . But in the end? Now I understand we have only done something harmful, we have dragged these young people down our old paths. The sort of sentimentalism, individualism, grumblings, and sorrows with no way out! . . . Where is the way out for them? They can only sink deeper and deeper day by day into their own gloom, not seeing the connection between society and their sufferings. Even if they could improve their language and produce some essays and poems that may win praise from some old writers, what good, I ask you, is it to them? And what good to society? Therefore with regard to writing, personally I am ready to give it up.[62]

The quotation is from "Yijiusanlingnian chun Shanghai" (Shanghai in the spring of 1930), a story from her "love and revolution" phase. This reflection acts as a catalyst in transforming the heroine from the love object of an unprogressive writer into an active revolutionary.

The novelette *Wei Hu* (1930)[63] is a more extended treatment of the "love and revolution" conflict, but could appropriately be subtitled "portrait of the revolutionary as an artist." A romantic figure just back from the Soviet Union whose revolutionary activities are quite hazy when compared with his literary interests, Wei Hu, in his blue cotton worker's clothes, dazzles the girls with talk about Chopin and Turgenev. Before departing for Canton to organize revolutionary activities, he writes a final letter to his beloved, symbolically leaving her with his diary, his literary collection, and manuscripts of his poems. Art and literature, as well as love and sentiment, had to be renounced for revolutionary commitment.

Wei Hu is an overblown romance, yet elsewhere Ding Ling was quite capable of seeing through the pose of the would-be revolutionary poet:

On that melancholy street he would feel indignant, indignant against those capitalists; at that moment he could very well become a revolutionary hero. It was not entirely because he had no money to frequent brothels, no money to marry that he felt revolution was necessary, but because there were many rickshaw men wearing only their tattered quilted clothes, still afraid to go home to face their wives and children, still loitering on the street. Truly the idea that the moneyed class had to be eradicated was mostly formed from these rickshaw men. He could not of course be utterly different from those many other people who shared his feelings. Only after he heard others say that rickshaw men were pitiable did he see rickshaw men and could before long write a vernacular poem in a certain magazine singing about them. However, it was fortunate that they themselves did not realize how important they were.[64]

One could compile an anthology entitled "Writers and Rickshaw Men," with stories by Lu Xun, Yu Dafu, Ba Jin, Lao She, Zhang Tianyi, and others, in order to test Ding Ling's point that writers had only a shallow understanding of revolution and indulged in self-serving sentimentalism toward the only representative of the "proletariat" with whom they in their relatively privileged existence had any contact. She wrote a few more stories with the writer as the central figure, struggling to overcome his own defects and affirm his faith in his new revolutionary role. But in her later works, writers are portrayed as self-important, weak, prone to abstraction, divorced from reality, and far removed from the people. After her political conversion, the writer is taken down from his pedestal and given a new and humbler role. Her advice in 1931 is: "Do not let yourself be isolated from the masses, do not consider yourself a writer. Remember, you are one of the masses, you are speaking for them, speaking for yourself."[65] This and several other "Concrete Opinions on Creative Writing" appear in an editorial in the magazine *Beidou (Big dipper)*, one of the short-lived journals of the League of Left-Wing Writers, which Ding Ling edited in 1931.

With the explicit politicization of literature, the problem of the relationship between literature and life in Ding Ling's career entered a new phase. The challenge, which became increasingly severe, was to reconcile her acceptance of literature's assigned position in the overall revolutionary scheme with the need to uphold the idea of literature itself. While she certainly did not think of literature as autonomous, she had the professional writer's belief in its distinct nature and value, which she continually tried to define. She recognized the writer's responsibility to struggle against the influence of his petty bourgeois origins, to live among and learn from the masses, to proceed always from a Marxist world view, and to use the methodology of socialist realism. But through countless reiterations, she also relentlessly sought to answer the question of how one can in the end come up with a good piece of literary work. The party bureaucrats only dimly understood the nature of the problem, if they recognized its existence at all. Most other veteran writers made only perfunctory gestures toward its solution. It is because Ding Ling failed that one realizes the elusive nature of her search.

Even after her commitment to Marxism, while she began to adapt her writing to her new role as spokesman for the masses, the strain of satisfying ideological preconceptions in literary practice was already evident. "Flood" was hailed as a forward step in leftist literature when it was published in 1931, but it was also criticized as being only "a small budding sprout of the new fiction we should have," because it did not adequately reflect the situation of the revolutionary leadership.[66] Inevitably, from then on, her literary writings would always be enmeshed in political events or party developments and would be evaluated on those terms. An extreme example occurs in an essay about her unfinished novel, *Mother*. It had been planned as an account of the story of her mother and of "the changes of a social system in historical process." Only the first third was published in 1933, after Ding Ling had been arrested and presumed executed. An obviously emotional response to this report, the article on the novel concludes with the following eulogy in which the word "mother" refers to Ding Ling's actual mother, the book about her, and Ding Ling's own nurturing, sacrificial "motherly" role as a writer:

> *Mother* is unfinished, it is only a fragment; the author of *Mother* has sacrificed her everything for light [*guangming*]; how forcefully does this show that our times are in the midst of a violent storm! The mother of the first generation "embodied the future aspirations of the people." The "mother" of the second generation has burst through "aspiration" and entered into "reality." In form *Mother* may be a fragment, but in fact, Ding Ling has used her blood to complete this book; can there be any book more valuable, more precious than this? Be content, Ding Ling! Your blood even more forcefully than your pen has instructed the masses; even those who are weak, because of your sacrifice have awakened and stood up![67]

Here is the perfect, ultimate fusion of the personal life and the literary vocation; blood will take up where ink leaves off. Although the rumor of her "sacrifice" turned out to be false, Ding Ling may have been unique among writers in the singular intensity and dedication with which she practiced what she wrote. Fate or choice always seemed to place her at the very center of what was happening. She lived through and acted upon each moment of experience with the full force of her personality. She evaded execution, and, under obscure circumstances, escaped to Yenan in 1936, arriving in the disguise of a Manchurian soldier. There, she devoted her energies and writings to serving the war and revolutionary effort. When the war with Japan broke out, she went to the front as a secretary to the Eighth Route Army. Later she became director of the Northwestern Front Service Corps, a propaganda team that wrote and produced plays and skits. She worked to carry the message of resistance to towns and villages in the guerrilla areas and send back reports from the front.[68] Her own efforts at dramatic writing look extremely crude on paper. But it was the effectiveness of her efforts and those of others like her in mobilizing the people that confirmed for the Communist party the importance of art and literature as an integral part of the "mass line" revolutionary technique. In spite of these successes, she was beginning to get into difficulties with the party leadership over how that part should be played.

When literature was given a specific function to perform for the revolution, it seemed that the self-questionings of Ding Ling and others in the 1930s about the worth of their writings to society were immediately answered. The actual devaluation of the writer's role was not readily apparent. It was not until Mao Zedong's "Talks at the Yenan Forum on Literature and Art" in 1942 and the subsequent application of the talks as doctrine that the ominous implications for literature became plain. Henceforth, Philistine moralism and utilitarianism, both of which had been the traditional enemies of art everywhere, would find a powerful ally in a fundamentalist political ideology. The talks, part of the great thought-reform campaign that was to mold the Communist party into the distinctive and effective instrument it became for carrying out revolution, were specifically a rebuke against Ding Ling and several other writers. Their critical essays, published in the months before Mao's talks in the *Liberation Daily*, edited by Ding Ling, revealed that they had been under the illusion that they could continue to play the adversary role against established society that had initially drawn them to literature in the twenties. But it was not until 1957–1958, during the massive antirightist campaign, that Ding Ling's "crimes" in the Yenan period were made public.

The antirightist drive was motivated by several factors — literary factionalism dating from the quarrels in the 1930s, struggles for power within the cultural hierarchy, political maneuvers that expediently made an example of a prestigious writer. One may well wonder whether it was just Ding Ling's ideas on literature that posed such a threat in themselves to socialist construction. Certainly the total mobilization of mass opinion and the vehemence of the attacks seem out of proportion to the seriousness of her offenses. The major problem with Ding Ling was that even though she believed that literature must always be subservient to a cause larger than itself, she also believed it must still keep its distinct character of being literature. She sought to define this distinction through the special relationship between literature and life. Her lectures constantly urged writers to broaden their scope and "get deeper into life" (*shen ru shenghuo*), so as to avoid superficiality and writing by formula (*gongshihua*).[69] By life, she meant, of course, the life of the masses. The writer might not live permanently in a village but should spiritually "make his dwelling among the masses," the title of a talk given to literary workers in 1953.[70] Just as "Diary of Miss Sophie," "When I was in Xia Village," "In the Hospital," and "Thoughts on March 8" were the target pieces for the attacks on her ideas about the individual and women, regardless of what she might have said elsewhere on these subjects, this 1953 lecture was singled out for what it revealed about her pernicious ideas about literature. She began by saying that literary creation is very complex labor. To write a good piece requires many prior conditions. Some have overemphasized the need for analysis and study, thinking that it is all a matter of understanding Marxist-Leninist policy and thought. But the problem in creative writing is "connecting it with life," not just seeing something on the surface and using it as material:

> What they [Cao Xueqin, Shi Naian, Tolstoy, Gorky] wrote was about the people and events that had been most meaningful to them in their lives, their whole lives. These people and events were used to express a lifetime's summation of feeling and life. From life they established and discovered certain truths, which they wanted to propagate. In order to do it well, they used the form of literature; they did not write because they were writers, nor did they search for a subject because they wanted to write, or go search for material because they had a subject. This is the opposite of what we do.[71]

Writers, she continued, now are living in a wonderful time; never in history have they had such good fortune, have they been regarded so highly.

> In such a heroic time . . . we should have a goal to struggle for, to write a good book, not a slovenly book, but a book that has a high degree of consciousness and art, not just for one's own enjoyment, or the praise of a few friends, but to be cherished by thousands and thousands of readers, pondered over and forever imprinted in their hearts, a book they are happy to refer to, not just popular for a time, but lasting into the future. . . I do not oppose the writing groups and such organizations that we have now. But I believe it is wrong for a writer never to be without guidance. A writer is not like a child who cannot leave his nurse, he should grow independently. Because no matter how literary creation is guided, a work is created through the individual.

The lecture ended:

> Let me now secretly tell you, I still have some ambition, I still would like
> to write a good book. I ask you to help me.[72]

Her main argument is for fuller participation in the life of the masses, but the passages quoted above were among the most damning. She was attacked because she saw literature as the creation of the individual genius and as a means to achieve profit and fame, both marks of "bourgeois individualism." Worse still, she was accused of setting up this "one-bookism"[73] — the achieved literary work — to oppose the party leadership. Thus, the antirightist campaign against Ding Ling was waged as a "struggle to protect the socialist line in art and literature."[74]

Writers do tend to have grandiose views of themselves and their work, which may be necessary for the risks they have to take. Yet, in spite of the animated, semiconfidential tone in her talk, Ding Ling was not referring to her own immortality among the company of great writers. She was talking about the transcendent possibilities of literature as a tradition, about the personal vision of life and truth communicated in an enduring form. But her critics believed that literature should serve only the urgent needs of the present. In a situation where the margin between economic viability and starvation was still so close, literature should be restricted to what it could do to inspire collective efforts toward fulfilling practical goals. The issue was not so much artistic autonomy versus party control as it was between two different views of literature.

The limited, short-range view of literature was not just born with the socialist revolution. It is also one consequence of the lack of faith in *all* literary tradition that has occurred in modern political history. For this lack of faith, Ding Ling and the whole iconoclastic impulse of the May Fourth generation, inevitable as it had been, were partly responsible. During that literary revolution, traditional literature, the ornament and support of the evil past, had been utterly discredited. But the new literature, born of a sense of cultural loss and personal despair, soon began to express a basic disillusionment with itself. Under the new order, the relevance of a serious literature to the solution of urgent social problems has yet to be defined. The May Fourth period began with great expectations for literature, but in a time of cataclysmic social transformation and cultural crisis such as marks modern China's history, one may question whether an assured role for the serious literary writer is indeed possible.

14.

Yu Dafu and the Transition to Modern Chinese Literature

Michael Egan

The May Fourth period was as much a watershed for Chinese literature as for politics. A new generation of authors seemed to spring up almost simultaneously to the call of Chen Duxiu and Hu Shi for a new Chinese literature, and by the 1920s the novel and short story no longer occupied the low position they held for earlier, Confucian generations. Though the twenties were a transitional period for Chinese fiction and saw the introduction of innovative literary techniques, many devices and themes that had been established in earlier literature, and may therefore be considered traditional, can be found even in the most adventurous works of the literary revolution. This mixture of old and new is a characteristic feature of May Fourth literature.

Unfortunately, genre theory has been a rather neglected area of Chinese literary studies. A scale or system for judging traditional and modern aspects of fiction has not yet been worked out.[1] Nonetheless, a closely read and carefully considered analysis of a literary text can reveal both old (pre-literary revolution) and new (elements that are not found in traditional literature) phenomena. Analyzing texts with an eye to the novelty of the literary devices they use will add to our awareness of the development of Chinese fiction as well as enhance our appreciation of the individual works.

The texts of a pivotal writer such as Yu Dafu provide some distinctive features that will give evidence of an evolving literary genre. The logical place to look for clues would be in his first two stories, "Chenlun" (Sinking) and "Yinhuisede si" (Silver-gray death), completed in January and May of 1921. It would be in these early stories that some incongruous elements would probably appear — elements characteristic of a passage from traditional to modern.

Yu, one of the leading figures of modern Chinese literature, was both typical of a major literary movement and a highly individualistic artist. He was a leading writer of fiction in the Creation Society and a literary stylist of unique and original ability. An innovator both in his prose style and in his choice and organization of themes, Yu is often regarded as the archetypal "modern" author of the twenties — heavily influenced by Western literature and self-consciously at odds with the Chinese tradition. If Yu's reputation as one of the most avant-garde writers of the twenties is justified, concrete evidence of literary change will be found in "Sinking" and "Silver-gray death." Just as the origins of modern Chinese fiction are to be sought much earlier than the generally accepted dates of the May Fourth movement,[2] so too will traditional elements be found even in the work of the most experimental author.

First it is necessary to reconsider a commonly held but incorrect opinion regarding Yu's fiction: that it is sentimental. Reading Yu's stories as sentimental will prevent the perception of an extremely important and subtle innovation, the use of irony.[3]

Critics as different as Jaroslav Průšek and C. T. Hsia have both held that an outstanding feature of Yu's stories is the subjective inclusion of personal details of the author's own life. Průšek writes:

> we can speak of the markedly subjective coloring of Yü's work, for the author — or his representative — is almost always the principal hero of the story, the plot being based as a rule on his personal experiences and the subjects of his narratives are his own spiritual processes, everything being described from his subjective angle.[4]

Hsia writes:

> Though a third-person narrative, "Sinking" is unabashedly autobiographical. The familial and educational backgrounds of author and hero are almost identical, and the story is told in an intimate fashion. In that sense, the whole body of Yü's fiction, with the few exceptions in the proletarian mode, constitute a Rousseauist confession.[5]

Both Průšek and Hsia accept the conventional opinion that Yu and the protagonist of "Sinking" are one and the same person. If this is true, Yu might well be guilty of, as Hsia puts it, "Wertherian self-pity" and "the worst sentimental affectation."[6]

This view of the personal basis of Yu's fiction is held by no less an authority than the author himself. As Leo Ou-fan Lee points out, "For Yü Ta-fu, all literature is autobiography; the reverse seems also applicable, that all autobiography — at least his autobiography — is literature. This autobiographical impulse is the motivating force for most of his creative output."[7] Yu himself wrote in the preface to "Sinking," "I feel that the statement 'all literature is nothing but the autobiography of the author who wrote it' is absolutely true."

But authors make notoriously poor critics, especially of their own work, and Lee wisely takes Yu's view of his own writings with a grain of salt. Lee further comments, "precisely because Yü identified art with life, and life with art, biographers of Yü must be constantly on guard: *behind the simple unity of his life and works lies a maze of ambiguities between reality and appearance, between the self and visions of the self.*"[8]

This is a distinction that must always be made. To consider "Sinking" subjective and autobiographical, based on the author's own word or on similarities between its plot and events in Yu's own life, is to commit what critic William Wimsatt has called the "intentional fallacy." That is, falling into the trap of believing that "in order to judge an author's performance, we must know *what he intended.*"[9] Wimsatt spells out what Lee has already implied: "We ought to impute the thoughts and attitudes of the work to the dramatic speaker, and if to the author at all, only by an act of biographical inference."[10] The intentional fallacy "begins by trying to derive the standard of criticism from the psychological *causes* of a [text] and ends in biography and relativism."[11]

Though Yu was beyond question a writer who broke new ground, most criticism of his work has centered around its autobiographical nature and thus is unsatisfactory on two counts: it implies that the subjective element is a new one in Chinese literature when it is not, and excessive identification of author with protagonist has resulted in misinterpretation of Yu's stories.

Of course, Yu's fiction was based upon subjective experience, as any artist's must be. But surely an author, while relying to some degree on personal experience, can freely use imagination to temper that experience without being confused with everything and everyone he writes about. Kafka was never actually a cockroach, no matter how movingly he wrote about a man who underwent metamorphosis into one. Yu is often misread in this way. When C. T. Hsia, in one of his typically interesting and informative sketches of Chinese writers, informs us that Yu's fictional characters are "by turns voyeur, fetishist, homosexual, masochist, and kleptomaniac,"[12] we may assume that he is talking of individual characters in individual stories. Hsia has perceptively pointed out that a single fictional character could not possess all these personality traits without putting a severe strain on his believability. And it is even more unlikely that a real person, even an affected author like Yu Dafu, could have such a fantastic personality.

Yu has suffered a case of mistaken identity. The real author, Yu Dafu the person, has been confused with the implied author, or narrative persona, of the work. And beyond this mix-up over what Wayne Booth would call the "rhetoric of fiction," there is an even more basic misunderstanding that "Sinking" is subjective, naïve, and sentimental. This misunderstanding comes from the aforementioned fallacy: the confusing of the author with the story's self-pitying protagonist on the rather flimsy evidence that both happened to be melancholy exchange students in Japan, and the implicit assumption that the author would thus have to treat "himself" sentimentally and sympathetically. Melancholy author equals self-pitying protagonist equals sentimental narrative. A rather neat tautology, but an untrue one. A close reading of "Sinking" will reveal anything but a narrative based upon mawkish sentimentality. Indeed, the exact opposite is true.

By separating narrative from dialogue, it can be seen that the story (which deals with the adventures of a young, alienated, homesick, and somewhat paranoid Chinese exchange student living in Japan) is told exclusively in strict third-person objective form. That is, the narrator is not an active or intrusive character in the story. He suppresses all subjective commentary on characters and their actions. Further, "the narrator is no 'deputy' of the author in the narrative text; rather it is a *narrative technique* created and applied by the author more or less consciously and consistently."[13] Very rarely does the narrative of "Sinking" reveal sentimental traces (such as when the patriotic theme is raised). On the whole, it is objective. Rather than empathize with the protagonist's self-pity, the objective narrative technique serves instead as an ironic counterpoint that undercuts the hero's sentimental view of himself, emphasizing the basic absurdity of his self-image. The great advance made by this story should not be seen in the mistaken identification of author with protagonist but rather in the ironic treatment of the "hero," which makes us see him coldly and dispassionately, as a character who stands alone and not as the author's alter ego, despite what Yu wrote about his own story.

Examples of such narrative detachment are legion. The story opens with the protagonist getting a rather pompous self-satisfaction from his own sensitivity and the fact that he is able to read Wordsworth in English. Yet the objective narrative quite coolly punctures this bubble. It matter-of-factly informs the reader that the hero, though he makes great pretense of collecting and gushing over English literature, lacks the concentration and determination to read even the thinnest volume from cover to cover, and indeed has read only two stanzas of the four-stanza poem cited:

> It had been his recent habit to read nonconsecutively . . . even slender volumes he never bothered to read from beginning to end . . . Most of the time, when he picked up a book, he would be so moved by its opening lines . . . that he literally wanted to swallow the whole volume. But after three or four pages, he . . . would say to himself: "I must not gulp down such a marvelous book as this at one sitting. Instead I should chew it over a period of time . . ." Every time he closed a book, he made excuses for himself in this way. The real reason was that he had grown a little tired of it.[14]

The choice of the poem cited is itself ironic. It is "The Solitary Reaper," a poem that perhaps more than any other typifies the Wordsworth of popular imagination. The speaker of the poem is in the Highlands of Scotland communing with nature when he comes upon a woman singing a beautiful melody. But he cannot understand her — a line of the poem reads, "Will no one tell me what she sings." The woman is singing in Gaelic, which the speaker of the poem cannot understand. He is incapable of any genuine empathy with her, with nature, or with her experience of nature. Likewise, the student in Yu's story is cut off from the countryside he professes to admire. The episode ends, "While standing there in a daze, a cough from behind signaled the arrival of a peasant. He turned around and immediately assumed a melancholy expression, as if afraid to show his smile before strangers."[15] It is the peasant who has the true experience of nature, and the student is as far removed from him as the speaker of "The Solitary Reaper" is from the Highlands lass.

Another theme that contradicts a sentimental reading of this text is that of the protagonist's relationship with his classmates. He feels sorry for himself as a lonely Chinese living in Japan, and much has been made of the fact that he finds himself constantly at odds with his Japanese fellow students. He feels isolated, is suspicious of them, and thinks that they are mocking him. Indeed, this is regarded as a

313

manifestation of Japanese prejudice against Chinese. But the fact that the protagonist's relationship with his *Chinese* schoolmates is equally bad, though it cannot have been caused by racism, immediately leads the reader to doubt our hero's self-perception. He is just as separated from his fellow Chinese; this leads to the unsentimental conclusion that his loneliness is his own fault and not the result of hatred or prejudice:

> At school he had the feeling that his Japanese classmates were avoiding him. And he no longer wanted to visit his Chinese classmates . . . [who] couldn't understand his state of mind . . . He wanted to avenge himself on these few Chinese friends as on his Japanese schoolmates . . . He was finally so alienated from the Chinese that he wouldn't even greet them when he met them . . . He didn't attend any of the meetings for Chinese students, so that he and they became virtual enemies.[16]

The protagonist has forfeited his credibility with the reader; if his self-image of alienation from the Chinese was false, his view of himself as a victim of Japanese prejudice is also suspect.

This contradiction between the narrator's view of the hero and the hero's view of himself is again brought out in a scene that treats the relationship of the protagonist with women. He is drinking alone in an inn, and he feels himself deserted by the hostess. He begins the following diatribe against women in general, and the hostess in particular: "Bastards! Pigs! How dare you bully me like this? Revenge! Revenge! I'll revenge myself on you! Can there be any truehearted girl in the world? You faithless waitress, how dare you desert me like this? Oh, let it be, let it be, for from now on I shall care nothing about women, absolutely nothing."[17] He composes a poem and falls into a drunken sleep. Yet when he wakes up he finds that the hostess has not deserted him, indeed, she has shut the window to close out a draft, and covered him with her own quilt. She is unfailingly friendly, courteous, and sympathetic to him. This helps to emphasize to the reader just how inaccurate the hero's perceptions really are.

The same scene squelches the protagonist's view of himself as a victim of Japanese prejudice. He tries to communicate with the waitress:

> The more he wanted to talk to her, the more tongue-tied he became. His embarrassment was apparently making the waitress a little impatient, for she asked, "Where are you from?" At this, his pallid face reddened

again; he stammered and stammered, but couldn't give a forthright answer. He was once again standing on the guillotine. For the Japanese look down upon Chinese just as we look down upon pigs and dogs. They call us Shinajin, "Chinamen," a term more derogatory than "knave" in Chinese. And now he had to confess before this pretty girl that he was a Shinajin.[18]

He *had* to do nothing of the sort. The waitress asked him this question to put him at his ease by making conversation, not to humiliate him. He, and not the waitress, calls himself a Chinaman, and he could have chosen any other term. The reader feels more contempt than sympathy for him and his self-imposed degradation.

These examples illustrate that the narrative mode, far from romanticizing or sentimentalizing the protagonist of the story as a surrogate for the author, always shows him as the rather pathetic figure he really is. Clearly, the impression that emerges is not one of identification of author with protagonist, as Průšek and Hsia have claimed, but rather of separation. What has been mistaken for an innovative, "modern," sentimental, and self-revealing mode of writing is really an objective and ironic presentation of a *character* with a mistaken and sentimental view of *himself*. Any empathy or feeling for the character comes from a response to the protagonist's personality as revealed by his actions or interior monologues, not narrative comment. This is what marks the story as truly modern — its use of irony.

Earlier fiction had often been satirical or had presented characters whose actions might have been reprehensible or ludicrous. But the reader was always given sufficient data with which to judge the character, even to classify him according to Confucian morality. The breakthrough in "Sinking" is not the autobiographical nature of the fiction but that no standards are given against which the protagonist's conduct may be judged. Thus, the surface characterization presents a sentimentalized "hero" who is, upon close inspection, not a hero at all. This is something quite new in Chinese literature.

It is also the source of the story's irony. The objective situation is exactly the reverse of what the participant thinks it is. There is a clear contrast between the situation revealed by our "hero's" thoughts and what is more or less wryly hinted at by the narrative text. Unknown to himself, the hero's thoughts and deeds conflict with facts known to the reader. This produces results directly opposite to those the protagonist might have wanted. Such tension, or opposition, between surface meaning and deeper reality approaches a textbook definition of irony — language is used that has a special inner meaning for the audience and an outer or surface meaning for the speaker or person most directly concerned — the protagonist. That the attempt to convey irony might be on occasion clumsy is irrelevant. It is not surprising that this innovation has gone unnoticed in the smoke screen created by the intentional fallacy. As Booth has written with regard to this type of irony, "Wherever explicit judgment has been unavailable, critical troubles . . . have ensued."[19]

Sex is a major theme of the story, and its treatment has been considered modern. The hero is obsessed with women. Though the women in the story treat him normally and are friendly to him, he cannot respond to them and suffers in a bitter isolation of his own making. He battles against masturbation, which he fears is driving him insane.

Lee writes, "Thematically the story was among the first works in Chinese literature in which the author had brought forth with all seriousness a problem which had been treated as a subject of either social taboo or secretive and often flippant fun."[20] Hsia also recognizes this important facet of the story. "To its contemporary student readers the story represents the discovery of sex as a serious concern."[21]

While these assessments are accurate and acute, the use of sex per se as a theme does not make the story modern. Certainly, sex had no novelty as a theme in serious vernacular Chinese fiction. The famous novels *Jin ping mei* (Golden lotus) and *Rou putuan* (Prayer mat of flesh) are saturated with sex. There is at least one scene in *Hong lou meng* (Dream of the red chamber) that deals explicitly with masturbation. The entire plot of the late Qing novel *Hen hai* (Sea of woe), while not specifically concerned with physical sex, consists of the depiction, through psychological characterization, of the disintegration of two persons' love. These examples are in addition to the so-called Butterfly fiction, which was, in the coastal provinces at any rate, a sensual literature of considerable extent. Undoubtedly, Yu's story caused quite a sensation when first published, but perhaps this was more due to what its readers perceived to be its confessional nature than any genuine innovation in its sexual theme.

"Sinking" is neither particularly daring nor explicit when compared to previous works in Chinese fiction. What makes the story modern is not its erotic dimension but the fact that sexual acts are important not as plot or actions in themselves, as had been the case in the past, but for their effect on the psychology of the hero. The protagonist's mental response to his sexual activities is the true subject of the narrative. The sexual adventures themselves are far less important than those of, say, Ximen Qing in *Jin ping mei.*

Thus, the two supposedly "modern" facets of the story that have been considered have both been based on misunderstandings and have obscured genuine advances made by Yu Dafu. Is there anything in his early fiction that is clearly and unambiguously modern, that is unquestionably a product of the time when it was written?

Certainly. His first two stories contain very obvious, even transparent devices that are distinctly modern. Some are present in both stories, others are used to good effect in only one of them. Some are more subtle and more successful than others, while some are artistic failures, and still others are merely clumsy.

Generally, the more subtle of these techniques, such as Yu's innovative use of time, the emphasis upon psychology as a mainstay of the plot, and the impressionistic use of color to establish mood are the ones that succeed. The more blatantly obvious devices, like nomenclature or the theme of patriotism, work less well.

Yu uses the modern technique of the manipulation of time to great advantage not only in "Sinking" but especially in another story, "Silver-gray Death." The action of that story may be divided into separate scenes. These are presented in a sequence completely different from the way Chinese fiction had unfolded in the past.

An outstanding feature of older novels and stories was that chronologically they consisted either of semi-independent episodes, narrated in the simple past and within a single time frame, or of longer narratives in which the plot proceeded in a single continuous chronological line from beginning to end. The focus might shift to auxiliary or subplots, but the time pattern remained linear and conventional. Even simple flashbacks were quite rare. When the narrative called for revealing past events, they were put into the direct speech of the characters and thus took place in the text's linear present. For example, the characters in *Lao Can youji* (The travels of Lao Can) take turns telling about their past experiences, but always in direct speech; thus, the past is always part of the chronological "present" of the text.

But the events of "Silver-gray Death" shift through various strata of time in a way that is quite far removed from the traditional linear sequence. The action that makes up the "present" in the narrative is quite simple: a young man awakens, washes up, and goes out to a small wineshop owned by the girl he is in love with and her mother. He gets drunk, pawns some books, and buys her a wedding gift, for she is getting married to another man. A few days later his body is discovered in a schoolyard, presumably a suicide. But a complex series of past events is interspersed with these few actions in the narrative present. Each of the past events occurs in a different time frame. The chronology of the story forms a recurring pattern that is quite intricate. The narrative shifts from the present to the past actions of the protagonist that are general yet habitual (his drunkenness) to a specific incident in his past (one particular time when he got drunk). This pattern repeats itself three times in exactly the same manner. This innovative manipulation of time is achieved with great artistry and indicates a mastery of literary craftsmanship in so young an author.

Another modern feature of Yu's early stories is their psychological dimension, easily the most important aspect of their plots. The stories are concerned almost exclusively with the mental states of their protagonists. Their actions, feelings, and emotions are what the reader responds to most readily. This is obvious right from the very first sentence in "Sinking": "Lately he had felt pitifully lonesome. His emotional precocity had placed him at constant odds with his fellowmen and inevitably the wall separating him from them had gradually become thicker and thicker."[22] And this is merely the starting point of the protagonist's mental state, which then proceeds from alienation through self-pity and paranoia to despair. "Silver-gray Death" also concerns itself with the mental state of its protagonist, though in a different way. Instead of relying on authorial omniscience for a direct depiction of the mental traits of the hero, the reader must infer them from indirect characterization via action or physical externals. Thus, the protagonist's mental deterioration is reflected by his declining physical state — his poverty, drunkenness, and finally death.

In "Sinking" the technique used to convey the story's psychological content is quite similar to the technique Yu used in his treatment of time — the alteration and manipulation of different aspects of the plot. After the opening description of emotion just quoted, there is a passage describing nature and the protagonist's actions as he reads Wordsworth. Then we get his psychological response to what he has just read. He says to himself, "You have no further need to join the world of the shallow and flippant. You might as well spend the rest of your life in this simple countryside, in the bosom of nature."[23] And so the story goes, alternating event or action with psychological reaction. Events and action intensify until the story ends in a veritable crescendo of emotion. Driven to the brink of suicide by what he considers to be the insults of the waitress, he utters the words, "O China, my China, you are the cause of my death! . . . I wish you could become rich and strong soon! . . . Many, many of your children are still suffering!"[24]

Thus, though there are relatively few events in the story, tension is built by alternating these events with glimpses of the protagonist's emotions and thoughts. The total effect, decidedly modern, could almost be called impressionistic. It is built up through the accumulation of minor but structurally crucial detail, much as a painting might be composed of daubs of paint.

In "Silver-gray Death" Yu actually uses color to establish the mood of the story: it is possible to infer the mental state of the protagonist from the physical description of his milieu. The story opens with a description of Tokyo after a snowstorm. The landscape is covered with a cold whiteness, but this cannot chill the people's warm holiday spirits — all except for our hero. For him the snow is a metaphor for his psychological state. Human emotions are frozen out of him, and white is the color of death for the Chinese. His room is described as a den of "lacquerlike blackness." When a single ray of sunlight penetrates the closed shutters, it serves only to emphasize the ashen pallor of his face. When he goes out at night, the moonlight and the electric sparks of the streetcars make the rooftops seem as if they are covered with frost, and this continues the motif begun with the opening snowstorm. Brighter colors such as red are associated with his dear dead wife and his current hopeless love. This is a cruel twist, because red is the color of joy and is worn by Chinese brides. When he warms himself before a stove, its cozy red glow seems to mock him.

The use of color is repeated throughout the story at intervals. Thus, the technique is similar to Yu's use of psychological depiction (of both the direct and indirect type) and time. All are recurring motifs — continually shifting, abandoned, and returned to. Taken together, they create an impression that is both modern and a tribute to Yu's artistic ability.

Color, time, and the psychological element mark these stories as modern not because they are lacking in earlier fiction but because Yu uses them in a way that is qualitatively as well as quantitatively different from their use before. Direct description in fiction had always given the color of things. But the symbolic or metaphoric use of color to show mood had been used chiefly in poetry and was almost unknown in vernacular prose. *Dream of the Red Chamber* is a masterpiece of psychological realism because its characters always act as we expect them to act. Still, their psychological traits must be inferred exclusively from their actions. The text of *Dream of the Red Chamber* ignores the mental makeup of its characters, except to explain on a superficial level that so-and-so is worried, or happy, or brokenhearted. Similarly, the events of previous fiction all took place in time, but time as it exists in Yu's stories is a different experience entirely.

A less successful innovation is the use of nomenclature and the rather ponderous, if fashionable, adoption of Western vocabulary wherever possible.

The hero of "Sinking" is nameless. There is precedent for this in the late Qing, *Guanchang xianxing ji* (The bureaucrats), for example, but in "Sinking," except for the cities Peking and Hangchow, Tokyo and Yokohama, all other place and personal names are expressed in very affected fashion by the use of the first initial of their names in the Roman alphabet. Thus, the hero goes to H school and battles his enemy, the missionary Mr. M. In Japan, he travels to N city to attend X preparatory school. Consistent with his pretensions to sensitivity and good taste, he quotes Wordsworth in English and Heine in German. Though it may have been questionable narrative strategy for Yu to present large chunks of English and German to a readership presumably incapable of reading them, at least it was justified by the story. His use of the English words "megalomania" and "hypochondria" in the narrative text to describe the protagonist's state of mind, however, is both unsatisfactory and annoying. Furthermore, words are used incorrectly and out of context. Clouds appear in the shape of Cupids, and the protagonist compares himself to Zarathustra. These are difficult, if not inappropriate allusions, especially for a Chinese readership.

All these devices jar the contemporary reader, and any novelty that they might once have had has long since dissipated. They may have been fashionable techniques in 1921, and thus have had a modish appeal, but they are still bad writing. Nonetheless, they are traits that enable us to date the stories fairly accurately. They are signs of the modern, and only the modern, era.

Likewise, a subplot of "Sinking," the protagonist's concern with the plight of China and his equating of his own problems with his country's debasement — each an innocent and passive victim — typifies the intellectual temper of the times. The subplot reflects the increasing politicization of writers and anticipates the overt and self-conscious use of literature as a political weapon as well as the organization of writers for political purposes.

Unfortunately, the analogy between the respective conditions of China and the story's protagonist is not a good one. The attempt to make nationalism and anti-imperialism issues in a story that is a pathological character study must be considered a failure. From the internal evidence of the story, nationalism and anti-imperialism have no bearing on the psychological deterioration of the protagonist. They are introduced almost as an afterthought and are irrelevant to the development of the story. As issues, they are resolved ambivalently, if at all, by the story's ending — the implied suicide of the protagonist. If the analogy is a true one, does he, and by implication China, lack the strength to continue? Is the situation hopeless? However, if on the basis of the objective narrator's text, the hero's self-image is the product of delusion, the analogy is false and the presentation of the plight of China must undergo the same ironic reevaluation as the plight of the protagonist.

The political theme is not successful, perhaps because it is tacked on, as if out of obligation, to a story that deals with a single isolated person. The plot of "Sinking" is essentially apolitical and individualistic, as opposed to social and ideological. In one respect, Yu typifies the writers of the twenties, whose revolutionary fervor was as yet mostly emotional. Even Lu Xun's short stories, while plainly not apolitical, tend to the allegorical rather than the programmatic. Members of the Literary Association, concerned as they were with the modernization of letters and the development of fiction, were not yet overtly political or ideological. Ye Shengtao's early short stories are perhaps the most clearly "leftist" fiction contemporaneous to "Sinking," but they owe what "political success" they have to the fact that by and large their themes are social rather than individual. Thus, they can be read as "social realism," as opposed to Yu's more bourgeois output.

Nonetheless, even Ye's stories lack the tone of ideological urgency that momentarily was to develop in Chinese fiction. Yu's apolitical approach alone does not make him unique at this time, inasmuch as Chinese fiction was not yet the activist force it later became. Rather, it is the individualistic nature of his subject matter that creates a background against which an outward-looking theme stands out as garish and clashing.

When Yu raises the political issue in a way that cannot but detract from the story, he is perhaps wearing his heart on his sleeve in response to an issue too big to be ignored. The difference between the political theme in "Sinking" and in the stories of Lu Xun is one of subtlety, the difference between telling and showing fiction. In Yu's story the political theme fails because it is too obvious, but satisfactory or not, it is there — and from the late Qing onward, political literature has been a sign of the times.

Futher clues to the modernity of these stories are found in the very words in which they are written. As the subject matter of Chinese fiction changed from plots based upon action to plots based upon psychological character revelation, there was a concomitant switch from "static" to "dynamic" modes of characterization, to use the terms of Scholes and Kellogg.[25] This change necessarily involved revealing the characters' thoughts and actions through such narrative devices as interior monologue, first in its marked form as direct discourse, and later as unmarked indirect discourse. Understandably, a certain amount of clumsiness distinguished their use in the early stages of this transition. Often, passages of thought were set off by the use of stock phrases and clichés to alert the reader to what was going on. These phrases seem to be a carry-over from the old techniques of oral storytellers used in the early Chinese novels.[26] They are still present to some degree in Yu's stories, which indicates that the facile use of these devices for revealing characters' thoughts had not yet been realized. In "Silver-gray Death" there are passages of marked interior monologue followed by the redundant stock phrase "having thought thus far" (*xiangdao zheli*)[27] and preceded by something that might be translated "he thought in his bosom" (*ta xinli xiang shuo*).[28] The weight of these seems to be more than just plain "he thought." A course of action is decided upon in interior monologue and the reader is needlessly told afterward that "he reached this conclusion" (*xiangdingle zhuyi*).[29]

Yu's use of these stock phrases, however, is not nearly as widespread as in earlier texts of vernacular literature. And his use of them declines quite noticeably in his later stories, which might indicate increasing familiarity with the device of interior monologue. While it is true that this development may have been due to his increasing skill as a writer, it seems that the decline in usage of such stock phrases was a general one, occurring throughout Chinese literature.

A striking example of a clear admixture of traditional and modern elements can be seen in Yu's use of symbol and metaphor. It has been established that the plot of "Silver-gray Death" is a very modern one, concerning as it does the psychological deterioration and death of a young Chinese widower living in Japan and his intermittent relationship with the daughter of a woman who owns a small wineshop. Advanced as this plot is, however, its language sometimes seems appropriate to a more genteel subject matter. Women are sometimes described with classical phrases that hark back to earlier literature. They have lips like "rose blossoms" (*qiangwei huabao*),[30] "slender fingers that are delicate and snowy white" (*xueyang nende xian shou*),[31] and "soft and warm" (*wenruan*) bosoms.[32] The protagonist's dead wife was a beauty worthy of description by the great poet Li Bo. Indeed, we learn of his wife in a flashback that occurs while he is gazing at the moon. The sight reminds him of an idyllic moonlit night he spent with her in happier times — a device so common as to be almost a cliché in classical poetry.

At the same time, he wanders around the city of N against a background of sparking streetcars, electric lights, telephone lines, and railroad stations. The descriptive passages present an interesting and very successful blend of nature combined with the workings of a modern city, which have a mechanical beauty all their own. Descriptions and metaphors from old and new sources are mingled almost indiscriminately.

Occasionally this use of old and new is humorous or even grotesque in the original sense of an incongruous juxtaposition of unlikely elements. A few paragraphs after the daughter's eyes are described with a classical allusion as being like "autumn water" (*qiu shui*),[33] she glares at the protagonist and her eyes "flash like electric sparks" (*tong dian-guang side shanfale yixia*).[34] Writing such as this is clearly transitional and draws its language from both traditional and modern sources.

The basic theme of both stories, a scholar in difficult straits who is befriended by a woman who might be a singing girl, hostess, or prostitute, is also quite common in earlier traditional literature. But it is clear that Yu's treatment of this theme is anything but traditional.

First evidence of the modernity of these two stories can be found in the debt they obviously owe to Western literature. Yu's use of English and the Roman alphabet has already been noted. More importantly, it is quite possible that some of the outstanding and important features of his work, his use of psychology, time, and color, were a direct result of foreign influence. Such writers as Yu Dafu appear to have been quite impressed by Russian and European sources, and it should be apparent that "Sinking" and "Silver-gray Death" could possibly owe a large debt to Dostoevsky, for example. Such one-to-one relationships are difficult to prove, however, beyond saying that Yu was widely read in Western literature. To trace direct stylistic (as opposed to intellectual) relationships with Western authors is nearly impossible.

If writers turned to Western sources, it seems logical to believe that they did so in response to issues they had already internalized. That is, they made the decision (probably consciously and deliberately) to expand the subject matter of Chinese fiction to include these that were commonly dealt with in Western literature. The Europeans were looked to because they had already dealt with themes such as alienation, which were attractive to the new generation of Chinese writers. Thus, it might be said that their influence, if present, is an effect and not a cause.

Nonetheless, it is safe to say that foreign influence is definitely present in Yu's fiction, obviously placing it in the modern period.

Purely on the basis of the internal evidence of Yu Dafu's first two short stories, it can be seen that there was indeed a transitional period between the old vernacular fiction and the "modern" literature written after the literary revolution had produced its full effects. It can also be seen that Yu, despite his deserved reputation as an innovative writer who did much to modernize Chinese fiction, owes a debt to tradition that has perhaps been underestimated. In the early fiction of Yu Dafu, an evolving literary genre can clearly be seen in a transitional state, with all the elements of both old and new that one would expect to find plainly in view.

Part Three

Continuities and Discontinuities

China's popular old-style culture persisted in the May Fourth era alongside the radically new culture of the May Fourth writers that emerged with the Western impact. Perry Link shows that the widely read Butterfly literature was closely connected with the traditional vernacular literature. Not only were there similarities of style and language but also of content in its expression of a conservative attitude toward popular traditional values and in its rejection of Westernization and social change.

The May Fourth writers had a smaller audience than the Butterfly writers and were regarded with ambivalence and even hostility by the general public. This phenomenon was pointed out by the Communist literary theorist Qu Qiubai, whose attack on the May Fourth writers is analyzed by Paul Pickowicz. Qu charged that the May Fourth writers had even less connection with the Chinese masses than the old Confucian literati because their Westernized culture was more alien than that of the old literati. He urged the May Fourth writers to participate in the lives of the ordinary workers and peasants in order to depict their lives.

Cyril Birch's "Change and Continuity in Chinese Fiction," which concludes the book, demonstrates that May Fourth literature was indeed a radical departure as Qu charged. Birch compares three pieces of literature from three eras: the traditional, May Fourth, and Chinese People's Republic. He finds striking similarities between the traditional and post-1949 writings. In fact, he regards the post-1949 literary work as a return to the didacticism that characterized traditional Chinese literature. By contrast, he finds that May Fourth literature in both content and form was a radical change in the Chinese context, a change that was more in tune with the mainstream of Western culture than with Chinese culture.

May Fourth literature certainly had continuities with China's traditional culture, but it was revolutionary when viewed from the perspective of what existed before and what was to come after.

15.

Traditional-Style Popular Urban Fiction in the Teens and Twenties

Perry Link

In 1932 Qu Qiubai observed that the May Fourth movement, for all its spectacular ferment, had hardly affected the popular culture of Chinese cities. While the educated classes, stimulated by the modern West, were busy campaigning to inspire nationalism, promote science, instill democracy, liberate women, boycott imperialism, examine traditions, and write all about it in the new vernacular, "the laboring masses of China," according to Qu, "were still in the Middle Ages in their cultural life."[1] Qu's feeling of intense frustration with this condition was only one more symptom of the May Fourth generation's long-standing hope to reach China's common people and to lead them out of those "Middle Ages."

Their efforts placed the May Fourth writers in direct competition with a large number of "old school" novelists, who continued throughout the teens and twenties to produce the very stuff of backward consciousness in popular traditional-style novels. This fiction flooded the market in Shanghai and spread rapidly to Tientsin, Peking, and other major cities. In sharp contrast to the May Fourth writers' impassioned search for new social visions, in general, these popular writers sought only to entertain the reading public. Instead of raising consciousness, most of them strove to raise only their weekly word total, which directly correlated with their pay.

The writers of this group are known by a colorful and distinctive name, the "Mandarin Duck and Butterfly School" (*yuanyang hudie pai*), whose origins need some explanation. One of the early best sellers of the type was Xu Zhenya's *Yu li hun* (Jade pear spirit), which was first published in 1912 and achieved a circulation of several hundred thousand.[2] An intense love story written in clever, semiclassical parallel prose, it is generously padded with sentimental poems in

327

which lovers are compared to pairs of butterflies and mandarin ducks. Though the metaphors are traditional, Xu's prominent use of them led, during the late teens, to the convention of calling the authors of this kind of sentimental love story the "Mandarin Duck and Butterfly School." The label was pejorative, and originally was limited quite narrowly to Xu, Li Dingyi, Wu Shuangre, and a few others.

With the advent of the May Fourth movement, the scope of the term "Mandarin Duck and Butterfly" became dramatically enlarged. Zheng Zhenduo, Mao Dun, and many other new writers of the early twenties used the term to lead an attack on *all* kinds of current old-style fiction. This included not only the love stories but also "social" novels, "knight-errant" novels, "scandal" novels, "detective" novels, "ideal" (fantasy) novels, "comic" novels, and many other kinds. The consequent ambiguity in applying the term has persisted to the present. Communist writings have meant it to include every kind of "old-style" fiction, while non-Communist writings generally use it to mean love stories only. Here, the broader definition (abbreviated to "Butterfly") is used, but simply as a matter of convenience. It is intended that the reference be value-free, as the question of quality in Butterfly fiction must await research and appraisal on a case-by-case basis.

The May Fourth writers argued in the pages of *Wenxue xunkan* (The literary ten-daily) that since literature should serve social progress, Butterfly works were at best useless, at worst pernicious. Their authors thrived in Shanghai's festering "three-mile foreign mall" (*shili yangchang*) and were comparable, said Zheng Zhenduo, to "intellectual bats."[3] They were accused of being motivated by unscrupulous greed: "literary prostitutes" in Zheng's phrase, "gold worshipers" in Mao Dun's.[4] Perhaps worst of all, these writers monopolized the fiction market and poisoned the minds of youth — "stole the show," as Guo Moruo saw it[5] — thereby depriving May Fourth of its audience. The issue was so urgent and clear-cut that all the early May Fourth groups, despite their interfactional differences, enthusiastically joined in the attack.

By the late twenties, however, factional strife among the May Fourth writers had diverted most of their attention from the persisting problem of Butterfly fiction. In 1931 Lu Xun told the League of Left-Wing Writers that: "Last year and the year before, the scope of the literary war . . . really has been too small. None of the old-style literature and ideology has received notice from the new-style people. Quite the contrary: we have a situation where the new literature people are off in one corner fighting among themselves, leaving the old-style people free to stand comfortably by as spectators to the struggle."[6] What basically disturbed Lu Xun was not, of course, that Butterfly writers were free to be spectators but that they were also free to continue spreading "feudal" social mores. His observation was essentially the same as Qu Qiubai's: that the May Fourth writers had not yet fulfilled their own earnest pledge to reach the common reader. The result of this failure was that most readers continued to prefer traditional tales and Butterfly novels, as well as all sorts of comic strips, peep shows, movies, and storytelling based on these. In what seems clearly to be exaggeration born of despair, Qu Qiubai concluded, still in 1932, that: "The working peoples' knowledge of their own existence, their view of social phenomena, in general their world view and life view, is practically all gained from this sort of reactionary popular literature."[7]

The Growth of Butterfly Fiction

For the May Fourth authors, part of the discomfort in recognizing Butterfly fiction's genuine popularity was their assumption that this kind of "bad" literature was a peculiarly *Chinese* malady. This of course was not so. Popular fiction very much like the Butterfly type had grown up in England along with the Industrial Revolution. It had spread to western Europe and America contemporaneously with industrialism. In East Asia, Japan (primarily in Tokyo and Osaka) was first to see English and French popular novels translated and imitated for consumption by the new urban classes. Beginning in the early twentieth century, Shanghai, as the first Chinese city to undergo "modern urbanization," also produced an outpouring of entertainment fiction. First came Western stories, translated via Japanese, and then original creations drawn mostly from models in China's own vernacular tradition.

The spread of modern urban fiction to cities such as Tokyo and Shanghai was not simply a matter of borrowing one more item from the West. Nor was it merely the result of rapid growth in the printing industry, which expanded sixfold in Shanghai from the beginning of the century to the early thirties,[8] or rising literacy rates, which appear to have doubled or more in Shanghai during the same years.[9] One of the essential causes, in China and Japan no less than in the West, appears to have arisen from the psychological needs of urban dwellers confronted with the "modernizing" environment and all that that implied: the transition away from traditional, rural-based values toward the nuclear family, "universalistic" public intercourse, and what sociologists know as *Gesellschaft* culture generally. An early characteristic of this shifting environment was the stream of new scientific information that accompanied technological change and demanded the attention of anyone who would thrive and advance in the city. The forerunners of popular reading material both East and West were not novels but journals and magazines that offered self-taught science, practical know-how, and whatever information was necessary to keep up with expanding popular knowledge. Early examples of Shanghai fiction were created in the reformist atmosphere of the late Qing decade. Liang Qichao's advocacy in 1902 of a "new fiction" — aimed at nation building — served also as a mantle that lent social respectability to fantastic "science novels" (*kexue xiaoshuo*) and "novels of ideals" (*lixiang xiaoshuo*). The psychological function of most of this protopopular fiction can be broadly characterized as one of *orientation* to present and new, or future and imagined, conditions of life.

In what might be called the "second stage" (the end of the first decade and the second decade of the century) in the development of popular urban fiction, the reader of science news and seeker of practical improvement found that the new press could be fun. It told of strange customs and marvelous happenings in distant parts of the world, and its main function gradually became one of *amusement*. The readership's thirst for amusement was intensified by the modern phenomenon of a weekend day off — time that the new urban living seemed to schedule for such things as fiction reading. Thus, just as the nineteenth-century West saw weekend magazines and Sunday newspapers swell with light fiction, jokes, and puzzles, Shanghai produced a welter of tabloids and magazines of comparable interest. More than a hundred magazines appeared in the teens alone, though many of them were short-lived.[10] The best-known magazine was called, significantly, *Libailiu* (The Saturday magazine) and explicitly declared its intention to "help pass the time."[11]

In a third stage in Shanghai fiction (late teens and twenties), the pursuit of amusement turned increasingly toward *escape*. As the exigencies of the new urban environment became burdensome, the reader's desire to keep up with the world gave way to the desire to forget that he could not keep up. Novels of ideals and discovery declined and were replaced by scandal stories, detective stories, and fantastic "knight-errant" (*wuxia*) stories.

In the teens and early twenties, the price of fiction was a greater impediment to circulation than was literacy. Magazines normally cost from .10 to .40 yuan apiece, and books .30 to .80 yuan. These were high prices for a population that spent an average of one yuan per family per year on all entertainment.[12]

The teens readership may be analyzed, in fact, according to those who could afford fiction with ease and those who could not. Those who could pay included well-to-do merchants, landlords, bankers, industrialists, and the leisured women of their households; a portion of the reform-generation intellectuals, many of whom were now government officials; a group of what might be called "full-time amusement seekers" — degenerates who were attracted to Shanghai for opium, adventure, and night life; and a considerable number of rural gentry who, though choosing not to live in the city, were fascinated by what issued from it and ordered fiction magazines by mail.[13] For many of these readers, especially the women, an important aspect of fiction's appeal was that it could be consumed in private. Other available amusements — theater, teahouses, dance halls — exposed one to possible public scorn for overindulgence. But no social pressures could limit the duration or intensity with which one read a book at home.

The second group of readers — those who could not easily afford fiction — was much more important in its growth potential. They were students and white-collar workers who sacrificed the luxury of fiction-in-private for the economy of openly sharing their resources. Books and magazines were passed around in offices and shops, where word-of-mouth previews were also exchanged. Clerks and shop assistants would read during a meal break or a slow period on the job. New schools, despite their lofty aims, were even more important in the spread of popular fiction, a fact as ironic in China as it had been in the West. In England, Sunday schools had pioneered the spread of literacy to increasing numbers of town and city youth; in China, the way was led by the reform-movement "new schools" (*xin xuetang*), whose numbers appear to have increased from around 4,000 in 1905 to more than 120,000 by the late teens.[14] In neither case had it been foreseen that an ability to read about God or national self-strengthening would also afford youngsters access to love and scandal stories. By the mid-teens, though, Shanghai high school students had become enthusiastic readers of Xu Zhenya's *Jade Pear Spirit* and its train of sequels and imitations. The fame of these love stories spread contagiously in Shanghai, reached to other cities, and eventually created the first major wave of popular fiction in modern China.

In both China and the West, popular urban fiction bore distinctive characteristics that seem to have attracted the common reader. The stories tell of strange, unusual events; their plots take unexpected turns; most of their leading characters are flatly all good or all bad; they are expressed in simple, direct language and are filled with action, sparse with description.

Even the major themes of Butterfly fiction bear remarkable similarities to those of Western popular urban fiction, and seldom is this accountable to direct borrowing. In both cases, the (1) romantic love story, (2) righteous-hero adventure story, (3) scandal, or "muckraking" story, and (4) crime detection story were the leading types (listed here in order of popularity in Shanghai). Each of these themes, however distorted by modern circumstances, had strong roots in the Chinese vernacular tradition, which were, respectively: (1) The love story tradition of *Hong lou meng* (Dream of the red chamber) and *caizi jiaren* or "talent-meets-beauty" stories; (2) *Shuihu zhuan* (The water margin), *Ernü yingxiong zhuan* (Tale of heroic young lovers) and the whole "knight-errant" tradition; (3) *Rulin waishi* (Informal history of scholars) and the late Qing "blame" novels; and (4) Qing "public case" (*gongan*) stories, such as *Peng gongan* (The cases of Judge Peng) plus the admixture of late Qing translations of Sherlock Holmes, the outstanding example of borrowing from the West.

The tendency toward similarity in the themes of popular fiction East and West suggests a similarity of concerns among its nascent popular audiences. The likeness is particularly striking between the female protagonists of two leading love stories, Li Niang of *Jade Pear Spirit* and Clarissa Harlowe of Samuel Richardson's *Clarissa*. Both women are scrupulously virtuous, at least in their intentions. Li Niang is a chaste widow and Clarissa a virgin; yet each is trapped, by circumstances and a handsome young lover, in what they and society agree to be the "fallen condition" of illicit love (sex in Clarissa's case, affection in Li Niang's); both resolve that suicide is the only solution and literally *think* themselves first to sickness, then to death.

Throughout the teens and twenties, popular fiction arrived in "waves" — some large, some small. Each wave consisted of one type of story. When a type had begun to "catch on," the fact of its popularity became a great stimulus to further popularity. But if we ask why a particular kind of story would "catch on" in the first place, it clearly appears that more than chance was involved. In general terms, the themes of fiction waves correlate with social issues that were prominent in the urban public. For example, the first of the major waves — the love stories of the early teens — took freedom of marriage as their common theme. Expectations that under the new regime of the republic young people would suddenly be free of the old family system were, however unrealistic, a key ingredient in the popularity of these stories. A young person could read them as a way of trying out new ideas without risking his or her own destiny in the experiment.

The next major wave, which crested in the later teens, appears to have stemmed from the troubles with Yuan Shikai and general disillusionment with the revolution. The wave consisted of three major strands. First, there was an increase in the popularity of satirical "social novels" (*shehui xiaoshuo*), of which Li Hanqiu's *Guangling chao* (Tides of Yangchow), a multilevel portrait of Yangchow society, was the leading example. Second, the Western-style detective story was widely imitated, most successfully in a series by Cheng Xiaoqing under the general title *Zhongguo Fuermosi Huosang tan'an* (Cases of the Chinese Sherlock Holmes, Huosang). Third, there was a great outpouring of what was called "scandal fiction" (*heimu xiaoshuo*), which exposed corruption and depravity in the worlds of officialdom, business, education, journalism, entertainment, diplomacy, religion, and almost every other walk of urban life. Powerful people hired writers to discredit their enemies with scandal stories. Such efforts appeared most commonly in the "mosquito" papers — single-sheet tabloids of which there were dozens in Shanghai, the best known of them called *Jing bao* (The three-day crystal).

A third popularity wave, which may be generally viewed as a reflection of antiwarlord sentiment, was touched off by Xiang Kairan's "knight-errant" novel *Jianghu qixia zhuan* (Chronicle of the strange roving knights). Though originally serialized in 1923–1924, this novel and the wave of imitations it inspired reached a peak of popularity from 1927 to 1930, at a time when the Northern Expedition's struggle against warlordism had a strong hold on the public imagination.

Butterfly authors dominated China's literary scene in the teens, but with the May Fourth movement they were displaced from several prominent positions by the new May Fourth writers. The most dramatic example of this changeover came in December 1920, when the Commercial Press took the editorship of *Xiaoshuo yuebao* (Short story monthly) from the Butterfly group and gave it to Mao Dun and Zheng Zhenduo. But as pointed out at the beginning of the present essay, May Fourth writers had only a small and transient effect in curtailing Butterfly popularity during the twenties. Far more important in Butterfly fiction's development during the decade was its increased commercialization and its new media of distribution. Together these made it possible to reach an audience much broader, and less literate than its audience of the teens.

Before the twenties nearly all Butterfly stories had been published in expensive fiction magazines, with the most popular works later appearing as books. Publishers in the teens normally operated with a target figure of only 3,000 copies for books and magazines, which was the minimum sale necessary to recover costs.[15] A circulation of more than 50,000 was rare. In the twenties, however, the most popular stories were also made into movies, comic strips, stage plays, and even scripts for traditional-style drum singing. The importance of these new media lay not only in their understandability by the barely literate and illiterate but also in their lower cost to the individual. Instead of paying .5 yuan for a book, one could see a movie for .02 yuan or less.[16] Comic books could be rented for even smaller amounts, or, if bought, traded and passed around among friends.

Besides the Butterfly magazines, which lowered their prices somewhat and continued to flourish, the leading commercial newspapers ran daily Butterfly columns that serialized some of the biggest hit novels of the twenties. In Shanghai, *Xinwen bao*'s "Kuaihuo lin" (Forest of lightheartedness) and *Shenbao*'s "Ziyou tan" (Unfettered talk) were the leading Butterfly columns. Newspaper serialization of fiction had important implications for publisher, author, and reader alike. For publishers, it provided the chance to sell newspapers with more regularity by hooking readers on a story line. For authors, it created the necessity to develop a small climax at the end of each installment to ensure the reader's interest in the next day's continuation. (The practice came naturally to most writers because of the similar custom — though with longer spaces between climaxes — that had prevailed in China's vernacular tradition.) And for readers, serialization meant one more inexpensive source of fiction. The small daily outlay in buying a newspaper, .04 yuan at most, plus the fact that one was getting the news as well, made the fiction seem like a kind of bonus. Some newspapers even printed their fiction installments in a form ready to be stitched between homemade book covers. Newspapers could also be literally free, because they were posted on bulletin boards or could be picked up secondhand. News lost its value after a day in a way that fiction did not.

The new media of the twenties helped Butterfly fiction reach the families of factory workers, rickshaw pullers, and manual laborers of several sorts. Observing in particular the impact of comic books, May Fourth writers first began to use the term "the masses" to describe the Butterfly audience. Mao Dun wrote that:

It goes without saying that the contents of all comic strip fiction are poisonous, but it is worth noticing the strong influence of comics on the general masses and on children. We cannot, moreover, deny that the form of these circulating comic strips . . . is worthy of adoption. The comic strip portion not only can attract barely literate readers, but also can help the barely literate, by "self-cultivation," to read and understand the written portion.[17]

And Qu Qiubai observed:

These things, at the bookstalls on alley corners, and so on . . . have they a certain, in fact a very great influence? Of course they have . . . the literate masses read them day by day, and the illiterate masses often hear them spoken about in casual ways by others . . . and unconsciously absorb the "instruction" of the stuff.[18]

By 1930 the enjoyment of Butterfly fiction, which during the teens had usually been a private affair, moved conspicuously into public. Hit novels, such as Zhang Henshui's *Tixiao yinyuan* (Fate in tears and laughter [1929]), became multimedia crazes. The book, two movies, several stage plays, and many comic books of this novel were all in circulation at once; the author was suing for his copyright; and a leading actress in the movie was reported (falsely, as a commercial device to spur interest) to have committed suicide. The story's characters gained a kind of suprafictional reality, as if they were "friends" of the public. Popular magazines referred to them as if they were real people. Sequels telling of their latest adventures came from many quarters, and readers besieged the author with letters asking for more of the true story. Clearly, word of mouth had become an important new "medium" of Butterfly culture.

The new media and expanded market of the twenties had a significant impact on the literary and personal styles of Butterfly authors. Many of their stories in the teens had been translations, but in the twenties almost all were original. Most short stories had been in a kind of classical, or quasi-classical language; now most were in vernacular style. Besides being more readable, the vernacular style had become more respectable thanks to the May Fourth movement.

Most of the authors of the teens had come to Shanghai during the first decade of the century from gentry backgrounds in interior cities, primarily Soochow. Many had lost their fathers in childhood and had lost also the traditional route to success when the civil service examinations were abolished in 1905. Looking for new alternatives in life, they had hit upon fiction writing partly because, around 1900, Shanghai publishers began paying for manuscripts. These authors generally stood on the fringes of the reform-and-revolution ferment of the first decade of the century and the early teens. Though following events closely, they stayed detached and lighthearted, fashioning for themselves a variety of eccentric life-styles. Even in treating tragic themes, their main aim was entertainment. They would couch their tragedies in expansive Buddhist metaphors about the pain and evil of mundane life, the inexorable hand of retribution, and so on. In the secular sphere they were firmly grounded in Confucian morality, though at the same time they stylishly adorned their stories with a few of the progressive "new-style" ideas of the time. They were friendly with one another and frequently came together for banquets, merry-making, and literary games.[19] Though paid for their fiction, most of them had other sources of income and did not rely primarily upon fiction to support themselves.

In the twenties, however, the opportunity to sell fiction to large newspapers, even sometimes to film companies, turned these authors into commercial writers. Payment for popular fiction, up from the standard rate in the teens of 2 yuan per 1,000 characters, now reached 4 or 6 yuan, sometimes higher. Leading authors would contract in more than one city to write serialized novels for as many as six or seven newspapers simultaneously. Some were hired as regular newspaper staff. In short, writing fiction could now realize a substantial living, and the Butterfly group spirit diminished as individual enterprise grew. They used Buddhist metaphors less often, and their topics became more "modern." Between the traditional images of the lettered gentleman on the one hand and the street-corner storyteller on the other, they had created a new literary identity: this was the producer of mass commercial fiction, who wrote for the appetite of "average readers" he could not see and did not know, but to whom he could become a popular hero and in whose numbers he measured his success.

"His," by the way, may be taken literally here. Of hundreds of better-known Butterfly writers, not one was a woman. Even stories in magazines ostensibly by, for, and about women were in fact written by men using female pseudonyms. The rare contribution actually written by a woman usually came from the wife or a daughter of a well-known author.

Butterfly fiction began to lose its predominant hold on the urban readership in the early thirties. By then, the May Fourth readership had grown and matured enough to give writers such as Ba Jin, Mao Dun, and Cao Yu a substantial following among students and other "new-style" readers who in the teens and twenties might have been exclusively Butterfly readers. Of even greater importance in reducing the Butterfly appeal were the Japanese attacks on China, which implanted in the urban populace a feeling of national urgency quite incompatible with the Butterfly mood. The question that had been placed before the reading public in the twenties of whether modern fiction should be serious and aim at social transformation, as many May Fourth writers proposed, or continue to be designed primarily for amusement, as the Butterfly example suggested, had been resolved by history and the Japanese in favor of the May Fourth side.

Many Butterfly writers did speak for the new ethic and wrote anti-Japanese stories. But most of them continued in their old ways, and the result was a splitting of levels within Butterfly fiction: a "higher" level, exemplified by Zhang Henshui, approached the May Fourth tradition (though still writing in the traditional style); while a "lower" level, exemplified by Feng Yuqi, reached new depths of artlessness, hackneyed content, and even bad grammar. This "lower" level produced hundreds of novels throughout the thirties and forties, and Butterfly publication remained high until the Communist victory in 1949. Even then it was not wholly eradicated. Butterfly books, and even stage plays of *Fate in Tears and Laughter*, were available until the eve of the Cultural Revolution.

The index of Wei Shaochang's volume entitled *Yuanyang nudie pai yanjiu ziliao* (Research materials on the Mandarin Duck and Butterfly School) lists 2,215 Butterfly novels, plus 113 magazines and 49 newspapers and tabloids that carried Butterfly fiction. The list of 2,215 does not include most of the magazine and newspaper novels, nor does it include short stories (which easily outnumbered the long novels), most translation novels (hundreds or more in the teens),[20] many sequels to the popular novels, or the many novels by unknown writers who, trying to sell, would take a famous writer's pen name. Based on these considerations, one might safely estimate that the volume of published Butterfly fiction between 1912 and 1949 (including translations) reached an equivalent of at least 5,000 average-length novels, or somewhere upwards of half a billion characters. The question of the circulation of this vast stock is very difficult. Publishers would inflate figures (or not have them), copyrights were not observed, geographical

337

distribution was seldom recorded, and most books in circulation had multiple readership. One can only guess at the numbers of people reached through movies, comic strips, and word of mouth. Calculating roughly from what we do know, though, it would appear that in one form or another, the most popular stories, such as *Jade Pear Spirit* and *Fate in Tears and Laughter*, must have reached between four hundred thousand to a million people in Shanghai during years when that city's population is estimated to have grown from around 1.4 to around 3.3 million.[21]

Butterfly Fiction and Westernization

Explaining the remarkable growth of Butterfly fiction in terms of technological innovations, increased literacy rates, new urban readerships, and so on is only a partial explanation. For one may ask why the new writings of May Fourth, which had equal or better access to the urban media, did not achieve similar popularity during the twenties. Certainly, their young authors eagerly wanted this. Just as certainly, though, they did not begin achieving it until the thirties. What differences between May Fourth and Butterfly fiction explain the difference in popularity?

This question was discussed by May Fourth writers themselves in the early thirties. Some theorized that the syntax, diction, and narrative style of traditional storytelling simply felt more "natural" to the common reader; it was "the masses' own." By contrast, the new vernacular of May Fourth seemed foreign (Western-influenced) and hard to grasp.[22] Others, including Qu Qiubai, rejected this explanation and had a different theory: "One cannot say popular fiction is 'the masses' own'; all one can say is that it is an elaborate snare laid out by the ruling classes to tie the masses down."[23] Certainly, there is some truth in the theory that less Westernized readers found themselves more at home with the idiom of traditional-style fiction. And Qu Qiubai's "snare" theory, farfetched as it may seem, can also be documented in the record of the warlord governments of the teens and twenties.[24] But there is a third and more important explanation: that, in various ways, Butterfly fiction expressed genuinely felt concerns of its readership. So explosive was its growth in Shanghai, and so great its popularity, that it is difficult to believe that it was foisted upon the public or that its appeal was merely a matter of style.

There were, in fact, many aspects to its appeal, and they cannot be briefly listed. In addition to providing amusement and escape, as mentioned above, one major factor seems clearly to have been

Butterfly fiction's *conservative attitude toward popular Chinese values and its expression of protest against the West and social "modernization."* Here it differed markedly from May Fourth writing.

This "protest" can best be understood by recalling certain aspects of the literary tradition from which Butterfly fiction arose. The vernacular tradition that finds its origins among Tang *bianwen* and the storytelling of Song and Yuan cities has often been considered "popular" for at least two reasons: first, it was less formal and more easily accessible than either classical literature or bureaucratic prose; second, it frequently built its stories around the lives of ordinary urban people — handicraftsmen, shop assistants, petty officials, even loafers and bandits.

It can further be argued, as Jaroslav Průšek and his students have done, that in addition to providing entertainment for and about the urban common classes, vernacular fiction also served to advocate their point of view. In "public case" (*gongan*) stories, for example, interest often shifts from the apprehension and judging of thieves to the activities of the thieves themselves, who, like the *Water Margin* heroes, are revealed as basically sympathetic characters who sometimes rob the rich to help the poor. Justice in the end could be turned upside down: the thieves not only escape punishment but receive rewards for merit.[25]

Other strains within the "popular" tradition offer numerous examples where the lowly and downtrodden were, if not exalted, at least taken seriously. As during the Enlightenment in the West, a kind of populist notion thrived in which common people and daily life came to supplement, or even replace, the aristocracy and its idealized forms as legitimate sources of good, of truth, and of human drama. In interpersonal relations, where Confucian orthodoxy elevated one person to the higher pole of a social relationship, popular fiction would give attention and dignity to the one who stood at the lower. For example, not only do female characters predominate in *Dream of the Red Chamber*, but female psychology is given more serious and differentiated exploration than male-dominated orthodoxy might have considered worthwhile; nor is it accidental, perhaps, that Bao Yu lets slip his opinion that women are better than men, though they can be "contaminated" after marriage "and be just as evil."[26] Youth versus age offers another example. While Bao Yu draws attention to the strains and tribulations imposed upon youth by the expectations of orthodox elders, his resistance of them also introduces the idea of escape from such pressures. Similarly, the young protagonists of *Tale*

339

of Heroic Young Lovers may be viewed as expressing youth's fanciful wish for a way to glory that avoids the orthodox examination system as the only route. Even the irreverent spirit of Sun Wukong can be viewed, in its broadest sense, as typifying youth's naughty impulse to dance in the sun rather than memorize the classics.

Besides upholding those who were looked down on, traditional vernacular fiction often debunked those on top. While helping the poor may have been the knight-errant's basic purpose, his means to that end, which would occupy most of a story, often lay in disposing spectacularly of corrupt officials and wicked potentates. The well-known satires of officialdom and orthodoxy contained in *The Scholars*, *Jing hua yuan* (Flowers in the mirror), and the late Qing "blame" novels are — though not as extensively popular as "knight-errant" and "public case" stories — further examples of a willingness in the larger vernacular tradition to question who it is among the high and low in Confucian society who really deserve one's respect.

But was this element of "protest" in vernacular fiction a protest against the Confucian value system? Or was it only a protest against abusers of power, in behalf of the abused, asking that they be given fair account within what was basically the same value system? Most of the evidence suggests that the latter view is nearer the truth. To oversimplify, the orthodox view held that social good originated from the top, through good government; the popular view held that it could also originate from "below" and even be used to correct evil in higher places. But the conception in the two viewpoints of what constitutes moral behavior and the proper organization of society showed very few differences. The popular hero who destroyed corrupt officials did so because they were corrupt, not because they were officials. Good officials remained safe, were even protected, by the popular hero; and a story could end happily, the hero disappearing into the hills, when all evil power holders had been replaced by ones who exercised traditional virtues in the correct manner. Anti-Manchu stories left no suggestion that anyone or anything but a true Chinese emperor should replace the Manchus. In the formulaic "talent-meets-beauty" love stories, a poor and unappreciated scholar would be helped by a beautiful young woman to overcome all odds, become a *zhuangyuan*, and live happily ever after — with no suggestion that his mobility should take any but the standard path.

The fabulous young heroine Shisan Mei of *Tale of Heroic Young Lovers* is another, and most dramatic example. While her victories over evil implicitly express the unorthodox notions that both women and youth can perform great acts, she turns out in the end to fall solidly within the confinements of Confucian propriety. When she decides to become the second wife of the young gentleman whose family she has rescued from plunderers, she does so on grounds that it is her filial duty to produce offspring. Besides, having been so close to the young man during the various rescues, she fears it might appear improper if they do not marry.

If, therefore, the vernacular tradition is seen to contain a component of "protest," it was not radical protest that favored an alternative social order. Without attacking the Confucian system, it simply provided an outlet and forum for certain human feelings the system left underaccounted. We might call it "remedial protest." Its expression in fiction was not only natural but also quite probably necessary for the stability of the social order.

It is significant that Butterfly fiction, in its twentieth-century context, inherited a tradition that allowed for this type of "remedial protest." Butterfly love stories protested some of the constraints of the traditional marriage system, while the social novels, scandal novels, and modern knight-errant novels continued to attack abusive members of society's elite quite in the style of past traditions.

But interestingly enough, not all "remedial protest" in Butterfly fiction was directed against traditional targets. Besides corrupt officials and restrictive orthodoxy, Western influences of the twentieth century brought new targets within popular fiction's range. Sentiment against Westernization shows up in a great number of ways: in the tragic collapse of Western-style love affairs, in the uncultured amorality of new-style school graduates, or in the flaunting of Western gadgets as status symbols. These anti-Westernization sentiments are seldom overtly labeled as such but can be easily inferred as one follows the "line of sympathy" — who is good, who is evil — that Butterfly novels clearly lay out for their readers. (For the best-selling novels, we must assume that large numbers of urban readers followed these lines of sympathy and concurred in their basic values and attitudes. They could not possibly have enjoyed the stories were this not so.) The process of identifying particular behavior as either Western or non-Western is facilitated by the fact that most novels divide their characters into clearly labeled "new" (Western-influenced) and "old" types. Though Western-influenced characters are common in the fiction, Westerners themselves are rare.

In Butterfly fiction's view, the West was objectionable for fundamentally the same reasons corrupt officials of the past had been. Both tended to upset the proper functioning of society and to adulterate those time-honored values that were felt intuitively to be correct and upon which such proper functioning rested. Both, furthermore, were targets that sat atop the social scale (the West was associated with the modernizing elite), and this suggested to the Butterfly reader that — as "remedial protest" had always shown — society could easily be restored to health and normalcy if only the offending elements were removed.

One crucial difference between traditional protest and anti-Western protest concerned the role of the elite. Opposing corrupt officials in traditional fiction had the full backing of good officials and of orthodox principle. There was scant moral leadership from any source that recommended supporting forces that undermined the traditional order. But the issue of Westernization appeared to the popular mind in a far less clear-cut form. On the one hand, Westernization's assault upon cherished values was undeniable; yet on the other, it was not only rapacious warlords who exalted the West. Social leaders, and many others among the wealthy and the glamorous, seemed equally eager for it. This contradiction produced in the popular outlook a kind of traumatic tension. The external pressure to accept Western ways and enjoy the security that comes from concurring with social authority could in no way make its peace with a visceral reaction against the very idea of pursuing anything so outrageously untraditional.

Consequently, certain aspects of Westernization could become widespread in urban culture but were superficial. Among both fictional characters and the real-life attitudes of most readers, superficial Westernization consisted mainly of stylishness, such as owning a fountain pen, wearing a tie, shaking hands in greeting, or using an occasional Western phrase in speech. Such behavior was not only acceptable but often signified social status and mobility. But on a deeper level — on questions such as what person, from what generation, should one find a young woman's husband — modern Western ideas were firmly rejected. In *Jade Pear Spirit* a young woman returns from a "new-style" women's school in the provincial capital stridently proclaiming that in modern times no woman should accept a traditional marriage: "In the old days, one had to obey the wishes of one's parents . . . but now the tides of the West have surged across eastern Asia and every single one of the new-style experts regards freedom of marriage as the most important thing in one's life."[27] But when the issue draws near for this young woman's beloved sister-in-law, she suddenly abandons her Western veneer and reverts to a strong — and, to the reader, much more sympathetic — espousal of traditional morality. Alone in her room, she is overheard singing a song that expresses sweet and appropriate Confucian regard for each member of her immediate family: her father, "gray-haired" and "lonely"; her deceased mother, "bones grown cold, bringing grief to my heart"; and so on.[28]

As Western ideas were rejected, so were many aspects of life in the modern city. A country bumpkin in one story comes to Shanghai for the first time and finds it expensive, foreign, "irrational," "petty-minded," impersonal, depraved, and chaotic. A pot of tea costs a preposterous sum. Women show their legs. The streetcars, for no reason, have a first class and a third class but no second class, and run on hopelessly intricate routes. The avenues have crazy, foreign-sounding names. Asking directions to a friend's house, the bumpkin finds that nobody knows anybody else.[29] (The Butterfly reader understands these facts of urban life, yet sympathizes with the bumpkin's viewpoint.) Despite the attractions of the city's glitter and wealth, a person is at the mercy of large, dark forces that operate there.

The pressures to accept Western ways superficially yet reject them fundamentally were most often mishandled by persons who let their superficial acceptance go too far. Rich people in Western-style mansions exemplify such excess, as do young women who drive cars. The reader's sympathy is drawn only to those fictional characters who keep their Westernization in *correct proportion* by confining it to a superficial level.

The principle of "correct proportion in Westernization" applied to many aspects of life. On the issue of superstition, for example, one of the West's messages as perceived by Butterfly culture was that many of China's traditional beliefs were superstitious and that superstitions were bad. Enough elite attention was given this idea to oblige Butterfly culture to consider it stylish at a superficial level. But on a deeper level, no sympathetic character would tolerate such an attack on old China. In one instance, a young teacher who has been exposed to "the tides from the West" notices peasants burning money in supplication for a rich autumn harvest. He "laughs at their superstition" and thinks how unfortunate it is that "the tides have not arrived here."[30] Yet no sooner has he completed his new-style duty to decry superstition than he adds a heartfelt plea for excusing it. The country folk after all are "pure and sincere," in touch with the source of their livelihood. They are vastly preferable to the modern city slicker, and their superstitions — though no doubt "backward" — reflect their simplicity and sincerity. Another case in point is the question of whether or not dreams foretell the future. A young man confides to a friend that he is worried because he has dreamed that his girlfriend is being tortured. The friend chides him: do you mean a "civilized" [euphemism for "Westernized"] person like yourself still believes that dreams come true? The young man concedes that such notions about dreams are indeed antiscientific. But then, not allowing Westernization more than its due, he objects that this particular dream has been *persistent,* and hence must be taken more seriously.[31]

The problem of correct proportion arose most frequently in cases of young people facing "modern" sex roles. As we have already seen, the "new-style" young woman could easily be an unsympathetic character if her Westernization were more than skin-deep. The over-Westernized Helena in *Fate in Tears and Laughter* frequents nightclubs, spends extravagantly, and uses English to order beer, which she gulps rudely. She wears a revealing dress, silk stockings, and rouge, because she wants "Western beauty," which comes from "Western civilization."[32] A young woman such as Fengxi in the same novel attains the reader's sympathy when she owns no Western objects except a pair of "no prescription" glasses — just to wear for looks; when she asks for education but then wilts in the effort of pursuing it; or when she states a preference for new-style courtship yet feels unbearably embarrassed when any sign of her interest in a young man is detected by others.

For the young Chinese man, the problem of handling a new-style role, though less obvious than the woman's problem, was just as troublesome. In the woman's case, the content of a new-style role was clear. It included education, free social association outside the household, and other kinds of equality with men. But men in China already enjoyed these privileges and could hardly pursue them as part of the "new style." What, then, were they to pursue? They felt they should cut at least as bold an image as the "modern woman" did. But except for such things as ties and handshakes, the image of the "modern man" was elusive. One could only grope for it, and the result was confusion, uneasiness, and inhibition. On a date with the aforesaid Helena, a young man sits in frustrated silence, observing her make all the decisions he would have made quite easily for himself had there been no West and no new-style date.

The traditional premise of male superiority greatly aggravated the young man's burden. It made any of his moves seem weightier, less revocable. A young woman who overdid a Western-style dance and later felt embarrassed at her crassness could always revert to a recessive, nondancing, "old-style" role. Her error would be overlooked by others as the impulsive excess of a soft creature who knew no better. But when a young man experimented with Western dance, he imperiled his traditional male image. Should he overdo himself, there would be no recourse to the guise of well-intentioned dunce. His fear of appearing ridiculous added a paralyzing weight to his inhibitions about new-style behavior. It could prevent him from acting in the new style even when there was little chance of failure or embarrassment. The male protagonist of *Jade Pear Spirit*, for example, has the opportunity to study in Japan. He knows this is socially acceptable, and knows it is a route to success, but somehow — for no reason he can articulate — feels profoundly uncomfortable with the idea and refrains for a long time from going. As in the simpler examples we have seen, the reader's sympathy concurs in his skepticism of the West.

Butterfly Culture and the May Fourth Movement

The impulse in Butterfly fiction to keep Westernization at arm's length and to "protest" against its deviations from proper values provides more than an explanation of the fiction's popularity. It also offers an insight into May Fourth's own relatively small readership during the twenties. For, no matter how intense and undeniable the patriotism of May Fourth leaders from their own point of view, from the Butterfly perspective their advocacy of Western ideas was cause for great suspicion. The tradition of "remedial protest" in vernacular fiction had consistently attacked abusive authority and sympathized with its victims; now that the May Fourth generation was abusing its leadership position by peddling Westernisms, they too were viewed as having strayed from the path.

Viewing May Fourth's "literary renaissance" from the perspective of Butterfly fiction, it appears as a highly elite movement in many of its basic features. (This is to deny only the efficacy, not the sincerity, of May Fourth's attempts to reach the common people in the twenties.) The magazine *Xin qingnian* (*New youth*) was written and read almost exclusively by a tiny number of China's most privileged young intellectuals, many of whom had studied in Japan or the West and spent their time in China clustered around leading universities. In a new and different way, they seemed as far removed from the mainstream of popular culture as the advocates of eight-legged essays whom they sought to overthrow. Even the name *Xin qingnian* had elite overtones to the popular ear, since the term *qingnian* had traditionally been used only in reference to young males of upper-class households. To the ordinary person the name went halfway toward suggesting "new young gentlemen."

While May Fourth authors had studied abroad and were Western-oriented, Butterfly authors — to say nothing of their readership — had scarcely an impression of life outside China. Li Hanqiu, for example, grew up and lived only in Yangchow, from whose society the abundant detail of his ten-volume *Tides of Yangchow* was drawn; it is said that on his first trip to Shanghai in the early twenties, Li was brought to a Western-style hotel and shown to the elevator, which he immediately took to be his room and objected that it was too small.[33] Few Butterfly authors studied abroad, and these exceptions only prove the rule that overseas study did not mix with Butterfly culture. Chen Shenyan and Xiang Kairan explicitly repudiated their foreign study as they took up careers in popular fiction. Xiang actually began by writing a best-selling novel called *Liudong waishi* (Informal history of overseas study in Japan [1916]), which exposed and bitterly satirized the profligate lives of Chinese students in Japan.

If the main barrier between early May Fourth fiction and the common reader was the issue of new Western ideas, an associated barrier, certainly, was the difference between traditional vernacular (*baihua*) style and the Western-influenced style of most May Fourth writing. It is important to recall that May Fourth writing was by no means the first baihua in twentieth-century China. Baihua newspapers had appeared twenty years before May Fourth,[34] and a great deal of baihua fiction in the traditional style had appeared since 1900. In 1915 the Butterfly magazine *Xiaoshuo huabao* (Fiction pictorial) began a policy of publishing fiction exclusively in baihua.[35] The first May Fourth vernacular fiction appeared more than three years later.

Butterfly baihua had survived in the teens in spite of the stigma that orthodoxy still placed upon vernacular fiction. Viewed in this context, the landmark contribution of May Fourth leaders such as Hu Shi and Chen Duxiu was not to create vernacular writing but to venture the audacious opinion that the elite should stoop to it.

But even among Hu's and Chen's colleagues, few were really prepared to accept baihua in its vulgar forms, either oral or written. Appropriate to their elite and Westernized backgrounds, they created something that looked to the Butterfly reader like an elite and Westernized language. It was an entirely new baihua that borrowed heavily from Western styles and made frequent use of Western grammar and vocabulary. To most urban readers, it was impenetrable. True, May Fourth fiction frequently drew its themes from lower-class life and expressed great sympathy for the common people. But May Fourth readers — the ones who found these portraits of the lower classes appealing — were not the lower classes themselves but a privileged and Western-influenced minority. And the sympathetic feelings of the privileged classes toward the humbler classes were by no means always the same as the feelings of the humbler classes themselves.

Qu Qiubai, realizing in the early thirties that a gulf between May Fourth authors and the common people still existed, chose his words carefully in calling May Fourth writing "a new classical language" (*xin wenyan*).[36] From the popular viewpoint, the new elite of May Fourth was in many respects simply attempting to replace the old elite in its former role. Were not both elites drawn from the wealthy and well educated? Did not both seek to govern society and enshrine their thoughts in occult language? Did not both express scorn for such things as popular fiction?

But despite the gap between Butterfly and May Fourth writing, their differences narrowed somewhat as the twenties and thirties progressed. A few authors from each side chose to join the other. Ye Shengtao and Liu Bannong, who had begun their careers in the Butterfly journals of the teens, became stalwarts of May Fourth. Zhang Ziping, an example of the reverse, began writing with the Creation Society in Japan but by the late twenties had turned to stories of love triangles and pornography.

The crossover among authors was more than matched by crossover among readers. Some May Fourth readers admitted to having read Butterfly fiction in their "lighter" moments. Conversely, there is no doubt that shopkeepers, clerks, high school students, and other Butterfly readers participated in the campaigns and boycotts of the larger May Fourth movement. On the question of opposing Western imperialism, a rather wide unanimity was possible in the cities. It was only with regard to opposing the West in areas we might call cultural or ideological that popular doubts about the West differed markedly from May Fourth's readiness to adopt new Western ideas.

Even in the strictly cultural sphere, though, the two sides drew closer together in the early thirties. With the Japanese attacks on Manchuria in 1931 and on Shanghai in 1932, Butterfly authors set aside entertainment themes and wrote patriotic resist-Japan stories. Still very different from May Fourth fiction, these stories at least had adopted

May Fourth's premise that national needs should take precedence over amusement. For their part May Fourth authors, though without acknowledging Butterfly fiction, began to expand their readership by adopting some of its traits. The great popularity of the romantic theme in Ba Jin's *Jia* (Family) is much easier to explain in terms of the similar popularity of Butterfly love stories and of traditional fiction like *Dream of the Red Chamber* than in terms of May Fourth precedents. Another and most interesting element in the popularity of some May Fourth works of the early thirties was an increased tendency to express skepticism about Western culture. Cao Yu's very popular play *Richu* (Sunrise [1935]), for example, sharply satirizes the over-Westernized returned student "Georgy" Zhang, a fop who praises all that is Western and scorns all that is Chinese.

In one crucial respect the expanded May Fourth audience of the thirties and forties outstripped the Butterfly audience. Butterfly fiction had always been an urban phenomenon. To the extent that it had a rural readership, this readership was strictly of gentry background. When modern Chinese literature finally began to reach the peasantry, it was not Butterfly fiction that accomplished this but the patriotic wartime plays and stories of the developing May Fourth tradition. May Fourth writers joined this effort themselves by traveling in the countryside. Under increasingly leftist leadership, they sought broad appeal while at the same time excising all the backward and "feudal" elements that had constituted part of the attraction of Butterfly stories. Though their works never became "hits" as Butterfly stories did, their quest to reach the peasants made these heirs of May Fourth the first writers in modern China to achieve what may be properly called a "mass" audience.

As this new "mass" literature continued to grow and develop in the fifties and beyond, it took on a special character easily distinguishable from both the May Fourth and the Butterfly literature of the twenties. Yet it is best understood as an outgrowth of both these traditions. Roughly speaking, it preserved the basic political orientation of the May Fourth tradition but gave up May Fourth's pursuit of Western-style art. This it replaced with a more popular art, which in certain ways (but *only* in certain ways) resembled traditional vernacular fiction and Butterfly fiction. In terms of politics and themes, the differences between the new mass fiction and Butterfly fiction remained tremendous. But in terms of the standard literary features that always have given popular fiction its popularity (in the West as well), unmistakable similarities emerge: one finds the predominance of action over description, unambiguously good and bad characters, the victory of good over evil, the recounting of unusual events, and so on. From rural surveys of the sixties, there is evidence that stories that include the extraordinary in both persons and events were still the most widely read in China.[37] Of traditional stories, *The Water Margin* and *Romance of the Three Kingdoms* were favorites. The most popular of contemporary stories — *Taking Tiger Mountain by Strategy* and *The White-haired Girl* — were likewise ones that involve unusual happenings and dashing characters who stand out from the crowd for their capabilities and moral perfection.

The similarity between the new mass fiction and certain aspects of traditional-style fiction raises questions about the problem of continuity in modern Chinese literature. Can Butterfly fiction possibly be viewed as an intermediary? There is certainly no explicit imitation of Butterfly writing in China today, since all aspects of Butterfly culture have been consciously repudiated. Yet May Fourth fiction, the only other possible "intermediary" between Qing times and the present, has now also been largely rejected. May Fourth, moreover, grew in considerable degree from foreign origins and consciously rejected the Chinese past.

Seemingly discontinuous on both ends, then, May Fourth writing may eventually appear as a kind of Western-influenced detour in the course of Chinese literature. Certainly this seems likely if one speaks of popular literature. Butterfly fiction was of course also transitory, and also is distinguishable both from what it followed and what it preceded. But the continuity of popular literary features that it appears to preserve may allow us to conclude that it fits the role of modern "intermediary" somewhat less uncomfortably than do the Western-style writings of May Fourth. The question of continuity remains difficult and no doubt is too early to decide. But however it is decided in the future, account will surely have to be taken of Butterfly as well as May Fourth writing.

16.

Qu Qiubai's Critique of the May Fourth Generation: Early Chinese Marxist Literary Criticism

Paul G. Pickowicz

It is well known that by 1930 there were a large number of revolutionary writers in China, many of whom knew and strongly supported a variety of foreign Marxist literary theories. Despite this activity, no distinctively Chinese school of Marxist criticism had emerged that approached the unique problems of literature and revolution in China from a Marxist perspective. Marxist literary thought had not been "Sinified." Further, the revolutionary aspirations of these literary activists had been repeatedly thwarted by their endless internal feuding and by their failure to make meaningful contact with the masses for whom they so often spoke. The fact that the revolutionary writers did not make a comprehensive and self-critical evaluation of the history and development of the modern literary movement also helped perpetuate their practical difficulties.

The attempt in 1931 by Qu Qiubai, leader of the League of Left-Wing Writers, to analyze the problems of the left-wing literary movement marks the first appearance of a characteristically Chinese form of Marxist literary criticism. Unusual in its time, Qu's work remains significant today for several reasons. First, Qu's most innovative writings did not focus on the enemies of the revolution but rather on the left-wing literary camp itself. Indeed, Qu's search for a convincing explanation of left-wing literary failures required that he make a rather harsh critique of the celebrated May Fourth generation of revolutionary writers. This particular aspect of Qu's diverse literary activities is interesting precisely because he raised new and unusual questions that affected the Chinese literary scene for decades, perhaps even up to the present. Qu, like others then and now, recognized the great contributions of the May Fourth period to the revolutionary literary movement. But to what extent, he asked, did this same heritage contribute to the problems of the revolutionary camp? In what ways had the May Fourth experience conditioned Chinese responses to foreign Marxist literary theories? Why had the introduction of Marxist criticism in the early twenties not resulted in a clear delineation of the major failings of the revolutionary literary movement? Were these theories misinterpreted or were some unsuited to Chinese conditions?

Qu's probing reflected more than an intellectual and political concern for the destiny of the literary movement. There is an intensely personal side to the Qu Qiubai story. It was people with backgrounds like his own whom Qu castigated in the early thirties for having uncritically embraced foreign literary theories without having explained their relevance to the special problems of the Chinese scene. Qu's rigorous critique of his closest friends seems to have been based partly on an awareness that he had committed many of the same mistakes in an earlier period. For this reason, his analysis contains a number of revealing introspective and self-critical qualities.

The New Culture and May Fourth Pattern

The Russian Literary Masters It is somewhat ironic that Qu Qiubai became known in his later years as an uncompromising critic of the May Fourth generation of Westernized intellectuals because there is no more typical a product of that momentous movement than Qu himself. As with numerous other May Fourth activists of gentry origin (such as Guo Moruo and Lu Xun) who were born in the last years of the troubled nineteenth century, the affluence and privilege of Qu's childhood soon disappeared with the rapid disintegration and eventual destruction of his family, a process that resulted in the tragic suicide of Qu's mother.[1] And like the other young people who had been schooled both in the ancient literary and historical classics and the new ideas of Confucian reformers such as Tan Sitong and Liang Qichao, the young Qu drifted to Peking at precisely the time the iconoclastic forces of the New Culture movement were mercilessly ridiculing the hypocrisy and irrelevance of traditional values and society. The collapse of his family was an agonizing and crushing personal experience; but, typical of his generation, Qu gradually came to view the downfall of his family as a microcosm of the disintegration of the whole Chinese civilization.

Qu's celebrated participation in the May Fourth movement after his arrival in Peking in 1916 was by no means immediate. Quiet, introverted, and still recovering from the brutal destruction of his feuding family, the studious Qu audited literature classes at Peking University for several months while privately studying neo-Confucianism, Lao Zi, Zhuang Zi, and Mahayana Buddhism late into the evening. Ironically, his decision to enter the tuition-free National Institute of Russian Language in the summer of 1917 had nothing to do with his prior interest in literature or any particular attraction to Russian culture or politics. Qu knew nothing about either the glories of Russian literature or the Russian Revolution. Rather, it was the promise of employment in the Ministry of Foreign Affairs or by the Chinese Eastern Railway that drew the talented but virtually penniless Qu to these "modern studies." Nevertheless, Qu distinguished carefully between the mundane "worldly" duty of preparing for a career and the need to prepare himself for the "unworldly" duty of "saving China by cultural means."[2] His secluded cultural studies continued late at night.

Like so many other young people in his situation, Qu was ripe for recruitment into the iconoclastic New Culture movement. As he later put it, "The May Fourth movement sucked me in like a whirlpool."[3] Not only did the new ideas contained in *Xin qingnian* (New youth) seem relevant to the collapse of his own family, they also explained the collapse and weakness of China. Spontaneously, small groups of students emerged to discuss the issues of the day. Qu's closest associates included Geng Jizhi, Qu Shiying, Xu Dishan, and Zheng Zhenduo, all of whom were later instrumental in the formation of the famous Literary Association. Typically, their concerns included not only an examination of the failures of traditional Chinese culture and a search for new cultural models but also a deep patriotic concern for China's plight. For them, ridiculing the cultural tradition was a precondition for saving the nation.

Because he was articulate and bright, Qu was selected by his friends to represent them at the meetings of Peking student leaders prior to the May Fourth Incident. On the day of the incident Qu actually led the institute delegation on the historic march from Tian An Men to the home of Cao Rulin. Following his election as a representative to the Peking Student Union, Qu was arrested and jailed on June 5. As public support for the patriotic students increased, the authorities relented. On June 8, Qu was among the freed students who triumphantly marched amid the cheers of hundreds who gathered for the occasion.[4] In the following months Qu and his close friends, many of whom he would criticize in later years, founded new magazines such as *Xin shehui* (New society) and *Rendao (L'humanité)* and wrote typical May

353

Fourth articles on iconoclastic and patriotic themes in a variety of other magazines. In his search for new ideas Qu (and other obscure students like Zhou Enlai and Mao Zedong) joined the various Marxist study groups founded by Li Dazhao in 1919 and 1920.

In this New Culture and May Fourth context the modern literary movement blossomed. As with others of his generation, the pursuit of a modern professional career introduced Qu to a Western language. Coincidentally, a small portion of his language curriculum included reading selections of nineteenth-century Russian literature. Just as others enthusiastically proclaimed the "obvious" relevance of German, English, or French literature, Qu, Geng Jizhi, Jiang Baili, and others became May Fourth standard-bearers of "their" foreign model, despite their superficial understanding of Russian language and literature.

In the following months these eager "experts" published a variety of translations and commentaries on Russian literature as part of their May Fourth activity.[5] Qu had great interest in Leo Tolstoy, one of the foreign writers who had the most influence on the May Fourth period. In all, Qu translated four works by Tolstoy and wrote two reviews of Tolstoy's views. In later years Qu commented, "When I published *New Society* . . . the ideology to which I felt closest was anarchism of the Tolstoy type."[6] Many other Chinese radicals, like the youthful Mao Zedong, were influenced during this period by anarchistic utopian ideals. Suspicious of politics and government, Tolstoy was an inspirational moral leader and cultural revolutionary.

Generally, Qu's early attraction to Russian literature fits the May Fourth pattern. Like many interested in modern literature, he was attracted to the eighteenth- and nineteenth-century bourgeois tradition, not the avant-garde symbolist and futurist trends. While some were inspired by the works of the great romantics, Qu was drawn more to realism. Its language was direct and clear, and its content confronted the key social issues, although often melodramatically. The progressive nineteenth-century ideas in these works appeared to these socially conscious Chinese youths to be extraordinarily relevant to the problems of Chinese society in its transition from the traditional to the modern. This was the beginning of what Qu would later call China's "bourgeois-democratic cultural revolution." These alienated and outraged intellectuals were demanding both the liberation of the individual and social reform. As cultural revolutionaries, they were drawn to literature as a vehicle for their protest.

It is significant that while Qu, like many others, was somewhat attracted to Marxist *political* theories (among other things), his interest in Russian *literature* remained focused exclusively on the "bourgeois" masters of prerevolutionary times, not on the postrevolutionary "proletarian" schools. Events at Versailles may have shaken New Culture faith in the morality of Western liberal politics, but young intellectuals continued to believe Western cultural models were relevant to China's needs. The acceptance of Marxist literary theory eventually accompanied Qu's own formal conversion to Marxism after 1920, but many others continued to be attracted to various "bourgeois" foreign cultural models long after they had become staunch anti-imperialists and Marxists. Unrecognized by Qu at the time, the implications of this unusual phenomenon were to be an overriding concern of his after 1930.

The Soviet Model   Certainly, Qu's rare chance to visit the Soviet Union fundamentally changed his perception of the significance of his foreign model. But in light of developments in later years, it would appear that the most noteworthy aspect of the shift in Qu's emphasis from nineteenth-century Russian literary modes to Marxist literary thought was his failure to depart from the May Fourth literary pattern of imitative, uncritical borrowing. Of course, what distinguishes Qu in this new period from his old May Fourth colleagues was his discovery that his foreign cultural model could be updated and placed alone in the "vanguard." Formerly, Qu had been attracted to prerevolutionary Russian literature as one of many modern foreign literary traditions relevant to China. Later, his personal experience in the Soviet Union convinced him that the new socialist literature and criticism were truly unique and not to be compared to the modern but decidedly prerevolutionary traditions of either western Europe or Russia. In both cases (and in typical May Fourth fashion), Qu was not particularly creative or critical in his interpretations of these models.

This is not the place to recount the details of Qu Qiubai's pioneering two-year visit to the Soviet Union. But the trip was a typical May Fourth "spiritual pilgrimage" to a progressive foreign society. Although he was intensely curious about the new experiment, Qu knew exceedingly little about the Bolshevik Revolution when he departed in October 1920. Like others who visited the West, he polished his language skills, immersed himself in cultural and literary studies, and came into contact with leading cultural figures — Mayakovsky, Lunacharsky, Lenin, and members of the Tolstoy family. This experience made a profound impact on the impressionable Qu. Soon he began to write glowing reports that celebrated the cultural and spiritual brilliance of the new Soviet society.

Qu's new ideas about the significance of his foreign model reflected a clear understanding of the uniqueness of the historical era into which Russian society had entered. His New Culture interest in prerevolutionary Russian literature had been based on an appreciation of the general struggle between modernity and tradition reflected in its content. But Qu's views on Soviet culture and literature revealed a new interest in the more specific struggle between declining bourgeois-capitalist society (then identified with western Europe) and emerging socialism. As an Asian revolutionary, Qu believed that it was highly significant that socialist revolution had first occurred in such a backward corner of Europe. The same "shortcuts" (*jiejing*) to socialism taken by Russia might also be taken by an even less developed China. For this reason, Qu tended to view the Soviet Union as an important cultural bridge between East and West.[7]

Yet many of Qu's views about postrevolutionary Russia were conditioned by various already deeply engrained New Culture and May Fourth ideas about the significance of "cultural revolution." Qu was, for example, acutely aware of the general underdevelopment of Russia and the material hardships of everyday Soviet life. But he was not depressed by these hard realities. Instead he became excited by the spiritual strength and will of the Russian people. His belief in the decisive role of subjective factors in human development was dramatically confirmed, thus making the Soviet model all the more relevant for a nation as backward as China. In fact, it was during midwinter spells of tuberculosis that Qu joined the CCP in Moscow. He proclaimed, "I have enrolled myself in the ranks of the world's cultural movement, which will open new avenues for the whole of human culture."[8] Thus, when he returned to China in January 1923, Qu was no less determined than he had been during the May Fourth movement to "save China by cultural means."

Obviously, Qu's various efforts to introduce Soviet literary trends and Marxist literary criticism into China in 1923 most clearly reveal what he had learned about literature in the Soviet Union. As a member of the Literary Association, as a professor at Shanghai University, and as a leader in Communist publishing circles from January 1923 to mid-1924, Qu made a variety of pioneering efforts to introduce Marxist theories of literary criticism, popularize postrevolutionary Russian literary trends, and evaluate the condition of the May Fourth literary revolution. It is well known that interest in Marxist political thought grew in China after 1919, but, interestingly, nothing was known about Marxist literary theory in the early twenties.

After returning to Shanghai, the new center of modern intellectual activity, Qu was able to observe how much the literary movement had changed in the two years of his absence. By successfully challenging traditional assumptions about the form, content, and purposes of literature, the struggling and vigorous modern literary movement had clearly won some major victories after 1920. Yet consolidating these triumphs cost the movement much of its vitality. The unity of the early May Fourth period had given way to divisiveness within the movement (especially between the Literary Association and the Creation Society) as powerful and elite literary organizations were founded. Perhaps more importantly, the formation of these societies indicated the rupture of the tenuous but dynamic link between intellectuals and the urban masses that had been forged so successfully during the 1919 national crisis. During the May Fourth movement, the literary revolution and social activism in general were indistinguishable. But by 1923, when the political crisis seemed less urgent, this link between literature and society began to weaken in the face of increasing literary professionalism. The returning Qu Qiubai was deeply disturbed by some of these developments, but his criticisms were vague. While he ascribed these developments to the "bourgeois Westernization" of the literary movement, Qu still could not do more than substitute a Marxist, but still thoroughly foreign, alternative. Qu may have been unique as the earliest advocate of Marxist criticism, but he stayed well within the May Fourth literary tradition of uncritical adoption of foreign models.

An excellent example of this imitative pattern was Qu's brief and very elementary introduction of the rudiments of Marxist literary theory in his popular book *Shehui kexue gailun* (Outline of the social sciences), a text he used at Shanghai University. The main purpose of this sketchy discussion was to establish the validity of the materialist conception of literature and art. Thus, at the beginning of the chapter on art, Qu posited that an economic and social base (mode of production and corresponding social relations of production) existed as the foundation of society in any historical era. Built upon this base, and related to it, is a superstructure composed of social institutions and organizations, cultural patterns, and a variety of religious, philosophic, artistic, and ideological beliefs. Consequently, argued Qu, art of any period is best understood as an expression of various aspects of economic relations in a given society. Art is "organically" rooted in the material conditions of society, not a free-floating force that transcends society.

357

The study of history reveals the nature of this relationship between art and society. In "primitive societies," where the economic base and art forms are quite simple, the relationship is rather direct. "In primitive society," Qu explained, "singing, dancing, and drawing all had a close relationship to the mode of production at the time."[9] But as modes of production and societies become more complex and as the division of labor increases, the interrelationship between art and the economic base becomes more complex, especially in bourgeois society. Nevertheless, in complex class societies, the prevailing aesthetic standards are always the standards of the ruling class. Qu, then, stressed the phenomenon of contending, class-related artistic development in advanced societies. Bourgeois art becomes increasingly important in the late feudal period as class struggle intensifies. Furthermore, Qu insisted, "there has been art of the masses in every era." Some of it was in the healthy folk and handicraft tradition, but in the bourgeois period much of it was degenerate, commercialized art forced on the masses.

Perhaps the most interesting section of Qu's discussion was entitled "Art and Social Reform." There he discussed the function of art in bourgeois society by identifying four major trends: early antifeudal literature and art in support of modern bourgeois revolution; reformist literature exposing the evils of bourgeois society; decadent literature of despair in the period of bourgeois decline; and, finally, emerging proletarian literature.[10] Qu clearly favored "proletarian" literature, but he recognized certain difficulties confronting the new proletarian literary movement in the period before bourgeois rule was completely overthrown. First, bourgeois artistic standards continued to exert a very strong influence in the period of bourgeois decline, causing many writers and artists otherwise sympathetic to the working-class movement to dismiss folk and proletarian art. Second, because of its cultural deprivation, the proletariat could not develop "its own thoroughly independent art." Thus, a small group of radical intellectuals had to take the lead in expressing and representing the views of the working class in the world of letters.

The weakness of Qu's simplistic introduction of Marxist concepts was his total failure to relate this framework to the Chinese context. Were these remarks to be understood as a call for a Chinese "proletarian" literary movement? Was he appealing to the inflated egos of progressive intellectuals by assigning them a vanguard position? Was the Chinese bourgeois literary movement in the antifeudal, reformist, or declining-decadent stage? Were his warnings about the pitfalls of the "art for art's sake" and "art for life's sake" approaches meant to be oblique references to the powerful Creation Society and Literary Association respectively? It is impossible to answer these questions definitively, for nowhere in this early discussion of theory is China mentioned. This is not surprising, because Qu's book, like so many May Fourth volumes, was little more than a summary of a foreign original — in this case Bukharin's *Historical Materialism.*

More specific and exciting, but no more relevant to current Chinese conditions, were Qu's pioneering efforts to introduce Chinese readers to postrevolutionary Soviet literary trends. As an active member of the Literary Association, Qu did as much as he could to direct his old May Fourth friends away from bourgeois Western literary models and toward the new trends produced by the Russian Revolution. Indeed, the evidence suggests that in 1923, six years after the Bolshevik Revolution, cosmopolitan Chinese intellectuals knew almost nothing of the truly dynamic literary developments taking place in the Soviet Union. *Xiaoshuo yuebao* (Short story monthly), the most distinguished journal of the modern literary movement and the most oriented toward foreign developments, was devoted almost exclusively to western Europe and America. Its translations and commentaries on Russian literature concentrated on the great nineteenth-century tradition Qu helped to introduce years before. While fragmentary and imitative, Qu's *Short Story Monthly* articles, such as "Laodong Eguode xin zuojia" (New writers of workers' and peasants' Russia) and "Chi E xin wenyi shidaide diyi yan" (The first swallows of red Russia's new literary and artistic period), were a serious effort to bring progressive Chinese writers up to date.

In these works, Qu concerned himself primarily with the nature of revolutionary literature and the possibility of "proletarian culture." In "New Writers" he discussed Vladimir Mayakovsky, Sergey Semyonov, and the proletarian writers of Proletkult as examples of the various strains in the new Russian literature of the twenties. Qu correctly pointed out that the early futurist and symbolist writings of Mayakovsky and other cultural activists were revolutionary because of their iconoclastic rejection of traditional literary forms and language. He saw Mayakovsky and the young Boris Pasternak as cultural revolutionaries whose work had the effect of undermining the old order.[11]

Undoubtedly, this account of the revolutionary role of Soviet cultural activists impressed Chinese readers who were themselves veteran cultural revolutionaries. But it must have been disconcerting for these products of the May Fourth movement to discover that some of the Russian iconoclastic and proletarian artistic activists were preoccupied with experiments in artistic forms, and that the "tradition" these young enthusiasts rejected was the very same nineteenth-century bourgeois Western tradition so enthusiastically embraced by Chinese iconoclasts.

While there may have been agreement in Soviet literary circles on the need for an iconoclastic rupture with the bourgeois past and rapid development of a new "proletarian" art, Qu's articles revealed there were significant differences on other questions. First among these, according to Qu, was the problem of the class origin of "proletarian" cultural activists, and the issue of whether the "proletarian" movement should focus primarily on artistic form or on content. Qu presented Semyonov, in contrast to Mayakovsky, as a proletarian literary figure of genuine working-class origin and Bolshevik party membership. In Semyonov's well-known novel *Hunger,* Qu saw the first fruit of a new and truly proletarian literary movement — that is, a literature produced by proletarian intellectuals for working-class consumption rather than a literature produced for them by petty bourgeois intellectuals. Unlike the "proletarian" cultural activists who experimented with futurist and symbolist forms, Semyonov's work was realistic and easy to read — so colloquial that it was comprehensible to illiterate workers when read aloud.[12]

In fact, a central theme in Qu's early writings on the Soviet proletarian cultural movement was the split between futurist artists who viewed the revolution (and the revolution in art) as a rare opportunity to experiment with new forms and anti-intellectual but equally iconoclastic working-class artists who insisted on straightforward mass-based art. Qu ended "New Writers" with a discussion of several avant-garde writers, such as Nickolai Poletaev, Vasily Kazin, Mikhail Gerasimov, Vasily Aleksandrovsky, Il'ya Sadofiev, and Aleksey Gastev, who were associated with Proletkult in its early days. For Qu, they had radical new ideas in style but remained close to the old bourgeois order in content. But in his second article, "The First Swallows of Red Russia's New Literary and Artistic Period," Qu featured the "pure" proletarian, antiformalist strains in the revolutionary literary movement, as reflected in the lives of Feodor Kalinin and Pavel Bessalko. A student of Alexander Bogdanov's and head of Proletkult in Petrograd, Bessalko was as iconoclastic as the futurists, but ridiculed their literary theories. A former factory worker himself, Bessalko insisted on genuine proletarian leadership in cultural affairs and wrote in simple Russian for mass consumption.[13] Kalinin, also a former worker and cofounder of Proletkult with Bogdanov, was presented by Qu in much the same way. Kalinin argued that the working class could expect no help from the old intelligentsia in creating its own art and culture because artistic expression is class-based and principally subconscious, therefore "an intellectual can never be a proletarian in his subconscious mind."[14]

Significantly, Qu Qiubai did not make any startling conclusions about the meaning of postrevolutionary Russian literature for a distinctively prerevolutionary China. In fact, nowhere in these reports is China even mentioned. These and other essays written by Qu merely describe developments in this most "progressive" foreign nation. Nowhere is the relevance of these trends for particularly Chinese conditions spelled out. Again, there is evidence suggesting that, in typical May Fourth style, these reports were merely adapted from Soviet literary journals.[15] Whereas radical Chinese writers of the May Fourth generation were certainly disturbed by the general rejection of the great bourgeois literary tradition and the anti-intellectualism contained in the Soviet movement, Qu chose not to confront these problems. He seems to have been unaware that Lenin and Trotsky were highly skeptical of both the "futurist" and "pure" proletarian directions of the proletarian cultural movement. Both men were unwilling to accept such a radical break with the bourgeois literary past, and neither could see the complex futurist experiments in form, or the often simplistic content and form of "pure" working-class literature, as manifestations of the coming proletarian culture.

Qu also apparently did not realize that the rather deterministic account of Marxist literary theory he presented in his Shanghai University lectures contradicted not only the assumptions of early Soviet proletarian cultural activists but also his own deeply rooted faith in the vanguard role of cultural revolution. While the theoretical views he expressed allowed for the *possibility* that the superstructure of society (including art and literature) might have an impact on the economic substructure, the overall direction of Qu's brief remarks (entirely in keeping with Plekhanov's pioneering work in Marxist literary theory) was that cultural change always followed fundamental economic transformation. Despite their differences, the early Soviet proletarian cultural groups discussed above tended to assume that certain basic changes in the superstructure could be accomplished before, and presumably independently of the transformation of the economic base. Lenin and Trotsky, conservatives on matters of literature and art, disagreed with both proletarian schools on this question. In any case, Qu's early reports on the Soviet scene were oblivious to these issues and their implications in China.

More relevant to the Chinese literary scene, but not nearly as detailed as his articles on Russia, was Qu's work with Yun Daiying, Deng Zhongxia, and Xiao Chunü in well-known Communist publications such as *Zhongguo qingnian* (Chinese youth) and a reorganized *New Youth*, which Qu edited. Only in short articles, such as "Gao yanjiu wenxue de qingnian" (To young people studying literature) and "Huangmoli — yijiuersannian zhi Zhongguo wenxue" (In the wasteland — Chinese literature in 1923), did Qu hint at the direction he felt the modern literary movement should move in. In doing so, he made some perceptive, if sketchy observations about the problems of the literary revolution.

Their writings conceded that the old May Fourth literary revolution to undermine the classical tradition by introducing modern Western literature and using a more vernacular literary language had been largely successful. But unless further progress was made, Qu and his associates warned that there was a danger that the trends of forming elite literary groups and "conserving" early victories of the literary revolution might increase. As cultural revolutionaries, they were afraid that the modern cultural movement might fall behind and stagnate. Impatient for the next stage to begin, their call for "revolutionary literature" was simply an attempt to place the literary movement in the mainstream of the emerging nationalist and labor movements of the twenties and thereby reestablish the organic link between literature and society so pronounced at the time of the May Fourth Incident.[16]

While Qu recognized the need for more use of colloquial language, he saw the transition to the new stage largely as a problem of literary content. The struggle for the supremacy of *baihua* (vernacular Chinese) over *wenyan* (literary Chinese) had been won; now it was a question of what the new literature should say. In "Wasteland," Qu asserted that only a few Chinese writers were interested primarily in form.[17] Instead, Qu and others were far more concerned with those works whose content was overly sentimental, egocentric, escapist, or simply decadent. They tried persuading writers to adopt a Marxist world view and reflect it in their writing, which, in 1923, meant attention to the labor movement, support for anti-imperialist nationalism, and condemnation of the feudal power of landlords and warlords. To get the content of the new literature out of the clouds and onto the streets, the *Chinese Youth* group urged more direct contact between writers and the masses, and even direct participation in the revolutionary struggle. "It is a disgrace to the literati," Qu wrote, "not to have writers going into the coal pits." To write realistically, writers "must taste every human bitterness, endure every human ignominy."[18]

Nowhere in his 1923 writings did Qu relate the failure of writers to maintain direct contact with the masses to the impact to Westernization on the literary world. Still, in "Wasteland" Qu made some intriguing but vague references to the influences of something he chose to call "foreign classicism" (*wai gudianzhuyi*).[19] This term seems to satirize the tendency of modern writers to imitate stylish Western bourgeois literary models, life-styles, and language, implying that this trend was somehow an obstacle to the *political* shifts necessary for the emergence of "revolutionary literature." Qu had touched on something rather important in "Wasteland," but he failed to develop this theme until the early thirties. He simply assumes that if the *political* consciousness of revolutionary writers undergoes the appropriate transformation, the literary movement will automatically shift from the bourgeois "literary revolution" to "revolutionary literature." Later he would realize he had been wrong: the political radicalization of writers had not resulted in the abandonment of the bourgeois Western cultural model. The problems of the literary movement involved more than one's political perspective. Ironically, he would also see that his own advocacy of Marxist literary criticism in 1923 also fit the pattern of "foreign classicism."

Despite Qu's early efforts to introduce Marxist literary theory and Soviet trends and to promote a shift from "literary revolution" to "revolutionary literature," the Shanghai literary world was unreceptive to these new ideas in 1923. What factors account for this failure at a time when the CCP was beginning to have a significant impact in political circles? Qu had been fairly creative in analyzing the condition of the literary movement, and Marxist criticism would seem more relevant to Chinese writers in later years, when the political situation worsened. But the major reason for Qu's lack of success lies in his failure to demonstrate clearly the relevance of Marxist theory or Soviet trends to the Chinese literary scene. Indeed, Marxist criticism and Soviet trends did not appear to be very relevant. For example, Qu's introduction of the concept of "proletarian" literature implicitly reflected his conviction that the proletarian movement should begin in China at some point, yet as a member of the Central Committee of the CCP he enthusiastically endorsed the party's position that the Chinese revolution was at present bourgeois-democratic in nature and that its leading political force was the Guomindang. Furthermore, certain features of the postrevolutionary Soviet literary scene introduced by Qu, such as the antibourgeois and anti-intellectual strains in some proletarian groups, could hardly have appealed to the May Fourth literary mind. In fact, the domination of Western bourgeois literary theories was a major obstacle blocking early efforts to promote Marxist concepts in Chinese literature. Introducing Marxism into politics was much easier because Western liberalism had been discredited long before 1923, but ironically, despite the appeal of Marxist politics, the influence of Western bourgeois culture and literature became increasingly powerful after the May Fourth Incident. By 1923 it was deeply entrenched in the modern cultural sphere. Finally, it must be recognized that Qu did not present a very cohesive picture of Marxist aesthetics, partially because there is no systematic body of literature that Western Marxists consider authoritative, orthodox texts on the Marxist approach to art. In any event, Qu had grasped only fragments of this amorphous tradition. Not only did some of his remarks contradict others but also he seems to have been unaware that the Western tradition of Marxist criticism contained elements decidedly less hostile to the bourgeois tradition and to bourgeois literary experts themselves, elements that might have appeared, and later did appear more attractive to May Fourth writers.

Qu's early efforts may have failed, but his attempts to introduce Marxist theory and Soviet trends were in the familiar May Fourth pattern of introducing foreign literary schools. In the first place, "Russia" was Qu's foreign model. Because the model had changed to "Soviet Russia" by 1923 should not obscure the fact that, like other May Fourth activists, Qu was first interested in the modern bourgeois literary tradition and did not intend to abandon his love of prerevolutionary literature. His lifelong commitment to Marxist literary theory grew out of his early study of the Russian language, his reading of the nineteenth-century Russian masters, and his travel experience in that most "advanced" foreign nation. And in typical May Fourth fashion, his grasp of the Marxist and Soviet literary model was both imitative and superficial. Ironically, in essays such as "Wasteland" and "To Young People Studying Literature," which show touches of originality in Qu's work, it is fairly difficult to trace his indebtedness to either Marxist criticism or Soviet proletarian models. In later years, he would criticize — with considerable justification — the failure of May Fourth writers to relate their foreign literary models to specific Chinese conditions, but Qu was guilty of that offense himself in 1923.

It is important to place the origins of Marxist literary criticism *within* the May Fourth literary tradition. For, despite its early lack of appeal, under different conditions in later years, Marxist literary theory would hold interest for many of those May Fourth writers who had rejected it in 1923. Under new conditions, the "Western" Marxist model suddenly would appear to be quite compatible with the May Fourth tradition.

In any event, Qu's lack of success in the Shanghai literary world helped transform his initial concern with the literary revolution into serious disillusion with the prospects for further cultural revolution. Already deeply involved in CCP activities, Qu soon focused his attention on the labor movement and "national" revolution. To him, these events promised more than the disintegrating literary movement. Forced underground, Qu wrote absolutely nothing on literary and cultural subjects from mid-1924 to early 1931. Instead, he became absorbed in the political development of the CCP. As one of the CCP's most prominent leaders, he was involved in the spectacular successes of the United Front period of the mid-1920s, as well as the crushing defeats that followed the disastrous counterrevolution of 1927.

Critique of Westernization, Marxism, and the Revolutionary Literary Movement

The Setting There is no need to detail Qu's political activities here, except to note the circumstances under which he left the inner circles of CCP leaders and reemerged as a powerful force in the left-wing literary movement in Shanghai. Generally, Qu became more and more disillusioned with aspects of Chinese Communist and Comintern politics in the last two or three years of his involvement. For instance, just as Qu had been instrumental in making Chen Duxiu the scapegoat for Comintern failures in 1927, so too did the Comintern hold Qu accountable for the "insurrectionist" disasters that followed. Qu remained in Moscow as a Chinese representative to the Comintern for two years after the Sixth CCP Congress of 1928. There he became increasingly suspicious of Stalin's China expert, Pavel Mif, who repeatedly attempted to manipulate CCP politics by supporting the rise to power of Wang Ming and the 28 Bolsheviks group, first at Moscow's Sun Yat-sen University and later within the Central Committee of the CCP itself. The first clash between Qu and Mif in early 1930 in Moscow caused Qu's dismissal from the Chinese delegation to the Comintern. The second and more decisive struggle, which occurred in Shanghai from the summer of 1930 to early 1931, concerned the question of who was to succeed Li Lisan as leader of the CCP. Qu had been instructed to support Mif and the repudiation of the Li Lisan line. But he rallied his old supporters in China at the Third Plenum, overruling the objections of Mif and his Chinese followers by temporarily assuming control of the CCP himself and pursuing a fairly conciliatory policy toward Li's errors. Incensed at Qu's rebelliousness and armed with Stalin's full support, Mif himself took over the Fourth Plenum in January 1931. Apparently powerless, Qu was denounced and dismissed from the Politburo and other key positions within the CCP. As might be expected, Qu remained disaffected with the new Wang Ming leadership group throughout the early thirties. Isolated from the center of political power and personally embittered, Qu turned to literature, where the prospects for "cultural revolution" once again appeared great.

Qu's break with both the Comintern and the Wang Ming leadership led to his disillusionment with foreign "theories" about the Chinese revolution and with the revolutionary leadership's uncritical acceptance of foreign "wisdom." It is at this moment that Qu independently and creatively investigated the impact of "Westernization," both bourgeois and Marxist, on the left-wing literary movement. This investigation became a logical first step in formulating a distinctively Chinese approach to Marxist literary thought. Qu's estrangement from the CCP leadership probably made his work a bit easier because no restraints were placed on his intellectual activity due to political obligations. Also, there is no evidence that the Central Committee under Wang Ming had an "official" policy on the arts or directed the activities of left-wing writers. Still, it would be wrong to suggest that Qu had rejected Marxism. He remained an active revolutionary. What he did reject was dogmatic, uncritical acceptance of foreign ideas about politics or literature.

When he returned to literary circles, Qu could hardly avoid noticing that during his absence the literary world had changed in some ways, yet in other ways had not resolved old problems. Most notable among the changes was the new interest shown in two major schools of Western Marxist literary theory, in part caused by the revolutionary upsurge of the mid-twenties. By 1925 the call for transition from "literary revolution" to "revolutionary literature" made much earlier by Qu and others was finally being heard in some quarters. Romantics like Guo Moruo and Cheng Fangwu probably were motivated more by a voluntarist desire to take decisive revolutionary steps than by any scholarly encounter with Marxist literary theory. In the mid-twenties very little was known about the Western tradition of Marxist literary criticism, but this did not prevent some romantics from declaring themselves Marxists. The interests of realist writers who had been radicalized politically in this period were at first more theoretical and, therefore, less explicitly political than those of the romantics. Thus, they attempted to make available translations of Western Marxist literary theory that stressed the materialist tradition rather than the voluntarist tradition. For example, Lu Xun and other members of the Unnamed Society translated Trotsky's *Literature and Revolution.*

The radicalization of writers and interest in Marxism increased rather than decreased after the counterrevolution of 1927 as the civil war stepped up and Guomindang suppression of its intellectual critics intensified. But despite this new interest in revolution and Marxism, several old problems, such as the isolation of writers from the masses and the factionalism that separated the various literary groups, continued to haunt the movement.

Nothing reflected the development of the contradictory trends of increased radicalism and greater divisiveness more than the debate on the nature of revolutionary literature that took place in Shanghai from 1928 to the beginning of 1930.[20] This was a debate among revolutionary writers who were already interested in Marxism. The liberal Crescent Moon Society had become involved at an early stage, but the significant clash was among the left-wing writers themselves. They agreed that there should be revolutionary literature, but they fought over the nature of revolutionary literature and the role of socially conscious writers.

On one side, there was a dynamic coalition of two romantic groups, the Sun Society and a transformed Creation Society, which called for a specifically proletarian literary movement. Some "veteran" romantics, such as Cheng Fangwu and Jiang Guangci, and especially some younger romantics, such as Qian Xingcun, Zheng Boqi, and Feng Naichao, apparently were influenced not only by certain strains of the "proletarian" literary tradition of Russia discussed above but also by the proletarian cultural movement in Japan, where many of the romantics had studied.[21] Bursting with optimism, they argued that the new proletarian literary movement should concentrate almost exclusively on the condition of the broad masses and should agitate on their behalf. Characteristically, however, they had no illusions that the working class could produce proletarian literature. Instead, they advocated that proletarian literature be written by intellectuals with a genuine "proletarian consciousness." Finally, these romantic Marxists had a very high estimation of the role of literature and artists in the revolutionary struggle. In sharp contrast to Plekhanov and Trotsky, they unabashedly placed the proletarian literary and cultural movement they led in the vanguard of the overall struggle for proletarian revolution. But in spite of accepting certain key aspects of foreign proletarian literary movements, the Chinese romantics accepted neither the antibourgeois and formalist thrusts of the futurist groups nor the anti-intellectual bias of the "pure" proletarian groups in Russia.

On the other side, a much looser coalition of writers emerged from the realist tradition of the Literary Association and its various splinter groups. Led by Lu Xun and some of his young followers, such as Rou Shi, Bai Mang, and Feng Xuefeng, these writers were also revolutionaries who shared a new interest in Western Marxist criticism, but the tradition they studied was the decidedly "nonproletarian" literary tradition of Plekhanov, Trotsky, and the "late" Lunacharsky. It would be misleading to suggest that these writers were not revolutionaries or that their views represented a categorical rejection of the concept of proletarian literature, as in the case of the Crescent Moon Society. Rather, they rejected the romantic Marxists' premature demand for "proletarian" literature. The defeat of 1927 made the realists more pessimistic about an immediate and heroic solution to China's problems. As Lu Xun put it, revolutionary literature in China did not arise from the high tide of revolution, but developed because of a setback in revolution.[22] They rejected the idea that the romantics were uniquely equipped to write about and on behalf of a proletariat with whom they had little direct contact. Further, consistent with the views of Plekhanov, Trotsky, and Lenin, the "realist" Marxists were reluctant to place the literary movement in the vanguard of the revolution. They thought that revolutionary writers should reflect, accurately and honestly, the condition of society from a revolutionary perspective rather than portray heroic and inspiring social relations that did not yet exist.

While these debates reflect the increasing attraction of Chinese writers to different schools of Marxist theory, they also point up the ongoing impact of the May Fourth experience on both these groups. There were important substantive issues in the debates between "bourgeois" romantics and realists in the early twenties, but in both cases the debates often degenerated into totally unconstructive and bitter personal attacks. This May Fourth legacy tended to perpetuate divisiveness among revolutionary writers. And despite the revolutionary rhetoric of both groups, neither could honestly claim it had a base in the masses. Like the "romantic" Marxists, the "realist" Marxists were quite prepared to retain the exclusively intellectual leadership of the revolutionary literary movement and were unwilling to break with the Western bourgeois literary tradition. Thus, in addition to divisiveness, another May Fourth legacy — social isolation — was perpetuated.

The formation of the League of Left-Wing Writers in March 1930 was an extraordinarily significant event. It signaled an end to the hostilities related to the debate on revolutionary literature. The league membership included the most distinguished literary figures brought together in a single group during the Chinese revolution, and as such it represented one of the most unified and dynamic periods of the modern literary scene. Nevertheless, although political and social circumstances brought these luminaries together, their serious differences were not suddenly resolved. The league organization was clearly dominated by the "romantic" Marxists, but Lu Xun was its leading personality. The inaugural resolution, written by romantics, spoke of poets as "prophets" and "leaders of humankind" who stood "in the forefront" of the proletarian struggle.[23] But the sober Lu Xun, in his speech at the first meeting, warned against writers becoming "salon socialists" and expecting special treatment when the revolution was successful.[24]

Despite these obvious difficulties, Qu Qiubai was excited by the new potential of the literary movement. An adviser to the league before January 1931, Qu became its chief policy maker in the three years after his expulsion from the Politburo. As Qu saw it, 1931 was a turning point for the left-wing cultural movement. Alarmed by the intensified internal suppression symbolized by the Guomindang's secret execution of five writers in early February and by the Japanese invasion of China in September, he demanded that radical writers either recognize their mistakes and begin a new period of struggle or risk becoming permanently ineffective and isolated from the revolutionary movement. The league could implement practical programs designed to put revolutionary writers into contact with the people only if its members first examined their own conduct. Inevitably, this process called for an analysis of the May Fourth experience.

Principal Contradictions   In several of his critical essays of this period, Qu used a dialectical analytic method to identify what he considered the primary contradictions of the modern literary movement at various stages of its development. In the first stage of his three-part outline, the 1915–1925 New Culture and May Fourth period, he described the main contradiction in these terms: "Chinese intellectuals of the literati type quite clearly formed into two camps: the tradition-alists and the Westernized school."[25] As a bourgeois-democratic cultural movement, this struggle pitted the die-hard defenders of the decaying traditional culture against iconoclastic young intellectuals advocating Western literary models. But contrary to the beliefs of his old May Fourth colleagues, Qu emphasized repeatedly in the early thirties that the bourgeois-democratic literary revolution had never been completed and concentrated on the failures rather than the successes of the early May Fourth period.

The second period of the modern literary movement, the 1925–1927 stage of "national" revolution, was not dominated by efforts to complete the bourgeois-democratic literary revolution but rather by revolutionary political considerations. "For approximately the period between the May Fourth movement and the May Thirtieth Incident," Qu explained, "thinking circles in China were gradually preparing for the second 'great split.' This was no longer a rupture between retrogression and the new culture, but a *split within the ranks of the new culture* . . . This split, although not completed until the end of 1927, was under way between 1925 and 1926."[26] In literature, this political struggle did not involve further literary reform, but literary content. Believing that the "literary revolution" had been successfully completed, modern writers were now split on the question of whether the new literature should be explicitly political. Whereas most conservative writers defended the literary world's autonomy and resisted the politicization of literature, after 1925 most radical writers asserted that literature could fulfill its social responsibility only by advocating revolutionary change. As shown earlier, Qu himself had been among those who incorrectly assumed that a shift in the political thrust of the literary movement would automatically resolve the purely literary problems that remained.

The most interesting of Qu's stages was certainly the last, from 1928 to the early thirties. The main contradiction in the literary movement was no longer between old culture and new culture as in the first stage, or between revolutionary and nonrevolutionary political orientations within the New Culture movement as in the second stage. The majority of prominent modern writers had become staunchly opposed to Guomindang rule by the thirties. Hence, the main contradictions were between forces in the revolutionary camp itself — particularly between contending factions in progressive literary circles such as the "romantic" Marxists and the "realist" Marxists, and between the masses and Westernized revolutionary intellectuals in general. In fact, Qu argued that past failures precluded an independent bourgeois-democratic revolution in the literary world. Instead, current conditions will require the bourgeois-democratic revolution in literature and art led by intellectuals to merge with the beginnings of a socialist revolution in literature and culture involving the masses themselves.[27] But before the alliance between revolutionary intellectuals and the masses could be achieved, radical writers had to confront the barriers that separated then from the people — especially the intellectuals' extreme iconoclasm and extensive ties to Western literary models. Hoping for open discussions like those of 1928, Qu wrote, "The fact that this debate and conflict have led to a study of principles and theory, and the introduction of genuine revolutionary theories of literature and art, marks a genuinely new chapter in revolutionary proletarian literature."[28]

Consequences of "Westernization": Social Isolation As soon as he returned to the literary world, Qu began to publish articles in league magazines concerning the last of these contradictions — the distance between revolutionary writers and the masses. How could the failure of the dynamic left-wing literary movement to place itself solidly on a mass base be satisfactorily explained? What precisely were the failures of the Westernized May Fourth generation of writers in this regard? In a variety of articles, including " 'Women' shi shui?" (Who are "we"?) and "Ouhua wenyi" (Europeanized literature and art), both written appropriately on the thirteenth anniversary of the May Fourth Incident, Qu gave some fascinating answers to these questions.

Qu believed the problem of social isolation was as old as the literary revolution itself. For a time, the Westernized literary revolution had a political role to play in the social revolution. But he tried to show that by the mid-twenties, May Fourth literary thought no longer had revolutionary political implications. Once the literary revolution had gained its initial victories over traditional culture, the further introduction of Western literature had a decidedly conservative effect. It preserved early triumphs when the rising mass political movement was making entirely new demands on the literary world.

Further, Qu charged that the bourgeois-democratic literary revolution was never fully achieved,[29] because it never really reached beyond exclusive literary societies and because its leaders never sufficiently recognized that what was "bourgeois-democratic" in the West was not necessarily "bourgeois-democratic" in China. Consequently, a major outcome of the literary revolution was that many writers had become "Westernized" and thus isolated from the "non-Westernized" masses who were mostly illiterate and knew nothing of the foreign literary and cultural heritage upon which this literary revolution had been based. In effect, Qu argued that there had been no indigenous bourgeois-democratic literary and cultural revolution in China, merely a transfer of the major features of nineteenth-century bourgeois European culture to Chinese soil. In the process, the age-old scholar-gentry monopoly of traditional literature was replaced by a new Europeanized literature monopolized by a Europeanized intelligentsia — without upsetting the structure of elitism. Particularly disturbing to Qu was his realization that the Western culture these staunchly anti-imperialist writers embraced was that of China's imperialist enemies. May Fourth cultural iconoclasm led early revolutionary writers to the West. But it also cut them off not only from China's despised classical tradition but, more importantly, from China's popular and folk tradition — without which there could be no meaningful link with the masses.

In the West, Qu pointed out, bourgeois-democratic cultural revolution had meant the end of aristocratic monopoly on literature and art and the emergence of a vernacular literature accessible to the broad public. In China, he suggested, neither of these things had happened.[30] Not only did the social stratum that had monopolized literature and reading in traditional times continue to monopolize it after the May Fourth period, but its vernacular (*baihua*) was nothing more than a "new classical" (*xin wenyan*).[31] Qu wrote:

> A Great Wall surrounds the working people, forming a barricade that completely cuts them off from cultural life. What is this Great Wall? It is simply the new classical language of the May Fourth period (the so-called *baihua* literature of today). Regardless of how much it is popularized, so long as it rests on the foundation of new classical language, all the scientific and artistic knowledge of the new period will only be able to reach ten or twenty thousand intellectual youth.[32]

Not only did the "new classical" retain a considerable amount of old classical expressions and structure but it also borrowed heavily from European grammar and vocabulary.[33] New words were invented by writers, and, frequently, untranslated European words were simply inserted in the Chinese text — all of which hampered the spread of the new culture.

Particularly disturbing to Qu's revolutionary colleagues of the early thirties was his assertion that the radicalization of the literary world after 1925 had done nothing to resolve the related problems of the relatively difficult literary style of revolutionary art and its lack of a mass audience. Qu obviously approved of the increasingly revolutionary political posture assumed by modern writers in the mid-twenties, but this political transformation occurred in the framework of the abortive May Fourth bourgeois literary tradition. While Qu did feel that social isolation restricted the diversity of the content (*neirong*) of writing, he was more concerned with questions of form (*xingshi*). One of Qu's most interesting arguments was that the "literary revolution" or revolution in form had not been completed, and as a consequence, the increasingly militant message of modern writers simply was not reaching the masses. In a truly remarkable statement on the effects of Europeanization on radical writers Qu pointed out:

> The indifference of the revolutionary front in Chinese literature to this question [of the masses] is due to the fact that the cadres of revolutionary literature are captives of the bourgeois "May Fourth cultural movement"; the majority of them are standing on the other side of the Great Wall — they do not have a common language with the Chinese working people, and *to the middle and lower ranks of the people they are almost "foreigners." They live in "their own country of intellectual youth" and in the stationery stores of Europeanized gentry.*[34]

In "Europeanized Literature and Art," Qu proclaimed that even the transition to "proletarian literature" had occurred within the framework of the abortive bourgeois-democratic cultural movement. From the outset, intellectuals alone were the leaders in the left-wing literary movement. The leadership and audience for "proletarian literature" remained basically unchanged — the movement had become merely the latest phase of Europeanization. "From the beginning," remarked Qu, "the proletarian literary movement was the recipient of this bourgeois heritage. Consequently, for the longest time it has been separated from the broad masses."[35]

In "Who Are 'We'?" Qu pointed out that the formation of the League of Left-Wing Writers had by no means automatically solved these problems. By openly criticizing the elitist attitude of Zheng Boqi, who was a prominent league member and a participant in a conference on popular literature and art held in 1930 in Shanghai, Qu hoped to focus attention on several romantic pretensions that characterized early efforts to promote a "proletarian literary movement" within the Westernized May Fourth framework. Reflecting on the failures of that movement after 1928, Qu wrote:

> Aside from empty talk, nothing has been accomplished in the last few few years! Of course, the most significant reason is that the proletarian literary movement has not yet gone beyond the stage of "research societies"; it is still an intellectual clique, and not a mass movement. These revolutionary intellectuals — the petty bourgeoisie — have still not resolved to go among the ranks of the working class. They still view themselves as teachers of the people and dare not "go to the people to learn" [*xiang dazhong qu xuexi*]. Consequently, in word they advocate "popularization," but in fact they oppose "popularization."[36]

Further, Qu suggested that Zheng Boqi and other "literary youth" active in the early proletarian literary movement perpetuated the dichotomy between "we," the intellectual leadership, and "they," the masses of followers. The majority of revolutionary writers and "literary youth," he charged, "stand *outside* the people, intent on positioning themselves above the people and instructing the people."[37] Consequently, not only did the masses not read the nonrevolutionary writings of May Fourth writers like Xu Zhimo, they were also unfamiliar with the revolutionary writing of "Europeanized" radicals.[38] "The movement of popularization launched in the past two and a half years has accomplished absolutely nothing," he observed, "yet they still claim that their method is not mistaken!"[39] Qu believed that the real obstacle to establishing a mass base for the literary movement was not the low cultural level of the masses but rather the "Europeanized" attitudes of literary intellectuals. *"The source of this malady,"* he cautioned, *"must be completely uprooted,* otherwise the movement for the popularization of literature and art will be obstructed in a very serious way."[40] What is particularly significant about these remarks is the unmistakable implication that the acceptance of Western Marxist literary theories did not resolve this and other contradictions but only perpetuated them.

Consequences of "Westernization": Internal Conflict Another unique feature of Qu's critical writings of the early thirties is his suggestion that "Westernization" also created a certain amount of factionalism within the league. His articles suggest that "Westernization" had given rise to different views within the May Fourth tradition on the nature of literature and the writer's role. While there were strengths and weaknesses (and potentially revolutionary implications) to many of the views, the cooperation and unity necessary for an effective revolutionary literary movement had not been achieved. These substantive differences among Westernized writers quite often degenerated into bitter personal feuds.

Qu's critical writings dealt mostly with the familiar tension between romanticism and realism, the two most identifiable trends within the league. In fact, his awareness of these general categories can be traced to December 1921, when he rather eloquently expressed the following sentiment:

> Alas, I was born a romantic, who always wanted to transcend the environment and accomplish some miraculous deed that would amaze and move the people. Acts of impulse know no limit, no limit. Yet, since my childhood, I have had a strong bent for the inner strength of realism. I must carefully study reality and do things one by one. The power of reason imposes its dictatorship over me ... If one can reconcile these two streams his efforts may benefit Chinese culture.[41]

Just what were these various strains that Qu saw in romanticism and realism? With regard to romanticism, Qu was concerned with the implications of its fundamentally subjective, idealist, and emotionalist orientation. He was profoundly impressed by certain voluntarist and even social revolutionary tendencies characteristic of romantic thought. This "social" variety of romanticism might supply the literary movement with the spiritual strength necessary to overcome seemingly overwhelming objective restraints. Still, "individual" romanticism might permit the writer's escape from society by transcending and mystifying reality. Such a potentially self-indulgent and decadent path would eventually lead the writer away from revolution. With regard to the realist tradition, Qu was generally attracted to its materialist and scientist tendencies. But while he deeply appreciated the need for revolutionaries to study and understand the infinite complexities of an ever-changing objective reality, Qu was also sensitive to the "naturalist" implications of bourgeois realism. Extreme scientism might give rise to a rigidly deterministic view of the historical process, fatalism, and finally despair — the antithesis of revolutionary zeal. In any case, in his references to these divisive tendencies, Qu never meant that individual writers could be easily identified with the revolutionary or nonrevolutionary portions of the romantic or realist tradition. Romantics were influenced by both the revolutionary and nonrevolutionary strains of bourgeois romanticism as realists were influenced by both the revolutionary and nonrevolutionary strains of bourgeois realism.

An excellent example of Qu's criticism of combined literary and political romanticism occurs in an article entitled "Gemingde lanmandike" (Revolutionary romantic), written as an introduction to *Diquan* (Spring), a novel by the well-known "proletarian" writer and league member Hua Han (Yang Hansheng). Qu's essay is noteworthy precisely because it focuses on the weaknesses rather than the strengths of a close colleague and fellow Marxist. (Interestingly, it is not included in the 1953 Peking edition of Qu's collected literary writings.) Without question, Qu approved of Hua Han's revolutionary intentions. Yet, though he recognized that *Spring* was the "product of a period of difficult times" for the proletarian cultural movement, he regarded the work as a failure caused by romantic excesses. As Qu put it:

> Without question *Spring* contains new ideals and assumes a determination to "transform this world." But *Spring* does not even achieve the goal of commonplace realism. The extremely superficial description obviously reveals that not only is *Spring* incapable of helping to "transform the affairs of this world" but also incapable of even "understanding this world." Thus, *Spring* should be studied by the newly rising literature movement — *as a model of how not to write.*[42]

In Qu's opinion, the language and interrelations of the characters bore little resemblance to reality, and the activities of revolutionaries were not based on any clear analysis of current conditions. The revolution did not advance by sudden change and "heroic individualism" but rather by protracted struggle of the masses — with whom the romantics had very little contact.

In brief, Qu's introduction to Hua Han's novel is not a rejection of the romantic spirit in general but rather of the conception that romantic Chinese Marxists had of proletarian culture. "This sort of romanticism," he stated bluntly, "is an obstacle to the newly rising literature."[43] To league writers he proclaimed, "All these mistakes are worthy of research. We should take the path of dialectical-materialist realism, profoundly recognize objective reality, abandon all self-deceiving romanticism, and correctly reflect the great struggle; only when this occurs will we genuinely be able to help transform the affairs of the world."[44]

Qu's critiques of romanticism by no means suggest that he could find no fault with realist "excesses." In his translation of "Zola's *L'argent*" by the French Marxist Paul LaFargue, and in his review of Mao Dun's *Ziye* (Midnight), Qu was eager to expose the shortcomings of "naturalism" as well.

Qu carefully pointed out that LaFargue's essay was "a Marxist literary critique of 'naturalism'" and the first of its kind to be translated into Chinese. LaFargue strongly approved of Zola's intention of painstakingly and scientifically "analyzing the colossal economic organisms of the modern era," and he regarded this effort as an important departure from familiar European literary accounts of blundering romantic heroes.[45] The proletariat was actually in the best position to expose capitalism, but its cultural backwardness prevented it from articulating this critique. Thus, the task fell to well-intentioned intellectuals who did not themselves "participate in the life of the working class." Despite his admiration for *L'argent*, a novel about the French stock exchange, LaFargue believed Zola had failed in many respects. In a comment that must have impressed Qu as especially relevant to the situation among Westernized realists and naturalists in China, LaFargue proclaimed:

> The novelists of our time, who call themselves naturalists and realists, and who pretend to follow nature, lock themselves up in their workshops and amass veritable mountains of scribbled and printed matter in which they imagine they can detect throbs of real life; they emerge from their comfortable abodes only occasionally for dilettante investigations in order to bring back from excursions the most elementary and superficial sensations ... They claimed that a writer must not only hold himself aloof from the political struggles of his time, but must even remain above human passions, in order the better to describe them.[46]

Qu, of course, objected to the views of those realist writers who maintained that society could be analyzed "objectively" and "scientifically" only by investigators who were not directly involved in the movement for social change. He argued that it was this distance between intellectuals and the masses that required writers to participate in the people's struggle.

LaFargue criticized another important characteristic of naturalist writing — the tendency of these laboratory writers to catalog objectively every detail of social phenomena without drawing any general conclusions about the nature of historical change. A work like *L'argent*, LaFargue observed, "which sets out to describe and analyze social phenomena, ought to express a definite conception of society. However, it does nothing of the sort."[47]

The main thrust of Qu's 1933 review of *Midnight*, a novel about the Shanghai stock exchange, was to identify Mao Dun as a realist who had avoided the dangers of the ahistorical, clinical, naturalist method. *Midnight* was neither a romantic fantasy nor a fatalistic description of "natural" forces. In his novel Mao Dun argued that a truly independent national capitalism had no future in China because of imperialist penetration and competition. In praising the novel, Qu stated:

> This is China's first successful realist novel. Quite obviously it bears the influence of Zola's *L'argent*. Naturally, it has many shortcomings and even mistakes. But in its use of genuine social science, and in its literary expressions of China's social relations and class relations, it cannot be denied that this work represents a great accomplishment. Mao Dun is not Zola; at least he is not a victim of Zola's Proudhonist foolishness.[48]

Qu's admiration for the realist tendencies of Mao Dun and Lu Xun should not obscure the fact that he continued throughout the early thirties to stress the revolutionary and nonrevolutionary implications of both the romantic and realistic schools. Although he probably leaned toward the realist tradition (partly as a result of romantic domination of left-wing literary circles in the late twenties), he had close contacts with both romantics and realists throughout the twenties and thirties. The old Creation Society had published a number of his books in the early twenties, and he had been an official member of the old Literary Association. Acting as an arbiter in the early thirties, he hoped to reconcile the two traditions and end factional strife by identifying the strengths and weaknesses of each school. The romantic spirit of social voluntarism was not incompatible with realist materialism. Indeed, the "convergence" of these two "streams" was essential to the unity and success of the revolutionary literary front. At the same time, the nonrevolutionary aspects of these two bourgeois schools should be openly opposed.

Marxism and the Revolutionary Literary Movement The implications of Qu's critique of the Westernized May Fourth generation were far-reaching for Marxist writers in the early thirties. In effect, Qu was saying that conversion to Marxism among romantics and realists alike had not resolved the two main contradictions of the literary movement: the distance between writers and the masses and the divisiveness among revolutionary writers themselves. Accepting Marxist criticism was within the bourgeois May Fourth literary tradition, he implied, and thus actually perpetuated these problems. In this important sense the introduction of Marxist theory was a "conservative" political trend in the literary world. Western bourgeois romanticism had conditioned romantic responses to Marxism while bourgeois realism had conditioned realist responses. Although both Marxist schools had something to offer, neither had been interpreted with uniquely Chinese conditions in mind. Despite important differences in emphasis between romantic and realist Marxist criticism, neither school questioned the need to preserve the glorious bourgeois "heritage" or the assumption that it was essential to keep the leadership of the literary movement in intellectual hands. Western Marxist ideas in China reaffirmed what was felt to be the fundamental validity of Westernized May Fourth literary values.

While it is true that even by the early thirties relatively little was known about the Western tradition of Marxist literary criticism, two unmistakable trends were emerging among radical Westernized writers. "Realist" Marxists, including Lu Xun, Feng Xuefeng, and others, took a keen interest in the more "conservative" Marxist literary tradition with which Plekhanov, Trotsky, and Lunacharsky were identified, and they busied themselves translating important writings such as Plekhanov's *Unaddressed Letters* and *Art and Social Life,* and two collections of Lunacharsky's works published in China under the titles of *On Art* and *Art and Criticism.*[49] Consistent with aspects of bourgeois realism and naturalism, this Marxist tradition had a rather "conservative" notion of the function of art and the artist. This school did not assign to literature or the writer a leading revolutionary role in society. Stressing the "reflective" nature of literature as part of the superstructure, this tradition saw the arts following history, and reflecting social conditions at a given moment. Writers should study actual conditions. While they may be sympathetic to revolution, scientific and objective observation of reality require that artists not be direct participants and there be no direct link between literature and party politics.[50]

Less studious and more attracted to the "radical" Western tradition of Marxist criticism, the "romantic" Marxists seem to have been influenced more by the various proletarian artistic groups that flourished in Russia and Japan. Consistent with the thrust of bourgeois romanticism, this tradition obviously stressed subjective emotional factors in its promotion of "proletarian" literature and art. Trying to overcome a sometimes restrictive objective reality, romantic Marxists saw literature and writers as leaders in the historical process and in the center of political struggle (although not necessarily under the direction of a political party).

Many of Qu's ideas on the conservative political implication of these Western Marxist schools are contained in remarks on Hu Qiuyuan, a "realist" Marxist, and Qian Xingcun, a "romantic" Marxist, made by him during the brief 1932 debate on the "Third Category" of writers. On this occasion, Qu (and Lu Xun) defended romantics and other league members by fiercely criticizing the demand of Hu Qiuyuan (an early league member and advocate of Plekhanov's aesthetics) and other "Third Category" writers for the total separation of literature and art from partisan politics of the right and left.[51] In essays written in May and October 1932, " 'Ziyu ren' de wenhua yundong" (The "free man" culture movement) and "Wenyide ziyu he wenxuejiade bu ziyu" (Artistic freedom and the writer's lack of freedom), Qu does not merely accuse Hu of misinterpreting Marxist theory. He openly states that Hu advanced Marxist ideas held by Plekhanov, ideas that were inapplicable to China. Qu's articles cautioned left-wing writers about the nonrevolutionary implications of approaching Marxism from the narrow perspective of the "Westernized" May Fourth literary tradition. Left unchallenged, this tradition could easily lead away from revolution.

In essence, Qu objected to Hu's (and Plekhanov's) interpretation of the materialist conception of literature and his conservative view of the role of literature and the artist in society. Following Plekhanov, Hu saw literary works as historical documents that mechanically reflect social conditions. Neither literature nor the writer help make history; rather they consciously or unconsciously reflect class relations in society. To do the job correctly the artist must be a detached observer, not a participant. For Qu, who advocated the writer's political commitment and activism and who believed in literature's revolutionary function, Hu's perspective was far too deterministic. Rejecting the idea that writers could transcend class and remain detached from the process of historical change, Qu observed:

> Hu Qiuyuan's theory is a kind of hypocritical objectivism; he has washed away the strong points of Plekhanov's theory and maximized Plekhanov's Menshevist development to an extreme — transforming it into a hypocritical bourgeois *on-lookerism. In fact he refuses to admit the*

positive uses of art, and refuses to recognize that art can influence social life . . . Of course art cannot effect a transformation of the social system, and must be regarded from beginning to end as being regulated by the mode of production and class relations. But art can also influence social life, and *to a certain degree* advance or block the development of class struggle, changing somewhat the conditions of this struggle, and adding to or weakening the power of a given class.[52]

In Qu's view, the abortive bourgeois-democratic literary movement had failed precisely because it remained "detached" from the masses. Qu repeatedly insisted that such detachment, far from being "objective" and "apolitical," was entirely consistent with Western bourgeois literary values.

While defending Qian Xingcun in his attack on the "realist" Marxist Hu, Qu also pointed out that radical "romantics" had also approached Marxism from their particular May Fourth perspective. Qian, a Creation and Sun Society activist in the "proletarian" literary movement after 1928, was a member of the league's standing committee and a leading spokesman for radical proletarian cultural programs in 1931. Inspired by Russian proletarian cultural groups, Qian, in contrast with Hu, overestimated the importance of literature and art in the revolutionary movement, according to Qu. Noting the tendency of both men to accept uncritically foreign Marxist theories, Qu remarked:

He [Hu] states that Qian Xingcun's theoretical base is confused, that Qian has randomly picked up and integrated aspects of Bogdanov, [the early] Lunacharsky, and the futurists. What about him? He has integrated aspects of Plekhanov, Andreev, and the Art Supremacist Group. *Superficial students of Marxism like Qian Xingcun pick and choose, and manifest petty bourgeois wavering in matters of literary theory and criticism, and do not understand dialectical materialism. I definitely do not want to minimize the mistakes of Qian Xingcun.*[53]

Qu welcomed Qian's voluntaristic interpretation of literature, but he remained mindful of the dangers of extreme subjectivism among romantics and the failure of all May Fourth writers to relate foreign theories to Chinese conditions.

The speed with which the "Third Category" of writers disappeared from the literary scene indicates the increasing politicization of the literary world in the early thirties — in response to the total crisis of Chinese society produced by the Japanese and Guomindang threats. Yet Qu was still alarmed at Hu's attempt to "usurp the title of a true

Marxist" and to put Marxist criticism in the service of bourgeois liberalism at the expense of the politically committed proletarian literary movement.[54] Speaking of Hu's use of Plekhanov, Qu asserted, "Originally Plekhanov's theory contained ingredients of objectivism and a distaste for class orientation, as well as the sprouts of negativist art theory. In the hands of Hu Qiuyuan this theory is mixed with Andriev's thesis and Hu's own thesis with the result that it is transformed into 100 percent *bourgeois liberalism*."[55] Joining Qu's attack on writers who remained politically uncommitted during a severe national crisis, Lu Xun, a Marxist critic himself by 1932, wrote, "No writer living in a class society can transcend class, no one living in a time of wars can leave the battlefield and stand alone."[56]

Perhaps more important, even among the politically committed, was the tendency of both romantic Marxists and realist Marxists to retain the elitist structure of the literary movement. Like Hu Qiuyuan, radical writers did this by focusing on important strains in the Western tradition of Marxist literary criticism. One was the tendency in Western Marxist writings to assume that only experts and professionals were qualified to engage in literary activities. Another was reflected in the writings of revolutionaries from Marx to Lenin — the notion that the proletariat should inherit the splendid cultural "heritage" of the bourgeoisie.[57] As Lenin so succinctly put this noniconoclastic view, "All the culture that capitalism has left us must be carefully preserved and it is on this basis that Socialism must be built; otherwise it will be impossible for us to create the life of Communist Society. And this science, this technique, and this art are in the hands and minds of specialists."[58] This was a reasonable view for Western Marxists, but it did not, of course, have the same meaning in China. Originally attracted to Western bourgeois culture, Chinese iconoclasts found this to be a most welcome element in Marxist literary theory. They tended to interpret its meaning rather literally: the *Western* bourgeois tradition was to be preserved by these Chinese Marxist experts, not their own Chinese cultural tradition. This, Qu believed, was a consequence of early "Westernization," and as such it helped rob the left-wing literary movement of a mass base by ignoring the rich, popular, folk "heritage" of the Chinese people. Many writers had become Marxists, but few of the old Western values had been abandoned. The "heritage" upon which the revolutionary literary movement was based was alien to the Chinese people.

"Westernization" and the May Fourth Generation While Qu's critique of the Westernized May Fourth generation of leftist writers is undoubtedly significant, his writings should not be interpreted as a wholesale rejection of either Western Marxist or bourgeois literary schools. Qu continued to write of Zola, Hugo, Pushkin, and others, and to translate the theoretical writings of Marxists such as LaFargue and Plekhanov. Although he pointed to the failings of writers like Zola and Plekhanov in order to identify the source of May Fourth errors, Qu also recognized and appreciated their contributions, and thus continued to call for Chinese receptivity to foreign ideas. But he was not primarily interested in reminding May Fourth writers of the rich legacy of foreign literature and criticism. On the contrary, Qu's perspective was new precisely because he dwelled upon the tendency of May Fourth writers to embrace foreign schools uncritically and sometimes dogmatically, a tendency that characterized Qu's own early attraction to Marxist aesthetics.

Qu's critique was not a mere intellectual exercise. It came from a practical political concern with the problems and destiny of the leftist literary movement. He focused on May Fourth values and intellectual trends simply because he regarded them as the real source of contemporary literary problems. But the political implications of Qu's work are also important. He was the first Chinese Marxist to analyze the politically conservative aspects of New Culture and May Fourth cultural iconoclasm. The New Culture rejection of various domestic literary traditions was linked to the search for appropriate foreign models upon which to base the modern literary movement. The literary revolution was quite successful, but it continued to be monopolized by the Westernized literary elite, and the "trickling down" of modern culture and literacy never really happened, as it had in the West. The heritage valued by the Westernized May Fourth generation was literally "foreign" to the Chinese people. After the initial New Culture victories, May Fourth writers tended increasingly to "conserve" and "defend" the new values.

Qu was also the first Chinese Marxist to discuss the history of Chinese interest in Marxist aesthetics. His main point was that while May Fourth *political* thinking had been radicalized in the mid-1920s, Chinese interest in Marxist literary theory was shaped by old May Fourth values. Consequently, the revolutionary literary movement, like its New Culture forerunner, never had a mass base. Qu was himself a Marxist critic, but he believed Western Marxist literary theory should be interpreted in light of distinctively Chinese conditions. He argued that aspects of Western Marxist aesthetics tended to perpetuate conservative May Fourth literary values, while other aspects were simply unrelated to Chinese needs.

Finally, in assessing the significance of Qu's critique, it must be pointed out that his concerns continued to be expressed in left-wing literary circles long after his death in 1935. This suggests that the problems he raised were by no means resolved at the time. It is well known that in the forties and later Mao Zedong continued to warn Marxist cultural workers of the dangers of "complete Westernization" and "national nihilism." Indeed, in many ways the cases made against Zhou Yang, Hua Han, and other prominent members of the "Westernized" generation during the spectacular proletarian Cultural Revolution of the sixties were a continuation of arguments made by Qu thirty-five years earlier.[59]

17.

Change and Continuity in Chinese Fiction

Cyril Birch

To assess the role of the May Fourth writers in the development of Chinese literature we need to test the nature of their writings against those of the premodern period and those of the post-Yenan years. A comparison of three portraits from novels of successive generations will reveal not only the unique contribution of May Fourth literature to modern China but also the continuities and changes in Chinese literature between the late Qing and the People's Republic. The continuities are within indigenous traditions, the changes largely in the direction of Westernization.

The three portraits represent men from the late Qing, the republican period, and the People's Republic who are in the same sort of predicament, figures of authority who have aroused antagonism. The first is Prefect Fu, whom we observe hopping half-shod through a hostile mob in chapter 11 of *Wenming xiaoshi* (A brief history of enlightenment, 1906), by Li Boyuan (1867–1906). The second is manufacturer Zhou Zhongwei, playing with dollhouse furniture as his workers clamor outside in chapter 16 of *Ziye* (Midnight, 1933), by Mao Dun (1896–). The third of our beleaguered bosses is village head Zhang Jinfa, staring defiantly at his plow in chapter 34 of *Jinguang dadao* (Golden highway, 1972), by Hao Ran (1932–).

Each of these portraits occurs in an episode about five to seven thousand characters long. The novels from which they are drawn are roughly comparable in length, scope, and literary quality, and exhibit a similar breadth of social concern. If the May Fourth period had been represented by a work of a more obviously subjective, individualistic kind (by Yu Dafu, for example, or even Ba Jin), the experiment might have looked somewhat different, but the results would have shown little change. Most important for the experiment was the selection and analysis of episodes involving situations of a single general kind, the confrontation of an authority figure.

Traditional Fiction and *A Brief History of Enlightenment*

The kind of work that through its unitary structure defines a whole world of human relationships is certainly rare in pre–twentieth-century China. *Hong lou meng* (Dream of the red chamber) is the egregious exception, the creation of genius that put an end to the line of development, as Shakespeare did to poetic drama or *Paradise Lost* to the epic in England. Much more common is the episodic narrative: *Shuihu zhuan* (The water margin), *Rulin waishi* (The scholars), *A Brief History of Enlightenment*. Such works sometimes strike us as little more than collections of tales on a single theme or set of themes. One of the early terms for "short story" was *chuanqi*, "relating the remarkable," and in fact, the great cycles share with the traditional kind of story the emphasis on *qi*, the "remarkable." In the longer works, the very accumulation of episodes and personages creates a "world": there is a "world" of *The Water Margin* in the sense that there is a "world" of Dickens. But on examination we find this world to be only a segment of society and not an organic whole with its full complement of inter-relations such as we derive from *War and Peace* or *Middlemarch* — or *Dream of the Red Chamber*, with its representation of all social levels, from court officer to bond maid.

The traditional narrator functions as technician-demonstrator. He openly avows his technique, constantly telling us "we won't go on with this matter . . . our story forks at this point," and so forth. What he is demonstrating, by and large, is the working out of the laws of destiny, *yinguo*. He shares the norms of his assumed audience, norms marked by common humanity, the distrust of any kind of excess, of evil or even of good (for example, in the late Ming story *Zhen zhushan* (Pearl-sewn shirt), "excess of good" — strict adherence to the moral code — would demand the death of the transgressing wife; in *The Scholars*, there is nothing but ridicule for the man who welcomes his widowed daughter's proposal to immolate herself).

A prevalent mode of traditional fiction is comic-satiric. Underlying all is the sense of social order, which may be disrupted by an ambitious scoundrel, a lustful ne'er-do-well, or a shrewish woman, but will be restored as retribution runs its course. Drama has characteristics of its own but shares much with fiction, both in materials and in modes, and offers the clearest evidence of this "restoration of order" in the obligatory "grand reunion" scene that concludes the Ming southern-style play.

The tragic vision of vain but pitiable strife against overwhelming forces is more rare but is found in a number of works of the highest quality: Tang stories like *Huo Xiaoyu,* Yuan plays like *Dou E yuan* (Sorrows of Dou E) or *Hangong qiu* (Autumn in the Han palace), southern plays like *Pipa ji* (Lute song) and *Taohua shan* (The peach blossom fan), promptbook stories like *Shen Xiaoguan* (The canary murders), and a handful of the greatest romances. The quality of these works is heightened often by the author's superior grasp of the transcendental religious dimension, usually Buddhist-Taoist but Confucian in such an example as *Lute Song,* an early Ming play that of all Chinese works most closely resembles certain Western manifestations of tragic dividedness in the face of conflicting imperatives. There is still the basic urge toward the restoration of order, but this may be possible on the mundane plane only in terms of revenge; otherwise, completion of the action must take place in the next world. The various sequels to *Dream of the Red Chamber* reveal this principle in terms that seem quite ludicrous to modern eyes, by resurrecting the heroine and so on.

In 1905 the traditional system of examinations was abolished. *A Brief History of Enlightenment,* like several other novels of the period, pillories the products of that system as incompetent and venal pedants. The "enlightenment" is primarily the introduction of Western learning in pious hope of modernization. Li Boyuan's novel pokes endless fun at self-styled reformers whose Western learning consists of a couple of misunderstood phrases like "constitutional monarchy," and a penchant for wearing straw hats. A cavalcade of these fools and knaves constitutes the main body of the novel in a minimally structured series of episodes. Chapter 60 halfheartedly imposes a sort of retrospective structure — rather in the manner of Jin Shengtan's "truncated" *The Water Margin* — by having a positive figure, the model administrator Ping Zheng, reject all applicants for the post of assistant in his projected overseas study of constitutional monarchy. The applicants comprise virtually the entire preceding cast of the novel.

The first eleven chapters are much more unitary. Essentially in this lively section the author seems to be pronouncing the bankruptcy of the imperial system of administration. Unrest and catastrophe result from the opening incident, an innkeeper's breaking of a teacup that happens to belong to an Italian mining prospector. The local prefect, Liu, is an honest and humane man, but hopelessly indecisive and incompetent. He is replaced by our man, Prefect Fu, a self-proclaimed martinet whose prescription for the troubles is to flog the ringleader until the court runs with blood. "First try soft, then try hard"; but neither Liu's soft way nor Fu's hard way can restore harmony to this corner of China at the turn of the century, and Prefect Fu in his turn is recalled. In chapter 11, the "spontaneous" demonstration of popular affection he organizes for himself backfires as the mob turns hostile.

The mode of narration of the *Brief History* is, in Patrick Hanan's useful phrase, the "simulated context" of the storyteller addressing his audience. Consequently, there is much intrusion on the part of the narrator, a good deal of commentary, a continuing dialogue with the postulated listener. At least six interpolations in this short episode explain plot developments: one is introduced by "formerly . . .," two more by direct question of the audience. When the hostile crowd confronts the prefect, the narrator describes the targets of their hostility, then asks the audience, "What do you think caused this?"

Though he is one of the more important characters in the novel, Prefect Fu is presented as little more than a humor, a caricature of the splenetic. He establishes his own character in a speech in chapter 6:

> The people of the region are obstinately set in their ways. After taking up my duties as magistrate there, I attempted to lead the populace in the right way, but whenever I came up against individuals who refused to accept my instructions, I would treat one or two with the greatest severity and make examples of them. The result was that the people were afraid to misbehave.

The principal method of depiction is "killing with borrowed blade": in a long dialogue discussing Prefect Fu, his secretary is a straight man, and the local magistrate, a very effective cynic with a low view of Fu's character. The revelation of the prefect's true cowardice is withheld to the end of the episode, when he cowers in a peasant hut. The author shows us very little else of Fu's physical or moral individuality.

It is difficult to see any kind of narrative flow in this episode. The technique gives rather a kind of scattershot effect. Each new sentence seems to have a different subject. Loose or unstated subject-predicate relationships allied with the lack of any consistent center of vision further dissipate the shifting focus. An example is the following passage, summarizing the preparations for the "spontaneous" demonstration:

> The secretary followed the instructions of the district magistrate by

handing over some money, finding a tailor, and having the farewell umbrellas made up. Discussion with his attendants elicited the names of a couple of clerks who had formerly received favors at the hands of the prefect, and they were instructed to organize the rest of the clerks so that they would all appear at the appropriate time, wearing official hats and gowns, to present the umbrellas. On this day, Prefect Fu allowed the clerks to put on this show without ever seeing through the pretense; though if [they?] [he?] had seen through it, [they?] [he?] could hardly have let on out of concern for face.

The rapidly switching subjects of the first part of the passage depict a riot of delegated authority, a glorious general irresponsibility — obviously it is never going to be possible to identify the agent of any particular action. In the final sentence of commentary, the ambiguity of reference of the ungoverned verbs lends a sense of all-around duplicity.

Throughout, the narrative is studded with formally ungoverned verbs, *dengdao* (wait till), *yao* (wanting to), *nianqilai* (reading this). The actual subject of each seems to be narrator plus reader. A distancing effect and an ironical tone are achieved by this alliance to observe "from above" the activities of these clownish creatures.

In these ways the narrative method is appropriate for the satirical purpose. In other ways a certain primitiveness is observable: in the opening of almost each new section, for example, with a time phrase, "wait till," "at that time," "on this day."

The language of the episode shows few features worth particular comment, but the inevitable classical tags and allusions that crept into the late vernacular novels are often used here to special effect. Use of examination slang (*jiao juan*, hand in paper) in a quite nonspecific context to mean simply "finish," or the description of a beating (*da ta yige buyilehu*, walloped him a not-indeed-delightful) serves very well to underline the pedantic absurdity of the prefect and his associates. The endemic concern for face is indicated by many examples of a very concrete kind of vocabulary: *koubei* (reputation), *fengwen* (rumor), *yan ermu* (bamboozle), *bubian chu kou* (indiscreet).

The message of the episode, in fact of the whole of the opening section (chapters 1–11), is obliquely summarized by the opening commentary of chapter 12, when Fu is replaced by another prefect. Whether this man is benevolent and beloved or ferocious and feared, "the author of this book cannot spare the time to elaborate."

At the time Li Boyuan is writing, the dynasty has finally been discredited by its association with the xenophobic Boxers. Reform seems to be stymied; revolution is in the air, but there is little faith that even revolution can save China from being "carved like a melon" by the foreign powers. The troubles that have brought down both Prefect Liu and Prefect Fu originated in a mischance involving an Italian mining prospector, perfect epitome of foreign exploitation. The situation is desperate, and when the man in charge is fundamentally concerned only with his own face, then it makes little difference what his personal qualities might be: the author "cannot spare the time to elaborate." All he can do is express, through the mouth of Ping Zheng in the last chapter of the novel, a basic moral stance: "In our classics we are told that one should delight in establishing his virtue, his merit, and his words, and that these three things shall endure imperishably. Nowhere is there any mention of wealth and honor, failure or success."

The May Fourth Writers and *Midnight*

The most startling new feature of the fiction published just after the literary revolution of 1917–1919 was not its Westernized syntax nor its tone of gloom but the emergence of a new authorial persona. The storyteller pose was dropped, and the narrator became one with the implied author and often with the author himself. The prime example is Yu Dafu, and "Chenlun" (Sinking) is the clearest illustration of the self-revelation, almost the exhibitionism of the romantic rebel.

"A Q zhengzhuan" (The true story of A Q), with all its brilliant irony, does not seem quite so characteristic of Lu Xun as "Zhufu" (Benediction) or "Guxiang" (Native place). The first-person narrator of these stories is heavily autobiographical, Lu Xun in his persona as a superfluous man, silent and useless before the old woman's urgent question ("Is there such a thing as a soul?") in "Benediction," appalled by realization of the barrier that separates him from his boyhood peasant companion in "Native Place."

Jia (Family) eliminates the first-person narrator but is still avowedly autobiographical. In the third brother, Juehui, Ba Jin offers us a self-portrait of the revolutionary in quest of a better world. Ding Ling in her romantic, preproletarian phase offers us the feminine counterpart in "Shafei nüshi de riji" (Diary of Miss Sophie).

Works of this kind introduce a new seriousness into Chinese fiction and still impress us as the heart-cry of a generation that felt itself to be deracinated and its culture bankrupt. But seriousness can be a double-edged sword. Fiction began, and at its very best succeeds, as entertainment. One of the reasons we read *War and Peace* is to find out what happens next — will Natasha *never* marry Pierre? Plot is a positive virtue in *The Mayor of Casterbridge* or *Intruder in the Dust;* would we really accuse Hardy or Faulkner of pandering to popular whim by actually telling a story?

The "good stories" were told by those May Fourth writers who largely eschewed the autobiographical, Lao She, Zhang Tianyi, and the like. (Shen Congwen had the advantage of an extraordinarily fertile personal past, so that his own autobiography reads with an excitement superior to most of his fiction.). Yet in Lao She, we find a vision no less individual. The new respect, gained from Western models, for unitary structure permits the presentation of a total "world" when it combines with a truly inventive fictional imagination. This kind of fictional world is specifically *not* the "real world." Maxim Gorky has a story, "The Cemetery," in which a scheme is proposed to record every significant fact about every living individual. But neither all-inclusiveness nor random selection will suit the novelist's purpose. He must fall back some distance in the direction of the remarkable (*qi*), at least as far as the outstandingly representative: he must to some extent choose types (*dianxing*), figures that are heightened and thus more typical, as Mao Zedong tells us in a frequently quoted passage.

This was the great achievement of the May Fourth writers, to establish unforgettable types like the tycoon Wu Sunfu in *Midnight,* the old woman Xianglinsao in Lu Xun's "Benediction," Lao She's rickshaw boy and the rest. Mao Dun came closest to totally objectifying his individual vision: it is much easier to recognize the lyricism of Shen Congwen, the hard-bitten naturalism of Zhang Tianyi, the claustrophobia of Zhang Ailing.

If we had to characterize an overall mode, we might call it tragic-ironic in comparison with the comic-satiric of the past. Irony provided some defense against nihilism for Lao She contemplating his hypocritical philanthropists or Zhang Tianyi his petty bullies. The old feeling of order disrupted and restored is gone: order itself is gone, the world is in chaos, any kind of happy ending unthinkable. If in traditional fiction we can distinguish two dominant attitudes, one of them norm-sharing and communal celebration (*Pearl-Sewn Shirt, The Scholars*), and one more individual, relatively alienated (*Huo Xiaoyu, Dream of the Red Chamber*), then it is the latter attitude that characterizes the May Fourth writer. The "communal" waits in the wings — waits for Liberation.

The writer chosen to represent the May Fourth period in this experiment is Mao Dun. His major novel *Midnight*, in sharp contrast with the rambling *A Brief History of Enlightenment,* presents a tight overall dramatic structure. The magnificent opening chapter (the old man's ride through the streets of Shanghai) is both a microcosm of the whole novel in the manner of the Zhen Shiyin episode in the first chapter of *Dream of the Red Chamber* and an allegory comparable with the opening dream of *Lao Can youji* (Travels of Lao Can). The death of the old man sets up the funeral gathering of chapters 2 and 3, where dialogues among changing groups, prefiguring future plots and subplots, recall the kaleidoscope of Anna Pavlovna's soiree at the beginning of *War and Peace.*

Zhou Zhongwei, match manufacturer, associate, and unsuccessful rival of Wu Sunfu, is a minor figure in the total scheme, but the central protagonist of chapter 16. The subplot built about him effectively demonstrates the plight of the native Chinese industrialist. Zhou Zhongwei is spotlighted, an isolated and harassed figure, on the balcony of his residence. From the alley below he is badgered by locked-out workers angered by the closing of the match factory, which has been losing to Swedish competition. Inside his house, two financier acquaintances wait to advise him to sell out to the Japanese. Caught between the devil of exploited labor and the deep blue sea of foreign capital, this Chinese industrialist vividly personifies one of the most profound dilemmas of modern, pre-Communist China as Mao Dun perceived it.

The setting for Zhou's big scene is cleverly crafted. All action through a sequence of some seven thousand characters takes place at Zhou's residence. The guarded alley is the outside world where the workers wait, chafing under police control; Zhou's sitting room is his private dream world of toys, to which his favored financier friends are admitted; the balcony symbolizes Zhou's attempted mediation between labor without and capital within. Tensions are exacerbated by the hot weather, from the workers' delegates baking on the concrete sidewalk at the start of the sequence to the beads of sweat on Zhou's forehead as he ends his negotiations with them.

Notable developments in the dramatic buildup of the sequence are the effective first indication of Zhou's presence, a burst of laughter from up on the balcony; the hasty entrance of Zhou's rickshaw man to report the delegates' second visit; the heads suddenly visible at the window as Zhou and the financiers discuss strategy; and the final confrontation when the workers have gained admission to the house and Zhou makes his last desperate gamble to con them out of their strike threat. The entire development alternates between two foci,

Zhou on the one hand and the workers on the other. All is objectively rendered; at no point does Mao Dun as narrator intrude upon the action; when background information is required, it is presented in documentary form (Zhou shows his associates the letter from the Manufacturers' Association).

As the central figure of this subplot, Zhou Zhongwei is fully individualized. We know his height, features, complexion, gait, voice, and manner. He is ugly, toadlike (this is a recurrent image for him: in chapter 3 he "squats on the floor and hops about like a frog, clicking his tongue and balancing Xu Manli's shoes on his head"). He has a nickname, "the Red-Tipped Match." A fake from start to finish, he reveals the increasing strain of his pretended casualness by an increasing shortness of breath. His toys symbolize his divorce from reality. Turning from the impending collapse of his enterprise, he devotes himself in his den to reconstruction of "the rituals of the defunct Qing dynasty." With enormous care and gusto, he arranges a set of dollhouse furniture, tiny chairs and a three-inch white curtain, in rehearsal of the anticipated funeral of his wife, who lies sick in the next room. It is a perfect image of make-believe, the essential symbol contrasting Zhou with the novel's central protagonist, Wu Sunfu, who is "ambitious, adventurous, and plucky, and . . . hates to see good industries go to rack and ruin in the hands of inexperienced, inefficient, timorous, or mediocre men" (chapter 3).

Syntactical relations, such as the explicitness of the sentence subject and its link with the predicate, are conspicuously tighter and more logical in Mao Dun's prose than in Li Boyuan's. Logic governs the development of the paragraph, as for example when the workers first reach Zhou's house: the narrowness of the alley restricts the number who can approach nearer, therefore delegates must be chosen. It may be worth investigating whether the import of paragraphing from the West did not impose a new discipline on writers like Mao Dun. Where the traditional "paragraph" (unmarked) was often coterminous with the meandering sentence itself, we now have a carefully constructed unit with a single center of vision. The action, sentence by sentence, of *Midnight* flows much more explicably from the situation and the characters; there is less of the sense that anything may happen next.

Since Mao Dun is moving in the modern world of delegates, insurance companies, stockbrokers, his extensive vocabulary inevitably contrasts with the more tradition-bound terms of *A Brief History of Enlightenment*. Some of his neologisms are oddly dated now, such as "Huaqiren" for Americans and "Jiamenren" for Germans. What seems surprising, until we recall the essentially old-fashioned mentality of characters like Zhou Zhongwei, is the number of highly traditional metaphors. Zhou is a *laihama* (scabby toad — seeking a taste of swan's flesh, as the old cliché runs); at the end of the episode, his past prosperity seems to be *yichang meng, yige xunhuan* (a dream, a revolving wheel). In an apt allusion to popular tradition, Zhou hoodwinking his workers is compared with Zhuge Liang's ruse of the empty city in *San guo yanyi* (Romance of the three kingdoms).

Compared to Li Boyuan, Mao Dun presents a highly individualized authorial persona. He is not merely a sniper taking potshots at targets that every reader will immediately recognize as ridiculous but an analyst offering a fully integrated interpretation of the ills of his society. The portrayal of Zhou Zhongwei is rounded, realistic, and convincing. Mao Dun demonstrates exactly how Zhou, the would-be tycoon, is forced by external pressures and by his own incompetence to retreat from reality into a make-believe realm of his own. *Midnight*, the novel of which the Zhou episode forms a small part, uses the techniques of Western realism to depict the total "world" of Shanghai facing the menace of the depression years. In these ways, Mao Dun effectively represents the achievements of the May Fourth writers.

Post-Yenan Writers and *Golden Highway*

Mainland fiction of the last thirty years reveals many traditional features underlying the surface newness. Most conspicuous is the renewed sense of a social order. Zhao Shuli's character Li Youcai is an outstanding example of the storyteller quite in the traditional style and deliberately recalling the old popular forms, who identifies himself with the norms of his presumed audience (though, of course, the audience itself has changed from urban to peasant). The predominant mode reverts to comic, as destiny works itself out through the Marxist dialectic of struggle that takes the place of the old karma process. The satiric tone is much softened. *Foibles* (the satirist's prime target) in positive characters seem less and less permissible as time goes on; *faults* must be seriously identified and corrected, and this is not a function of satire. As the society becomes more consolidated, the emphasis shifts from "antagonistic" to "nonantagonistic" contradictions; in consequence, the black villain — counterrevolutionary, Japanese officer, landlord — has given place to the revisionist or individualist waverer. This is why the middle peasant Zhang Jinfa is much more conspicuous than the landlord in Hao Ran's *Golden Highway*. As class distinctions blur and conflicts become more subtle, the type portraits take on sharper edges. Most revisions of model operas like *Hong deng ji* (Red lantern) tend in this direction.

With the shift of gears from karma to dialectic, we are shown not so much a restoration of order as an advance to a new and superior order. But the means of demonstration is the same: the formula. The "cooperative story" (individual holdout tries to go it alone, fails, realizes the benefits of cooperation, joins, celebration) is as explicit a formula as one can find even in Ming drama (lovers are betrothed, reduced to mutual distrust by machinations of rich young wastrel, reunited when truth is brought to light, celebration). A formula once identified is difficult to describe without seeming to denigrate the quality of the work concerned. Yet this is an unnecessary consequence of our modern Western obsession with originality. A story like Zhou Libo's *Shanxiang jubian* (Great changes in a mountain village) manages to invest the co-op formula with a strong sense of reality and considerable interest.

In conscious reaction to the May Fourth writers, the new men strive to entertain. We see this in the wealth of incident of war stories like *Lüliang yingxiong zhuan* (Heroes of Lüliang), in Hao Ran's vivid characterization and fondness for suspense, and clearest of all, in the sparkling uniforms, acrobatic leaps, and tense situations of model operas like *Shajiabang.*

Where the May Fourth writers were committed to the antihero, the explicit aim now is the creation of heroic models. Often this takes the form of legend building, as it did in the past in works like *Three Kingdoms. Bai mao nü* (The white-haired girl) is a fair candidate for legendary, even mythical status — there is something quite blood-chilling in her movie image, poised in a lightning flash against a background of jagged peaks. Gao Daquan in Hao Ran's *Golden Highway* is the fictional equivalent of the real life Lei Feng or other subjects of deliberate legendization.

The return to the more public or communal manner has naturally meant the abandonment of individual style, that hallmark of the May Fourth writer. Though the process is not yet complete and complex Westernized syntax still occurs where the writer's control has slackened for a moment, the preference is clearly for the short, blunt sentence enriched by earthy and picturesque metaphor. That such a style may be rich and vivid should be apparent from the illustration from Hao Ran, below.

At this point, we should bear in mind some aspects of the political control of literature in China. We know that a great deal of the traditional literature survived frequent and large-scale proscription. It is ironic that *Jin ping mei* (Golden lotus) is more accessible now in English than it has ever been in Chinese. To avoid proscription on political (rather than moral) grounds, writers of the past developed numerous techniques. They might circulate their works privately, as happened with *Dream of the Red Chamber* and *The Scholars,* or they might edit drastically, as Jin Shengtan edited *The Water Margin.* Best of all were the many subtle devices of allusion and the use of historical time settings, for example vilifying the Song dynasty traitor Qin Gui in order to arouse public sentiment against Ming appeasers of the Mongols or the Manchus.

Government censorship of the May Fourth writers was sufficiently ruthless to make martyrs of Hu Yepin and Rou Shi but insufficiently organized to establish anything like national control. The Guomindang never effectively governed more that a few provinces, and even there, the foreign concessions played an important role in protecting antiestablishment writers from Lu Xun down.

Probably all of the above safety precautions are being observed in China at present, though it is impossible to tell from outside whether much private circulation of works goes on. Most prevalent is the historical time setting. Wu Han's play *Hai Rui ba guan* (Hai Rui withdraws from office) is a good example, though the attempt to avoid proscription failed spectacularly. The play, set in the Ming dynasty, was interpreted as an attack on Mao and served to spark the Cultural Revolution. Few new works go back so far into the past. The safe period, favored by novelists and the revolutionary model operas alike, seems about 1930 to 1950. The short story, on the other hand, seems to be a much more ephemeral and disposable kind of vehicle in present-day mainland use and is more likely to have a contemporary setting.

Editing to bring into line with current policy is most conspicuous in the model operas, which offer so many advantages. Since their form is never to be regarded as final, they can be continuously trimmed to eliminate any trace of bourgeois revisionism, as *Red Lantern* has been pruned of excess family sentiment or materialistic concerns. They are hospitable to elements from local traditions, Peking Opera or other.

Finally, we must emphasize that we have been speaking almost exclusively of the mass manner of the new writers. A case could be made for the existence of a cadre (*ganbu*) literature that clings like moss to a dry wall, becoming visible only with the occasional, perhaps increasingly rare, relaxations of national tension. The 1956–1957 issues of *Renmin wenxue* (People's literature) contained pieces of a very peculiar interest, which may have reposed in desk drawers until that brief, halcyon Hundred Flowers interlude.

This "peculiar interest" of pieces like "Meili" (Beauty), "Zuzhibu xinlaide qingnian" (The young newcomer to the organization section), or "Benbao neibu xiaoxi" (Inside story), is not from any cynical glee on our part that they dig the dirt, nor even that they seem more real, less idealized, but that they seem specifically to be addressed to the cadre community rather than to the masses. This is the only conclusion we can draw from their complex language and from their themes of cadre life: how to cope with bureaucracy, how to maintain enthusiasm in the face of apathy and physical weariness, how to detect and expose the frauds. They were "revisionist" and were condemned as such; but the "revision" was strictly in accordance with Mao's directive to handle contradictions among the people (in this case, within the party) by means of criticism and education.

In contrast with such cadre-oriented, revisionist works, Hao Ran's stories represent the mass style. Hao Ran was born in 1932, son of poor peasants in Hopei. He became an editor of the party organ *Hong qi* (Red flag) at thirty and is the most prolific writer to have sailed over the dam of the Cultural Revolution.

The first part of his new novel took almost all of 1971 to write. The "golden highway" is the road toward organization and socialist cooperation, which, in 1951, a year after the land reform in Hopei province, the peasants are just beginning to discover. The party leadership has issued the slogan, "Labor to Develop the Home, Produce for Prosperity." Backsliders have significantly shortened this to "Develop Home Prosperity." Zhang Jinfa, village head and party member, even announces a "Home Development Contest." Under this banner he leads the more affluent villagers on a campaign for self-enrichment that threatens to exploit their poorer neighbors.

Gao Daquan, fellow party member, heads the opposition to this group and leads the activists and the poor of the village onto the golden highway by working selflessly for the common good, especially by helping the poorest peasants complete their spring sowing. This is at a time, in the earliest years of the new republic, when the fruits of the revolution and of the land reform are threatened by a cruel shortage of the means of production, especially of draft animals for the spring plowing.

Chapter 34 of *Golden Highway* develops a confrontation between Gao Daquan and Zhang Jinfa who, rather than freely helping out a poor neighbor, is exploiting the latter's dilemma by renting his plowing team to him. In building the confrontation, Hao Ran uses a characteristic trick, a misapprehension to develop suspense. Gao mistakenly thinks Zhang is donating his labor, and stands admiring the excellence of Zhang's plowing, until he discovers the truth of the situation. He harangues Zhang, who defends himself, and the episode ends with long propagandistic speeches from Gao on the virtues of the new ethic of selflessness in cooperation for communal advance.

Use of the poor peasant activist Gao Daquan as principal center of vision is consistent with the biographical structure of *Golden Highway* and with its dominant theme of Gao's expanding political consciousness. As compared with works of the fifties, *Golden Highway* stresses mass self-reliance; there is much less preaching by party seniors. Gao makes his own discoveries; he has some guidance, but even the mutual-aid team is "independently" invented by villagers before advice on large-scale application is provided by the leadership. Gao is our guide whenever he is present. "From the look of the plot, they had started plowing that morning" — that's the way it looks to *Gao*, not to the narrator. The earth's scent is smelled by *Gao*, not "one." Yet authorial intrusion is not rare, for example, "These words seems to hit Zhang Jinfa like the sudden discovery of some subtle mystery" — seemed to whom? To the narrator. When Gao has berated Zhang, "unfortunately Zhang couldn't think of anything to say for the moment, and never would." The "unfortunately" is authorial sarcasm, the "never would," authorial prediction.

Gao Daquan is the supreme new type of the poor peasant who owes everything to the revolution, who dedicates himself to the service of the community and accepts with alacrity leadership and guidance from the Communist party. He is physically strong, personally frugal, a tireless worker, thoughtful, and patient with those less perceptive than himself. His rising level of political consciousness is revealed in his words. In the dispute with Zhang Jinfa, the "new phrases" all come from Gao's lips: "people's government," "serve the people," "sacrifices of the revolutionary martyrs," "strengthen industrial development," and so on. The village head doesn't use this language, unless in sarcastic echo of Gao. The obligatory quotations from Chairman Mao, set in boldface type, are all spoken in Gao's presence and find in him their most enthusiastic reception.

Zhang Jinfa is not exactly colorless as a negative character, though only a flat sketch when compared with Mao Dun's rounded portrait of Zhou Zhongwei. He is a man of force and initiative: a skillful farmer, as his plowing indicates; and a born leader, appointed village head in recognition of his active role at the time of Liberation when he single-handedly tracked down and brought to book the villainous landlord, his former employer. The problem is that he is using his formidable energy and authority to reintroduce all those bourgeois values the new society has renounced: self-help for personal enrichment, scorn for those less fortunately situated, and even the willingness to exploit one's fellows, to "squeeze a bit of fat out of your poor brothers," as Gao Daquan puts it.

An interesting contrast with the able farmer Zhang Jinfa occurs in chapter 42, when Gao Daquan observes the pathetic efforts of a poor peasant neighbor to plow unassisted his newly acquired land. Here is Hao Ran's style at its happiest:

> Suddenly Gao Daquan spotted an unplowed plot in the midst of the fields of newly turned earth. The ground was as hard as a plastered wall, layered white with alkaline salts, salt grass piercing up like knife blades amid the mildewed corn stubble.
>
> Gao's heart started to thump like a drum as he tried to work out whose land this must be. A few steps further on he found some furrows newly turned along one edge of the field. They were shallow, littered down their length with clods big and small, their surface dotted with specks of seed corn in full view. Whose land was this not properly plowed, just peppered with seed in furrows still half stubble? How could you grow a crop out of this? With these questions going through his mind, he looked up, and something in his head went "bam" like a thunderclap.
>
> It was nobody else's field but Deng Jiukuan's. There was Deng himself driving Fifth Song's little donkey and guiding a broken plow, sketching a faint line across the rock-hard, white-crusted salt grass field. Leading the beast was his boy Black Ox, and his wife followed behind sowing from a wicker basker.

The passage merits comment in some detail. There is still an air of the traditional storyteller about it, fostered by the short sentences, the step-by-step progression, the rhetorical questions, and also by specific phrases, "thump like a drum," "something . . . went 'bam' like a thunderclap," "nobody else's but" But actually Hao Ran is not posing as a storyteller here. His center of consciousness is still Gao Daquan. The norms of the novel are his, and it is because we have accepted them that we respond to his sense of shock at such a shoddy piece of farming. We see through his eyes, in cinematic detail, the poorly plowed field, down to the telling last close-up of the seed lying exposed on the salt soil. We look up and see Deng's family team with the pathetic borrowed donkey. It is another extraordinarily effective buildup to a dramatic confrontation.

If it has this effect on us, we can easily imagine the responses of the primary audience, the peasant readership who would almost tangibly feel the rock-hard unyielding earth and the heartbreak of the wife, vainly going through the motions of sowing, actually throwing away the precious seed corn. With biblical simplicity, Hao Ran brings home two major lessons: what poverty the peasants faced a generation ago (the time is the first years after Liberation), and how futile were the attempts to conquer this poverty until the peasants organized for collective effort.

This brief confrontation itself is one of the most satisfying things in the book, for it reveals human weakness in the paragon Gao Daquan. Frustration and chagrin (he has been driving himself to the limits to urge his fellow villagers to cooperate in the plowing) lead Gao to burst out in a tirade against his friend Deng. His rage is misdirected, of course, and he regrets it later. But he becomes more believable for this fault, which is the consequence of an excess of generous concern.

Hao Ran's vivid images are drawn from the heart of peasant life. The house built by the backsliding village head Zhang stands out against those of his poorer neighbors "like a camel among sheep"; approaching the house, Gao smells frying onions (luxurious diet) and sees dogbane in bloom (purely ornamental, and poisonous). But Zhang is a good farmer: the earth he has plowed has "risen like bread." His fault is his mercenary mentality — he "shakes his head like a peddler's drum."

Hao Ran loves symbols — the ax that roots out an obstructive tree, the rope that gains strength from the union of many strands — that recall the old storytellers and dramatists. He can go to excess, for example by his overuse of the master image of redness (black heart, red heart) or by such an inflated image of Gao Daquan's righteous anger as "sparks seemed to come from his eyes as they widened into an angry glare." Perhaps the obligation to reflect revolutionary fervor forces such exaggerations. He is after all producing a kind of official literature. Yet, he has not entirely freed himself from the complex syntax of the petty bourgeois: it is not exactly proletarian to write "*Gao Daquan conglai meiyou ba ta digu dao xiang ta jintian ziji biaoxianchulaide zhezhong beixiade chengdu*" "Gao Daquan had never held [Jinfa] at as low a level as today he had proclaimed for himself").

The really distinctive new feature of *Golden Highway* is surely the portrait of the positive model of socialist manhood, Gao Daquan. This must be the explanation of the novel's enthusiastic reception in this post–Cultural Revolution period. Almost two decades earlier Zhao Shuli wrote a major novel, *Sanliwan* (Three-mile bend), similar in theme and furnished with a parallel set of representative characters, young activists, selfish rich peasants, backsliding village head, and so on. But Zhao Shuli himself recognized that the success of *Three-Mile Bend* was vitiated by the weakness of the positive characters. The villains were so much more lively. As Zhao explained, he had lived longer in the old society and knew its people better. Like so many other established writers, Zhao Shuli was discredited during the Cultural Revolution. Hao Ran has replaced him, and Hao Ran, in his teens at the time of Liberation, is solving the problem set by the theory of revolutionary romanticism — how to move forward from exposing old abuses to celebrating the new ethic without losing your readers in the process. *Golden Highway* is his solution.

Holding in mind the figures of these three beleaguered bosses, Prefect Fu, Zhou Zhongwei and Zhang Jinfa, we may note some further contrasts. Each of these men represents sociopolitical concerns that predominated in their respective eras: Prefect Fu, the problem of educating administrators; Zhou Zhongwei, the possible role of private enterprise in China's historical development; Zhang Jinfa, the question of organizing the peasant masses. Through the three works, there is a significant descent in the social level of the protagonist, from prefect to private industrialist to village head.

Conversely, the role of the mass figure gains in weight. The prefect's charges, the members of the populace, in *A Brief History of Enlightenment* remain faceless. No names are given — not even to the peasant owner of the hut in which Prefect Fu shelters in his final predicament. The workers and their delegates in Mao Dun's *Midnight* function essentially as a group: only two are actually named. In *Golden Highway*, there is no unnamed character. Hao Ran often uses an interesting schematic device to list multiple reactions to an event or a speech: when Gao Daquan upbraids Zhang Jinfa, X is enthusiastic, Y bewildered, Z unconcerned, but no one in the group of characters is left without at least this minimal degree of participation or left unnamed.

Overall, we may see the incident of Prefect Fu in *A Brief History of Enlightenment* as intriguing but meretricious. Li Boyuan's targets are comprehensive but superficial, because of his limited understanding of the historical situation. Everything is going wrong, but he doesn't know why. So he can only erect a rickety structure of ridicule.

In presenting his great panorama, *Midnight*, Mao Dun is as doctrinaire as Hao Ran in his analysis but remains unhampered by the need to promote any specific political program. His thoroughly researched understanding of contemporary society and his firm grasp of the methods of social realism permit convincing characterization and a thoroughly dramatic presentation of the incident concerning Zhou Zhongwei, as of all other incidents. He takes no explicit stand on Zhou's faults but shows us the man's inevitable defeat and his retreat into his private world of make-believe.

There is an interval of close to seventy years between *A Brief History of Enlightenment* and *Golden Highway* — about the same length of time that separates *Bleak House* and Joyce's *Ulysses*. Hao Ran enjoys large technical advantages: the colorful saws and symbols of the old vernacular tradition plus the more systematic narrative flow developed by the modernizers. He is modern in his manipulation of centers of vision, cinematic in his close-up shots and fondness for the flashback (always useful to recall the bad old days of poverty and oppression).

Underneath the surface newness, however, we find the old bugbear of predictability. The laws of dialectics turn Zhang Jinfa into just the same kind of straw figure as Prefect Fu. The demands of the positive hero rob Hao Ran's story of its tension and steer it toward melodrama as the incident stiffens into a mere scaffolding for Gao Daquan's oratory.

Realist Fiction in China

However much we may admire and be indebted to C. T. Hsia's excellent book *The Classic Chinese Novel*, it may be necessary at some time to ask whether any of the works he discusses is actually a novel. Certainly the term "novel" is elastic in the extreme; it is as Henry James said, the "prodigious" form. But if we turn from consideration of the realist fiction of nineteenth-century Europe and apply this same term "novel" to *Three Kingdoms, Dream of the Red Chamber*, and so on, surely we obscure more than we clarify and reduce our critical vocabulary almost to meaninglessness. We are lured into doing this by the powerful doses of formal realism we find even so far back as *The Water Margin*, the superfine skill of the Chinese narrative art developed by the union of historian and marketplace storyteller. But we shall understand these works more fully if we begin by defining them not as novels but as romances. (*Dream of the Red Chamber* is a classic instance of the romance defined in Northrop Frye's "Theory of Myths"), allegories (*Xiyou ji*, [Journey to the west]), or perhaps as something sui generis for which we must borrow an indigenous label (such as *jiangshi*, exposition of history, for *Three Kingdoms*) or coin a new one.

Even *Golden Lotus*, the best candidate, if we insist on calling it a realistic (or naturalistic) novel, runs the risk of being evaluated as just a masterpiece of pornography. When we see it as allegory, take seriously its homiletics and Buddhist underpinnings, we come closer to its true greatness as a work of literature. It is easier to see *The Scholars* and the many turn-of-the century works, including *A Brief History of Enlightenment*, as galleries of satirical portraits rather than as novels in any strict sense.

By restricting the scope of the term in this way, we shall be able to speak of the novel's emergence in China with the May Fourth writers — and to observe its submergence again after Mao's 1942 "Talks at the Yenan Forum on Literature and Art." With few exceptions, the May Fourth story or novel belongs to the realist mode. Its author may be highly visible, whether through a filmy disguise as the central character (Yu Dafu, Ba Jin) or as intrusive narrator (Lao She). Or he may withdraw into the background, as Mao Dun preferred to do. But even in *Midnight*, with its minimal authorial intrusion or commentary, we are conscious of the implied author as an individual taking an independent stand. Unlike Li Boyuan or Hao Ran, Mao Dun completely dissociates himself from commonly held principles of behavior. He is neither celebrating commonly agreed heroes nor castigating commonly agreed villains. He is analyzing a world from whose power structure he feels himself to be alienated. His vision owes much to the Marxist social and economic models, but he goes beyond these to ask and answer the question, "What is the reality that confounds both a mediocre dreamer like Zhou Zongwei and a born leader like Wu Sunfu?"

When we move on from this kind of independent critical stance to the post-Yenan writers, we see a return to didacticism as a very obvious phenomenon. The post-1942 work of fiction can be assigned to the realist mode only if we accept the arrival of the millennium on the mainland. It is not enough just to admire and welcome the spectacular improvement in the lot of the vast majority of the Chinese people. We would have to believe that human nature itself has been fundamentally changed there before we could find realism in fiction where all behavior patterns are dictated by class origin, where the motivations of positive types can be paralleled only by the lives of epic heroes or saints in other literatures, and where the happy ending is mandatory, a formal requirement. What Hao Ran offers us is allegory. Zhang Jinfa is as much an allegorical figure as Prefect Fu is a "humor"; Gao Daquan's return to the village has the mythic quality of Yu's work on the Flood (in chapter 20, Gao Daquan returns with his fellow villagers from a construction stint of some months in Peking, but not until chapter 25, late in the moonlit night, does he enter his own house and greet his wife; the selfless devotion of the great Yu of the flood myths was symbolized when he "thrice passed his own door but never entered").

We have defined and compared three successive periods, and are concerned now with the opposition between change and continuity among them. The opposition may often be superficial or even artificial. Change *in* continuity is a phenomenon we observe throughout our studies. The May Fourth writers, despite their conscious rejection of indigenous forms in favor of massive borrowings from the West, still constantly hark back to their own Chinese literary tradition in their vocabulary, allusions, use of dialogue, modes of characterization, and love of the lyrical. In terms of their literary public, they are an important stage in an evolutionary process. They greatly expanded the readership of fiction, and though they themselves never reached mass circulation, they paved the way for the unified, classless, and nation-wide reading public of the post-Yenan period.

In the end, we see the May Fourth period as discrete, a stage not so much in evolutionary process as in a dialectical progress. The May Fourth writers were the genuine revolutionaries. Writers like Lu Xun, Lao She, and Mao Dun brought China into the mainstream of world literature, and at the same time, made possible the technical advances of their mainland successors, who have left the stream again. These new writers of the People's Republic are engaged in a kind of Great Return. Whatever comparative value judgments we may wish to make, we are bound to find the new mainland fiction "more Chinese," and it is demonstrably more popular. In all of Chinese narrative and dramatic literature, there is a strong urge toward the exemplary. We must be prepared to see this urge expressed again and again in writings of the future. There is, after all, no reason why the realist phase, which so dominated the literature of nineteenth-century Europe, should occupy China for any more than the space this paper has indicated, the brief decades subsequent to May 4, 1919.

Contributors
Notes
Index

Contributors

John Berninghausen teaches Chinese language and modern Chinese literature at Middlebury College. He edited a special issue of the *Bulletin of Concerned Asian Scholars* on modern Chinese literature and is completing his doctoral dissertation on Mao Dun's fiction at Stanford University.

Cyril Birch is a professor of Chinese and comparative literature at the University of California, Berkeley. He has published articles on Xu Zhimo, Lao She, and writers of the Communist period. His books include *Stories from a Ming Collection, Anthology of Chinese Literature,* and *Studies in Chinese Literary Genres.*

Yü-shih Chen is an assistant professor of Chinese at Hunter College. She has written several articles on Tang-Song classical prose and is now working on a book on Mao Dun's fiction.

Ching-mao Cheng is an associate professor of Chinese and Japanese literature and chairman of the Asian studies program at the University of Massachusetts, Amherst. He has published several studies in English, Chinese, and Japanese on Chinese-Japanese literary relations, including a book, *Chinese Literature in Japan.*

Milena Doleželová-Velingerová is a professor of Chinese literature at the University of Toronto. She is a coauthor of *Ballad of the Hidden Dragon* and has written articles on Guo Moruo, Shen Fu, and Chinese storyteller literature.

Irene Eber is a lecturer at the Hebrew University of Jerusalem.

Michael Egan is completing his doctorate in modern Chinese literature at the University of Toronto. His dissertation is a study of the short stories of Yu Dafu.

Yi-tsi M. Feuerwerker (Mei I-tzu) teaches at the Residential College, University of Michigan, and writes about modern Chinese literature.

Douwe W. Fokkema is an associate professor of comparative literature at the University of Utrecht. His works include *Literary Doctrine in China and Soviet Influence, 1956–1960* and *Report from Peking: Observations of a Western Diplomat on the Cultural Revolution.*

Merle Goldman is a professor of history at Boston University and an associate of the Harvard University East Asian Research Center. She is the author of *Literary Dissent in Communist China.*

Leo Ou-fan Lee is an associate professor of East Asian Languages and Cultures at Indiana University. He is the author of *The Romantic Generation of Modern Chinese Writers* and articles on modern Chinese literature and history in English and Chinese.

Perry Link is an assistant professor of East Asian studies at Princeton University. He teaches modern Chinese language and the social and cultural history of China.

Bonnie S. McDougall is a research fellow at Harvard University East Asian Research Center and writes on modern Chinese poetry and literary criticism. She is the author of *The Introduction of Western Literary Theories into Modern China*.

Harriet C. Mills teaches modern Chinese language and literature at the University of Michigan. She has written the *Intermediate Reader in Modern Chinese* and published articles in *The Atlantic Monthly, China Quarterly*, and *Far Eastern Quarterly*.

Paul Pickowicz is an assistant professor of history at the University of California, San Diego. His articles and reviews have appeared in *The China Quarterly, The Journal of Asian Studies, Modern China*, and *Literature East and West*. He is currently writing a book on Qu Qiubai and Chinese Marxist literary thought.

Ezra F. Vogel is a professor of sociology and director of the East Asian Research Center at Harvard University. His books include *Canton under Communism: Programs and Politics in a Provincial Capital, 1949–1968* and *Japan's New Middle Class*.

Ellen Widmer is a Ph.D. candidate at Harvard University in the department of East Asian languages and civilizations, specializing in Chinese vernacular fiction. Her dissertation is on the *Shuihu zhuan* [The Water Margin].

Notes

Introduction

1. *Straw Sandals: Chinese Short Stories, 1918–1933*, Harold R. Isaacs (Cambridge, Mass., MIT Press, 1974), pp. xi–xlviii.

2. Ibid., p. xxxiii.

3. See Patrick D. Hanan, "The Technique of Lu Hsün's Fiction," *Harvard Journal of Asiatic Studies* 34:53–96 (1974).

4. Ibid., p. 65.

5. Paul Cohen, "The New Coastal Reformers," in *Reform in Nineteenth-Century China*, ed. Paul A. Cohen and John E. Schrecker (Cambridge, Mass.: East Asian Research Center, Harvard University, 1976), p. 263.

1. The Origins of Modern Chinese Literature

MILENA DOLEŽELOVÁ-VELINGEROVÁ

1. Hu Shi, "Wenxue gailiang chuyi" (A preliminary discussion of literary reform), *Xin qingnian* (New youth) 2.5:1–11 (January 1, 1917); Chen Duxiu, "Wenxue geming lun" (On literary revolution), *Xin qingnian* 2.6:1–4 (February 1, 1917).

2. In 1932, in his book *Zhongguo xin wenxuede yuanliu* (The origins of new Chinese literature), the modern writer Zhou Zuoren explained the new literature movement in the framework of the evolution of Chinese literature as a whole. Although his interpretation was exceptional at that time, he took into consideration only the development of orthodox genres and neglected completely literature written in the vernacular. J. Průšek's article, "Subjectivism and Individualism in Modern Chinese Literature," *Archiv Orientální* 25:261–283 (1957), and C. Birch's study, "English and Chinese Metres in Hsü Chih-mo," *Asia Major* n.s. 8.2:258–293 (1961), were the first attempts to discover connections between the various streams of traditional and modern literature. The following works can also be regarded as major contributions to this new trend: V. I. Semanov, *Lu Sin' i ego predshestvenniki* (Moscow, Nauka, 1967); J. Průšek, *Three Sketches of Chinese Literature* (Prague, Academia, 1969); the three-volume collection *Contributions to the Study of the Rise and Development of Modern Literatures in Asia* (Prague, Academia, 1965, 1969, 1970); and Leo Ou-fan Lee, *The Romantic Generation of Modern Chinese Writers* (Cambridge, Mass., Harvard University Press, 1973).

3. *Zhongguo xin wenxue daxi* (Comprehensive anthology of new Chinese literature), ed. Zhao Jiabi (Shanghai, 1935–1936; Hong Kong reprint, 1963) I, II, X. These discussions

were also briefly summarized in J. de Francis, *Nationalism and Language Reform in China* (Princeton, Princeton University Press, 1950), pp. 68–78.

4. To my knowledge, no extensive analytical studies about the rise of modern standard Chinese have yet been undertaken. The picture of the language situation in nineteenth-century China as discussed in this article is therefore a hypothetical one. My major sources for this topic are: Liu Fu, *Les mouvements de la langue nationale en Chine* (Paris, Les Belles Lettres, 1925); Li Jinxi, *Guoyu yundong shi gang* (A history of the movement for national language: an outline), 2nd ed. (Shanghai, 1935); Tan Bi'an, *Wan Qingde baihuawen yundong* (The late Qing written vernacular movement) (Wuhan, 1956), *Wenxue yuyan wenti taolun ji* (Discussions on the problem of literary language), ed. Beijing daxue, Zhongguo yuyan wenxue xi, Yuyanxue Hanyu jiaoyan shi (Peking University, Faculty of languages and literatures of China, Department of linguistics and Chinese language) (Peking, 1957); N. I. Konrad, "O literaturnom iazyke v Kitae i Iaponii," *Trudy Instituta iazykoznaniia AN SSSR* 10:11–49 (1960); R. S. Britton, *The Chinese Periodical Press, 1800–1912,* reprint (Taipei, 1966); A. and M. Cartier and J. Kalousková, "Les aspects linguistiques du mouvement du 4 Mai," in *Major Papers Prepared for the XX International Congress of Chinese Studies* (Prague, Academia, 1968), pp. 165–187; and V. M. Solntsiev, "Lingvisticheskij aspekt Dvizheniia 4 maia," in *Dvizhenie 4 maia 1919 goda v Kitae* (Moscow, Nauka, 1971), pp. 321–330.

5. Britton, *Chinese Periodical Press,* p. 57.

6. *Zhongguo xinwen shi* (A history of Chinese journalism) ed. Zeng Xubai (Taipei, 1966), pp. 146, 149.

7. Britton, *Chinese Periodical Press,* pp. 115–116. See also *The Revolutionary Movement during the Late Ch'ing: A Guide to Chinese Periodicals,* Yü Ping-chüan, Li Yu-ming, Chang Yü-fa, comp. (Washington, D.C., Center for Chinese Research Materials, Association of Research Libraries, 1970).

8. A. H. Mateer, *New Terms for New Ideas: A Study of Chinese Newspapers* (Shanghai, 1913). According to the author's preface, the terms were collected from newspapers written in the vernacular during the period from 1900 to 1913.

9. P. Kratochvíl, *The Chinese Language Today* (London, Hutchinson University Library, 1968), p. 67.

10. *Revolutionary Movement,* pp. x–xi.

11. Huang Zunxian, *Riben guozhi* (Records from Japan), section *Xueshu zhi* (Records on learning), in Wu Tianren, *Huang Gongdu xiansheng chuan gao* (Published manuscripts of Mr. Huang Gongdu [Zunxian]) (Hong Kong, 1972), pp. 349–357.

12. Qiu Tingliang's article, "Lun baihua wei weixinzhi ben" (On vernacular as the basis for modernization), was originally published in the journal *Wuxi baihuabao* (Wuxi vernacular journal). It was reprinted in *Zhongguo jindai lunwenxuan* (Selected modern Chinese essays) ed. Jian Yizhi et al. (Peking, 1959), I, 176–180.

13. Lo Chan-pei and Liui Shu-sian (Luo Changbei and Lü Shuxiang), "Vopros o normakh sovremennogo kitaiskogo iazyka," *Sovetskoe vostokovedenie* 1:(1956); Li Jinxi, pp. 13–14.

14. Wang Zhao's *guanhua zimu* ("alphabetization" of Mandarin) in 1900 was the most successful of the schemes proposed by various Chinese scholars in the years 1892–1910, and it was the only one that gained some support from the authorities. Compare Li Jinxi, pp. 23–48.

15. Li Jinxi, introduction and *juan* 1.

16. B. I. Schwartz, *In Search of Wealth and Power: Yen Fu and the West* (Cambridge, Mass., Harvard University Press, 1964), pp. 92–98.

17. Hong Shen, "Cong Zhongguode xin xi shuo dao huaju" (From Chinese new drama to spoken drama), originally published in February 1929 in the journal *Guangzhou minguo ribao* (Canton republican daily). My quotation is from Hong Shen's introduction to *Zhongguo xin wenxue daxi*, IX, 14. There the original article appears in excerpts.

18. This is my English paraphrase of A. and M. Cartier's and J. Kalousková's description of the document as found in their article, pp. 175–176.

19. Ibid., p. 175.

20. Their short stories were originally published in various short-lived literary magazines and later reprinted in *Zhongguo xin wenxue daxi*, III. In his preface to this volume Mao Dun refers to these writers as "meteoric."

21. J. Průšek, introduction to *Studies in Modern Chinese Literature* (Berlin, Akademie-Verlag, 1964), pp. 1–43. See especially pp. 11–12.

22. My two major sources for this topic are: Chen Zizhan, *Zhongguo jindai wenxuezhi bianqian* (Changes in modern Chinese literature) (Shanghai, 1929), chap. 2, "Shijie geming" (Revolution in poetry); Lü Meisheng, "Shi lun wan Qing shijie gemingde yiyi" (Preliminary discussion about the significance of late Qing revolution in poetry) in *Wenxue yichan zengkan* (Supplements to *Literary Heritage*) (Peking, 1961), VIII, 73–94.

23. Huang Zunxian, *Renjinglu shi cao* (Verses from the [studio] Renjinglu), in *Wanyou wenku* (A compendium of literary works) (Shanghai, 1937), pp. 60–62, 70.

24. Ramon L. Y. Woon and Irving Y. Lo, "Poets and Poetry of China's Last Empire," *Literature East and West* 9.4:331–361 (1965).

25. For example, Huang Zunxian's "The Formosan Tragedy," "The Yielding General," and "The Bluffing General," discussed in Woon and Lo, "Poets and Poetry."

26. Huang Zunxian, *Zagan wushou* (Five poems of mixed feelings) (quoted from Liu Xinhuang, *Xiandai Zhongguo wenxue shi hua* [Discussions on the history of modern Chinese literature] [Taipei, 1971], p. 2).

27. Woon and Lo, "Poets and Poetry," p. 356.

28. Lü Meisheng, "Shi lun wan Qing shijie gemingde yiyi," pp. 75–76.

29. Quoted from Liu Xinhuang, p. 2.

30. Woon and Lo, "Poets and Poetry," p. 356.

31. See *Zhongguo huaju yundong wushinian shiliao ji* (Documentary materials on fifty years of the Chinese drama movement, 1907–1957) ed. Tian Han, Ouyang Yuqian, et al. (Peking, 1958); Hong Shen, introduction to *Zhongguo xin wenxue daxi*, IX; S. A. Serova, "Pervye shagi novogo teatra i revoliutsionnoe dvizhenie v Kitae (konets XIX–nachalo XXv.)," in *Kratkie soobscheniya Instituta Narodov Azii* (Moscow, Nauka, 1965), LXXXIV, 117–125.

32. Its members were future renowned actors and directors, such as Ouyang Yuqian, Lu Jingre, Ma Jiangshi, and others.

33. Ouyang Yuqian, "Huiyi Chun liu" (Recalling the Spring Willow [Society]), in *Zhongguo huaju*, pp. 13–47; Ouyang Yuqian, "Tan wenming xi" (On civilized drama), in *Zhongguo huaju*, pp. 48–108.

34. Hong Shen, introduction to *Zhongguo xin wenxue daxi*, IX, 15.

35. Ibid., p. 14.

36. The article was originally published in the first issues (October 16 to November 18, 1897) of the Tientsin *Guowenbao* (National News). It is reprinted in A Ying, *Wan Qing wenxue congchao: Xiaoshuo xiqu yanjiu juan* (Collected documents on late Qing literature: research materials on fiction and drama) (Peking, 1960), pp. 1–13.

37. This article was originally published in the first issue of *Qingyi bao* (The China discussion) (December 23, 1898). It was used as a preface to the Chinese translation of

Shiba Shirō's *Kajin no kigū* (Romantic encounters with beautiful ladies), the first political novel translated into Chinese at the end of the nineteenth century. Liang Qichao's article was later reprinted in A Ying, *Wan Qing wenxue congchao: Xiaoshuo xiqu yanjiu juan*, pp. 13–14.

38. This article was originally published in the first issue of the journal *Xin xiaoshuo* (New fiction), and was reprinted in A Ying, *Wan Qing wenxue congchao: Xiaoshuo xiqu yanjiu juan*, pp. 14–19. M. Gálik has pointed out the foreign and Buddhist influences on Liang Qichao's theory in his article "On the Influence of Foreign Ideas on Chinese Literary Criticism (1898–1904)," *Asian and African Studies* (Bratislava) 2:38–48 (1966).

39. See A Ying, *Wan Qing xiaoshuo shi* (A history of late Qing fiction) (Peking, 1955).

40. In my unpublished article "Typology of Plot Structures in Late Qing Novels."

41. Information drawn from the extensive and valuable list of Western fiction translated into Chinese during the late Qing period, compiled by V. I. Semanov, "Inostrannaia literatura v Kitae na rubezhe XIX–XX vekov," in *Iz istorii literaturnykh sviazei XIX veka* (Moscow, Izdatel'stvo Akademii nauk SSSR, 1962), pp. 267–311.

42. Three representative authors of the political novel, Yano Ryūkei, Shiba Shirō, and Suehiro Tetchō, were translated at the beginning of the twentieth century. Soon thereafter came translations of Japanese "romantics," such as Ozaki Kōyō. See V. I. Semanov, "Iaponskaia proza v Kitae na rubezhe XIX–XX vekov," in *Iz istorii literaturnykh sviazei XIX veka*, pp. 312–334.

2. The Impact of Western Literary Trends

BONNIE S. McDOUGALL

1. See forum page and reviews in *Wenxue* (Literature) during 1934 and 1935, especially Ma Zongrong's reviews in 3.5 (November 1934) and the forum page in 4.2 (February 1935). The comments on the decline in demand for translations since 1926 and on the present need for a new wave to improve the quality of Chinese writing are by *Literature* contributors and do not necessarily represent my own opinions.

2. Mabel Lee, "Liang Ch'i-ch'ao (1873–1929) and the Literary Revolution of Late-Ch'ing," in *Search for Identity: Modern Literature and the Creative Arts in Asia*, ed. A. R. Davis (Sydney, Angus & Robertson, 1974), pp. 203–224.

3. Lu Xun, "Moluo shi li shuo" (The power of Mara poetry), in *Lu Xun quanji* (Complete works of Lu Xun) (Peking, 1956), I, 194–234.

4. See also Leo Ou-fan Lee, *The Romantic Generation of Modern Chinese Writers* Cambridge, Mass., Harvard University Press, 1973). pp. 6–7, 28–40.

5. *Moruo wenji* (Collected works of Guo Moruo) (Peking, 1959), X, 204–213.

6. "Yishujia yu gemingjia" (Artists and revolutionares), *Moruo wenji* X, 76–78.

7. "Wenyijiade juewu" (The writer's consciousness) and "Wenxue yu geming" (Literature and revolution), *Moruo wenji*, X, 302–311, 312–323.

8. M. Gálik, *Mao Tun and Modern Chinese Literary Criticism* (Wiesbaden, Franz Steiner, 1969), pp. 111–116; and Fritz Gruner, "Some Remarks on the Cultural-Political Significance of the Chinese League of Left-Wing Writers at the Beginning of the 1930s,"

in *Search for Identity*, pp. 255–259.

9. "Zai Yan'an wenyi zuotanhuishangde jianghua" (Talks at the Yenan Forum on literature and art) in *Mao Zedong xuanji* (Selected works of Mao Zedong) (Peking, 1969), III, 807.

10. Mao Dun, "Wenxue yu rensheng" (Literature and life), in *Zhongguo xin wenxue daxi* (Comprehensive anthology of new Chinese literature), ed. Zhao Jiabi (Shanghai, 1935-1936), II, 149–153.

11. See Gálik, especially the conclusion.

12. *Ba Jin wenji* (Collected works of Ba Jin) (Peking, 1961), X, 91–97, 101; and Olga Lang, *Pa Chin and His Writings* (Cambridge, Mass., Harvard University Press, 1967), pp. 44–46.

13. "Yishujia yu gemingjia", p. 77.

14. For Yu Dafu's views, see 'Wenxueshangde jieji douzheng" (Class struggle in literature), *Dafu quanji* (Complete works of Yu Dafu) (Shanghai, 1930), V, 147–157.

15. Compare Guo's 1923 "Yishude pingjia" (The value of art), *Moruo wenji*, X, 79–82, with his 1926 "Wenxue yu geming."

16. Lee, *Romantic Generation*, pp. 103–105.

17. See "A Statement by the *Critical Review*," *Xueheng* 13 (January 1923); see also Hu Xiansu, "Lun pipingjiazhi zeren" (The Responsibility of Critics), *Xueheng* 3: (March 1922).

18. Zhu Guangqian, *Wo yu wenxue ji qita* (Literature and I and other essays) (Shanghai, 1947), pp. 14–20; compare I. A. Richards, *Principles of Literary Criticism* (London, Routledge & Kegan Paul, 1926), chap. 7, 8.

19. Zhu Guangqian, pp. 29, 40, 46.

20. Ibid., pp. 67–69; compare Edward Bullough, " 'Psychical Distance' as a Factor in Art and an Aesthetic Principle," *British Journal of Psychology* 5.2:87–118 (June 1912).

21. He Qifang, "Chimude hua" (Twilight flowers), in his *Keyi ji* (Painstaking work) (Shanghai, 1948), pp. 96–108, especially p. 99. (This is the fifth edition of the title *Keyi ji*. "Chimude hua" is not included in the first or second editions, nor do the essays referred to in note 22 appear in the third or subsequent editions.)

22. He Qifang, "*Yanni ji huo hua*" (Afterword to the *Yanni Collection*) and "Mengzhong daolu" (Paths in dreams) in *Keyi ji* (Shanghai, 1938), pp. 63–67, 67–69.

23. He Qifang, "Chimude hua," pp. 98–99.

24. He Qifang, "Wo he sanwen" (The essay and I), in his *Huanxiang riji* (Diary of a visit home) (Shanghai, 1939), pp. 1–14, especially pp. 9–12.

25. *Chuangzao yuekan* 3: (Creation monthly) (May 1926); see also note 7 above.

26. It has been suggested that Chinese writers may have considered the native literature to be irrelevant to China's political and social problems rather than inferior; however, much of the Western literature being read was also irrelevant in style and content, except to Westernization itself.

27. Ernst Wolff, *Chou Tso-jen* (New York, Twayne, 1971), pp. 41–42, 62. The first monograph on Chinese mythology in a non-Chinese language' was E. T. C. Werner's *Myths and Legends of China* (London, Harraps, 1922).

28. John Dewey, for example, described literature as one of the great "transnational" forces that may yet unite the separate countries of the world and overcome the present state of international anarchy. See his *Lectures in China, 1919–1920*, ed. and tr. Robert W. Clopton and Tsuin-chen Ou (Honolulu, East-West Center, 1973), p. 159. Bertrand Russell was another famous internationalist.

29. University extension lectures began in 1873 and grew considerably in the 1880s

and 1890s, appealing mainly to the middle classes, especially to women, and the Workers' Educational Association was founded in 1903. One important series of textbooks was Short Histories of the Literatures of the World, edited by Edmund Gosse for Heinemann around the turn of the century; Herbert A. Giles's *A History of Chinese Literature* (1901) was one of those commissioned. The need for simple, concise textbooks on every subject in the humanities and dealing with every country in the world was also present in China. *Outline History of the World* by H. G. Wells (1920; abridged version, 1922), and *Outline of World Literature* by John Drinkwater (1923–1924) are two examples popular in China and the West.

30. Two notable examples popular in China were Georg Brandes's *Main Currents in Nineteenth Century Literature* (1923; first published in German, 1871–1890), and R. G. Moulton's *The Modern Study of Literature* (1915).

31. The compilation of anthologies of world literature was a popular occupation in the twenties and thirties. Some well-known examples: *Great Short Stories of the World,* ed. B. H. Clark (1926); *Great Short Novels of the World,* ed. B. H. Clark (1929); *A Book of Modern Short Stories,* ed. Dorothy Brewster (1928); *A Book of Contemporary Short Stories,* ed. Dorothy Brewster (1936); *Great Essays of All Nations,* ed. F. H. Pritchard (1929); *From Confucius to Mencken,* ed. F. H. Pritchard (1929); *Masterpiece Library of Short Stories,* ed. J. A. Hammerton (1927); *Fifty Contemporary One-Act Plays,* ed. F. Shay and P. Loving (1928); and *International Tales of War and Revolution,* ed. Martin Lawrence (1932–1933).

32. *Xinyue* (Crescent) on the front cover but *Xinyue yuekan* (Crescent monthly) in the colophon.

33. Jerome B. Grieder, *Hu Shih and the Chinese Renaissance: Liberalism in the Chinese Revolution, 1917–1937* (Cambridge, Mass., Harvard University Press, 1970), and Lee, *Romantic Generation.*

34. Hu Shi, "Xin wenhua yundong yu Guomindang" (The New Culture movement and the Guomindang) *Xinyue* 2.6,7:5 (September 1929); see also Grieder, p. 229. Hu's article is dated November 29, 1929.

35. "The English novelists of roughly her own generation were Compton Mackenzie, Aldous Huxley, J. B. Priestly, Hugh Walpole, David Garnett and Rose Macauley; none of them seemed to be carrying forward the revolution which, in 1924, she had believed to be imminent. Having lost both her adversaries [Wells, Bennett, Galsworthy], and her collaborators [Forster, Lawrence, Eliot, Strachey, Joyce], she stood very much alone." Quentin Bell, *Virginia Woolf: A Biography* (London, Hogarth Press, 1972), II, 185.

36. George Orwell, "Inside the Whale," in *The Collected Essays, Journalism and Letters of George Orwell* (London, Secker & Warburg, 1968), I, 493–527. Quotation from p. 509.

37. Orwell, p. 510. Cyril Connolly, a contemporary of Orwell who does not share his left-wing views, sees the "modern movement" in a wider perspective but also grants that its peak period was from 1910 to 1925. "The Great War cut across the Movement, deflecting it but unable to stem its vitality. The late twenties show a falling off but the angry thirties introduce the political themes which sent many writers back to realism . . . Yeats (b. 1865), Joyce, Virginia Woolf (both b. 1882) are gone within six months of each other, and everything the Movement stood for is dubbed 'degenerate art' or converted into propaganda. The Titans depart, the theses begin." *The Modern Movement: One Hundred Key Books from England, France and America 1880–1950* (London, Deutsch & Hamilton, 1965), pp. 4–5.

38. See *"Nüshen* zhi difang secai" (Local color in *The Goddesses*) and "Shide gelü" (Form in poetry), in *Wen Yiduo quanji* (Complete works of Wen Yiduo) (Shanghai, 1948), III, *ding,* 195–201, 245–253.

39. Lu Xun, "Yi Wei Suyuan jun" (In memory of Wei Suyuan), in *Wenxue* 3.4 (October 1934); reprinted in *Lu Xun quanji,* VI, 49–54.

40. *Benliu* (Torrent) 1.1 (June 1928). Brooks's article was published in Irving Babbitt, et al., *Criticism in America* (New York, Harcourt, Brace, 1924). Italics added.

41. The left-wing writers in England were rather late in emerging, and poets like Auden and Spender did not really form a political group until after the publication of *New Signatures* in 1932. The first issue of *New Writing,* an internationalist and socialist journal established by John Lehmann in 1936, contained a short story by Zhang Tianyi, translated from the French by Lehmann himself. Lehmann, *The Whispering Gallery* (London, Longmans & Green, 1955), pp. 172-182, 231-241.

42. For the growth of left-wing literature around the world in the thirties, see Jürgen Rühle, *Literature and Revolution: A Critical Study of the Writer and Communism in the Twentieth Century* (London, Pall Mall Press, 1969). Dorothy Brewster's *East-West Passage: A Study in Literary Relationships* (London, Allen & Unwin, 1954) has some interesting passages on Soviet literature in America and England during the "Pink Decade."

43. Lu Xun, "Zhongguo wentanshangde guimo" (Devils of the Chinese literary scene), *Lu Xun quanji,* VI, 119–125.

44. C. T. Hsia, *A History of Modern Chinese Fiction, 1917–1957* (New Haven, Yale University Press, 1961), pp. 125, 618–619. According to its editor, Fu Donghua, *Wenxue* was established as a successor to *Xiaoshuo yuebao* (Short story monthly).

45. Apart from the short story collections, the English-language material in this series consisted of Carlyle's *On Heroes and Hero-Worship* (1841), Thackeray's *Vanity Fair* (1847–1848), Charlotte Brönte's *Jane Eyre* (1847), J. M. Barrie's *Peter Pan* (1904), John Drinkwater's *Abraham Lincoln* (1918), Hardy's *The Dynasts* (1904–1908), Galsworthy's *Justice* (1910), Hawthorne's *The Scarlet Letter* (1850), and O. Henry's *The Four Million* (1906).

46. Several of the examples of apparently "irrelevant" reference to Western literature come close to the "bourgeois cosmopolitanism" Levenson sees as characterizing one strain in the new literary movement. I think, however, that the examples of cosmopolitanism given by Levenson, such as the distinction made between Shakespeare and Corneille, are not representative of the general tendency. See J. R. Levenson, *Revolution and Cosmopolitanism: The Western Stage and the Chinese Stages* (Berkeley, University of California Press, 1971.

47. For example, in 3.1, Ma made a detailed report on literary journals in France, in a way reminiscent of the early *Short Story Monthly;* he discussed at length about ten of the large-circulation journals and briefly mentioned another dozen smaller ones.

48. See, for example, Irene Eber, "Translation Literature in Modern China: The Yiddish Author and His Tale," *Asian and African Studies* (Jerusalem) 3.3:291–314 (1972).

49. Zhu Guangqian, "Jindai meixue yu wenxue pipan" (Modern aesthetics and literary criticism), in *Wo yu wenxue ji qita,* pp. 104–144.

3. The Impact of Japanese Literary Trends on Modern Chinese Writers

CHING-MAO CHENG

1. Guo Moruo, "Zhuozide tiaowu" (Dance of the table [1928]), in *Zhongguo xin wenxue daxi xubian* (Sequel to comprehensive anthology of new Chinese literature, hereafter *Xubian*), 10 vols., Hong Kong Literary Research Association, comp. (Hong Kong, 1968), I, 139.

2. See, for example, Sanetō Keishū, *Kindai Nisshi bunka ron* (Recent Japanese-Chinese cultural relations) (Tokyo, 1941), pp. 237–241.

3. Ibid., pp. 18–19. See also Robert Scalapino, "Prelude to Marxism: The Chinese Student Movement in Japan, 1900–1910," in *Approaches to Modern Chinese History* ed. Albert Feuerwerker, et al. (Berkeley, University of California Press, 1967), p. 192.

4. Quoted in Sanetō Keishū, p. 254.

5. "Zhuzuozhe zixuzhuan lüe" (A brief autobiography of the author [1915]), in *Lu Xun quanji* (Complete works of Lu Xun, hereafter *LXQJ*) 20 vols. (Peking, 1973), VII, 448.

6. Preface to *Nahan* (A call to arms [1923]), in *LXQJ*, I, 271–272.

7. "Dianlun lunwen" (On literature) in *Wenxuan* (Anthology of literature), Xiao Tong (501–531), comp. (Hong Kong, 1965), *juan* 52:1128.

8. *"Mengxue bao Yanyi bao hexu"* (Joint preface to *Mengxue* and *Yanyi* journals), *Shiwu bao* 44 (October 1897), collected in *Yinbingshi wenji leibian* (Classified writings from the ice-drinker's studio), reprint, 2 vols. (Taiwan 1974), I, 787.

9. "Yi yin zhengzhi xiaoshuo xu" (Preface to the translation and publication of political fiction), *Qingyi bao* 1 (December 23, 1898), collected in *Yinbingshi wenji leibian*, I, 742–743.

10. Yanagida Izumi, *Seiji shōsetsu kenkyū* (A study of political fiction), 2 vols. (Tokyo, 1947), I, 381.

11. "Lun xiaoshuo yu qunzhi zhi guanxi" (On the relationship between fiction and the rule of the masses), *Xin xiaoshuo* (New fiction) 1 (winter 1902), collected in *Yinbingshi wenji leibian*, I, pp. 382–386.

12. Masuda Wataru, in his article "Ryo Keichō ni tsuite" (On Liang Qichao), gives a concise, well-documented account of Liang's tremendous influence on modern Chinese intellectual and poltical leaders. He quotes acknowledgments from Hu Shi, Lu Xun, Zhou Zuoren, Guo Moruo, and Mao Zedong. See his *Chūgoku bungakushi kenkyū* (A study of Chinese literary history) (Tokyo, 1967), pp. 147–172.

13. Qian Xuantong, "Ji Chen Duxiu" (A letter to Chen Duxiu [1917]), in *Zhongguo xin wenxue daxi* (Comprehensive anthology of new Chinese literature, hereafter *Daxi*), ed. Zhao Jiabi, 10 vols. (Shanghai, 1935–1936; Hong Kong reprint, 1962), I, 80.

14. "Riben jin sanshinian xiaoshuo zhifada" (Advancement of Japanese fiction in the past thirty years [1918]), in *Daxi*, I, 309.

15. Masuda, p. 152.

16. For details, see A Ying (Qian Xingcun), *Wan Qing xiaoshuo shi* (History of late Qing fiction) (Hong Kong, 1966), especially chap. 2, 3, and 11. See also a discussion in Masuda Wataru, pp. 327–346; and Lu Hsun [Xun], *A Brief History of Chinese Fiction*, tr. Yang

Hsien-yi and Gladys Yang (Peking, 1964), pp. 372–388.

17. For details, see Yanagida Izumi, *Meiji shoki honyaku bungaku kenkyū* (A study of the translated literature of early Meiji) (Tokyo, 1961), especially pp. 165–189, 461–493.

18. "Dongji yuedan" (Comments on Japanese books [1902]), in *Yinbingshi wenji leibian*, I, 761.

19. Zhou Zuoren, "Riben jin sanshinian xiaoshuozhi fada," in *Daxi*, I, 308–319.

20. Ibid., p. 319. Italics in original.

21. Ibid., p. 309.

22. "Wenxue geming lun" (On literary revolution [1917]), in *Daxi*, I, 44.

23. See, for example, Zhu Ziqing, "*Xiandai shige* daolun" (An introduction to the *Anthology of Modern Poetry* [1935]), in *Daxi*, VIII, 15, where he states: "Toward the end of the Qing dynasty, Xia Zengyou, Tan Sitong, and others were already inspired toward a 'revolution in poetry' . . . Though that 'revolution' ended in failure, it actually exerted a great influence on the 1918 new poetry movement with regard to ideas, though not skills." The "others" he refers to include Huang Zunxian and Liang Qichao.

24. "Jianshede wenxue geming lun" (On constructive literary revolution [1918]), in *Daxi*, I, 155–168.

25. "Dongji yuedan," p. 760.

26. Preface to his book, *Jin ershinian Zhongguo wenyi sichao lun* (On the Chinese literary trends of the past twenty years) (Shanghai, 1939), p. 1. For details, see Bonnie S. McDougall, *The Introduction of Western Literary Theories into China, 1919–1925* (Tokyo, 1971).

27. "*Benliu* bianjiao houji" (Editorial comments on the *Torrent* magazine), in *LXQJ*, VII, 554.

28. "Shehui beijing yu chuangzuo" (Social conditions and literary creation), published under the name of Lang Sun, in *Daxi*, II, 406–408.

29. "Xin wenxuezhi shiming" (Mission of the new literature), in *Daxi*, II, 608–609.

30. "Zai zhongloushang" (Up the bell tower [1927]), in *LXQJ*, IV, 48.

31. "Wo zenme zuoqi xiaoshuo lai" (How I started writing fiction [1933]), in *LXQJ*, V, 107.

32. Takeda Taijun, "Chūgoku no shōsetsu to Nihon no shōsetsu" (Chinese fiction and Japanese fiction), in his *Kōga umi ni irite nagaruru* (Yellow river flowing forever into the sea) (Tokyo, 1966), p. 238.

33. "Bungaku wa shimetsu suruka" (Is literature going to die? [1963]), in *Bungei hyōron shū* (An anthology of literary criticism), Chikuma Shobō, comp., *Gendai bungaku taikei* (Tokyo, 1966), XCVI, 370.

34. *Meiji bungakushi* (A history of Meiji literature) (Tokyo, 1963) p. 184.

35. *Kafū zenshū* (Complete works of Nagai Kafū), 28 vols. (Tokyo, 1962–1965), II, 171.

36. "Some General Comments on *Watakushi shōsetsu*," in *International Conference on Japanese Studies Report*, ed. The Japan P.E.N. Club (Tokyo, 1974) I, 174–177.

37. See McDougall, pp. 149–168.

38. *LXQJ*, XVI, 13–43.

39. "*Nahan* pinglun" (A critique of *A Call to Arms* [1924]), quoted in Imamura Yoshio, *Ro Jin to dentō* (Lu Xun and tradition) (Tokyo, 1967), p. 319.

40. See, for example, Imamura Yoshio, pp. 243–245, 317–320. Also, Takeda Taijun, "Shū Sakujin to Nihon bungei" (Zhou Zuoren and Japanese literature and art) in his *Kōga umi ni irite nagaruru*, pp. 177–178.

41. "Guanyu Lu Xun zhi er" (More on Lu Xun [1936]), *Guadou ji* (Shanghai, 1937;

Hong Kong, 1969), p. 239. Zhou Zuoren's statement here requires some clarification. Though not enthusiastic about Tōson, Lu Xun actually translated part of the author's *Asakusa dayori* (Tides from Asakusa) in 1924 into Chinese, entitled *Cong Qiancao lai*. Also to be remembered is his translation of Katayama Koson's article on naturalism, which has been mentioned earlier in this chapter.

42. "Daoqi Tengcun xiansheng" (Mr. Shimazaki Tōson [1943]), in *Yaotang zawen* (Miscellanea from the Medication Studio) (Hong Kong, 1943), pp. 111–114.

43. "Ziranzhuyi yu xiandai Zhongguo xiaoshuo" (Naturalism and modern Chinese fiction [1922]), in *Daxi*, II, 386–399.

44. "Daoyan" (Introduction) to *Daxi*, V, 12.

45. Ibid., pp. 11–12.

46. There is one scene in this story where the heroine, "I," lying in a quilt after her lover left the house without bidding her farewell, tells herself, "Right now, indeed only this quilt can understand my true feelings." This is reminiscent of the last scene in Katai's *Futon* (Quilt). *Daxi*, V, 418.

47. C. T. Hsia, *A History of Modern Chinese Fiction, 1917–1957*, rev. ed. (New Haven, Yale University Press, 1971), p. 102.

48. "Liuqinian lai chuangzuo shenghuode huigu" (My literary life in the past six to seven years in retrospect [1925]), in his *Guoqiji* (Taiwan reprint, 1968), pp. 6–7.

49. Quoted in Zhou Zuoren, "Chenlun" (On "Sinking"), in *Zijide yuandi* (My own garden) (Shanghai, 1929; Hong Kong reprint, 1972), p. 22.

50. Quoted in Zheng Boqi, "Daoyan," in *Daxi*, V, 21–22.

51. "Shenme shi wenxue" (What is literature?), in *Daxi*, II, 172.

52. Guo Moruo, "Zhuozide tiaowu," pp. 139–140.

53. "Ruzan no rakudo," *Kafū zenshū*, XIII, 49.

54. "Chenlun" pp. 75–80.

55. *Daxi*, V, 99.

56. *Kumō no shōchō*, chap. 4.

57. *LXQJ*, XIII, 379.

58. "Liangdi shu" (Correspondence between two places), a letter dated April 28, 1925, in *LXQJ*, VII, 81.

59. Part of the text is quoted in Lu Xun, "Ti weiding cao" (The untitled, a draft [no. 5, 1935]), in *LXQJ*, VI, 167–169.

60. "Guanyu Lu Xun zhi er," p. 239. Lu Xun said of himself that he was fond of reading Sōseki and Ōgai in his essay "Wo zenme zuoqi xiaoshuo lai," in *LXQJ*, V, 105.

61. See Lu Xun, "Huran xiangdao" (Suddenly remember [1925]), in *LXQJ*, III, 21; "Geming shidaide wenxue" (Literature of revolutionary age [1927]), in *LXQJ*, III, 410; and "Zai zhongloushang," in *LXQJ*, IV, 47.

62. Imamura Yoshio, p. 246.

4. Lu Xun: The Impact of Russian Literature

Douwe W. Fokkema

1. For example, Chow Tse-tsung, *The May Fourth Movement: Intellectual Revolution in Modern China* (Cambridge, Mass., Harvard University Press, 1960); Marián Gálik, *Mao Tun and Modern Chinese Literary Criticism* (Wiesbaden, Franz Steiner, 1969); Bonnie S. McDougall, *The Introduction of Western Literary Theories into Modern China, 1919–1925* (Tokyo, 1971).

2. Like a language (*langue*), a code is a construct based on speech or the extant texts (*parole*). It is a generalization that cannot do justice to all particulars of the available texts but still has its roots in empirical facts and, therefore, may have explanatory power.

3. References in square brackets indicate volume and pages of Lu Xun, *Quanji* (Complete works) (Peking, 1973).

4. Compare *Kratkaya literaturnaya entsiklopedia*, ed. A. A. Surkov (Moscow, Sovetskaya Entsiklopedia, 1962–1972). So far seven volumes have appeared.

5. Dmitrij Chizhevskij, *On Romanticism in Slavic Literature* ('s-Gravenhage, Mouton, 1957); René Wellek, "The Concept of Romanticism in Literary History," in his *Concepts of Criticism*, ed. Stephen G. Nichols (New Haven and London, Yale University Press, 1963), pp. 128–199.

6. Quoted by Huang Sung-k'ang, *Lu Hsün and the New Culture Movement of Modern China* (Amsterdam, Djambatan, 1957), p. 36 [I,58–59]. Also, V. I. Semanov deals with "The Power of Mara Poetry" in his *Lu Sin' i ego predshestvenniki* (Moscow, Nauka, 1967), pp. 21–24.

7. Huang Sung-k'ang, p. 52.

8. Tsi-an Hsia, "Aspects of the Power of Darkness in Lu Hsün," in his *The Gate of Darkness: Studies on the Leftist Literary Movement in China* (Seattle and London, University of Washington Press, 1968), pp. 146–163.

9. "Zhu Zhong E wenzizhi jiao" (China's debt to Russian literature), 1932 [V, 53–59], translated in Lu Hsun, *Selected Works* (Peking, 1956–1960), III, 180–185. Lu Xun wrote an introduction to the Chinese translation of *Poor Folk* [VII,460–465] and translated an essay by L'vov-Rogachevsky on Tolstoy into Chinese [XVI,345–396].

10. René Wellek, "The Concept of Realism in Literary Scholarship," in *Concepts of Criticism*, pp. 222–256.

11. Peter Demetz, "Zur Definition des Realismus," *Literatur und Kritik* 2:333–345 (1967).

12. See Gálik.

13. See Demetz, "Zur Definition."

14. René Wellek, "The Term and Concept of Symbolism in Literary History," in his *Discriminations: Further Concepts of Criticism* (New Haven and London, Yale University Press, 1970), pp. 90–122.

15. See M. Ye. Shneider, "V poiskakh 'literatury dlja zhizni': proizvedeniya Leonida Andreyeva," *Izucheniye kitaiskoi literatury v SSSR*, Sbornik statei k shestidesyatiletiyu chlena-korrespondenta AN SSSR N. T. Fedorenko (Moscow, Nauka, 1973), pp.

206–234.

16. Anna Balakian, *The Symbolist Movement: A Critical Appraisal* (New York, Random House, 1967), p. 10.

17. Siegfried Behrsing, "Nekotoriye soobrazheniya otnositelnosti Lu Sinya kak perevodchika," *Teoreticheskiye problemy vostochnykh literatur* (Moscow, Nauka, 1969), pp. 227–232.

18. Jurij M. Lotman, *Die Struktur literarischer Texte*, übersetzt von Rolf-Dieter Keil (Munich, Fink, 1972).

19. Chizhevskij, p. 51.

20. N. V. Gogol, *Polnoye sobraniye sochinenii* (Moscow, Ak. Nauk SSSR, 1937–1952), III, 234.

21. T. A. Hsia.

22. Lotman, p. 414.

23. Quoted by Huang Sung-kang, p. 52 [VI,242].

24. D. W. Fokkema, *Literary Doctrine in China and Soviet Influence, 1956–1960* (The Hague, Mouton, 1965), pp. 253–255.

5. Qu Qiubai and Russian Literature

Ellen Widmer

1. "Ch'ü Ch'iu-po: The Making and Destruction of a Tenderhearted Communist," in his *The Gate of Darkness: Studies on the Leftist Literary Movement in China* (Seattle and London, University of Washington Press, 1968).

2. *Qu Qiubai wenji* (Collected works of Qu Qiubai) (Peking, 1953-1954), II, 861. On the central importance of this article, see Maeda Tosiaki, "Kushūhaku to Saren" (Qu Qiubai and the League of Left-Wing Writers), *Tōyō bunka* (Eastern culture) 52:133–156 (March 1972).

3. From "Zai lun dazhong wenyi da Zhijing" (More on mass literature, a reply to Zhijing [Mao Dun]), in *Qu Qiubai wenji*, II, 910.

4. Translation in T. A. Hsia, p. 15. See also M. F. Shneider, *Tvorcheskii put' Tsiui Tsiubo* (Moscow, Publishing House of the Academy of Sciences, 1964), p. 12; and Yang Zhihua (Mrs. Qu Qiubai), "Yi Qiubai" (Remembering Qiubai), *Hongqi piaopiao* (Red flag fluttering) 8:26 (July 1958).

5. Maurice Meisner, *Li Ta-chao and the Origins of Chinese Marxism* (New York, Atheneum, 1973), p. 73.

6. See *Qu Qiubai zhuyi xinian mulu* (A chronological listing of Qu Qiubai's writings and translations) ed. Ding Jingtang and Wen Cao (Shanghai, 1959); pp. 102–103 discuss which of the Tolstoy translations in *Qu Qiubai wenji* are actually by Qu. See also Shneider, pp. 21, 227. I have used D. S. Mirsky, *A History of Russian Literature* (New York, Knopf, 1964) for background on Russian literature.

7. "Lun Puxijinde *Bianerjin xiaoshuo ji*" (A discussion of Pushkin's *Belkin's Tales*), in *Qu Qiubai wenji*, II, 541–543; "Eluosi mingjia duanpian xiaoshuo ji, xu" (Preface to Collected short stories by famous Russian writers), in *Qu Qiubai wenji*, II, 543–545; untitled note accompanying translation of Gogol's *The Servants' Room*, in *Qiu Qiubai wenji*, III, 1304–1305.

8. Meisner, especially pp. 46 and 64. On "Asian spirituality" in Qu's work also see

note 26 below.

9. *Qu Qiubai wenji*, II, 543–544.

10. *Qu Qiubai wenji*, III, 1304–1305.

11. *Qu Qiubai wenji*, II, 461–539.

12. Shneider, pp. 52–53. See also Nījima Atsuyoshi, "Pekin de mita Kushūhaku hihan" (The criticism of Qu Qiubai as viewed from Peking), *Tōyō bunka* 44:107–118 (February 1968). Both refer to Qu's habit of borrowing from Russian authors without acknowledgment.

13. P. 473.

14. Ibid.

15. On "superfluity," see Leo Ou-fan Lee, *The Romantic Generation of Modern Chinese Writers* (Cambridge, Mass., Harvard University Press, 1973), pp. 250 ff.

16. P. 485.

17. P. 525.

18. P. 526.

19. "Chidu xinshi," in *Qu Qiubai wenji*, I, 117.

20. Pp. 473, 479, 492, and 503 respectively.

21. P. 485 on language. This point is mentioned under the discussion of Lermontov, not of Pushkin. P. 512 on collapse.

22. Translated by Almyer Maude (New York and Indianapolis, Bobbs Merrill, 1960), pp. 163–164.

23. V. I. Lenin, "Leo Tolstoy as the Mirror of the Russian Revolution," in *Collected Works* (Moscow, Foreign Languages Publishing House, 1963), XV, 202–209; Peter Kropotkin, *Russian Literature* (New York, McClure, Phillips, 1905), pp. 117–119.

24. " 'Women' shi shui?" (Who are "we"?), in *Qu Qiubai wenji*, II, 875–879.

25. P. 126.

26. See especially pp. 162–175.

27. Pp. 165–166.

28. P. 139.

29. P. 175.

30. P. 171. Translated in T. A. Hsia, p. 40.

31. Pp. 166, 169.

32. Lee, pp. 110–123.

33. Ibid., p. 192; David Roy, *Kuo Mo-jo: The Early Years* (Cambridge, Mass., Harvard University Press, 1971), pp. 162–171.

34. Some of the differences may also be explained by Jiang Guangci's editing of Qu's manuscript in 1927. In either case, Qu's private concerns have been revised to conform better to proletarian interests.

35. "Huangmoli" (In the wasteland) in *Qu Qiubai wenji*, I, 233.

36. Shneider, p. 41.

37. According to C. T. Hsia, *A History of Modern Chinese Fiction, 1917–1957*, rev. ed. (New Haven, Yale University Press, 1971), pp. 127–131, Qu was actual head of the league in 1931–1933 and Lu Xun was its nominal spokesman. See also Maeda, "Kushūhaku to Saren."

38. P. 864. Russian term used in the original.

39. P. 873.

40. *Qu Qiubai wenji*, IV, 2025. See "Amituofo," I, 186–187.

41. "Lun fanyi" (On translation), *Qu Qiubai wenji*, II, 919. On the reference to "common people," see note 44.

42. *Qu Qiubai wenji*, II, 977–1002.

43. P. 861.

44. Pp. 857–858.

45. D. S. Mirsky, *Pushkin* (New York, Dutton, 1963), pp. 69–72. I am indebted to Madeline G. Levine for assistance on this point.

46. See Nījima, "Pekin de mita Kushūhaku hihan"; also Zhao Cong, "Tan Qu Qiubai" (Remarks on Qu Qiubai), *Mingbao yuekan* (Mingbao monthly) 2:66–68 (December 1967).

47. "Duoyude hua" (Superfluous wods, in Sima Lu, *Qu Qiubai zhuan* (Biography of Qu Qiubai) (Hong Kong, 1962), pp. 147, 155–156.

48. Pp. 135–136.

49. P. 154. Translated in T. A. Hsia, p. 53.

50. P. 161.

51. Yang Zhihua, "Yi Qiubai," p. 52.

6. Images of Oppressed Peoples and Modern Chinese Literature

IRENE EBER

This article is part of a larger study on oppressed people's literature in Chinese translation. I would like to express my gratitude to the Center for Chinese Studies of the University of Michigan for the grant that has supported this study. Special thanks are due to Harriet Mills and Yi-tsi Feuerwerker for giving their constructive criticism. I am, of course, responsible for any errors and all interpretations.

1. According to A Ying, there were eighty publishers who printed translations before 1912, among them the well-known Commercial Press and Kaiming. See his *Wan Qing xiqu xiaoshuo mu* (Theater and fiction at the end of the Qing) (Shanghai, 1959), pp. 109–172.

2. Yan Fu and Xia Zengyou, "*Guowen bao* fuyin shuobu yuanqi," in A Ying, *Wan Qing wenxue congchao* (Collection of late Qing literary documents) (Peking, 1960), pp. 1–13. This essay first appeared in serial form between November 10 and December 11, 1897, in *Guowen bao* (Tientsin).

3. Zhou Zuoren, *Zhongguo xin wenxuede yuanliu* (The origins of the new Chinese literature) (Hong Kong, 1972), preface dated 1932.

4. "Zhongguo yu Bolan zhi bijiao" (China and Poland compared), *Dongfang zazhi* (Eastern miscellany, hereafter *DFZZ*) 1.8:163–164 (August 1904).

5. "Lun Youtairen sandu bu yi ban xin" (Concerning the continuous scattering of Jews), *Wanguo gongbao* (The globe magazine, henceforth *WGGB*) 10:305b–306 (1878); "Geguo zaji" (Miscellany from all countries), *WGGB* 15.7:28a–b (August 1903), mistakenly numbered 157; "Baoniu guozhi lai ganyu" (Intervention in a country's oppression), *WGGB* 14.11 (no. 167):18a–b (December 1902). Also *Minli bao* 337:2226 (September 19, 1902), where Jewish persecutions in Russia are noted.

6. "Youtairenzhi xianzhuang" (Unrest among the Jews), *WGGB* 17.8 (no. 200):24–25 (August 1905).

7. "Meiguo datong lingba yong heiren" (America's high command seeks to use

Blacks), *Xinmin congbao* (no. 29), in *Yiwen yinshu* (Taiwan reprint, 1966), V, 74–75.

8. Dong Wufan Yishu [original author?], "Meiguo heirenzhi jinzhuang" (Present affairs of American Blacks), tr. Ji Lifei, *WGGB* 18.6:13–17 (July 1906).

9. Liang Qichao, "Lun xiaoshuo yu qunzhi zhi guanxi" (On the relationship between fiction and the rule of the masses), in *Yinbingshi heji*, part 1, IV, 6, 1932 edition. This essay was first published in *Xin xiaoshuo*, 1, 1902.

10. Zhou Zuoren, *Zhongguo xin wenxuede yuanliu*, pp. 95–97.

11. Ibid., p. 21.

12. This is a brief summary of Lu Xun's essay "Fen" (The grave), in *Lu Xun sanshi-nian ji* (Lu Xun's thirty-year collection) (1907–1925, 1937), pp. 53–100.

13. "*Wenxue xunkan* xuanyan" (Manifesto of the *Literary Ten-Daily*), in *Zhongguo xin wenxue daxi* (Collection of China's new literature) ed. Zhao Jiabi (Shanghai, 1935–1936; Hong Kong reprint, 1963), X, 82–83.

14. Shen Yanbing (Mao Dun), "Xin wenxue yanjiuzhede zeren yu nuli" (The duties and strivings of researchers in new literature), *Xiaoshuo yuebao* (Short story monthly), hereafter *XSYB*) 10.2:2,4 (February 1921). Published under the pseudonym Lang Sun.

15. Shen Yanbing (Mao Dun), "Jindai wenxuede fanliu — Aierlande xin wenxue" (Countercurrent in modern literature — Ireland's new literature), *DFZZ* 17.7:66 (April 1920).

16. Zheng Zhenduo, "Aierlande wenyi fuxing" (Renaissance of Irish literature), in *Wenxue dagang* (Outlines of literature) (Shanghai), IV, 523.

17. Lang Sun (pseud.), "Shehui beijing yu chuangzao" (Social background and creativity), *XSYB* 12.7:14–17 (July 1921).

18. Shen Yanbing (Mao Dun), "Bolan jindai wenxue taidou Xiankeweizhi" (Poland's contemporary notable writer Sienkiewicz), *XSYB* 12.2:1 (February 1921).

19. Lang Sunao, "Shehui beijing yu chuangz," p. 18.

20. "Bolan wenxue tiyao" (Important points of Polish literature), tr. Zheng Zhaolin and Zhu Sunglu, *Xueyi zazhi* (Wissen und Wissenschaft) 3.10:2–5 (March 1922). Translated from Emile Faguet, *Initiation littéraire* (Paris, 1913).

21. Shen Yanbing (Mao Dun), "Xin Youtai wenxue gaiguan" (A brief look at Yiddish literature), *XSYB* 12.10:61 (October 1921).

22. Zhao Jingshen, "Heirende shi" (Black poetry), *XSYB* 19.11:1359 (November 1928).

23. Lu Xun, "Aierlan wenxuezhi huigu" (Looking back at Irish literature), in *Lu Xun quanji* (Complete works of Lu Xun) (1938), XVI, 440. First published in 1929. Translation of an essay from the Japanese by Noguchi Yonejirō.

24. Zheng Zhenduo, "Shijiushijide Bolan wenxue" (Nineteenth-century Polish literature), *XSYB* 17.10:1–2 (October 1926). With few modifications this article was also published in *Wenxue dagang*, IV.

25. "Youtai wenxue yu Pinsiqi" (Jewish literature and Pinski), tr. Han Jing, *XSYB* 12.7:3–7 (July 1921).

26. Translation according to Bonnie S. McDougall, *The Introduction of Western Literary Theories into Modern China, 1919–1925* (Tokyo, 1971), pp. 178–179. This is the final paragraph in Shen Yanbing, "Jindai wenxuede fanliu — Aierlande xin wenxue," p. 66.

27. Zheng Zhenduo, "Aierlande wenyi fuxing," p. 539.

28. Shen Yanbing, "Bolan jindai wenxue taidou Xiankeweizhi," pp. 1–4.

29. Translation according to Marián Gálik, *Mao Tun and Modern Chinese Literary Criticism* (Wiesbaden, Franz Steiner, 1969), p. 38. First published in *Xuesheng zazhi* 6.4–6:23–32, 33–41, 43–52 (April–June 1919).

30. Jaroslav Průšek, "Einige Bemerkungen zur Chinesischen Literatur in dem

Zeitraum 1919–1937," *Acta Orientalia* 15:231 (1962).

31. Zhou Yang, "Dui jiu xingshi liyong zai wenxueshangde yige kanfa" (A view on the utilization of old forms in literature), in *Zhongguo xiandai wenxue shi cankao ziliao* (Research Materials on the history of modern Chinese literature) (Peking, 1959-1960), I, 734.

32. "Beixing wangquede renmen," tr. Zhou Zuoren, *Xin qingnian* (New youth, hereafter *XQN*) 8.3:427–438 (November 1920). The play was published a second time in Zhou's *Kong da gu* (Empty drums) (Shanghai, 1928). Translated from *Six Plays of the Yiddish Theatre*, tr. Isaac Goldberg (Boston, Luce, 1916). Translated a second time by Wang Xinqing, "Beiwang juede linghun," *Pingmin.*

33. "Jin wang . . . ," *XSYB* 12.10:104–105 (October 1921). Translated from *Anthology of Modern Slavonic Literature in Prose and Verse*, tr. Paul Selver (London, Kegan Paul, 1919), p. 211.

34. "Huanghun," tr. Zhou Zuoren, *XQN* 7.3:89–94 (February 1920). Also in *Tiandi* (Drops) (Shanghai, 1920), pp. 221–236. Translated from *Tales by Polish Authors*, tr. Else C. M. Benecke (Oxford, 1915).

35. "Shenpan," tr. Zhongchi *XSYB* 12.2:23–35 (February 1921); and *Bolan duanpian xiaoshuo ji* (Collection of Polish short stories), tr. Shi Zhicun, (Shanghai, 1936), vol. D (500) in Wanyou wenku series. Translated from *More Tales by Polish Authors*, tr. Else C. M. Benecke and Marie Busch (New York, 1916).

36. "Canfeizhe," tr. Hu Yuzhi, *Mintuo* 3.2: (February 1, 1922). Translated from *David Pinski; Ten Plays*, tr. Isaac Goldberg (New York, 1920).

37. "Yige erende gushi," tr. Chen Gu, *XSYB* 16.2:1–14 (February 1925). Also translated by Wang Luyan in his *Pinsiqi ji* (Pinski collection) (Shanghai, n.d. [published before 1929]). Chen Gu's translation was taken from *Temptations: A Book of Short Stories by David Pinski*, tr. Isaac Goldberg (London, 1919).

38. "Cibei", tr. Zhou Zuoren, *Yusi* (Thread of talk) 5.12:647–656 (May 1929). Translated under the pseudonym of Nanming. Translated from *Jewish Children*, tr. Hannah Berman (New York, 1920).

39. "Yuan ni you fu le," tr. Zhou Zuoren, *XQN* 8.6:839–842 (April 1921). Reprinted in Zhou Zuoren, *Xiandai xiaoshuo yicong* (Shanghai, 1922). Translated from Esperanto of *Antologia Internacia*, tr. A. Grabowski (1904). Translated again by Xing Zhen, "Xushi sifu de," in *Xuehui* 52 [1920s]. Published again in *Chenbao fujian* (1923), probably from *Antologia Internacia*. Translated a third time by Sun Yong, "Shou zhufude," *Yiwen* (2.4:890–894) (1936).

40. Feng Yi, "Yingwende ruoxiao minzu wenxue shizhi lei" (Histories of small and weak people's literature in English), *Wenxue* (Literature) 2.5:941–945 (May 1934).

41. Hua Lu, "Xian shijie ruoxiao minzu ji qi gaikuang" (Survey of the world's small and weak peoples), ibid., p. 790.

42. Ibid.

43. René Wellek, "The Concept of Realism in Literary Scholarship," in *Concepts of Criticism* (New Haven and London: Yale University Press, 1964), p. 242.

44. Zheng Zhang, *Shijie ruoxiao minzu wenti* (The problem of the world's small and weak peoples) (Shanghai, 1940), pp. 14–15, 2–3. First published in 1936.

45. For example, Sean O'Faolain, "Sullivan's Trousers," translated by Xu Tianhong, "Suliwende kuzi," *Wenyi* 1:969–992 (1936); J. Kaden-Bandrowski, "The Sentence," translated as "Sixing panjue," in *Bolan duanpian xiaoshuo ji*, pp. 101–145, *Selected Polish Tales*, tr. Else C. M. Benecke and Marie Busch (London, 1921).

46. "Jiaru women bu neng bu si," tr. Gu Feng, *Wenxue* 2.5:929 (May 1934).

47. Claude McKay, *Harlem Shadows: The Poems of Claude McKay* (New York, Harcourt,

Brace, 1922), p. 53.

8. Genesis of a Writer: Notes on Lu Xun's Educational Experience, 1881–1909

LEO OU-FAN LEE

1. *Lu Xun quanji* (The complete works of Lu Xun, hereafter *LXQJ*) (Peking, 1973), I, 269.

2. Zhou Xiashou (Zuoren), *Lu Xun de gujia* (Lu Xun's old home) (Hong Kong, 1962), p. 7.

3. Qiao Feng (Zhou Jianren), *Lüejiang guanyu Lu Xun de shiqing* (A brief account of matters concerning Lu Xun) (Peking, 1954), p. 12.

4. For a list of titles and brief explanations of their contents, see William R. Schultz, "Lu Hsün: The Creative Years" (Ph.D. dissertation, University of Washington, 1955), pp. 17–19, 43–47.

5. Ibid., p. 17.

6. *LXQJ*, I, 264.

7. *LXQJ*, III, 136–137.

8. Wang Yao, *Lu Xun yu Zhongguo wenxue* (Lu Xun and Chinese literature) (Shanghai, 1952), pp. 18–19.

9. *LXQJ*, I, 264.

10. For Lu Xun's intellectual debt to Six Dynasties literature and to Zhang Binglin, see Wang Yao, "Lu Xun zuopin yu Zhongguo gudian wenxuede lishi guanxi" (On the historical relationship of Lu Xun's works with classical Chinese literature), *Wenyi bao* (Literary gazette) 19:11–18 (October 1956).

11. Tsi-an Hsia, *The Gate of Darkness: Studies on the Leftist Literary Movement in China* (Seattle and London, University of Washington Press, 1968), pp. 146–162.

12. *LXQJ*, II, 386.

13. Ibid., p. 357. English translation from *Silent China: Selected Writings of Lu Xun*, ed. and tr. Gladys Yang (New York, Oxford University Press, 1973), p. 102.

14. Zhou Xiashou, *Lu Xun de gujia*, p. 29.

15. Xu Qinwen, "Lu Xun xiansheng yu guxiang" (Mr. Lu Xun and his old home), *Wenyi bao* 20:25 (October 1956).

16. T. A. Hsia, p. 157.

17. Cao Juren, *Lu Xun nianpu* (Chronology of Lu Xun) (Hong Kong, 1970), p. 11.

18. *LXQJ*, I, 270.

19. Ibid., p. 269.

20. Zhou Zuoren, *Zhitang huixiang lu* (Memoirs of Zhou Zuoren) (Hong Kong, 1970), I, 12, 36.

21. Zhou Xiashou, *Lu Xun de gujia*, pp. 39–40.

22. Ibid., p. 155.

23. Erik H. Erikson, "In Search of Gandhi," *Daedelus* (Summer 1968), p. 726. See also his *Gandhi's Truth* (New York, Norton, 1969), p. 132.

24. *LXQJ*, II, 371–373.

25. See Zhou Xiashou, *Lu Xun xiaoshuolide renwu* (Characters in Lu Xun's short stories) (Shanghai, 1954), pp. 212–213; and Qiao Feng, p. 8.

26. Erik H. Erikson, *Insight and Responsibility* (New York, Norton, 1964), pp. 202–203.

27. Zhou Xiashou, *Lu Xun xiaoshuolide renwu*, p. 5.

28. *LXQJ*, I, 269–270. See also *Selected Stories of Lu Hsun*, tr. Yang Hsien-yi and Gladys Yang (Peking, 1960), p. 20.

29. Zhou Xiashou, *Lu Xunde gujia*, p. 92.

30. *LXQJ*, II, 397–398.

31. Zhou Zuoren, *Zhitang huixiang lu*, I, 31.

32. See Erikson, *Gandhi's Truth*, pp. 123–133. Erikson's analysis of Lu Xun, based on material supplied by this author, can be found on pp. 130–131.

33. Ibid., p. 132. The leading Japanese scholar on Lu Xun, Takeuchi Yoshimi, has likewise characterized Lu Xun's creative life as stemming from a sense of "atonement." See his *Ro Jin* (Lu Xun) (Tokyo, 1961), p. 11.

34. Erikson, *Gandhi's Truth*, p. 132.

35. For more theoretical explications of these terms see Erikson, *Identity, Youth and Crisis* (New York, Norton, 1968), especially pp. 159–188.

36. Zhou Zuoren, *Zhitang huixiang lu*, I, 52.

37. *LXQJ*, I, 270.

38. Zhou Zuoren, *Zhitang huixiang lu*, I, 41, 90.

39. Zhou Xiashou, *Lu Xun xiaoshuolide renwu*, pp. 249–250.

40. *LXQJ*, II, 405.

41. Ibid.

42. See Xu Shoushang, preface to Wang Yeqiu, *Minyuanqiande Lu Xun xiansheng* (Lu Xun before 1912) (Shanghai, 1947), p. 10.

43. Zhou Xiashou, *Lu Xun xiaoshuolide renwu*, pp. 268–269.

44. Ibid., pp. 266, 273.

45. *LXQJ*, II, 405. Huxley's original reads: "It may be safely assumed that two thousand years ago, before Caesar set foot in southern Britian, the whole countryside visible from the windows of the room in which I write, was in what is called 'the state of nature.' ' See Thomas H. Huxley, *Evolution and Ethics* (New York, Appleton, 1914), p. 1.

46. *LXQJ*, II, 405–406.

47. Zhou Xiashou, *Lu Xunde gujia*, pp. 183, 192–193.

48. Ibid., p. 177.

49. Schultz, p. 79.

50. Quoted in Wang Yeqiu, p. 79.

51. Included in *Lu Xun shijian xuanji* (Selected poetry of Lu Xun) (Hong Kong, 1967), pp. 2–3. English translation is my own.

52. Ibid., p. 3.

53. Chinese and Japanese scholars have argued ad nauseam on the issue of Lu Xun's relationship with the Restoration Society. The majority opinion tends to agree that Lu Xun did join, but the scholars disagree on the date. For a summary of the various views, see Ozaki Hideki, *Ro Jin no taiwa* (Dialogue with Lu Xun) (Tokyo, 1963), pp. 49–55. Ozaki puts the date between the end of 1903 and the fall of 1904. Given the amorphousness of Lu Xun's political attitude, Ozaki's date seems too early.

54. Schultz, p. 79.

55. See Benjamin I. Schwartz, *In Search of Wealth and Power: Yen Fu and the West*

(Cambridge, Mass., Harvard University Press, 1964), pp. 55–56; and Leo Ou-fan Lee, *The Romantic Generation of Modern Chinese Writers* (Cambridge, Mass., Harvard University Press, 1973), pp. 51–56.

56. Xu Shoushang, *Wo suo renshi de Lu Xun* (The Lu Xun I knew) (Peking, 1952), p. 8.

57. Ibid.

58. Lin Yü-sheng, "Radical Iconoclasm in the May Fourth Period and the Future of Chinese Liberalism," in *Reflections on the May Fourth Movement: A Symposium* ed. Benjamin I. Schwartz (Cambridge, Mass., Harvard East Asian Monographs, 1972), p. 29.

59. *LXQJ*, I, 270; *Selected Stories of Lu Hsun*, p. 21.

60. *LXQJ*, I, 271; *Selected Stories of Lu Hsun*, p. 21.

61. Zhou Xiashou, *Lu Xun xiaoshuolide renwu*, p. 230.

62. Yamada Norio, *Ro Jin den sono shisō to henreki* (Biography of Lu Xun, his thought and experience) (Tokyo, 1964), p. 44.

63. Xu Shoushang, *Wangyou Lu Xun yinxiang ji* (Impressions of my late friend Lu Xun) (Peking, 1955), p. 9.

64. Quoted in Yamada Norio, pp. 69–70.

65. For Lu Xun's grades, see Yamada Norio, p. 55.

66. Ibid., p. 65.

67. Hosoya Kusako, "Fujino Gonkyūro sensei ni tsuite" (About Mr. Fujino Gonkyuro), *Daien* 12.10:41–43 (October 1966).

68. *LXQJ*, II, 416.

69. Quoted in Yamada Norio, pp. 66–69. I am indebted to Ian Levy of Princeton University for translation from the Japanese in this and other Japanese sources.

70. Yamada Norio, p. 62.

71. *LXQJ*, I, 271.

72. *LXQJ*, II, 412.

73. Yamada Norio, p. 61.

74. Xu Shoushang, *Wangyou Lu Xun yinxiang ji*, p. 17.

75. *LXQJ*, I, 35, 30, 37. See also Harriet C. Mills, "Lu Hsün: The Years on the Left, 1927–1936" (Ph.D. dissertation, Columbia University, 1963), p. 18.

76. English translation in Mills, p. 18.

77. Ibid.

78. *LXQJ*, I, 44–51.

79. Ibid., p. 41; Mills, p. 20.

80. Ibid., p. 61; Mills, p. 20.

81. Ibid., pp. 99–101; Mills, pp. 20–21.

82. Lin Zhen, *Lu Xun shiji kao* (Research on Lu Xun's record) (Shanghai, 1948), p. 43.

83. Zhou Xiashou, *Lu Xunde gujia*, p. 198.

84. *LXQJ*, I, 272; *Selected Stories of Lu Hsun*, p. 22.

85. Zhou Zuoren, *Zhitang huixiang lu*, I, 196.

86. Ibid., pp. 197–198, 208, 210–211.

87. Zhitang (Zhou Zuoren), "Guanyu Lu Xun zhi er" (More on Lu Xun) in *Lu Xun xiansheng jinian ji* (Memorial collection on Lu Xun) (Shanghai, 1937), I, 30; *Zhitang huixiang lu*, I, 210. While Lu Xun relied on these works for much of the basic information, the interpretation of European literary trends still reflected his own thinking.

88. Schultz, p. 99.

89. Ibid.

90. Mills, p. 22.

91. Zhitang, "Guanyu Lu Xun zhi er," pp. 30–31.

92. The author is much indebted to Patrick Hanan's comments made at the conference, which significantly enriched this part of the paper. For more details on Lu Xun's choices of European literature, see Hanan, "The Technique of Lu Hsün's Fiction," *Harvard Journal of Asiatic Studies* 34:55–96 (1974).

93. Zhitang, "Guanyu Lu Xun zhi er," p. 31. Lu Xun's predilection for symbolist literature is discussed in chapter 4, "Lu Xun: The Impact of Russian Literature" by Douwe Fokkema.

94. See chapter 4.

95. The description of these three stories is based on Lu Xun's own assessments, quoted in Wang Yeqiu, pp. 101–104. Certain motifs in "Silence" — such as the canary bird representing the soul of the dead daughter and the graveyard scene near the end of the story — may have had an artistic impact on Lu Xun's conception of the story "Medicine." See Hanan, "The Technique of Lu Hsün's Fiction," pp. 62–63. The two stories by Andreyev can be found in *Silence and Other Stories,* tr. W. H. Lowe (London, Francis Griffiths, 1910), pp. 46–61, 77–99.

96. Quoted in Wang Yeqiu, p. 103.

97. *LXQJ*, V, 106.

98. Wang Yeqiu, p. 101.

99. Zhou Zuoren, *Zhitang huixiang lu*, I, 232.

100. *LXQJ*, I, 272, *Selected Stories of Lu Hsun*, p. 23.

101. Zhou Xiashou, *Lu Xun xiaoshoulide renwu*, p. 10.

102. *LXQJ*, I, 277; *Selected Stories of Lu Hsun*, p. 26.

103. For detailed analysis, see Hanan, "The Technique of Lu Hsün's Fiction," pp. 66–68; see also J. D. Chinnery, "The Influence of Western Literature on Lu Xun's 'Diary of a Madman,'" *Bulletin of the School of Oriental and African Studies* 23.2:309–322 (1960).

104. Erikson, "In Search of Gandhi," p. 276.

9. Lu Xun: Literature and Revolution from Mara to Marx

HARRIET C. MILLS

1. For an imaginative treatment of Lu Xun's first twenty-eight years, see Chapter 8, "Genesis of a Writer: Notes on Lu Xun's Education Experience, 1881–1909" byy Leo Ou-fan Lee. Material discussed there has been cut from my remarks which can be filled out by — if not always reconciled with — Lee's fuller treatment. No attempt will be made here to cite the standard iographies and biographical tables for Lu Xun. For the early years, the most helpful source is Zhou Zuoren (Zhou Xiashou): *Lu Xunde gujia* (Lu Xun's old home) (Shanghai, 1953); *Lu Xun xiaoshuolide renwu* (Characters in Lu Xun's short stories) (Shanghai, 1954); *Zhitang huixiang lu* (Memoirs of Zhou Zuoren) (Hong Kong, 1970).

2. Zhou Zuoren, *Lu Xunde gujia*, pp. 128–142, 159–161, offers an introduction to his reading in this period.

3. *Lu Xun quanji* (Complete works of Lu Xun) (Shanghai, 1938), hereafter cited as *1938 CW*, VI, 189. On the eve of his departure for Japan, he was reading the violently anti-Manchu *Su bao* (Kiangsu journal).

4. *1938 CW*, I, 270.

5. For the Japan period, note especially the works of Xu Shoushang: *wangyou Lu Xun yinxiang ji* (Impressions of my late friend Lu Xun) (Shanghai, 1947); *Wo suo renshi de Lu Xun* (The Lu Xun I knew) (Peking, 1952). See also Robert Scalapino, "Prelude to Marxism," in Albert Feuerwerker, Rhoads Murphey, and Mary C. Wright, eds., *Approaches to Modern Chinese History* (Berkeley, 1967), p. 194.

6. *Lu Xun quanji* (Complete works of Lu Xun) (Peking, 1957), hereafter cited as *1957 CW*, VII, 18–23.

7. *1938 CW*, I, 270; translation in *Selected works of Lu Hsun (Peking, 1956-1960, hereafter cited as SW)*, I, 2.

8. *Lu Xun quanji buyi xubian* (Supplement to Lu Xun's complete works) (Shanghai, 1953), hereafter cited as *1953 Supp.*, pp. 465-585.

9. *1938 CW*, XI, 10.

10. Lu Xun's relations with the Restoration Society and the Chekiang revolutionaries in Tokyo is complicated. Basic materials include: Mary Backhus Rankin, "The Revolutionary Movement in Chekiang: A Study in the Tenacity of Tradition," in *China in Revolution*, ed. Mary C. Wright (New Haven, Yale University Press, 1968), pp. 319-361; Shen Diemin, "Ji Guangfu hui er san shi" (A few recollections of the Restoration Society), in *Xinhai geming huiyi lu* (Reminiscences of the 1911 revolution), ed. Zhongguo renmin zhengzhi xieshang huiyi quanguo weiyuanhui wenshi ziliao yanjiu weiyuanhui (Peking, 1962), IV, 131-142; Lin Zhen, *Lu Xun shiji kao* (Research on Lu Xun's record) (Shanghai, 1948), pp. 1-11; *1938 CW*, XX, 617. The Taos, uncle and nephew, were from Shaohsing. See also Lee, "Genesis of a Writer," note 55.

11. The most perceptive study available on the influence of Lu Xun's early reading in Western sources on his own literary development, particularly on the development of his fiction, is Patrick D. Hanan, "The Technique of Lu Hsün's Fiction," *Harvard Journal of Asiatic Studies* 34:53-96 (1974).

12. *1938 CW*, I, 24-37, 13-23, 38-54, 55-102.

13. Ibid., p. 40.

14. Ibid., p. 101.

15. Ibid., pp. 48-49.

16. *1957 CW*, VII, 235-247, 240.

17. *1938 CW*, I, 49.

18. Ibid., p. 54.

19. Ibid., p. 53. Translation by William Schultz, "Lu Hsün: The Creative Years" (Ph.D. dissertation, University of Washington, 1955), p. 94.

20. *1938 CW*, I, 41.

21. *1957 CW*, VII, 240.

22. Ibid., pp. 244-245, 247.

23. Ibid., pp. 257-264.

24. *1938 CW*, II, 423 (*SW*, I, 415).

25. Zhou Zuoren, *Lu Xunde gujia*, pp. 418-419, and *Zhitang huixiang lu*, pp. 332-334.

26. *1938 CW*, I, 21, 274 (*SW*, I, 5-6; II, 58).

27. Chen Duxiu, "Wo duiyu Lu Xun de renshi" (My acquaintance with Lu Xun), in *Lu Xun xin lun* (New discussions on Lu Xun), ed. Wang Ming et al. (n.p., 1938), pp. 101-102.

28. *1938 CW*, V, 50.

29. Xu Shoushang, *Wo suo renshi de Lu Xun*, p. 38; O. V. [Feng Xuefeng], "Lu Xun xiansheng jihua er weicheng de jiezuo" (Mr. Lu Xun's planned but unfinished works), in *Lu Xun xin lun*, pp. 129–136; Feng Xuefeng, *Dang geiyu Lu Xun yi liliang* (The party gave Lu Xun strength) (Honan, 1951), p. 9; Xu Guangping, *Lu Xun huiyi* (Remembrances of Lu Xun) (Peking, 1961), p. 139.

30. *1938 CW*, II, 450; *Old Tales Retold,* tr. Yang Hsien-yi and Gladys Yang (Peking, 1972), p. 2.

31. *1957 CW*, I, 369.

32. *1938 CW*, II, 14–16, 24–25, 49–50 (*SW*, II, 25–30, 37–38).

33. *1938 CW*, I, 274–275 (*SW*, I, 6).

34. *1957 CW*, IX, 286; 8/20/18 to Xu Shoushang.

35. *1957 CW*, IX, 299–300; 5/4/20 to Song Chongyi.

36. *1938 CW*, IV, 459; VI, 279 (*SW*, III, 225; IV, 169).

37. *1938 CW*, VI, 323 (*SW* IV, 183-184).

38. *1938 CW*, I, 178-179; VI, 323, 327; *1957 CW*, I, 371 (*SW*, II, 97; IV, 183, 185).

39. Chen Duxiu, "Wo duiyu Lu Xun de renshi," pp. 101–102.

40. *1957 CW*, I, 451–452, 274.

41. *1938 CW*, I, 208.

42. *1957 CW*, VII, 333.

43. Paragraph based on *1937 CW*, I, 177, 181, 200–220; II, 24–25 (*SW*, II, 95–96, 99, 108–109, 139–141).

44. *1957 CW*, III, 12–13.

45. *1938 CW*, III, 43–44 (*SW*, II, 115). See also *1957 CW*, VII, 364, 393–394.

46. *1938 CW*, III, 48–49; I, 195–196 (*SW*, II, 133–134).

47. *1938 CW*, III, 249 (*SW*, II, 250).

48. *1938 CW*, V, 48 (*SW*, III, 171).

49. *1938 CW*, I, 199, 201, 252; III, 50–51, 237, 245–262; *1957 CW*, III, 70–71, 237; (*SW*, II, 123, 138, 140, 211, 248–266). For a brief background on Weimingshe, see Mills, pp. 65-68.

50. *1938 CW*, I, 221–222 (*SW*, II, 190–191).

51. *1938 CW*, III, 79, 24, 48–49 (*SW*, II, 161, 108, 120).

52. *1957 CW*, I, 370; *1938 CW*, I, 264.

53. *1938 CW*, VII, 81; I, 10, 260; III, 150 (*SW*, II, 196).

54. *1938 CW*, I, 528–531, 479 (*SW*, I, 353–355, 335).

55. *1938 CW*, VII, 97, 30.

56. This and the remaining quotes are from *1938 CW*, VII, 96–98.

57. For background bibliography on Amoy, see Harriet Mills, "Lu Hsün: The Years on the Left, 1927–1936" (Ph.D. dissertation, Columbia University, 1963), p. 70.

58. *1938 CW*, II, 449–452, 467–483.

59. Ibid., III, 368 (*SW*, II, 311).

60. Paragraph based on *1938 CW*, VII, 1–354, esp. pp. 156–160, 205–206, 256–257, 308, 316.

61. For Canton bibliography, see Mills, pp. 76–77.

62. *1938 CW*, III, 407 (*SW*, II, 326–333).

63. *1938 CW*, III, 393–396.

64. *1957 CW*, VII, 429–430.

65. *1938 CW*, III, 402–410 (*SW*, II, 326–333).

66. *1938 CW*, III, 433–449, 457–461, 477–478.

67. Ibid., pp. 466, 473–476, 509–510 (*SW*, II, 338).

68. Paragraph and quotes from *1938 CW*, III, 441, 465, 508.

69. Ibid., VII, 287.

70. Ibid., III, 441.

71. Ibid., IV, 44 (*SW*, II, 359).

72. *1938 CW*, III, 445–446.

73. The most detailed study of this period remains Mills.

74. *1938 CW*, IV, 213–214 (*SW*, III, 74).

75. See Mills, pp. 123–128, for brief discussion.

76. Paragraph based on *1938 CW*, IV, 73–74, 78–79, 94–95, 135–136, 214–220 (*SW*, II, 363–364, III, 12–13, 16, 21–22, 45, 76–77, 81).

77. *1938 CW*, IV, 138; VII, 526.

78. Feng Xuefeng, *Huiyi Lu Xun* (Remembering Lu Xun) (Peking, 1952), p. 161.

79. Zheng Boqi, "Zuoyi huiyi pianduan" (A memory of the League of Left-Wing Writers) *Wenxue pinglun* (Literary review) (February 1960), pp. 74–76.

80. *1938 CW*, V, 49–50 (*SW*, III, 172–174).

81. *1938 CW*, IV, 283–284 (*SW*, III, 120).

82. For background on Rou Shi and the other martyrs and the possibility that party rivalry was responsible for their sacrifice, see T. A. Hsia, "Enigma of the Five Martyrs," in his *The Gate of Darkness: Studies on the Leftist Literary Movement in China* (Seattle and London, University of Washington Press, 1968), pp. 163–233.

83. For example, Lu Xun addressed meetings arranged through the league and the party on a 1932 trip to Peking.

84. *1938 CW*, IV, 236–242 (*SW*, III, 93–98).

85. This and balance of paragraph based on *1938 CW*, IV, 243, 250; *1957 CW*, VII, 757–758.

86. *1938 CW*, VII, 772–773.

87. Paragraph based on *1938 CW*, IV, 268–269, 283–285; V, 29–30, 34–35 (*SW*, III, 108, 120–122, 153–155, 161–162).

88. Paragraph based on *1938 CW*, IV, 267–275, 280–288 (*SW*, III, 107–113, 118–124).

89. Paragraph based on *1938 CW*, IV, 197, 286–289, 357–359 (*SW*, III, 124–125, 159).

90. Paragraph based on *1938 CW*, IV, 361–373, 376–380.

91. Paragraph based on *1938 CW*, IV, 276–292; V, 45–46 (*SW*, III, 114–128, 169). Quotation, *1938 CW*, IV, 289 (*SW*, III, 125).

92. Mills, pp. 191–331, presents the most detailed analysis available on Lu Xun's major themes and activities in these years.

93. *1957 CW*, IX, 301–302; 8/2/36 to Cao Bai.

94. *Lu Xun quanji buyi* (Supplement to Lu Xun's complete works, Shanghai, 1946), pp. 327–328.

95. Best quick treatment is T. A. Hsia, pp. 101–145.

96. For background, see Mills, pp. 280–283.

97. *Lu Xun shujian* (Lu Xun's correspondence) (Shanghai, 1948), p. 849; 12/6/34 to Meng Shihuan.

98. *1957 CW*, X, 163–164; 10/7/33 to Hu Jinxu.

99. Rest of paragraph and quotes from *1938 CW*, III, 53–54; IV, 453–455; V, 172–173, 642–643; VI, 13–14 (*SW*, II, 143, III, 226, 308; *Chinese Literature*, May, 1973, p. 20.)

100. *1957 CW*, X, 214–215; 5/6/34 to Yang Jiyun.

101. *1938 CW*, V, 169–173, 554.

102. Paragraph and quotes from *1938 CW*, II, 11, III, 179–180, 228–229; VI, 14, 222.

103. *1938 CW*, V, 229; VI, 615 (*SW*, IV, 296).

10. Lu Xun's "Medicine"

MILENA DOLEŽELOVÁ-VELINGEROVÁ

1. The story first appeared in *Xin qingnian* (New youth) 6.5:479–484 (May 1919) and was later included in Lu Xun's short story collection *Nahan* (A call to arms) (1923). I use the edition published by Renmin wenxue chubanshe (Peking, 1973). Unless stated otherwise, quotations from "Medicine" are based on Yang Hsien-yi and Gladys Yang's translation in *Selected Stories of Lu Hsun*, rev. ed. (Peking, 1972), pp. 25–33.

2. The autobiographical sources are described in Wu Benxing's essay, "Lu Xun 'Yao'" (Lu Xun's "Medicine"), in his *Wenxue zuopin yanjiu* (Studies of literary works) (Shanghai, 1954), I, 93–123.

3. In contrast to Lu Xun's other famous stories, relatively few studies have been devoted to "Medicine." To my knowledge, there are only four: Xu Qinwen, "Du 'Yao' xin gan" (New impressions when reading "Medicine"), *Renmin wenxue* (People's literature) 4.6:66 (1951); Feng Xuefeng, "Yao" (Medicine), *Wenyi xuexi* (Literary studies) 1.1:5–7 (April 1954); a brief analysis of "Medicine" by C. T. Hsia in *A History of Modern Chinese Fiction, 1917–1957*, 2nd ed. (New Haven, Yale University Press, 1971), pp. 34–76; and the aforementioned article by Wu Benxing, "Lu Xun 'Yao.'"

4. Several narrative techniques for the portrayal of characters, the depiction of milieu, and parallelism were analyzed by Wu Benxing in his study, "Lu Xun 'Yao.'" Recently, Patrick Hanan has also published an article, "The Technique of Lu Hsün's Fiction," *Harvard Journal of Asiatic Studies* 34:53–96 (1974). However, he deals with only one aspect of Lu Xun's narrative technique, namely, his devices of irony.

5. See Lu Xun's preface to his *A Call to Arms* and his essay "Fuqinde bing," (Father's illness) in the collection *Zhao hua xi shi* (Morning blossoms plucked at dusk) (Hong Kong, n.d.), pp. 48–53.

6. For further information, see *Eminent Chinese of the Ch'ing Period* ed. Arthur W. Hummel (Washington, D.C., Library of Congress, 1943–1944), pp. 169–171.

7. This description of Uncle Kang is strikingly similar to that of the "butcher" from chapter 27 of the classic novel *Shuihu zhuan* (The water margin). Like Uncle Kang, "he was dressed in a white coarse cotton shirt, fastened by a long sash at his waist," and "his face was heavy-jowled." The "butcher" is a dealer in human flesh (he and his wife rob and kill bypassers and sell the human "meat" as beef), not unlike Uncle Kang, who profits from selling the belongings of those who are executed. There is also a startling correspondence with the motif of the mantou. The only difference between the mantou served in the teahouse and that served in the wineshop is that in *Shuihu zhuan*, the mantou is filled with human "meat." These similarities, of course, open up a more general problem of Lu Xun's relationship to the Chinese literary and folklore traditions. Compare his later collection, *Gu shi xin bian* (Old tales retold), and Berta Krebsová's

study, "Lu Hsün and His Collection *Old Tales Retold,*" *Archiv Orientální* 28.2:225–281 (1960); 28.4:640–656 (1960); 29.2:268–310 (1961).

8. Lu Xun's wording, "*Tamen kengle ni,*" is rendered in the Yangs' tranlation as "They murdered you." Since the word *keng* means "to hard, to entrap," and only the compound, *kengsha,* is rendered as "to murder," I prefer the closer translation, "to trap." In this version Mother Xia is referring to her treacherous relaive. I wish to express my thanks to Yü-shih Chen for her suggestion of this translation.

9. As with other symbols in this story, the meaning of the names is intricately hidden in the text. In the first three sections, the name Hua is introduced only once, at the very beginning of the story, when the full name of Old Shuan is given. It reappears consistently only in section four, in association with Mother Hua (Hua *dama*). The name Xia is disclsoed at the end of section three by Uncle Kang. In the Yang's tranlation the name Hua disappears completely from the text (Mother Hua is referred to as Old Shuan's wife), and no attempt is made to indicate the symbolic meaning of either name.

10. Lu Xun, preface to *A Call to Arms.*

11. The Central Contradiction in Mao Dun's Earliest Fiction

JOHN BERNINGHAUSEN

1. Georg Lukács, "Franz Kafka or Thomas Mann?," in his *Realism in Our Time: Literature and the Class Struggle* (New York: Harper Torchbooks, 1971), p. 75.

2. Mao Dun, *Shi* (Corrosion) (Shanghai, 1930), p. 4.

3. See Georg Lukács, "Art and Objective Truth" in his *Writer and Critic and Other Essays* (New York, Grosset & Dunlop, 1970).

4. "Cong Guling dao Dongjing" (From Guling to Tokyo, hereafter "CGDD"), dated July 16, 1928, originally published in *Xiaoshuo yuebao* (Short story monthly), also in *Mao Dun pingzhuan* (Selected critical writings on Mao Dun, hereafter *MDPZ*), ed. Fu Zhiying (Hong Kong, 1968), p. 345.

5. The revolutionary regime in Wuhan at this time was made up of the left-wing elements of the GMD (Guomindang) in coalition with the CCP (Chinese Communist party or Gongchandang) operating under the banner of the recently deceased Sun Yatsen's GMD party.

6. Mao Dun, *Zhuiqiu* (Searching), in *Shi,* p. 261.

7. Ibid., p. 266.

8. I have relied on Ye Ziming, *Lun Mao Dun sishiniande wenxue daolu* (Discussing Mao Dun's forty-year literary path) (Shanghai, 1959), pp. 3–6, for biographical data. Also see *Straw Sandals: Chinese Short Stories, 1918–1933,* ed. Harold R. Isaacs (Cambridge, Mass., MIT Press, 1974), pp. lxiii–lxv. For a detailed exposition of Mao Dun's career as a critic, editor, translator, see Marián Gálik, *Mao Tun and Modern Chinese Literary Criticism* (Wiesbaden, Franz Steiner, 1969).

9. See note 4 above; also see "Gulingzhi qiu" (Autumn in Kuling), one of several early stories omitted from the ten-volume collection of Mao Dun's writings, the *Mao Dun wenji* (hereafter *MDWJ*) (Peking, 1958). Although Gálik has mentioned that it first

appears in the magazine *Wenxue* (Literature) in 1933, from the content and certain stylistic elements, I suspect it was actually written during Mao Dun's stay in Tokyo and that it is unique among his early stories in that it represents an *autobiographical* account of his escape from Wuhan in late July 1927. It is included in several anthologies of his short stories, including one published under its title.

10. Mao Dun, "Xie zai *Ye qiangwei* de qianmian" (A preface to *Wild Roses*), dated May 9, 1929 in *Ye qiangwei*, p. iii.

11. Ye Ziming, p. 82. See also Georg Lukács, "Critical Realism and Socialist Realism" in his *Realism in Our Time*.

12. Ernst Fischer, *The Necessity of Art* (New York, Penguin Books, 1963), p. 102.

13. *MDWJ*, VII, 68.

14. Wang Yao, *Zhongguo xin wenxue shi gao* (A draft of the history of new Chinese literature), I, 225.

15. Mao Dun, *Huanmie* (Disillusionment), in *Shi*, p. 9.

16. Mao Dun, *Lu* (The road) (Shanghai, 1935), p. 6.

17. Jaroslav Průšek, "Basic Problems of the History of Modern Chinese Literature and C. T. Hsia, *A History of Modern Chinese Fiction*," *T'oung pao*, 49.4–5:396.

18. *MDWJ*, VII, 24–25.

19. Mao Dun, *Dongyao* (Vacillation), in *Shi*, p. 128.

20. Ibid., p. 154.

21. *MDWJ*, VII, 53–54.

22. *MDWJ*, II, 463.

23. Ibid., p. 468.

24. Ibid., p. 471.

25. Gálik, pp. 49–50.

26. *MDWJ*, VII, 3.

27. Mao Dun, *Hong* (The rainbow) (Shanghai, 1930) p. 111.

28. Ibid., pp. 113–114.

29. *MDWJ*, VII, 79.

30. Mao Dun, "Zisha" (Suicide), in *Zhongqiuzhi ye* (Mid-autumn night) (Shanghai, 1937), p. 62.

31. Ye Ziming, p. 65 ff.

32. Mao Dun, *Dongyao*, in *Shi*, p. 164.

33. Mao Dun, *Zhuiqiu*, in *Shi*, p. 276.

34. Mao Dun, "Shi yu sanwen" (Poetry and prose) in *Zhongqiuzhi ye*, p. 72.

35. "CGDD," sect. 2, in *MDPZ*, p. 345.

36. Qian Xingcun, "Mao Dun yu xianshi" (Mao Dun and reality), in *MDPZ*, p. 212.

37. Mao Dun, "Xie zai *Ye Qiangwei* de qianmian", pp. iv–v.

38. Ibid., p. v.

39. Mao Dun, *Huanmie*, in *Shi*, p. 53.

40. *MDWJ*, VII, 84.

12. Mao Dun and the Use of Political Allegory in Fiction: A Case Study of His "Autumn in Kuling"

Yü-shih Chen

1. Contrary to what many believe, Mao Dun was not "purged" in 1965. He was not even criticized during the Cultural Revolution. It may be said that he was under pressure after Mao Zedong criticized the management of cultural affairs in 1964 (see Chou En-lai's "Report on the Government Administration," *Renmin ribao* [People's daily], December 31, 1964). Mao Dun was removed from the Ministry of Culture, but he was officially appointed to the National Committee of the Political Consultative Conference on January 4 (see the announcement of appointments, *Renmin ribao*, January 5, 1965). His removal from the Ministry of Culture was probably due to some sort of mistake in the management of cultural affairs that was brought to light during the socialist education campaign in late 1964. It remains an open question, however, whether that was in fact an official removal — it could have been a transfer or a resignation (see announcements about the Third National People's Congress, *Renmin ribao*, December 30, 1964, to January 6, 1965). He was criticized in some wall posters put up by Red Guards, but the fact that the film based on his short story "Lin jia puzi" (Lin's store) was withheld from release may be due to production delays. Neither action necessarily stands for the party's policy.

2. To date there are two collections of Mao Dun's works, both comprehensive but neither complete. *Mao Dun wenji* (Collected writings of Mao Dun), 10 vols. (Peking, 1958–1961), and *Mao Dun pinglun ji* (Collection of Mao Dun's critical works) (Tokyo, 1957–1960).

3. They include the incomplete *Hong* (The rainbow [1929]), the often ignored *Lu* (The road [1930–1931]), and *San ren xing* (Of Three Friends [1931]). There are also many baffling short stories in the collection titled *Ye Qiangwei* (Wild roses). Among his best individual stories are: "Semang" (Color-blind [1929]), "Nining" (Mud [1929]), "Tuoluo" (The top [1929]), and the historical tales "Shi jie" (Stone tablet), "Baozitou Lin Chong" (Lin Chong and the leopard head), "Daze hsiang" (Tatse county [1930]) and "Gulingzhi qiu" (Autumn in Kuling [1933]).

4. Zhang Guotao, *Wo de huiyi* (Memoirs) (Hong Kong, 1971), p. 101. Also A. Farien, "Mao Zedongde wenyi zhengce ji wenhua geming" (The literary policy of Mao Zedong and the Cultural Revolution), tr. Guo Xiong, *Mingbao yuekan* (Mingbao Monthly) 21:22–27 (September 1967).

5. Mao Dun, "Wode xiao zhuan" (My brief biography), in *Mao Dun xuanji* (Selected works of Mao Dun) (Shanghai, 1940), p. 265.

6. Zhang Guotao, p. 97.

7. The impression that Mao Dun was a prudent person was derived from the comments Chen Bilan made in her interview with A. Farien (see note 4). Chen Bilan joined the Chinese Communist party in October 1922, and was a leader of the women's movement in the 1920s, and knew Mao Dun well. Zhang Guotao, on the other hand,

shows us a different facet of Mao Dun's character when he makes the incidental remark that Mao Dun supported Chen Wangdao in the latter's protest against the party resolution to increase discipline and ideological training made at a meeting in Shanghai in 1922. See Zhang Guotao, p. 217.

8. Chen Bilan, for instance, mentioned in the interview with A. Farien (see note 4 above) that she had known Mao Dun well since the early 1920s. She and Ding Ling were roommates at Shanghai University in 1923-1924 when Mao Dun was teaching fiction there. Deng Yinchao at that time was the chairman of the Committee for Women's Movement. Chen Bilan, Ding Ling, and Kong Dezhi (Mao Dun's wife) were all members of the committee. Mao Dun knew them all since he and they all worked for the May Thirtieth movement.

9. Mao Dun, "Du Ni Huanzhi" (On reading Ni Huanzhi), Wenxue zhoubao (Literature weekly) 8.20 (May 1929). The article was collected in Mao Dun pinglun ji, I, 64–80.

10. Ibid., p. 69.

11. The announced reason for the decision was that he wanted to devote more time to social movements. But the pressure from the board of directors of the Commercial Press, which had suffered considerable embarrassment from Mao Dun's political outspokenness and his radical stand on the antifeudalism and anti-imperialism movements, must have contributed it. See Ye Ziming, Lun Mao Dun sishiniande wenxue daolu (On Mao Dun's forty-year literary path) (Shanghai, 1959), p. 13.

12. Ibid., p. 39.

13. Mao Dun, "Ji ju jiu hua" (Remarks on the past), in Mao Dun xuanji, pp. 1–5.

14. Xingshi (Awakened lion) is the title of a periodical published during 1905-1907. The main theme of the periodical is national revolution. While it is difficult to prove whether the ship that took Mao Dun and his companions to Canton actually had the name Xingshi, the association of a national, patriotic, and revolutionary cause is unmistakably there.

15. Italics added.

16. Martin Wilbur and Julie Lien-ying How, Documents on Communism, Nationalism and Soviet Advisers in China 1918-1927 (New York, Columbia University Press, 1956). For a detailed account of the duties and activities of a party propagandist, see pp. 97–98.

17. For training programs in the party schools and activities of party cells, see ibid., pp. 97–98.

18. Qian Xingcun, "Cong Dongjing huidao Guling" (Returning from Tokyo to Kuling), Xiandai Zhongguo wenxuejia (Contemporary Chinese literary writers) (Shanghai, 1929), II, 121. In chapter 5 of Disillusionment, a group of students in S College calls a meeting to discuss and pass a resolution on a triangle love relationship among three classmates.

19. Ibid., pp. 153–154:

> As to the respected and sympathetic character Wang Shitao, her desperate recourse to prostitution certainly moves one's heart. But that is definitely not the way of life for someone who has truly grasped the meaning of life, nor a revolutionary in the revolutionary camp. I do not dare to say that there do not exist today people like Wang . . . If her career is the author's way of portraying her attitude toward sex, then that is altogether another matter. Or if the author was using her to hint at one way of coming to terms with life, that is also acceptable. However, if she is meant to demonstrate the revolutionary spirit of women, then it becomes as ridiculous as what he attempted to show with Cao Chifang's behavior.

20. Mao Dun, *Mao Dun xuanji* (Selected works of Mao Dun) (Peking, 1951), p. 7 (please note that this is not the same *Selected Works of Mao Dun* as in notes 5 and 13. This volume was published by the Kaiming shudian in Peking and is a title in the collection Xin wenxue xuanji [Selections from new literature], while the 1940 *Selected Works of Mao Dun* was published by the Wanxiang shuwo in Shanghai and is a title in the Xiandai chuangzuo wenku [Library of contemporary creative writings]).

21. The "devastating defeat" here refers to the series of events that culminated in the catastrophic Canton Commune in December 1927.

22. Mao Dun, "Cong Guling dao Dongjing" (From Kuling to Tokyo), *Xiaoshuo yuebao* (*Short Story Monthly*) 19.10:1138–1147 (October 1928).

23. Wu Tien-wei, "Chiang Kai-shek's March Twentieth Coup d'Etat of 1926," *Journal of Asian Studies* 27.3:585–602 (May 1968).

24. For general reference on the Comintern-CCP relationship in the 1920s, see Harold R. Isaacs, *The Tragedy of the Chinese Revolution* (New York, Atheneum, 1968); Conrad Brandt, *Stalin's Failure in China, 1924–1927* (Cambridge, Mass., Harvard University Press, 1958); Zhang Guotao.

25. Mao Dun, "Gulingzhi qiu" *Wenxue* (Literature) 3:371–374, 5:752–761, 6:922–925 (September, November, December 1933).

26. The story was later added to a collection of Mao Dun's short stories bearing the title *Gulingzhi qiu* (Shanghai, 1957), pp. 1–64. This is the text used in this chapter.

27. Ibid., p. 64.

28. It has been suggested that these sections were never written, since Mao Dun seemed to have a certain predilection for incomplete works — *Hong*, for example. But there is another deliberate deletion on a similar subject by Qian Xingcun in his polemical attack on Mao Dun at that time. Qian acknowledged the deletion and the reason for it in his appended note to "Cong Dongjing huidao Guling":

> The content of section four in this article was originally divided into two parts . . . But at the time of publication, I felt that this was not a suitable place or time for the latter part of the article to appear, so I withdrew that part, added the section "On *Wild Roses*" instead, and also rearranged the preface.

29. Mao Dun, *Gulingzhi qiu*, pp. 58–59.

30. "Zhongyang fukan" (Literary supplement to the *Central Daily*) 125:227–228 (Hankow, July 29, 1927).

31. The date August 8 is inferred from Yun's remarks about Fuchow. The retreating troops arrived in Fuchow on or around August 8, 1927. See for instance, "Chou Yi-ch'un's Report," in Martin Wilbur, *Ashes of Defeat* (New York, Institute of East Asian Studies, Columbia University, 1964), reprinted from *The China Quarterly* 18:3–54 (April-June 1964).

32. Ibid., p. 9.

33. See note 31.

34. Zhang Guotao, "Wode huiyi" (Memoirs), *Mingbao Monthly* 20:87–96, 21:85–91, 22:88–94, 23:88–94, 24:89–98 (August through December 1967).

35. *Mao Dun pinglun ji*, I, 72–73.

36. Mao Dun, "Tan wode yanjiu" (On my studies), *Mao Dun pinglun ji*, II, 132.

37. Mao Dun, *Gulingzhi qiu*, p. 9.

38. It has been suggested by Marián Gálik to the author that Master Yun in "Autumn in Kuling" was Sun Yunbing, a leftist who was quite active at the time. There might be a

number of local resemblances between Master Yun and Sun Yunbing to support the identification. For example, they both have the character *yun* in their names, and Sun Yunbing might also have been on board the same ship to Kuling with Mao Dun. But then which one in the story is Mao Dun?

Mao Dun had insisted on the fact that the characters in his stories and novels are types, composite pictures of men and women he knew. Considering the character and action Master Yun represents against the "collective background" of the passengers on board the ship, he seems not to represent a specific individual.

39. In July 1927 Lushan was a meeting ground for political negotiations, intrigues, and party reorganization. For example, the Nanchang Uprising was partly planned there, Borodin and Qu Qiubai met there to discuss the August 7 conference, and Wang Jingwei, Sun Ke, and Zhang Fakui also went there in late July to plan their countermeasure against the anticipated Nanchang Uprising.

In "Autumn in Kuling," Yun bought a travel guide to Lushan and studied it with great care. But once he got there, all he could do was to play chess in a hotel. His situation serves as an ironic comment on the general futility of the CCP activities in that area.

40. Mao Dun, *Gulingzhi qiu,* p. 15

41. See the reconstruction and description of the Nanchang Uprising by Colonel J. Guillermaz, *The China Quarterly* 11:161–169 (July–September 1962).

42. A comparable portrayal can be found in Zhang Guotao, "Memoirs," *Mingbao Monthly,* 25:90–96 (January 1968).

13. The Changing Relationship Between Literature and Life: Aspects of the Writer's Role in Ding Ling

Yɪ-Tsɪ M. Feuerwerker

1. Ding Ling, "Zenyang duidai 'Wusi' shidal zuopin — wei *Zhongguo qingnian bao* xie" (How to regard the works of the May Fourth period — written for *The China Youth Gazette),* in *Dao qunzhongzhong qu luohu* (Go make your dwelling among the masses) (Peking, 1954), pp. 104–108.

2. Ibid., p. 107.

3. Shen Congwen, *Ji Ding Ling, Ji Ding Ling xuji* (Reminiscences of Ding Ling, Further reminiscences of Ding Ling) (Shanghai, 1940); Yao Pengzi, "Womende pengyou Ding Ling" (Our friend Ding Ling), in *Ding Ling xuanji* (Selected Works of Ding Ling) ed. [Yao] Pengzi (Shanghai, 1939), pp. 1–42.

4. Gunther Stein, *The Challenge of Red China* (New York, McGraw Hill, 1945), pp. 251–259; Helen F. Sow, *Women in Modern China* (The Hague, Mouton, 1967), pp. 190–221; Robert Elegant, *China's Red Masters: Political Biographies of the Chinese Communist*

Leaders (New York, Twayne, 1951), pp. 145–162; Robert Payne, *China Awake* (New York, Dodd, Mead, 1947), pp. 381–386; E. H. Leaf, "Ting Ling, Herald of a New China," *T'ien Hsia Monthly* 5:225–236 (October 1937).

5. The major category in Ding Ling's writings is *xiaoshuo*, which covers short stories and novels. Unlike the English term "fiction," it does not in itself imply a created, imagined world. But Ding Ling clearly distinguished *xiaoshuo* from "records" (*shilu*) and "reportage" (*baogao wenxue*), which she also wrote and labeled as such.

6. Ding Ling, "Mouye" (A certain night), in *Yehui* (Night meeting) (Shanghai, 1933), pp. 1–11. It was first published in the June 1932 issue of *Wenxue yuebao* (Literature monthly), and dated May 1932.

7. This would not have been unusual. Agnes Smedley records the account of a "neurotic" German pilot who saw a dozen Communists beheaded in Hankow as they sang "The Internationale" in "high shrill voices." See her *Battle Hymn of China* (New York, Knopf, 1943), p. 76.

8. Ding Ling, "Yige zhenshirende yisheng — ji Hu Yepin" (The life of an upright man — reminiscences of Hu Yepin), in *Hu Yepin xiaoshuo xuanji* (Selected stories of Hu Yepin) (Peking, 1955), pp. 1–21.

9. Ding Ling, "Mouye," p. 4.

10. Ibid., p. 11.

11. Ding Ling, "Cong yewan dao tianliang" (From night till daybreak), in *Shui* (Flood) (Hong Kong, 1954), pp. 129–139.

12. Ding Ling makes claims for both "truth" and imaginative leeway in her postscript to the story: "These are probably all facts [*zhe dayue dou shi zhenshi*], written in memory of a friend. I started to write this piece last July but put it aside for other things. Not until today did I finish it in a hurry. I feel there are still many new ideas and compositional matters [*yisi he buju*] but I can't write them out now."

13. The effectiveness of conscious images of martyrdom may depend on the reader's ideological predisposition. To Harold Isaacs, "A Certain Night" "shows what effect the Communist political conversion could have on the gifts of a creative writer." The assumption is that the effect could only be negative. See *Straw Sandals: Chinese Short Stories, 1918–1933*, ed. Harold R. Isaacs (Cambridge, Mass., MIT Press, 1974), p. lviii. Other readers, closer to the events described in the story, found it "powerfully moving." See, for example, the editor's note by [Yao] Pengzi in *Wenxue yuebao* 1.1 (June 1932). The abstract character of Ding Ling's story was what qualified it to become part of the legendary material on the five martyrs. T. A. Hsia's chapter "Enigma of the Five Martyrs," in his *The Gate of Darkness: Studies on the Leftist Literary Movement in China* (Seattle and London, University of Washington Press, 1968), does not mention "A Certain Night" but suggests that the lack of precise information about the circumstances surrounding the arrest and execution of the young revolutionaries (intraparty strife and betrayal are strongly suspected) enhanced the symbolic usefulness of their martyrdom.

14. For the terminology and discussion of this type of narration, see Lubomír Doležel, "The Typology of the Narrator: Point of View in Fiction," in *To Honor Roman Jakobson, Essays on the Occasion of His Seventieth Birthday, 11 October, 1966*, Janua linguarum series maior (The Hague, Mouton, 1967) XXXI, 549–550; and Wayne C. Booth, *The Rhetoric of Fiction* (Chicago, University of Chicago Press, 1961), p. 153.

15. Excluding the stories in diary or letter form in which the act of writing is presumably concurrent with the narration, these stories include the following: "Yitian" (One day), "Nianqiande yitian" (The day before New Year's) (the title is given here as

"Nianqiande yinian"), both in Ding Ling, *Shui,* pp. 113–127, 142–157; "Suimu" (The end of the year), in *Zisha riji* (A suicide's diary) (Shanghai, 1937), pp. 71–89; "Yecao," in *Yige nüren* (A woman) (n.p., 1930), pp. 95–107.

16. Most sources give 1907 as the date for Ding Ling's birth. Like all other "facts" of her life, this is disputable, though she *was* unquestionably a young and already prolific writer at the time.

17. Ding Ling, "Wo zenyang fei xiang le ziyoude tiandi" (How I flew towards a free heaven and earth), in *Kuadao xinde shidai lai* (Stride into the new era) (Peking, 1953), pp. 157–162.

18. Ding Ling, "Yige zhenshirende yisheng," p. 7.

19. Shen Congwen, *Ji Ding Ling,* p. 87.

20. Ding Ling, "Mengke," in *Zai heianzhong* (In the darkness) (Shanghai, 1933), pp. 1–71.

21. Ibid., p. 71.

22. Ding Ling, "Wode chuangzuo shenghuo" (My life in creative writing), in *Ding Ling xuanji* (Selected works of Ding Ling), ed. Xu Chensi and Ye Wangyou (Shanghai, 1935), pp. 134–138.

23. Ding Ling, "Yige zhenshirende yisheng," p. 8.

24. Ding Ling, "Shenghuo, sixiang yu renwu" (Life, thought, and characters), *Renmin wenxue* (People's literature) 3:120–128 (1955).

25. Ding Ling, "Shafei nüshi de riji" (Diary of Miss Sophie), in *Zai heianzhong,* pp. 74–135.

26. Ibid., p. 135.

27. For a discussion of the influence of this book, see Leo Ou-fan Lee, *The Romantic Generation of Modern Chinese Writers* (Cambridge, Mass., Harvard University Press, 1973), pp. 283–286. With certain qualifications, the early Ding Ling could probably be admitted as a female member to Lee's "romantic generation."

28. David Goldknopf, *The Life of the Novel* (Chicago, University of Chicago Press, 1972), p. 11.

29. Ding Ling, "Amao guniang" (Miss Amao), "Shujiazhong" (During summer vacation), in *Zai heianzhong,* pp. 203–270; "Zisha riji" (A suicide's diary), "Qingyunlide yijian xiaofangli" (A small room in Qingyun Lane), "Xiao huolunshang" (On a small steamer), in *Zisha riji,* pp. 15–31, 33–46, 91–107.

30. Ding Ling, "Shui" (Flood), in *Shui,* pp. 1–55.

31. Lecture on Ding Ling in Ann Arbor, February 10, 1969.

32. See C. T. Hsia's devastating criticism in his *A History of Modern Chinese Fiction,* rev. ed. (New Haven, Yale University Press, 1971), pp. 268–272.

33. I have benefited from consulting English translations of both these works, "Diary of Miss Sophia," tr. A. L. Chin, in *Straw Sandals,* pp. 152–153, *The Sun Shines over the Sangkan River,* tr. Yang Hsien-yi and Gladys Yang (Peking, 1954), pp. 25–26. I have tried for more literal versions to get across the stylistic differences.

34. Ding Ling, *Zai heianzhong,* p. 109.

35. This "implied" author is no less a creation than the characters within the novel. See Booth, pp. 70–76. Ding Ling's version of herself as author here is very different from the one presented in "Diary of Miss Sophie."

36. Ding Ling, *Taiyang zhaozai Sangganheshang* (The sun shines over the Sangkan River) (Peking, 1955), pp. 24–25.

37. Parzival as a *developmental* character is discussed in Robert Scholes and Robert Kellogg, *The Nature of Narrative* (New York, Oxford University Press, 1966), pp.

167–169.

38. For historical accounts of the antirightist drive, see D. W. Fokkema, *Literary Doctrine in China and Soviet Influence, 1956–1960* (The Hague, Mouton, 1965), pp. 160–163; Merle Goldman, *Literary Dissent in Communist China* (Cambridge, Mass., Harvard University Press, 1967), pp. 203–242; and C. T. Hsia, pp. 341–349.

39. For example, see Zhou Yang, *Wenyi zhanxianshangde yichang da bianlun* (A great debate on the literary front) (Peking, 1960), p. 14; and Yao Wenyuan, *Wenyi sixiang lunzheng ji* (Polemics in literary ideas) (Shanghai, 1965), p. 218. Ding Ling has denied that she was writing about herself in Miss Sophie. See "Shenghuo, sixiang yu renwu," p. 120. How this applies to the sequel to the "Diary of Miss Sophie" is less clear. That consists of two entries purportedly made the day of and the day after the sixth anniversary of her meeting with Hu Yepin. "Shafei nüshi riji dierbu" (Diary of Miss Sophie, part II), in *Yiwai ji* (The unexpected collection) (Shanghai, 1936), pp. 189–202.

40. Two problems must be clarified in discussing feminism in literature. First, the label "women's writing" has often condescendingly implied a distinct mode of writing subsidiary to the dominant masculine mode, to be judged by different criteria. Although certain generalizations can be made about the women writers of Ding Ling's generation, they do not begin to cover the characteristics of any individual writer, particularly one of Ding Ling's range. A writer's sex may provide one useful context for understanding his or her work, but is irrelevant to its aesthetic evaluation.

Second, feminism is of little use in the analysis of the inherent workings of literary texts as *literary* texts; what it offers here is an important perspective on the life-literature relationship in Ding Ling's ideas about the writer's role.

41. Ding Ling, *Muqin* (Mother) (Shanghai, 1933).

42. Shen Congwen, *Ji Ding Ling xuji*, p. 145.

43. Shen Congwen, *Ji Ding Ling*, p. 83.

44. Ibid., pp. 67–68.

45. Ibid., pp. 101–102.

46. Ding Ling, "Yige nüren he yige nanren" (A woman and a man), in *Yige nüren*, pp. 1–40.

47. Ding Ling, "Ta zou hou" (After he left), in *Yige nüren*, pp. 41–62.

48. Ding Ling, "Yecao," in *Yige nüren*.

49. Ding Ling, "Nianqiande yitian," in *Shui*.

50. Ding Ling, "Bu suan qingshu" (Not a love letter), in *Yiwai ji*, pp. 205–223.

51. "Wode chuangzuo jingyan" (My experience in writing), in *Ding Ling xuanji*, ed. Xu and Ye, p. 142.

52. Ding Ling, "Yecao," p. 96.

53. Reprinted during the antirightist campaign in *Wenyi bao* (Literary gazette) 2:8–10 (1958).

54. Originally published in the Yenan journal *Guyu* (Grain rain) in 1941, it was revised and published in *Wenyi zhendi* (Literary base) 7.1 (1942). This version was copied and printed in *Wenyi bao* 2:11–16 (1958).

55. Ding Ling, "Wo zai Xiacun de shihou" (When I was in Xia village), in *Wo zai Xiacun de shihou* (Peking, 1951), pp. 13–41.

56. Hua Fu, "Ding Lingde 'fuchoude nüshen' — ping 'wo zai Xiacun de shihou' " (The "vengeful goddess" of Ding Ling — a criticism of "When I Was in Xia Village"), *Wenyi bao* 3:22–25.

57. Zhang Guangnian, "Shafei nüshi zai Yan'an" (Miss Sophie in Yenan), *Wenyi bao* 2:9–11 (1958).

58. Yao Wenyuan, "Shafei nüshimende ziyou wangguo — Ding Ling bufen zaoqi zuopin pipan, bing lun Ding Ling chuangzuo sixiang he chuangzuo qingxiang fazhan de yige xiansuo" (The free kingdom of the Miss Sophies — a criticism of some of Ding Ling's early works, and a discussion of a clue to the thought and direction of development in Ding Ling's creative writing), in his *Wenyi sixiang lunzheng ji*, p. 212.

59. Ibid., p. 218.

60. Ding Ling, "Amao guniang," p. 243.

61. Shen Congwen believes that Hu Yepin's unjust treatment in the hands of book editors "nurtured his will and courage to oppose present conditions." See *Ji Ding Ling*, p. 84.

62. Ding Ling, "Yijiusanlingnian chun Shanghai" (Shanghai in the spring of 1930), in *Ding Ling wenji* (Shanghai, 1936), pp. 190–191. This passage is quoted and translated in Lee, pp. 271–272, and in T. A. Hsia, p. 188.

63. Ding Ling, *Wei Hu* (Wei Hu) (Hong Kong, 1953).

64. Ding Ling, "Yige nüren he yige nanren" (A woman and a man), in *Ding Ling wenji*, p. 549. This story is also in *Yige nüren*, pp. 1–40.

65. "Duiyu chuangzuoshangde jitiao juti yijian" (A few concrete opinions on creative writing), in *Ding Ling xuanji*, ed. Xu and Ye, pp. 139–141.

66. He Danren, "Guanyu xin xiaoshuode dansheng — ping Ding Lingde 'Shui'" (Concerning the birth of the new fiction — a criticism of Ding Ling's "Flood"), in *Ding Ling xuanji*, ed. Xu and Ye, pp. 54–60.

67. Qian Xingcun, "Guanyu *Muqin*" (About *Mother*), in *Ding Ling xuanji*, ed. Pengzi, pp. 314–315.

68. Her accounts of these activities can be read in Ding Ling, *Yinian* (One year) (n.p., 1939).

69. These phrases were common in many writings on literature at the time and are by no means original with Ding Ling. What invited attack was the way she stretched them into personal statements about literature, as the quoted passages show.

70. "Dao qunzhongzhong qu luohu" (Go make your dwelling among the masses), in *Dao qunzhongzhong qu luohu*, pp. 88–103.

71. Ibid., p. 95.

72. Ibid., pp. 101–103.

73. The charge of "one-bookism" referred also to her arrogance on the basis of one successful book, *The Sun Shines over the Sangkan River*. See Wang Ziye, "Fengming xiezuo" (Writing to order), *Renmin wenxue* 10:8–9 (1957).

74. "Jianchi shehuizhuyide wenyi luxian" (Hold fast to the socialist line in literature), editorial in *Wenyi yuebao* (Literary monthly) 10:3–5 (1957).

14. Yu Dafu and the Transition to Modern Chinese Literature

Michael Egan

1. The outstanding work of this type comprises a series of volumes, *Contributions to the Study of the Rise and Development of Modern Literatures in Asia* (Prague, Academia, 1965, 1969, 1970).

2. This was one of the conclusions drawn by the 1972 University of Toronto Conference on the Late Qing Novel. A volume, *The Late Qing Novel: Antecedents of Modern Chinese Fiction* is now in preparation, edited by Milena Doleželová-Velingerová.

3. This chapter concentrates on what the noted scholars C. T. Hsia and Jaroslav Průšek have written about Yu. Anna Doleželová's *Yü Ta-fu: Specific Traits of his Literary Creation* (New York, Paragon, 1971), despite its title, devotes itself chiefly to plot summation and biographical material. Most of the Chinese and Japanese works on Yu are biographical or personal reminiscences about him.

4. Jaroslav Průšek, *Three Sketches of Chinese Literature* (Prague, Academia, 1969), p. 69.

5. C. T. Hsia, *A History of Modern Chinese Fiction 1917-1957* (New Haven, Yale University Press, 1961), p. 105.

6. Ibid., pp. 104–105.

7. Leo Ou-fan Lee, *The Romantic Generation of Modern Chinese Writers* (Cambridge, Mass., Harvard University Press, 1973), p. 110.

8. Ibid., p. 110. Italics added.

9. William W. K. Wimsatt, Jr., *The Verbal Icon: Studies in the Meaning of Poetry* (Lexington, University of Kentucky Press, 1954), p. 4.

10. Ibid.

11. Ibid., 21.

12. C. T. Hsia, p. 109.

13. Lubomír Doležel, *Narrative Modes in Czech Literature* (Toronto, University of Toronto Press, 1973), p. 73.

14. Yu Dafu, "Chenlun" (Sinking), *Twentieth Century Chinese Short Stories* ed. C. T. Hsia, (New York, Columbia University Press, 1971), p. 5.

15. Ibid., p. 6.

16. Ibid., p. 18.

17. Ibid., p. 29.

18. Ibid., pp. 28-29.

19. Wayne C. Booth, *The Rhetoric of Fiction* (Chicago, University of Chicago Press, 1961), p. 316.

20. Lee, p. 111.

21. C. T. Hsia, p. 105.

22. Yu Dafu, "Chenlun," p. 3.

23. Ibid., p. 4.

24. Ibid., p. 33.

25. Robert Scholes and Robert Kellogg, *The Nature of Narrative* (New York, Oxford

University Press, 1966), p. 164ff.

26. Stock phrases are used ingeniously to date early vernacular stories in Patrick Hanan, *The Chinese Short Story: Studies in Dating, Authorship and Composition* (Cambridge, Mass., Harvard University Pres, 1973).

27. Yu Dafu, "Yinhuisede si" (Silver-gray death), in *Yu Dafu xuanji* (A Yu Dafu anthology) (Hong Kong, 1973), p. 49.

28. Ibid., p. 49.

29. Yu Dafu, "Chenlun," in *Yu Dafu xuanji*, p. 27.

30. Yu Dafu, "Yinhuisede si," p. 43.

31. Ibid.

32. Ibid.

33. Ibid., p. 47.

34. Ibid., p. 51.

15. Traditional-Style Popular Urban Fiction in the Teens and Twenties

PERRY LINK

1. Qu Qiubai, *Qu Qiubai wenji* (Collected works of Qu Qiubai) (Peking, 1953), II, 885.

2. *Yuanyang hudie pai yanjiu ziliao* (Research materials on the Mandarin Duck and Butterfly School), ed. Wei Shaochang, (Shanghai, 1962), p. 462.

3. Zheng Zhenduo, "Sixiangde fanliu" (The backward current in thought), *Wenxue xunkan* (The literary ten-daily) 4 (June 10, 1921).

4. Zheng Zhenduo, "Wenchang" (Literary prostitutes), *Wenxue xunkan* 49 (September 11, 1922); Mao Dun, "Ziranzhuyi yu Zhongguo xiandai xiaoshuo" (Naturalism and modern Chinese fiction), *Xiaoshuo yuebao* (Short story monthly), 13.7 (July 1922).

5. Guo Moruo, "Zhi Zheng Zhenduo xiansheng xin" (A letter to Mr. Zheng Zhenduo), *Wenxue xunkan* 6 (June 30, 1921).

6. Address at the inauguration of the League of Left-Wing Writers, March 2, 1931, quoted in Chen Jiying, "Sanshi niandai wentan huigu" (A look back at the literary scene in the thirties), *Zhuanji wenxue* (Biographical literature) 22.5:27 (May 1963).

7. Qu Qiubai, *Qu Qiubai wenji*, p. 885.

8. Zhang Jinglu, *Zhongguo chuban shiliao bubian* (Supplement to Materials on the History of Chinese Publishing) (Peking, 1957), p. 279.

9. This approximation is based on: (1) the estimates of Butterfly publishers in Shanghai during these years, specifically Bao Tianxiao, Chen Dingshan, and Cheng Shewo, who were interviewed by the author; and (2) evidence on primary school enrollment in all Kiangsu province, as listed in Bell and Woodhead, *The China Year Book 1912* (London, Routledge & Sons, 1912), p. 323; and Woodhead, *The China Year Book 1924* (Tientsin, 1925), p. 252.

10. Ninety-two titles are listed for the teens in *Yuanyang hudie pai yanjiu ziliao* pp. 277–451, and this listing is far from complete.

11. Wang Dungen, "*Libailiu* chuban zhuiyan" (Useless talk about the publication of *The Saturday Magazine*), *Libailiu* 1:–(June 6, 1914).

12. L. K. Tao, *The Standard of Living Among Chinese Workers* (Shanghai, 1931), p. 25; Sung-ho Lin, *Factory Workers in Tungku* (Peking, 1928), pp. 64, 83.

13. Interviews with Bao Tianxiao, December 6, 1972; Chen Dingshan, July 25, 1973; Cheng Shewo, July 26, 1973; Zheng Yimei, May 9, 1973. Also Gao Zhenbai, "Ji Bao Tianxiao xiansheng" (On Mr. Bao Tianxiao), in Bao Tianxiao, *Yishi zhuxingde bainian bianqian* (Changes in daily life over a hundred years) (Hong Kong, 1974), pp. 86–90.

14. Chow Tse-tsung, *The May Fourth Movement* (Stanford, Stanford University Press, 1967), p. 379.

15. Bao Tianxiao, *Chuanyinglou huiyi lu* (Reminiscences of the residence of bracelet shadows) (Hong Kong, 1971), p. 377.

16. William J. Reilly, "China Kicks in with a Champion," *Moving Picture World* (New York), April 26, 1919, as quoted in Jay Leyda, *Dianying: Electric Shadows* (Cambridge, Mass., MIT Press, 1972), p. 25.

17. Zhang Jinglu, p. 292.

18. Qu Qiubai, *Qu Qiubai wenji*, pp. 898–899.

19. Stimulated by May Fourth writers' bent for forming associations, Butterfly writers formalized two of their own in 1922, the Star Society (Xing she) and the Green Society (Qing she).

20. A Ying has estimated there were at least four to five hundred translation novels in the late Qing period alone. (See Ning Yuan, *Xiaoshuo xin hua* [New talk about fiction] [Hong Kong, 1961], p. 62). Though there are no estimates of the number of translation novels and short stories in the teens, there would appear to be at least as many as in the late Qing period.

21. Rhoads Murphey, *Shanghai: Key to Modern China* (Cambridge, Mass., Harvard University Press, 1953), pp. 20, 22.

22. Zhi Jing, "Wentizhongde dazhong wenyi" (The controversial mass art), in *Zhongguo xin wenxue daxi xubian* (Sequel to Comprehensive anthology of new Chinese literature) (Hong Kong, 1968), I, 507–509.

23. Qu Qiubai, *Qu Qiubai wenji*, pp. 897–898.

24. Examples are Yuan Shikai's closing of the political newspaper *Minquan bao* (People's rights) and his sly substitution of it with a hard-core Butterfly magazine called, preposterously enough, *Minquan su* (Essence of people's rights) (see *Yuanyang hudie pai yanjiu ziliao*, pp. 287–288); and the awarding of public prizes to Butterfly writers by *beiyang* warlords for their literary efforts on behalf of continence and chastity (ibid., p. 109).

25. Jaroslav Průšek, "The Beginnings of Popular Chinese Literature: Urban Centers — the Cradle of Popular Fiction," *Archiv Orientální* 36:107 (1968).

26. Cao Xueqin, *Hong lou meng*, trans. C. C. Wang, *Dream of the Red Chamber* (New York, Twayne, 1958), p. 490.

27. Xu Zhenya, *Yu li hun* (Jade pear spirit) (Shanghai, 1914), pp. 70–71.

28. Ibid., p. 124.

29. Bao Tianxiao, *Xiangxiaren you dao Shanghai* (The countryman revisits Shanghai), Shanghai *Shenbao* (November 4, 10, and 11, 1931).

30. Xu Zhenya, pp. 86–87.

31. Zhang Henshui, *Tixiao yinyuan* (Fate in tears and laughter) (Shanghai, 1930), III, 6–7.

32. Ibid., I, 34.

33. Bao Tianxiao, *Chuanyinglou huiyi lu xubian* (Supplement to Reminiscences of the

residence of bracelet shadows) (Hong Kong, 1973) p. 60.

34. Bao Tianxiao, *Chuanyinglou huiyi lu*, p. 168; Roswell S. Britton, *The Chinese Periodical Press, 1800–1912* (Shanghai, 1933), p. 115.

35. Bao Tianxiao, *Chuanyinglou huiyi lu*, p. 380.

36. Qu Qiubai, *Qu Qiubai wenji*, p. 885ff.

37. Joe C. Huang, *Heroes and Villains in Communist China* (London, C. Hurst, 1973), pp. 323–326.

16. Qu Qiubai's Critique of the May Fourth Generation: Early Chinese Marxist Literary Criticism

PAUL G. PICKOWICZ

1. For biographical details on Qu, see Paul G. Pickowicz, "Ch'ü Ch'iu-pai: Die Verbindung von Politik und Kunst in der chinesischen Revolution," in *Die Söhne des Drachen* ed. Peter J. Opitz (Munich, Paul List Verlag, 1974), pp. 292–321; Paul G. Pickowicz, "Ch'ü Ch'iu-pai and the Origins of Marxist Literary Criticism in China" (Ph.D. dissertation, University of Wisconsin, 1973); Mark F. Shneider, *Tvorcheskii put' Tsiui Tsiu-bo* (Moscow, Publishing House of the Academy of Sciences, 1964); Bernadette Yu-ning Li, "A Biography of Ch'ü Ch'iu-pai: From Youth to Party Leadership (1899–1928)" (Ph.D. dissertation, Columbia University, 1967); Sima Lu, *Qu Qiubai zhuan* (A biography of Qu Qiubai) (Hong Kong, 1962); Cao Zuxi, *Qu Qiubaide wenxue huodong* (Qu Qiubai's literary activities) (Shanghai, 1958); and T. A. Hsia, "Ch'ü Ch'iu-pai's Autobiographical Writings: The Making and Destruction of a 'Tender-hearted' Communist," *China Quarterly* 25:176–212 (January–March 1966).

2. Qu Qiubai, *Qu Qiubai wenji* (Collected works of Qu Qiubai, hereafter *QQBWJ*) (Peking, 1953–1954), I, 22.

3. Ibid.

4. For details on Qu's May Fourth Activities, see Li Anbao, "Wusi shiqide Qu Qiubai" (Qu Qiubai during the May Fourth period), *Jiaoxue yu yanjiu* (Teaching and research) 5:66–72 (May 1959); Zheng Zhenduo, "Ji Qu Qiubai tongzhi zaonian ersan shi" (A few anecdotes in Comrade Qu Qiubai's early life), *Xin guancha* (New observer) 12:26–28 (June 16, 1955); and Ding Jingtang, *Xuexi Lu Xun he Qu Qiubai zuopinde zhaji* (Learn from the message of Lu Xun and Qu Qiubai's works) (Shanghai, 1961), pp. 121–144.

5. Qu's complete May Fourth publication record can be found in *Qu Qiubai zhuyi xinian mulu* (A chronological listing of Qu Qiubai's writings and translations) ed. Ding Jingtang and Wen Cao (Shanghai, 1959), pp. 1–5. Qu and his friends compiled a volume of Tolstoy short stories that was published in 1921. He also contributed Tolstoy translations to *Xin Zhongguo* (New China) and *Jiefang yu gaizao* (Emancipation and reconstruction), two leading Peking magazines. His translation of Gogol's *The Servants' Room* appeared in *Shuguang* (Dawn). Finally, Qu was a major contributor to an anthology entitled *Eluosi mingjia duanpian xiaoshuo ji* (Collected short stories by famous Russian writers); he wrote a preface to the book, a short introduction to Pushkin's *Belkin's Tales*,

and a translation of Tolstoy's "Idle Talk."

6. Qu Qiubai, "Duoyude hua" (Superfluous words), in Sima Lu, p. 128. For an English version, see the translation used here: *The Chinese Revolution: 1911–1949* ed. D. J. Li (New York, Van Nostrand, 1970), p. 161.

7. *QQBWJ*, I, 91.

8. *QQBWJ*, I, 166, as quoted in Bernadette Yu-ning Li, p. 89.

9. Qu Qiubai, *Shehui kexue gailun* (Outline of the social sciences) (Shanghai, 1949), p. 47.

10. Ibid., p. 49.

11. Qu Qiubai, "Laodong Eguode xin zuojia" (New writers of workers' and peasants' Russia), *Xiaoshuo yuebao* (Short story monthly) 14.9 (September 1923); in *QQBWJ*, II, 546.

12. Ibid., p. 547.

13. Qu Qiubai, "Chi E xin wenyi shidaide diyi yan," (The first swallows of red Russia's new literary and artistic period), *Xiaoshuo yuebao* (Short story monthly) 15.6 (June 10, 1924); in *QQBWJ*, II, 556.

14. Quoted in Edward Brown, *The Proletarian Episode in Russian Literature, 1928–1932* (New York, Columbia University Press, 1953), p. 244.

15. Mark F. Shneider, *Tvorcheskii put' Tsiui Tsiu-bo*, p. 83.

16. For a discussion of the activities of this early Marxist literary group, see Zhang Bilai, "Yijiuersannian *Zhongguo qingnian* jige zuojiade wenxue zhuzhang" (The literary views of several writers of the 1923 *Chinese Youth* magazine), in *Zhongguo xin wenxue shi yanjiu* (Research on the history of modern Chinese literature) ed. Li Helin (Peking, 1951).

17. Qu Qiubai, "Huangmoli — yijiuersannianzhi Zhongguo wenxue," (In the wasteland — Chinese literature in 1923), *Xin qingnian* (New youth) 2 (December 20, 1923); in *QQBWJ*, I, 229–234.

18. Qu Qiubai, "Gao yanjiu wenxue de qingnian" (To young people studying literature), *Zhongguo qingnian* (Chinese youth) 5 (November 17, 1923); in *Zhongguo xiandai wenxue shi cankao ziliao* (Research materials on the history of modern Chinese literature) (Peking, 1959–1960), I, 195–197.

19. *QQBWJ*, I, 232.

20. The best collection of documents on the debate is *Zhongguo wenyi lunzhan* (Chinese literary polemics) ed. Li Helin (Peking, 1929).

21. For a discussion of the Japanese proletarian literary movement, see Tatsuo Arima, *The Failure of Freedom: A Portrait of Modern Japanese Intellectuals* (Cambridge, Mass., Harvard University Press, 1969).

22. Lu Hsun (Lu Xun), *Selected Works of Lu Hsun* (Peking, 1964), III, 120.

23. Quoted in Ting Yi, *A Short History of Modern Chinese Literature* (Peking, 1959), p. 27. In using the terms "realist" Marxist and "romantic" Marxist, I am trying to distinguish in a general way between materialists and voluntarists in the leftist literary camp. This combined use of literary and political terminology is necessary in analyzing a situation in which artists are in fact politically active, particularly when there seems to be a correlation between certain literary traditions and certain political styles. The use of this sort of terminology is justified because critics like Qu used it themselves to analyze the revolutionary literary scene.

24. Lu Hsun, III, 93.

25. Qu Qiubai, "Lu Xun zagan quanji xuyan" (Preface to *The Miscellaneous Writings of Lu Xun* [April 8, 1933]), in *QQBWJ*, II, 985. The passages from Qu's preface quoted here are

from an excellent translation of the whole essay that appears in *Chinese Literature* 5:40–68 (1959), under the title "Writing for a Great Cause."

26. Ibid., p. 988. Emphasis added.

27. Ibid., p. 882.

28. Ibid., pp. 996–997.

29. Qu Qiubai, "Ouhua wenyi" (Europeanized literature and art [May 5, 1932]), in *QQBWJ*, II, 881.

30. Qu Qiubai, "Dazhong wenyide wenti — chugao pianduan" (The question of popular literature and art — draft fragments" [1931?]), in *Dazhong wenyi lunji* (Essays on popular literature and art) ed. Ding Yi (Peking, 1951), p. 142.

31. Ibid., p. 143.

32. Ibid.

33. *QQBWJ*, II, 882.

34. Qu Qiubai, "Dazhong wenyide wenti — chugao pianduan," p. 145. Emphasis added.

35. *QQBWJ*, II, 880.

36. Qu Qiubai, " 'Women' shi shui?" (Who are "we"? [May 4, 1932]), in *QQBWJ*, II, 875. For a complete translation of this text, see my forthcoming contribution to a special issue of the *Bulletin of Concerned Asian Scholars* 8.2 (April–August 1976) entitled "The Development of Revolutionary Literature in China: A Selection of Source Materials."

37. *QQBWJ*, II, p. 875.

38. Ibid., p. 876.

39. Ibid.

40. Ibid., p. 878.

41. *QQBWJ*, I, 170–171. Quoted in Bernadette Yu-ning Li, pp. 90–91.

42. Qu Qiubai, "Gemingde lanmandike — Hua Han changpian xiaoshuo *Diquan* xu" (Revolutionary romantic — an introduction to Hua Han's novel *Spring* [April 22, 1932]), in Qu Qiubai, *Luan dan* (Random shots) (Shanghai, 1949), p. 314. Emphasis added.

43. Ibid., p. 317.

44. Ibid.

45. Paul LaFargue, "Zuolade Jinqian" (Zola's *L'argent*), translated by Qu Qiubai, in *QQBWJ*, II, 1138.

46. Ibid., 1144. The passage quoted here is from a partial translation of LaFargue's essay that appears in *Dialectics* 4:1–15 (1937), under the title "Emile Zola."

47. Ibid., p. 1168.

48. Qu Qiubai, "Ziye he guohuonian" (*Midnight* and the year of national products), *Ziyu tan* (Free discussion [April 8, 1933]), in *QQBWJ*, I, 438.

49. Mark F. Shneider, "Perevody Trudov po Markistskoy Estetike v Kitaye v 20-30ye Gody," *Narody Aziyi i Afrika* 5:188–194 (May 1961).

50. See Georg Plekhanov, *Unaddressed Letters and Art and Social Life* (Moscow, Foreign Languages Publishing House, 1957), p. 205.

51. Qu Qiubai, "'Ziyu ren' de wenhua yundong" (The "free man" cultural movement), *Wenyi xinwen* (Literature and art news [May 23, 1932]), in *QQBWJ*, II, 946–951. Also see: Harriet C. Mills, "Lu Hsün: The Years on the Left", 1927–1936 (Ph.D. dissertation, Columbia University, 1963), pp. 178–184; and Cao Zuxi, pp. 80–94.

52. Qu Qiubai, "Wenyide ziyu he wenxuejiade bu ziyu" (Artistic freedom and the writer's lack of freedom), *Xiandai* (Les contemporains), 1.6 (October 1, 1932), in *QQBWJ*, II, 954–955.

53. Ibid., p. 953. Emphasis added.

54. Quoted in A. Tagore, *Literary Debates in Modern China, 1918–1937* (Tokyo, 1967), p. 131.

55. *QQBWJ*, II, 956–957.

56. Lu Hsun, III, 162–163.

57. It is important to note that this notion was not accepted by all Western Marxists. The futurist proletarian artists and the "pure" proletarian writers were considerably more iconoclastic than Lenin.

58. Quoted in Henri Arvon, *Marxist Aesthetics* (Ithaca, N.Y., Cornell University Press, 1973), p. 58.

59. See Paul G. Pickowicz, "Modern China's Artistic and Cultural Life," *The Holy Cross Quarterly* 7.1–4:108–116 (1975), for a discussion of these developments.

INDEX

Aeschylus, 55

"Ah Q zhengzhuan," *see* "True Story of Ah Q"

Albov, M. N., 104

Aleichem, Sholem, 137

Aleksandrovsky, Vasily, 360

America, black literature in, 129, 133, 140

Analects, 43

Andersen, H. C., 57

Andreyev, L. N., 89; and Lu Xun, 10, 92-94, 99, 101, 183, 184, 187; and Hu Qiuyuan, 382; in Weiming congshu, 50

Anna Karenina, 100, 124

Archimedes, 43

Armenian literature, 140

Arnold, Matthew, 42, 44

Artsybashev, M. F., 92, 93, 94, 199

Asch, Sholem, 132

Ashes of Destruction, 32

Auden, W. H., 48

"Autumn in Kuling," 4, 254, 263, 269, 273-280

Autumn in the Han Palace, 387

Babbitt, Irving, 42, 44

Baerdishan, see *Partisan*

Baihua, 18-19; vs. wenyan, 17, 18-25, 34, 56, 362; in May Fourth literature, 17, 35, 56, 128-129, 217, 335, 362, 372; in Butterfly fiction, 346

Baihuawen, 9, 19, 35

Bai Mang, 368

Bai mao nü, see *White-Haired Girl*

Baitei, Tōjin, 66

Baiyu jing, see *Sutra of a Hundred Fables*

Ba Jin: and Western literature, 41, 50;

journal writing by, 52, 59; novels by, 92, 100, 146, 348, 390; Nobel Prize for, 262; and Butterfly fiction, 337

Barbusse, Henri, 51, 53

Barrie, J. M., 47, 55, 56

Baudelaire, Charles, 59

Bayuede xiangcun, see *Village in August*

Becher, J. R., 53

Behrsing, Siegfried, 95

Beidou, see *Big Dipper*

"Benbao neibu xiaoxi," *see* "Inside Story"

"Benediction," 99, 390, 391

Benliu, see *Torrents*

Bennett, Arnold, 47

Berninghausen, John, 3, 5, 7, 143, 156, 233-259

Besieged City, The, 146

Bessalko, Pavel, 360-361

Bian Zhilin, 59

Biaomeng, 21

Big Dipper, 53, 58, 303

Bing Xin, 25

Birch, Cyril, 13, 325, 385-405

Blake, William, 47

Bogdanov, Alexander, 360, 361

Booth, Wayne, 312, 316

Bourget, Paul, 44

Boxer Rebellion, 190

Brandes, Georg, 130, 183

Bridges, R. S., 47

Brief History of Enlightenment, 385, 386-390, 392, 393, 401-402, 403

Brooks, Van Wyck, 51

Browning, Robert, 47

Buddhism, 90, 104, 163, 353

Bukharin, N. I., 359

Bullough, Edward, 43

Bulwer-Lytton, Edward George, 68

451

Index

Index

Joyce, James, 61
Jūjigai o yuku, see *Toward the Crossroads*
Julius Caesar, 68
Jung, C. G., 45
Justice, 41

Kafka, Franz, 61, 311
Kalinin, Feodor, 360-361
Kang Youwei, 27, 169
Katayama Koson, 79
Kawakami Hajime, 87
Kazin, Vasily, 362
Keats, John, 57
Kenyū-sha, *see* Fellow Students' Society
Klim Samgin, 124
Konopnicka, Marya, 136
Korolenko, Vladimir, 184
Kropotkin, Peter, 41, 111
"Kuangren riji," *see* "Diary of a Madman"
Kumō no shōchō, see *Symbols of Agony*
Kuriyagawa Hakuson, 50, 84-86

La dame aux camélias, 29
LaFargue, Paul, 377-378
Lang, Andrew, 182
Language, Chinese, 18-25, 30, 121, 154-155, 217. *See also* Baihua; Baihuawen; Wenyan
Language, Polish, 133
Language, Russian, 107, 110, 121
Language, Yiddish, 133
Lao Can youji, see *Travels of Lao Can*
Lao She, 404; novels of, 42, 100, 146, 392; journal writing of, 50, 57, 59
Lao Zi, 353
L'argent, 377-378
Lawrence, D. H., 57
League of Left-Wing Writers: formation of, 40, 51, 86, 150-151, 155, 371; publications of, 51-55, 103; and Qu Qiubai, 118, 124, 351, 369, 373; and Lu Xun, 213-218, 328-329, 369; and Mao Dun, 256; and Ding Ling, 292, 303
League of Nations, 37
Lee, Leo Oufan, 5, 9, 143, 161-188, 311, 317
Leftism, *see* Communist party, Chinese;

League of Left-Wing Writers; Marxism; People's Republic
"Leifeng ta de diaodao," *see* "Collapse of the Leifeng Pagoda"
Lei Yu, 151
Lenin, V. I., 111, 355, 361, 368, 382
Lermontov, M. Y., 49, 108, 115, 116, 183
Lewis, C. Day, 48
Liang Qichao, 41; and fiction, 31-32, 65-69, 129, 332; and politics, 38, 67-69, 147, 169, 173-174; and Japanese influence, 65-69, 72; and language, 128; and Lu Xun, 170, 171, 172, 184, 185; journals of, 185, 190; and tradition, 352
Liang Shiqui, 44
Liang Zongdai, 55
Liaozhai zhiyi, see *Strange Stories from a Chinese Studio*
Libailiu, see *Saturday Magazine*
Liberation Daily, 298, 305
Li Boyuan, 28, 385, 387-390, 393-394, 401-403
Li Da, 264
Li Dazhao, 1, 104, 354
Li Dingyi, 328
"Life of an Upright Man—Reminiscences of Hu Yepin," 284
Li Hanqiu, 333, 346
Li He, 163
Li Helin, 73
Li Hun, see *Divorce*
Li Liewen, 219
Li Lisan, 213, 366
Li Min, 25
"Lin jia puzi," *see* "Lin's Store"
Link, Perry, 10, 12, 148, 325, 327-349
Lin Shu, 29, 31, 57, 129, 170, 174, 185
"Lin's Store," 261
Lin Yutang, 42-43, 51, 56, 157-158, 202, 206, 220
Literary Association, 72; journals of, 44, 131; and translations, 73, 79; and realism, 75, 80, 321; and Mao Dun, 92, 233, 264; and Qu Qiubai, 353, 356, 359, 368
Literary criticism, 12, 13, 135, 151, 325, 327, 329, 347, 351-384
Literary Gazette, 282
Literary Guide, 52, 215
Literary Research, 215

HARVARD EAST ASIAN SERIES

11.00
conference

X